GREEK HISTORY

GREEK HISTORY

Advisory Editor:

W. R. CONNOR

CHAIRMAN, DEPARTMENT OF CLASSICS
PROFESSOR OF GREEK
PRINCETON UNIVERSITY

THE HISTORY OF THE CHALCIDIC LEAGUE

BY

ALLEN BROWN WEST

ARNO PRESS
A New York Times Company
New York / 1973

85635

Reprint Edition 1973 by Arno Press Inc.

Reprinted from a copy in the
  Princeton University Library

Greek History
ISBN for complete set; 0-405-04775-4
See last pages of this volume for titles.

Manufactured in the United States of America

回回回

Library of Congress Cataloging in Publication Data

West, Allen Brown, 1886-1936.
  The history of the Chalcidic League.

    (Greek history)
    Reprint of the 1918 ed., which was issued as the
University of Wisconsin's Bulletin no. 969. History
series, v. 4, no. 2.
    Originally presented as the author's thesis,
University of Wisconsin, 1912.
    1. Chalcidic League. I. Title. II. Series:
Wisconsin. University. History series, v. 4, no. 2.
DF85.W47 1973   938'.1   72-7908
ISBN 0-405-04804-1

BULLETIN OF THE UNIVERSITY OF WISCONSIN

No, 969, History Series, Vol. 4, No 2, pp. 121-296

THE HISTORY OF THE CHALCIDIC LEAGUE

BY

ALLEN BROWN WEST

A THESIS SUBMITTED FOR THE DEGREE OF DOCTOR OF PHILOSOPHY
THE UNIVERSITY OF WISCONSIN
1912

MADISON, WISCONSIN
1918

PRICE, 40 CENTS

CONTENTS

THE CHALCIDIC LEAGUE

CHAPTER I

EARLY ATTEMPTS AT UNION

Jutting out in a south-easterly direction into the Thracian sea is the mountainous Chalcidic peninsula, ending in three finger-like promontories. Its area is approximately 4,000 sq. km., of which three fourths is found in the broad base of the peninsula. On the north it is shut off from the mainland by Mt. Cissos and Lake Bolbè, which extend across its whole width. The peninsula is almost entirely covered with forests, and along the coast and in the valleys between the mountains the country is very fertile. In the north-eastern corner there are deposits of iron and argentiferous lead. The rivers are small but comparatively numerous and there are many harbours upon the coast. Of the three promontories, Pallenè upon the west is the least mountainous and the most fertile. In size it is about equal to Sithonia, or the land of the Sithones, its neighbour upon the east. Actè, the third promontory, is the smallest and overtowers the others with its lofty Mt. Athos. The climate of Chalcidicè is less rigorous than that of the mainland and is suitable for the cultivation of the grape[1].

Thus the Chalcidic peninsula early came to the notice of the Greeks, as they sought places in which to plant their numerous colonies. The fertility of the country, its heavy forests furnishing material of all kinds for the building of ships, and its situation upon the sea, so favourable for the development of commerce,

---

[1] See the article upon Chalkidike in *Pauly-Wissowa*.

were advantages that attracted to it a large number of colonies from various states of Greece. The natives whom the Greeks found there were, so far as one can judge, of Thracian stock. In the fifth century remnants of this earlier population were still living upon the peninsula of Actè[2]. These were the Bisaltians, Crestonians, and Edonians. The Mygdonians, likewise a Thracian tribe, held the territory about Lake Bolbè.[3] In historical times the main body of the Bisaltians inhabited the country westward of the lower Strymon; the Paeonians were settled to the west of the upper Strymon; the Edonians held land in the neighbourhood of Amphipolis, while the Crestonians dwelt to the north of the Mygdonians[4]. These were the tribes that the Greeks found upon their arrival in the Chalcidic peninsula.

Many Greek cities participated in the colonization of the peninsula. Chalcis, Eretria, Corinth, and Andros sent colonies there and by the beginning of the fifth century the entire coast line was covered with their settlements, many of them large and flourishing towns.[5] But the Chalcidians from Euboea seem to have led the way in the colonization of this part of the Thracian coast. Sithonia, the central promontory, attracted their notice

---

[2] Thuc. IV, 109.

[3] Thuc. I, 58; II, 99; Hdt. VII, 123 f.

[4] Strabo, VII, 323, 4; 329, frg. 11; Thuc. II, 98–100; Hdt. VII, 113–115, 124.

[5] Thuc. I, 56ff; IV, 84, 88, 103, 109, 123; Theop. frg. 145; Steph. Byz. Φάρβηλος; Strabo, VII, 329, frg. 11; X, 447, 8. Chalcis was the founder of colonies, τὰς ὑπὸ 'Ολύνθῳ. This seems to refer to political subjection rather than to geographical position. The word ὑπό with the dative cannot mean around. Strabo may have thought of Olynthos as situated upon a hill and therefore above the other towns, or as inland. Harrison (Cl. Qu., 1912, p. 166) thinks that the number and area of the towns that could properly be said to lie under Olynthos in either sense would be small. For example they could not include Toronè, Assera, or Arnae. In VII, 329, 11, Strabo is more precise, for he says that the Chalcidians settled in the land of the Sithones. According to Herodotos, VII, 122, this included Toronè, Galepsos, Sermylia, Mecyperna, and Olynthos.

Thuc. IV, 109, speaks of the Chalcidic element in Actè, while Heracleides (F. H. G., II, 222) says that Cleonae was a foundation of Chalcidians from Elymynion which, according to Steph. Byz. was νῆσος Εὐβοίας πόλιν ἔχουσα. Cf. schol., Arist. Pax, 1126. Mela (II, 2, 30) mentions an Echinia near Acanthos, inter Strymona et Athon. The confusion between Λ and Χ is easy. Moreover, Plutarch, Aetia Graec., 30, refers to a Chalcidic element in the settlement of Sanè and Acanthos, and Dion. Hal., Ep. I ad Amm. 5, speaks of Chalcidian colonists in Stageiros. Scholiast, Arist. Eq., 237: εἰσὶ δὲ καὶ ἐπὶ Θρᾴκης οἱ Χαλκιδεῖς, ἄποικοι ὄντες ἀπὸ τῆς Εὐβοίας. Libanios on Olynthiac I, 1.

and there they planted many towns.   It was from these Chalcidic colonies that the peninsula has received its name.   Eretria took as her share Pallenè and Actè,[6] and Andros sent many colonies to the eastern shore.   Stageiros, Acanthos, Sanè and Argilos were all of her founding[7].   Finally about 600 B. C., Corinth founded the city of Potidaea upon the narrow neck of land that connects Pallenè with the mainland[8].

The new Greek population was, to a large extent, a homogeneous one, with a common tongue and similar commercial interests.   Conditions, therefore, were very favourable for the formation and continued existence of some form of political union. An external impulse alone was further necessary for the fusion of these independent Greek cities into a compact whole.   This impulse was to come with time and to thrust forward into prominence the little Chalcidic city of Olynthos.

At the time of the Persian expedition of Xerxes most of the cities of this peninsula submitted to him and furnished him ships or troops; many of the more important maritime cities sent both.   The Chalcidian and Bottiaean contingents are especially mentioned by Herodotos,[9] and this may be taken as evi-

---

[6] Strabo, X, 447, 8.   In Thucydides and other early writers the term Chalcidicè does not include the whole peninsula.   See Harrison, *Cl. Qu.*, 1912, pp. 93ff.   Scabala, Pharbelos, Mendè, Neapolis, Eion, Dicaea were directly or indirectly Eretrian colonies.   Theop. frg. 145: Σκάβαλα, χώρα Ἐρετριέων. Steph. Byz.: Φάρβηλος, πόλις Ἐρετριέων.   Thuc. IV, 7: Ἠιόνα τὴν ἐπὶ Θρᾴκης Μενδαίων ἀποικίαν.   Thuc. IV, 123: Μένδη . . . Ἐρετριῶν ἀποικία.   For Neapolis and Dicaea see tribute lists, *I. G.*, I, 230, 242.   Strabo credits Eretria with the settlement of Pallenè and Actè, but Thucydides fails to mention the Eretrian element in Actè.   The only pure Greek city of that peninsula, so far as we know, was Sanè and that was a colony of the Andrians.   In the other towns there was a certain mixture of Chalcidians.   Thuc. IV, 109; Hdt. VII, 22.   But in the opinion of Scylax, 66f, a writer of the fourth century, all of the cities of Actè are Hellenic.
[7] Thuc. IV, 84, 88, 103, 109.
[8] Thuc. I, 56ff; Nicol. Dam. 60 (*F. H. G.*, III, 393).
[9] Hdt. VII, 122-123, 185.   For Stageiros and Acanthos, cf. VII, 115. Troops alone were furnished by Assa, Piloros, Singos, Sartè, and the towns of Krossaia.   Toronè, Galepsos, Sermylia Mecyperna, Olynthos, Potidaea, Aphytis, Neapolis, Aegè, Therambos, Scionè, Mendè, and Sanè furnished ships and men.   In the summary (VII, 185) Herodotos says that the Greeks of Thrace furnished ships, and that among others the Paeonians, the Bottiaeans, the Chalcidic γένος, and such as dwelt on the sea-coast of Thrace furnished troops.   Harrison has attempted to prove that the Chalcidians were not originally colonists from Chalcis, but were a tribe similar to the Bottiaeans.   In part he relies upon the passages where Herodotos speaks of

dence that the Chalcidians and Bottiaeans were the most important peoples of the peninsula. Toronè was probably the largest Chalcidian city[10]. The evidence of Herodotos points to a union of some sort among the Chalcidians, the foundation for which was a consciousness of common descent[11]. Further evidence for this union is to be found in certain of the early coins of the Chalcidian peninsula. These coins, according to Head, probably were minted at Olynthos hardly later than the end of the sixth century B. C., although they have been assigned by others to Chalcis.[12] Herodotos, however, informs us that the Chalcidians first obtained possession of Olynthos about 479[13]. Since this is the case we can hardly ascribe these coins to Olynthos, for there is no reason to assign them to the Bottiaean city On the other hand, there is no need to deny their Chalcidian origin. It is fair to assume, then, that the coins were struck by the Chalcidians, settled in or near Sithonia. Numismatic evidence in this way corroborates and strengthens our assumption that the Chalcidians had united for certain purposes at least. They issued a common coinage and acted together in times of crisis[14].

---

the Chalcidic γένος. From those passages, however, we need not come to any such conclusion. If Herodotos had told us that the Chalcidians had furnished troops it would have been very easy for a reader to confuse the Chalcidians of Thrace with those of Euboea. This passage, taken by itself, cannot then be considered as conclusive evidence that Chalcis founded no colonies on the coast of Thrace, and the other evidence brought forward by Harrison is even more unsatisfactory. The fact that Eretria and Andros founded colonies in Thrace has not been questioned. It is hardly probable that Eretria's greatest rival, Chalcis, took no part in this colonization. Harrison, *Cl. Qu.*, vol. VI, 93ff, 165ff.

[10] Thuc. IV, 110, 114; Hdt. VIII, 127.
[11] This is expressed by the word γένος. For further discussion see below.
[12] *B. M. C. Mac.*, pp. XXXIV f.; Head, *Hist. Num.*,[2] *pp.* 207f.
[13] Hdt. VIII, 127. See below.
[14] When Olynthos commenced its coinage it remained true to Chalcidian tradition and adopted agonistic types similar to those in use during the previous century. The reverse type with its eagle points directly to Chalcis as the origin of the Chalcidian race. Harrison, *loc. cit.*, however, considers this as next to no evidence for a connection between Chalcis and the Chalcidians of Thrace. He bases his conclusion upon the well known fact that Elis also made use of the eagle type and says that the occurrence of agonistic types both on the earlier and the later coins of Olynthos makes it unnecessary to assume that the eagle type was borrowed by Olynthos from Chalcis. The evidence of a connection may be weak, but at least it cannot be lightly cast aside. When the similarity between names and coin types is so striking that confusion arises, we may assume that it is not so much the result of a coincidence as of premeditation. In either case, a hypothetical explanation of

Olynthos, about to play so great a part in the Chalcidic league, was originally settled by Bottiaeans[15]. Upon the defeat of the Persians at Salamis, Potidaea and the other cities of Pallenè revolted and a general uprising was feared by Artabazos. Olynthos was suspected of rebellious intentions and was captured. The city was then taken (480–479) from the Bottiaeans and was given by Artabazos to the Chalcidians under Critoboulos of Toronè[16].

this similarity of type, invented to suit a theory for which no positive evidence exists, must necessarily be viewed with suspicion.

Harrison has also attempted to show that the language of the Chalcidians resembled Eretrian, rather than Chalcidian. In his estimation the evidence points "not to Chalkis, nor to Euboea, at large, but to Eretria; though the Olynthian inscription lacks the most striking feature of Eretrian, the rhotacism of intervocalic σ." He goes on to say: "If, then, the Chalkidians of Thrace were derived from Chalkis, we must suppose that these features which at present connect Olynthos with Eretria were common to Eretria and Chalkis. If, as I suspect, the Chalkidians of Thrace were not derived from Chalkis, these features must be due to the influence of the neighboring colonies: Eretria's colonies, Mendè and Eion (and perhaps Dikaia), Mendè's colony, Nee-polis, and the Andrian colonies on the east coast." The weakness in this argument is pointed out by Harrison himself, the lack of inscriptions from Chalcis and her other colonies. Another difficulty is that the epigraphical evidence from Chalcidicè, except for coins, all dates from the fourth century, after many changes and much shifting of population had taken place. Harrison ought to have taken into consideration the evidence of the lettering on the early Olynthian coins. On one of them occurs the following inscription A↓ LK The form Ⴑ for Λ is peculiar to Chalcis and does not occur elsewhere in Euboea, and in Greece proper only in Boeotia and Attica. A later coin of the same type has the inscription ΟΛVN which points perhaps to Eretrian influence. *Numis. Chron.*, 1897, 276, pl. XIII, 6; cf. *Brit. Mus. Cat. Maced.*, p. 87, no. 2.

[15] Hdt. VIII, 127; Thuc. II, 99. The Bottiaeans were a Greek tribe and had once possessed territory on the lower Haliacmon and Ludias rivers, whence the growth of the Macedonian power had driven them to take refuge in what later became Botticè. Their two most important towns were Spartolos and Olynthos. Their migration to the Chalcidic peninsula probably took place in the sixth century, for the Macedonian power included this territory as early as the reign of Amyntas I. Thuc. II, 99; Hdt. V, 94; VII, 123, 127; Arist. *Ath. Pol.* 15; Köhler, *Sitz.-ber. d. Berl. Akad.* 1892, p. 345; 1897, p. 271; Strabo, VII, 329, frg. 11; 330, frgs. 20, 22, 23.

[16] Hdt. VIII, 126–129. It is worthy of note that the Chalcidians remained faithful to the Persians, while Pallenè, settled by Eretrians and Corinthians, revolted, and the Bottiaeans were suspected of disloyal intentions. The attempt to recapture Potidaea failed although a Scionaean captain within the town tried to betray it. In the battle at Plataea 300 Potidaeans took part. They were stationed with the Corinthians, by whom the city had been

The Greek settlement of Olynthos, then, did not take place until the first years of the fifth century. This is an indication of the tenacity with which the Greeks clung to the seaboard, only gradually moving into the interior. Thus Olynthos in 480–479 had become a Chalcidian city and this fact found expression in the coins of the town. Some of them show types that were common to the city of Chalcis, and one of them has the inscription A↓ LK upon its reverse. A later coin of the same type has in its stead an inscription showing that it was coined at Olynthos[17]. These coins then substantiate the account given by Herodotos and show that a feeling of kinship and unity existed among the Chalcidians of Thrace at the beginning of the fifth century.

The settlement of Olynthos by colonists taken from a number of related Chalcidian cities no doubt served to strengthen the union of these cities and to give to Olynthos special importance. It would be natural for the Chalcidians to regard it as a common possession in which all had a part. In time it became the center of Chalcidian interests, around which a closer and more permanent union grew up. This explains the importance of the

founded. No other city of the Chalcidic peninsula was represented. Hdt. IX, 28; Ditt. *Syll.*[2] 7.

The account given by Herodotos of the capture of Olynthos, however, is of greater importance. The expression τὸ Χαλκιδικὸν γένος is again used to describe the Chalcidians. From this passage it is clear that the Chalcidians, to a certain extent, at least, were united among themselves. They adopted a common policy and remained faithful to Persia. For this they were rewarded with the city of Olynthos, which they settled by joint action. The use of the term γένος in this passage is not so striking as in Hdt. VII, **185**, and it can not be taken as proof that the Chalcidians were a Greek tribe, in no way related to Chalcis. If any inference is to be drawn from these two passages, it is that the Chalcidians were conscious of their common origin to such an extent, perhaps, that a primitive union had been formed. The tribal theory, brought forward by Harrison, *loc. cit.*, would be adequate if we had evidence in its favour; but ancient writers fail even to suggest this, and the weight of their authority is on the other side. That there was an early Chalcidian union is not surprising, when we consider that the Chalcidians of the west acted together in times of crisis.

[17] *Numis. Chron.*, 1897, p. 276, pl. XIII, 6. Cf. *Brit. Mus. Cat. Maced.*, p. 87, no. 2. This coin might have been referred to Chalcis if the obverse had not contained the figure of a horse cantering, a type used by the Thracian Chalcidians. Hence we must ascribe it to a feeling of unity among them and to their settlement of Olynthos by united action.

city during the Peloponnesian War and the readiness with which the smaller Chalcidian towns upon the coast gave up their homes and migrated to it[18].

Shortly after the formation of the Delian Confederacy, Cimon besieged and took Eion on the Strymon, then in the hands of the Persians. Likewise the Persian garrisons were driven out of the cities on the Thracian coast, Doriscos alone excepted.[18a] Since no ancient authority tells us when the Greek cities of the Chalcidic peninsula enrolled themselves in the confederacy it is impossible to decide whether they waited until Cimon appeared in their neighbourhood with an armed force, or whether, even before this time, they had accepted membership in the new league and expressed their willingness to contribute their share in its expenses. We only know that they were admitted to the confederacy at an early date while Aristides was still acting as assessor.[18b] Aside from this, our knowledge of the history of the Chalcidic peninsula during the fifth century until the Peloponnesian War is almost entirely confined to what may be gleaned from the Attic Quota lists, which are in a very fragmentary condition and do not commence until 454. It is noteworthy that in some of the earlier lists cities which later became identified with the Chalcidian League are found combined. For example in 454, Olynthos, Scabla, and Assera are placed together; Mecyperna and Stolos also made a joint contribution.[19] In 445 mention is made of the

---

[18] Thuc. I, 58.

[18a] Thuc. I, 98; Hdt. VII, 106f.; Plut. *Cimon*, 7; Polyaen. VII, 24.

[18b] Thuc. V, 18. Cf. Beloch, *Rhein. Mus.*, 1888, p. 75; Busolt, *Griech. Geschichte*, III, 1, 228. Francotte, *Les Finances des Cités Grecques*, pp. 101f., while denying that the cities of Chalcidicè were assessed by Aristides, admits that they became members of the Delian League at an early date.

[19] *I. G.*, I, 226. 'Ολύνθ[ιοι]Σκα Μεκυπερ[να]ῖοι
βλαῖο[ι 'Ασ]σε Στόλιοι ⌈ᴴ . . . |
ρῖται H. . . . . Ⱶ.

Theop. frg. 145: Σκάβαλα, χώρα 'Ερετριέων. Theop. frg. 147 gives Assera to the Chalcidians. Arist., *Hist. An.*, 519 a 14, speaks of a river ἐν τῇ Χαλκιδκῇ τῇ ἐπὶ τῆς Θρᾳκης ἐν τῇ 'Ασσυρίτιδι. The passages, Hdt. VII, 122 f. and 185, do not necessarily exclude Assa from the Chalcidian tribe. Olynthos was of course Chalcidic. Thus we have the union of an Eretrian and two Chalcidian towns, so far as payment of tribute to Athens was concerned. Is not this an indication that there was no great difference between the two classes of towns? If Harrison's thesis were true, that the Chalcidians were a tribe like the Bottiaeans, and not colonists from Chalcis, there would

Sermylians and their συντελεῖs [20]. Athenian policy, however, seems to have been directed against such incipient unions and in the later lists each city is credited with its own individual contribution. The union of Olynthos with Scabla and Assera is of peculiar interest, for it is the first indication we have of a union among the Chalcidic cities in which Olynthos was the central and moving figure. It was probably at the time when this union was dissolved that a change was made in the

---

be no link to bind an Eretrian colony with two Chalcidic villages. On the other hand if the Chalcidic towns were also colonies of Euboea, similar conditions would prevail in Chalcidian and Eretrian towns and there would be no material difference between the two.

Stolos and Mecyperna, *I. G.*, I, 226, are also found in the list of 454 together. Stolos we know was a Chalcidian colony and Strabo calls Mecyperna the harbour (VII, 330, frg. 29) of Olynthos. Steph. Byz.: Στῶλος, πόλις μία τῶν ἐν Θράκῃ βαρβαρικῶν ἃς μετήνεγκαν ἐκ τῶν Ἡδοννῶν οἱ Χαλκιδεῖς εἰς τὰς αυτῶν πόλεις.

[20] *I. G.*, I, 235: | н Σερμυλιε̃ς κα[ὶ]συν. Who were the συντελεῖs of the Sermylians? Böhnecke has made the suggestion that Arnae, which was somewhere not far from Sermylia, was a colony of that town. *Dem. Lyk. Hyp.*, p. 398 and *Forschungen a. d. Gebiete d. Att. Redner*, p. 155. Steph. Byz. gives us the following information, Ἄρνη τῆς Ἐρασινίων πρὸς τῇ Θράκῃ. The name Ἐρασινίων has been a stumbling block to all editors and commentators, and various emendations have been suggested. Thucydides, IV, 103, definitely states that Arnae was Chalcidian and numismatic evidence confirms his statement. Böhnecke believes that the name Arnae is preserved in the modern Derna, which lies in the neighbourhood of Ormilia. *Dem. Hyp. Lyk.* p. 389. Ormilia without doubt is the ancient Sermylia. Thus he would emend by substituting Ἑρμυλίων or Σερμυλίων for Ἐρασινίων. This is a possible emendation and, if it is correct, we may assume that Arnae paid its tribute as a dependency of Sermylia. Thucydides shows that Arnae was in existence during the fifth century and that it was perhaps a day's march from Bromiskos. As it is not found in the tribute lists and was important enough to strike coins it is not at all improbable that its tribute was paid with that of the presumably Chalcidian Sermylia. I am inclined to question Böhnecke's location of Arnae at Derna. It seems more probable that the name of Calarnae of Mela, II, 2, 30, is to be identified with the Arnae of Thucydides. *Inter Strymona et Athon turris Calarnaea et portus* Κάπρου Λιμήν, *urbs Acanthos.* Steph. Byz.: Κάλαρνα, πόλις Μακεδονίας, ὡς Λούκιλλος ὁ Ταρραῖος.

The tribute of Sermylia presents several interesting problems. In 454 it amounted to the immense sum of 17.72 talents. Only Abdera and Aegina paid a higher tribute, so far as the accounts are preserved. In 451 the tribute was 5.91⅔ talents. In the years 449 and 447 Sermylia paid three talents. In 445 Sermylia and its συντελεῖs paid a tribute of five talents. In this year there is no possible doubt about the reading, Σερμυλι[ε̃s] κα[ὶ] συν. In the years 444 and 443 the tribute remained the same but the inscriptions have preserved no reference to συντελεῖs. Until the year 438 we have no record of the amount paid by Sermylia but in that year the tribute was lowered to four and one half talents. It was in that year that Athens was active in and around Chalcidicè. In 439 or thereabouts the tribute of several Chalcidian cities was raised. Thus the reduction of the tribute of Sermylia is

Olynthian coinage. The inscription ΟΛΥΝ took the place of $\frac{AL}{LK}$ which had been used heretofore. For many years nothing came of the early Chalcidian union. It is evident, however, that Athens was not able to destroy the feeling of unity that existed in the minds of the Olynthians and their Chalcidic neighbors. The crystalization of this feeling was due to an impulse from without. This came from Macedon.

----

noteworthy. It is also to be noted that in 438 several cities paid no tribute and that in the list of the following year ten new names are found for the first time. It was in 437 that Amphipolis was founded. Of these new tributaries, so far as their location is known, Piloros is the only one that could possibly have been subject to Sermylia. The year 436 saw discontent in Chalcidicè and for the first time, so far as we know, Sermylia paid no tribute. This may have been due to dissatisfaction because she had been deprived of her control over neighbouring towns. Other towns joined with Sermylia in refusing to pay their customary tribute and perhaps for the same reason, *I. G.*, I, 226–244.

CHAPTER II

FORMATION OF THE CHALCIDIC LEAGUE

Alexander I, the Philhellene, had extended the Macedonian sphere of influence on all sides, but by so doing he had made certain the coming conflict with the Greeks. These people then, settled upon the coasts that were necessary to Macedon if she was to obtain the power that was hers by every right, must, sooner or later, either become incorporated in the growing state of their powerful neighbour or make it commercially dependent upon them. Philip II realized this fully, when, conscious of his superiority, he replied to the Olynthian embassy that it was impossible for the Chalcidian power to exist side by side with that of Macedon[1].

Perdiccas, Alexander's successor as king of Macedon, had several rivals to contend with, and, for many years, was in no position to take an aggressive attitude. While he was strengthening his power, Athens was not idle. She fully realized the importance of maintaining her position and of putting every obstacle in the way of further Macedonian extension. When once she saw that the control of the Strymon was important for both states, she did not rest until Ἐννέα ὁδοί, the strategic point upon the river, was in her possession and she had founded the city of Amphipolis upon that site[2]. Then a policy, none too straightforward, was set into operation against Perdiccas. Athens supported pretenders to his throne and encouraged rebellious subjects in their attempts to break away from the authority of the Macedonian crown[3].

----

[1] Dem. IX, 11.
[2] The first attempt to found a Greek city on this important site was made by Aristagoras, 498–7. About thirty years later Athens made an unsuccessful attempt. Thuc. I, 100; IV, 102f; Diod. XII, 68; Schol. Aesch. II, 31; cf. Hdt. IX, 75; Paus. I, 29, 4.
[3] Thuc. I, 57, 59; II, 95.

In the years immediately preceding the Peloponnesian War more than forty cities of the Chalcidic peninsula were tributary to Athens. The richer and more important of them were situated upon the two peninsulas of Pallenè and Sithonia. In comparison with these, Olynthos and the other cities of the base of Chalcidicè were small and unimportant towns. Acanthos, the chief Andrian colony, and Spartolos, a Bottiaean city, both surpassed Olynthos in resources and importance[4].

At this time there seems to have been more or less discontent among the Athenian allies in the Chalcidic peninsula. In the year 440 several unknown Thracian cities paid no tribute[5] and in the list of 438-7 again there are a number of absentees.* It has been suggested that this is to be connected with the general feeling of unrest in the Athenian Empire, which found its expression in the revolt of Samos. In the next year, however, Athens was free to turn her attention to Chalcidicè. It was at this time that Amphipolis was founded† and that many new names were placed upon the Attic quota lists. In the quota

---

[4] *I. G.*, I, 237, 239, 242, 243, 244, 259. If we take the lists for the years 443. 441, 438, 437, 436, and 427 and compare the tribute of the various cities we can come to a rough estimate of their relative importance. The following table compiled from the lists of these years shows how small Olynthos was when compared with its neighbours:

City	Year	Tribute in talents	Year	Tribute
Aineia	443	3	427	⅙
Acanthos	443	3	427	3
Spartolos	436	$3^1/_{12}$		
Mendè	437	8	427	8
Olynthos	438	2		
Potidaea	436	15		
Sermylia	437	4½		
Scionè	438	15	427	9
Toronè	441	6	427	12

The combined tribute from the peninsula of Pallenè was about forty talents, that of Sithonia about fifteen, and that of Actè about five. The combined territory of these three peninsulas was approximately one-third of the area of the base of the larger peninsula, which paid roughly about twenty talents. Thus we see that Pallenè nearly equalled the combined wealth of the remainder of Chalcidicè, and that Olynthos was quite small at this time with its meagre two talents tribute.

[5] *I. G.*, I, 240.

* *I. G.*, I, 242-4. In 438-7 Galepsos, Scapsa, Stolos, and Argilos pay no tribute.

† Thuc. IV, 102f; Diod. XII, 32; Polyaen. VI, 53.

list for the year 437–6 about ten names are to be found for the
first time[6]. It is not probable that all of these were new members of the Athenian Empire. Without doubt, the majority of
them had paid tribute before through their wealthier and more
powerful neighbours, to whom they owed some sort of allegiance. In this way the allegiance of these towns was transferred
directly to Athens; and perhaps the cities that had failed to pay
their tribute during the preceding year were thus punished by
a loss of territory. It is noteworthy that there were no important reductions of tribute at this time. The tribute of Spartolos,
indeed, was increased, notwithstanding the fact that a Bottiaean
town appears as tributary to Athens for the first time[7]. The
most notable example of an increase in tribute occurred at Potidaea. There the original sum of six talents was increased to
fifteen. We know no special reason for this, since the Potidaean
tribute had been paid during the Samian revolt. Thus we see
that Athens was not idle and gained for the time being, at least,
both in tribute and in a widened sphere of direct commercial
influence. Her particularist tendencies, however, soon brought
about discontent in some of the leading cities, for in the year
436 several of them paid no tribute[8]. In Spartolos, Olynthos,
and Potidaea this same feeling of unrest was more slow in coming to a head. The final step was taken at the instigation of
Perdiccas.

We have seen that Perdiccas had good grounds for opposing
the Athenians and for trying to weaken their power, and that
it was good policy for him to encourage every movement by
which the Athenian allies might be severed from their allegiance. With these things in mind, he entered into negotiations

---

[6] *I. G.*, I, 243. In the list of 437 the names, Aioleion, Haisa, Gigonos,
Kithas, Cleonae, Piloros, Pistasos, Sartè, Sinos, Smilla, and Tindè are found
for the first time.

[7] Aioleion probably was Bottiaean, Theop. frg. 140, Oxford ed., (*ex coniec-
tura*), and perhaps Gigonos and Haisa were also. Sartè may have been tributary to Toronè and Piloros to Sermylia.

[8] *I. G.*, I, 238, 242, 243, 244. In the year 436, Stageiros, Stolos, Scionè, Sermylia, Mendè, Toronè, and Aphytis paid no tribute. The tribute of Potidaea
was raised from six talents in 438 to fifteen talents in 436. The tribute of
Spartolos was also raised during this period from two to three and one-
twelfth talents.

with the discontented cities[9]. It was greatly to his advantage
to persuade them to revolt; for if they did so, his hands would
be free to deal with the pretenders to his throne whom Athens
was supporting, and the Athenians would then be too busy in
crushing the revolt to put any large force into the field against
him.

Athens, learning of these negotiations and fearing for the
loyalty of the discontented Potidaea, commanded the city to raze
the walls on the side toward Pallenè, to give hostages, and to
sever all connections with its mother city Corinth[10]. Potidaea
immediately sent envoys to Athens in an attempt to avoid com-
pliance with these harsh commands. Furthermore it prepared
for the revolt, asking assistance from Corinth and the Peloponnese[11].

Perdiccas also sought to gain allies who were openly hostile to
Athens. In this way the winter of 433-2 passed[12]; and in the
following spring the Athenians decided that the time for action
had come if they were to forestall the revolt and the expected alliance between Macedon, Potidaea, the Bottiaeans, and the Chalcidians. Archestratos was sent against Perdiccas with thirty
ships and one thousand hoplites. He also was entrusted with
the task of taking hostages from the city of Potidaea, of demol-
ishing its wall, and of preventing any attempts at rebellion[13].

Influenced by promises of assistance from Sparta and a number of its own neighbours, Potidaea revolted early in 432, before
the arrival of the Athenian fleet. An alliance was formed with
the Chalcidians and the Bottiaeans, who also revolted. Perdiccas joined this alliance and persuaded the inhabitants of the
Chalcidic coast towns to emigrate to Olynthos, giving to them a
part of the Mygdonian territory for cultivation, so long as the
war with Athens should last[14].

The extent of the original revolt can be made out roughly from
an inspection of the quota lists. The names of many towns dis-

---

[9] Thuc. I, 57.
[10] Thuc. I, 56f.
[11] Thuc. I, 58.
[12] Thuc. I, 57.
[13] Ibid.
[14] Thuc. I, 58, 71.

2

appeared about this time, although the fragmentary condition of the tablets does not allow one to be at ,all certain about details. That the rebellion was general throughout Bottice, extending perhaps to the coast about Strepsa and Gigonos, the territory about Olynthos, southern Crousis, and the coasts of northern Sithonia can be clearly made out. Pallenè, except Potidaea, the greater part of Sithonia, Actè, and the eastern coast with its Andrian colonies remained loyal[15].

Thucydides tells us that an alliance was formed including Potidaea, the Chalcidians, and the Bottiaeans[16]. That this alliance culminated in a close union is attested by certain contemporary

---

[15] *I. G.*, I, 256. This list for the year 428 is complete in its Thracian part and is to be compared with the lists for the two following years, *I. G.*, I, 257, 426–5; *I. G.*, I, 259; cf. Cavaignac, *Le Trésor d'Athènes*, pp. XXXVI f.; *B. S. A.*, XV, 229–242. The latter has been assigned to the year 427–6. The list of Thracian tributaries is complete. The omissions are as follows, Potidaea, Olynthos, Spartolos, Strepsa, Stolos, Assera, Aioleion, Milkoros, Tindé, Scapsa, Cleonae, Haisa, Gigonos, Kithas, Smilla, Piloros, the Phegetioi, Dicaea, Pharbelos, Scabla, Mecyperna, Sermylia, and Singos. By comparing with *I. G.*, I, 257 (426–5) we are able to exclude from the list of revolting cities Dicaea, Cleonae, and Aioleion, a Bottiaean town (Theop. frg. 140). Sermylia and Scabla are found in *I. G.*, I, 255 which is to be placed early in the war. Of the remaining cities, Potidaea, Olynthos, Spartolos, and Stolos revolted, as we learn from Thucydides I, **56ff**; V, **18.** Assera (Theop.) frg. 147; Aristotle, *Hist. An.*, 519 a 14), Milkoros (Theop. frg. 150), Tindè (Steph. Byz. Τίνδιον), Scapsa (Steph. Byz., Κάψα; cf. Hdt. VII, **123**: Κάμψα) are known to have been Chalcidic at some time or other. Scapsa appears in *I. G.*, I, **263** (after 425–4) but this may only mean that it had returned to its Athenian allegiance. As it was near Aineia which did not revolt and situated in Crousis, I shall not include it in the list of revolting cities. Piloros and Mecyperna, the harbour of Olynthos, lay between Assera and Olynthos, both of which were Chalcidian, and Singos was not far distant from Piloros. Haisa, Gigonos, Kithas, and Smilla were situated in Crousis, south of Aineia. Steph. Byz.: Αἶσα, Σμίλα, Γίγωνος; Hdt. VII, **123**; Theop. frg. 338. They are bracketed with Tindè in a joint payment for the year 437 (*I. G.*, I, 243). Pharbelos was a colony of Eretria (Steph. Byz.), and perhaps was situated near Pallenè. Strepsa was a town on the borders of Macedon. Aesch. II, **27**; Thuc. I, **61** (?); Steph. Byz.: Στρέψα, πόλις Μακεδονίας. As it appears in the τάξις φόρου for 425, it may not have revolted, but its absence from the lists *I. G.*, I, 256, 257, and 259 is suspicious. The Phegetioi are otherwise unknown. From this list it is possible to judge as to the extent of the revolt. It must be remembered however that there is no evidence to prove that any of these towns revolted in 432. A part of Crousis, at least, including Aineia, remained faithful as we know from Thucydides (II, **79**) and the tribute lists. This limits the revolt on the north-west. In Pallenè the revolt did not extend beyond Potidaea. Sermylia in northern Sithonia did not take part in the revolt, which would make one hesitate before including Singos in our list of revolting towns. Acanthos and the Andrian colonies in the east remained faithful. Thus we have established the limits given in the text.

[16] Thuc. I, **58.**

coins[17]. Head has dated these coins in the early years of the fourth century, but they belong, no doubt, to this earlier period.[*] It has long been recognized that a change in the system of coinage was one of the accompaniments of the Chalcidic revolt from Athenian rule.   Until 432 the Attic standard was in common use in a great majority of the cities of this region, but this soon gave way to the Phoenician standard, then in use in Macedon.   Macedonian influence had been a powerful factor in bringing about separation from Athens, and Macedonian trade was growing more and more important.   Hence the change from the Attic to the Macedonian standard was a natural one for the Chalcidians to make as soon as possible after their separation from Athens.   According to the hitherto accepted classification of the Olynthian coin series a break occurred, extending from about 432 to the rise of the league of the Chalcidians in the first decade of the fourth century.   The Chalcidian adoption of the Phoenician standard is thus assigned to the fourth century, when Macedon had already ceased to use that standard.   This classification is based upon the assumption that the Chalcidian league did not come into existence until after the Peloponnesian War.   We would naturally expect Olynthos to have been one of the first to adopt the new standard; and as the leader of the Chalcidians in their revolt against Athens it had need of money for carrying on the war.   It is obvious that this was no time for a suspension of coinage[18].

Hence we must refer the ruder examples of the famous Chalcidic coinage to the years of the Peloponnesian War and not to the fourth century.   There are further reasons for placing the beginning of the Apollo series of Chalcidic coins at so early a

---

[17] The coins referred to are those of the Chalcidians, the Bottiaeans, the Acanthians, and the Arnaeans, having the figure of Apollo upon the obverse and with a cithara for the reverse type.   Cf. Head, *Historia Numorum*,[2] pp. 208f., 213; *B. M. C. Mac. p.* 63, nos. 2f; p. 36, nos. 40–41; p. 62, no. 1; p. 87, no. 5.   For a full discussion of these coins see *Classical Philology*, vol. IX, pp. 24–34.

[*] Walker has assigned these coins and the formation of the Chalcidic league to the end of the fifth century, 421–400.   Apparently Head has accepted this date.   See *Ency. Brit. Olynthus.*

[18] No other important city of the Chalcidic peninsula suspended its coinage during the war, excepting of course the ones destroyed or captured by Athens. On the other hand some of the revolting cities issued coins for the first time.

date. There were at least four states, the Chalcidian, the Bottiaean, Arnae, and Acanthos, that adopted the coin type bearing upon the obverse the head of Apollo Laureate and upon the reverse a cithara and the name of the state issuing the coinage. It is clear that this uniformity of coinage could not have existed unless there had been a close political alliance between the states issuing the coins, such as we find for example about the same time between Rhodes, Ephesos, Iasos, Cnidos, and Byzantion[19]. Therefore we can only assign these coins to a period in which the Bottiaeans, the Acanthians, and the Chalcidians were on very intimate and friendly terms. This was not the case in the early years of the fourth century. We have a treaty of about the year 390 or 389 between the Chalcidian League and Amyntas king of Macedon[20]. From this treaty we learn that the Chalcidians were at war with Acanthos and the Bottiaeans. This hostility, as we know, was due to the comprehensive plans that the Chalcidians were making for the expansion of their league[21]. Neither the Bottiaeans nor the Acanthians were willing to become members of this league. Acanthos, an important Andrian colony situated on the east coast of the Chalcidic peninsula, may have attempted to exercise a hegemony over the Andrian colonies or perhaps even to unite them as the Chalcidians and the Bottiaeans had united[22]. There is some slight evidence that these were her aims soon after her revolt to Brasidas in 424.* In any case she could not suffer with patience Chalcidic possession of strategic points in her immediate neighbourhood. Thus when the Chalcidians became masters of Thyssos in 420 and of Dion in 417, towns situated upon the peninsula of Actè[23], Acanthos began to feel jealous of the growing Chalcidian power. This jealousy became acute soon after the Peloponnesian War and continued until after the defeat of the Chalcidians by Sparta in 379. Thus it is impossible to conceive of any close alliance between Acanthos and the Chalcidians during this period.

---

[19] Hill, *Historical Greek Coins*, nos. 32 f.
[20] Ditt. *Syll.*,² 77.
[21] Xen. *Hell.*, V, 2, 11 ff.
[22] The Bottiaeans had a common coinage and made a joint treaty with Athens in 420. Hicks and Hill, no. 68; *B. M. C. Macedon*, p. 63.
* See pp. 78ff.
[23] Thuc. V, 35, 82.

As for the Bottiaeans, they enrolled themselves among the Athenian allies in 420 at the time of the peace between Athens and Sparta[24]. The Bottiaeans were close neighbours of the Chalcidians on the west. They had formed a loose confederation as an inscription and coins testify,[*] and looked askance at the growth of the Chalcidian league. As in the case of Acanthos, they were at war with the Chalcidians[25] about 390 but were conquered very soon after[26]. Thus we can date the beginning of the breach between the two states definitely in 420, when the Bottiaeans accepted the terms of the peace and became Athenian allies. The Chalcidians were at war with Athens for several years, at least, after this date.

Finally the coins that indicate an alliance between the Chalcidians and the Bottiaeans must have been struck before the year 420 and after the revolt in 432. Having seen that these coins belong to the first decade of the war we can have no hesitation in connecting them with the alliance which Thucydides says was concluded between these two states. The fact that the revolting states adopted a common coin type is an indication that the alliance was very close indeed, and the further fact that the coins were struck upon the standard in use in Macedon seems to point to the influence of Perdiccas. It was largely through his efforts that the revolt had taken place. The Bottiaean state and the Chalcidians were the first members of this monetary alliance. Acanthos must have joined soon after 424 when it revolted to Brasidas[27]. The fourth state to adopt this coinage was the little place of Arnae. Thucydides does not tell of its revolt, but he mentions it as a Chalcidic town in the winter of 424–3[28]. Of the other cities that we might expect to find in this league, Potidaea, Toronè, Mendè, and Scionè fell to Athens soon after their revolt. Except for Mendè, almost no coins of these cities, struck on the Phoenician standard—the standard recently adopted by the revolting states—are in existence and these are of small value.

[24] Note 22; *I. G.*, I, 260; cf. notes 5 and 9, chap. VIII.
[*] See note 22.
[25] Ditt. *Syll.*,[2] 77.
[26] Isaeos, V. 42: τῆς Ὀλυνθίας ἐν Σπαρτώλῳ; cf. Jebb, *Attic Orators*, II, p. 354.
[27] Thuc. IV. 84–88.
[28] Thuc. IV, 103.

This monetary league can not have existed for any length of time, as we see from the fact that the coins which have come down to us are few and small in value, a tetrobol from Olynthos, obols from Acanthos and Arnae and copper coins of the Bottiaeans. The gradual separation of Chalcidic and Bottiaean interests is shown by a coin of the latter state, retaining the cithara but having for the obverse type not the head of Apollo but that of Artemis[29]. The league had been formed in direct opposition to the Athenian power, and when once the purpose of the league had been gained, namely, freedom from the burdens imposed by Athens, and when the Bottiaeans became reconciled with the latter state, there was no bond strong enough to hold it together.

What bearing does the foregoing discussion have upon the question of the origin of the Chalcidic League? It is generally agreed that the Apollo coins issued from the Olynthian mint formed a league coinage and were not strictly speaking Olynthian coins at all. This is shown by the fact that all of the types that had been in use for the coinage of the city of Olynthos were laid aside in favor of one that had a more general application[30]. Moreover the name of the city gives way to that of the league. Upon the reverse of all of the new coins the inscription ΧΑΛΚΙΔΕΩΝ occurs. Upon the obverse of one of these Chalcidian coins is the inscription ΟΛΥΝΘ[Ι.[31] This coin is to be placed at the beginning of the series before the city had become entirely

---

[29] B. M. C. Maced., p. 63, nos. 1 and 4; Head, Hist. Num.,² p. 213. The next step was the rejection of the cithara for the reverse type and the adoption of the figure of a bull. We have a bronze coin of Pausanias, king of Macedon, which seems to have been struck upon a coin of this type. While the chronology of the Macedonian kings is very uncertain, we can date this coin at least before 390. Imhoof-Blumer, Monn. Gr., p. 66, no. 6.

[30] Thuc. I, 118. The account given by Thucydides in this passage is worthy of consideration here. We are told that the Delphian God gave his sanction to the war and promised to side with the Spartans. Without doubt the Chalcidians were acquainted with this oracle. After the revolt when the Chalcidians and their allies were considering the adoption of a new coin type, what one more satisfactory was to be found than the image of the God under whose protection they were fighting? Amphipolis too, when it revolted, adopted the head of Apollo for the obverse type on its coinage. It would seem probable then that there was some connection between the oracle given at Delphi and the adoption by the Chalcidians and their neighbours of the Apollo type for their new coinage.

[31] B. M. C. Maced., p. 87, no. 5; Head, Hist. Num.,² p. 209.

identified with the league, for the name of the city soon disappeared and was never replaced upon the coins. In conclusion, since the Apollo series of Chalcidic coins had its beginning about 432 and since it was distinctly the coinage of the Chalcidians and not merely of the city of Olynthos, we must then infer that there was a Chalcidian state at this early date. A consolidated currency is one of the surest signs of a close political union between states that have been hitherto autonomous and the fact that at so early a date there was this distinct Chalcidic coinage proves conclusively that the feeling of Chalcidic unity had crystalized into actual union in the administration of internal affairs.

Thus within the larger monetary league, we find a union of Chalcidic towns with a common coinage and headed by Olynthos[32]. We have seen traces of the beginnings of union even during the sixth and fifth centuries, extending down to the time of the Athenian supremacy. Even as the colonies of Chalcis in the west often acted together as a unit in times of crisis, so those upon the northern peninsula never lost that feeling of kinship which seems to have distinguished the Chalcidian colonies. Their interests were common ones and all things seemed to favour the formation of a state out of the autonomous Chalcidian towns. Now that Perdicas had persuaded many of the seacoast towns to move *en masse* to Olynthos, nothing could be more natural than that a closer political union should be formed[33]. It is impossible to state with certainty what towns were destroyed or how many of the Chalcidians joined the new league. Such places in the immediate vicinity of Olynthos as Stolos*, Mecyperna†, Milkoros, Assera, and Piloros, were undoubtedly among

---

[32] Xen. *Hell.*, V, 2, 12. Here we have a concise history of the Chalcidic league up to the year 383. In this account two steps are mentioned. The first naturally refers to the measures taken by Olynthos and the small seacoast towns. The second, introduced by ἔπειτα δέ and speaking of τῶν μειζόνων, gives us an account of the growth of the Chalcidian power that took place chiefly in the early years of the fourth century. Cf. Strabo, VII, 329, frg. 11; Polyb. IX, 28, 2.

[33] The fact that the inhabitants of the smaller Chalcidic towns were so willing to remove to Olynthos, destroying their old homes and leaving all that to a Greek was so dear, the political independence of his πόλις, shows conclusively that the tie between the colonies in the neighbourhood of Olynthos was generally recognized and was stronger than a mere feeling of relationship.

* Strabo, IX, 408, 23; Steph. Byz. Στῶλος.

† Strabo, VII, 330, frg. 29.

the constituent members.[34]   As the revolt became more general, a
larger portion of the Chalcidic peninsula was included in the
territory of the league[35].

We have the coins to show that there was a union among certain Chalcidian towns during the first years of the Peloponnesian War, and this is substantiated by the account that Thucydides gives of operations in Chalcidicè.   The coins give evidence
of internal union.   A careful reading of Thucydides will show
that as far as external affairs were concerned the Chalcidians
acted together and formed a distinct body[36].   The word
ΧΑΛΚΙΔΕΩΝ upon the coins shows that this was the official name
for the state.   Thus when Thucydides speaks of the Chalcidians,
we must infer *a priori* that he means the people as a state and
not as a race.   The narrative of Thucydides, however, presents
more cogent arguments than any *a priori* reasoning.   According
to him the Chalcidians carried on the war in the name of the
whole people, conducted negotiations, received embassies, declared truce, and made alliances.

After they had sworn alliance with the Bottiaeans and with
Potidaea, at the advice of Perdiccas, king of Macedon, they took
measures to enlarge Olynthos, their capital city, and to strengthen
the league generally by pulling down the smaller sea-coast
towns.   These small towns would have been nearly impossible
to defend during the long war that followed.   Their inhabitants
the Chalcidians transferred, in large part, to the metropolis.
This action is proof positive that there was in existence at that
time a close political union among these cities.   Otherwise such
an anoikism could never have taken place, for the foundation
of Megalopolis shows how unwilling even the Greek villages were

---

[34] *I. G.*, I, 256. This list belongs to 428 and is complete for the Thracian
district.   Hence one may conclude that the cities not found in that list were
not Athenian allies at that time, unless we know something to the contrary;
cf. *I. G.*, I, 259, (427–6) ; Cavaignac, *Le Trésor d' Athènes*, pp. XXXVI f.:
B. S. A., vol. XV, p. 240; cf. note 15, *sup*.

[35] It is not necessary to conclude that all members of the league shared
in the anoikism or that all of the Chalcidian cities were originally included
in the κοινόν.   Toronè is an example of a Chalcidian city that remained
master of its own affairs, and Stolos was a member of the league that was
not destroyed.   So we may judge from the fact that it receives special mention in the treaty of 421. Thuc. V, 18.

[36] Cf. Swoboda, *Arch.-epigr. Mitth.*, VII, pp. 55–59.

to merge their individualities in a larger union, how little they
wished to transfer their political rights to a body of which they
would form only a part. In the case of Megalopolis the destruction of the villages was decided upon by the Arcadian state for
protection against Sparta, both for the κοινόν and for the un-
protected villages that were to form the new city. In one respect conditions were more favorable for the synoikism of Megalopolis than for the anoikism at Olynthos. In the one case the
city was of new origin and the inhabitants, so far as citizenship
was concerned, were all on an equal footing from the beginning.
In Olynthos the citizens of the razed towns were not only to lose
their old rights but even to be absorbed into a long established
πόλις, where they would form but a small part of the citizen
body. This anoikism, then, could not have been brought about so
generally, with so little friction and unwillingness, if it had been
a measure suggested by Perdiccas, merely for the protection and
strengthening of Olynthos at the expense of the other Chalcidians. This is what Thucydides seems to suggest when he says,
ἀνοικίσασθαι ἐς "Ολυνθον μίαν τε πόλιν ταύτην ἰσχυρὰν ποιήσασθαι[37]. It must
have occurred, therefore, as a result of the action taken by a
Chalcidic κοινόν in which the principles of συμπολιτεία καὶ ἐπιγαμία
καὶ ἔγκτησις were expressed.[38] Without the employment of force,
no other conditions would have been sufficiently potent to bring
about such a thorough anoikism. We cannot know with certainty what cities took part in this movement to strengthen Olynthos. With the material at hand we must be content with the
knowledge that it is possible to trace the outlines of the process
which resulted in giving to Olynthos the power necessary for the
part she was to play during the next century until her final conquest by Philip of Macedon.

We have seen that the account of the anoikism, given by Thucydides, implies the existence of a union of some sort among the
Chalcidians. If we read him further, we will see that οἱ Χαλκιδῆς
οἱ ἐπὶ Θρᾳκης acted together as one body, just as any other state.
That this was the official title is most certain[39]. How then does

---

[37] Thuc. I, 58.
[38] Xen. Hell., V, 2, 12; 19.
[39] Ditt. Syll.,[2] 121; I. G., II, 17; F. H. G., II, 153; Arist. Pol., II, 12,
14; Strabo, VII, 329, frg. 11.

Thucydides use the term οἱ Χαλκιδῆς and what meaning does he
give to it? Does it mean to him the Chalcidian state? The answer will be in the affirmative. In the first place he tells us that
the Chalcidians swore alliances with the Bottiaeans and with
Potidaea[40]. It is important to notice that Thucydides says
that the Chalcidians did this ¡and not the Chalcidian cities.
Hence one must infer that this was the action of a union and
not of individual cities. In the battle before Potidaea, the Chalcidians[41] formed a distinct body of troops stationed at Olynthos with the Macedonian horse and the other allies. This is our
first indication of a Chalcidian army. After Aristeus made his
escape from Potidaea, he remained among the Chalcidians, aid-
ing them in the war[42]. Perdiccas in 431, after his reconciliation
with Athens, made an expedition ἐπὶ Χαλκιδέας with the Athenian
troops under Phormio[43]. In 430 Hagno lead another expedition
against the Chalcidians, τοὺς ἐπὶ Θρᾴκης, and against Potidaea.[44]
Phormio was no longer περὶ Χαλκιδέας. The next summer Xenophon led an expedition against the Thracian Chalcidians and
the Bottiaeans.[45] Spartolos was hard pressed, and traitors and
pro-Athenian sympathizers were already at work, but at the request of the revolutionary party, viz., the friends of the Chalcidians, assistance came from Olynthos. These reinforcements,
however, Thucydides calls Chalcidians and not Olynthians, although doubtless they were made up in large part of Olynthian
citizens. This is a noteworthy indication of the existence of a
Chalcidian army and speaks very strongly in favour of our contention that Thucydides constantly refers to a Chalcidian state
and not to an unorganized alliance between the Chalcidian cities.
Later in the same year Sitalces marched against the Chalcidians,
having in mind to end the war with the help of Athens.[46]
Athens, however, failed him and he did nothing more than to
ravage the country. In 425 Eion was betrayed to Athens but

---

[40] Thuc. I, 57–58.
[41] Thuc. I, 62–63.
[42] Thuc. I, 65.
[43] Thuc. II, 29.
[44] Thuc. II, 58.
[45] Thuc. II, 79.
[46] Thuc. II, 95 ff.

was recaptured by a force of Chalcidians and Bottiaeans.[47]   In
the following year, Strophacos, who was Chalcidian proxenos in
Thessaly, with several prominent Thessalians, conducted Brasidas through that country.[48]   The fact that a Chalcidian proxenos
had been appointed in Thessaly is added proof that the league
was a state, in the full sense of the word, and not a mere confederation of independent cities, allied for the time being to accomplish certain definite purposes, such as, for example, freedom
from Athenian rule.   In that case there would have been proxenoi of each of the more important cities of the union.   Olynthos
would probably have had its own foreign representatives.

Brasidas was invited by Perdiccas and the Athenian tributaries that had revolted to come with assistance from the Peloponnese[49].   Those who sent this invitation were, of course, the
Bottiaeans and the Chalcidians, although Thucydides mentions
only the latter by name.   Neighbouring cities that had not yet
revolted secretly joined in this request for Spartan aid.   The
contrast, implied by this statement of Thucydides, is that the
Chalcidians acted as a body while the others acted as individual
πόλεις. He does not say αἱ Χαλκιδικαὶ πόλεις as we would naturally
expect if the city still remained the political unit, and the
change is emphasized more strongly by the mention of the
action of those cities that still retained their old civic constitutions.   Here, then, we find that the league had charge of negotiations with foreign states.   This is an absolute essential to the
existence of any state composed of elements that have been
hitherto autonomous.   When this right has been conceded by
individual states to a central authority, true union has come
into being.   In almost the very next chapter, ambassadors of
the Chalcidians are mentioned as present with Perdiccas and
Brasidas in the expedition against Arrhibaeos[50].   This confirms
the statement that foreign relations were in the hands of the
league itself.

We next hear that the Chalcidians, knowing that there was a

[47] Thuc. IV, 7.
[48] Thuc. IV, 78.
[49] Thuc. IV, 79, 84.
[50] Thuc. IV, 83.

strong party in Acanthos favourable to them, took part in an expedition with Brasidas against the city[51]. Under the orders of Brasidas, some time later, a body of three hundred Chalcidian targeteers with Peloponnesian hoplites, all commanded by Polydamidas, was sent to the aid of Scionè and Mendè, as a defense against the expected Athenian attack[52]. In the second expedition against Arrhibaeos the allied forces had with them Chalcidians and Acanthians, besides contingents from the other cities in proportion to their strength[53]. Here again we have contrasted the Chalcidians on the one hand and individual cities on the other.

At the capture of Toronè by Cleon in 422, a few Chalcidians were taken prisoners and were sent to Athens. Later, however, they were exchanged[54]. At the time of Cleon's expedition against Amphipolis a body of Chalcidian peltasts was with the army of Brasidas protecting the city. In the battle that followed Chalcidic horse and light armed troops rendered good service[55]. After the treaty of peace in 421, Clearidas refused to give up the city of Amphipolis, acting as he was in the interests of the Chalcidians[56]. Although the treaty required Sparta to restore to the Athenians all that she had captured during the war, there was nothing to prevent continued resistance on the part of the quondam Athenian allies in Chalcidicè, and as was to be expected, the Chalcidians remained hostile and did not submit themselves to the conditions imposed upon them by the two contracting parties[57]. Corinth also was dissatisfied with the treaty and with the Spartan-Athenian alliance that followed, while Argos, seeing an opportunity to become a leading state in the Peloponnese once more, conducted negotiations with various disaffected cities, with a view to forming an Argive alliance

---

[51] Thuc. IV, 84.
[52] Thuc. IV, 123.
[53] Thuc. IV, 124.
[54] Thuc. V, 3. At the capture of Toronè, the Peloponnesians, the Toronaeans and the other Chalcidians were sent to Athens: αὐτοὺς δὲ καὶ Πελοποννησίους καὶ εἴ τις ἄλλος Χαλκιδέων ἦν, ἀπέπεμψαν ἐς τὰς ᾿Αθήνας. This shows that the Toronaeans were considered Chalcidians, probably as members of the league, for they were exchanged later through the kind offices of the Olynthians.
[55] Thuc. V, 6–10.
[56] Thuc. V, 21.
[57] Thuc. V, 26.

against Sparta and Athens. Among others the Chalcidians took this opportunity of gaining powerful friends in the hope of protecting themselves from Athenian aggression[58].

In 417, the Dians revolted from Athens to the Chalcidians[59], and later the Athenians attacked Perdiccas on the ground that he had failed to help them in an expedition under Nicias against the Chalcidians and Amphipolis[60]. In the following year, when Perdiccas found himself hard pressed by an Athenian force, the Chalcidians received orders from Sparta to assist him, but as they had made a truce with Athens and were unwilling to break it, they refused.[61]

Throughout all these years the Chalcidians had been the moving spirits in the rebellion against Athenian authority in Thrace and in resistance to all attempts to reassert that authority. Since they acted with a united front towards all foreign powers, we are forced to conclude that the Chalcidic κοινόν which existed in the early years of the fourth century had already been formed and, moreover, even during the first decade of the Peloponnesian War was working in complete harmony.

So complete was the union that Olynthos, the leading city among the Chalcidians, received but scant mention at the hands of Thucydides. On only two occasions did the Olynthians undertake anything of importance,—once when they exchanged prisoners at Athens[62] thereby obtaining the freedom of the Chalcidians and Toronaeans captured in Toronè, and a second time when they captured Mecyperna[63]. The raid upon this town, the harbour of Olynthos, was undoubtedly carried out in the main by those most concerned, the Olynthians. We may well be surprised by the small part that they played in the general history of the league, as presented by Thucydides, but, nevertheless, the explanation is a simple one. Thucydides was interested only in

---

[58] Thuc. V, 29–31. Walker cites this as evidence for the formation of the Chalcidic league after the Peace of Nicias; but as I have shown, an earlier date is more in accordance with the known facts. See the article, *Olynthus, Ency. Brit.*

[59] Thuc. V, 82.

[60] Thuc. V, 83.

[61] Thuc. VI, 7.

[62] Thuc. V, 3.

[63] Thuc. V, 39.

the history of the league as a whole and not in the actions of any
of its parts, nor did he confuse the part with the whole. Although Olynthos was the most important member of the Chalcidic union, he did not make the mistake of crediting that city
with the deeds of the state of which it formed a part. His consistent preference for the term Chalcidian is shown by his description of the attack on Spartolos by Xenophon[64]. Then, if
ever, one would have expected him to speak of the Olynthians.
As the story goes, the inhabitants of Spartolos sent to Olynthos
for aid. This was sent, but it consisted of Chalcidian troops.
If, however, this hasty call for assistance had been made to Olynthos at a time when there was no thoroughly centralized power
but only a loose alliance of the Chalcidians, the reinforcements
that came from Olynthos would have been Olynthians, and
Thucydides would probably have called them such. There
would have been no time to call out troops from the other members of the league.

The care that Thucydides showed in constantly using the
term Χαλκιδῆς goes a long way to prove that he was speaking of
them as members of a κοινόν having a distinct corporate existence. This becomes clearer if we review the functions that we
have seen were performed by that body. The control of the
army was in its hands. This was always called Chalcidian. No
mention is made of a contingent from Olynthos nor from any
other of the revolting Chalcidic cities[65]. Negotiations were carried on by ambassadors of the κοινόν and treaties were made in
its name. It had its foreign representatives and maintained
a well defined and straightforward policy throughout all this period. This policy was, of course, resistance to Athens. It was
against the Chalcidians that Athenian expeditions were so often
sent and for them that Clearidas refused to return to Athens
that important vantage point, Amphipolis. In fact, so far as it
is possible to judge, externally the Chalcidic cities were but one
body exercising all the functions of statehood.

---

[64] Thuc. II, 79.
[65] I do not mean that no contingent from Acanthos is mentioned by
Thucydides, for Acanthos was not a Chalcidian city nor a member of the
Chalcidic league. This applies to other cities in a similar position.

Thucydides has shown us that the Chalcidians managed their foreign affairs as one people. The coins we have discussed show that the administration of internal affairs to a certain extent had been consolidated. Thus we have only to combine the information given by these two sources and we will see that a Chalcidic κοινόν was formed about the time of the revolt of the Chalcidians from Athens in 432.

CHAPTER III

TO THE CAPTURE OF POTIDAEA

Now that we have considered the evidence of the coins and of Thucydides concerning the formation and existence of the Chalcidic league, we can with profit take up the narrative of events in these regions in greater detail.

The revolt of the Potidaeans, the Bottiaeans, and the Chalcidians had been anticipated by the Athenians and measures had been taken to prevent it. Athens promptly fitted out an expedition against Perdiccas, whom she suspected of being the prime mover in all the disturbances on the borders of Macedonia and Thrace. Early in 432, thirty ships and one thousand hoplites were sent under the command of Archéstratos, the son of Lycomedes, with orders to take hostages from Potidaea, to raze the wall of that city, and, in addition, to watch closely affairs in the neighbouring cities[1]. During the previous winter a Potidaean embassy at Athens had been unable to gain any concession, but at Sparta promises were given that, if Potidaea were attacked, the Peloponnesians would invade Attica[2]. In March of the year 432, the revolt took place[3]. Two separate alliances were sworn, one by the revolting states with Corinth[4] and the other with Perdiccas.[5]

All of this happened before the arrival of Archestratos.[6] As

---

[1] Thuc. I, 57. With Archestratos went colleagues, probably two, although the text of Thucydides gives the number as ten. Cf. Busolt, III, 2, p. 795, note 2. The chronology of this period is involved in several difficulties. Cf. Busolt, III, 2, p. 799, note, and my article published in *Classical Philology*, vol. X, pp. 34–53.

[2] Thuc. I, 58, 71.

[3] Cf. note 1.

[4] Thuc. V, 30.

[5] Thucydides does not expressly state that an alliance was made with Perdiccas but the course of events clearly shows that such was the case. Thuc. I, 57ff.

[6] Thuc. I, 59.

his forces were all too insufficient to subdue the cities that had
risen, he turned his attention towards Macedonia with the intention of humbling Perdiccas and of placing upon the throne his
brother Philip. This Philip and a certain Derdas, another
enemy of Perdiccas, held independent principalities in upper
Macedonia and had been in league with Athens for some time
previous; and now Philip and the brother of Derdas were working in conjunction with the army of Archestratos.[7] Notwithstanding the fact that Athens was officially on friendly terms
with Perdiccas, she had entered into relations with his enemies
and rivals, with a view to checking his power.[8] For this reason
Perdiccas, fearing what might happen next, had stirred up his
neighbours, allies of Athens, to rebel, and had sought alliance
with Corinth. All had happened as he had expected and now
open war was declared. Archestratos had some slight successes,
capturing Thermè and blockading Pydna.[9]

During the month of May, forty days after the revolt,[10] Aristeus, a Corinthian, arrived in Potidaea with assistance consisting of Corinthian volunteers and Peloponnesian mercenaries to
the number of one thousand heavy armed and four hundred light
armed troops. While this expedition was preparing, Athens,
greatly alarmed at the turn affairs were taking in the Chalcidic
peninsula, fitted out a second expedition against Potidaea, consisting of forty ships and two thousand Athenian hoplites under
the command of Callias and four colleagues. It was imperative
that she put forth the utmost efforts to quell the revolt before it
became widespread.[11]

Callias hastened to Macedonia, but, instead of proceeding at
once against Potidaea, he remained for a time besieging Pydna
without success. Meanwhile Potidaea and the Chalcidians were
by no means idle. They were making every preparation for the
coming of the Athenian army. The arrival of Aristeus finally
brought Callias and Archestratos to a realization of the danger
of further delay. They raised the siege of Pydna and came to

---

[7] Thuc. I, 57, 59; II, 95, 100.
[8] Thuc. I, 57.
[9] Thuc. I, 61.
[10] Thuc. I, 60.
[11] Thuc. I, 60f.

terms with Perdiccas, making an alliance with him.   They then
left Macedonia, taking with them six hundred Macedonian horse
under Philip and Pausanias, and proceeded by slow marches to
Gigonos, a town on the coast not far from Potidaea.[12]   Here
they encamped.

The allies had collected their forces in expectation of this
movement and in two divisions were awaiting the approach of
the Athenian army.   Now that Perdiccas had lured the enemy
away from Macedonia, thereby gaining all that he had desired
from the Athenian alliance, and now that there was every chance
of dealing a crushing blow to Athenian hopes in Chalcidicè, he
joined his former allies, receiving from them the position of
cavalry commander.   Aristeus had been given command of the
infantry.   The Potidaeans, the Peloponnesian mercenaries, and
the Corinthian contingent took up their position outside the
walls of Potidaea on the side towards Olynthos, while the rest of
the allies, Chalcidians, Bottiaeans, and two hundred horse furnished by Perdiccas, were stationed as a guard for the latter
place, ready to close in upon the Athenian rear if Potidaea
should prove to be the primary point of attack.[13]

Callias foresaw this movement and checked it with a counter
demonstration of Macedonian horse and allied troops.   Having
made these preparations to defend his rear, he broke camp at
Gigonos and marched forward to the attack of Potidaea.   An engagement followed in which the wing commanded by Aristeus
was successful.   It was not supported, however, by the rest of
the army.[14]   The Potidaean forces and the Peloponnesians fled
into the city, while the troops in Olynthos offered no support.[15]
Aristeus was almost cut off; with great difficulty he managed
to make his escape into Potidaea.   Callias, the Athenian general,

---

[12] Thuc. I, 61; Hdt. VII, 123; Steph. Byz.: Γίγωνος πόλις Θράκης, προσεχὴς
τῇ Παλλήνῃ.   I cannot here enter into a discussion of the geographical difficulties presented by Thucydides.   If the reading of the Oxford text is correct, ἐπὶ Στρέψαν instead of ἐπιστρέψαντες, a part of the difficulty is removed,
but this offers no satisfactory explanation for the attack upon Beroea, a
city so far inland.   If, however, there is a second Beroea a short three
days march from Gigonos, or if there is a corruption of the text, then it
can be easily explained.
[13] Thuc. I, 62.
[14] Thuc. I, 62.
[15] Thuc. I, 63.

was killed in the battle and with him one hundred and fifty Athenian hoplites. Of the enemy some three hundred fell. This battle took place in the second half of the month of May.[16]

Although the Athenians had gained a victory, they were in no position to carry out an effective siege. Their army at this time consisted of about three thousand hoplites and numerous allied troops. Potidaea, however, extended across the narrow isthmus and a complete blockade, conducted from both sides at once, would have entailed a division of forces. Since there was still a strong garrison within the city and a large army of Chalcidic troops and allies stationed in the Athenian rear at Olynthos, such a separation was not to be thought of. As it was, the Athenians took up a position upon the north side of Potidaea, outside the walls, and conducted a partial blockade, sending, meanwhile, to Athens for reinforcements. When the Athenians learned that the investment of Potidaea was but half complete and that it was free from attack on the side towards Pallenè, they sent out in June a further expedition of sixteen hundred hoplites under the command of Phormio. This made a total of some four thousand five hundred Athenian heavy armed soldiers engaged in the siege. Phormio landed at Aphytis on the east coast of Pallenè and marched thence to the revolted Potidaea, wasting the country as he advanced. He found no opposition and had no difficulty in making the investment complete, for the Athenian ships had already cut off all communication from the sea.[17]

Things were almost at a standstill in the Chalcidian peninsula. The Athenians did not have a force sufficiently strong to conduct extensive operations for the subjugation of the rebels. The troops in this region were fully engaged in their siege operations and had no time for campaigns far distant from Potidaea.[18] It was about this time that the original number of seventy ships

---

[16] *Ibid.; I. G.*, I, 442; Thuc. II, 2. The battle occurred in the tenth month before the attack on Plataea, i. e., Thargelion, May 15 to June 13. The reading of the MS ἕκτῳ can not stand. I place the attack on Plataea early in March 431. See *Class. Phil.*, vol. X, 34–53. Alcibiades and Socrates were present at the battle of Potidaea, as we learn from Plato, *Symposium*, 219ff.

[17] Thuc. I, 64.

[18] Thuc. I, 65.

was reduced to thirty. This number was sufficient to blockade Potidaea from the sea.[19]

The Chalcidians, moreover, without the assistance of the Corinthian and Peloponnesian troops shut up within the besieged city, were unable to gain further adherents for their cause. Aristeus saw that, unless sufficient aid came from the Peloponnese to raise the siege, the final capture was inevitable. Wishing to husband the provisions of the town, so that they might last until aid should arrive from without, and thinking that his forces were large enough to become troublesome to the besiegers if a part of them could escape and harass the Athenians, he tried to persuade the garrison to send away all except those that were necessary for the defense of the walls. This plan, however, was not accepted, and he with a chosen few made his escape and joined the Chalcidians, who at that time were defending themselves against the attacks of Phormio. After the completion of the siege works, Phormio had left the actual blockade to the troops sent out under Archestratos and Callias and had undertaken a campaign in the neighbourhood against the other revolted cities.[20] Each side gained a few victories. Phormio ravaged Botticè and western Chalcidicè and captured a few small places, while Aristeus defeated a body of Sermylians near their city.[21]

About this time, in the second prytany of the year 432–1, in the month of September, Eucrates was sent into Macedonia to harass Perdiccas and to keep him from interfering in the Chalcidic peninsula.[22] The plan seems to have been to divide the forces of the enemy. Eucrates was to keep Perdiccas in Macedonia, while Phormio kept the Chalcidians from giving assistance to Potidaea. The besieging army gave the Potidaeans no opportunity to help their allies.

Meanwhile Aristeus was engaged in trying to obtain further aid from Corinth and Sparta, and Corinth was using every means in her power to bring about a general war, by which she hoped to save Potidaea and her citizens besieged there.[23] Finally she

---

[19] Thuc. III, 17; Arist. *Ath. Pol.*, 24, 3; cf. Busolt, III, 2, p. 808, note 1.
[20] Thuc. I, 65.
[21] Thuc. I, 65.
[22] *I. G.*, I, Supp., 179a.
[23] Thuc. I, 65, 67.

carried her point. Sparta voted for war and called a synod of
the confederacy to lay the question before the allies, who, also,
were persuaded to declare war on Athens. In the year 431 this
war broke out.[24]

Conditions in the north were favourable to neither side.
Athens was at war with Perdiccas and had lost a greater part
of Botticè and Chalcidicè proper together with tribute, amounting roughly to about ten talents yearly.[25] Potidaea, it is true,
although lost to Athens, was thoroughly invested but, as results showed, leaving aside the possibility of assistance to the
besieged and the final liberation of the city, the Athenians had
a long siege ahead of them. Meanwhile they were being deprived of the Potidaean tribute of fifteen talents yearly and
were expending huge sums upon the siege, amounting to about
eight hundred talents per annum.[26] On the other hand, a large
body of picked Corinthian troops was in danger of capture and
an unsuccessful battle might easily lose for the Peloponnesians
all the allies that had been gained in these regions.

In the summer of 431, Nymphodoros, a native of Abdera was
invited to Athens and made Athenian Proxenos. Through his
agency an alliance was made with Sitalces, king of Thrace. To
cement this alliance Sadocos, the son of Sitalces, was given Athenian citizenship. Nymphodoros also brought about a reconciliation between Athens and Perdiccas. Athens then restored
Thermè and Perdiccas joined the Athenian army under Phormio,
who was then fighting against the Chalcidians.[27] Nymphodoros
also gave promises in the name of Sitalces that an army of
Thracian horsemen and peltasts would be sent to the aid of the
Athenian forces.

Later in the year Phormio was recalled and no troops were
sent to take his place.[28] The besieging force was not increased

[24] Thuc. I, 125; II, 2.
[25] The Attic quota lists. *I. G.*, I, 256, 428–7 B. C.; 257, 426–5 B. C.; 259,
427–6 B. C. See *B. S. A.*, vol. XV, pp. 229–242, and Cavaignac, *Le Trésor
d'Athènes*, pp. XXXVI f.
[26] Thuc. II, 70; III, 17.
[27] Thuc. II, 29, 95; Aristoph. *Acharn.*, 141ff.
[28] Thuc. II, 29, 31, 58. It is probable that Phormio was not reelected for
the year 431–0. He belonged to the tribe Pandinois (Paus. I, 23, 10),
Prosop. Attica, 14958, and we know that Hagno, also of that tribe, was gen-

and remained three thousand men. Athens was too busily engaged elsewhere to devote much additional attention to Chalcidicè. Payments for the army already there were made at irregular intervals. Early in the spring of 431 in the sixth or seventh
prytany one hundred and sixty-five talents were sent to the forces
in the north.[29] The size of the sum seems to indicate that activities were being renewed with increased vigour about this time.

Until the middle of May of the following year (430) there
were no troops in the field against the Chalcidians. At that
time, notwithstanding the fact that the plague had broken out in
Athens, Hagno and Cleopompos, taking the fleet that had returned from its Peloponnesian expedition,[30] sailed out to assist in
the reduction of Potidaea and to take the place of Phormio in
the war against the Chalcidians and Bottiaeans. This expedition was on a large scale, consisting of one hundred Athenian
triremes, fifty from Chios and Lesbos, four thousand Athenian
hoplites, three hundred horse, and many allies. They were well
equipped with siege engines which they put into use upon their
arrival, but all was of no avail. The new troops had been in-
fected with the plague before leaving Athens, and almost immediately the disease spread, working alike among the forces of
Hagno and Cleopompos and the original three thousand. In

---

eral in 431-0. Beloch, *Att. Pol.*, p. 323. At the time of the expedition
into Megara late in the summer of 431, only three thousand hoplites were
absent from Athens and these were engaged in the siege of Potidaea. Hence
Phormio with his troops must have already returned home.

[29] *I. G.*, I, 179a. The payments for the army at Potidaea were approximately as follows. Of the first two payments to the Hellenotamiai we know
neither the sum nor the date, but they were probably made in the third and
fourth prytanies. The third is to be dated on the twelfth day of probably
the fifth prytany, Jan. 2, 431. The amount was ten talents or more. The
fourth payment was made between the twentieth and twenty-ninth days of
a prytany, probably the sixth, Feb. 18-27. It amounted to one hundred and
sixty-five talents. The next payment, twenty talents, fell between the tenth
and the nineteenth days of a prytany, probably the seventh, March 19-28.
The sixth payment, of amount unknown, was probably made on the four-
teenth day of the eighth prytany, May 1. During the prytany of Hippo-
thontis, which was probably the ninth, two payments were made, one of
forty talents on the sixth or perhaps the sixteenth day, June 1 or June 11,
and the second of something over twenty talents on a day not known. The
last payment of sixteen talents was for the cavalry and was probably made
on the seventeenth day of the tenth prytany, July 21. For a discussion of
this inscription, see Kolbe, *Hermes*, 34, 380-394.

[30] Thuc. II, 58; VI, 31.

forty days more than a quarter of the army of four thousand hoplites that had set out from Athens had been carried off by the rapidity of the disease. About the first of July the rest took ship and returned home, leaving behind to prosecute the siege the depleted forces that had come out during the first year of the war.[31]

Meanwhile Aristeus had been trying every means to bring relief to Potidaea. Towards the end of the summer of 430 Corinth and Sparta despatched an embassy to Asia, in an attempt to persuade the king to assist them with money against the Athenians. Aristeus was made a member of this embassy. As Athens was master of the sea at that time, the ambassadors were forced to take the land route from Greece to Asia. This led them through Thrace, which had recently become an ally of Athens. Aristeus, however, persuaded the other members of the embassy to delay a short time and to do everything in their power to withdraw Sitalces from the Athenian alliance. He hoped that Sitalces would see fit to send an army to aid Potidaea and to raise the siege. When they arrived an embassy from Athens happened to be at the Thracian court. Sadocos, who had previously been honoured by grant of Athenian citizenship, gave to the Athenian ambassadors, Learchos and Ameiniades, a body of troops with which to capture Aristeus and his companions. This was done as they were preparing to cross the Hellespont. They were taken immediately to Athens and there executed without trial.[32] The strenuous efforts of Aristeus in behalf of Potidaea and the Chalcidians had created such fear and hatred in the hearts of his enemies that they meted this summary punishment upon the Peloponnesian embassy. The death of Aristeus deprived Potidaea of one of its most ardent supporters and greatly lessened its hopes of receiving Peloponnesian assistance, powerful enough to compel Athens to abandon the siege.

During the following winter, the garrison of the city was reduced to the last extremity. Starvation was imminent and no

---

[31] Thuc. II, **58.** They returned to Athens about the beginning of the new civil year. Hagno had not been reelected to office. He was followed by his predecessor Phormio. Cf. Beloch, *Att. Pol.*, pp. 290, 299f., 323; cf. 277.
[32] Thuc. II, **67.**

immediate relief could be expected. The annual Peloponnesian invasion of Attica had not sufficed to cause Athens to withdraw the blockading forces and the long continued siege had exhausted all the provisions of the defenders. Nothing remained but capitulation. Xenophon, Hestiodoros, and Phanomachos had been sent out from Athens to take charge of the siege. As winter was upon them and the army itself was in an exposed position, and since the Athenians had already spent two thousand talents upon the attempt to capture Potidaea, the generals did not wait for an unconditional surrender. The inhabitants with the Peloponnesian and Corinthian soldiers that had made up the garrison were allowed to leave the country, taking with them a small amount of money for ephodia and barely enough for themselves in the way of clothes. A large part of the Potidaeans joined their Chalcidian neighbours, thereby materially strengthening the latter. At Athens there was great displeasure and indignation at the leniency shown by Xenophon and his colleagues. An unconditional surrender must necessarily have taken place in a short time. The proceeds from the sale of prisoners would then have gone a long way towards recompensing the victors for the large sums of money expended by them upon the siege.[33]   Soon after the capture of the city a thousand colonists were sent out to take possession of it and the adjacent territory.[34]

---

[33] Thuc. II, 70; Isoc. XV, 113.
[34] Thuc. II, 70; Diod. XII, 46; *I. G.*, I, 340: Ἐποίκον ἐς Ποτείδαιαν.

CHAPTER IV

THE REVOLT SPREADS

The most important of the revolting Athenian allies had at last been captured at great expense. Perdiccas had been won over. Thrace had entered into a close alliance with Athens and things looked very favourable for the speedy reduction of the Chalcidians and the Bottiaeans. Now that the Corinthian garrison was no longer in danger, and since Aristeus, the active ally of Chalcidian interests, had been executed, there was but little reason to expect that the Peloponnesians would send assistance to the north, so far from the base of operations.

In the early summer of 429, Xenophon and two colleagues recommenced operations in Chalcidicè. They had with them an army of two thousand Athenian hoplites and two hundred horse[1]. Their first attempt was against Spartolos, the chief town of Botticè, for they thought that in it they would find sufficient Athenian sympathizers to deliver it into their hands. The capture of the city would soon put a stop to the revolt throughout the whole of the Bottiaean territory, and the Chalcidians, forced to stand alone, would, in time, be compelled to return to their former allegiance. While Xenophon was wasting the country round about Spartolos, a request for aid was sent to Olynthos. A part of the Chalcidian troops were collected there, expecting an attack, but they quickly marched to the assistance of the endangered town, arriving there with a force of cavalry, hoplites, and light armed soldiers. Battle was immediately offered near the city. The engagement resulted in a victory for one part of the troops and in defeat for the other. The strength of the Chalcidians lay in their cavalry and light armed troops, and in this part of the engagement the

---

[1] Thuc. II, 79.

Athenians were overcome. A second body of peltasts arrived
from Olynthos too late for the battle; but encouraged by their
previous victory and strengthened by the reinforcements, the
Chalcidian light armed troops, supported by the cavalry, sallied
out again from Spartolos. Their peculiarly harassing tactics
proved disconcerting for the Athenians and soon put them to
flight. The remnants of the Athenian army made their escape
to Potidaea and returned to Athens with less than nothing accomplished, having lost more than one-fifth of the army, including Xenophon and his two colleagues.

This battle showed Athens the strength that she had to meet
and to overcome if she was to regain her former authority. The
Chalcidians and the Bottiaeans had been in revolt more than
three years and yet were no nearer subjection than before.
Sooner or later, unless the revolt could be quickly checked, the
other allies in that neighbourhood would take encouragement
and would join the movement. While the Chalcidic tribute was
but a small fraction of the total, if the rebellion should spread
and become general, as would probably be the case, Athens
would be face to face with a revenue largely decreased and with
her expenses proportionately increased. The two thousand talents spent upon the siege of Potidaea would be multiplied many
times. On this account it was necessary to take urgent measures against the Chalcidians before their neighbours should join
them. About this time, however, Pericles died, after which a
lull occurred in the Athenian operations in the north.

It was then that Perdiccas changed his colours again[2]. This
time he did not openly break with Athens but secretly assisted
her enemies in their western operations. Cnemos, the Spartan
admiral, undertook an expedition for the conquest of Acarnania, but in this he failed on account of a premature attack
made by a part of his barbarian allies. Perdiccas sent to him
a contingent of one thousand mercenaries, but these arrived too
late to be of any assistance in the campaign. Nevertheless, this
action showed that Perdiccas was none too faithful in his pro-
fessions of friendship for Athens.

Just as winter (429) was commencing, Sitalces undertook to

[2] Thuc. II, 80.

carry out his promise of 431, wishing to punish Perdiccas for his treachery and to subdue the Chalcidians[3]. For this purpose he collected a huge army of his subjects, amounting in all to one hundred and fifty thousand men. He had with him an Athenian general, Hagno, a number of Athenian ambassadors who had come to demand of him the fulfillment of his promise, and Amyntas, the son of Philip, whom he intended to put upon the Macedonian throne. With these forces he advanced into upper Macedonia, taking Eidomenè by storm and winning over several other towns that were loyal to Amyntas. His further operations were confined to ravaging Mygdonia, Crestonia, and the territory of Anthemos, for a short time only, since he was continually harassed by the Macedonian cavalry.

Notwithstanding the great size of his army, Sitalces was unable to accomplish anything of importance. Athens had failed him. The promised fleet had not arrived, for the Athenians, not expecting Sitalces to keep his promises, had sent nothing but envoys with gifts. Perdiccas, meanwhile, had not been idle but had been conducting negotiations with Seuthes, the son of Sparadocos, a man of great influence with Sitalces, and had finally won him over with the promise that he would give him his sister, Stratonicè, in marriage. Sitalces then left Macedonia and for a time ravaged the Chalcidian and Bottiaean territory; but his soldiers, having had enough of this winter campaign, deserted in large numbers and his army melted away. Then Seuthes, working in the interests of Perdiccas, persuaded Sitalces to return home. The expedition had accomplished almost nothing. A month had been spent in laying waste the country; but, owing to the inability of the Thracians to conduct siege operations, no important towns had been taken. Macedonia, in the end, had received the protection of Seuthes and the Chalcidians had been in no wise subjugated.[*]

The dilatory policy of Athens in the north was still pursued. Since her attention was fully engaged elsewhere, not thinking that the Spartan policy might change, she remained content with the recapture of Potidaea and postponed further opera-

---

[3] Thuc. II, 95–101.
[*] Thuc. II, 101.

tions against the Chalcidians until some more opportune time. Small bodies of troops may have been sent out occasionally or placed as garrisons in certain favourable spots[4], but no general movement was made. In individual instances conciliatory measures were adopted towards faithful allies[5]. Methonè, Aison, and Dicaea were allowed special privileges with regard to the payment of their tribute, being excused entirely except for the customary quota annually dedicated to the Goddess. In addition to this concession, negotiations were carried on with Perdiccas, asking him not to limit in any way the trade of the city, Methonè. Besides such conciliatory measures as these little was done.

Not long afterward, Sparta saw an excellent opportunity to make her power felt in the north[6]. The Trachinians and the Dorians appealed to Lacedaemon for protection against their neighbours of Oeta, from whom they had long been suffering severely. Their appeal was only too gladly received. A colony composed of Spartans, Perioeci, and other Greeks, excluding the Ionians and the Achaeans, was sent out in the summer of 426. The city of Heraclea, with a population of about ten thousand, was founded near Thermopylae. The site was favourable. It could be used as a base of operations not only against Euboea, but also against the northern allies of Athens, and was suitable for the conveyance of troops to Chalcidicè. Naturally the neighbouring peoples were particularly hostile, especially the Thessalians, who resented the foundation of Heraclea as an encroachment upon territory tributary to them and feared that it would be a means to their destruction and subjugation by Sparta. For this reason they made continual raids upon the new foundation, gradually wearing it out. In addition to these outside disturbances, the Spartan governors proved harsh and unjust in administration, thereby making Heraclea unpopular for further settlements. As a consequence it soon lost its early strength and never fulfilled its promise of an important future.

---

[4] *I. G.*, I, 40, l. 28; Thuc. IV, 7.
[5] *I. G.*, I, 40, 41; cf. *I. G.*, I, 257.   Privileges granted to Methonè, Aison, Dikaiopolis, and Aphytis.
[6] Thuc. III, 92f.

In the early summer of 425, operations on a small scale took
place in Chalcidicè.* An Athenian commander, Simonides, collected a force, consisting of a few Athenians from the neighbouring garrisons and of a multitude of allies, for the purpose
of recapturing the town of Eion.[7]

In this he was successful. The Athenian sympathizers in the
town acted in concert with him and betrayed the place to him.
He was not strong enough, however, to hold the place against
an attack of Bottiaeans and Chalcidians who came immediately
to its rescue and forced Simonides to leave, after having suffered considerable loss.

Early in the winter of this same year, Aristides, who had been
sent out in charge of a tribute-collecting ship, coming to Eion
on the Strymon, found there a Persian ambassador to Sparta by
the name of Artaphernes and arrested him[8]. He took him immediately to Athens where the despatches were read. This in-
terrupted correspondence between Persia and Sparta suggested
to the Athenians that they too should appeal to the king for
aid.

In the following year, 424, the conduct of the war was altered. Cleon had captured Sphacteria and with it a number of
Spartan prisoners. These the Athenians held as surety against
a repetition of the annual Peloponnesian raids into Attic territory. The Lacedaemonians could not run the risk of the loss
of these citizens, and so perforce, adopted new measures and
changed the scene of operations from Attica to Chalcidicè.
Brasidas, having shown himself a man of resource and ambition,
was entrusted with the task of weakening the Athenian power
still further in the Chalcidic peninsula[9]. Helots to the number
of seven hundred were sent out with him. At that time great

---

* *I. G.*, I, 446; Supp., p. 46. This inscription contains the names of
Athenians that had fallen in war at Potidaea, Amphipolis, ἐπὶ Θράκης, at
Pylos, at Singos, and at Sermylia, and has been referred to this year. The
small number of fatalities shows that we have to deal with a number of minor
engagements. The date of this inscription, however, is uncertain and thus it
may refer to minor engagements after the arrival of Brasidas.
[7] Thuc. IV, 7. This Eion, a colony of Mendè, is not the Eion upon the
Strymon, of which we hear so often. Cf. *Pauly-Wissowa*, p. 795, *s. v.* Bottike
and Eion, no. 2.; Eustath., *Comment., Il.*, II, 92.
[8] Thuc. IV, 50.
[9] Thuc. IV, 78–81.

anxiety was being felt in Sparta lest the Helots, instigated by
the Athenians at Pylos, should revolt. Hence it was thought
advisable to get some of the more dangerous of them out of the
way. There had been similar reasons for the choice of Brasidas. His ambition was thought to be dangerous to the Spartan
state. In Chalcidicè was found an opportunity to make use of
the energies of the discontented Helots and of the ambitious
Brasidas. There was the most favourable spot for dealing a
blow to Athens. A revolt was already in progress and even in
the cities supposedly favourable to Athens[10] there was a large
anti-Athenian party that had joined secretly in the invitation
sent by the Chalcidians to the Peloponnese for assistance.
Perdiccas, with the power of Macedon behind him, had expressed his willingness to break with Athens and had promised
to maintain half of the Spartan forces at his own expense.
The Chalcidians and the Bottiaeans were to furnish maintenance for the rest. Thus the Spartans were in a position to
inflict great damage upon Athens at little expense or trouble
to themselves, and they hoped to create such a diversion that
the Athenians would be forced to discontinue their attacks upon
the Peloponnese. Moreover, if they could win over the Chalcidic
peninsula and take Amphipolis, they would have an excellent
base for the equipment of a formidable navy, could hope to extend their operations to the other Athenian tributaries, and
might even persuade the islands to come under their hegemony.

Thus when the Chalcidians sent a special request that Brasidas
should be sent to their aid, he was chosen for the task and made
his preparations for a march to the north.[11] After collecting
seventeen hundred hoplites, of whom seven hundred were the
Helots already mentioned, he set out for Heraclea Trachinia.
The Thessalians were in the main hostile to Sparta at this time.
The foundation of Heraclea still rankled in their minds so that
Brasidas could not expect a quiet passage through Thessaly. The
Thessalians, however, were divided into factions and were not in

---

[10] Thuc. IV, **79, 84.** The oligarchic party of Acanthos joined with the
Chalcidians in petitioning the Lacedaemonians for assistance.
[11] Thuc. IV, **70, 74, 78.** Brasidas did not commence his march to the
north until after the affair at Megara, which took place about the month
of August, 424.

a position to unite in opposition to him. At Melitia in Achaea
Phthiotis, several of his friends from Pharsalos, including the
Chalcidic Proxenos, at his request met him to give him and his
troops safe escort through Thessaly. Perdiccas, also, used his influence upon his Thessalian friends and sent Niconidas from
Larissa to share in the escort. Notwithstanding these precautions, Brasidas was met at the river Euripos by a party of Thessalians who were opposed to the march. They stated, justly
enough, that Brasidas had no right to lead armed forces through
the country without the consent of the nation; and his escort
told him that they would not conduct him further if there was
any objection to the march. They excused themselves for what
they had done by saying that they had only acted as hosts should
act towards guests. Brasidas, however, met the hostile Thessalians with tactful words and sent them away; whereupon he made
all haste to finish his march through Thessaly before a force collected large enough to stop him. In this he was successful, reaching Dion, a Macedonian city, without trouble. Shortly afterwards he joined Perdiccas for an expedition against Arrhibaeos,
king of the Lyncestians.[12] The desire of Perdiccas to gain help
for this undertaking was the chief reason for his open break with
Athens and for his requests to Sparta for assistance. His envoys
had promised that Brasidas would gain many allies for the Lacedaemonians among the neighbouring tribes. Therefore, when
Brasidas received word from Arrhibaeos that he was ready to
submit the affair to him for arbitration, he was unwilling to make
the king of Lyncestis a permanent enemy by going further with
Perdiccas in his plans for subjugation. The Chalcidian envoys
who were present with the expedition advised against the complete subjugation of the enemies of Perdiccas, on the ground that
it would not be well to remove all difficulties from his path lest
Perdiccas should be found wanting when they in turn were in
need of his promised assistance. So Brasidas left Perdiccas to
his own devices, thereby vexing him so greatly that he refused
to pay the half of the maintenance of the Peloponnesian troops,

---

[12] Thuc. IV, 79, 83.

as he had promised. A third was all that he was willing to provide.[13]

Athens little realized the danger threatening her and sent no forces sufficient to cope with a general uprising in Thrace.[14] Her attention was at that time fully taken up with the expedition into Boeotia and few men could be spared for the war in the Chalcidic peninsula. Athens merely declared war on Perdiccas and decided to keep closer watch over her allies in that region. Thucydides and Eucles were sent to take charge of affairs there, but they were provided with a very insufficient force, consisting of seven ships. Eucles, being without troops, took up his head-quarters at Amphipolis and Thucydides remained at Thasos with the fleet. This island was suspected of harbouring feelings of disloyalty, and for this reason the presence of Athenian forces was thought necessary for the protection of Thasos and the ad-jacent mainland with its rich deposits of gold. Thus Athens thought to hold the places most important for the maintenance of her position among the Thracian allies, Amphipolis controlling the valley of the Strymon and guarding the roads from Chalci-dicè to the Thracian coast, and Thasos, the most important island in that neighbourhood. Otherwise the Athenian allies were left almost without protection.[15] Argilos had no garrison at the time of its revolt and this is probably true of the other cities. It was not until after the capture of the city of Amphipolis that Athens realized the importance of placing garrisons in its allied cities.

Brasidas, after having entered into a truce with Arrhibaeos, left Macedonia and entered Chalcidicè where he joined forces with his allies, the Chalcidians.[16] They had asked for his aid, fearing that the recent successes of Athens would leave her free to turn her attention towards them.[17] The combined army, with Brasidas in command, advanced upon Acanthos, an Andrian col-ony, situated not far from the canal of Xerxes on the east coast of the Chalcidic peninsula. Hitherto this city had been a faith-ful member of the Athenian empire and one of the most impor-

---

[13] Thuc. IV, 83.
[14] Thuc. IV, 82, 104.
[15] Thuc. IV, 108.
[16] Thuc. IV, 84.
[17] Thuc. IV, 79.

tant upon the base of the peninsula, paying an annual tribute of three talents.[18] With the successful revolt of their Chalcidic neighbours before their eyes, the oligarchic party within the city had acted in concert with its friends, the Chalcidians, and had secretly invited Brasidas to come to their assistance. Being only a minority, however, they were unable of themselves to admit him into the city without prolonged discussion. The demos feared that the constitution would be changed in the interests of the oligarchic party. For this reason, Acanthos and the other cities which later came over to Brasidas hesitated at first to admit him. This hesitation shows that, in the main, Athenian rule had not been oppressive in these regions.

In the autumn, just before the vintage, Acanthos was face to face with the question whether she should adhere to Athens, thereby endangering her harvest, or whether she should join the Chalcidians at the demand of Brasidas and the oligarchic party of the city.[19] As the democratic party was in the majority, it seemed doubtful whether the revolt could be brought about without a struggle, but the fear of losing the vintage persuaded the people to admit the Spartan general alone and to hear what arguments he had to bring forward in favour of his demands. He told them that he had come to free them and others from the Athenian yoke, as had been promised at the beginning of the war. He had no intention of freeing them from one master to make them slaves of another, nor did he come in the interests of any party. No constitutional changes were contemplated and the democracy was still to remain. This he promised with solemn oaths, both for himself and for the Spartan government at home. His speech ended with a threat as to what they might expect if they were to persist in opposing him. His promises and threats were effective and the revolt of the city was voted by secret ballot. Soon afterward, the Acanthians entered into alliance with the Chalcidians and the Bottiaeans. This fact is shown by the similarity of coin type used by these three states. The new type was adopted by Acanthos at the time when it first struck coins of the Phoenician standard soon after its revolt from Athens.

---

[18] *I. G.*, I, 259.
[19] Thuc. IV, 84–88.

This alliance probably lasted only a few years, for Acanthos and the Chalcidians became rivals a short time later.[20]

Stageiros, another Andrian colony not far from Acanthos, influenced by the revolt of the latter city, offered no opposition to the demands of Brasidas and revolted from Athens during the same summer.[21] Meanwhile, the Athenians were still lax in their efforts to protect their faithful allies. No army was sent to Chalcidicè. The summer was ended, and a winter campaign in Thrace was a thing to be avoided, if possible, by the Athenian citizen troops. Moreover, the attack on Boeotia was in preparation and no force could be spared for so distant a campaign. About this time Seuthes inherited the kingdom of Thrace from his uncle Sitalces.[22] This meant that Thracian sympathy was no longer to be counted upon, and it might easily be that Seuthes, who was an ally of Perdiccas, would take active part with Brasidas in bringing about the revolt of the Athenian allies upon the borders of his country. Hence, affairs were in a very critical position for Athens.

Amphipolis, the connecting link between the Athenian allies in the Chalcidic peninsula and those east of the river Strymon, was destined next to feel the power of Brasidas. With great difficulty, the city had been settled by Athens thirteen years before,[23] but it had already become very important, for it commanded the bridge across the Strymon and the passage into Thrace. One would think that the Athenian generals would have taken every precaution to guard the place, but, on the contrary, no forces were placed in the city and Eucles had nothing to depend upon but the loyalty of the citizens, the majority of whom were bound to Athens by no ties, for only a small portion of them were Athenian citizens. The remainder of the population consisted of foreigners who had been attracted to the spot by its commercial advantages. Some were Chalcidians, whose sympathies lay with the revolted Chalcidians. Some were from Argilos, a neighbouring town across the Strymon that had suffered greatly in impor-

[20] Ibid.; Ditt. Syll.,[2] 77; cf. Chap. II.
[21] Thuc. IV, 88.
[22] Thuc. IV, 101.
[23] Thuc. IV, 102.

tance because of the foundation of Amphipolis. The Argilians, therefore, were hostile. Macedonian settlers, instigated by Perdiccas, also formed a part of the discontented element.[24] Thus, unless energetic measures were taken by the Athenian generals, conditions were very favourable for the success of Brasidas.

In November or December of the year 424 the attack was made.[25] The conspirators within the city were warned and all preparations were made. Brasidas, relying partly on them, partly on the suddenness of the attack, expected an easy victory. Starting from the Chalcidic town of Arnae one wintry day, he commenced his march towards Amphipolis. During the night he arrived at Argilos. The Argilians had been awaiting his coming and revolted to him upon his approach. Without hesitation they joined forces with him and led him to the bridge across the Strymon. This bridge gave access to the territory of Amphipolis and was watched by a small guard of volunteers, placed there by Eucles. This guard, however, offered no resistance and was quickly overpowered. The intrigues of the conspirators within the city, the unexpectedness of the attack, and the difficulty of keeping a body of citizen soldiers on faithful guard during a wintry night, all played their part in this preliminary success. After the capture of the bridge and the guard upon it, Brasidas took possession of everything outside the city, capturing many citizens whom he found without the walls. When news of the attack came to Eucles, he sent a request to Thucydides for assistance, but the consternation within and the favourable terms offered by the Spartan general caused even the loyal citizens to waver and, before Thucydides could bring up his fleet from Thasos where he was stationed, Amphipolis had capitulated. Those that wished, whether Athenians or not, departed with their goods, while the others remained in peaceful possession of their rights and property, without any interference on the part of Brasidas.

[24] Thuc. IV, 103; *I. G.*, I, 237, 244. In 443 the tribute paid by Argilos was one talent. In 436, after the founding of Amphipolis, it had dropped to one-sixth of that amount. This shows the influence the new city had on the fortunes of the older town. In all probability some of the territory of Argilos had been confiscated for the foundation of Amphipolis. For Chalcidians in Amphipolis, cf. Aristotle, *Pol.*, VIII, 3, 13, 1303B.
[25] Thuc. IV, 102–106.

Thucydides got no farther than Eion at the mouth of the Strymon before the fall of Amphipolis.[26] This place he put in a position for defence. It commanded the river and was of great importance to any one holding Amphipolis. Without it the way to the sea was blocked. Thus Brasidas had succeeded only in part. He lost no time, however, in attacking Eion but he failed both in gaining command of the entrance to the harbour and in capturing the city from the landward side. Could he have taken it, he would have used it as a base for the fitting out of a Spartan fleet. Notwithstanding his failure here, he commenced to build triremes on the upper Strymon, hoping that his urgent messages to Sparta would bring him sufficient forces to capture the city by siege.[27]

Returning from Eion to Amphipolis, with the assistance of Perdiccas he took measures for the settlement of affairs in that city.[28] Almost immediately he found that his hopes of further successes were well founded. Cities beyond the Strymon eagerly joined him. Myrcinos of Edonia was among the first. A little later, two colonies of Thasos on the coast came over to his side, Oesymè and Galepsos. Brasidas had now a free approach to the Athenian tributaries on the Thracian coast, and great fear was entertained at Athens lest he should extend his operations in this direction. A rapid march might even put the Athenian holdings upon the Hellespont in danger and, if successful, would cut off the grain supply from the Black Sea, so necessary for the life of Athens. The loss of Amphipolis, the threatening dangers, taken together with the disheartening defeat at Delion, caused serious alarm among the Athenians and made them fear that a general revolt among their allies might break out at any moment, now that their prestige had suffered so heavy a blow. Notwithstanding all this, they merely sent out a few small garrisons for the most important posts.[29] The season of the year and the unexpectedness of the blow united to cause delay.

The Athenian fears were well founded. The oligarchic anti-Athenian parties in the cities that were still faithful grew more

[26] Thuc. IV, 106f.
[27] Thuc. IV, 108.
[28] Thuc. IV, 107.
[29] Thuc. IV, 108.

powerful and secretly sent messages to Brasidas asking for assistance in their rebellious projects.   His many successes had inspired in all a conviction that Sparta, at last, was willing to help
them and could be trusted to keep its promises towards them.[30]
In this they were to be disappointed, for, as it proved, Brasidas
was their only support.   The Lacedaemonians were more eager
for peace than for the good of their newly gained allies.

The next campaign of Brasidas, in the winter of 424–3, was
against Actè, the easternmost peninsula on the Chalcidic coast.[31]
It contained many small towns with inhabitants of many nation-
alities.   Some were Greek, among whom were a small number of
Chalcidians, but the greater part belonged to various Thracian
tribes, Edonians, Crestonians, and Bisaltians.   Others Thucydides calls Pelasgians.   Most of the towns of Actè revolted to
Brasidas upon his approach, but Dion and Sanè remained faithful to Athens.   Brasidas did not have an army sufficiently strong
to compel them to join him and so, after wasting their territory,
he left them and crossed over into Sithonia.   It was more important to forestall any measures on the part of Athens and to capture this peninsula before the arrival of garrisons to defend it.

The most important city situated upon Sithonia was the Chalcidian Toronè.   It had paid in the year 427–6 a tribute of twelve
talents, exactly twice as much as had been hitherto demanded.
The general increase of tribute seems to have rested upon the Toronaeans more heavily than upon others in that region.[32]   For
this reason they were discontented and ready for revolt.   Toronè,
moreover, was a Chalcidic city and had many citizens who were
in sympathy with the revolted Chalcidians, their neighbours.
The recent successes of Brasidas had served to increase the
strength of the oligarchic party in the town.   Athens had placed
there a small garrison with two guard-ships, but, owing to the

---

[30] Thuc. IV, 108.
[31] Thuc. IV, 109.
[32] *I. G.*, I, 259, 427 B. C.; Cavaignac, *Le Trésor d'Athènes*, pp. XXXVI ff;
B. S. A., XV, pp. 229–242; *I. G.*, I, 256, 428 B. C.; *I. G.*, I, 237, 443 B. C.;
I. G., I, 239, 441 B. C.   Athens may already have commenced further oppres-
sions of her allies, trying to fill her empty coffers by means of the confiscated
estates of rich citizens in the subject cities.   This would naturally create feeling among the richer classes and would favor the formation of an aristocratic
party with Lacedaemonian leanings.   Cf. Aristoph. *Vesp.*, 286ff; *Pax.*, 639ff.

lateness of the season, the city had not been put in a state of complete defence, the walls being decayed and, moreover, carelessly guarded. Brasidas, acting in concert with the Chalcidian or oligarchic party in the town, suddenly appeared before the walls during the night. As the majority of the citizens had no suspicion of his presence, the conspirators introduced into the city a body of seven light armed soldiers under the command of Lysistratos, an Olynthian. These men killed the sentinels on guard and with the help of their Toronaean friends opened the gates to a company of chosen targeteers. Thereupon a signal was given to Brasidas, and he led the remainder of the army into the city. The Athenian soldiers were taken by surprise and with some of the citizens fled to the fort Lecythos, situated near the town upon a narrow peninsula that was connected with the mainland by an isthmus. The city itself was completely in the hands of the enemy, but those who had taken refuge in Lecythos refused to surrender. Brasidas made many fair promises to the main body of citizens, after the manner of his speech at Acanthos, and told them that he had come to liberate and not to enslave, that no Toronaean need fear ill treatment at his hands, and that it was to their advantage, as well as their duty, to be faithful allies of the Spartans.

After the expiration of a two days' truce, spent in making preparations for the attack upon Lecythos, Brasidas advanced, and, owing to an accident within the fort, became master of the place. Many of the Athenians escaped to Pallenè by means of their ships, but all that were captured were put to death.[33]

During the remainder of the winter, Brasidas was engaged in putting to rights the affairs of his newly made allies and in placing Toronè in a position to defend itself against the expected Athenian attack, tearing down the old walls and rebuilding them to include more of the town.[34] Probably in some of the captured cities, notwithstanding the promises of Brasidas, aristocratic governments were established.[35] We know this to have been the case later at Mendè, and it is rather significant that at Acanthos and

[33] Thuc. IV, 110–116.
[34] Thuc. IV, 116; V, 2.
[35] Thuc. IV, 107, 116, 130; cf. Chap. XIV.

the other towns "the few" were the ones who were actively interested in the Lacedaemonian plans.[36] We have no means of judging as to the newly established constitutions of Toronè and
Scionè, but it is safe to assert that the tendency was aristocratic
and that some change was carried out, presumably in that direction.

In the year 423 politics in Athens and Sparta were more favourable to peace than they had been at any time before. The
Spartan successes in Thrace had made both sides eager for a truce.
This would give time for the negotiations necessary for the conclusion of peace or would afford both sides an opportunity to
strengthen their respective positions. Instead of continuing in the
way into which Brasidas had led them, the Spartans desired nothing better than to use what he had gained for them, as a means
for obtaining favourable terms from Athens. Athens, for her
part, wished to put an end to further inroads into her empire and
to put herself in a stronger position, where she could, if peace
failed, regain that which she had lost. Sparta and Brasidas, however, went their different ways, neither troubling about what the
other was doing or wished to do. While the Lacedaemonians
were using all their means to bring about a truce, Brasidas, their
general, was trying to bring about a revolt upon the peninsula
of Pallenè. This with a few scattered cities was all that was left
of the Athenian empire in these parts. Methonè, on the Macedonian coast, Eion on the Strymon, and Dion and Sanè, upon the
peninsula of Actè, were still faithful, but Pallenè was more
important than any of these for the plans of Brasidas. Being cut
off, as it was, from the mainland by the city of Potidaea, Pallenè
was, in effect, an island and could only be approached by sea, so
long as Potidaea remained an Athenian possession. An attack
on Pallenè would show Athens that her dominion over the islands was soon to be threatened, and it would show the island
communities that they might rely upon Sparta in case they saw
fit to revolt. It may be questioned whether Brasidas was justified in thinking that his power was sufficient to maintain Pallenè
against the combined attack of Athens by sea and by land.

---

[36] Thuc. IV, 84, 110, 123.

CHAPTER V

BRASIDAS AND CLEON DURING THE TRUCE

In the month of April, 423, truce was declared between Athens and Sparta, the terms of which were that the '*status quo*' should be maintained and that neither side should receive deserters from the other.[1] Unfortunately for all who were desirous of a peaceful settlement of affairs, Brasidas did not make his arrangements for the revolt. of Scionè before the ratification of the truce. Scionè, next to Potidaea, was the most important city of Pallenè. At the time of its revolt it was paying to Athens a tribute of nine talents yearly.[2] Together with its neighbour, Mendè, it seems to have owed its commercial importance, in large part, to the wine produced in that region.[3] The revolt of Scionè occurred almost immediately after the oaths for the truce had been sworn.[4] It was carried through without the presence or intimidation of Brasidas. When he heard what had happened, he crossed over to Pallenè to encourage the citizens of Scionè, and, in an assembly called to welcome him, he praised them for their action. After he had finished speaking he was received with great honours. The whole affair redounds greatly to his credit and shows to what a height of popularity he had reached, by means of his moderation and justice, and, moreover, what confidence was placed in him and his plans.

Now that he had an important foothold upon Pallenè, he wished to anticipate the Athenian attack by winning over the remainder of the peninsula and if possible to recapture Potidaea. This would afford him access to the peninsula by land and he

---

[1] Thuc. IV, 117–119.
[2] *I. G.*, I, 259.
[3] [Dem.] XXXV, 10, 20, 35.
[4] Thuc. IV, 120–122.

could then more easily defend his recent acquisitions. It is not strange that he should have had hopes for the revolt of Mendè, another very important city, situated near Scionè, but that he should expect co-operation from Potidaea, a recently founded Athenian colony, strikes one as peculiar. Nevertheless, even there he had friends with whom he had entered into negotiations for the delivery of the city.[5]

Leaving the city of Scionè temporarily to the protection of a small garrison, he returned to Toronè to fit out an expedition to carry out his further plans. With these forces he sailed across again to Scionè, intending to use this as his base of operations in Pallenè.[6] Soon after his arrival, ambassadors came from Athens and from Sparta to announce the truce, Aristonymos the Athenian and Athenaeos the Lacedaemonian. Except for Scionè, there was no disagreement as to the application of the terms of the truce. All of the other revolted allies agreed to accept them, but Aristonymos, learning that Scionè had been guilty of rebelling two days after the cessation of hostilities had been agreed upon, refused to allow it to remain in the alliance with Sparta or to share in the truce itself. Brasidas protested, but to no avail, and arbitration was refused by the Athenians.[7]

At Athens Cleon and his supporters, hostile to any proposals for peace, were only too glad to have this instance of Spartan perfidy to use for party ends; and the indignation aroused among the Athenians was such that Cleon had no difficulty in persuading them to fit out an expedition for the recapture of Scionè and to vote the massacre of the Scionaeans, as punishment for their rebellion. Notwithstanding this hitch in the operation of the truce, both sides abstained from general hostility. In Pallenè alone was the war carried on.[8]

While preparations were being made in Athens for the recapture of Scionè, the oligarchic party in Mendè took measures to put their city in line with Scionè. Immediate action alone could

---

[5] Thuc. IV, 121.
[6] Thuc. IV, 121f. After the arrival of the ambassadors Brasidas sent back his army to Toronè.
[7] Thuc. IV, 122.
[8] Thuc. IV, 122, 134; cf. the following account.

free them from Athens, for if once peace was declared and
Spartan support withdrawn they could have no hope of resisting
the Athenian power.   They saw, moreover, that Brasidas was
willing to help them, although it was contrary to the terms of the
truce, and for this reason they trusted him to do all in his
power for their protection.   Having had it in mind for some time
to take this step, the conspirators compelled the majority to ac-
cede to their wishes.   That the people, as a whole, were against
this step, is clearly shown by their actions later during the siege;
but we do not know what means the oligarchic party took to gain
their ends.   Brasidas did not hesitate to receive them into alliance with him, claiming that the Athenians had violated the
terms of the truce.   Next he took measures to put both Mendè
and Scionè in readiness for a siege.   The women and children
were conveyed to the Chalcidic city Olynthos for safety and Polydamidas with five hundred Peloponnesian hoplites and three hundred Chalcidian peltasts was sent to their assistance.[9]   Hearing
of this, Athens increased her preparations with a view to the recovery of both cities. Fifty ships were manned, including ten from
Chios, and sent out under the command of Nicias and Nicostratos.
One thousand Athenian hoplites, six hundred archers, and one
thousand mercenaries from Thrace, together with a body of allies
to be recruited from the neighbourhood of the Chalcidian peninsula, were included in the expedition.[10]

When Brasidas had done all that could be done for Scionè and
Mendè, he turned his attention towards the affairs of Perdiccas,
who was still at war with Arrhibaeos.[11]   We are not informed
what reasons Brasidas had for leaving Chalcidicè when an Athenian attack was expected to come at any moment.   He may have
relied overmuch upon the tardiness of Athenian action and
the ease with which Arrhibaeos and the Lyncestians could be conquered.   In any case it would have been dangerous for him to
coop himself up in Pallenè with all his troops; for even should
he be successful in defeating the Athenians on land, the superiority of the hostile fleet would keep him shut up, as it were,

---

[9] Thuc. IV, **123.**
[10] Thuc. IV, **123, 129.**
[11] Thuc. IV, **124–128.**

upon an island, and would render his troops useless for further operations outside that peninsula, whether of an offensive or of a defensive nature. Perdiccas had been importunate in his demands for assistance and may even have threatened to go over to the Athenian side, unless he received aid from Brasidas immediately. Perdiccas had been helping in the maintenance of the Peloponnesian forces and felt that he had a right to some return for this expense.[12]

One thousand Chalcidian and Macedonian horse, three thousand hoplites, and an unorganized mass of Macedonians made up the combined army of Brasidas and Perdiccas. The hoplites were recruited from various sources. Besides the Peloponnesians serving under Brasidas, there were Greeks settled in Macedonia, Chalcidians, Acanthians, and soldiers furnished by other allied cities. In the battle that followed their entry into the territory of the Lyncestians, Arrhibaeos was defeated and his army was put to flight. Brasidas now wished to return, feeling apprehensive about the fate of Mendè. The expected Illyrian reinforcements then joined Arrhibaeos, the news of which so frightened the Macedonian army that it took flight immediately, carrying Perdiccas along with it. This precipitous movement left the Greek contingent alone in the enemy's country, surrounded by forces superior to them in number and in knowledge of the lay of the land. There was nothing to do but to retreat; but this retreat was so well conducted that after a few skirmishes the Barbarians ceased their attacks in the open country and tried to seize the pass through which it was necessary for the Greeks to go before leaving the territory of Arrhibaeos. Here Brasidas forestalled them, thereby reaching Macedonia in safety. But since he was unable to restrain the anger of his soldiers at their desertion by Perdiccas, and could not keep them from ruthlessly plundering the baggage train of the Macedonian army which they found at Arnissa[13], the enraged Perdiccas executed another right about face and came to terms with the Athenian generals, using all his influence against the Peloponnesians[14].

---

[12] Thuc. IV, 83.
[13] Thuc. IV, 124–128.
[14] Thuc. IV, 132; .V, 6, 80.

When he entered into negotiations with them, they required
proofs of his newly formed friendship for Athens. Thereupon
he persuaded his Thessalian friends to allow no more Spartan
forces to pass through their country to the aid of Brasidas and
the Chalcidians. This informal agreement with the Athenian
generals was later ratified and became an alliance for offensive
purposes against the Chalcidians and the other revolted allies[15].
In every way the second expedition against Arrhibaeos had
proved disastrous to the hopes and plans of Brasidas, for upon
his return to Toronè he found that Mendè had already fallen to
Athens[16]. While Brasidas was absent, the expected Athenian
expedition had arrived upon the scene of action. Nicias had
first turned his attention to Mendè. The first attack upon the
town had ended in the defeat of the Athenian troops; for the
Mendaeans, with three hundred Scionaeans and the Peloponnesians under Polydamidas, had taken their position upon a steep
hill outside the city and could not be dislodged. The next day
the Athenians changed their position, sailing around Mendè to
the south, where they took a part of the suburbs and devastated
the fields without opposition. The democratic party meanwhile
grew discontented and desirous of surrendering to Athens. The
Scionaeans, fearing that this would be done, returned to their
homes. The Athenian army divided its forces. Nicias wasted
the country as far as the Scionaean border, while Nicostratos took
up his position outside the northern gates of the city. Polydamidas, wishing to attack Nicostratos, exhorted the Mendaeans to
go out and offer battle. In repressing insubordination that broke
out among the dissatisfied members of the popular party, Polydamidas so angered the already discontented democrats that they
attacked the aristocratic party and the Peloponnesians and then
threw open the gates for the entry of the Athenians. The Peloponnesians rushed to the citadel for refuge and Nicias, who had returned, entered the town with his whole army. The place was
plundered, but, through the efforts of the generals, the lives of the
citizens were spared. Clemency was shown to the city as a whole.
Its old constitution was reestablished and the conspirators were

---

[15] *I. G.*, I, Supp., 42, p. 141.
[16] Thuc. IV, 129.

handed over to the Mendaeans for trial. The citadel with its
Peloponnesian garrison was placed in a state of siege by means of
a wall and guard.[17]

After the settlement of affairs in Mendè, the main body of
the army left the city and marched against Scionè. The defenders took their stand upon a hill outside the city but were
soon dislodged and were forced to retire into the town, where
they were joined shortly by the Peloponnesian garrison of
Mendè, which had escaped from the acropolis by night and had
eluded the Athenian guards outside Scionè. The Athenians
then proceeded to invest the city, surrounding it with a wall and
establishing a blocade[18]. Towards the end of the summer the
investment was completed and the main body of troops returned
home, leaving a guard sufficient to keep up the siege[19]. During
this time Brasidas had returned to Toronè, but, feeling that he
could not help his friends of Pallenè, he kept quiet and did nothing[20]. Perdiccas had come to terms with Nicias and as a proof
of his friendship, through his influence in Thessaly, he put a
stop to a Lacedaemonian expedition under Ischagoras that was
then fitting out for the aid of Brasidas[21]. Ischagoras, nevertheless, with Ameinias and another Spartan came through to Chalcidicè. They had been sent out by the Lacedaemonian government to learn how things stood with the Spartan allies in the
north. They brought with them certain Spartans of military
age who were intended as harmosts for the captured cities. As
there were no Spartans under the command of Brasidas, the
Lacedaemonians deemed it necessary, for the proper protection
of Spartan interests, to send reliable men to act as governors
and commanders in the newly acquired towns. Although it was
contrary to Lacedamonian custom to appoint men of age for
military service to such positions, Clearidas was made harmost
at Amphipolis and Pastelidas received a similar appointment at
Toronè.[22]

---

[17] Thuc. IV, 129f.
[18] Thuc. IV, 130f.
[19] Thuc. IV, 133.
[20] Thuc. IV, 129.
[21] Thuc. IV, 132.
[22] Thuc. IV, 132.

It seems that the Spartan commissioners used all their power and influence to make Brasidas abide by the terms of the truce, for he undertook no further operations during that summer. After they returned, towards the spring of the year 422, he made a night attack upon Potidaea, but he was detected before he had managed to scale the wall and withdrew hastily.[23].

---

[23] Thuc. IV, 135.

CHAPTER VI

CLEON'S CAMPAIGN AGAINST AMPHIPOLIS

In April of 422, the truce expired but it was not until after the Pythian games in September that hostilities actually commenced. No peace had been agreed upon[1]. Sparta sent a second body of nine hundred troops to the aid of Brasidas, but they went no further than Heraclea, being detained there by the necessity of placing affairs in that colony in a more healthy condition[2]. In Athens, Cleon was insisting constantly upon the departure of an expedition against Amphipolis. The hopes of the peace party had received a blow. The Athenians had trusted Sparta; but she had proven herself either unable or unwilling to keep the promises that she had made. So it seemed advisable to repair the breaches made in the Athenian empire by the campaigns of Brasidas. Cleon was entrusted with this task.[3] His military qualifications were few; but it was necessary to have some one in charge of the affair who was an ardent

---

[1] Thuc. V, 1. The reason for this delay was as follows. Cleon was not a member of the board of strategoi when the truce ended in April 422. At that time his political opponents held office. Laches, Nicostratos, and Nicias were the leaders of the opposition. Evidently it was not thought advisable to entrust anything of importance to men who were opposed to a continuation of the war. Cleon came into office towards the end of July, but instead of immediately setting sail for Chalcidicè he waited until after the Pythian games which came in September. How are we to explain this inactivity and to reconcile it with Cleon's eagerness to renew the war in the north? It would be inexplicable but for the fact that the Etesian winds during the summer months make voyages northward almost impossible. They commence about the 22nd of July and blow for forty days until about the first of September. This explains the whole course of events. Cleon was unable to sail before September, but his eagerness to renew the war was such that he persuaded the Athenians to undertake an autumn campaign. Autumn campaigns were greatly disliked by the citizen soldiery of Athens, and to this may be due a part of the dis content of Cleon's troops.

[2] Thuc. V, 12.
[3] Thuc. V, 2.

supporter of the war policy. Although a majority of the citizens were in favour of the undertaking, a large minority, consisting of the middle classes, had no sympathy with it. From this minority came, in large part, the hoplites to whom the carrying out of the affair must necessarily be entrusted. This fact, taken together with the popular Athenian distrust of Cleon's ability as a general, created a general unwillingness to serve under him on the part of those chosen for the expedition[4]. He had under his command thirty ships carrying twelve hundred Athenian hoplites, three hundred horse, and a body of allies. In addition to these forces, he expected Perdiccas to send reinforcements, in accordance with the alliance of the previous year. Polles also was called upon to bring to the aid of the Athenian army as many Thracian mercenaries as possible[5]. Brasidas, by this time, had left Toronè, his headquarters, and had gone to Amphipolis to assist Clearidas in making all necessary preparations for its defence; for it was no secret that Athens wished to regain this city above all others[6].

Cleon touched first at Scionè, still under siege, but, finding that its capture was only a matter of time, he did not delay long there. Taking with him as many of the besieging hoplites as could well be spared, he crossed to the peninsula of Sithonia, landing in the so-called harbour of the Colophonians near Toronè. When he learned that Brasidas had left the city, he made an attack upon it, both by land and by sea. The new fortifications, of much larger extent than the old, were still unfinished and the garrison of the city was not large enough to guard the full length of the walls and to defend the harbour. Thus while Pastelidas was busily engaged protecting the new wall enclosing the suburbs, the Athenian fleet sailed into the port and took the town. The citizens of Toronè, together with the Peloponnesians and the Chalcidians engaged in the defence of the place were sent as prisoners to Athens, while the women and children were

[4] Thuc. V, 7.
[5] Thuc. V, 2, 6.
[6] Ibid.

sold into slavery. Cleon left a garrison in the city and sailed around Mt. Athos, on his way towards Amphipolis[7].

As soon as Brasidas learned that Cleon had arrived in the Chalcidic peninsula, fearing for the safety of Toronè and knowing its weaknesses, he hastened to its aid. Cleon, however, had anticipated him and the capture of the city took place when he was still four and a half miles from it[8]. When he heard that it had fallen he returned with all speed towards Amphipolis. Cleon made Eion his headquarters, where he awaited the arrival of expected reinforcements from Perdiccas and Polles, king of the Odomantes.[9] During this time the towns of Actè were readmitted into the Athenian empire, probably at their own request. Cleon also attacked Stageiros but failed in his attempt to take it. Galepsos, however, which had submitted to Brasidas after the capture of Amphipolis, was retaken[10].

Brasidas took a position upon a high hill called Cerdylion, across the river from Amphipolis in the territory of Argilos. Here he was able to keep a close watch upon the movements of the enemy. His army, in addition to his own forces, included one thousand Edonian and Chalcidian peltasts and three hundred horse. He had summoned, as well, fifteen hundred mercenaries from Thrace and the whole body of Edonian troops. His heavy armed forces amounted in all to two thousand men. Of these, he kept with himself upon Cerdylion fifteen hundred, while the rest remained under the command of Clearidas in the city[11].

The armies of the two commanders were about equal in num-

---

[7] Thuc. V, 2f; Müller-Strübung, *Thuk. Forsch.*, pp. 262f. It is probable that many of the women and children had been sent into safety in the interior, perhaps to Olynthos. The prisoners were exchanged later through the kind offices of the Olynthians. The women and children of Scionè had been sent to Olynthos at the time of the expected Athenian attack. Cf. Thuc. IV, 123.

[8] Thuc. V, 3.

[9] Thuc. V, 6.

[10] Thuc. V, 6. If the towns of Actè had been captured by Cleon the probabilities are that Thucydides would have mentioned the fact, or they would have been included with Toronè, Scionè, and Sermylia in the treaty of the following year. That Cleon recovered them is seen from the fact that Cleonae is in the tribute list of 421 and that Thyssos revolted to the Chalcidians soon after the peace. Thuc. V, 35; *I. G.*, I, Supp., p. 141, no. 37; cf. Kirchoff, *Thuk. u. s. Urkundenmaterial*, pp. 42ff and *infra* Chap. VIII, note 9.

[11] Thuc. V, 6.

bers, but the insubordination of the Athenian soldiers, due to their distrust of Cleon, here manifested itself. Their impatience forced Cleon to act. Drawing out his whole army to investigate the lay of the land, he was led into a trap that cost him his life and lost the battle for Athens. He had no intention, whatever, of fighting before the arrival of his reinforcements. Thus when he saw the enemy within the city preparing to sally out against him, he gave the order to retreat. This retreat he managed so unskilfully that he left his center open to the attack of the enemy. Brasidas attacked with a handful of men and found the Athenians so unprepared that he routed their center and left wing easily. Clearidas with his troops sallied out against the right wing where Cleon was stationed, and after a short resistance here, the Athenians turned and fled, Cleon himself being the first to leave the field of battle. Those that escaped slaughter made their way to Eion and from there they took ship for Athens. Six hundred Athenians lost their lives in the battle, among which number was their general, Cleon.[12]

On the other side the loss was small in numbers, but Brasidas was among the slain. He was buried in the city of Amphipolis with great ceremony. The services that he had rendered the city seemed so great in the eyes of the citizens that he was given the title of "Founder" and all the honours pertaining to that title, games, and annual sacrifices. The real founder, Hagno, the Athenian, was thus degraded and displaced[13].

[12] Thuc. V, 7–11. Perhaps the impatience of the Athenian soldiers was due in part to a desire to put an end to the autumn campaign, so that they could return home or at least go into winter quarters in Amphipolis.
[13] Thuc. V, 11.

CHAPTER VII

THE PEACE OF NICIAS

Now that in both Athens and Sparta the war party had lost its leader everything seemed favourable to a rapid consummation of peace. Each side had something to offer in exchange for that which it desired to receive. Sparta wanted most of all the return of the prisoners held by Athens and the evacuation of the places held upon its coast. Athens wished the return of the colonies it had lost in the north. Other reasons for peace were not lacking. Towards the end of the winter of 422 Athens and Sparta entered into negotiations which resulted in an agreement that each side should give up all that it had gained by force of arms. This caused much dissatisfaction among the Peloponnesian allies, but early in 421 Sparta, together with a majority of allies, accepted peace for a period of fifty years upon these terms[1].

So far as the history of the Chalcidic league and of its neighbours is concerned the conditions were as follows. First of all, the Lacedaemonians and their allies, i. e., the Chalcidians, Acanthians, etc., were to restore Amphipolis to Athens.[2] This was the most important item, without which the Athenians would never have consented to a peace. The Chalcidians as Spartan allies were then included in the treaty whether they wished it or not. Sparta was willing enough to pledge their obedience to the terms she had made; but when it came to fulfilling these terms she found herself unable to enforce them without recourse to arms. At Amphipolis there was a Lacedaemonian harmost with a Peloponnesian garrison and Athens trusted that Sparta would be able to hand the city over to her. Moreover, it was

---

[1] Thuc. V, 14ff.
[2] Thuc. V, 18, 5.

undoubtedly an Athenian colony and had been captured from
her during the war. The right of Athens to the place was un-
questionable. The only difficulty was that the Amphipolitans
were unwilling to return to their allegiance. The Chalcidians
seem to have had considerable influence in the town, for Thucydides tells us that Clearidas, working in their interests, refused to give up Amphipolis to the Athenians[3].

The conditions with regard to Argilos, Stageiros, Acanthos,
Stolos, Olynthos, and Spartolos were different[4]. The first three
were Andrian colonies that had come over to Brasidas at his request. None of them had been taken by actual force of arms.
Olynthos, Spartolos, and Stolos, likewise, had not been captured
by Sparta but had been Lacedaemonian allies from the very beginning of the war. These six, therefore, were to receive a sem-
blance of autonomy for which they were to pay to Athens the
tribute as it had been assessed by Aristides[5]. They were to have
the right of entry into alliance with Athens if they so desired;
but she could not use force upon them, except in default of payment of tribute. Sparta renounced all claims to alliance with
them. It was not possible for her literally to hand them over to
Athens. These cities were only her allies and not dependencies
and she had no garrisons in them by which she could force them
to do as she chose. Athens, however, had gained her point. By
the treaty, these cities had become members of her empire. If
they proved refractory, Sparta had promised not to interfere
when they refused to pay the tribute. In that case she could attack them and do with them as she chose. If they became dis-
couraged because of their desertion by Sparta and paid their
tribute, Athens would be saved the trouble of more forceful
measures. Another fact is to be noted here. No mention of

---

[3] Thuc. V, 21.
[4] Thuc. V, 18, 5.
[5] The word used in the treaty for the action of the Lacedaemonians is
παρέδοσαν. This can only mean that Sparta renounced all claims to alliance with these cities. It can not mean that she promised literally to
give them up, for, except possibly for Amphipolis, which had a Lacedaemonian garrison, these cities were only her allies and not dependencies.
Hence Sparta had no authority over them. Moreover, she had her promises made to them to perform and if she failed in this, she could expect
nothing more nor less than a rejection of the treaty by these allies. The
Chalcidians, in fact, did refuse to accept the treaty.

the Chalcidians by name is found in the treaty. The same thing
is true of the Bottiaeans. In place of this occur the names of
the cities, Spartolos, the chief city of the Bottiaeans, and Olynthos and Stolos, two Chalcidian cities. It is definitely stated,
moreover, that the Spartan allies were to take the oaths κατὰ
πόλεις. This warrants us in the conclusion that Athens was
unwilling to recognize the newly formed states and wished to
weaken their prestige, as far as possible, by making individual
cities swear to the treaty. This would form another objection
to the peace from the standpoint of the Chalcidians.

Mecyperna, Sanè, and Singos were to be autonomous just as
Olynthos and Acanthos.[6] The fact that these three towns come
under a separate classification is of peculiar interest here. Various conflicting explanations of this state of affairs have been
given. Why was a separate category formed for these three
cities, and how did they differ from those in the preceding list?
It can be taken for granted that the article which refers to Sanè,
Singos, and Mecyperna was not put in as an afterthought. There
is still another question that must be answered. What have
Olynthos and Acanthos to do with these cities, that their names
should be inserted here? Are they to be considered merely examples, chosen because they happened to be the most important
cities, or are they of special significance? Before we enter upon
a discussion of the explanation of this clause of the treaty, it is
necessary for us to pass in review what we know of the histories
of these three cities. Sanè was an Andrian colony, situated upon
the peninsula of Actè near the place where Xerxes dug his famous canal.[7] Plutarch tells an interesting story of its foundation
and of the part it played in the settlement of Acanthos.[8] According to his version of the story it was founded by Andrians and
Chalcidians acting in concert. This is borne out to a certain
slight extent by Thucydides, who says that part of the inhabitants of Actè were of the Chalcidic race.[9] After Sanè had been
captured from its original inhabitants it was learned that Acan-

[6] Thuc. V, 18.
[7] Thuc. IV, 109.
[8] Plutarch, *Aetia Gr.*, 30. It is to be remembered that Andros was at an
early date an Eretrian dependency.
[9] Thuc. IV, 109.

thos was deserted; whereupon scouts were sent out to ascertain the truth of the matter. These scouts learned that the rumor was correct; and one of them, a Chalcidian, conceived the idea of claiming the city for the Chalcidians. When they were near the city he broke into a run, hoping to enter Acanthos first and then lay claim to it by right of priority of arrival. An Andrian scout guessed his purpose and, being unable to overtake him, cast his spear ahead of the Chalcidian into the Acanthian territory. Both parties then asserted their rights to the city and it was referred to the arbitration of the Erythraeans, Samians, and Parians. The first two decided in favour of the Andrians, but the Parians upheld the Chalcidian claim. The interesting thing about this story is the fact that, in the time of Plutarch, there was a tradition connecting Sanè and Acanthos. During the time of the Athenian empire, Sanè was one of the many minor cities of the Thracian district. Its tribute was raised from two-thirds of a talent to a talent. During the war, this was lowered to one-sixth, which it paid in 427.[10] In the winter of 424–3 it resisted the attack of Brasidas and was not captured by him.[11] After this we have no further mention of the city until its name occurs in the treaty of peace.

Of Singos little is known. It was situated upon the east coast of the neck of Sithonia. It is impossible to say by whom the city was founded, but as it lay in Sithonia where the Chalcidians settled, it is probable that it too was a Chalcidian colony.[12] Kirchoff[13] suggests that it, like Sanè, was Andrian; but his only proof for this hypothesis is that it is mentioned in the treaty after Sanè. He wishes to bring it into connection with Acanthos. The quota lists show that it was a more important city than Sanè, originally, but that it dwindled gradually, until in 436 it was paying but one talent tribute. Before that it had been paying four, three, and two talents per annum. After 436 it is found in no list. Thucydides fails completely to mention it in his account of the war in Chalcidicè. Its name occurs in the

---

[10] *I. G.*, I, 234, 446 B. C.; 244, 436 B. C.; 259, 427 B. C.
[11] Thuc. IV, 109.
[12] Strabo, VII, 329, frg. 11.
[13] Kirchoff, *Thuk. u. s. Urkundenmaterial*, p. 46.

treaty of 421 but nowhere else.   It is important to note, however,
that it was placed upon the τάξις φόρου of 421–0, but the tribute
assessed to it was the nominal one of ten drachmas.[14]

Mecyperna was upon the coast near Olynthos and was in fact
the harbour of that place.[15]   Thus probably it was a Chalcidian
town.   In the quota list of 454 it is found joined with the Chalcidian city Stolos, for some reason unknown.   After that, however, whenever it appears upon the lists, it is alone.   Its tribute
varied from two-thirds of a talent to a talent.   Like Singos it
appears in none of the extant lists after 436 and is not mentioned
by Thucydides until its name occurs in the treaty.   In the τάξις
φόρου of 421–0 it is also found and its assessment is the same
as that of Singos, ten drachmas.[16]   In the winter of that year, an
Athenian garrison was in the city, but a raid made upon it by
the Olynthians was successful and it was captured by them.[17]

In summing up, we find that Sanè was an Andrian colony, with
perhaps some Chalcidian elements.   Mecyperna was Chalcidian
and Singos was situated in territory settled by Chalcidians.
From 436 until 421 we have no knowledge as to whether Mecyperna and Singos were faithful to Athens or not.   Their names
are not found in the list of 428, which is complete for the Thracian district.[18]   This is purely negative evidence, for their names
may have occurred elsewhere in one of the appendices that are so
often found in the later lists.[19]   Sanè remained faithful until
424, but after that nothing is known.

The question resolves into the following.   Would there have
been any necessity or reason for making a separate provision in
the treaty of peace for these cities, if they had never revolted
from Athens, and for stating it as a corollary to the provision relating to Olynthos and Acanthos?   Furthermore is it possible

---

[14] *I. G.*, I, 226, 454 B. C.; 228, 452 B. C.; 230, 450 B. C.; 234, 446 B. C.; 242,
438 B. C.; 244, 436 B. C.; Supp., p. 141, no. 37.   This belongs with frg. z″
which has been wrongly dated in the year 425; cf. note 9, Chap. VIII.
[15] Strabo, VII, 330, frg. 29.
[16] *I. G.*, I, 226, 454 B. C.; 235, 445 B. C.; 242, 438 B. C.; 244, 436 B. C.;
Supp., p. 141, no. 37.
[17] Thuc. V, 39.
[18] *I. G.*, I, 256.
[19] This, however, is improbable, as the appendices usually contain the
names of towns of minor importance.

that two cities situated in the heart of the rebellion, such as were
Mecyperna and Singos, could have remained faithful to Athens?
If these cities revolted, did Sanè revolt between 424 and 421, or,
if it did not, why was it placed with the others in this treaty?
If they all remained faithful, why mention them at all?

These questions are very difficult to answer, and it is not surprising that so many differences of opinion have arisen. The
words of the treaty are as follows. The Mecypernaeans, the
Sanaeans, and the Singians are to inhabit their own cities just as
the Olynthians and the Acanthians. Does the word οἰκεῖν mean to
inhabit or to govern? It may even mean "to settle in." It is
evidently the crucial word of the passage and upon its interpretation depends, to a large extent, the meaning of this provision of
the treaty. If οἰκεῖν means, in this passage, "to govern", it is
clear that these three cities are to be autonomous, to pay the
Aristidean tribute and to become Athenian allies, if the Athenians could persuade them to take this step. These were the conditions that applied to Olynthos and Acanthos. The inference
is that the cities were not at that time Athenian allies and were
not paying tribute. To go further, is there any evidence that
they paid the Aristidean tribute or even were assessed the Aristidean tribute for the following year? As for Sanè, there is no
evidence whatever, but for the other two we are in a more fortunate position. According to the τάξις φόρου of 421 they were
assessed ten drachmas each. This is a mere nominal sum and
no one will deny the impossibility of so small a tribute having
been assessed by Aristides. There is no other case on record, so
far as I know, of such a sum, except in this τάξις φόρου of 421.*
It is, moreover, much less than that paid by these cities from
454 on. It is not probable that conditions had changed so materially in the twenty-five years since the first establishment of
the tribute. The change from ten drachmas to four talents in
the case of Singos and from ten drachmas to one talent in the
case of Mecyperna is scarcely conceivable under ordinary conditions.[20]

---

* But cf. *I. G.*, I, 37, where Keria is assessed ten and one-half drachmas.
[20] *I. G.*, I, 226–259; I, Supp., p. 141, 37.

If then οἰκεῖν means "to govern" and the cities of Mecyperna, Singos, and Sanè were not Athenian allies, as we have shown, how did they differ from Acanthos and Olynthos, that they should have a special article to themselves? From this alone, it is hard to see how they can have differed. We have shown, however, that the Aristidean tribute did not apply to them and the only conclusion is that οἰκεῖν does not refer to government at all. It must then refer to settlement or to habitation proper. If so, our inference is that the inhabitants had not been dwelling in their own cities. Where then had they been dwelling? We have seen that it was a policy of the Chalcidians from the very start of the revolt to concentrate themselves in their capital city, Olynthos. Stahl in his edition of Poppo's *Thucydides*[21] thinks that these are two of the cities upon the seacoast which participated in the anoikism of Olynthos. He thinks that the Sanè of the treaty is not the Sanè of Actè but another town of the same name situated upon the peninsula of Pallenè near Potidaea.[22] Steup, however, has shown that this assumption is inadmissible. If there had been two cities of any importance with the same name, it would have been necessary to distinguish them in some way in an important document like a treaty.[23] Moreover the fact that Acanthos is mentioned with Olynthos in this article shows that it had some connection with one of the three cities named therein. This necessitates the assumption that the Andrian Sanè is under discussion. To leave Sanè and Acanthos aside for a moment, let us consider the question of the others. As we have said, Mecyperna and Singos are not found in any extant tribute list after 436. This is of course no proof that they were not at that time faithful Athenian allies; but the complete preservation of the quota lists of 428 and 427 in their Thracian parts renders it probable that they had revolted. They were, moreover, right in the heart of the rebellion, Mecyperna from the beginning and Singos, if not then, at least after the capture of Sithonia by Brasidas. Mecyperna was less than two and a quarter miles from Olynthos and it is inconceivable that the Chalcidians should have allowed

---

[21] Stahl–Poppo, *Thuc.* V, **18**, note.
[22] Hdt. VII, **123**; Strabo, VII, 330, frg. 27; Steph. Byz., Σάνη.
[23] Steup, *Thuk. Stud.*, pp. 44ff; cf. Kirchoff, *op. cit.*, pp. 46f.

the Athenians to hold so important a post in the midst of their
territory. Hence we must conclude that this was one of the
cities which participated in the original revolt and most probably in the anoikism. It is not so certain that Singos was among
the number of the rebellious cities in 432; but its situation was
such that it must have joined in one of the following years, probably in the interval between 432 and 428. As it is not mentioned
in the account of Brasidas' exploits, which are given in such detail, and as the capture of it could not have been neglected by
him, one must assume that it had revolted at some previous time.
If it had been an Athenian ally, its position commanding the entrance to Sithonia would have made it necessary for Brasidas to
attempt its capture before advancing upon Toronè, and if he had
done so with success, or otherwise, one must assume that Thucydides would have mentioned it, since he takes pains to mention
the successful resistance of two small towns like Sanè and Dion
during this same campaign. On the other hand, if it had revolted of its own accord during the early years, Thucydides need
not have mentioned the fact of its union with the Chalcidians,
for he fails completely to give the names of the cities that joined
with Olynthos to make up the Chalcidian state. Hence we must
conclude that Singos revolted from Athens during the first years
of the war and moved the greater part of its inhabitants to Olynthos. There is no other satisfactory explanation of the οἰκεῖν
clause. If Mecyperna and Singos had remained faithful Athenian allies and had retained their inhabitants, why should they,
more than others, be mentioned in the treaty and why should
permission be granted to them to go on living where they had always lived? This permission is granted to no other city. Moreover, the tribute list of 421 shows that something had happened
to weaken them very materially, for otherwise they would have
been assessed more than ten drachmas tribute. This is the
strongest indication we have that Mecyperna and Singos had lost
the greater part of their inhabitants and we must connect this
loss of population with the well known Chalcidian policy of concentrating its power in Olynthos, especially since this policy was
concerned with sea-coast towns that would be hard to protect.
This is a further indication that the revolt of Singos occurred in

the early years before the arrival of Brasidas, for, after his arrival, such a policy was not so necessary. The power of Brasidas
was felt to be sufficient to protect the cities that rebelled. Except for the tribute list of 421 and this article of the treaty, our
proof is largely negative, but I think that it is clearly established,—first, that Mecyperna and Singos revolted during the
early part of the war, secondly, that their inhabitants moved to
Olynthos, and finally, that this article of the treaty provides for
the resettlement of these towns by the original inhabitants.

Steup and Kirchoff maintain that these cities were in the possession of Athens at the time of the treaty.[24] So far as one can
judge, their conclusions are based upon the possibility that Mecyperna and Singos were included in the appendices of the quota
list of 428, the fact that Sanè remained faithful to Athens up to
424, and the fact that in the winter of 421–0 Mecyperna was in
the hands of the Athenians, although Thucydides fails to mention
the fact of its capture. They think that, if it had been recaptured between the winter of 422–1 and 421–0, Thucydides would
certainly have mentioned it. As for the first argument, it is
weaker than pure negative evidence and can not be used against
the probability that these cities could not have remained in the
Athenian alliance while their neighbours, on all sides, were in
revolt. The history of Sanè up to 424 can prove nothing for
Mecyperna and Singos and the silence of Thucydides is entirely
negative.

As for Singos, Steup thinks that Thucydides' description of
the anoikism prevents one from assuming that this town participated in it. The word ἀνοικίσασθαι gives one the impression
that the cities to which the author is referring were separated
from Olynthos neither by ''Berghöhen'' nor by foreign territory. This eliminates Singos. This is confirmed, he thinks,
by the fact that Toronè, a Chalcidic city, did not take part in
the uprising. As we have shown, however, there is no necessity
for assuming that Singos revolted in 432 but only that the revolt
occurred in one of the early years of the war. Hence the de-

---

[24] Steup, pp. 40ff.; Kirchoff, *Thuk. u. s. Urkundenmaterial*, pp. 46ff. For
the capture of Mecyperna in the winter of 421–0 see Thuc. V, 39.

scription of the events of 432 need not have reference to Singos, and the use of the word ἀνοικίσασθαι can not be taken as an objection to the hypothesis that Singos followed the example of the other towns when she finally revolted.

What then about his other thesis that Olynthos and Acanthos had at some time or other claimed sovereignty over these three cities, the first over Mecyperna and the second over Sanè and Singos, and that this article was placed in the treaty at the request of Athens, in order to prevent any assertion of these claims? Athens feared that Olynthos and Acanthos would again assert this sovereignty and so had every reason for wishing it to be expressly stated that her allies Mecyperna, Singos, and Sanè were to be autonomous, just as were their former masters. Sparta in agreeing to this denies that Acanthos and Olynthos have any claims, whether old or new, upon these Athenian allies. Kirchoff goes a step further and says that the sovereignty dated from the times before the Athenian supremacy in the Chalcidic peninsula. In any case, in the quota lists, there is no sign of such dependence of Mecyperna, Singos, and Sanè upon Olynthos and Acanthos. Mecyperna may have been originally a dependency of Stolos or vice versa for they are found together in the list for 454, but there is no sign of any connection between it and Olynthos nor of the other cities with Acanthos.[25] It is not clear how Olynthos can have had any claim to Mecyperna before the time of the Athenian control in Chalcidicè for it did not receive its Chalcidian inhabitants until 479, almost immediately preceding the formation of the Delian League. Granted, however, that Olynthos and Acanthos had this supremacy at this early date, from 454 on it can only have been a theoretical supremacy and not an actual one; and if they were unable to assert this theoretical sovereignty during the time of the war,—that is to say, if these three cities remained faithful to Athens against the will of their masters,—Athens need have had little fear that they would be disloyal and would return to conditions existing more than fifty years before. If Olynthos and Acanthos had no part in the affairs of Mecyperna, Sanè, and Singos, and could not persuade them to revolt, their

[25] *I. G.*, I, 226.

claims were altogether too idle to cause Athens to think seriously
about them for a moment. As for Sanè, what we know of its
early history would seem to imply that it rather than Acanthos
would have, in theory at least, the sovereign position. If we are
to assume anything, it is this, that Mecyperna and possibly
Singos were members of some early Chalcidian union, and not
dependencies of a small town like Olynthos. We must remember that Olynthos was a very unimportant little village until the
revolt of 432.

We come back then to the point from which we started. The
sovereignty was an actual one and dates from the time of the
revolt of each of the cities, and probably not before. Steup
seems to have come near to the truth in his discussion of Mecyperna. He admits the possibility of its having been one of the
seacoast towns destroyed at the beginning of the war. He then
goes on. If the city had been actually deserted by its inhabitants and destroyed in 432, what conclusions can be drawn from
this as to the conditions existing in the winter of 422–1? Is it
not possible that the Mecypernaeans were induced to return
to their Athenian allegiance through discontent at the state
of affairs resulting from the synoecism or for some other reason? He closes by saying that the language of Thuc. V, 39, 1,
does not allow of a doubt that the city was in existence at that
time. Such a rebuilding of Mecyperna must be presupposed.
He thus admits that Mecyperna had taken part in the synoecism,
or as I have called it the anoikism. It seems probable to me
that the same thing later happened to Singos, but that the desertion of the sites was not so complete as Steup would have us
suppose. It is more than probable that many of the inhabitants
were averse from leaving their homes and for this reason remained
loyal to Athens, at least to the extent of being silent sympathizers in an enemy's country. If so, it may well be that some
of them stayed in the deserted towns. One can not tell whether
the citizens who had not wished it had been forced to take up
their abode in Olynthos. Probably this was not the case where
the town was fairly large and the dissenting minority considerable. If then a certain number of the inhabitants remained in
these two places, they would take care not to awaken the hos-

tility of the Chalcidians, unless they saw Athens in a position
to protect them. This was never the case from almost the first
day of the revolt until the year 421. Hence Thucydides had no
occasion to mention them until the treaty of that year.

At the time when the negotiations were being carried on, conditions probably were as follows. Mecyperna and Singos were
villages in the territory of the Chalcidic league. Most of their
population had moved to Olynthos. The citizens who remained,
and perhaps others as well mourned for the loss of the prestige
of their native cities, desiring to be freed from Chalcidian
domination and to return to the Athenian alliance once more
as autonomous cities. The Chalcidians of course were loath to
give them up, but they were not in a position to influence either
Sparta or Athens so as to be allowed to retain them in their possession. Athens wished above all to regain what she had lost
and to break up the Chalcidian power, while Sparta had no reason to object to the reestablishment of these cities upon their
former footing as Athenian allies. We may assume that affairs took approximately the following course. The few loyal
inhabitants of Mecyperna and Singos informed Athens of their
wishes to be freed from Chalcidian rule and to rebuild their
cities, asserting that they were ready to become allies of Athens.
This suggestion proved acceptable to the Athenians, for having
lost Olynthos and other allied cities once under her power, they
were only too happy to remove from Chalcidian influence towns
that desired protection and alliance. In this way they might
regain some of their lost ground and cripple their enemies.
Sparta had no objection to this. Both sides had agreed that the
Chalcidian league, as such, was to have no recognition in the
treaty and that the basis of city autonomy should be maintained.[26] Thus Sparta, after deserting Olynthos and her other
allies, could not very well object to the special terms given to
Mecyperna and Singos.

Unfortunately Sanè is difficult to fix in this category nor does

---

[26] The fact that Stolos and Olynthos are named in the treaty and not the
Chalcidians and that the oaths were to be sworn κατὰ πόλεις warrants us
in the conclusion that Athens was unwilling to recognize the newly formed
state and wished to ignore it by making the individual Chalcidian cities swear
to the treaty.

it appear in the fragmentary τάξις φόρου of 421.[27]   We can get no help from that quarter.   The episode of Plutarch already related shows that it was connected by tradition with Acanthos.   It remained faithful to Athens up to 424, and in 427 its tribute had been reduced from one talent to one-sixth.[28]   In 424 it had been able to repulse an attack of Brasidas, but after that nothing is known of it.   The fact that it occurs with Mecyperna and Singos in this article of the treaty seems to point to a revolt or to a capture by Acanthos.   At that time probably the Acanthians followed Chalcidian methods and removed most of the inhabitants to their own city.   We can perhaps date this capture between the battle of Amphipolis and the conclusion of the peace in the following spring.   Although Thucydides does not mention it, it is probable that it occurred at that time.   It has been shown that, before the battle of Amphipolis, Cleon had recovered the cities upon Actè that had gone over to Brasidas, and so there is no reason to suppose that Acanthos had taken Sanè before that time. We can not imagine that hostilities ceased in the Chalcidic peninsula during the interval between the battle and the final treaty of peace, even though Thucydides did not mention them.   Without doubt they were for the most part of little importance; but that they ceased entirely cannot be believed, since the Chalcidians and their allies were prompted by quite other motives than the Spartans.   Thucydides was busy narrating the progress of the peace negotiations and might easily have omitted to mention the capture of a small place like Sanè, as he omitted the recovery of Actè by Cleon.   Captured, then made subject to Acanthos, and deprived of its inhabitants, in part, at least, Sanè was in much the same position as were Mecyperna and Singos, and it could be included in the same article of the treaty.

This article gives a good picture of the methods employed by the Chalcidian state.   We are not to suppose, however, that all cities that entered the Chalcidian league were destroyed.   Stolos, as the treaty shows, had not lost its identity; but it is to be remembered that this town was situated in the interior, a little

---

[27] *I. G.*, I, Supp., p. 141, no. 37.
[28] *I. G.*, I, 256, 259.

to the north-east of Olynthos. Probably only the sea coast towns were evacuated. This agrees with the account of Thucydides for the first year of the revolt.[29] While Olynthos was uniting the neighbouring Chalcidians under her leadership, Spartolos seems to have been doing the same thing for the Bottiaeans as the coins of that nation show[30]. Thus it is not strange that Acanthos, the most important Andrian colony of the peninsula, should follow the example of Olynthos and Spartolos and attempt to form an Andrian state. Her first venture resulted in the capture of Sanè.

The other articles of the treaty were as follows.[31] All prisoners were to be returned, including those that would be taken at the capture of Scionè. The inhabitants of Scionè, Toronè, and Sermylia, and of any other city that Athens had recaptured or was besieging, were to be at the mercy of Athens. The treaty was to be sworn to by Athens, Sparta, and the allies, city by city.

It is clear from the wording of the treaty that Sermylia had at some time revolted and had been recovered by Athens. When this occurred Thucydides does not state. The city was still tributary in 430[32], although it had been an object of attack by Aristeus and the Chalcidians in the first year of the war. It seems probable that its revolt is to be placed at about the same time as that of Singos. Both names are lacking in the almost complete lists of 428 and 427.[33] Sermylia is situated at the base of Sithonia on the western side, while Singos was upon the side away from Olynthos. The more distant city would be likely to hesitate until the territory between it and Olynthos had been annexed to the Chalcidian state. By the time, at least, of Brasidas' activity, when the rest of Sithonia was in revolt, it had been forced to join in the movement. Athens had recaptured it before 421; but this again Thucydides passes over in silence. Scionè was not yet in the possession of Athens; but it was in a state of siege and its capture was only a question of time. The

---

[29] Thuc. I, 58.
[30] *B. M, C. Maced.*, p. 63, nos. 1–4. Coins two and three, as I have shown, are to be dated in the years 432–421 instead of in 392–379 as given.
[31] Thuc. V, **18**.
[32] *I. G.*, I, 255, B. c. 430(?).
[33] *I. G.*, I, 256, 259.

capture of Toronè has already been related. The other cities mentioned, but not named, were Mendè, Galepsos, and the cities upon Actè.[34]

---

[34] See Chapter VI.

CHAPTER VIII

CHALCIDIAN DIPLOMACY TO THE END OF THE FIFTH CENTURY

Sparta was vouching for the willingness of cities over which she had no control to accept the peace. The Chalcidians were not members of the Peloponnesian league and had no part in the negotiations for the peace. They were in a position to demand better terms. They were in alliance with Corinth and with Sparta, and the latter had no right to dictate to them nor to command them to become subjects of the Athenian Empire once more. The Chalcidians had revolted in order to be free from Athenian domination and had maintained their freedom against all that Athens could do. Acanthos and her neighbours also were allies of Sparta and had received promises of protection and freedom. Hence all had a just grievance against the Lacedaemonians for the readiness with which they had broken their promises when they accepted such terms as these.[1] It is true that they were not to be given absolutely into Athenian hands. The tribute was merely to be reimposed at the original figure. We are unable to go back of 454, but Argilos was paying in that year the immense sum of ten and one-half talents. By 445 this had been reduced to one, and, in 436 again, to one sixth of a talent. In 454 Stolos together with Mecyperna paid in excess of five talents, but in later years neither of them were assessed at more than a talent. We can tell little about Olynthos, for in 454 it was joined with Scabla and Assera, paying an uncertain amount that may have been as high as four and a fraction or as low as two talents. Thus if the tribute of 454 is any indication of the Aristidean tribute, Stolos and Argilos, and possibly Olynthos, would have fared worse under a renewal

---

[1] Thuc. V, 21, 35.

of the early tribute than they were faring at the time of the revolt. Hence they would have reason to be dissatisfied with the conditions imposed upon them.[2]

The treaty was to be sworn by the allies κατὰ πόλεις. This was another point with which the Chalcidians might well be dissatisfied, for it was an attempt to break up their recently formed state. All cities that had joined them, provided their existence had not been completely blotted out, were to be detached from the league and to be given the opportunity to take charge of their foreign relations once more. The κοινόν was to be deprived of the right of acting for the whole body of Chalcidians. Thus everything that the Chalcidians had gained during the revolt was to be taken away. They were again to become Athenian tributaries; the state for which they had laboured was to be dismembered; and the territory over which the Chalcidians had been ruling was to return to Athenian masters. In promising that the Chalcidians would acquiesce in such unjust conditions, Sparta had undertaken more than she could accomplish. Several of her allies refused to take the oaths and without general agreement between Sparta and her northern allies nothing could be done in carrying out the Lacedaemonian promises.[3]

The lot decided that Sparta was to make restitution first. The prisoners that she held were immediately released, and Ischagoras, Menas, and Philocharidas were sent as commissioners to the Chalcidic peninsula to see that Clearidas delivered Amphipolis to the Athenians and to persuade the other cities to accept the conditions of the peace that had reference to them. This they were unable to do, and a general protest against the treaty was raised by the Spartan allies in the north. Clearidas, imbued with the spirit of Brasidas and sympathizing with the Chalcidians, declared that he was unable to give Amphipolis to the Athenians against its will. Taking envoys with him from

---

[2] *I. G.*, I, 226, 235, 244. But cf. Francotte, *Les Finances des Cités Grecques*, pp. 101f., who contends that this article of the treaty does not require the payment of a fixed amount, but merely provides that the ratio between the tribute and the wealth of the town should be the same as that fixed by Aristides.

[3] Thuc. V, 21, 35.

the protesting cities, he hastened to Sparta to see what could be
done for them. Finding that the peace had been sworn and
persuading the Spartans that it was beyond his power to surrender a city belonging to others, he was ordered to return and
to withdraw all Peloponnesian forces from that region. This he
did.[4]

The Bottiaeans took this opportunity of making their peace
with Athens and soon afterwards an alliance was formed in accordance with the terms of the treaty.[5] In the spring of 420 we

---

[4] Thuc. V, 21, 34f.

[5] Hicks and Hill, no. 68. This inscription has been variously dated. Von
Scala, *Staatsverträge*, no. 82, and Busolt, III, 2, p. 1171, have assigned it to
the year 422 and think that this alliance was a direct result of the alliance
between Athens and Perdiccas. Meyer, *G. D. A.*, IV, pp. 494ff., thinks that
because of the orthography it belongs after the year 420, and so places it in
the year 417. It seems to me that this is an alliance between the Bottiaeans
and Athens in accordance with the terms of the treaty of peace of 421. The
Bottiaeans had grown tired of the war and were willing to return to their
original position as Athenian tributaries and allies. As evidence for this,
we have a fragment of a quota list for the year 421–0, *I. G.*, I, 260, bearing the names of two Bottiaean towns, Kamakai and Tripoiai. Sinos also
is probably Bottiaean. Köhler, *Sitz.-ber. d. Ber. Akad.*, 1891, 476. It
is to be noted, however, that the names [Τριπ]οαί Σίνος (in rasura) have been
found in frg. *y* of *I. G.*, I, 37, which has been assigned to the year 425, but
probably belongs to the τάξις φόρου of 421. Cf. Cavaignac, *Le Trésor
d'Athènes*, pp. XLVf, Pl. I, 3; and note 9, *infra*. Of these Kamakai and
Tripoiai are found in the fragmentary list of cities at the bottom of the inscription containing the alliance with Athens. Also the τάξις φόρου of 421
contains names of cities that may well be Bottiaean, Aioleion, for example.
Cf., Theop. frg. 140, Βοττικῆς (Meineke) and *Pauly-Wissowa*, III, p. 795.
There is no mention of tribute in the alliance and hence we must assume that
there were two steps in this reconciliation, first, the return of the Bottiaeans
as tributaries to Athens, and secondly, the formation of an alliance. Meyer's
statement, ''Von Tribut war nicht mehr die Rede,'' is somewhat misleading.
We are not to assume that the Bottiaeans were excused from paying tribute,
but that this had been satisfactorily arranged before the alliance was made.
Moreover there is no necessity for excluding Spartolos from the treaty, as
Meyer does. The list of cities is very fragmentary, and Spartolos may have
headed it so far as we can tell. The expression βουλήν seems to show that the
alliance was made with the Bottiaean state as a whole. Why then exclude
Spartolos, the chief city of the league? From a list that contains but three
out of the ten or fifteen names that were originally attached to the treaty, it
is impossible to say that Spartolos was not included. Thuc. II, 79 shows
that there was an Athenian party in that city in the early years of the war,
and it is probable that by 421 it came into power and was able to restore
Spartolos and the rest of the Bottiaeans to the Athenians.
The fact that Aioleion paid tribute in 426 makes it possible that the revolt
was not general throughout Bottice. *I. G.*, I, 257.
This inscription with the expression, Βοττια]ίων δὲ τὴν βου[λὴν καὶ, taken
together with the fact that the Bottiaeans had a common coinage at this
time, shows that the movement towards unity was not unique with the

find Bottiaean cities again paying tribute to Athens.[6]   The
Chalcidians, however, refused absolutely to agree to any conditions except freedom for themselves and possession of their
territory. Amphipolis, likewise, refused to surrender to
Athens, and the Athenians found that they had accomplished
little more than to withdraw Spartan assistance from the
rebels.[7]

Through the agency, as one must infer, of the Athenian sympathizers in Mecyperna,[8] a garrison was introduced into that
town by the Athenians, and it was placed upon the assessment
lists of the coming year. This probably also happened at Singos
as we find it likewise upon the τάξις φόρου for 421.[9] The fall

---

Chalcidians but that their neighbours were eagerly following their example.
No doubt the Bottiaean league was formed between 432 and 421. The coinage commences then and the Bottiaeans are mentioned in Thucydides as a
unit, just as the Chalcidians are. Thuc. I, 57, 58; II, 79, 101; IV, 7. Thus
it is evident that the union was perfected early. It is unfortunate that we
do not have the Πολιτεία Βοττιαίων, written by Aristotle.

We must conclude, therefore, that this is an alliance with the Bottiaean
state in accordance with the terms of the treaty of peace of 421 and that
instead of being with Spartolos alone, as the treaty reads, it includes the
rest of the Bottiaeans.

[6] *I. G.*, I, 260.
[7] Thuc. V. 35.
[8] Thuc. V, 39.
[9] *I. G.*, I, 37*yz*"; Supp., 543, p. 54; cf. 37, p. 141. These three fragments
can no longer be attributed to the τάξις φόρου of the year 425. E. Cavaignac,
Etudes sur l'histoire financière d'Athènes au Ve Siècle, pp. XLVf. and Adolf
Wilhelm in his *Urkunden des Attischen Reiches* published in the *Anzeiger der
phil. hist. Klasse der kais. Akad. der Wissensch.*, April 28, 1909, pp. 48–49
and 52–53. Of the twenty-two names from the Thracian assessment, eleven,
or perhaps twelve, appear for the first time as Attic tributaries. Of the others,
six had not appeared in any list after 436. These are Othoros, Pharbelos,
Singos, Pleumè, Sinos, and Mecyperna. Istasos is probably the same as
Pistasos which would make the number seven. It is noteworthy that Singos
and Mecyperna have their tribute reduced to the nominal sum of ten drachmas. It is probable that this assessment of ten drachmas has reference to
some decree excusing Mecyperna and Singos of all payment of tribute except
the customary quota to the goddess. A quota of ten drachmas ordinarily
means a tenth of a talent tribute, which is of course low for these two cities.
This is to be explained as a result of their partial destruction and incorporation with Olynthos. Cf. pp. 72–75. The tribute would naturally be increased
as soon as the cities recovered some of their lost strength. Hence it is necessary to place this in the first assessment after the peace of 421, i. e., in that
of 421–0. The cities Pistasos or Istasos and Othoros were perhaps Bottiaean,
as we know that about that time the Bottiaeans accepted the conditions of the
peace. Sinos and Tripoiai were undoubtedly Bottiaean. Cf. note 5, *supra*.
Pharbelos was an Eretrian colony, probably situated near Palenè, p. 132.
The mention of Mecyperna definitely places the date in the early months of

of Scionè took place during the summer of 421 after a protracted siege of nearly two years. The defenders were put to death in accordance with the Athenian decree, passed after the revolt of the city,[10] and the women and children were sold as slaves.[11] The city with its territory was given over to the Plataeans, who had been disappointed in their hopes of having their own city returned to them by Thebes.[12]

Athens was active in other places of this region and gained a number of new allies, and others that had been in revolt since the beginning of the war returned to their allegiance. These were no doubt in large part Bottiaean or disaffected Chalcidian towns.[13]

The Chalcidians, for their part, were not idle and continued hostilities wherever they were able. They succeeded in taking the town of Thyssos upon the peninsula of Actè, which was at

---

420 (Thuc. V, 39) for it was recaptured by the Chalcidians before the spring of that year.

Tragilos and Bromiscos, so far as we know, made their first appearance as Attic tributaries at this time. Thucydides makes no reference to their adherence to the Athenian cause. During the summer of 421, the Athenian force engaged in the siege of Scionè recaptured it and was thus freed for further operations. It is probable that these troops were used to strengthen the position of Athens in and round about Chalcidicè and, in addition to garrisoning towns like Mecyperna, were engaged in recovering old allies or gaining new ones. Bromiscos would be an important point for them to hold, commanding, as it did, the road between Chalcidicè and Amphipolis. By this move they severed connections between these allies. The few months immediately after the capture of Scionè seem to have been the only time when Bromiscos could have been won over, for the Athenian forces in Thrace during the next few years were too small in number to hold what Athens already had. These considerations have led me to place this inscription early in 420. It must belong, as Cavaignac says, *loc. cit.*, either to 420 or 416, but I can find no reason for placing it in the latter year. Moreover, Wilhelm in his article says that he finds the character of the writing extraordinarily similar to other inscriptions of 420.

[10] Thuc. IV, 122; V, 32.

[11] Thuc. IV, 123 says that the women and the children were removed from Scionè to Olynthos before the siege. There is an apparent contradiction here. It is probable, however, that some women remained in the town to cook for the defenders and to share their fate, but cf. Müller-Strübung, *Thuk. Forsch.*, pp. 138ff.

[12] Thuc. V, 17, 32.

[13] *I. G.*, I, 37y, Supp., 37, p. 141. Bromiscos, near the mouth of Lake Bolbè, and Tragilos, not far from the site of the later Philippi, were the two most important new allies of this immediate neighbourhood. Further east upon the coast, there were others.

that time in alliance with Athens.[14]   A few months later, about
April of the year 420, during the latter part of the winter, the
Olynthians made a sudden attack upon Mecyperna and captured
it, notwithstanding that an Athenian garrison held the place.[15]
The Chalcidian league probably now embraced nearly all of the
base of the peninsula, except Botticè on the west and the An-
drian colonies on the east.   In addition, it had a foothold upon
Actè and held some of the cities at the uppermost end of Sithonia.
Northward it extended to Mygdonia and Apollonia.

Meanwhile Athens and Sparta had formed an alliance,[16] much
to the disgust of the old Lacedaemonian allies, especially Corinth,
Megara, Elis, and Boeotia.   The Spartan peace with Argos was
soon to come to an end and the malcontents were looking towards
her for leadership.   Finally Argos, Corinth, Elis, and Mantinea
formed a defensive alliance, directed against the coalition of
Athens and Sparta.   This alliance the Chalcidians joined, having had friendly relations with Corinth since the revolt of Potidaea and the services that the Corinthian Aristeus had rendered
them.[17]

Sparta protested at this action of Corinth, saying that it was
against the fundamental principles of the Peloponnesian confederacy; but the Corinthians maintained that it was their sacred
duty to keep the promises made to the Chalcidians at the time
of their revolt.   Upon these promises the Chalcidians had put so
much reliance that they had dared the dangers of rebellion from
Athens.   The Corinthians further showed that the treaty of
peace was not at all in accord with promises made by Sparta to
their northern allies.   This argument the Spartans were unable
to answer, although they must have felt that Corinth was covering up her real motives with pious excuses.[18]

The Boeotians had held aloof from this new Peloponnesian
confederacy and had signed a truce with Athens, terminable at

---

[14] Thuc. V, 35.   The text here is corrupt, but inasmuch as the Dians did
not revolt until some time later (Thuc. V, 82), the suggestion of Poppo
seems to be the correct one.
[15] Thuc. V, 39.
[16] Thuc. V, 23–24.
[17] Thuc. V, 25, 27–31.
[18] Thuc. V, 30.

ten days' notice. A change of public opinion followed in Sparta
and this resulted in the election of ephors hostile to the Athenians and to the peace. They tried indirect means to come to an
agreement with Argos so that they could renounce their alliance with Athens, and they persuaded certain Boeotian ambassadors to do what they could to bring Boeotia into the Argive
alliance. This being done, the Boeotians were to use their influence to bring about an understanding between Argos and
Sparta[19]. The Corinthians and the Chalcidians also wished an
alliance with Boeotia for the same purpose and sent embassies to
Thebes to make the arrangements. The Boeotarchs were eager
to make these alliances, now that they had the permission of
Sparta back of them, but the negotiations failed through mis-
management in the public assembly.[20]

Then followed a time when every city fought diplomatically
for an advantage of position. Former alliances were disre-
garded ánd new ones made. Sparta made a separate treaty
with Boeotia.[21] In 420, Athens entered into an alliance, offensive and defensive, with Argos, Mantinea, and Elis. The
Corinthians and the Chalcidians refused to enter this.[22] In the
following year Athens repudiated her alliance with Sparta on
the ground that the treaty had been broken.[23] Not long after
war broke out between Argos and Sparta, ending in an Argive
and Spartan alliance of short duration.[24] Finally ambassadors,
sent to the Chalcidians of Thrace, brought about the reestablishment of the old Lacedaemonian friendship and the exchange of
new oaths. Perdiccas, although he did not openly break with
Athens, followed the example of the Chalcidians and entered into
friendship with Sparta.[25] In the very next year, 417, Argos renewed her friendship with the Athenians and in this position
things remained for some time.[26]

Throughout this period the policy of the Chalcidians had re-

---

[19] Thuc. V, 32, 36–38.
[20] Thuc. V, 38.
[21] Thuc. V, 39.
[22] Thuc. V, 47f.
[23] Thuc. V, 56.
[24] Thuc. V, 79.
[25] Thuc. V, 80.
[26] Thuc. V, 82.

mained thoroughly consistent, notwithstanding the constant political changes in southern Greece. Their friendly relations
with Corinth had not been broken and new affiliations had been
made with states that were at the time out of harmony with
Athens. In the first place, they had joined the Corinthian-
Argive alliance at the time when Sparta and Athens were working together. Then they had given assistance in the overtures
made to Boeotia, hoping thereby to cause an open break between
the Spartans and the Athenians again. After the failure of this
attempt, the Chalcidians were forced to be content with the Corinthian alliance. Then they broke off relations with Argos
when the Argives united with Athens, and still later renewed
them when Sparta gained Argos as an ally. Perdiccas at this
time entered into his old alliance with them; and when the Argives again made peace with Athens, the Chalcidic-Corinthian-
Lacedaemonian alliance was reformed.

During these years of diplomatic skirmishes neither the Chalcidians nor the Athenians accomplished much in the way of
military success. The Athenians contented themselves with
maintaining small garrisons in the towns that they held in the
north.

Late in the first prytany of the year 418–7 about the middle
of August, a payment was made to the Hellenotamiai for an expedition which was already ἐπὶ Θράκης under the command of
Euthydemos. Early in the year 417, the Athenians made preparations for the reconquest of their lost territory, intending to
subdue the Chalcidians and to recapture Amphipolis with the assistance of Perdiccas, who had not yet broken openly with
Athens. Perdiccas, however, gave them no assistance and the
expedition was disbanded.[27] During that summer, the Chalcidians gained an important point. Dion, having remained
faithful to Athens throughout the war, now came over to the
Chalcidians of its own accord.[28] A little later in this year,
Athens declared war upon Perdiccas who had betrayed her

---

[27] Ditt. *Syll.*,² 37, line 9. We know nothing of the activity of Euthydemos
except that he was present ἐπὶ Θράκης in 418. For the year 417 see line 19,
στρατεγοῖς Νικίαι Νικεράτ[ο Κυδαντ]ίδει Λ[υσιστρ]άτοι Ἐ[μ]πέδο Ὀέθεν;
Thuc. V, 83.
[28] Thuc. V, 82.

both in the expedition she had planned against the Chalcidic peninsula and in making an alliance with Argos and Lacedaemonia. In the winter an army was sent out, but nothing more than a blockade of Perdiccas and of the Macedonian coast was accomplished and nothing whatever was done against the Chalcidians.[29]

The vacillation of Perdiccas was a great vexation to every one with whom he had any connection and especially to Athens. This last defection of his proved to be a boon to the Chalcidians. The Athenians, greatly angered by his change of front, temporarily neglected the recovery of their revolted allies and directed all their attention to the punishment of Perdiccas. They felt that if he actively supported the Chalcidians, they could do nothing with the small forces they cared to send. Moreover, the disgust that the Athenians felt at his treachery reacted favourably for their straighforward opponents in Chalcidicè. The Chalcidians, since they knew how little the promises of the Macedonian king were to be trusted, felt themselves free to enter into negotiations with Athens with a view towards a cessation of hostilities, perhaps hoping for a final declaration of peace. These negotiations resulted in the conclusion of a truce terminable at ten days' notice, and Perdiccas was left to fight his battles alone[30].

In the following year, 416–5, Athens continued operations against Macedonia, making Methonè her headquarters. Reinforcements, consisting of Athenian cavalry and Macedonian exiles who had taken refuge in Athens, were sent out. For a time they ravaged the country, but they were able to accomplish nothing more. Sparta held aloof and sent no aid to the Macedonian king. When she commanded the Chalcidians to put an end to their armistice with Athens and to go to the assistance of Perdiccas, the Chalcidians flatly refused.[31]

---

[29] Thuc. V, 83; Ditt. *Syll.*,[2] 37, line 25. This is the record of a payment made directly to Chairemon for an expedition ἐπὶ Θρᾳκης. It is the first payment recorded for the year 417–6. The fact that the money did not go through the hands of the Hellenotamiai shows that it was paid to him before he left Athens. Chairemon was probably in command of the expedition sent out by Athens to blockade the Macedonian coast in the winter of 417–6.

[30] Thuc. VI, 7.

[31] Thuc. VI, 7. This happened in the winter of that year.

The Sicilian plans of Alcibiades so held the minds of the Athenians that Nicias was unable to persuade his fellow countrymen that their first duty was the conquest of the Chalcidians and the strengthening of their power over the disaffected allies.[32]   They had thoughts for Sicily alone, and time had accustomed them to look with comparative indifference upon all that they had lost in the north.   Moreover, the great expense to which they had been put for the recovery of Potidaea, Toronè, Scionè, and Mendè, the losses that had been sustained at Amphipolis, and the difficulties that they were certain to encounter in an expedition against the Chalcidians had long since put a damper upon any desire for extensive operations in those regions; and many Athenians, no doubt, were firmly convinced that the gain would not be worth the trouble.   It would be much better, they thought, to seek untried fields, where there was a promise of success more commensurate with the risk involved.   The suggestions of Nicias were laid aside and further operations against the Chalcidians were put off until a more favourable opportunity.

Perdiccas, however, was considered too important to be allowed to remain an enemy of Athens, and, early in the year 414, an expedition was sent out to the Thermaic Gulf.[33]   Probably operations had not ceased against him at any time.   Deserted by Sparta and with no help from his Chalcidian neighbours, his territory ravaged, Perdiccas had every reason to change sides again and late in the summer of this year we find him acting in co-operation with Athens once more.[34]   Mere alliance would not suffice the Athenians.   They had learned from former experience that his promises meant little or nothing and they now demanded proof of his renewed friendship, just as they had done before. Thereupon Perdiccas joined Euetion in an expedition against Amphipolis.   A large force of Thracians was collected to act in concert with them but the attack failed.   As Amphipolis was surrounded on three sides by the river Strymon, which was then in the power of the Athenians, and as they had a fleet of triremes

---

[32] Thuc. VI, 10.
[33] Ditt. *Syll.*,[2] 37, line 68, στρατεγοὶ ἐν τοῖ Θερμαίοι Κόλποι.   The date of this payment was the 22nd day of the eighth prytany or about the middle of April.
[34] Thuc. VII, 9; cf. VI, 7.

at their disposal, they still thought it possible to take the city, and so placed it in a state of siege. Notwithstanding the fact that they had good prospects of final success in their undertaking, they soon abandoned the siege. Thucydides is very brief in his account of this and one is left in doubt whether the Chalcidian truce was still in force.[35] As Amphipolis was at no time a member of the Chalcidic state, it was quite possible for Athens to attack the one while still at peace with the other.[36] Moreover, Bromiscos had been in the hands of Athens since the year 421, and this would shut off communication between the Chalcidians and Amphipolis.[37] Thus since it was difficult for the Chalcidians to give effective aid, the Chalcidians would have been the more willing not to arouse Athens by idle attempts to relieve the Amphipolitans.

No further mention is made of the Chalcidians during the course of the Peloponnesian War. The fact that this last Athenian expedition was directed, so far as one can tell, against Amphipolis alone, while the abortive one that preceded was against both the Chalcidians and Amphipolis, makes it probable that the earlier truce had resulted in a permanent peace with Athens. Amphipolis was really the important point. If that could be regained, Athens might rest content, notwithstanding the minor loss of the towns in the Chalcidic league. The Chalcidians had been in revolt so long and, except during the time of Brasidas, had accomplished so little in the way of enlarging their territory and of gaining fresh recruits at the expense of Athens, that she had little to fear from that quarter and might better conciliate them by a recognition of their independence and thereby prevent them from lending their assistance to Amphipolis. In this way the Athenian recovery of the town would be facilitated. We have seen how similar tactics worked against Perdiccas and we must

---

[35] Thuc. VII, 9.

[36] That Amphipolis remained independent is shown by what we know of the course of events in these regions and the long series of Amphipolitan coins.

[37] I. G., I, Supp., 37, p. 141. If the Ms. reading of Xen. Hell., I, 5, 15 is correct, the Athenians still held Eion on the Strymon as a base of operation. Cf. Schol. Aeschines, II, 31: πέμπτον (ἀτύχημα), οἱ ἐνοικοῦντες Ἠϊόνα Ἀθηναῖοι ἐξηλάθησαν. Dem. XXIII, 199. These passages are probably references to the events of 406.

remember that this happened at a time when the Athenians were about to put an end to the collection of tribute and when conciliatory measures had to be adopted.

For the remainder of the fifth century we are left to glean such facts as we can from isolated references to affairs Thraceward. Armies go there, generals are stationed there but the expression ἐπὶ Θρᾴκης is a very inclusive one. It would seem that Thasos, together with the opposite coast, became the scene of operations in that region and not the Chalcidic peninsula, as heretofore. Whether or not Athens was formally at peace with the Chalcidians is impossible to determine. It would seem that she was, for we know of no expedition against them after the year 417 when Perdiccas failed to aid Nicias as he had promised. The entire change in the scene of operations and the fact that the Chalcidians took no part in the affairs on the coast of Thrace show that they were keeping a neutral position. It is thus probable that the Chalcidians were at peace with Athens but did not care to become the ally of either side in the war. The part the Sermylians took in the affairs of Neapolis is in direct contrast to the inactivity of their neighbours.[38] We must remember that Sermylia was one of the towns that had revolted in the early years of the war but had been captured by Athens before the peace of 421. Thus we get from this somewhat doubtful mention of Sermylia a glimpse at conditions in the Chalcidic peninsula in some of the later years of the war. The Chalcidians had not been able to win back this city. This indicates that the expansion of the territory of the league had not been very great since the treaty of peace between Sparta and Athens; it may perhaps be taken as a further indication of the peaceful, if not friendly, relations existing between the Chalcidians and the Athenians.[39]

---

[38] Hicks and Hill, 75. If the Sermylians are really mentioned in this inscription, this is of interest for it shows the extent of the Chalcidic league at this time. It is an indication that the league had not made any headway in regaining the towns upon the peninsula of Sithonia. This may be because the Athenians and the Chalcidians had made peace. If the restoration of the name Sermylians is correct, we learn that they assisted the Neapolitans in maintaining the Athenian empire on the Thracian coast against Thasian attacks.

[39] If we can accept the Ms. reading of Xen. *Hell.*, I, 5, 15, the Lacedaemonians captured Eion in 406. This reading, however, has been questioned.

After the battle of Aegospotami and the final overthrow of the Athenian empire, Lysander sent Eteonicos, the former harmost in Thasos, to the Thracian region, where he was received with a general revolt of the Athenian allies.[40] This of course did not include the Chalcidians for although they may have been at peace with Athens, they were certainly not in alliance with her nor members of her empire. Before the capitulation of Athens, measures were taken for the expulsion of the Athenian colonists from Potidaea and Toronè and the Plataeans from Scionè. An attempt was also made to restore, as far as possible, the original inhabitants or their descendants.[41] Many of them were to be found among the Chalcidians. At the surrender of Potidaea the garrison and the citizens had been allowed to go where they wished and a great number of them had taken up their abode in Chalcidic territory. The prisoners captured in Toronè had been exchanged by their Chalcidic neighbours, although the women and children had been sold into slavery.[42] Scionè was more at a loss for inhabitants. At its capture in 421 a general massacre had taken place. Precautions, however, had been taken at the time of the revolt and a large part of the women and children had been sent to take refuge in Olynthos. These remained to furnish the population for the newly reestablished town.[43]

This enforced sojourn of the inhabitants of Toronè, Scionè, and Potidaea among the Chalcidians reacted very favourably upon the growth of Chalcidic influence and power. During the years of the war when assistance and support had been given so freely to the exiles from Pallenè and Sithonia who had found homes in Olynthos and had been freed by Olynthians from Athenian imprisonment, a strong feeling of friendship for the Chalcidians must have sprung up. This might lead to an incorporation of the restored towns in the Chalcidian league. Such an incorpora-

---

[40] Xen. *Hell.*, II, 2, 5. Here the expression, τὰ ἐπὶ Θρᾳκης χωρία, refers to the whole region, for Xenophon goes on, τὰ ἐκεῖ πάντα.

[41] Plutarch, *Lys.* 14; Xen. *Hell.*, II, 2, 9; cf. II, 2, 3.

[42] Perhaps some of them had sought refuge among the Chalcidians before the Athenian attack. Cf. Chap. VI, p. 65, note 7; Thuc. II, 70; V, 3.

[43] Thuc. II, IV, 123; V, 32.

tion did in fact occur some time during the first years of the fourth century, after the collapse of the Spartan empire.

After the capture of Athens, general measures were taken for the government of the new Spartan empire. Oligarchies and decarchies were established everywhere. Harmosts and garrisons were sent out to the cities that did not already have them, and protection was furnished the aristocratic governments against the outraged democrats. Bloodshed, banishment, and confiscation were used ruthlessly, very often for the personal gain of the decarchs themselves.[44] Such violence was probably not universal; nor were colleges of ten set up in all the cities. Sparta also imposed tribute upon her newly made allies just as Athens had done.[45] The position of the members of the Peloponnesian league remained the same. No tribute was levied upon them and wars were waged by the league and not by Sparta alone. Likewise allies outside the Peloponnesian confederacy with whom Sparta had been in alliance since the beginning of the war were left to manage their own affairs. No harmosts and no garrisons were sent them.[46] This was probably the case with the Chalcidians, as well as with the Boeotians, Phocians, and Locrians.

It was quite otherwise with some of the neighbouring cities.[47] Certain of them showed signs of disaffection and in the year 404-3 Lysander was sent to Thrace to regulate affairs. He found opposition in Aphytis upon the peninsula of Pallenè and besieged it. He was compelled, however, to withdraw because of a warning in a dream. His stay in Thasos was celebrated by the murder of democrats who had taken refuge in a temple.[48] From Thasos he continued his voyage, going to many of the cities and islands and establishing constitutions such as would fit in with his plans. Within a few years, however, the system of decarchies proved so unsatisfactory and so unpopular that the ephors were compelled to abolish them, without, however, withdrawing the garrisons and

[44] Diod. XIV, 3, 10, 13; Plut. *Lys.*, 13-14; cf. 19; Xen. *Hell.*, II, 2, 5; 3, 7.
[45] Diod. XIV, 10, 2; Aris. *Ath. Pol.*, 39.
[46] See Meyer, *Die Rede an die Larissaer, Theopmp's Hellenika*, pp. 266 ff.
[47] Diod. XIV, 10; Plut. *Lys.* 19-22.
[48] Polyaen. I, 45, 4; Nepos, *Lys.* 2; Plut. *Lys.* 19f. In this passage there seems to be a confusion between Thasos and Miletos.

harmosts.   Moderate aristocracies were set up in their place, such as that of the five thousand in Athens, in which full citizenship depended upon the possession of property to the amount of a hoplite census.   All of these changes applied to the cities grouped about Chalcidicè, but not to the Chalcidic state; for as we have shown, it was an independent ally of Sparta from the first and never a subject, and moreover it had already an aristocratic form of government.[49]   Thus like Boeotia, it probably remained throughout master of its own affairs and was not troubled with harmosts and garrisons.

[49] See Chap. XIV.

CHAPTER IX

PERIOD OF CHALCIDIC EXPANSION

During the years that followed, when Sparta was turning a longing eye towards Macedon and Thessaly, and when she was engaged in affairs nearer home and in Asia, an excellent opportunity was given the Chalcidians for strengthening their position. The years of peace gradually made them desirous of extending their sphere of influence beyond the cities that originally were of Chalcidic settlement. The reestablishment of those towns that had been destroyed by Athens and the relations of friendship existing between them and the Chalcidians gave a great impetus to this desire for aggrandizement. Other neighbours, such as the Bottiaeans and the Andrian colonies in the eastern part of the peninsula, were not so favourably disposed to this movement of expansion. Incorporation in another state was not to their liking, and the original bond that had united them with the Chalcidians and had caused them to make a close alliance had been broken since 421. As the Chalcidic league gained power upon the peninsula of Actè, upon which Acanthos also had designs, as we have seen from her attempt to hold Sanè, a feeling of jealousy sprang up. This antagonism increased from year to year until at last the two became avowed enemies.

Now that both the power and desire for expansion were at hand, only the opportunity was lacking. As long as Sparta encountered no opposition in Greece, it was hopeless for the Chalcidians to attempt to gain further members for their league from among their neighbours, who were Spartan allies. Peace, however, was not destined to be of long duration. Dissatisfaction was rife. Boeotia, Corinth, Argos, and Athens were waiting for an opportunity to gain that position which each thought was its own proper right and which Sparta resolutely refused to give

7   [217]

them. In the year 395 the trouble came to a head. Sparta was engaged in Asia, and the Persians at the suggestion of Conon, were busy preparing a fleet. As it was in their interest to create a diversion in Greece, they attempted to bring about an anti-Spartan coalition. First of all war broke out between Boeotia and Sparta but it was not long before Athens joined and an alliance of the disaffected cities was formed at Corinth. Every effort was put forth to make this as comprehensive as possible and many of the Spartan allies took this occasion to revolt. Euboea, Leucas, Ambracia, and Acarnania were among the number. The Chalcidians of Thrace felt that their oportunity had come. Influenced partly, no doubt, by the action of Corinth, their old established friend and ally, but chiefly led by a desire for further expansion, they joined the alliance.[1] Notwithstanding this alliance, they had no intention of embroiling themselves in the affairs of others and took little part in the campaigns of the war.[2] At the battle of Nemea, where nearly every other allied state was represented, no record of a Chalcidian contingent is to be found.[3]

Immediately upon the outbreak of the war, Agesilaos was called home from Asia. He encountered some opposition in Thrace but arrived in Amphipolis without great difficulty just in time to hear of the Spartan victory at Nemea. He did not trouble himself with a conquest of the Chalcidians but continued his march, crossing Macedonia without resistance. Thessaly, being then on friendly terms with Boeotia, gave him some difficulty but he finally reached his goal in safety.[4]

The Chalcidians eagerly seized this opportunity and persuaded Toronè, Potidaea, and perhaps Scionè to join them.[5] Mendè,

---

[1] Diod. XIV, 82.

[2] Isaeos, V, 46: τοσούτου καὶ τοιούτου γενομένου πολέμου, εἰς ὃν Ὀλύνθιοι μὲν καὶ νησιῶται ὑπὲρ τῆσδε τῆς γῆς ἀποθνήσκουσι μαχόμενοι τοῖς πολεμίοις. This is to be dated in 390 or 389. Cf. Jebb, *Attic Orators*, II. 350ff. This passage seems to indicate that the Chalcidians were active in the war, but to what extent it is impossible to tell.

[3] Xen. *Hell.*, 2, 17.

[4] Diod. XIV, 83, 3; Xen. *Hell.*, IV, 2, 8.

[5] Xen. *Hell.*, V, 2, 12, 15; 3, 18. After speaking of the original formation of the league out of small cities in 432, Cleigenes continues as follows, ἔπειτα δὲ καὶ τῶν μειζόνων προσέλαβόν τινας. It is difficult to tell which these cities were and when this development occurred. It is probable that Scionè was included, for it had always been friendly and it had had scarcely

which had a more independent position than these other cities, refused to become incorporated in the league.[6]   The Chalcidian plans were comprehensive, for they desired authority over the whole peninsula from the coast on the west to Amphipolis in the east. These designs, however, were not acceptable to the Bottiaeans, Acanthians, and the Amphipolitans.[7]   Each of these peoples felt that autonomy was more to be desired than participation in a league of which it would be but a part. The Bottiaeans were united among themselves and feared that union with a larger state would mean for them nothing less than loss of individuality and influence. Acanthos was jealous of the advance made by the Chalcidians in territory to which it had claims, and it hoped for a power in the eastern half of the peninsula over the Andrian colonies, similar to that of Olynthos over her Chalcidian neighbours. Amphipolis, the most important city of that region, was far removed from Olynthos and could not expect to be given its due share in the control of the affairs of the κοινόν. Its sympathies, moreover, were probably with the Andrian colonies rather than with the Chalcidian, although many of its inhabitants were of Chalcidian origin.[8]

During the time when the Chalcidians were members of the Corinthian league, Athens regained much of her lost influence in this region. Thrasybulos, in the year 389, operated upon the Thracian coast and with the help of two Thracian princes, Amedocos and Seuthes, regained Thasos and many other Greek cities, both upon the islands and upon the mainland.[9]

So matters stood with the Chalcidic union when Amyntas came to the throne of Macedon in 390. His power was insecure. On the one hand Argaeos was a rival claimant for the crown; on the other, the Illyrians were threatening an invasion. He turned immediately to his Chalcidian neighbours for assistance and a de-

---

enough time to become strong again since its restoration. It is significant, moreover, that the list of the Chalcidian enemies mentioned in the treaty with Amyntas (Ditt. *Syll.*,[2] 77) does not include Scionè, although it has Mendè, a near neighbour.

[6] Ditt. *Syll.*,[2] 77.
[7] *Ibid.*
[8] Aristotle, *Pol.*, VIII, 3, 13, 1303B; 6, 8, 1306A; Thuc. IV, **103**.
[9] Xen. *Hell.*, IV, **8**, 26; cf. V, **1**, 7; *I. G.*, II–III, 1, *editio minor*, 21, 22, 24, 25.

fensive alliance. This was readily granted him. In addition to certain commercial concessions that dealt chiefly with shipbuilding material and with the growing trade of the league, the treaty contained a mutual promise of aid against an attack upon either country. The Chalcidians gained a further guarantee that Amyntas would make neither peace nor alliance with their rivals and enemies, the Mendaeans, the Bottiaeans, Acanthians, and the Amphipolitans.[10] At this time there could have been little danger of attack upon the Chalcidians from any of these cities; but the Chalcidians desired to have a free hand to deal with them as they wished. This clause would allow them to go on with their plans of expansion without fear of objection and interference on the part of Macedon. Amyntas, however, did not wish to give the Chalcidians too free a rein and insisted that peace with any of these cities should be made with the consent of both. This condition was of little importance to the league. With its enemies once under its control, the κοινόν would be strong enough to break with Macedon, should Amyntas raise any objection to its course of action.

That the Chalcidian plans were large and comprehensive is shown by the fact that the construction of a navy was in their minds.[11] With Amphipolis and the Strymon valley under their control, it would have been possible for them to extend their authority to the east among the neighbouring Thracian tribes, win for themselves the Pangaean district with its rich gold mines, and perhaps spread out over the islands off the coast.[12] Hence it was to their interest to gain a free hand in their dealings with the cities that were opposing them and to be allowed the greatest possible liberty in the importation of shipbuilding materials.[13] For this they agreed to give assistance against the expected Illyrian attack, perhaps without meaning to put themselves to any great trouble to fulfil these promises. Later events give one the impression that the Chalcidians were aiming to get

---

[10] Ditt. *Syll.*,[2] 77. For a discussion of this inscription see Swoboda, *Arch. epigr. Mitth.*, VII, pp. 1–59.

[11] Xen. *Hell.*, V, 2, 16; cf. the articles relating to ship-building material in the treaty with Amyntas. Ditt. *Syll.*,[2] 77.

[12] Cf. Xen. *Hell.*, V, 2, 16–17.

[13] Ditt. Syll.,[2] 77.

as much as possible from Amyntas and to give the least possible
in return.

It was not long that Amyntas had to wait for the Illyrian invasion. When it came it proved too strong for him.[14] The Chalcidians offered him no help and he was forced to flee from the
country, satisfied merely if he could save his life. The Macedonian territory, adjacent to the Chalcidians, he ceded to them
as his allies.[15] This may have included the town Apollonia of
which we hear for the first time. It was situated in Mygdonia,
south of Lake Bolbè, which, at least during the reign of Perdiccas, was a part of the Macedonian territory.[16] Being inhabited by Greeks, however, it took this opportunity to gain its
freedom and resisted the attempts of the Chalcidians to conquer
it.[17] Other Macedonian towns looked with favour upon the Chal-

---

[14] Diod. XIV, 92; XV, 19; Isoc. VI, 46; Ael. *Var. His.*, IV, 8.

[15] Diod. XIV, 92; XV, 19; Xen. *Hell.*, V, 2, 12f. The account of Xenophon
differs from that of Diodoros in that it omits the Illyrian invasion and thereby gives an erroneous impression as to the Chalcidian possession of the Macedonian cities implying that they had been taken directly from Amyntas and
had not been rescued from the Illyrian power.

[16] Hegesandros, frg. 40 (*F. H. G.*, IV, p. 420); Thuc. I, 58; cf. note 17.

[17] Xen. *Hell.*, V, 2, 11. We have no information concerning the history of
Apollonia before the time of the Spartan attack upon Olynthos. It is possible, however, to reconstruct it in some of its more important details. In
432 Perdiccas gave to the inhabitants of the sea-coast towns a part of Mygdonia, south of Lake Bolbè, to inhabit (Thuc. I, 58,). Appollonia is nowhere
mentioned in the Attic quota lists; and either it was not in existence at that
time or it was under Macedonian rule. Its name may give some indication
of its origin. Thuc. I, 118 tells us that the Delphian God had given his
sanction to the war; and we know that the Chalcidians and their allies, including Amphipolis when it revolted, adopted Apollo for the obverse type
of the new coinage. It is natural to suppose that these Chalcidian settlers
in Mygdonia congregated into a town. This town they named Apollonia in
honour of Apollo under whose guidance they had been led to destroy their
original homes upon the seashore and to migrate inland. This settlement
was meant only as a temporary measure but, as time went on, and as the
settlers came to feel at home there, they had no inclination to change their
abode a second time. Their relations with Olynthos and the Chalcidians were
gradually severed as more and more Macedonians joined them. Under the
protection of Perdiccas and his successor the city grew. Perdiccas had not
meant that it should be a permanent gift to the Chalcidians and for this
reason it never became incorporated in their league but remained a part of
the Macedonian kingdom although its inhabitants were in large part
Chalcidian by birth.

As the city grew and the non-Chalcidian element became a continually increasing part of the whole body of citizens, it was no more willing to be
merged with Olynthos than the other cities of that region. Likewise, since
it was largely inhabited by Greeks, it was ready to free itself from Mace-

cidian designs and accepted union with the league as virtual
freedom. Hitherto they had been subjects of a king and had few
rights and privileges. Many Chalcidians and other Greek merchants were without doubt dwelling in them and these merchants
would probably welcome any step that would give them some of
the privileges that they had enjoyed at home. The fact that the
cities were in large part Macedonian in population, had never
known autonomy, and had always been a part of a large state
made them more ready to incorporate themselves in another state,
especially one where they would have political rights that had
been denied them before. Equality in all things was granted to
these new members of the Chalcidic state.

The Chalcidians, however, were not satisfied with their Macedonian accessions. With their strength came greater aspirations
and they went further afield until Pella was numbered among
their possessions.[18] During this time Amyntas had not been idle.
His attempts to gain assistance from without at last proved successful, and with a body of Thessalian troops he drove out the
Illyrians and unseated Argaeos from the throne.[19] His demands
that the Chalcidians should restore the Macedonian cities were
unavailing. These cities had not been in his power when they
joined the league and his flight and practical abdication had released them from all allegiance to him. If they could not protect themselves, there was nothing left for them to do but to put
themselves under the protection of the Chalcidians who could
protect them. Amyntas had deserted them and thereby forfeited
all claims upon their obedience; and now that he had returned,
the Chalcidians were unwilling, notwithstanding their former
alliance, to lose the new possessions which they had gained
with so much danger to themselves.

---

donia and to become a city state whenever the opportunity should present
itself. This it did, probably during the disturbances of the reign of Amyntas.
As further evidence for the comparatively late origin of the town, it had
no coinage before the fourth century, when we find it using an obverse type
imitated from that of the Chalcidians. I agree with Beloch, II, 224, note 5,
who says that there was one Apollonia only in the Chalcidic peninsula, the
Mygdonian city south of Lake Bolbè. See note 26, Chap. XIII.

[18] Xen. *Hell.*, V, 2, 12–13, 18: καὶ γὰρ ὁ θεὸς ἴσως ἐποίησεν ἅμα τῷ δύνασθαι
καὶ τὰ φρονήματα αὔξεσθαι τῶν ἀνθρώπων.

[19] Diod. XIV, **92.**

CHAPTER X

SPARTAN INTERVENTION

Meanwhile the Chalcidians made further endeavors to win over Acanthos, Apollonia, and other towns that were still holding out against them, such as, for example, Mendè and Aphytis in Pallenè and Spartolos in Botticè.[1] It is probable that they succeeded in their attempts upon Spartolos soon after their treaty with Amyntas, for a chance reference in Isaeos shows that about 390 it was a part of the Chalcidic state.[2] Acanthos and Apollonia, however, felt themselves too weak to resist. It is probable, moreover, that there was a Chalcidic party within their walls and that fears were entertained lest this party should prove strong enough to deliver the cities into the hands of the league. The treatment that the Chalcidians were giving the newly enrolled members was so generous that the supporters of city autonomy felt that a short period of participation in the privileges of union would be sufficient to win over a majority of the citizens and to dull any regrets that might at first be felt at the loss of their independence.[3]

With these things in mind, an embassy from Apollonia and Acanthos went to Sparta for the purpose of seeking protection there. Amyntas, likewise, turned to the Lacedaemonians for as-

---

[1] Xen. *Hell.*, V, 2, 11–19.

[2] Isaeos, V, 42. Spartolos (τῆς 'Ολυνθίας ἐν Σπαρτώλῳ) is mentioned in this passage as a part of the Olynthian state. It had been head of the Bottiaean league and as such it was a member of the Athenian league soon after 421. In 390 the Bottiaeans were hostile to the Chalcidians, but as this speech of Isaeos was delivered about 390, during the Corinthian war, Spartolos must have been conquered by the Chalcidians soon after their treaty with Amyntas. In 382, upon the arrival of the Peloponnesian forces it revolted and allied itself with Sparta. See Jebb, *Attic Orators*, II, 350 ff., 354.

[3] Xen. *Hell.*, V, 2, 19.

sistance in regaining his lost territory.[4] Circumstances combined
to render their requests acceptable.   Sparta's dominion in
Greece at this moment was unquestioned.   Nearly all opposition
had been crushed and the Peloponnesians were only too ready to
curry favour with the Spartans.[5] The peace of Antalcidas, with
its guarantee of autonomy to every Greek city, large and small,
was the moving force in Greek politics, and Sparta was making
use of it for her own advantage, to strengthen her position as the
leading state in Greece and to break the power of any union that
might in time prove dangerous to Lacedaemonian interests.   She
had here a clear case of attempted and accomplished violation of
the terms of the peace and it was to her own good to interfere
and to put a stop to the expansion of the Chalcidian κοινόν before it should gain too great a power in the politics of Greece.
Its strength was as yet not large in comparison with that which
Sparta could bring against it, but the principles upon which it
was·founded were proving themselves so powerful for winning
new adherents, even among the Greeks, whose one universal political ideal was that of a city state, that unless measures were
taken speedily, Sparta would soon find herself unable to cope
with the problem.   There was danger, moreover, that the league
would ally itself with Athens and Thebes.   Negotiations were
well under way.   Ambassadors from these cities were already at
Olynthos, and the Chalcidians had voted to send others in return
to complete the preliminary arrangements.[6] All this rendered
immediate action by Sparta necessary.   A synod of the Peloponnesian allies was called, and, almost without a dissenting vote,
it was decided to send an army of ten thousand hoplites to the
aid of Macedon, Acanthos, and Apollonia.   As speed was necessary and as much time would be consumed in the gathering of
so large a force, Eudamidas was sent forward with two thousand
men, Neodamodeis, Perioeci and Skiritans, to act as garrisons in
the cities that had need of them.[7] In the early summer of 382

---

[4] Xen. *Hell.*, V, 2, 11; Diod. XV, 19.
[5] Xen. *Hell.*, V., 2, 20.
[6] Xen. *Hell.*, V, 2, 15.
[7] Xen. *Hell.*, V, 2, 20–25; Diod. XV, 19; Isoc. IV, 126.

this advance contingent reached its destination.[8]   The anti-Chalcidian party in Potidaea proved strong enough to open the gates of that city to Eudamidas and he made the place his headquarters.[9]   To such towns as Spartolos, which also revolted to him, Acanthos, and Apollonia he sent small garrisons.[10]   His army was not numerous enough to conduct extensive operations and he contented himself with raids upon the Chalcidic territory until the arrival of reinforcements.   Phoebidas, who had been commissioned to follow with the troops left behind by Eudamidas, halted in Boeotia to capture the Cadmeon of Thebes.[11]   This enterprise proved successful, and the Spartans took up the war in the north with increased vigor.[12]   Teleutias, the brother of Agesilaos, was placed in command, and the full levy, strengthened by a force of cavalry and hoplites from Thebes, was put into the field.   Some time toward the end of the summer of 382, they arrived in Potidaea, after having been joined by Amyntas of Macedon and Derdas of Elimia with a few troops.

The Thebans and the Athenians sent no assistance to the Chalcidians.   Thebes itself was in the hands of the Spartans and could do nothing, while the Athenians were frightened by what had happened, and standing almost alone, they were unwilling to offend the Lacedaemonians.   The fact that Thebes had been negotiating an alliance had been used as a pretext against her; and Athens, as it would seem, did not wish a repetition of the affair directed against herself.[13]

A battle followed the arrival of Teleutias, but although the Peloponnesians gained a partial victory, Teleutias did not feel himself strong enough to attempt a siege of Olynthos.   The Chalcidians, meanwhile, were actively engaged in raids upon the hostile cities.[14]   In the spring of 381, a marauding expedition of six hundred Chalcidic horse set out from Olynthos against Apol-

---

[8] The chronology of this war is somewhat doubtful.   Cf. Meyer, *G. D. A.*, V, 894 A.

[9] Xen. *Hell.*, V, 2, 24.

[10] *Ibid.;* cf. note 2, *supra.*   Spartolos was in the hands of the Spartans at the time of the death of Teleutias in 381.   Xen. *Hell.*, V, 3, 6.

[11] Xen. *Hell.*, V, 2, 25–36.

[12] Xen. *Hell.*, V, 2, 37f.

[13] Xen. *Hell.*, V, 2, 34.

[14] Xen. *Hell.*, V, 2, 39–43.

lonia, but being surprised by Derdas, they turned in flight and were driven to the very walls of the city from which they had come.[15] During the summer, however, this defeat was atoned for by a much more serious one inflicted by them upon the Peloponnesians. Teleutias with his whole force marched against Olynthos, but outwitted by the Chalcidians, he was forced into battle, routed, and put to flight. The army scattered, seeking refuge in Potidaea, Spartolos, Acanthos, and Appolonia. Teleutias was killed with about twelve hundred of his army.[16]

It was necessary for Sparta to send out a new general with reinforcements. Agesipolis was given the command and volunteers came to him from all sides. Besides those from Sparta and the allied cities, there was Thessalian cavalry, and Amyntas and Derdas joined as before. The Chalcidians had made ready for a siege. Their troops were far outnumbered by the newly reinforced Peloponnesian army, and there was nothing for them to do but to retire behind their walls, while the enemy wasted their crops and those of their allies. Their strength was concentrated in Olynthos and they were even unable to prevent Toronè being taken from them by storm.[17]

In this way things went on till the summer of 380 when Agesipolis was taken with a fever and died in the temple of Dionysos at Aphytis. Polybiades was then placed in command and he maintained a close siege of the city of Olynthos until the food that had been collected in anticipation of this blockade had been exhausted. Thereupon the Chalcidians sent plenipotentiaries to Sparta, who made peace upon the condition that the Chalcidians join the Spartan alliance and render military service at Lacedaemonian behest. All of this took place in the year 379 before the revolt of Thebes.[18]

The accounts of the treatment meted out to the league are very unsatisfactory.[19] We may assume that the Macedonian boundaries were restored, that all of the cities recently gained by the

[15] Xen. Hell., V, 3, 1–2.
[16] Xen. Hell., V, 3, 3–6; Diod. XV, 21.
[17] Xen. Hell., V, 3, 8–9, 18; Diod. XV, 21f.
[18] Xen. Hell., V, 3, 19–20, 26; Diod. XV, 23.
[19] Xen. Hell., V, 3, 26; Diod. XV, 23. For military service under the Spartans in 377, cf. Xen. Hell., V, 4, 54.

Chalcidians were taken away, and that these cities also joined the Spartan alliance. This would leave the Chalcidian league almost as it stood after the close of the Peloponnesian War, restricted to the central portion of the base of the peninsula. This had been so long united and had become so identified with Olynthos, its capital city, that all thought of the original component elements had disappeared. The position of Olynthos in this territory is comparable to a certain extent with that of Athens in Attica. One sees, at least, that Xenophon used the word Olynthians to denote the Chalcidic κοινόν, while Thucydides, in whose memory remained the fact that the inhabitants of Olynthos had come from many Chalcidic towns and that the city was not coextensive with the state, did not use the name of the city for the nation but always spoke of the Chalcidians. Diodoros, who compiled his history from various sources, used both names.[20]

For a time the Chalcidians fulfilled the condition of the alliance and rendered faithful service to the Spartans. During the campaign of Agesilaos in Boeotia in the year 377, a body of Olynthian cavalry protected the rear of the Peloponnesian troops in their march to Thespiae.[21] In the same year a reorganization of the Spartan empire took place, according to which the Olynthians and the allies ἐπὶ Θράκης formed the tenth division.[22] We do not know how extensive an alliance the Spartans had in these parts, for Diodoros merely informs us that many of the other cities eagerly enrolled themselves under Sparta after the destruction of the Chalcidian power.[23]

---

[20] Diod. XIV, 82, 92; XV, 19–23.
[21] Xen. *Hell.*, V, 4, 54.
[22] Diod. XV, 31.
[23] Diod. XV, 23, 3.

CHAPTER XI

RELATIONS WITH ATHENS AND MACEDON UP TO
THE YEAR 360

This dependence of Chalcidicè upon Sparta was of short duration. Within four years, the Chalcidians commenced to regain
that of which they had been deprived during the last war. The
Lacedaemonians were not in a position to watch carefully their
actions nor could they have interfered if they had wished. The
Athenian power upon the sea had been reestablished and the
Spartans could not approach Chalcidicè by land, because of the
recent developments in central Greece. About this time, likewise, the Chalcidians probably regained Potidaea, Toronè, and
other towns upon the peninsulas of Sithonia and Pallenè.[1]
When Chabrias in 375 came to win over new recruits for the
second Athenian confederation, the Chalcidic league renewed its
alliance with Athens.[2] Friendly feeling had existed between the
two peoples since the outbreak of the Corinthian war, although
neither had felt itself in a position to render aid to the other.
One can not tell whether the projected alliance of the year 382
was made; but whether or no, Athenian sympathy must have
gone with the Chalcidians in their struggle against the overwhelming force of Sparta.

From the list of the members of the second Athenian confederation inscribed upon the stele that contains the provisions relat-

---

[1] During the operations of Timotheos in this region about fifteen years
later, these places were Chalcidian possessions. Diod. XV, 81; Isoc. XV,
108, 113; Dein. I, 14; Polyaen. III, 10, 15.
[2] *I. G.*, II, 17, 105. This latter inscription may well belong to this year
rather than to 352-1, to which it must otherwise be attributed. Cf. Ferguson, *Athenian Secretaries*, p. 38. I can not agree with Hill, *Classical Review*, 1900, pp. 279f, that it is the record of an Athenian alliance of 383
B. C. Cf. *infra*, p. 125, note 13.

ing to the formation of this confederation,[3] we can learn somewhat as to the extent of the Chalcidian power at this time.   Towards the end of the list occurs the name Διές ἀπὸ Θραίκης.   This
evidently refers to the town of Dion upon Actè.   The last record
we have of this city tells of its revolt from Athens during the
Peloponnesian War,[4] and of its union with the Chalcidians.   Join-
ing this with what we have learned concerning the rivalry between Acanthos and the Chalcidians and with a second inscription of a later date,[5] we may infer that Acanthos gained a hold
upon the easternmost peninsula, thereby supplanting the Chalcidians whose position there had never been strong.

The Chalcidian alliance with Athens, however, could only continue so long as Athenian interests did not clash with the long
cherished Chalcidian plans for expansion.   Should Athens prove
too powerful in the Thracian district and endeavor to put a limit
to the achievements of the league, the Chalcidians would feel no
hesitation about making other allies.   The bone of contention,
naturally enough, was Amphipolis, a town independent of both,
but one upon which each of them had claims and designs.   Athens
claimed it as her former colony, and the league, as an old ally
among whose inhabitants were many Chalcidians.[6]   The importance of the town to both claimants rendered the conflict certain
sooner or later.

The trouble came to a head soon after the congress at Sparta
in 371.[7]   Athens laid claim to Amphipolis,[8] and Amyntas, king
of Macedon, taking part in the meeting, used all of his influence
in favour of the ratification of the Athenian claim.   The relations of Amyntas with Jason, the powerful tyrant of Pherae and
the master of Thessaly, were such that it was important for the
Macedonian king to become as closely allied as possible with the
stronger of the Greek states.   Hence he was perfectly willing to

---

[3] *I. G.*, II, 17.
[4] Thuc. V, 82.
[5] *I. G.*, II, part 5, 108b.   See Chap. XIII, note 6.
[6] Arist. *Pol.*, VIII, 3, 13, 1303B; 6, 8, 1306A.
[7] Xen. *Hell.*, VI, 3, 2–20; Diod. XV, 50.
[8] Aesch. II, 32f.   That Athens and Amyntas were on good terms, Hicks and
Hill, 107, shows, and, as has been rightly conjectured, this inscription belongs to about the time of the congress at Sparta, perhaps in 370–69 as suggested by Ditt. *Syll.*,[2] 78.

renounce any dormant claims he might have had upon Amphipolis in exchange for Athenian protection. In this way the Athenian claim was ratified, to the great dissatisfaction of the Chalcidians.   Amyntas had pleased the Athenians and had gained their friendship. At the same time he probably wished to deliver a blow to the hopes of the Chalcidians, his old enemies and neighbours.

The Chalcidians awaited their opportunity. Amyntas died in 370–69[9] and the troubles following his death were eagerly watched by the league. In 368 the Athenians dispatched Iphicrates with a fleet for the recapture of Amphipolis.[10]   This brought about the actual break between the Chalcidians and Athens. About the same time, (368), Alexander of Macedon was murdered and there followed a contest among the claimants for the Macedonian crown.[11] The Chalcidians saw an opportunity to win influence and a close alliance. If a king, friendly to their interests, could be placed upon the throne, their position would be greatly strengthened and the Athenians would have fewer chances of success in their attempt to recapture Amphipolis. Pausanias, as it would seem, was the Chalcidian choice and they assisted him in his endeavour to gain the crown. He commenced operations at the Chalcidian frontier and for a time was successful, winning over one town after another. Anthemos, Thermè, Strepsa and other places fell into his hands and the prospects of final success were good.[12] Euridicè, the widow of Amyntas, and Ptolemy, to whom she had given the regency during the minority of Perdiccas and Philip, the younger brothers of Alexander, turned to Iphicrates, the Athenian general, for protection against Pausanias and his Chalcidian backers. This protection they claimed by reason of Iphicrates' previous friendly relations with Amyntas.* Iphicrates listened to their request and drove Pausanias out of the kingdom, hoping indeed to gain, in return, Macedonian assistance for his attack upon Amphipolis. This, however, proved to be a vain hope. Thebes

[9] Diod. XV, 60.
[10] Aesch. II, 27–29.
[11] Plut. Pel., 27; Diod. XV, 71.
[12] Aesch. II, 27–29, scholia.
* Aesch. II, 27–29; Nepos, Iph., 3, 2.

interfered and Ptolemy, who had no intention of allowing the Athenians to gain the city, was persuaded by Pelopidas to join the Theban alliance.[13]

The Chalcidians considered it more politic, for the time being at least, to recognize the independence of Amphipolis and so they made an alliance with it against the attacks of Iphicrates.[14] Ptolemy also joined in its protection. Iphicrates then was able to do nothing. For three years Iphicrates remained in charge of operations against Amphipolis but accomplished little.[15] It is told of him that he gained hostages from the Amphipolitans, but how this happened we do not know. He gave these hostages into the keeping of Charidemos, a certain captain of mercenaries in his employ. Charidemos, however, was not to be trusted and delivered them to Amphipolis. This happened after the recall of Iphicrates but is illustrative of the conditions prevailing in the Athenian army at that time.[16]

While Iphicrates was engaged against Amphipolis, the king of Persia was giving judgment upon the fate of the city.[17] Pelopidas at the time of his embassy to the Persian court in 367 received from the king a rescript, by which, among other things, the independence of Amphipolis was acknowledged. Some time later an embassy from Athens went up to protest, and it was then that the decision was reversed and the Athenian claims were recognized.[18]

In 364 Iphicrates was removed from his command and Timotheos took his place.[19] Feeling in need of as strong an army as possible, he attempted to re-engage Charidemos. This mercenary captain, however, was under the influence of Iphicrates, who had just been removed from his command, and of Kotys, who was openly hostile to Athens. Instead of taking service under the newly appointed Athenian commander, he restored the Amphipolitan hostages, whom he had in charge, to their friends in Am-

---

[13] Plut. *Pel.*, 27; Aesch. II, 27–29.
[14] Dem. XXIII, 149–150.
[15] Dem. XXIII, 149; Aesch. II, 29.
[16] Dem. XXIII, 149–150.
[17] Dem. XIX, 137; Xen. *Hell.*, VII, 1, 36; Diod. XV, 81, 3.
[18] Dem. XIX, 137, 253; Hegesippos, *de Hal.*, 29.
[19] Dem. XXIII, 149–150; schol., Aesch., II, 31; Polyaen. III, 10, 7, 8, 14f.

phipolis, and taking a number of Athenian ships, he sailed off to
serve under the Thracian Kotys in his war against Athens.[20]
Timotheos felt that the recent murder of Ptolemy Alorites[21] and
the accession of Perdiccas III to the Macedonian throne offered
him a splendid opportunity to obtain revenge for the ungrateful
manner in which the Athenians had been treated at the time
when Iphicrates had established Ptolemy in his regency.   Turning his attention to Macedon and especially to the Thermaic
Gulf[22] he captured the coast towns, Pydna and Methonè, and persuaded Perdiccas[23] to enter an alliance with Athens and to assist
in the war against the Chalcidians.   Perdiccas was willing
enough to aid Athens in her attempts to weaken the Chalcidian
league, for it had been a menace to Macedonian unity since the
time when the Chalcidians had snatched so many Macedonian
towns from the hands of the Illyrians and had taken the territory
that Amyntas was powerless to hold.   A second time they had
interfered in the affairs of Macedon and had almost succeeded in
placing their candidate upon the throne.   Hence it was that
Perdiccas entered eagerly into the plan of humbling a neighbour
that might again become dangerous.   With this assistance Timotheos was able to capture Potidaea and Toronè, together with
many Chalcidian towns of less importance.[24]   Although he was
successful in gaining Macedonian aid and in taking from the
league much of its outlying territory, such as the peninsulas of
Sithonia and Pallenè, he could not capture Olynthos nor do more
than weaken its power.   One must remember, however, that he
was ill supported by Athens and for supplies and men he was
dependent in great part upon his own resources.   Isocrates considered it as one of his greatest merits that he was able to do so
much at so little expense to Athens.[25]   He raised his money in
various ways.   Part of it he collected from the Athenian allies
about Thrace; part he furnished himself; and the rest came from

[20] Dem. XXIII, 149–150.
[21] Diod. XV, 77, 5.
[22] Deinarch. I, 14.
[23] Dem. II, 14; Polyaen. III, 10, 14.
[24] Diod. XV, 81, 364–3; Isoc. XV, 108, 113; Polyaen. III, 10, 15; Deinarch. I, 14.
[25] Isoc. XV, 113.

miscellaneous sources, from the profits of debasing coinage, for example, and from the gifts of friendly princes.[26] His eager-ness to enlist Charidemos and his willingness to pardon him for his previous treachery show that the problem of maintaining an army sufficiently large to be effective was one that was difficult of solution.[27] Another mercenary captain serving under Timo-theos was Menelaos. Later he was honoured by Athens and given Athenian citizenship.[28]

In his attempts to capture Amphipolis, Timotheos was even less successful than he was against Olynthos. The details of the war have not been preserved for the most part and those that re-main cannot be dated with any degree of certainty.[29] It would seem that Alcimachos, a lieutenant of Timotheos, received a sev-ere repulse and that soon after Callisthenes was sent to replace Timotheos in his command.[30] This probably happened in the spring of 362.[31] During the time when Callisthenes was in com-mand in these regions, the loyal citizens of Potidaea preferred a request to Athens that cleruchs be sent out to take possession of the city. The request was granted and Potidaea was made an Athenian cleruchy.[32] Callisthenes, however, had as little success against Amphipolis as his predecessor.[33] Perdiccas III, follow-ing in the footsteps of the second Macedonian king of that name, deserted the Athenian cause and offered his assistance to the Amphipolitans. He had been willing to assist Athens so long as she was busily engaged in weakening the power of his enemies and potential rivals, the Chalcidians; but when it came to de-livering into the hands of the Athenians a city so favourably situated as Amphipolis and giving them so strong a foothold in the neighbourhood of Macedonia, Perdiccas decided to dispense with Athenian alliance and to throw the weight of his power on

---

[26] Ditt. *Syll.*,[2] 102, (362 B. C.); Polyaen. III, 10, 14; Arist. *Oecon.*, II, 23, 1350a.

[27] Dem. XXIII, 150.

[28] Ditt. *Syll*[2]., 102, 103.

[29] Schol., Aesch. II, 31.

[30] Aesch. II, 30; Arist. *Rhet.*, II, 3, 13, 1380b.

[31] Timotheos was still in command in the early months of 362, as we learn from Ditt. *Syll*[2]., 102.

[32] Ditt. *Syll.*,[2] 104; Dem. VI, 20, schol.; Hegesippos, *de Hal.*, 10; Diod. XVI, 8.

[33] Aesch. II, 30.

the side of Amphipolis. Presumably a Macedonian garrison was given to the city for its protection.[34] At least Callisthenes for some unknown reason not acceptable to Athens, thought it wise to conclude an armistice with Perdiccas, and for this he was tried and condemned to death.[35] In 360, Timotheos again took the command against Amphipolis but he fared worse than before. His attack was repulsed and the triremes that he had transported by land so that he could use them above the town had to be burned, in order that they might not fall into the hands of the enemy.[36] In the interval between Callisthenes and the return of Timotheos, so far as one can judge, no operations were undertaken against the Amphipolitans.

[34] Diod. XVI, 3; Aesch. II, 29.
[35] Aesch. II, 30.
[36] Schol., Aesch. II, 31; Polyaen. III, 10, 8.

CHAPTER XII

CHALCIDIAN ALLIANCE WITH PHILIP

Late in the year 360, Perdiccas III fell in battle with a horde of invading Illyrians.[1] Macedonia then became the scene of a many sided struggle for succession. Pretenders to the throne arose from all sides. While these claimants, however, were fighting among themselves for supremacy, it seemed quite likely that Macedonia would fall a prey to the attacks of its restless neighbours, the Illyrians and the Paeonians, who were seizing this opportunity to overrun as much of the country as possible. Athens again tried the doubtful experiment of interfering in Macedonian domestic quarrels by supporting Argaeos, one of the many claimants to the crown. Mantias was sent out to Macedon in command of three thousand hoplites and a fleet of considerable size. Landing at Methonè, Mantias sent Argaeos with the mercenary troops to Aegae, the ancient capital of Macedonia. At this place Argaeos called upon the citizens to enlist themselves under his banner, but as few favoured his cause, he returned to Methonè.

Philip, the son of Amyntas, showed himself the most powerful claimant for the throne. The Paeonians he had caused to withdraw by the payment of a sum of money. Pausanias and Archelaos, two other pretenders, he had disposed of easily. There was no one left to deal with except Argaeos. Having made these preparations, Philip appeared before Methonè where Mantias and his troops were stationed. In the battle that followed the Athenian forces were defeated and many prisoners were taken by Philip.[2]

Philip saw that friendship with Athens was necessary for his

---

[1] Diod. XVI, 2, 4.
[2] *Ibid.* 2f.

purpose and took such measures as he could to heal the breach between them.   Knowing that the Athenians were eager to gain possession of Amphipolis and that they had been willing to support Argaeos so that they might have upon the Macedonian throne a king friendly to their interests and one that would grant to them this city, Philip withdrew his garrison from the place and left it free and autonomous.[3]   Upon the capture of the Athenian troops at Methonè, he had another opportunity to show his good will toward Athens, and so instead of holding the prisoners for ransom or exchange, he freely liberated them.[4]

After Philip had made these friendly advances, he entered into negotiations for the conclusion of peace.   Now that he had given up all claims to that for which the Athenians had been struggling for so long a time, the city of Amphipolis, and had shown his friendship to them in other ways, he had no difficulty in persuading them to come to a peaceful understanding with him.[5]   The Athenians, however, desired him to guarantee to them the possession of Amphipolis.   It was not enough for him to have surrendered all claims upon it.   Consequently a bargain was struck by which, in return for this favour, the Athenians were to deliver into his possession the seacoast town of Pydna, which was then an Athenian ally.   This agreement was so far from being just to the inhabitants of Pydna that the Athenian ambassadors in charge of the negotiations hesitated to bring it before the assembly.   It came up before the Boulè alone and was there ratified.[6]

This secret agreement, however, Philip almost immediately broke.   His chief end had been gained when he had lulled the suspicions of Athens and had induced it to lay aside its hostility for him.   He could now turn his attention to his more dangerous neighbours, the Paeonians and Illyrians.   During the year 358, his hands were occupied with the pacification of these peoples.[7]   When he had accomplished this and had removed the barbarian menace, he was free to extend Macedonian power and influence.

---

[3] Diod. XVI, 3.
[4] Dem. XXIII, 121.
[5] Diod. XVI, 4; Dem. II, 6–7; XXIII, 121.
[6] Theop. frg. 165a–d.
[7] Diod. XVI, 2–4.

For this extension of power it was essential that Philip gain a foothold upon the seacoast and make Macedon a maritime nation. Since the time of Amyntas the Macedonian seacoast had been greatly lessened. Pydna was in the hands of Athens. Philip, however, did not first direct his attention to the shores of the Thermaic Gulf, but to the country commanded by the river Strymon. Here was situated the flourishing city of Amphipolis and near it lay the rich mining region of Mt. Pangaeos. The valley of the Strymon could furnish wood in abundance for the building of a fleet; and Lake Bolbe and the lower river formed an excellent place for the headquarters of a large navy. The gold mines would furnish the money for equipping and manning it. Thus there were many reasons why Philip should try to become master of Amphipolis. To incorporate it, however, in the Macedonian kingdom, meant nothing more nor less than to sever all relations with Athens. The Athenians still asserted that Amphipolis was theirs, because of its original settlement by them. Philip, moreover, had promised to deliver it to them in exchange for Pydna. It is impossible to tell whether Philip ever had any intention of keeping his bargain. It would seem that from the first he realized the importance of the extension of Macedonian power to the sea; but that his original aim had been to regain the lost Macedonian territory upon the Thermaic Gulf. As his power grew and as he felt himself more safely seated upon the Macedonian throne, his plans widened; and the importance of the possession of Amphipolis grew upon him to such an extent that he was willing to enter into open hostility with Athens. The success of the Thasian colony, Krenides, situated upon Mt. Pangaeos, and the development of the neighbouring mines undoubtedly exerted their full share of influence upon him.[8] Whatever may have been his full purpose in promising to deliver the city of Amphipolis into Athenian hands, in the year 357, he took measures to get it into his power.[9]

In the city, however, notwithstanding its long and determined

---

[8] Diod. XVI, 3.

[9] Diod. XVI, 8. The date of the capture can be made out from a comparison of Dem. I, 8 with an Athenian inscription of the Archonship of Agathocles, 357-6, Ditt. *Syll.*,[2] 109.

resistance to Athens, there was a strong Athenian party, and, when the purpose of Philip began to become patent, the strength of this party increased to such an extent that it controlled the affairs of the city. Accordingly Hierax and Stratocles were sent to Athens to ask for aid against Philip and to offer their submission to Athens. For some reason Athens would have nothing to do with this offer.[10] She may still have had faith in the promise of Philip, expecting to receive the city from his hands. It is certain, at least that during the siege Philip sent an embassy to Athens renewing his promises and saying that when Amphipolis was captured it would be restored to the Athenians.[11] On the other hand Athens may have thought it impossible to save the city from Philip and for this reason was unwilling to risk a body of men in its defence. After a short siege Philip was successful and the city fell[12]. The leaders of the Athenian party were exiled and the town and its territory was incorporated in the Macedonian kingdom[13]. Theoretically Philip allowed the town to retain its autonomy but actually he had the control of affairs in his own hand[14].

While the Athenians were wondering what Philip would do next, whether he meant to keep his promise or not; and before they could recover from their surprise at his failure to do so, Pydna also was in his possession[15]. His foothold upon the coast was now well established and it was only necessary for him to extend it and to develop his navy. Although he had found it advisable to break with Athens, he did not feel himself strong enough to stand entirely alone while the formation of his navy was in progress. It was necessary, moreover, that Athens should have no base of operations in his immediate neighbourhood. For this reason the Chalcidians were to be reckoned with. Not-

---

[10] Dem. I, 8; Theop. frg. 43.
[11] Dem. XXIII, 116; Hegesippos, *de Hal.*, 27.
[12] Diod. XVI, 8.
[13] Diod. XVI, 8.
[14] Ditt. *Syll.*,² 113. This shows that the city was theoretically in charge of its own affairs and autonomous; but the statement of Diodoros expresses the actual state of affairs, that it was subject to Philip. It is noteworthy that one of the exiles, Stratocles by name, was a member of the Amphipolitan embassy to Athens.
[15] Diod. XVI, 8; Dem. I, 9, 12; XX, 63.

withstanding the fact that Timotheos had greatly weakened them, they still formed a powerful state, naval and commercial, so far as the Thracian coast was concerned. If Athens should persuade them to enter an alliance with her, for the purpose of waging war against Philip, the position of the Macedonian king would become precarious. The Chalcidians, however, were ready to enter into an alliance with Philip. This he offered in order that he might forestall any understanding with Athens and that he might have no fear of Chalcidian opposition to his plans. Hostility to Athens was the common interest that bound the two together, and it was agreed that neither party should conclude a peace without the consent of the other[16]. In return for this alliance the Chalcidians received the city of Anthemos, to which they had claims. Philip, moreover, captured Potidaea from the Athenians and gave it and its territory back again into the possession of the league. The Athenian colonists were sent home unharmed. This happened in the early part of the year 356[17]. Pydna and Amphipolis had slipped out of the hands of the Athenians because of their too ready confidence in the word of Philip and because of their unwillingness to undertake any risks in the defence of these cities. With Potidaea it was not far otherwise. Procrastination and dilatory methods characterized Athenian movements in and about Chalcidicè. Although Philip spent considerable time upon the siege of Potidaea, the army sent out by Athens for its relief did not arrive before the final capitulation of the place[18].

In this way Philip had gained what Athens had lost. The Athenians had had this very opportunity of an alliance with the Chalcidians, but hoodwinked by the fair promises of Philip, they had refused to listen to the requests made to them by Chalcidian ambassadors[19]. The political insight of the Chalcidians detected

---

[16] Diod. XVI, 8; Dem. II, 6f; VI, 20; XXIII, 108; Liban. on Dem. I; Scala, no. 185. Dem. II, 6 shows that the Chalcidians would have made terms with Athens if it had been possible. Their hostility to Athens gave way to their fear of Philip. When Athens refused they were forced to make the best of their position and to turn to Philip. This refusal of Athens must have made them more hostile than ever to her.

[17] Plut. *Alex*. 3; Dem. II, 7.

[18] Dem. IV, 35; cf. 4f.

[19] Dem. II, 6.

the quarter from which the danger was to come and they were
willing to lay aside their quarrel with Athens in order to have
her protection against Philip. When they found themselves
unable to persuade Athens of the correctness of their views,
there was nothing left to do but to make their hostility to Athens
a means of gaining better treatment from Philip. They were
unable to stand alone and it was then essential for them to make
an alliance with Philip, as it were, to protect themselves against
him, or at least to delay as long as possible the struggle that they
felt to be impending. Philip, for his part, not only needed their
assistance and most of all their good-will; but he felt that they
were in a position to inflict damage upon him and to hinder him
in the furtherance of his plans. Having assured himself of the
Chalcidian friendship, he saw that it was worth while for him
to deprive Athens of Potidaea, her most important station in this
region. As he could not hold it for himself, so long as the Chalcidic state intervened, breaking the continuity of the Macedonian
coast line between Amphipolis and the Thermaic Gulf, it was to
his distinct advantage to hand it over to the Chalcidians.
Thereby he would gain their good-will and lull any suspicions
that they might have concerning his ultimate intentions.

Philip could now turn his attention in other directions. He
made use of Amphipolis to enter Thrace, where he founded the
city of Philippi and caused the gold mines of the neighbourhood
to be worked on a greater scale[20]. Neither the town nor the
mines were new, but they were taken over by him and enlarged.
The name of the town had been Krenides, but Philip departed
from Greek custom and named it after himself[21]. We are told
by Diodoros that the mines of the city furnished him an annual
revenue of one thousand talents. At least Philip was able to put
into circulation a very large quantity of new gold coins. Having
crossed the Strymon, he came into contact with the Thracian
prince, Ketriporis, who together with Lyppeios of Paeonia and
Grabos of Illyria, made an alliance with Athens. These princes
were defeated, without great difficulty, before they could receive

---

[20] Diod. XVI, 8.
[21] Diod. XVI, 3, 8.

assistance from Athens[22]. In the next few years Philip was actively engaged in extending his power in every direction. On the Thracian coast he captured Abdera and Maronea[23]. On the Thermaic Gulf he deprived Athens of Methonè, her last possession[24]. Likewise he was active in Thessaly and upon the Propontis. It would seem that Philip was waiting only for an opportunity or an excuse for attacking and destroying the Chalcidic league.

---

[22] Hicks and Hill, 131; Diod. XVI, 22; Plut. *Alex.*, 3.
[23] Polyaen. IV, 2, 22.
[24] Diod. XVI, 34, 353–2 B. C. Also wrongly given under 354–3, XVI, 31; Dem. I, 9, 12, 13; IV, 35.

CHAPTER XIII

DESTRUCTION OF THE LEAGUE BY PHILIP

The league, however, was on its guard, strengthening itself in every possible way. Its territory was probably as great in extent as it had been at any time during its history, except perhaps for a short period just before its humiliation by the Lacedaemonians.[1] Towards Macedonia, Anthemos, by a recent gift of Philip, was within its boundaries.[2] Botticè by this time had certainly become a part of the Chalcidic league[3] for its territory was confiscated later for settlement by Macedonian nobles, as was that of Olynthos.

---

[1] Some indications of the extent of the Chalcidic league during the fourth century can be gained from a consideration of the coinage of the Chalcidic peninsula. The cities issuing coins must have been independent at some time during this period. Acanthos, Olophyxos, Orthagoreia, Aphytis, Mendè, Potidaea, Aineia, and the Bottiaeans were the only states issuing coins during the fourth century. The coinage of Apollonia is rather doubtful. Orthagoreia may be identical with Stageiros, but evidence on this point is somewhat conflicting. In any case other evidence shows that Stageiros was a member of the Chalcidian league at the time of its destruction by Philip. Thus its coinage can be assigned only to the first quarter of the fourth century. The fact that Olophyxos struck coins about 350 corroborates our assumption that the league had little or no hold on the peninsula of Actè. The coins of Potidaea are probably contemporary with its reestablishment by Sparta about 400. Those of Mendè and Aphytis show that the Chalcidians made little headway in Pallenè. As for Aineia, we have no reason for assuming that it remained independent when places such as Anthemos were in Chalcidian hands, and thus we must assign the coins of that city to a date antecedent to its incorporation in the league. The Bottiaean coinage ceased, probably about 490. It is to be noted that none of the cities of Sithonia issued coins during the fourth century, which fact may be taken as an indication of Chalcidian influence in that peninsula. Head, *Historia Num².*, pp. 203–214.

[2] Dem. VI, 20; Arrian, *Anab.* II, 9, 3; cf. note 3.

[3] Arrian, *Anab.* I, 2, 5. This shows that Bottiaean territory was confiscated for the benefit of the Macedonian nobles at the time of the destruction of the league. Also cf. Theop. frg. 140. Meineke's conjecture Βοττικῆς for 'Αττικῆς is very probable and would show that Botticè was a part of the Chalcidic league. One can not tell when this union was brought about. Arrian confirms this conjecture.

It is doubtful whether Apollonia on the northern frontier was ever incorporated in the league, although its territory was later confiscated by Philip.[4] On the east the Chalcidic territory was limited, not by the coast, but by the territory of Acanthos[5]. Of the three peninsulas the easternmost was under Acanthian influence rather than Chalcidian.[6] Sithonia and at least the northern portion of Pallenè formed a part of the possessions of the league[7]. Demosthenes, speaking of the league,[8] says that it could put into the field one thousand horsemen and that the number of its citizens was ten thousand. This gives one a certain idea of the extent and power of the Chalcidian league in the period immediately preceding its final struggle with Philip.

Although it seemed strong and prosperous, Philip had really weakened its powers of resistance in many insidious ways. Bordering so closely upon Macedonia, Chalcidicè was in a position to be easily influenced by Philip's newly acquired wealth. The relations between the two countries were friendly and there must have been a great deal of communication from one to the other. Of all this Philip made use in his attempts to cement the friendship between the Chalcidians and the Macedonians. He did not hesitate to use bribery for the purpose of attaching to himself important citizens of the various cities of the league. Wood for house-building, cattle, sheep, and horses were given in abundance with this end in view[9]. Demosthenes may possibly have indulged in rhetorical exaggeration in his accounts of the importance of these measures of Philip, but other less tangible forces were at work. The Chalcidians were to a large extent interested in commercial enterprises. Macedonia was their nearest neighbour and

---

[4] *I. G.*, II, 70, 355–4 B. C. This is a decree giving honours to a citizen of Apollonia for services rendered to Athens during the Social War. Arrian, *Anab.* I, 12, 7; cf. note 26, p. 128.

[5] (Dem.) XXXIV, 36. In 326 Acanthos was still in existence and had not been destroyed. Hence in all probability it had not been a member of the league.

[6] *I. G.*, II, part 5, 108b; cf. Köhler, *Sitz.-ber. d. Berl. Akad.*, 1891, p. 475. This shows that Acanthos and Dion were connected and not joined with the Chalcidians.

[7] Diod. XVI, 53; Hegesippos, *de Hal.*, 28. Toronè was captured by Philip with the other cities of the league.

[8] Dem. XIX, 266. See chapter on population.

[9] Dem. XIX, 265.

it is fair to assume that Chalcidian traders were found throughout the country. A large proportion of the Macedonian trade must have gone through their hands. Hence everything that tended to promote this trade tended to exert a pro-Macedonian influence upon the merchant princes of Chalcidicè. Philip's alteration in the standard of weight in use for Macedonian coins was a judicious one;[10] for when he adopted the standard used by the Chalcidians he gave a great impulse to this commerce. This worked more effectively than all the direct bribery mentioned by Demosthenes. Many of the leading Chalcidian citizens must have seen that the fate of their peninsula was bound up with that of Macedon and felt that commercial interests demanded friendship with Philip at all costs, even to the sacrifice of their national independence. That the Macedonian party was strong later developments showed[11].

In many ways the Chalcidians could look upon loss of autonomy with better grace than most of the other Greeks. Their training for the last eighty years had been in the direction of union. The cities that had joined the league had given up the prevalent Greek idea that the city was the political unit and had united themselves to form a common state. Hence the idea of union with a still larger power, thereby forming a still larger unit, was not a novel one nor in itself essentially objectionable. When one takes into consideration the energy shown by Philip and the growing power of Macedon, the hopelessness of a struggle against it, and the manifold commercial advantages of remaining on friendly terms with a neighbour so powerful and so necessary to their welfare, one will hesitate to condemn the so-called traitors. The Chalcidians had shown political sagacity in advance of their time. Conditions now were altered and it remained to be seen whether they would take the next step toward union with Macedon of their own accord or by force. The last few years had shown which way things were moving and those who were far-sighted enough to read the signs of the times probably realized that there was nothing for the Chalcidians to do

---

[10] Hill, *Historical Greek Coins*, nos. 43–44.
[11] Dem. IX, 56, 66. Apollonides was exiled for opposition to Philip.

but sooner or later to become a part of Macedon. The conservative party, however, was in the majority, except perhaps for short periods of time; and it was the stubborn resistance to union with Macedon, offered by this party, that in reality brought down upon the Chalcidic cities the terrible punishment meted out to them by Philip.

It was irksome indeed for the Chalcidic or nationalistic party to feel that they were hemmed in on all sides by the power of Philip and that only by reason of his favour could they be at all secure. He had become too great to keep faith with them[12]. They were full of foreboding for the future and their fears were well justified. If they should insist upon breaking with him and seeking assistance from Athens, there could be no hope for them. The Chalcidian treaty with Philip required that neither party should make peace with the Athenians without the consent of the other. Violation of this provision by the Chalcidians meant the wrath of Philip and almost certain punishment; for this would give him an excuse and an opportunity for attacking and subduing them, the very thing for which he was waiting.

But notwithstanding the dangerous possibilities attendant upon alliance with Athens, the Chalcidians decided to come to terms with her in hopes that they could thereby maintain their independence against Philip. Having come to this conclusion they waited for an opportunity for action, and in the summer of 352, when Philip was busily engaged in Thessaly, ambassadors were sent to Athens to conclude a peace[13]. There was even talk of forming an alliance, but this was probably postponed on account of the Chalcidian fear and dread of Philip. Although

---

[12] Dem. XXIII, 108.

[13] Libanios, *Hypoth.*, *Olynth.* I; Dem. III, 7; XXIII, 108f.; *I. G.*, II, 105. This inscription, a treaty between Athens and the Chalcidians, has been dated by various editors in various years. If the treaty was made at this time, Ferguson, *Athenian Secretaries*, p. 38, is the only one that has dated it correctly, *i. e.*, in the year 352–1, in the archonship of Aristodemos. It seems to me quite improbable that this treaty refers to the so-called Olynthian war. Philochoros, frg. 132, says that the alliance was made in the Archonship of Callimachos (349–8). This fits in better with the facts. If there had been an alliance existing between Athens and the Chalcidians at the time of Philip's expedition of intimidation in 351, Philip would not have let matters rest with a warning. Thus it seems best to date it in the archonship of Charisandros, when the Chalcidians joined the second Athenian confederacy.

this peace with Athens was displeasing to Philip, and moreover, contrary to the Macedonian alliance, he did not feel himself ready to take active measures against them. After his return from Thrace in 351 he threatened them with an invasion, entering Bisaltia and going to the very borders of the Chalcidic territory.[14] The Chalcidians were not ready to engage in a struggle with him at that time and sent an embassy to persuade him of their friendship.[15] Evidently this was successful for nothing further was done by Philip. What is more, he sent word that his intention was a peaceful one,[16] and he seems to have tried to gain his end without compulsion and the horrors of war.

The two parties in the Chalcidic towns were evenly divided. A few months before this time the national or independence party had been strong enough to make peace with Athens. Now, after the peaceful designs of Philip had been seen, the Macedonian party was in the majority and Apollonides, a leader of the opposite party, was sent into exile[17].

After having assured himself of many adherents in all the Chalcidian towns, in the year 349, Philip advanced into Chalcidicè. Since he thought that he had sufficient sympathizers among the Chalcidians to make a resort to force and arms unnecessary, and since he wished to quiet the fears of his opponents,[18] he let it be understood that his errand was a peaceful one;[19] but when he arrived in the vicinity of Olynthos, he demanded the restoration of his stepbrother Arrhidaeos, who had escaped him and had taken refuge among the Chalcidians.[20] Upon their refusal to comply with his demand, he laid aside his mask of friendship and commenced the war in earnest.

This refusal of the Chalcidians shows plainly how evenly the parties were divided. Not long before the Macedonian party had been strong enough to exile Apollonides, presumably for the purpose of pleasing Philip. Now that Philip had attempted to

---

[14] Dem. I, 13; IV, 17; cf. Theop. frg. 124.
[15] Theop. frg. 124.
[16] Dem. IX, 11.
[17] Dem. IX, 56, 66; [Dem.] LIX, 91.
[18] Dem. I, 21.
[19] Dem. VIII, 59.
[20] Schol., Dem. I, 5; Justinus, VIII, 3, 10.

dictate to them, the balance swung in the other direction and it was decided to undergo the risk of war rather than to submit to this dictation. Probably the Chalcidians saw the real purpose of Philip and felt that his demand for the restoration of Arrhidaeos was only a pretext made use of to justify himself in the eyes of the world. Immediately they sent an embassy to Athens asking for an alliance, and this was granted them in the archonship of Callimachos (349–8)[21].

In accordance with this alliance the Athenians sent a body of mercenary troops to Chalcidicè to assist in carrying on the war against Philip. These troops were under the command of Chares and consisted of two thousand peltasts and thirty triremes. As results proved, these forces were insufficient[22]. Demosthenes, who saw the danger, was unable to convince the Athenians of the critical position in which the Chalcidians were placed and of the need of more strenuous measures. Probably the Chalcidian ambassadors had hesitated to depict conditions in their true colours. They were offering Athens an alliance and it was to their interest to make their offering seem as valuable as possible. The soldiers for which they were asking were not for their protection, but were for the purpose of carrying on the Athenian war against Philip from more advantageous headquarters.

The details of the war are more or less uncertain, but it seems clear that neither side accomplished much during the first campaign. Diodoros tells us that Philip in his expedition against the Chalcidian cities captured a fort called Geira and destroyed it, and at the same time so frightened certain of the other towns that they submitted to him evidently without opposition[23].

---

[21] Philochoros, frg. 132.

[22] Philochoros, frg. 132; Diod. XVI, 52, 9; cf. Dem. XIX, 266.

[23] Diod. XVI, 52, 9. I have given the manuscript reading. Beloch (*Gr. Gesch.*, II, p. 502, note 1) and others have thought that Stageiros is meant. This seems to me to be impossible, for Stageiros was a city, not a fort. Certain of the manuscripts read Ζειρά, and the suggestion has been made that this is the same as Ζειρηνία, Theop. frg. 45. It is not impossible that the name Ζέρεια, found in the τάξις φόρου of 421, *I. G.*, I, Supp, 37, p. 141, is a variant of the manuscript reading. I prefer this explanation to that given by Beloch. Chytropolis, perhaps, came over to Philip during this campaign. Theop. frg. 134. Of its history we know nothing except that it was a colony of Aphytis.

So far as we know nothing else was accomplished during this year. It is probable that in the autumn Chares and his troops returned to Athens. As for Philip, he was busy putting down opposition in Thessaly.

In the spring of 348 a second embassy came from the Chalcidians to Athens asking assistance. In answer to this Charidemos was sent out in command of a larger expedition. Four thousand peltasts, one hundred and fifty horsemen, and eighteen triremes accompanied him.[24] The ambassadors had been insistent and had pictured the Chalcidians as hard pressed by the war. Probably Philip had already commenced his campaign of 348. In the preceding year he had won over several Chalcidian towns. Where these were we do not know. They may have been Bottiaean or Pallenan, for the first efforts of Charidemos were spent in ravaging this territory. This may have been the time when Derdas of Macedon was taken prisoner; but of this one can not be certain. Little of real value was accomplished, for the incidents recorded of Charidemos refer to his insolence and dissoluteness rather than to his military exploits.[25]

During this time, Philip had not been idle. Among the towns that came into his hands, either by force or persuasion, were Apollonia (?)[26], Toronè, Mecyperna, and Sanè.[27] With these he

---

[24] Philochoros, frg. 132; Justinius, VIII, 3, 10. Philip's step brother Menelaos may have accompanied this expedition. His brother Arrhidaeos had found refuge in Olynthos, and had been the ostensible cause for the war. Later the two suffered the same fate at the hands of Philip. Cf. Schaefer, *Demosthenes u. s. Zeit*, II, pp. 17, 124, notes.

[25] Theop. frg. 139; cf. Ael. *Var. His.*, II, 41. For successes of Charidemos see Dem. III, 1, 85, and Liban. *Hypoth., Ol.* III, 27.

[26] Dem. IX, 26; Hegesippos, *de Hal.*, 28–9.
To which Apollonia was Demosthenes referring in IX, 26, when he says that Olynthos, Methonè (?), Apollonia, and thirty-two towns ἐπὶ Ορᾳκης were completely destroyed by Philip? We have two or perhaps four cities of that name from which to choose. See *Pauly-Wissowa*, nos. 3–6. The existence of an Apolllonia on Actè, Pliny, *N. H.*, IV, 10, 37, is very questionable and the other Apollonias seem to have possessed many lives. I need not go into the question as to whether there were two Apollonias in the Chalcidic peninsula or not. The fact remains that except for this passage of Demosthenes no ancient writer tells us of the destruction of either of them by Philip. One of them, no. 3, existed for several centuries after Philip's time and is mentioned by several writers. Livy, 45, 28; Pliny, *N. H.*, IV, 10, 38; Ptol. III, 12, 33; *Acts of the Apostles*, 17, 1; *Itineraries*. Apollonia no. 4 is supposed to have been the Apollonia mentioned by Xenophon and destroyed by Philip. If so its destruction was not complete, for Strabo, VII, 330, frg. 21, tells us that it

had little difficulty. The Chalcidians had concentrated all their
efforts upon the protection of their capital Olynthos. Philip was
now ready to attack them where they were the strongest. All
of their other possessions were in his hands. Even Mecyperna,
the Olynthian harbour, had fallen to him. Advancing upon the
city, he met the Chalcidians in two battles and defeated them.*
When he was within a short distance of the city, the Chalcidians
tried to come to terms, but it was too late and their attempt was
in vain. Philip replied that the time had come when one or the
other must give way.[28] With this he commenced the siege of the
town and in an attempt to storm it he lost many men. Finally,
however, he managed to cut off from the town a body of five hundred horse, weakening the garrison so that the city was captured
a short time afterwards. This cavalry success was due, in all
probability, to the treachery of two prominent Olynthians, Lasthenes and Euthycrates, who having been elected hipparchs, betrayed their trust and allowed their command to fall into the
hands of Philip.[29]

Upon the refusal of Philip to come to terms, the Chalcidians
had sent an urgent request to Athens for more assistance. This
was granted them and Chares was put in command of a body of
citizen hoplites under orders to sail to Chalcidicè and to raise

participated in the synoecism of Thessalonica. Thus the identification of the
Apollonia of Demosthenes with no. 3 or no. 4 is not without difficulty. On
the other hand Strabo, VII, 331, 35, tells us that the eastern Apollonia was
destroyed by Philip. As Demosthenes does not tell us where Apollonia was
except that it was ἐπὶ Θρᾴκης, and as the two Apollonias of the Chalcidian
peninsula, if there were two, existed until much later times, it seems better
to assume that Strabo and Demosthenes refer to the same city, except that
Livy, 38, 41, mentions the existence of an eastern Apollonia in the year 188
B. C. His account places it between Maronea and Abdera, while the Apollonia of Strabo was situated west of the Nestos river. Thus the whole question is involved in numerous difficulties which make a positive answer out of
the question. It seems probable, however, that there were but two Appollonias,
the one in Mygdonia, surviving until later times and the other near the eastern Galepsos, destroyed by Philip. This seems to be confirmed by Steph.
Byz.: Ἀπολλωνία, γ, Μακεδονίας.....κβ, τῶν ἐπὶ Θρᾴκης Ἰώνων ἣν Δημοσθένης
φησίν.

[27] Diod. XVI, 53; Front. Strat., III, 3, 5.
*Diod. XVI, 53.
[28] Dem. IX, 11.
[29] Diod. XVI, 53; Dem. IX, 56, 66; XIX, 267; Suidas, Κάρανος; Hyperides, frg. 76 (Blass, 3d ed.)

the siege.[30] Philip's movements were too rapid for them and so,
hindered by the Etesian winds, upon their arrival they found
that Olynthos had been taken.[31] This happened early in the
archonship of Theophilos (348–7) some time after the Olympic
festival.[32]

The fate of the Chalcidians was a hard one. Olynthos and
many other cities, according to Demosthenes, were destroyed so
thoroughly that it was difficult to tell that their sites had ever
been inhabited. He mentions Olynthos and Apollonia and says
that there were thirty-two besides.[33] The number is large and it
has been generally regarded as an example of rhetorical exaggeration.* This of course may well be, but the definiteness of the
number would seem to speak against this supposition; moreover,
we must not fail to remember that Demosthenes does not say
that all of the cities destroyed were Chalcidian. On the contrary, he used the more general term ἐπὶ Θρᾳκης and definitely
mentions Apollonia, which we have seen was certainly not a
member of the Chalcidic league. The exaggeration is probably
not in the number but in the importance of the places described
by the term πόλεις. Many of them could have been more accurately called πολίσματα or towns. It would be an almost hopeless task to attempt to give an accurate list of these thirty-two
ruined cities and towns. Our evidence is very scanty and we are
forced to fall back to a large extent upon pure conjecture. In
the extant fragments of Theopompos[34] are found the names of a
number of Chalcidic towns. Many of these, no doubt, suffered
a fate similar to that of Olynthos. From Arrian, we learn that
the Bottiaean territory furnished to the army of Alexander a

---

[30] Philochoros, frg. 132.
[31] Suidas, Κάρανος.
[32] Philochoros, frg. 132; Aesch. II, 12–15; Diod. XVI, 53.
[33] Dem. IX, 26; Strabo, VII, 329, frg. 11; Suidas, Κάρανος.
* See Köhler, Sitz.-ber. d. Berl. Ak., 1891, pp. 473ff.
[34] Skithai, Theop. frg. 338; Assera, Theop. frg. 147; Milkoros, Theop. frg.
150; Aioleion, Theop. frg. 140; Thermè, Theop. frg. 135. It is doubtful
whether Thermè was included in the Chalcidic league. The fact that Theopompos does not call it a Macedonian city might go to show that it was not
considered a part of Macedon. Hence it may very well have been in Chalcidic territory, although neither Theopompos nor Scylax, 66, calls it Greek.
Chytropolis, Theop. frg. 134. This town is otherwise unknown, but its
settlement by Aphytis and surrender to Philip might place it within or at
least near the Chalcidic borders. This town is also called Thracian.

troop of cavalry.[35] The natural inference from this is that the
lands of the Bottiaeans were apportioned among the favourites of
Philip. Botticè, however, included a large number of small
towns, as we learn from an inscription of the preceding century.[36] The Chalcidian territory proper and the three peninsulas supported other groups of towns and these with places such
as Anthemos would go far in making up the number mentioned
by Demosthenes. If we add to these the other towns outside the
Chalcidic peninsula that were destroyed by Philip, the list will
probably be complete.[37]

---

[35] Arrian, *Anab.*, I, 2, 5; Ditt. *Syll².*, 178.

[36] Hicks and Hill, 68.

[37] A list of the towns destroyed by Philip is a difficult thing to make with
the evidence at hand. Demosthenes says that, exclusive of Olynthos, Methonè, and Appollonia, there were thirty-two in all ἐπὶ Θρᾴκης. To make
up this list we must use the indirect evidence of many authors and include
Chalcidian towns that may be presumed to have survived the ravages of the
Peloponnesian War. There can be little doubt that most of the cities and
villages in the Chalcidic territory were destroyed and their possessions given
over to Macedonian nobles or to other favorites of Philip, so that if we can
show that a town was Chalcidian and existed in Philip's time, we can assert
that in all probability it was destroyed by him. Strabo, X, 447, 8; cf.
Theop. frg. 217b. First of all I shall mention the places for which there is
some definite evidence. Diodoros says that Philip in his expedition against
the Chalcidian cities captured Geira, a φρούριον, and destroyed it. Diod.
XVI, 52, 9. In his next campaign he captured Toronè and Mecyperna.
Diod. XVI, 53, 2. We may assume that Mecyperna was destroyed, although
it is mentioned by Mela II, 3, 34, as follows: *In litore flexus Megybernaeus
........(unde ipsi nomen est) Megybernam incingit.* Pliny, *N. H.* IV, 10,
36, says merely, *sinus Mecyberna,* and Scymnos, 640f, definitely states that
it no longer existed when he wrote, c. 147–75 B. C. Εἶτ' ἔστι κόλπος λεγόμενος
Τορωνικός, οὗ πρότερον ἦν τις Μεκύβερνα κειμένη.
    Southern Sithonia, however, seems to have been spared by Philip, for
Toronè is mentioned by three writers, Pomponius Mela II, 3, 34; Pliny, *N.
H.,* IV, 10, 36, and Scymnos, 642. Theopompos, in the books that deal with
the Chalcidians and Philip's campaigns against them, mentions the names of
several Chalcidian towns that probably were attacked and destroyed by Philip.
Chytropolis, a colony of Aphytis, and Thermè, which is called a Thracian and
not a Macedonian town, are mentioned in the twenty-second book. Theop.
frgs. 134, 135; cf. note 34.
    It is probable, however, that Thermè was not destroyed by Philip for it,
together with Aineia, Garescos, Cissos, and Apollonia, according to Strabo,
VII, 330, frgs. 21, 24, were in existence at the time when Cassander founded
Thessalonica. Twenty-six towns in all, situated in Crousis, participated in
the synoecism which resulted in the establishment of this new city on the
site or in the neighbourhood of Thermè. Thus it would seem as though
northern Crousis had been spared in the general destruction meted out to
the Chalcidian cities. In this connection it is interesting to note that Aineia
was still in existence as late as 182, Livy, XL, 4; XLIV, 10, and also that
Apollonia is mentioned in the *Acts of the Apostles,* 17, 1.

In this same book Theopompos mentions Thestoros, πόλις Θράκης, frg. 136. As book 22 deals largely with the Chalcidians and as Thestoros occurs in the tribute list of 421, *I. G.*, I, 37y, with other cities situated in or near Chalcidicè it may be possible to consider Thestoros one of the outlying possessions of the Chalcidian league. Other towns mentioned in this list, as we know, later became Chalcidian. In his next book Theopompos speaks of an expedition against Aioleion, probably a Bottiaean town included in the Chalcidic league. Frg. 140. Aioleion is also known to us from the tribute lists, and the fact that it appears in the τάξις φόρου of 421, *I. G.*, I, 37, Supp. p. 141, shows that it was not at that time a member of the Chalcidian league. It is probable that it entered the league with the rest of Botticè, for Theopompos definitely states that it was a member of the league; cf. chap. XIII, note 3. We know that the Bottiaean territory was confiscated from other sources, Ditt. *Syll².*, 178; Arrian, *Anab.*, I, 2, 5. Assera, a Chalcidian town, and Skabala or Scabla, an Eretrian colony, known also from the quota lists of the fifth century are named in the twenty-fourth book, frgs. 145, 147. Pliny, however, IV, 10, 38, names a certain Cassera, which has been generally identified with Assera, and Ptol. *Geog.*, III, 12, 33, gives us the location of an Asseros in Mygdonia. The value of this evidence is questionable, for the Cassera of Pliny seems to have been situated on the peninsula of Actè, near an unknown and somewhat doubtful Apollonia, while the Asseros in most manuscripts is called Assoros and is evidently situated in the interior, near the Mygdonian Apollonia. The Assera of the quota lists was situated on the east coast of Sithonia and in the district known to Ptolemy as Chalcidicè. Cf. Hdt. VII, 122. Herodotos knows Assera as Assa but there is little question of the identity of this place with the Assera mentioned by Theopompos, as πόλις Χαλκιδέων and by Aristotle, *Hist. An.*, 519a, 14. Therefore I think it rather probable that the mistake of Ptolemy and Pliny was due to the fact that the city was no longer in existence and its location unknown. Frg. 338 speaks of Skithai as a place near Potidaea. This is probably to be identified with the Kithas of *I. G.*, I, 243. Frg. 150 definitely assigns Milkoros to the Chalcidians. Frg. 141 mentions Brea, originally a colony of Athens, and frg. 144 mentions an Okolon, a colony of Eretria and as these fragments come from the same book as the reference to Skabala, cited above, it is possible that Okolon was also ἐπὶ Θράκης, and that the two towns were destroyed by Philip. In this connection we may perhaps mention Pharbelos, called by Stephanus Byz. a settlement of the Eretrians. It is also found in the quota lists. *I. G.*, I, Supp., p. 141, no. 37. Stolos, Tindè, and Scapsa were all Chalcidian towns according to Stephanus. Kampsa, which is to be identified with Scapsa, is called by Herodotos, VII, 123, Krossaian. The passage of Pliny, IV, 10, 37, which has been amended to read *Torone, Siggos, Stolos, fretum quo montem Atho Xerxes * * * abscidit, etc.*, can hardly be taken as evidence for the existence of Stolos in his time. Stolos was not situated on the coast between Singos and the peninsula of Actè, but somewhere in the interior. The very mention of Singos in conjunction with Stolos throws Pliny's evidence out of court, for in Strabo's time Singos had been long destroyed. Strabo, VII, 330, frg. 31. It is hardly probable, moreover, that a city in the heart of Chalcidicè should have been left standing by Philip, even though he spared others on the coast for commercial reasons. As for Singos, Strabo states that it had been destroyed. Although he does not say by whom we may assume that Philip was responsible for its ruin.

Having mentioned the fact that Singos occurs in Pliny, I may state that Ptolemy, III, 12, 9, also gives its location. We may take this as a warning not to lay too much stress upon the evidence of these two writers, for the fact that they give us the names of cities long destroyed shows that towns mentioned by them were not necessarily in existence when they wrote. The men tion of Mecyperna by Mela, cited above, and that of Potidaea, II, **2**, 33, indicates that the same thing is true of him.

The confiscation of the territories of Sinos and Spartolos is shown by Ditt. *Syll.*,[2] 178. Arrian tells us that Anthemos as well as Apollonia and the Bottiaeans furnished a troop of cavalry to the Macedonian army, *Anab.*, II, **9**, 3. We know that it formed a part of the Chalcidian league at this time and it is probable that it is another of the ruined cities. The fact that Anthemos is mentioned by Pliny, IV, **10**, 36, proves nothing as to its existence in his time, as I have shown above, especially as he locates it in or near Pallenè, *in Pallenensi Isthmo quondam Potidaea, nunc Cassandrea colonia, Anthemus, Olophyxus, sinus Mecyberna*, etc. Potidaea also is to be included in our list of cities destroyed by Philip. It was first captured by Philip and then handed over to the Chalcidians after it had been destroyed and the Athenian colonists had been driven out. Diod. XVI, **8**; Dem. VI, **20** and scholion, ἄψας; Strabo, VII, 330, frg. 25. The destruction of Stageiros is mentioned by Plut. *Alex.*, 7, and we know from other sources that it was a member of the Chalcidian league, Strabo, VII, 331, frg. 35; Dion Chrys., XLVII, 9. Whether Sanè was a member of the league is not known, but Frontinus, *Strat.*, III, **3**, 5, says that it was captured by Philip. The destruction of the eastern Apollonia and of the eastern Galepsos is mentioned by Strabo, VII, 331, frg. 35. When the town of Philippi was founded, inhabitants were taken from the neighbouring cities. Daton suffered in this way, Philoch. frg. 127; and it is probable that Apollonia and Galepsos were also dismantled for the same reason.

In this connection Pliny and Mela are to be considered again. Both mention Apollonia. Mela II, **2**, 30: *Ultra Nestos fluit, interque eum et Strymona urbes sunt Philippi, Apollonia, Amphipolis.* Pliny, *N. H.*, IV, **11**, 42: *In ora a Strymone Apollonia, Oesyma, Neapolis, Datos. Intus Philippi colonia.* Of these Ptolemy, *Geog.*, III, **12**, 7, 28, names only the maritime cities Oesymè and Neapolis together with Amphipolis and Philippi in the interior. The same is true of the metrical geography of Scymnos, vs. 656-9. For Daton, cf. the following additional references: Theop. frgs. 44a, b; Scylax, **67**; Strabo, VII, 331, frgs. 33, 36; Diod. XVI, **8**; Appian, *B. C.*, IV, **13**, 105; Harpocration, Δάτος; Steph. Byz., Φίλιπποι. On the whole while the evidence as to the destruction of Daton, Galepsos, and Apollonia is not absolutely certain, I think that we can include them in our list.

So far we have only mentioned cities for which there is some evidence. Now I wish to consider a number of towns that survived the ravages of the Peloponnesian War and probably existed until the time of Philip, then to be destroyed by him. The existence of Sermylia about the middle of the fourth century is proved by the fact that Scylax, **66**, mentions it. That Sermylia lay on the west coast of the base of Sithonia in the very heart of the league and is nowhere even mentioned by later geographers makes it probable that it too was destroyed.

We know that Strepsa was in existence during the first half of the fourth century, Aesch. II, **27**, but beyond that our evidence does not go. We have now to consider certain Bottiaean towns, whose existence in 420 makes it probable that they survived into the fourth century, for after the Peace of Nicias there were no great disturbances in Chalcidicè during the Peloponnesian War. These towns are Kamakai, (*I. G.*, I, 260; Hicks and Hill, 68), Tripoiai, (*I. G.*, I, 37y; Hicks and Hill, 68), Kalindoiai, (Hicks and Hill, 68). A Kalindoiai of Mygdonia is mentioned by Ptolemy, III, **12**, 33, but this can not be identical with the Bottiaean town of that name. To these I would add, Pistasos or Istasos, Othoros, Pleumè, and Sermè, although we are not certain that all of these places were in the Chalcidic peninsula, *I. G.*, I, 37, frg. yz″, Supp., p. 141. Bromsikos was also tributary to Athens at this time, but whether it existed until the time of Philip is open to question

In addition to the complete destruction of Olynthos and its Chalcidic neighbours, the inhabitants were sold into slavery, given away by Philip to his friends, or sent to work upon the royal domains.[38] Perhaps some of them were transported to upper Macedonia and there compelled to assist Philip in his scheme of colonization by swelling the population of his newly established towns. A number of Athenians were taken prisoners in Olynthos[39] and with them Menelaos and Arrhidaeos, the stepbrothers of Philip.[40] These latter Philip immediately put to

---

for it is not mentioned in the contemporary geography of Scylax, *loc. cit.* Alapta otherwise unknown, is mentioned by Scylax as a town seemingly north of Acanthos and as his work preceded the destruction of the Chalcidian cities, and as Alapta is nowhere mentioned by a later writer we may add it to our list.

I have omitted all towns from the foregoing list mentioned in the Athenian quota lists, unless there is evidence that they survived the period of transition during the first years of the Peloponnesian War, likewise all towns of Pallenè, except Potidaea, all places of southern Sithonia, cities on the peninsula of Actè together with Acanthos, and certain towns in the neighbourhood of Thermè. In this point I have differed with the list offered by Böhnecke, *Forschungen auf dem gebiete d. Attisch. Redner*, pp. 154ff.; *Dem. Lyk. Hyp.* p. 398. That Toronè, Mendè, Scionè, Aphytis, Acanthos, and the towns of Actè existed until later times can be readily shown. Pliny, IV, 10, 36f.; Mela, II, 2, 30ff.; Livy, XXXI, 45; (Dem.) XXXIV, 36; XXXV, 10, 35; Strabo, VII, 330, frg. 27. The towns of northern Crousis, Thermè, Aineia, Garescos, and Cissos have been omitted because of the fact that they survived to participate in the foundation of Thescalonica. Livy, XL, 4; XLIV, 10; Strabo, VII, 330, frgs. 21, 24.

The smaller towns of southern Crousis, such as Smilla, Gigonos, Haisa, Kombreia, and Lipaxos, seem to have disappeared before the fourth century, for they are not mentioned by Scylax nor any later writers except the lexicographers. Hdt. VII, 123; Steph. Byz. Αἶσα, Σμίλα, Λίπαξος. Dicaea may still have been in existence when Pliny wrote, IV, 10, 36. The other towns of this region I have considered above.

It is noteworthy that our list contains the names of thirty-six cities and villages on the borders of Thrace that probably existed during the fourth century, but of whose later existence we have no proof. This list is offered only by way of suggestion and no finality is claimed for it; for the evidence upon which it is based is largely negative and therefore inconclusive. Towns have probably been included that were not destroyed by Philip or perhaps perished before his time. In fact the very location of many of these places is unknown or doubtful. It is also possible that the names of other cities that should appear in our list have been omitted. In one respect, however, the list is of value, for it shows clearly that there were a great many towns and villages on the Chalcidic peninsula during the fourth century and therefore makes it probable that the number thirty-two given by Demosthenes is not an exaggeration but an actual statement of fact.

[38] Diod. XVI, 53; Aesch. II, 156; Hyperides, frg. 76; Dem. VI, 21; XIX, 145, 305f, 309; cf. 139.

[39] Aesch. II, 15.

[40] Justinus, VIII, 3.

death. Some of the Chalcidians, however, managed to flee and
make their way to Athens and to these the Athenians gave the
privileges of ἀτέλεια.[41] The lands of the Chalcidic cities were
confiscated and given with a lavish hand to all who had been
able to please the fancy of Philip. A few Macedonian nobles
came into the possession of the farms of many Greeks.[42] It
would seem that these grants were not made in fee-simple but
depended upon the rendering of some service, military or otherwise.[43] Thus the whole of the Chalcidian territory was made a
part of Macedonia, inhabited in large part by Macedonians and
enjoying the same rights and privileges as the rest of the country.
The Chalcidian league had made its last stand and had suc-
cumbed to the same force that was later to conquer the remaining Greek cities.

The career of the league had been eventful. Almost from the
very day of its foundation it had to encounter strenuous opposition and a large part of its eighty-five years of existence had been
spent in fighting for its life. It had shown itself to be founded
upon sound political principles. Its adherents had remained
faithful until an outside power gave them their freedom and
even then rejoined the league when the trouble had blown over.
Greek cities and Barbarian were alike appreciative of the generous terms upon which they had been admitted. There was opposition, of course, but the gradual extension of the Chalcidian
boundaries shows that the innate force of the league, the justice
of the conditions it offered for admission, and the satisfactory
way in which the government was managed, were able in the
end to convince the majority of the opposing party. Absolute
annihilation was the only thing that could keep the Chalcidians
from extending their league. Time after time they received a
check such as other unions have not been able to overcome. Its
members were taken from it and it still survived and grew, in a
short time winning back more than it had lost. Beset with en-

---

[41] Suidas, Κάρανος; cf. Aesch. II, 155; Harpocration, s. v. ἰσοτελής; Hicks
and Hill, 138a.
[42] Diod. XVI, 53; Dem. XIX, 145; Ditt. Syll.,[2] 178; Koehler, Sitz.-ber. d.
Berl. Ak., 1891, pp. 473ff; Theop. frg. 217b.
[43] Arrian, Anab., I, 2, 5; 12, 7; II, 9, 3. These passages refer to troops
of cavalry recruited from the territory confiscated.

emies that wished to stop its growth, the league had become a power to be reckoned with.

The history of the fourth century shows that the Greek city state had reached the limit of its usefulness. If Greece was to remain a force in the world politically or to resist the encroachments of her neighbours, it was necessary for her to enter into some form of permanent union. Conditions were such that the πόλις was unfitted for the duties of statehood. The growing restlessness of the Greek people, their development towards individualism, and the consequent impatience under authority and refusal to undertake the duties of citizenship made it impossible for Greece to remain an aggregate of independent cities and survive. Greek wealth and commerce was one of the chief factors in bringing about this state of affairs. No longer was the state regarded as of prime importance, for which it was the duty of every citizen to sacrifice his own pleasure and interests. The rights of the individual were becoming paramount; and with this change of thought went an unwillingness to undertake personal military service and other political burdens. This naturally resulted in the employment of an increasing number of mercenaries and in the creation of bodies of free-lances, ready at all times to create disturbances, to desert to a master offering better pay, and to embarass the whole Greek world generally. With such problems to solve, Greece was in need of all her political acumen. As a body of independent cities, it found the problem too difficult to solve. Union would have given it greater stability and greater strength to use in maintaining order within its territories. This, however, was distasteful to nearly the whole Greek people and every effort was made to maintain the principle of local city autonomy. This same particularism had proved ruinous to the Chalcidians and in turn was to prove ruinous for the remainder of Greece.

The Chalcidians, however, had solved the problem and were making the experiment on a small scale, gradually extending it as the union proved to be successful and in working order. It is true that their union was the result of the necessity of combination, so that they might be able to resist Athens with success; but the fact that their form of confederation was so popular in their immediate neighbourhood and existed with them until the whole country became an integral part of Macedonia shows that it was admirably suited to the conditions. Although the problem that faced the Chalcidians was by no means as large or as difficult as that of the Greek cities in the south, it was essentially the same problem. Conditions were very similar. These cities, conservative and adhering to their worn out political theories, could not be expected to appreciate the excellent example placed before their eyes by the Chalcidic league, and so allowed it to go to its ruin without even gaining a lesson from its history.

CHAPTER XIV

THE CONSTITUTION OF THE CHALCIDIC LEAGUE

It will be interesting, I think, to consider how the Chalcidians
solved so satisfactorily the internal problems of union. Our materials for this are of the scantiest, but nevertheless the attempt
must be made to put into some sort of coherent relation the
scattered information that we possess. It is extremely unfortunate that the treatise on the polity of the Thracian Chalcidians,
written by the Stagirite Aristotle, has not come down to us.[1]
He was in a position to know from personal observation what the
constitution was and how it was administered. He was born at
a time when the Chalcidians were expanding and it is possible
that Stageiros then became a member of the league. In any case
the aims of the league and its ideals, its political experiments,
successful or otherwise, must have been a matter of common
talk in the birthplace of Aristotle, less than thirty miles distant
from the center of the movement.

---

[1] *F. H. G.*, II, 153, Χαλκιδέων τῶν ἐπὶ Θράκης πολιτεία. For Stageiros,
see Strabo, VII, 331, frg. 35: ἐν δὲ τῷ κόλπῳ πρώτη μετὰ τὸν 'Ακανθίων λιμένα
Στάγειρα, ἔρημος, καὶ αὐτὴ τῶν Χαλκιδικῶν, 'Αριστοτέλους πατρίς. Dion. Hall.,
ep. I, ad *Amm.*, 5, calls Aristotle's mother a descendant τινὸς τῶν ἐκ Χαλκίδος
τὴν ἀποικίαν ἀγαγόντων εἰς Στάγειρα. Dio. Chrys., *Or.* XLVII, 9. Philip
and Alexander at the request of Aristotle allowed the restoration of Stageiros,
τὰ δὲ Στάγειρα κώμη τῆς 'Ολυνθίας ἦν. Cf. Plut. *Alex.*, 7; Ael. *Var. His.*, XII,
54. This may be a mistake but it is noteworthy that Aristotle was born in
384 just when the Chalcidians were extending their power in the peninsula
and even in Macedon. Probably Stageiros became one of the members of the
league at that time. If it is true that it had a Chalcidian element in its
population, this is not at all unlikely. We know moreover that Aristotle had
relations in Olynthos. Callisthenes, born about 360, the historian of Alexander's court, was his nephew or cousin and an Olynthian by birth. If the
city was destroyed by Philip, we have additional evidence that it belonged to
the league in the time of Philip. Strabo definitely states that it was Chalcidian and we may assume not that it was a Chalcidian settlement primarily,
although with perhaps some Chalcidian elements, but that it later became a
member of the κοινὸν τῶν Χαλκιδέων.

Political union was by no means unknown to the Greeks at the time when the Chalcidic league came into existence in 432.   It had already appeared in various forms.   For religious political unions the Greeks had their Amphictyonic leagues.   Sparta had her loose but effective Peloponnesian Confederacy and Athens her Delian Empire.   These were none of them entirely satisfactory.   The bond of union was either too weak or too artificial to be permanently effective; and this condition of affairs naturally resulted in the employment of force against the unwilling and dissatisfied members.   Still another form of political union was found in Boeotia.   Although even here coercion was at times necessary to maintain the existence of the Boeotian State, the ties binding the members together were real ones and in large part dependent upon lasting community of interests.   Thebes, moreover, did not have so powerful a control over the other Boeotian cities as did Sparta and Athens over their followers.   Thus the relations of the states participating in the Boeotian league more nearly approached equality and for that reason it tended to be more stable.   A further and more primitive form of union was to be found in Attica, viz., the synoecism.   This had proved so strong that all thought of the original component elements had been lost.   A city had been formed and not a federal state.   The primitive κοινόν of the Aetolians may be used as another type. In this the tie was racial.   Thus we see that race, natural geographical boundaries, necessity, policy, and fear, all played their part in bringing about union among the Greeks.

Which of these forces or what combination of them was active in bringing about union among the Chalcidians and what was the form of union produced?   According to the ordinary view the city of Chalcis founded many colonies upon the peninsula jutting out from the Thracian coast and these colonies, as it would seem, maintained, throughout their existence, a consciousness of their common origin and relationship.   So numerous were these colonies and so strong was this feeling of kinship that the place in which they were settled has become known as Chalcidicè.   Even with conditions favourable for union, it was impossible for the Chalcidians to accomplish anything in that line so long as Athens kept a firm hand upon the reins and held them

as tributaries to the Athenian league. All early attempts at
union, however small, proved futile. We find traces of such a
primitive union in the early coins, in Herodotos, and perhaps in
the quota lists, but under Athenian supremacy every effort was
made to resolve this union into its elements. Freedom from
Athens was necessary for union and conversely union was necessary for the maintenance of this freedom. Aside from Athenian opposition, however, nothing stood in the way. The Chalcidians were of the same race and were engaged in similar pursuits.

The revolt of Potidaea and the encouragement and support
offered by Perdiccas gave the Chalcidians the very opportunity
they needed.[2] Not content with a mere union of cities, weak because of its excessive division, they decided to dismantle many
of their seacoast towns and remove the inhabitants of these towns
inland to Olynthos or to a place to be loaned them by Perdiccas.
In this we see that the Chalcidians recognized the value of synoecism and were determined to make use of it as a foundation for
their nascent state. Their purpose, however, was not to create
a city state nor to make the position of Olynthos in Chalcidicè
analagous to that of Athens in Attica. This is made plainly evident by the history of the league in the early years of the fourth
century. Cities and towns were then incorporated in the Chalcidic κοινόν without losing their corporate individuality. The
same thing is shown just as clearly in the fact that the name
given to the state was not that of the city, Olynthos, but that of
the race. Inscriptions, coins, and Thucydides prove that the
state was officially known as the κοινόν of the Chalcidians on the
borders of Thrace.

It is clear, however, that Demosthenes believed the league to
be in reality Olynthos.[3] With one exception he always speaks of
the Olynthians, never even mentioning the Chalcidians.[4] The
explanation is simple. He has confused the synoecism of Olyn-

---

[2] Thuc. I, 58ff.

[3] Dem. XIX, 263ff. This passage speaks of the strength of the Chalcidic
league, calling it Olynthos.

[4] *Ibid.* The phrase οὔπω Χαλκιδέων πάντων εἰς ἓν συνῳκισμένων shows that
he confounds the city with the league.

thos with the formation of the state and has given Olynthos a
position in Chalcidicè similar to that of Athens in Attica.   This,
however, is not borne out by the facts we know concerning the
league.   The analogy of Athens applies only in a very limited
degree.   None but seacoast towns, and these of no great size,
participated in the synoecism.   Therefore, if the formation of
the Chalcidic state had confined itself to these, there could have
been no valid reason for choosing the more general term, Chalcidian, in preference to the name of the city to which the strength
of the small seacoast towns had been added.   From the words of
Thucydides,[5] moreover, we infer that there were Chalcidic towns
inland and from the history of the league and from the use of
the name Chalcidian we see that these inland towns also were
members of the κοινόν.   Stolos, a town of approximately half
the importance of Olynthos before the war, is perhaps the most
noteworthy example of a Chalcidian inland town, not destroyed,
but still a member of the newly formed state.   Hence one can
say that Demosthenes is wrong in describing the formation of
the Chalcidic state as a synoecism.   It was more than that.

We must now inquire as to the manner in which this union was
perfected and what were the principles upon which it was based.
We have noticed before that the Chalcidians were conscious of a
racial unity and that this was one of the factors which tended
to promote political unity among the Greeks.   Our typical example of a league in which the ethnical element exerted a powerful influence for unification is that of Aetolia.   The Aetolian
league, however, in its early stages was not a union of cities but
rather a federation of clans, dwelling in small and unimportant
villages.   Thus if we accept the traditional view as to the origin
of the Chalcidians we cannot consider the Aetolian league analogous to the κοινόν of the Chalcidians, for the Chalcidians
had reached a higher degree of civilization and were settled in
cities, each with its own highly developed political life and its
feeling of independence.

If then we are to find an early analogy in Greek history, we
must look for it in some union of city states.   Of the unions we

---

[5] Thuc. I, 58.

have mentioned, the Peloponnesian and Delian leagues and the Boeotian state are yet to be considered. The first was not a state in any sense of the word but merely a loose organization. The Delian league, or in its later form, the Athenian Empire, was practically an hegemony in which Athens was the center and held the executive power. In its developed form, it was composed of cities bound to Athens by separate treaties and owing allegiance to Athens and not to the league. Such a position for Olynthos among the Chalcidians is scarcely conceivable. Such a union results not in the formation of a state but in that of an empire. In an empire, however, centrifugal tendencies are always apparent, and these must be counteracted by the superior force of the hegemonic state. With such tendencies at work stability is almost impossible to maintain. If the rule is mild and just, a gradual loosening of the bonds takes place, resulting finally in a loose confederation as in the second Athenian empire. If, however, the rule is autocratic, discontent will break out and rebellions are bound to occur, as happened in the first Athenian empire. Stability was one of the most noticeable qualities of the Chalcidic league and for this reason it seems best to look elsewhere for the pattern of the Chalcidian constitution. In considering the question of the confederation of Greek cities, one must constantly keep in mind the universal attitude of the Greeks towards the city state, and one must always expect to find in the various cities of any league a reactionary party, favouring separation and city autonomy. Hence it is remarkable that this party in the cities of the Chalcidic league was of no greater consequence. Only once did it show its head, and then only for a short time under the influence of external pressure and in cities that had been recently united with the league. This happened in the year 382, at the time when Peloponnesian troops entered the Chalcidic peninsula for the purpose of breaking up the power of the κοινόν[6]. Success, however, was only temporary. In a few years' time the league regained all that it had lost. This recuperative power of the Chalcidian state proves its stability and shows that it was based upon sound political principles. Equal-

---

[6] See Chap. X.

ity and some form of states rights are thus to be looked for in the Chalcidic constitution.

As our sources give us little direct knowledge concerning the organization of the Chalcidic league, it is advisable to make use of the principle of analogy as far as possible. The constitution of Boeotia at the time of the Peloponnesian War may be taken as the general type of a confederation, embodying the principles of equality and of states rights. Local city autonomy and proportional representation were two important elements in this constitution.[7] Now Xenophon tells us that the cities of the Chalcidic league used the same laws and had sympolity[8] or in other words, were members of one state. From this statement of Xenophon that the Chalcidic state was composed of cities using the same law, we may infer that local administration was entrusted to the cities, as in Boeotia, but was carried out in accordance with principles laid down by the state itself. The words of the Acanthian envoys at Sparta state this in a different way, viz., from the standpoint of the cities that refused to join the league. The reason given for this refusal is that they wished to use their own ancestral laws and to be αὐτοπολῖται. Included in this body of common law in common use among all the cities of the league we find ἐπιγαμία and ἔγκτησις παρ' ἀλλήλοις, i. e., connubium and commercium. This clearly amounts to the establishment of a national citizenship.

There can be no doubt that the πόλις still remained the unit of administration, even though its sphere was more limited than that of the city in the later leagues, e. g., Arcadian, Aetolian, and Achaean, or than that of the state in the constitution of the United States. Xenophon's description of the principles upon which the Chalcidic league was based is so very cursory that it is impossible to tell within what limits the local city government was restricted. The use of common laws, however, does not necessarily mean that there was no freedom of action in city affairs. The constitution of the United States makes certain things obligatory upon each of the states and requires of them constitutions

---

[7] *Hell. Oxyrhynch., Oxon.*, Chap. **11.** For a discussion of the Boeotian constitution see Bonner, *Cl. Ph.*, 1910, Vol. V, 405–417.

[8] Xen. *Hell.*, V, 2, 12, 14, 19.

conforming to a certain general type, and yet there remains to them a large amount of freedom in the choice of details. One can still say of the people of the United States, in the words of Xenophon, that they are using common laws. Some such arrangement as this probably existed among the cities of the Chalcidic κοινόν. The constitutions of the many πόλεις were made to conform to a certain type, beyond which there was a field, large or small, in which their autonomy was not restricted. In this way then the constitution of Boeotia seems to have been followed, either consciously or otherwise, by the Chalcidian statesmen in organizing their newly formed state.

When several city states unite to form a federation, the question immediately comes up, what shall be the executive and law making bodies, how they shall be composed and what shall be the method of representation. For one educated in a Greek πόλις and imbued with the idea that the citizen body alone has the right to make the laws, it is difficult to conceive of government by duly elected plenipotentiary representatives. Two ways were ordinarily used by the leagues to free them from this difficulty. In the more loosely organized, the acts passed by the council of delegates were afterwards ratified κατὰ πόλεις. In the later confederations, except perhaps the Achaean, a primary assembly passed upon all important measures. In this all citizens who were present might cast their votes. Here, however, the voting was usually by cities, each city casting one ballot. The first method caused delay and was unsatisfactory. The second was unwieldy and gave an undue influence to the smaller cities and the richer citizens, who alone could afford to attend the meetings of the assembly, especially if it was held at a distance from their home towns. Both of these methods were theoretically democratic, giving to the people the ultimate control of affairs.

The Boeotians, however, proverbially stupid as they were, used neither of these methods. Their senate or Boulè was purely elective and representative, and to it and the Boeotarchs was entrusted practically sovereign power. The Boeotians had found a substitute for the national primary assembly and for the referendum. Boeotia, moreover, was divided into constituencies and each of these was represented in the national assembly in proportion to its size and importance. Thus we find in Boeotia the forerunner of the modern parliament. While the Achaean and Aetolian leagues were essentially democratic and embodied democratic principles in their constitution, Boeotia was a limited aristocracy; and it is to this difference that we must look for an explanation of the fact that the sovereign assemblies of the first were primary, and that of Boeotia representative.

Unfortunately our sources for the Chalcidic league are so scanty that it is impossible to tell how closely its constitution followed that of Boeotia. The relations existing between the two states were from the beginning friendly ones. Before the Peloponnesian War, Boeotia was as hostile to Athens as were the Chalcidians and we have seen how the latter at various times, sought alliance with the Boeotians. Their interests were common during the first years of the war. After the treaty of 421 and the ensuing alliance between Athens and Sparta, Chalcidian ambassadors endeavoured to draw Boeotia into a coalition with Corinth and Argos, but this attempt failed, not so much because of unwillingness on the part of the Boeotians as because of a misunderstanding of the Lacedaemonian position.[9] In the following years Boeotia was again with the Chalcidians in their hostility towards Athens. Later during the Corinthian War the two were in alliance,[10] and again in 382 attempts were made to cement more closely the friendship of the two peoples.[11] This, however, was forestalled by the Spartan attack upon the Cadmeon. Thus we see that the relations existing between the Chalcidians and the Boeotians were very close indeed. It is worth while, moreover, to note that the Athenian oligarchs at the time of their supremacy in 411 set up a constitution in Athens modelled in certain particulars after that of Boeotia. This goes to show the high regard in which the Boeotian constitution was held. Thus, inasmuch as we know that Boeotia and the Chalcidians were on very friendly terms indeed and since the Boeotian constitution served as a model to be copied by the moderate aristocratical gov-

[9] See Chap. VIII.
[10] See Chap. IX.
[11] See Chap. X.

ernment of Athens, we will not be surprised if we find resemblances in the constitution of the aristocratic Chalcidian state to the contemporary constitution of Boeotia. It has already been mentioned that both states were confederations of cities. It remains to be shown that the government of the Chalcidians was aristocratic.

Boeotia, as we have seen, was governed by a mild form of aristocracy. This government made use of the principles of proportional representation, which is to be explained, perhaps, by the fact that representative institutions are more in accord with an aristocratic form of government than with a democratic one. The reason for this is that the citizen body is more homogeneous. Its interests, therefore, are common; its political and commercial views are more likely to be harmonious; and the chances are that the opinions of any given number of individuals will coincide with those of the citizen body as a whole. Hence there can be but little objection to a representative assembly. Wherever the interests of the individual coincide with those of the community to which he belongs, the community will have little hesitation in allowing any collection of members to represent it. In a democracy one always finds the demos in opposition to the few. Their interests are not the same and for this reason delegation of power to individuals is by no means so satisfactory.

Even before the time of the formation of the Chalcidic league, political theorists were beginning to feel that the pure democracy of Athens was not the best possible form of government. People were realizing the unreliability of the demos in political affairs, and thinkers of the time were turning their minds towards a consideration of the advantages of aristocracy. Scarcely a writer, except the Athenian orators, had a favourable opinion to express concerning democracy. Even in Athens, the very bulwark of democracy, this aristocratic tendency was strong. Distrust of the demos is shown only too clearly in the pseudo-Xenophontic Constitution of Athens and in the oligarchic revolution of 411.[12]

It is not surprising, then, that the Chalcidians adopted a limited form of aristocracy at the time of their revolt from Athens.

---

[12] Cf. Beloch, *Att. Pol.*, p. 11.

That they did this is not directly stated in any ancient authority, but several considerations lead one to this conclusion. First of all there is the natural supposition that a revolt from Athens would be followed by a change in government from democracy to aristocracy. Various passages in Thucydides[13] show plainly that this was the general tendency and that, on the one hand, Sparta encouraged the movement and, on the other, that the oligarchically minded were almost universally those who desired separation from Athens and alliance with the Lacedaemonians. In the second place, while we have no definite evidence as to what happened in the Chalcidic state, there are plain indications that the aristocrats of the neighbouring cities worked in harmony with the Chalcidians and that revolt from Athens was followed by a change in the government of the revolting cities. When Brasidas came into Chalcidicè, it was at the invitation of the Chalcidians and of Chalcidian partizans in the neighbouring cities.[14] When he made his attempt to win over Acanthos, Thucydides tells us that there was a stasis in the city between the demos and those who, together with the Chalcidians, had invited Brasidas to come to their assistance.[15] From the speech of Brasidas it is evident that the division was upon the question of democracy versus aristocracy.[16] This is also clear from the fact that it was the "few" who were opposed to the demos. Acanthos finally revolted and allied herself closely with the Chalcidians. At Toronè and Scionè there was the same feeling,[17] but from the troubles at Mendè we can see best how affairs stood in the rest of the peninsula.[18] The oligarchs, either by force or persuasion, brought about the revolt, and forced the democrats to act contrary to their wishes. After the revolt, however, the stasis continued and finally the demos rose against the Peloponnesian commander and the oligarchic party. Opening the gates of the city the people handed it over to the attacking Athenian forces. Because of this they were treated with clemency by Athens and were allowed to

---

[13] Thuc. I, 19; III, 82.
[14] Thuc. IV, 79.
[15] Thuc. IV, 84.
[16] Thuc. IV, 86.
[17] Thuc. IV, 110.
[18] Thuc. IV, 123, 130.

bring to trial the oligarchs who had been the cause of the revolt. In no other case was such clemency shown. It is distinctly stated, moreover, that the old constitution was restored. Thus it is clear, that in Mendè, at least, an oligarchic or aristocratic constitution had been set up at the time of the revolt. We may consider this a typical example of the course of events in the other cities of that region. First the oligarchic party, aided from without, and working with the Chalcidians, forced the city to withdraw from the Athenian alliance. After this had been accomplished, the next step was the formation of an aristocratic government. We have evidence that this was done in Mendè and the supposition is strong that Brasidas established aristocracies, when he reorganized the constitutions of the cities newly acquired by him.[19] Taking into consideration all these facts, we are forced to come to the conclusion that the oligarchic party in the cities of the Chalcidic peninsula, working at the suggestion of the Chalcidians, in reorganizing the constitution, merely followed the example set at the time of the establishment of the Chalcidic league, and conversely, that the Chalcidians adopted an aristocratic form of government at the beginning.

To the question, what were the qualifications for full citizenship, we can only give a probable answer. In Boeotia a property qualification had been established,[20] with probably a hoplite census as the lowest limit. Certain considerations lead us to believe that in the Chalcidic state, likewise, the possession of a certain definite amount of property carried with it, *ceteris paribus*, the rights and duties of citizenship, and that the same limit, *viz.*, the hoplite census, was adopted. The aristocratic government founded by the Chalcidians must have been a moderate one. Otherwise its stability could not have been maintained as successfully as it was during the many periods of disturbance through which the Chalcidians passed. A limited aristocratic form of government of this nature does not differ radically from a democracy and satisfies all except the lowest classes, those who, having little at stake, are lacking in that sense of responsibility which is so necessary a qualification for good citizenship.

---

[19] Thuc. IV, **107, 116.**
[20] Cf. Bonner, *Cl. Ph.*, 1910, p. 407.

In a Greek state, where citizen soldiery was the rule and mercenaries the exception, service in the army played a much more important part than at present; and ability to take part in the protection of the state was a more necessary qualification for citizenship.   Those that could not provide themselves with a suit of hoplite armour were neither able to fulfill the chief duty of the citizen, nor had they sufficient at stake to be entrusted with the responsibilities of government.   Thus the citizens of the state, in the first instance, were those who had something to protect and could share in its protection.   In the fifth century Boeotian citizenship was based upon these principles, and in Athens[21] at the time of the overthrow of the Four Hundred, they were further employed for the selection of the Five Thousand.   Thus it would be not at all strange if the moderate aristocracy in Chalcidicè should adopt them as a part of its constitution.   For evidence we must go to Demosthenes who gives us some figures for the Chalcidic league at the time of Philip.[22]   In speaking of the strength of Olynthos, he says that the Olynthians were in all more than ten thousand in number, and had a body of one thousand horse.   It is evident from the context that this refers to the fighting strength of the town; and yet the wording would imply that the number of citizens is meant.   This would go to show that our previous suggestions were correct, and that the citizen body was coextensive with the army.   Now the proportion between hoplites and cavalry was ten to one in the Boeotian army and we have every reason for supposing that the Chalcidians used approximately the same ratio.[23]   Thus Demosthenes is probably speaking of the hoplite levy.   We have just seen that the citizen body was limited to approximately ten or eleven thousand, and since this was probably the number of the hoplites, we can not be far wrong in assuming that citizenship was possessed only by those who could provide themselves with hoplite equipment.

In this passage of Demosthenes, Olynthos is credited with the impossible number of 11,000 of hoplite census.   The total levy

---

[21] Thuc. VIII, 97.
[22] Dem. XIX, 266.
[23] Cf. note 30, Chap. XV.

of Boeotia early in the fourth century was only 11,000 hoplites and 1,100 cavalry.[24] Taking this into consideration and also the fact that Demosthenes almost invariably speaks not of the Chalcidians but of the Olynthians when he is patently referring to the whole state, we are forced to the conclusion that the numbers given in this passage are applicable not to Olynthos but to the κοινόν itself. One more reference is to be considered. Theopompos[25] tells us that eight hundred Macedonian ἐταῖροι possessed as much land as ten thousand Greeks, τοὺς τὴν ἀρίστην καὶ πλείστην χώραν κεκτημένους. It has been suggested and with good reason that this is a reference to the Chalcidic confiscations after the destruction of Olynthos and the other cities of the league. The wording may be significant. The Greeks mentioned were those that held the best and the most land, that is to say, the richest. The others were not taken into consideration. It is noteworthy that the numbers given by Demosthenes and Theopompos are approximately the same and we may assume that the ten thousand of the latter were the full citizens of the league, those who held sufficient property to make up the required census and to be enrolled in the army as hoplites. This is additional evidence in support of our interpretation of Demosthenes.[26]

We have shown to all probability that the Chalcidic state was aristocratic and that either unconsciously or consciously in this it had followed that principle on which the Boeotian constitution was based. In Boeotia, moreover, we have seen that there was a logical connection between the moderate form of aristocracy and the principles of representation expressed in the formation of its national assembly. Inasmuch as the Chalcidic state had similar problems to face, being a union of Greek cities, homo-

---

[24] *Hell. Oxyrhynch*, Chap. 11. Eleven thousand is too great a number for Olynthos alone and would be more nearly what we would expect from the league as a whole.

[25] Theop. frg. 217b; Cf. Koehler, *Sitz.-ber. d. Berlin. Akad.*, 1891, pp. 473 ff. In Diod. XXXII, 4, Olynthos is called πόλις μυριάνδρος.

[26] Only once does Demosthenes use the term Chalcidian (XIX, 263). This is a difficult passage. It speaks of the strength of Olynthos at the time of the Spartan invasion in 382 and says that the synoecism of the Chalcidians had not yet taken place. This is a confusion of the city with the league and places Olynthos and the Chalcidic territory in an analogous position to that of Athens and Attica.

geneous in race, civilization, government, and economic life, it
would not be strange if it had followed the example of its southern ally and had formed its national assembly or Boulè by means
of a system of proportional representation. For a centralized
government of any wide territorial extent, primary assemblies
are unsatisfactory; and such assemblies, moreover, are in accord
with democratic rather than aristocratic principles.

Unfortunately, however, the constitution of the κοινόν can be
made out only in its broadest outline. As to the details of organization, we are left in almost complete ignorance and can
only make suggestions here and there. One would like to know
whether the Chalcidians had the political acumen to recognize
the fitness of a representative assembly for their peculiar conditions. Likewise it would be interesting to learn more of their
legislative and administrative bodies. A chance remark of Theopompos tells of a Boulè of the Olynthians.[27] This, in all probability, refers to the assembly or the Boulè of the κοινόν, inasmuch as the question concerns a prisoner of war. Even so, from
such a statement no information can be gained. Concerning offices of the state we have again as little knowledge. Euthycrates
and Lasthenes held the military post of Hipparch.[28] On the
Chalcidic coins we have the names of a number of magistrates,
but what the magistracy was or what duties fell to its lot it is impossible to say.[29]

Finally a summary of the rights of the central government will
be advantageous for our discussion. All foreign relations were
in its charge, the making of treaties and alliances, and the appointment of ambassadors and proxenoi.[30] It also had control
of exports and imports.[31] From Thucydides we see that the
army was centralized. Coinage also was under the control of
the central government. Thus there was a national and not a

---

[27] Theop. frg. 139.
[28] Hyp. frg. 76; Dem. IX, 66. Demosthenes here confuses the Olynthians
with the Chalcidians. The hipparch would naturally be an officer of the
state and not of the city. Hyperides makes the same mistake. Heraclides
(F. H. G., II, 222) tells us that no one was allowed to become a Chalcidian
magistrate or ambassador until he had reached the age of fifty years.
[29] B. M. C. Maced., pp. 66ff., nos. 2, 8, 9, 10, 11, 12, 25.
[30] Ditt. Syll.,² 77, 121; I. G., II, 17; Thuc. IV, 78–79, 83.
[31] Ditt. Syll²., 77.

city coinage.   The admission of new members was likewise controlled by the state under uniform regulations.   We may even
assume that a national court existed, although Demosthenes with
his usual metonomy, speaks of the Olynthian court in this connection.[32]   At least we know from Aristotle that there were federal laws concerning murder and inheritance.[33]   This is the best
confirmation of Xenophon[34] that the Chalcidians had a common
body of law, and it shows to what extent the centralization had
been developed.   The fact that ἔγκτησις and ἐπιγαμία παρ' ἀλλήλοις
were allowed suggests that the laws concerning property and
marriage were also under state control.

Thus the Chalcidic state was, in its elements, a union of cities,
but a union so close and centralized that it approached very near
to the territorial state in form, such as Great Britain or Canada
for example.   Its government was stable and aristocratic, and
the league, although beset with vicissitudes, showed so great and
inherent a power of resiliency as can only be found in a state
based not only upon justice and equality, but also upon sound
political principles.

---

[32] Dem. IX, 56, 66.
[33] Arist. *Pol.*, II, 12, 14.   Androdamas of Rhegium, otherwise unknown,
was the νομοθέτης for the Chalcidians.
[34] Xen. *Hell.*, V, 2, 12; 19.

CHAPTER XV

POPULATION OF THE CHALCIDIC PENINSULA

The base of the Chalcidic peninsula during the fifth century was fringed with Greek settlements. The country inland had not been developed to any great extent; but the three promontories had offered themselves to the Euboeans as places suitable for colonization. Eretrian colonies were planted on Pallenè and later on Actè, and the land of the Sithonians, or Sithonia, was chosen by the Chalcidians.[1] On the eastern coast Andrian colonies found a home for themselves.[2] In the west the Bottiaeans had settled, after having been driven out from their original home on the Thermaic gulf.[3] The colonists, however, seem to have kept fairly close to the sea. There the land was fertile and the harbours were good, while the interior was more or less hilly and covered with heavy forests. It was not until the time of the Persian wars that the Chalcidians obtained possession of Olynthos. Before that time the Bottiaeans had held the city and the adjacent territory.[4]

That the mainland at the time of the Peloponnesian War was relatively sparsely settled can be seen from an inspection of the Attic tribute lists. The area of the mainland is approximately three times as great as that of the three peninsulas, and yet it paid only one third as much tribute.[5] No city, moreover, at the base of the peninsula was large enough to pay the small sum of four talents, while upon Pallenè alone there were cities paying six, eight, and fifteen talents. Finally, if the country had been

---

[1] Strabo, VII, 329, frg. 11; X, 447, 8.
[2] Strabo, VII, 330, frg. 31; Thuc. IV, 84, 88, 103. Andros was at an early date an Eretrian possession. When Eretria began to decline Andros sent out her colonies.
[3] Hdt. VII, 123, 127; VIII, 127; Thuc. II, 99.
[4] Hdt. VIII, 127.
[5] *I. G.*, I, 242–244.

at all developed, Perdiccas could not have thrown open to Chalcidic settlement a large tract of land south of Lake Bolbè.[6]   The
reason for the scarcity of towns in the interior of Chalcidicè is not
hard to find.   Pallenè, Sithonia, and the shores of the mainland
were capable of supporting a large population.   The Greeks,
moreover, preferred the seacoast for the purposes of commerce.
Their settlements were thus placed wherever they could find good
harbours.   It was only as time went on that the Greek population spread into the fertile territory inland.   Before the Peloponnesian War, as we have seen, this movement towards the interior had taken place only to a small degree.   However, when the
seacoast towns were destroyed and the inhabitants moved to
Olynthos and to the region in Mygdonia, given to them by Perdiccas, the development of the "Hinterland" commenced.   Later,
the capture of Potidaea in 429 and that of Scionè in 420 placed
a large number of the inhabitants of these towns in a position
where it was necessary for them to seek new homes.   Without
doubt many of them settled in the sparsely settled Chalcidic territory.[7]

Beloch has estimated the number of the citizens of the whole
Chalcidic peninsula at about twenty-five thousand at the time of
the revolt in 432.[8]   This number seems to be excessively large for
that period.   Attica at the time of her greatest prosperity had
only about ten thousand more.   Beloch has based his figures, in
part, upon those given by Xenophon and Demosthenes for a
much later date.[9]   According to this estimate Olynthos alone had
five thousand citizens.   This number is manifestly far too great
for the period of the Peloponnesian War.   For the three small
peninsulas Pallenè, Sithonia, and Actè, we can accept Beloch's
figures as more nearly correct, since they are based upon contemporary evidence.   Beloch estimates that Pallenè had approximately seven thousand citizens; but this number is but two thousand more than he ascribes to the city of Olynthos alone.   Pal-

---

[6] Thuc. I, 58.
[7] Thuc. II, 70; IV, 123.   The women and children of Scionè had been
conveyed to Olynthos for safety at the time of the revolt.
[8] Beloch, Bevölkerung d. Griech. Rom. Welt, pp. 202–206.
[9] Xen. Hell., V, 2, 14; 3, 1; Dem. XIX, 263–266.

lenè, however, had four cities, each of which paid more tribute
than Olynthos, and the total tribute of Pallenè was fifteen or
twenty times as great as that of Olynthos. It is evident that a
city paying only two talents tribute can not support a population five-sevenths as great as the combined population of other
neighbouring cities which pay thirty to forty talents.[10] Five
thousand, moreover, for the combined forces of Apollonia and
Acanthos is equally preposterous.[11] Apollonia was not yet in
existence, or, if so, was of no size nor importance,[12] and Acanthos,
judging from the tribute lists again, was about as large as Olynthos.[13] For the peninsulas Beloch has worked out a ratio between the amount of tribute paid and the number of citizens in
any given city or territory. The conditions could not have been
so very different in the base of the Chalcidic peninsula and approximately the same ratio ought to hold good for both. This
ratio, however, Beloch has failed to use for the mainland. According to this ratio the thirty-five or forty talents tribute of
Pallenè was paid by a citizen body of about six or seven thousand. Sithonia,[14] paying about fifteen talents, would then have
from two thousand five hundred to three thousand citizens, and
one thousand more were found in Actè. Thus for the three
peninsulas we obtain the rough average of from five to five and

---

[10] The amount varied from year to year as the following table shows:

Potidaea	15 T.	436	*I. G.* I, 244.
"	6 T.	438	" 242.
Scionè	9 T.	427	" 259.
"	4 T.	428	" 256.
"	15 T.	438	" 242.
"	6 T.	443	" 237.
Mendè	8 T.	437–428	" 243–256.
Aphytis	3 T.	428	" 256.
"	1 T.(?)	438	" 242.

[11] From the cavalry estimate in Xenophon, *Hell.*, V, 2, 14 and 3, 1, Beloch
assumes that Apollonia and Acanthos together were about equal to Olynthos.
Op. cit., p. 205.

[12] See note 17, Chap. IX.

[13] The tribute of Acanthos in 427–6 was three talents. *I. G.*, I, 259.

[14]Sermylia	4½ T.	437	*I. G.*, I, 243.
"	1 T.	430(?)	" 255.
Toronè	6 T.	428	" 256.
"	12 T.	427	" 259.
Singos	3 T.	438	" 242.
"	2 T.	437	" 243.
"	1 T.	436	" 244.

one-half talents per one thousand citizens. We may use this as a basis for attacking the problem of the population in the rest of the Chalcidic peninsula. Conditions were very similar so that the results obtained by using this ratio, up to a certain degree of accuracy, will be correct. The whole base of the peninsula paid about eighteen talents tribute, about a third as much as Pallenè, Sithonia, and Actè combined.[15] The citizen body of these three peninsulas numbered about eleven thousand. Using our ratio then, we may assume that the remainder of the peninsula held no more than four thousand citizens. If we include northern Sithonia with the cities Singos and Sermylia we must add one thousand to this number.[16] This is in accord with what has just been said concerning the sparsely settled condition of the greater part of that region. The hills and the woods and the distance from the sea acted as a hindrance to dense settlement. We may conclude, therefore, that, both relatively and absolutely, there were no towns of any size upon the mainland.

Five thousand citizens in a country such as Chalcidicè would be able to maintain about two thousand hoplites.[17] How does this compare with what we know of the forces of the Chalcidians and their neighbours? Taking part in the expedition against Arrhibaeos there were three thousand Greek hoplites.[18]

[15] Aineia	3 T.	428	*I. G.,* I,	256.
Acanthos	3 T.	428	"	256.
Spartolos	3 $\frac{1}{12}$ T.	436	"	244.
Olynthos	2 T.	438	"	242.
Mecyperna	1 T.	436	"	244.
Stolos	1 T.	437	"	243.
Strepsa	1 T.	437	"	243.

The smaller towns of this region contributed together three or four talents more.

[16] I have included Singos and Sermylia in this discussion for the sake of completeness. These two cities were at this time members of the Chalcidian league and their military levies were a part of the Chalcidian forces. Thus when we speak of Chalcidian hoplites or peltasts we have to reckon with contingents from all of the members of the league.

[17] Of five thousand citizens about 90% ordinarily would be subject to military service. The ratio between hoplites and light armed soldiers is approximately 43–57. Thus of five thousand citizens, four thousand five hundred are enrolled in the army. Of these four thousand five hundred nearly two thousand are able to supply themselves with the heavy armour of a hoplite. Cf. Beloch, *Bevölkerung*, pp. 53–54 and p. 25.

[18] Thuc. IV, 124. The Chalcidians also sent a body of cavalry upon this expedition.

These were Peloponnesians, Greeks settled in Macedonia, Chalcidians, Acanthians, and others κατὰ πόλεις. We may assume that, of these, about one thousand were from the Peloponnese under Brasidas. He had brought with him about seventeen hundred but had detached some for garrison duty.[19] Five hundred he had left for the protection of Scionè and Mendè under the command of Polydamidas.[20] Macedonia probably furnished one thousand and Chalcidicè the other. The expedition was Macedonian and one would expect to find that the Macedonian contingent formed a large part of the whole. The Chalcidians, moreover, would send only a part of their troops away for foreign service. A little later, at the time of the battle at Amphipolis, nearly two thousand hoplites were present.[21] The Macedonian contingent was absent, and this fact explains why the number was smaller. Of these two thousand, perhaps one-half came from the Chalcidic peninsula. There is no reason for thinking that Brasidas did not have with him all of the available Peloponnesian forces, probably about one thousand hoplites, and hence we must conclude that the native hoplite forces made up about half of the whole number. Thus in both expeditions there was a body of about one thousand hoplites from the Chalcidic state, Acanthos, and the neighbouring allied cities. It is not to be expected, however, that these cities would put into the field, for such expeditions away from home, more than half of their full strength. Beloch shows us that the age for military service in the field was between twenty and fifty years and that youths between eighteen and twenty and men between fifty and sixty were reserved for garrison duty. He estimates that 63 per cent of the males over eighteen years were between twenty and fifty years of age.[22] Thus out of two thousand hoplites about twelve hundred might have been with Brasidas. Probably, however, the full levy was not called out. Cities on the western coast would

---

[19] Thuc. IV, 78.
[20] Thuc. IV, 123.
[21] Thuc. V, 6. We have assumed one thousand as the number of the Macedonian contingent in the first expedition, because of the fact that at Amphipolis where that contingent was absent the hoplite forces numbered approximately one thousand less.
[22] Beloch, Bevölkerung, pp. 53f, and p. 163.

be loath to send a large proportion of their forces to Amphipolis. The Chalcidians needed soldiers to protect themselves against surprise from Pallenè and Sithonia. On the other hand full quotas from Acanthos and Amphipolis were probably with Brasidas on this occasion. Thus, knowing that the population of the base of Chalcidicè was large enough to support about two thousand hoplites, we are not surprised when we find one-half of this number under Brasidas in the Macedonian expedition and at Amphipolis. Besides the hoplite forces at Amphipolis, there was a body of three hundred Greek horse and one thousand Myrcinian and Chalcidian peltasts.[23] In Greek warfare, it must be remembered, a man's property determined whether he should serve as a horseman, a hoplite, or as a light armed soldier, and in an army serving $\pi\alpha\nu\delta\eta\mu\epsilon\iota$ the usual ratio between light and heavy armed troops was about 57–43.[24] In this ratio the cavalry is included among the heavy armed troops, inasmuch as the horsemen came from the richest class in the state. At Amphipolis, as we have seen, there were about thirteen hundred of hoplite census, not counting the troops of Brasidas. Of the other class, there were one thousand, Chalcidians and Myrcinians. Of these probably not many came from Myrcinus. Thus the Chalcidian peltasts were about eight hundred in number. Of the hoplites and the cavalry, probably, not more than one-half were Chalcidians, making about six hundred in all.[25] Our ratio would therefore be eight hundred light armed troops to six hundred hoplites and cavalry. This, however, is almost equal to the ratio given above, 57–43.

---

[23] Thuc. V, 6.

[24] Cf. note 17.

[25] By this time Sermylia and Singos had probably enrolled themselves in the Chalcidian league. With these two cities the Chalcidians could easily have furnished as many troops as the rest of the peninsula. The other half came from the Bottiaeans, Acanthians, Argilians, Amphipolitans and other cities. At this time Mendè had renewed its allegiance to Athens. Toronè had been recaptured and Scionè was in a state of siege. In the Macedonian expedition small contingents from Toronè and from Actè may have been included. On the other hand the levies from the cities in the eastern part of Chalcidicè were probably greater than at the battle of Amphipolis. Thus the two counterbalance one another. It is to be noted also that at the time of the Macedonian expedition 300 Chalcidian peltasts were acting as a garrison for Mendè and that Chalcidian horsemen were serving with the Macedonian cavalry. Thuc. IV, 123f; cf. note 16.

The battle of Amphipolis was a very important one and every effort was made by both sides to increase their armies. Hence we may assume that all of the Chalcidian troops that could be spared were with Brasidas. It is not too much to suppose that one-half of the army had been sent on this expedition. One thousand hoplites from the cities at the base of the Chalcidic peninsula is not too large a number for a citizen body of five thousand and fits in with our hypothesis. If then by using Beloch's ratio between tribute and population, we come to the conclusion that the citizens of the cities of the mainland numbered five thousand, and if we gain the same impression from a consideration of the allied troops at Amphipolis and in Macedonia, our estimates can not be very far wrong. Five thousand then is amply sufficient for the period of the Peloponnesian War.[26] A citizen body of five thousand represents approximately a population of fifteen thousand, metics and slaves excluded. We can distribute the population approximately as follows. Spartolos which was the chief Bottiaean city paid a tribute of about three talents. The Bottiaeans then numbered perhaps two thousand. Aineia as we learn from the quota list was about equal in importance to Spartolos and probably had about the same number of inhabitants. The other towns of the western coast paid about three talents in all. Thus we see that about three eighths of the population was centered to the west of the territory held by the Chalcidian league. Olynthos, Mecyperna, and Stolos with the smaller towns in their neighbourhood paid five or six talents, and probably numbered about four thousand inhabitants. With the Chalcidians we must include Mecyperna and Singos. Their combined population was perhaps four thousand and more. Another two or three thousand were to be found in Acanthos and the other Andrian settlements on the east coast.[27]

In the next century conditions were changed. Olynthos, as the capital of a flourishing league, had increased materially. At

---

[26] Beloch estimates the citizen body of the whole peninsula at about twenty-five thousand. My estimate is five thousand for the base of the peninsula, including Sermylia and Singos, and six thousand for Pallenè, Sithonia, and Actè, not including the two cities of northern Sithonia already mentioned. This makes a total of eleven thousand citizens.

[27] Cf. notes 15–16.

the beginning of the Peloponnesian War, before its enlargement, a citizen body of four or five hundred is all that can be assumed for it. This would make it a little village of about two thousand inhabitants, slaves and metics included. By the time of the Spartan invasion in 382, it had grown larger. For this period we have two puzzling statements of Xenophon and Demosthenes. Demosthenes states that the citizen body was five thousand,[28] while Xenophon says that it could put into the field eight hundred hoplites and many more peltasts, besides a body of six hundred cavalry.[29] According to Demosthenes the cavalry was not more than four hundred in number, but this discrepancy of two hundred is a small matter and need cause us no trouble. How are we to reconcile the five thousand citizens of Demosthenes with the eight hundred hoplites of Xenophon, and is one true and the other false, or are both true?

Xenophon, without exception, makes no distinction between Olynthians and Chalcidians. He always speaks of the Olynthians, even when he is patently referring to the whole body of Chalcidians. Except for the context, we have no means of distinguishing in any given passage whether the word Olynthians refers to the inhabitants of the city alone or whether it has a wider meaning and embraces all of the Chalcidian state. Since we have these two meanings for the term it is not surprising if confusion results. Such carelessness can not fail to lead to faulty interpretation. This is probably what has happened with regard to the passage under discussion. Editors have generally questioned the manuscript reading, thinking that the number eight hundred is far too small. They were unable to reconcile it with the five thousand of Demosthenes, and they felt that the number of the cavalry was too great in proportion to the rest of the army. Are we to reject the figures of Xenophon because they seem too small or are we to analyze them further and see whether they can not readily be explained?

First, let us turn to the eight hundred hoplites with which Olynthos is accredited by Xenophon. No one will question for

---

[28] Dem. XIX, 263.
[29] Xen. *Hell.*, V, 2, 14; 3, 1.

a moment that this is too small a number for the army of the whole Chalcidic state, for if the Chalcidians had had no more than this in 382, the Peloponnesians would not have had such difficulty in conquering them. Editors, moreover, have generally made this assumption and have therefore been forced to question the reading as it stands. If, however, we assume that Xenophon is speaking of the military force of the city of Olynthos alone, we come to an entirely different conclusion, and it is quite unnecessary to suppose that we have a corrupted text. A body of eight hundred hoplites means a city of from six to eight thousand people. This would make the city three or four times as great as it was during the early period of the Peloponnesian War and would give it a reasonable and fairly rapid rate of increase in population. There is then no objection to taking Xenophon's statement as correct and applying it to Olynthos alone.

With regard to the cavalry the case is different. It is worthy of mention here that the raising of horses was one of the important pursuits of the Olynthians, if one may judge from their early coin types; and from this one might expect to find in the army a comparatively large proportion of cavalry.[30] This, however, does not seem to be the true explanation. Too much stress can not be laid upon the fact that Xenophon confuses the Olynthians and the Chalcidians. His universal use of the term Olynthians, now in the narrow sense, and now in its wider application, was bound to lead to confusion and to mistakes, even in the mind of the writer. It is not surprising, then, that in one and the same passage he uses it in the two senses. We have seen that his hoplite estimate referred to the city. Evidently he knew no figures for the league as a whole. He did know that, in one engagement, six hundred Chalcidian cavalry took part.[31] Inasmuch, however, as he did not distinguish between the forces of the league and the city, it was natural for him to connect the six hundred cavalry with the eight hundred hoplites. This he did

---

[30] The theoretical ratio between cavalry and hoplites in the Boeotian army is about 1–10. Cf. Boeotian army at Delion, Thuc. IV, 93; Boeotian levies, *Hell. Oxyrhynchia*, 11, 4; Athenian levies, Thuc. II, 13. The Chalcidian cavalry seems to have followed the Boeotian ratio, for in both countries cavalry seems to have played a rather important part in military operations.

[31] Xen. *Hell.*, V, 3, 1.

in a more or less rhetorical way; for he says, in the words of Cleigenes, the Acanthian envoy to Sparta, that if the Acanthians and Apollonians should join Olynthos, the combined cavalry would amount to one thousand in number. Xenophon realizes that the number is unduly large compared with that of the hoplite forces, for he seems to place his emphasis upon the cavalry. The whole context of the two passages where Xenophon mentions the Olynthian cavalry and especially the fact that he speaks of the hypothetical addition of the cavalry of Acanthos and Apollonia shows that he is referring to the cavalry levy of the whole Chalcidic κοινόν. To conclude, it is fair to presume that Xenophon has given us the figures as he knew them; but that his lack of knowledge of the political conditions existing in the Chalcidic state and his supposition that the city of Olynthos was the state has caused him to combine two different sets of figures. He knew the hoplite estimates for the city, but not those for the league. In the same way he knew the cavalry estimates for the league, but not for the city. Thus, not realizing that his information was faulty, he combined the two. If the cavalry of the league numbered six hundred, the hoplites probably numbered about six thousand. Assuming then that Xenophon is correct, and that the Chalcidian army mustered six hundred horse and ten times that number of hoplites, let us now consider the figures offered by Demosthenes.[32] At a first glance they will seem highly inflated.

He assumes for Olynthos a citizen body of five thousand and a cavalry force of four hundred. The numbers of the cavalry agree nearly enough with those given by Xenophon, and one may assume that Demosthenes, just as Xenophon, is here speaking of the cavalry levy of the Chalcidian league.[33] We must remember that Demosthenes when speaking of the Olynthians is subject to the same inaccuracy which we have detected in Xenophon. He uses the name in both senses and in this case he seems

---

[32] Dem. XIX, 263.

[33] The numbers given by Demosthenes for the cavalry and for the hoplites are only approximately in the ratio of 1–10; but this small divergence need not disturb us. He is writing many years after the occurrences mentioned, and the ratio is not absolutely fixed and unalterable.

to mean the whole body of the Chalcidians, for he goes on to say that the synoecism of the Chalcidians was not entirely complete. He shows by this not only that he was ignorant of the true condition of affairs in the league but also that he confused Olynthos with the league itself. Further proof is unnecessary, for in no other case does he ever speak of the Chalcidians by name, although he refers to their affairs many times. To him the Olynthians are the Chalcidians. If my previous assumption is correct, that a moderate aristocracy was formed in the Chalcidic κοινόν and that the citizen body is made up of those possessing a hoplite census, we may assume, from the five thousand citizens of Demosthenes,[34] a Chalcidic army of approximately eleven or twelve thousand, of which about five thousand were hoplites and cavalry and the rest peltasts. Considering that it took a Peloponnesian army of ten thousand men to conquer it, one could not expect to find a smaller Chalcidic army. That Olynthos should furnish eight hundred hoplites out of a little more than four thousand is not surprising; but it is scarcely conceivable that there were five thousand citizens of the town at this time. It is improbable that a town of two thousand inhabitants, as it was in 432, should have become in 380 a city of at least forty thousand.[35] Beloch has recognized the confusion shown by Demosthenes between the part and the whole, that is to say, between Olynthos and the league, but he has failed to see that in this case Demosthenes was perfectly consistent with himself and is referring both to the citizen body of the league and to the cavalry of

---

[34] In this passage he is speaking of the strength of the Chalcidians. He says that they only possessed four hundred horse and all told were no more than five thousand in number. It is evident from the context that this refers to the fighting strength of the town, and yet the wording, by itself, merely gives the number of Olynthian citizens. These figures are probably a rather conservative estimate. In my chapter on the constitution I have given my reasons for believing that we are dealing with a citizenship based on a hoplite census. I wish to add that a body of four hundred cavalry is consistent with a hoplite force of five thousand but not with one of less than half that number. Thus it seems that the five thousand of Demosthenes refers only to the hoplites, or perhaps to the men of hoplite census.

[35] If we take the number five thousand to be the free men of Chalcidian birth in the city, the population of Olynthos would be about twenty thousand. Even this is a greater growth than the facts seem to warrant.

the league.[36]   Beloch saw that the cavalry figures given by Demosthenes belonged to the κοινόν, but he did not consider the
possibility that the five thousand citizens were Chalcidian and
not merely Olynthian.

The explanation that has been given harmonizes the contemporary statement of Xenophon with the later one of Demosthenes and fits the facts of the case.   The figures to which we have
arrived give to the Chalcidian territories for this period a population of approximately forty thousand free inhabitants, excluding metics.[37]   Its territory included the western part of the
Chalcidic peninsula, Potidaea, most of Sithonia, and a small part
of the Macedonian country.   Considering the ravages to which
all this territory had been exposed, the transfer of inhabitants
from Sithonia to the interior and back again, and the foundation
and rapid growth of Apollonia, such a population is almost what
one would expect.   What was the population for the rest of the
peninsula not included in the league?   We have but little on
which an estimate can be based.   Using Xenophon's estimate of the
cavalry which the Acanthians, Apollonians, and Chalcidians mustered,[38] we may assume that Acanthos and Apollonia numbered
with their dependencies about two thirds as many inhabitants as
the Chalcidians, or about twenty-five or thirty thousand.   Thus
we have a total for the Chalcidian peninsula of about seventy
thousand free inhabitants not including metics.[39]   The population had doubled since the beginning of the Peloponnesian War.

By the time of Philip, according to Demosthenes, the population had again doubled.   There were then ten thousand Chalcid-

---

[36] Beloch, *Bevölkerung*, p. 205, note 3 on Dem. XIX, **266**. See p. 206.
The cavalry of the Bocotian league was theoretically one hundred for every
thousand hoplites.   Thus, using the same ratio, the four hundred cavalry of
the Chalcidian state is about what we would expect for a force of five thousand hoplites.   This is further evidence that Demosthenes has in mind
merely the heavy armed forces of the Chalcidian army.

[37] If Olynthos furnished eight hundred hoplites it must have had a population of Chalcidian birth of about six or seven thousand.

[38] Xen. *Hell.*, V, 2, 14; 3, 1.

[39] Acanthos seems to have exercised some sort of hegemony on the eastern
coast and in Actè; the Chalcidians held most of the territory, if not all, in
the south and west, and Apollonia was the only important city of the interior.
Thus our estimates for these three states give approximately the population
of the whole Chalcidian peninsula.

ian citizens with full franchise.[40]   This shows a great increase
in prosperity and commercial importance. Beloch's estimate for
this time of about thirty thousand citizens for the whole extent
of the Chalcidic peninsula seems to be more nearly correct. Even
here we are without sufficient data; and we must remember that
the number ten thousand does not refer to Olynthos alone and
that this is the number of the hoplite census or of the citizens
with full franchise. Doubling this will give us twenty thousand
for the number of free men of Chalcidian birth in the territory
of the league. We may conjecture that the remainder of the
Chalcidic peninsula had about five thousand more. This, however, is very uncertain. Beloch estimates that one hundred thousand free inhabitants lived in the Chalcidian peninsula at the
time of its conquest by Philip.[41]   This gives an average density
of twenty-five to the square kilometer. If we include slaves we
may estimate it at thirty or forty.

Between 380 and 350 an era of development had taken place[42]
in Chalcidic territory. The "Hinterland" had been settled, the
forests cut down and agriculture more widely extended. Thus
the increase in population is merely due to the natural development of a rich country. The fact that Philip considered it worth
while to make presents of wood for house-building purposes to
Chalcidians shows that the forests of Chalcidicè had been ruthlessly cut out, as in every new and rich country, and the country
was now forced to rely upon imports, to some degree, at least,
for its building material.[43]   This is indicative of the state of the
forests and of the spread of agriculture in that period.

The inhabitants of Chalcidicè were mostly Greeks, although in
certain parts of the peninsula there was a considerable part of
native intermixture. The Bottiaeans in the west were presumably of Greek extraction with a strong admixture of Thracian

---

[40] Dem. XIX, 266.
[41] Beloch's figures for Attica, excluding the population of the city, are
fifty to the square kilometer. The free population of Boeotia in 424 was
approximately one hundred thousand, inhabiting about 2500 square kilo-
meters. Thus it was more densely populated than Chalcidicè. Beloch,
Bevölkerung, pp. 101, 161ff, 212.
[42] See chapter on the economic condition of Chalcidicè.
[43] Dem. XIX, 265.

blood. They had originally been settled in Macedonia near the
Axios river, but the growing Macedonian power had driven them
out to take refuge in Chalcidice.[44] In Mygdonia a Thracian stock
was to be found, while upon Actè[45] there were remnants of the
original population, the so-called Pelasgians and Thracians from
the tribes of the Bisaltians, Crestontians, and Edonians. These
had kept their native tongue but used the Greek language as
well. Euboeans and Andrians had shared in the settlement of
the peninsula. The latter had kept to the east and had founded
Sanè, Acanthos, Stageiros, and Argilos.[46] Of the Euboeans, the
Eretrians had been responsible for the settlement of Pallenè, and
the Chalcidians had placed the majority of her colonies upon
Sithonia.[47] The western coast also came into the possession of
Greek settlers. Thus we see that the peninsulas of Pallenè and
Sithonia, together with most of the coast-line, were completely
Hellenized at an early date. Actè and the interior kept its native
inhabitants and only gradually did the Greeks encroach upon
their territory.[48]

The official dialect of the Chalcidic league was a form of Ionic,
as we see from the treaty with Amyntas.[49] That the Ionic dialect was quite generally adopted in this region is shown by an
Amphipolitan inscription of the time of Philip.[50] This Amphipolitan decree is especially noteworthy, since Amphipolis was
originally an Athenian colony, and the adoption of the Ionic
shows that it was in general use in the cities of that neighbour-

---

[44] Cf. Köhler, *Ber. d. Berl. Akad.*, 1897, p. 271; cf. notes 3 and 4 *supra*.
[45] Thuc. IV, 109. In Atke there was a slight mixture of Chalcidian blood.
[46] Thuc. IV, 84, 88, 103, 109.
[47] Thuc. IV, 110, 114, 123; Strabo, VII, 329, frg. 11; X, 447, 8.
[48] By the time when the geography of Scylax was written, about the middle of the fourth century, even the cities on the peninsula of Actè were considered Greek. In fact all of the cities on the coast of Chalci-dicè commencing with Aineia are called by him Hellenic. Thermè, how-ever, on the north western border was evidently in his estimation not a Greek city. The cities mentioned by him are as follows: Aineia, Poti-daea, Mendè, Aphytis, Thrambeis, Scionè, Olynthos, Mecyperna, Sermylia, Toronè, Dion, Thyssos, Cleonae, Acrothooi, Charadrous, Olophyxos, Acanthos, Alapta, and Arethousa. He goes on to say that there were many more towns inland which he does not mention. Scylax, 66.
[49] Ditt. *Syll*²., 77.
[50] Ditt. *Syll*²., 113. Aristotle tells us that there had been considerable emigration of Chalcidians to Amphipolis, *Pol.*, VIII, 3, 13, 1303B; 6, 8, 1306A.

hood. Both of these inscriptions are of the fourth century and give little information as to the usage of the fifth.[51] We have, however, a number of fifth century coins from Chalcidicè that must be noted here. The use of the Ionic omega was introduced at the time of the revolt from Athens in the coins of almost every city of the Chalcidic peninsula. The coins of Acanthos alone retain the older omicron, and this use continues throughout the coinage of the city. The other cities, however, when they gave up the Euboic-Attic standard, adopted the Ionic alphabet. The Bottiaeans and Chalcidians did this about 432, Amphipolis about 424, and Toronè a little later. Toronè is a very interesting example, for its coinage ceases practically at its destruction by Athens in 422.[52] Thus we may say that the use of the Ionic alphabet was officially adopted in Chalcidicè about thirty years before it came into general use in the rest of continental Greece.

---

[51] The dialect of these inscriptions has certain affinities with that of Eretria and Oropos, though it lacks the most striking feature of Eretrian, the rhotacism of intervocalic σ. On the fifth century coins of Mendè and Toronè we find the inscriptions Μινδάον and Τερωνάον with the suppression of ι. This reduction of αι to α is found in many forms of Ionic and occurs in names from the Euboean Styra. See Harrison, *Cl. Qu.*, 1912, pp. 169f. An early fifth century coin of the Chalcidians shows the form for Λ. This form is peculiar to Chalcis and does not occur elsewhere in Euboea, and in Greece proper only in Boeotia and Attica, *Numis. Chron.*, 1897, p. 276, pl. XIII, 6. Taking everything into consideration it is highly probable that the features which show a connection between Olynthos and Eretria were common to Eretria and Chalcis.

[52] *B. M. C. Mac.*, p. xxxiii. Coins minted after the restoration of Toronè are few and do not concern us here.

CHAPTER XVI

ECONOMIC CONDITIONS

The strength of the Chalcidic league was upon a sound economic basis. The country was rich and could supply the needs of a large population. Its position, moreover, was excellent for the maintenance of a large trade, for its three peninsulas offered good harbours and its proximity to Macedon gave the Chalcidians an opportunity to exploit that country to their own profit. They were quick to see the advantages which they had, and prosperity was a natural consequence.

Agriculture was one of the most favoured of occupations.[1] The country was fertile, capable of producing much grain, and hence it was possible for it to sustain a fairly dense population. Pallenè was the first to be brought into a high degree of cultivation. It was the least hilly of all the peninsulas and the most suited for agriculture, and for this reason it soon became a rival, so far as numbers were concerned, of the more densely populated districts of Greece. An interesting statement of Aristotle concerning Aphytis may be taken as illustrative of the conditions in the rest of the peninsula.[2] He says that although the citizens of the town were many, and its territory small in extent, nevertheless all of them were tillers of the soil.

The mildness of the climate allowed the cultivation of the olive and the fig.[3] Another of the chief products of the region was wine.[4] Mendè was the center of its production and the Men-

---

[1] Xen. *Hell.*, V, 2, 16; Appian, *B. C.*, IV, 13, 102.
[2] Arist. *Pol.*, VII, 4, 9f, 1319A.
[3] Theop. frg. 230.
[4] [Dem.] XXXV, 10, 20, 35; *F. H. G.*, II, 301, 30; Athen. I, 41, 53; IV, 4; VIII, 67; Hippocrates, *de intern. affect.*, 17; Hesychios, Μίσκελλος οἶνος; Steph. Byz., Mendè; Varro, *R. R.*, I, 14. The coins of Mendè and other cities of Chalcidicè show Dionysiac types.

dean wine was famous for its peculiar flavour. Scionè also was
a wine producing city, but the culture of the vine was by no
means confined to Pallenè. In Sithonia there was a promontory
called Ampelos,[5] and at the time of the expedition of Brasidas
against Acanthos, as we are told, the vintage had not yet occurred, and fear for the destruction of the crop was one of the
determining factors in the revolt.[6] Pallenè also had a reputation for the production of honey, as the name Melissurgis shows.[7]
Besides all this, however, the Chalcidic peninsula was a great
grain producing region,[8] and Egyptian beans seem to have
thrived well in the region about Toronè.[9]

Grazing must have been important in the less settled portions
of Chalcidicè. On the early Olynthian coins we find the horse
portrayed and throughout the history of the Chalcidian league,
cavalry plays an important part in the operations of the army.[10]
Later, after the destruction of the league, Macedonian cavalry
was recruited from this territory.[11] The bribes given to various
Chalcidians by Philip show us something of the nature of agriculture in the later years of the league.[12] Horses, cattle, and
sheep are among the gifts mentioned, and we may assume from
this that stock-raising was an important part of Chalcidic farming, although it was by no means so important as to exclude the
more intensive side of agriculture. Grazing goes hand in hand
with the formation of large estates; but the rapid increase in
population and the general prosperity of Chalcidicè show that
the formation of large estates had not, in the fourth century,
increased to such an extent that it was detrimental to the country. The plateaus and hills of the interior were well suited to
grazing and probably it was chiefly confined to that part of the
peninsula. After the conquest of Philip grazing and large
estates became the rule. The country was parcelled out among

---

[5] Hdt. VII, 123; Steph. Byz., "Ἄμπελος.
[6] Thuc. IV, 84, 88; Athen. I, 56.
[7] Cf. Dionys. *Orbis Descriptio*, 327 ff.
[8] Xen. *Hell.*, V, 2, 16.
[9] Athen. III, 2.
[10] Thuc. IV, 124; V, 6, 10; Xen. *Hell.*, V, 2, 14; 3, 1; Polyaen. III, 10, 7;
Dem. XIX, 263–6 *et al.*
[11] Arrian, *Anab.*, I, 2, 5; 12, 7; II, 9, 3.
[12] Dem. XIX, 265.

his favourites in large blocks and the raising of grain fell off so that it had to be imported.[13]

The natural resources of Chalcidicè were great. In the north-eastern portion of the peninsula there were rich deposits of iron, silver, and lead.[14] The region about Acanthos was noted for its salt[15] and Pallenè had a reputation for the peculiar stones found there.[16] The base of the peninsula was heavily wooded and Athens was dependent upon this region for the wood necessary for the maintenance of its fleets. After the revolt of Amphipolis, Athens was at a loss for ship-building material. Brasidas immediately turned the forests of the country to good account and commenced the formation of a navy.[17] Xenophon also tells us that there was plenty of wood in the country, of which the Chalcidians were not slow to take advantage.[18] In the period of the Chalcidian growth, when the league had expectations of becoming an important power in Greek politics and was planning to establish a navy, it took into its hands the forests and restricted the exportation of wood. This is shown by the Chalcidian treaty with Amyntas.[19] According to this treaty no timber could be exported to Macedon unless the κοινόν had no need of it.

We learn also that there was an abundance of fish in a little stream that flowed by the cities of Olynthos and Apollonia into Lake Bolbè.[20] In certain months of the year the fish went up the river as far as Olynthos and were caught in quantities sufficient to supply the needs of the inhabitants.

The fact that Philip used wood for house building as bribes for the Chalcidians gives one an interesting sidelight upon the conditions existing in the years immediately preceding the destruction of the league.[21] This shows that at that time wood was a valuable commodity and the natural inference is that much of

---

[13] (Dem.) XXXIV, 36; Theop. frg. 217b.
[14] *Pauly-Wissowa*, Chalkidike. May not the mineral resources of the country have had something to do with its early settlement by the Chalcidians?
[15] Pliny, *N. H.*, XXXI, 85.
[16] Dionys., *Orbis Descriptio*, 327 ff.
[17] Thuc. IV, 108.
[18] Xen. *Hell.*, V, 2, 16.
[19] Ditt. *Syll².*, 77.
[20] *F. H. G.*, IV, 420, Hegesandros of Delphi.
[21] Dem. XIX, 265.

the forest had been cut down and the country given over to grazing and agriculture.   This would be the natural consequence of
the increase in population and the consequent extension of the
settlements in the interior.

The trade of Chalcidicè also played a very important part in
its development.   The Chalcidian relations with Macedon were
on the whole intimate and every effort was made to increase the
commerce between the two countries.   Without doubt, from the
very first settlement of the Chalcidic peninsula, the Greeks settled there had their share of the trade to and from the neighbouring parts of Macedonia.   This, however, was hampered, to
a certain extent, by a difference in the coin standards in use in
the two countries.   During the period of her supremacy, Athens
favoured a uniform coinage throughout her empire.[22]   Hence up
to 432 the cities of Chalcidicè employed, for the most part, the
Attic standard, while in Macedonia the Pheonician standard was
in use.   When the revolt from Athens occurred in 432, the Chalcidians, without any hesitation, changed from one to the other.
This is an indication of the fact that they saw the importance of
friendly commercial relations with the interior and looked upon
Macedon as their chief market.   Towards the end of the Peloponnesian War, the Macedonian Archelaos I espoused the side of
Athens, and, as it would seem, broke off relations with the Chalcidians.   Archelaos was desirous of strengthening Macedonia,
unifying it, and extending its influence.   Among other things
he wished to make it commercially independent of the Chalcidians.   To do this he changed his system of coinage so as to
handicap the Chalcidian traders.[23]   This went hand in hand
with his development of the roads and the sea-coast towns, and
all of this must have reacted unfavourably upon the trade with
Chalcidicè.

Early in the fourth century, after the murder of Archelaos
and the abandonment of his plans, friendly relations were renewed with the Chalcidians and commerce once more went on
uninterrupted.   For this period we are fortunate enough to have

---

[22] Cf. Weil, *Zeitschr. f. Numis.*, XXV, pp. 52 f.
[23] Archelaos gave up the Phoenician standard and adopted a Persic stater
of 170 gr.

a commercial-political treaty between Amyntas and the Chalcidic league.[24] In addition to the clause relating to timber and
ship-building material, there was one that guaranteed to each
party the right of export, import, and transport of all goods
through the country of the other upon the payment of the usual
duties. In this way Amyntas gained the use of the Chalcidic
harbours and a market for the raw products of Macedonia, while
the Chalcidians obtained the necessary means for an increase in
trading operations among the less civilized inhabitants of the
interior. Without doubt they reaped a rich harvest from the
trade. Besides the fact that the Chalcidians became the mid-
dlemen for the Macedonian trade and increased their individual profits thereby, the revenues of the state were greatly
benefited. This was not free trade.[25] Export and import duties
were collected on the articles of commerce destined for Macedonian use and a greatly increased revenue must have resulted.

Although the treaty was not of long duration, the supremacy
in Macedonian trade probably remained, to a greater or less extent, until the time of Philip. Demosthenes speaks of the Macedonian discontent at being shut off from the Chalcidian markets
because of the war.[26] So important was this trade to the Chalcidians that at one time (368) they interfered in Macedonian
politics and attempted to place upon the throne a king that
would be favourable to their interests.[27] Under Philip, however,
friendly relations were renewed and their commerce received a
new lease of life. For a time in the early part of Philip's reign
he did all in his power to conciliate the Chalcidians and to win
their favour. It was at this time that he entered into an alliance
with them and gave them Anthemos and Potidaea. The change
that Philip introduced into the Macedonian coinage is indicative
of the importance of the Chalcidians in the commerce of Macedon. Since the time of Archelaos I, the two countries had maintained different coin standards, but now Philip returned to the

[24] Ditt. *Syll²*., 77.
[25] Cf. Xen. *Hell.*, V, 2, 16. This indicates the importance of Chalcidian commerce.
[26] Dem. II, 16; cf. Appian, *B. C.*, IV, 13, 102. This passage tells us of the mutual benefit derived from the Chalcidic trade with the Thracians.
[27] Cf. Chap. XIII.

standard in use in Chalcidicè. The reason for this change has been referred to a desire on the part of Philip to regulate the ratio between gold and silver.[28] Without doubt, he purposely adopted the coinage that was in use by the merchants who held the balance of Macedonian trade. Whatever may have been his reasons this change simplified and expedited commerce with Chalcidicè and tended to increase it. Considering these evidences of friendship on the part of Philip and the profits that accrued to the Chalcidians from Macedonian trade, it is no wonder that a strong pro-Macedonian party was formed in the league. The causes that are given by Demosthenes for the formation of this party are unimportant in comparison with the perfectly legitimate economic factors at work.[29] Bribery works very well with individuals, but commercial opportunities, given or taken away, influence the attitude of whole classes. The economic union of Macedonia and Chalcidicè had already taken place, and the merchants, realizing that a break with Macedon would deprive them of their logical market, were quick to resent any attempt on the part of the national party to renew relations with Athens. They saw that, so far as the prosperity of the country was concerned, a peaceful incorporation in the Macedonian kingdom was preferable to independence with a consequent diminution of the Chalcidian trade. The land-holding elements in the state, naturally conservative and nationalistic, were not influenced by these commercial considerations. Their interest lay chiefly in agriculture; and without doubt they could not be brought to see the economic importance of trade with Macedon. Thus it was natural for them to be influenced by patriotism and to strive to maintain the independence of the

---

[28] Hill, *Hist. Greek Coins*, p. 81. The fact that after the destruction of the Chalcidian league the Phoenician standard in Macedonia gave way to the Attic seems to be an added reason for supposing that commercial grounds were at the bottom of the change made by Philip. After the Chalcidian coinage ceased when the towns were razed, the reasons that had impelled Philip to maintain the Phoenecian standard disappeared. The commercial activity of the Chalcidians was no longer to be considered and the change to the Attic standard was dictated by a desire to place Macedonian trade in touch and competition with that of the great commercial cities of Greece.

[29] Dem. XIX, 265.

Chalcidian state.   In the end, patriotic considerations won the day and dictated the policy of the country to its destruction.

Little more is to be said of the economic side of Chalcidic life. In the Chalcidian territory, two elements, agriculture and trade, played almost equal parts and their development progressed side by side.   As the country became more thickly settled and more generally cultivated, commerce increased.   There was room for both and neither infringed upon the other until the end, when the commercial party was forced to sacrifice itself to patriotism, and when, as a result both commerce and agriculture were almost completely destroyed in the territory of the league.

BIBLIOGRAPHY

Beloch, Julius,—*Die attische Politik seit Pericles.* Leipzig: 1884.
Bevölkerung der griechisch-römischen Welt. Leipzig: 1886.
Griechische Geschichte. Vols. I, II. Strassburg: 1893–1897.
Böhnecke, Karl Georg,—*Forschungen auf dem Gebiete der Attischen Redner und der Geschichte ihrer Zeit.* Berlin: 1843.
Demosthenes, Lykurgos, Hyperides und ihr Zeitalter. Berlin: 1864.
Bonner, Robert J.,—*The Boeotian Federal Constitution. Classical Philology,* vol. V, 405–417, Chicago: 1910.
Busolt, Georg,—*Griechische Geschichte,* Band III, Teil 2. Gotha: 1904.
Cavaignac, E.,—*Etudes sur l'histoire financière d'Athènes au* VE siècle: *le Trésor d' Athènes de 480 à 404.* Paris: 1908.
Dittenberger, Guilelmus,—*Sylloge Inscriptionum Graecarum.* Leipzig: 1898–1900.
Ferguson, William Scott,—*The Athenian Secretaries. Cornell Studies in Classical Philology:* 1898.
Francotte, Henri,—*Les Finances des Cités Grecques.* Liege: 1909.
Greenwell, the Rev. Canon,—*On Some Rare Greek Coins. Numismatic Chronicle,* vol. 17, new series, 276. London: 1897.
Harrison, E,—*Chalkidike, Classical Quarterly,* vol. VI, 13–103, 165–178. London: 1912.
Head, B. V.,—*British Museum Catalogue of Greek Coins, Macedon.* London: 1899.
Historia Numorum. Oxford: 1911.
Hicks, E. L. and Hill, G. F.,—*A Manual of Greek Historical Inscriptions.* Oxford: 1901.
Hill, G. F.,—*Athens and Olynthos in 384–3* B. C., *The Classical Review,* vol. XV, 279f. London: 1889.
Handbook of Greek and Roman Coins. London: 1889.
Historical Greek Coins. London: 1906.
Imhoof-Blumer, Fred.,—*Monnaie Grecques.* L'Académie royale Néerlandaise des sciences: 1883.
Jebb, R. C.,—*Attic Orators from Antiphon to Isaeos.* London: 1893.
Kirchoff, A.,—*Inscriptiones Graecae. Inscriptiones Atticae Euclidis anno vetustiores.* Berlin: 1873. *Supplementa.* Berlin: 1877–1891.
Thukydides und sein Urkundenmaterial. Berlin: 1895.
Kirchner, J.,—*Prosopographia Attica.* Berlin: 1901–1903.
Köhler, Ulrich,—*Inscriptiones Graecae. Inscriptiones Atticae aetatis quae est inter Euclidis annum et Augusti tempora.* Berlin: 1877–1895.
Ueber Probleme der griechischen Vorzeit. Sitzungsberichte der königlich preussischen Akademie der Wissenschaften zu Berlin, 1897, 258–274.
Die Zeiten der Herrschaft des Peisistratos in der Πολιτεία ᾿Αθηναίων. *Sitzungsberichte der königlich preussischen Akademie der Wissenschaften zu Berlin,* 1892, 339–345.
Philip II und die chalkidischen Städte. Sitzungsberichte der königlich preussischen Akademie der Wissenschaften zu Berlin, 1897, 258–274.
Kolbe, Walter,—*Ein chronologischer Beitrag zur Vorgeschichte des peloponnesischen Krieges. Hermes,* vol. 34, 380–394. Berlin: 1899.
Meyer, Eduard,—*Geschichte des Altertums.* Books III and IV. Stuttgart und Berlin: 1901–1902.
Theopomp's Hellenika mit e. Beilage über die Rede an die Larissaer und die Verfassung Thessaliens. Halle: 1909.

Müller-Strübung, Hermann, *Thukydideische Forschungen.* Wien: 1882.

Wissowa, Georg,—*Pauly's Real Encyclopadie der Classichen Altertums-wissenschaft. Neue Bearbeitung.* Stuttgart: 1894–1914.

Schaefer, Arnold,—*Demosthenes und seine Zeit.* Vols. I–III, Leipzig: 1885–1887.

Steup, Julius,—*Thukydideische Studien.* Freiburg I. B. und Tübingen: 1881.

Swoboda,—*Vertrag des Amyntas mit dem Chalkidiern. Archäolog.-epigraph. Mitth. aus Oest.,* vol. VII, 1–59, 1883.

Wilhelm, Adolf,—*Urkunden des Attischen Reiches. Anzeiger der phil.-hist. Klasse der kais. Akad. der Wissenschaften.* Wien: April 28, 1909.

Woodward, A. M.,—*An Attic Quota List. The Annual of the British School at Athens,* vol. XV, 229–242. London: 1908–1909.

GREEK HISTORY

AN ARNO PRESS COLLECTION

Aeschinis. **Aeschinis Orationes.** E Codicibus Partim Nunc Primum Excussis, Edidit Scholia ex Parte Inedita, Adiecit Ferdinandus Schultz. 1865.

Athenian Studies; Presented to William Scott Ferguson (*Harvard Studies in Classical Philology,* Supplement Vol. I). 1940.

Austin, R[eginald] P. **The Stoichedon Style in Greek Inscriptions.** 1938.

Berve, Helmut. **Das Alexanderreich:** Auf Prosopographischer Grundlage. Ersterband: Darstellung; Zweiterband: Prosopoghaphie. 1926. 2 volumes in one.

Croiset, Maurice. **Aristophanes and the Political Parties at Athens.** Translated by James Loeb. 1909.

Day, John. **An Economic History of Athens Under Roman Domination.** 1942.

Demosthenes. **Demosthenes,** Volumina VIII et IX: Scholia Graeca ex Codicibus Aucta et Emendata, ex recensione Gulielmi Dindorfii. 2 volumes. 1851.

Ehrenberg, Victor. **Aspects of the Ancient World:** Essays and Reviews. 1946.

Finley, Moses I. **Studies in Land and Credit in Ancient Athens, 500-200 B.C.:** The Horos Inscriptions. 1952.

Glotz, Gustave. **La Solidarité de la Famille dans le Droit Criminel en Grèce.** 1904.

Graindor, Paul, **Athènes Sous Hadrien.** 1934.

Grosmann, Gustav. **Politische Schlagwörter aus der Zeit des Peloponnesischen Krieges.** 1950.

Henderson, Bernard W. **The Great War Between Athens and Sparta.** 1927.

Herodotus. **Herodotus: The Fourth, Fifth, and Sixth Books.** With Introduction, Notes, Appendices, Indices, Maps by Reginald Walter Macan. 1895. 2 volumes in one.

Herodotus. **Herodotus: The Seventh, Eighth, and Ninth Books.** With Introduction, Text, Apparatus, Commentary, Appendices, Indices, Maps by Reginald Walter Macan. 1908. 3 volumes in two.

Jacoby, Felix. **Apollodors Chronik.** Eine Sammlung der Fragmente (*Philologische Untersuchungen*, Herausgegeben von A. Kiessling und U. v. Wilamowitz-Moellendorff. Sechzehntes Heft). 1902.

Jacoby, Felix. **Atthis: The Local Chronicles of Ancient Athens.** 1949.

Ledl, Artur. **Studien zur Alteren Athenischen Verfassungsgeschichte.** 1914.

Lesky, Albin. **Thalatta:** Der Weg der Griechen Zum Meer. 1947.

Ollier, Francois. **Le Mirage Spartiate.** Etude sur l'idéalisation de Sparte dans l'antiquité Greque de l'origine Jusqu'aux Cyniques and Etude sur l'idéalisation de Sparte dans l'antiquité Greque du Début de l'école Cynique Jusqu'à la Fin de la Cité. 1933/1934. 2 volumes in one.

Ryffel, Heinrich. ΜΕΤΑΒΟΛΗ ΠΟΛΙΤΕΙΩΝ Der Wandel der Staatsverfassungen (*Noctes Romanae*. Forschungen Uber die Kultur der Antike, Herausgegeben von Walter Wili, #2). 1949.

Thucydides. **Scholia in Thucydidem:** Ad Optimos Codices Collata, edidit Carolus Hude. 1927.

Toepffer, Iohannes. **Attische Genealogie.** 1889.

Tscherikower, V. **Die Hellenistischen Städtegründungen von Alexander dem Grossen bis auf die Römerzeit** (*Philologus*, Zeitschrift fur das Klassische Alterum, Herausgegeben von Albert Rehm. Supplementband XIX, Heft 1). 1927.

West, Allen Brown. **The History of the Chalcidic League** (*Bulletin of the University of Wisconsin*, No. 969, History Series, Vol. 4, No. 2). 1918.

Woodhouse, William J. **Aetolia:** Its Geography, Topography, and Antiquities. 1897.

Wüst, Fritz R. **Philipp II. von Makedonien und Griechenland in den Jahren von 346 bis 338** (*Münchener Historische Abhandlungen*. Erste Reihe: Allgemeine und Politische Geschichte, Herausgegeben von H. Günter, A. O. Meyer und K. A. v. Müller. 14, Heft). 1938.

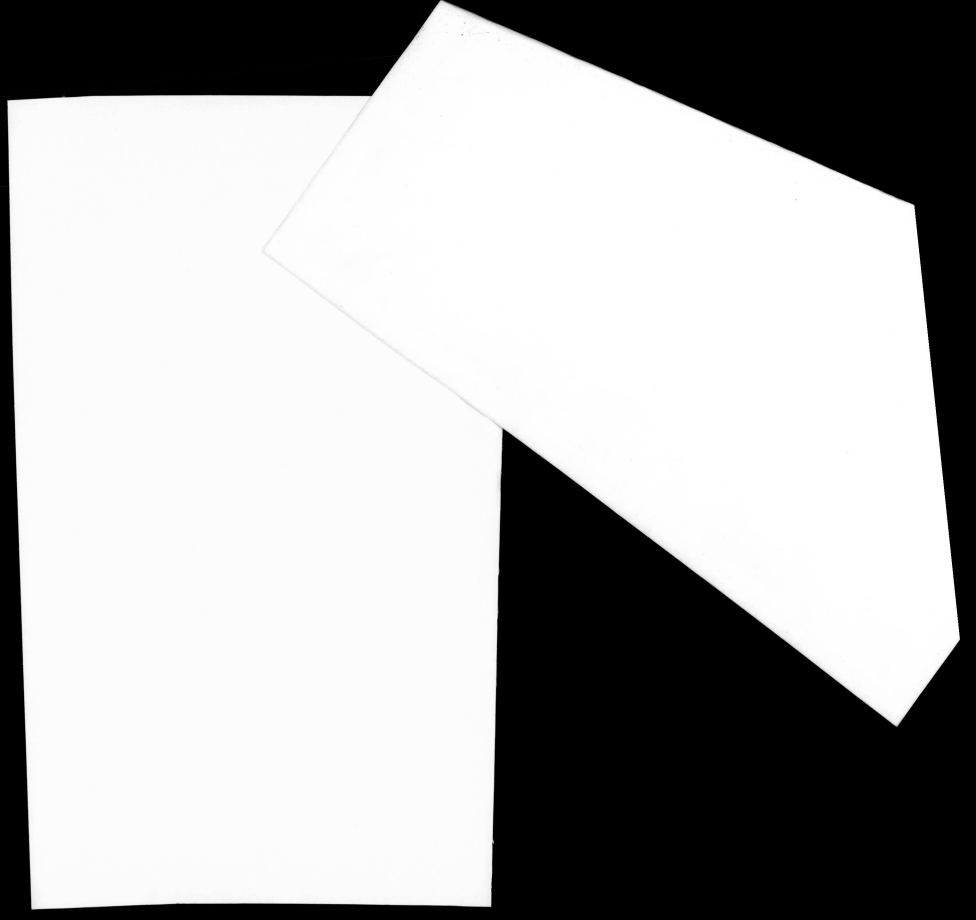

Ancestor Masks
and Aristocratic Power in
Roman Culture

HARRIET I. FLOWER

CLARENDON PRESS · OXFORD
1996

Oxford University Press, Great Clarendon Street, Oxford ox2 6dp

Oxford New York

Athens Auckland Bangkok Bogota Bombay
Buenos Aires Calcutta Cape Town Dar es Salaam Delhi
Florence Hong Kong Istanbul Karachi
Kuala Lumpur Madras Madrid Melbourne
Mexico City Nairobi Paris Singapore
Taipei Tokyo Toronto

and associated companies in
Berlin Ibadan

Oxford is a trade mark of Oxford University Press

Published in the United States
by Oxford University Press Inc., New York

British Library Cataloguing in Publication Data
Data available

Library of Congress Cataloging in Publication Data
Ancestor masks and aristocratic power in Roman culture
Harriet Flower
Revision of the author's thesis (doctoral—University of
Pennsylvania, 1993) presented under the title: Imagines Maiorum:
ancestral masks as symbols of ideology and power.
Includes bibliographical references and index. `
1. Funeral rites and ceremonies—Rome. 2. Masks—Rome.
3. Nobility—Rome. 4. Elite (Social sciences)—Rome. 5. Power
(Social sciences)—Rome. I. Title
DG103.F56 1996 393'.9—dc20 96-8168
ISBN 0-19-815018-0

1 3 5 7 9 10 8 6 4 2

Typeset by Hope Services (Abingdon) Ltd.
Printed in Great Britain on acid-free paper by
Biddles Ltd.,
Guildford and King's Lynn

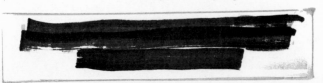

To My Parents
Margaret H. and Michael G. Dealtry

ACKNOWLEDGEMENTS

I WOULD like to take this opportunity of thanking everyone who helped me with this project, which originated as a 1993 Ph.D. dissertation at the University of Pennsylvania under the title '*Imagines Maiorum*: Ancestral Masks as Symbols of Ideology and Power'. My dissertation adviser, Robert E. A. Palmer, was unfailing in his encouragement and support while being thoughtful and clear-sighted in addressing problems as they arose. I also received advice from my readers J. Farrell and J. J. O'Donnell. As a graduate student I was the grateful recipient of four years of support from an Annenberg Fellowship, and two years of funding as a Mellon Dissertation Fellow.

I embarked on researching Roman ancestor masks in the Autumn of 1990 while resident at the Center for Hellenic Studies in Washington, DC. I owe a special debt to all there during that time and especially to the Director Zeph Stewart and to his wife Diana. I benefited greatly from the resources of the Center and from its own characteristic ambiance.

After receiving my degree, I revised and rewrote my manuscript substantially during the 1993/4 academic year in Oxford, where I was affiliated with both University College and Wolfson College. While at Oxford I was particularly helped by the insight and enthusiasm of my former tutor Chris Pelling of University College. In August 1993 I was able to visit and photograph the Casa del Menandro at Pompeii for which I am grateful to the Soprintendenza Archeologica and especially to the soprintendente Dr B. Conticello. The book took on its final form in 1994/5 which was my first year of teaching at Franklin and Marshall College. I was fortunate in the many forms of support I received from my colleagues in the Classics Department: Joel Farber, Robert Barnett, and Ann Steiner. I am grateful to Franklin and Marshall College for a generous Faculty Research Grant to cover the cost of the illustrations, as well as for a new computer, which greatly facilitated the production of the manuscript.

vii

I am greatly indebted to Werner Eck of the University of Köln and to Miriam T. Griffin of Somerville College, Oxford, who made it possible for me to read and use the important new *S.C. de Cn. Pisone patre* before its publication. Chris Pelling, Miriam Griffin, and Richard Brilliant all read and commented on the entire manuscript while saving me from numerous pitfalls. In addition I would like to thank the following for suggestions or help with specific topics or chapters: Ernst Badian, John Bodel, Birgitte Ginge, John Graham, Guy Hedreen, Geneviève Hoffmann, Christopher Howgego, Diana Kleiner, Ann Kuttner, David Langslow, Scot McKendrick, Silvio Panciera, John Penney, Gloria F. Pinney, David Potter, Nicholas Purcell, Eric Robinson, Frank Ryan, Christiane Sourvinou-Inwood, and Rudolf Wachter. Any errors of fact or of interpretation remain strictly my own.

I owe a special debt to Ellen Roth, Librarian of the Center for Hellenic Studies and to Mary Shelly of the Franklin and Marshall College Library for obtaining many bibliographical items for me. I have been able to consult only a few select works after 1994. Carmella Dixon, secretary of the Ancient History Graduate Group at Penn, was constant in her assistance. Janet Stone, the secretary of the Classics Department at Franklin and Marshall College, typed the family trees in Appendix E and helped in many other ways. Judy Homan, slide librarian of the Franklin and Marshall Art Department, helped to make the photographs for plates 4a and b.

I received many useful suggestions from the anonymous readers for Oxford University Press. I would also like to thank Hilary O'Shea, the classics editor for the Press, and her assistants Liz Alsop and Jenny Wagstaffe for all their help, especially with the illustrations.

My family supported me in many ways throughout these years. I am especially appreciative of my mother's encouragement and of her care for Isabel during my trips to Italy. My father, Michael G. Dealtry, has been invaluable in reading and criticizing everything I wrote at the dissertation stage. I am deeply grateful to my husband Michael A. Flower for his cheerfulness, patience, and common sense, and for his careful reading of the manuscript. I have also been inspired as well as being distracted by our daughters Isabel and Rosalind. I hope that they will choose to read this book one day.

H.I.F.

Lancaster, Pennsylvania
August 1995

CONTENTS

ix

Contents

Contents

LIST OF PLATES

1. Marble grave relief showing busts of a man and a woman facing each other in profile in open cupboards, Copenhagen.
   Photograph courtesy of the Department of Near Eastern and Classical Antiquities, National Museum, Copenhagen (inv. no. 1187).

2. Busts of ancestors in exedra 25, Casa del Menandro, Pompeii.
   Photograph by the author.

3. *a*. Minucius' column, reverse of denarius of C. Minucius Augurinus, 135 BC (Crawford 242.1).
   b. Elephant, reverse of denarius of C. Metellus, 125 BC (Crawford 269.1).
   c. Basilica Aemilia, reverse of denarius of M. Aemilius Lepidus, 58 BC (Crawford 419.3*a*).
   d. Busts of Brutus and Ahala, obverse and reverse of denarius of M. Junius Brutus, 54 BC (Crawford 433.2).
   Photographs courtesy of the Ashmolean Museum, Oxford.

4. *a*. Aeneas with Anchises and Ascanius.
   b. Romulus dressed as a general carrying spoils taken from an enemy general (*spolia opima*), wall-paintings from the façade of a house in Pompeii.
   After Zanker (1968) pls. 40, 41. Courtesy of Ernst Wasmuth Verlag, Tübingen.

5. Marble relief showing a woman lying in state, Tomb of the Haterii, Rome, late Flavian/early Trajanic, Vatican Museum.
   Photograph courtesy of the German Archaeological Institute in Rome, DAI Inst. Neg. 81.2858.

6. Marble relief showing a funeral procession, Amiternum, late Republic (?), Museo Aquilano, Aquila.
   Photograph courtesy of Alinari/Art Resource, New York, 36101.

7. Sarcophagus of Lucius Cornelius Scipio Barbatus, Museo Pio-Clementino, Vatican.
   Photograph courtesy of the Vatican Museums, XVIII. 19. 12.

LIST OF FIGURES

ABBREVIATIONS

AArch	*Acta Archaeologica*
ACS	American Classical Studies
AHAW	Abhandlungen der Heidelberger Akademie der Wissenschaften, Heidelberg
AJA	*American Journal of Archaeology*
AJP	*American Journal of Philology*
AK	*Antike Kunst*
AncSoc	*Ancient Society*
Annales ESC	*Annales: économies, sociétés, civilisations*
ANRW	*Aufstieg und Niedergang der Römischen Welt*
ANSMusN	*American Numismatic Society Museum Notes*
AntJ	*Antiquaries Journal*
ARom	*Analecta Romana Instituti Danici*
ASNP	*Annali della Scuola Normale Superiore di Pisa*
BCAR	*Bulletino della Commissione Archeologica Communale di Roma*
BICS	*Bulletin of the Institute for Classical Studies*
C&M	*Classica et Medievalia*
CA	*Classical Antiquity*
CCSL	Corpus Christianorum. Series Latina
CISA	*Contributi dell'Istituto di Storia antica dell' Università del Sacre Cuore, Milan*
CJ	*Classical Journal*
CPh	*Classical Philology*
CQ	*Classical Quarterly*
CR	*Classical Review*
DArch	*Dialoghi di Archeologia*
EA	*Epigraphica Anatolica*
G&R	*Greece and Rome*
GMusJ	*The J. Paul Getty Museum Journal*
HSCP	*Harvard Studies in Classical Philology*
ICS	*Illinois Classical Studies*
JbKS Wien	*Jahrbuch der Kunsthistorischen Sammlungen des Allerhöchsten Kaiserhauses, Wien*
JDAI	*Jahrbuch des Deutschen Archäologischen Instituts*
JHS	*Journal of Hellenic Studies*

JRA	Journal of Roman Archaeology
JRGZ	Jahrbuch des Römisch-Germanischen Zentralmuseums, Bonn
JRS	Journal of Roman Studies
LCM	Liverpool Classical Monthly
LEC	Les Études Classiques
MAAR	Memoirs of the American Academy in Rome
MDAI(R)	Mitteilungen des Deutschen Archäologischen Instituts, Römische Abteilung
MEFRA	Mélanges d'Archéologie et d'Histoire de l'École Française de Rome, Antiquité
MH	Museum Helveticum
MJBK	Münchner Jahrbuch der bildenden Kunst
NC	Numismatic Chronicle
ORF⁴	Oratorum Romanorum Fragmenta Liberae Rei Publicae (= Malcovati 1976)
ORom	Opuscula Romana
PBSR	Papers of the British School at Rome
PCPS	Proceedings of the Cambridge Philological Society
PP	Parola del Passato
RA	Revue Archéologique
RdA	Rivista di Archeologia
RE	Pauly's Real-Encyclopädie der classischen Altertumswissenschaft
REA	Revue des Études Anciennes
RFIC	Rivista di Filiologia e di Istruzione Classica, Turin
RhM	Rheinisches Museum
RIA	Rivista dell'Istituto Nazionale di Archeologia e Storia dell'Arte, Rome
RN	Revue numismatique
RPh	Revue de Philologie
SBMünchen	Sitzungsberichte der Bayerischen Akademie der Wissenschaften, München
SE	Studi Etruschi
SBHeidelberg	Sitzungsberichte der Heidelberger Akademie der Wissenschaften, Heidelberg
SO	Symbolae Osloenses
TAPA	Transactions of the American Philological Association
WZJena	Wissenschaftliche Zeitschrift der Friedrich-Schiller-Universität, Jena
ZPE	Zeitschrift für Papyrologie und Epigrafik

INTRODUCTION

> The true aristocrat does not feel the need to learn of his past
> through reading; his methods of acculturation are familial,
> institutional, and traditional.
>
> (Bloomer (1992) 259)

IT is now around sixty years since a book was dedicated largely or
wholly to Roman ancestor masks (*imagines*) with the result that the
present re-examination is not in need of a lengthy justification.[1]
Since then new evidence has come to light and critical methods
have changed considerably. Much has been written about the *imagines* more recently, but either in brief or as part of larger studies
with their own, separate concerns.[2] Most attention has come from
archaeologists and students of Roman portraiture. However, the
evidence we have for the *imagines* is not physical, and their relationship with Roman portraits in other media remains obscure and
disputed. Historians, meanwhile, are in general agreement that the
imagines were indeed a vital part of Roman culture. Usually this fact
is simply noted without further elaboration. The present study aims
to explore why and how the *imagines* were important in Roman
society. I have tried to be as comprehensive as possible in treating
the development of the *imagines* from their first mention in Plautus
to their last in Boethius over 700 years later.

By way of an introduction, it is relevant to emphasize that this
study will not be using the approach of an art historian, but of
social history. My aim is to elucidate the role of the *imagines* against
a wide cultural background. This is not an archaeological study but
an historical one which integrates the evidence of material culture
with literary sources. Answers will be sought to the following questions. What were the *imagines*? How did their function develop?
What can they tell us about the society that produced them? Such

---

[1] See Zadoks (1932) and Bethe (1935).
[2] On the *imagines* themselves, see esp. Rowell (1940), Boethius (1942), Brommer
(1953–4), Drerup (1980), Lahusen (1985*b*), Lucrezi (1986), and Dupont (1987).

questions arise partly because the *imagines* are not obviously paralleled elsewhere in the Mediterranean world.

No other ancient culture we know of made realistic wax masks of office-holding family members and kept them in the home, or used them for actors to wear at funerals. Dramatic impersonation of ancestors in civic or family ritual can be found in a number of traditional societies, but nowhere does it involve the realistic representation of ancestors of special political significance for the sake of offices they held.[3] The *imagines* have no connections with magic or the spirit world, and they were not used to conjure up the spirits of ancestors from the dead. Their secular and civic character can, therefore, be used to reveal the particular culture created by Rome's leading families.

Unlike death masks, the *imagines* were made during a person's lifetime and could be worn as real masks.[4] *Imagines* were never deposited in tombs. Previous studies have been hampered by the mistaken assumption that they were necessarily connected with death masks or that they developed from a mask used to cover the face of the dead man at his funeral.[5] In fact, there is no evidence to suggest any connection between *imagines* and death masks.[6]

The *imagines* were clearly designed for use by the living members of the family. They had no role to play in cult or commemoration of the dead at the tomb.[7] They represented only family members who had held at least the office of aedile. Their function is, therefore, overtly political, and is not related to beliefs about life after death.[8] Their use by actors to impersonate the ancestors at family funerals served to politicize such occasions.[9] They proceeded before the corpse to the Forum where they formed part of the audience for the funeral eulogy delivered from the speaker's platform (*rostra*). The presence of the ancestors in full magisterial costume and seated on ivory curule chairs provided the context for the speaker's words.

It is remarkable that studies of the fragments of Latin funeral

---

[3] See Breckenridge (1968) 28 for comparative material.

[4] The *S.C. de Cn. Pisone patre* = I16 suggests that the *imago* was made during a man's lifetime.

[5] For the origin of this view, see Benndorf (1878).

[6] This has been proved by Drerup (1980), who gives a catalogue of extant Roman death masks.

[7] *Imagines* and the cult of the ancestors is discussed in Ch. 7 § 4.

[8] See Breckenridge (1973) 840.

[9] The funeral procession is discussed in detail in Ch. 4. Our best evidence is Polybius 6. 53–4 = T61.

speeches (*laudationes*) have not taken any account of the *imagines* as the setting for the speech.[10] The flavour and character of Roman funeral rhetoric can only be fully appreciated once its proper context has been reconstructed, just as the dramatic setting helps to explain the nature of Greek tragedy.[11]

The main characteristics of Roman ancestor masks were their political function and their public use. Consequently, they can tell us about the nature of political culture in Rome and the role of spectacle within the city-state. These broad themes have not been properly addressed before in discussions of the *imagines*.[12] The emphasis of the present examination is on the function and cultural significance of *imagines* and of the dynamic representation of the ancestors which they made possible.

I. *Sources*

The basis of this study is the references to *imagines* found in ancient authors. No satisfactory collection of these references has been made previously.[13] A new catalogue can be found in Appendix A, which represents all definitely identifiable references to the *imagines maiorum* in ancient authors. I provide my own translation of each text throughout the book since most standard translations do not bring out the meaning 'ancestor mask' for *imago*. Many of these references are very brief or come as an aside. However, evidence from a wide variety of sources can be combined to give a much more complete picture of the *imagines* and their milieu than has been attempted before.

Appendix B contains references to the *imagines* in legal texts and in inscriptions, as well as epitaphs from tombs (*elogia*) which are of related interest. The fragments of Roman funeral orations (*laudationes*) have been collected and edited by Kierdorf.[14] Surprisingly, funeral speeches and epitaphs have not previously been used to

[10] The *laudationes* have been edited most recently by Kierdorf (1980), but see also Martha (1883), and Durry (1942) and (1950).

[11] For a comparison, see the discussions of how Greek tragedy was performed in Taplin (1977) and (1978).

[12] Dupont (1985) and (1987) is most useful here, although many of her conclusions about the *imagines* are not supported by ancient evidence.

[13] Vessberg (1941) is brief while Lahusen (1984) is uncritical and inaccurate. He omits a number of mentions while including many dubious passages. His reproduction of texts contains errors and standard editions are not used consistently.

[14] Kierdorf (1980).

reconstruct the labels (*tituli*) to be found under the *imagines* in the *atrium*.[15] The *imagines* were always explained, either by a written label in the house or by the speech of a family member at a funeral.

Most of the conclusions offered here about the ancestor masks themselves rely purely on literary evidence. However, a wide variety of information derived from the material culture and the art of the Romans is referred to in recreating the setting of the masks and of their owners. The aim is to understand them as products of a whole culture, and to appreciate their development with the evolution of that culture. The masks were originally made to fulfil certain specific functions within the aristocratic society of the Republic, but their continued use shaped Roman ways of thinking about the past and about the nature of valour and service to the state.

The architecture and decoration of Roman town houses (*domus*) is given consideration as the setting for the *imagines*, which were usually kept in cupboards (*armaria*) in the *atrium*.[16] Their presence in the most public part of the house gave the ancestors a role in the reception of visitors and in the life of the family and of the whole household. The *imagines* also had a central place in a rich vocabulary of ancestral iconography to be found in the city of Rome.[17] Statues of ancestors were put up in public places both in the city and outside its walls. Direct copies of ancestral portraits from domestic settings were sometimes made for public buildings, such as the shield portraits to be found on some temples. Augustus created the most extensive display of statues of famous Romans from the past in his Forum of Augustus.[18] The inscriptions which accompanied his gallery of Roman heroes are specially suggestive of the type of text to be found associated with ancestral images. Furthermore, ancestors came to be represented on coins, mostly in the last century of the Republic, and these can be found listed in Appendix C. They also appear on gems which were widely used as seals on public and private documents. Busts, apparently of ancestors, can be found as a regular feature of the relief decoration on curule chairs, which were the seats used exclusively by magistrates during their term of office.

In addition, Appendix D examines new evidence for Etruscan por-

---

[15] For the *tituli*, see Ch. 6 § 2.
[16] For the *imagines* in the *atrium*, see Ch. 7 § 1.
[17] Ancestral iconography is treated in Ch. 3 § 2a–c.
[18] For Augustus and the *imagines*, see Ch. 8.

traits of ancestors which suggests that ancestor statues were known in Italy well before the foundation of the Roman Republic. The origins of wax masks of ancestors is obscure, but their function connects them closely with the nobility of office which emerged in Rome after the conflict of the orders. Nevertheless, the recent discovery of monumental statues of ancestors from the seventh century BC, which were apparently also kept in the *atrium* of the Etruscan house, raises questions about the kinds of ancestral images to be found in Rome during the regal period.[19]

2. *Representations of the* Imagines *in Art*

A basic premise for the present study of the *imagines* is that we do not have any surviving representation of them: our knowledge must, therefore, come from written sources. Much recent comment on the *imagines* is marred by the unsubstantiated assumption that they are faithfully reproduced by portraits in other media.[20] The *imagines* are described by all our ancient sources as being wax masks.[21] Attempts to assimilate them to busts, especially those from the early imperial period, must be dismissed as unsound.[22] The result has been ingenious theories which try to accomodate all the literary evidence and physical remains in the same scheme.[23] These approaches have failed because none of the physical evidence we have corresponds in any significant way to the main literary *testimonia* about the appearance of the *imagines maiorum*. The following portraits will not, therefore, be discussed in the chapters which follow.

The most popular 'representation' of the *imagines* is the so-called Barberini statue from the Barberini Palace in Rome.[24] Assigned to

---

[19] The present examination depends on the publication of the Tomba delle Statue in Ceri by Colonna and von Hase (1986).

[20] Most recently, see Gruen (1992) 152–82 who has special insight about the *imagines*, but accepts the so-called representations of them without discussion.

[21] The two most important sources are Polybius 6. 53–4 = T61 and Pliny *Nat.* 35. 4–14 = T54. For a detailed discussion see Ch. 2 § 1*b*.

[22] See Boethius (1942) 229 ff. and Bianchi Bandinelli (1970) 76.

[23] Most notoriously, Zadoks (1932), whose artificial construct of dating different ancestral portraits has been criticized by Horn (1933) and most effectively by Rowell (1940) 137 ff.

[24] See Altmann (1905) 204, Zadoks (1932) 45–6, Boethius (1942) 234, Bianchi Bandinelli (1970) 80, Toynbee (1971) 48 no. 192, Lahusen (1985*b*) 281 ff., Hofter (1988) 341–2, Kleiner (1992) 36–7, and Gruen (1992) 155.

the early Augustan period for stylistic reasons, the statue shows a man in senatorial dress holding two busts of what appear to be his ancestors. It is important to note that the head of the statue is not original. The generally accepted argument is that the busts appear so light in his hands that they could have been made of wax. From this inference there follows much unwarranted speculation about what the *imagines* looked like, and the theory that they had become busts by this date. The circularity of such an argument is evident.

In fact, the man is only holding one bust, as the other is fixed to a column and appears as a type of herm, which he has put his right arm around.[25] Such portrait herms are a common Roman genre, and several depicting relatives or present owners have been found in houses at Pompeii.[26] The busts were usually made of bronze, or sometimes of stone. The other portrait, held in his left hand, is also a bust and not a mask. It may be of terracotta, or of wax, if it is made of a light material.[27] Wax was also used for portrait busts made during a person's lifetime.[28]

The fact that the man is associated with what seem to be portraits of ancestors, but not with *imagines*, perhaps indicates that he is a *novus homo* with no ancestors who were magistrates. In any case, the overall style of the piece has recently led scholars to suggest that it comes from an Italian municipal context, rather than from Rome itself.[29] Although the statue is interesting in its own right, it can tell us little about the wax funeral masks used by families of office-holders in Rome.

The only extant wax bust was found in a tomb at Cumae in 1852 and is now in the National Museum in Naples.[30] It provides valuable evidence for the degree of realism achieved in wax, and the effect is heightened by the glass eyes. However, this is also a bust rather than a mask, and it comes from a tomb. The whole point of the *imago*-mask was that it stayed in the house to recall the deceased in the realm of the living members of the family. The

[25] Note also the static character of the main figure, who is clearly not part of a funeral procession.

[26] See Dwyer (1982) 127–8 and (1991) figs. 1–2 with Ch. 7 § 1.

[27] See esp. Kleiner (1992) 36–7 for the most acute recent discussion.

[28] For examples, see Ovid *Ep.* 13. 149–56; *Rem.* 723–4; Martial 11. 102; Servius *A.* 8. 634 and Ch. 2 n. 2.

[29] See Zanker (1983) and Hofter (1988) 341–2.

[30] See Naples National Museum room 97, Swift (1923) 293, Adriani (1970) 107 n. 159, and esp. Drerup (1980) 93–4 with Taf. 49.1.

Cumae head, and another like it which has not survived, were found accompanying the burial of two persons who had been decapitated.[31] The circumstances of the burial are most untypical; the wax bust seems intended to replace the missing head. Nothing about the usual practices of Roman aristocratic families is revealed by the Cumae head.

A number of grave reliefs are extant which show portraits in cupboards with open doors. These have been taken as references to the *imagines* and their cupboards, which were opened to mark special occasions and celebrations.[32] The most well-known and the best example of the genre is now in the National Museum in Copenhagen (see Pl. 1).[33] It depicts two cupboards, with pediments and open doors, containing portraits of a man and a woman facing each other in profile. Again a comparison with the *imagines* as described in literary sources reveals many differences and only a few similarities. The iconography of the relief shows that we are not dealing with *imagines* here. Both portraits are clearly busts and not masks. Moreover, the bust on the right is of a woman although women could not be represented by *imagines* as they were not able to hold magisterial office. Further confirmation comes from the context as the stone was set up in memory of a married couple, both freedmen, at their grave.[34]

There is a wide range of funeral reliefs from the late Republic and early imperial period depicting freedmen and freedwomen in traditional poses which stress their new status as Roman citizens.[35] Naturally, these reliefs do make reference to the art and customs of the élite families, and especially of the imperial family with its particular iconography. The appearance of cupboards on freedmen's reliefs can be interpreted as such a reference.[36] The cupboards on

[31] The tomb was built before the end of the 2nd cent. AD but a coin of Diocletian found inside shows that it continued to be reused.

[32] This argument has been specially stressed by Lahusen (1985*b*) 282 ff., who provides a recent bibliography.

[33] National Museum, Ny Carlsberg Glyptotek, Copenhagen no. 1187, Zadoks (1932) 26, 43, pl. 4a, Toynbee (1971) no. 13, and Gruen (1992) 155.

[34] The inscription reads *A. Aemilius A. || L. | Aristomachus | Aemilia A.) L. | (Hilara* ('Aulus Aemilius Aristomachus, freedman of Aulus, Aemilia Hilara, freedwoman of Aulus'). This reading was kindly supplied by the Department of Near Eastern and Classical Antiquities, National Museum of Denmark.

[35] For a general discussion of freedmen's reliefs, see Altmann (1905) 196–7, Zanker (1975), Kleiner (1977), and Frenz (1977).

[36] Cf. Zanker (1975) 310: 'Die Kenntnis der Ahnengalerien in vornehmen Häusern mag mitgespielt haben.'

the reliefs can give an idea of what the *armaria* for the *imagines* looked like.[37] However, the busts inside, which sometimes appear as truncated versions of statues, are not *imagines*. Claims that busts on freedmen's reliefs consistently depict people who have died earlier and therefore closely imitate the *imagines* cannot be substantiated.[38] Such busts are often used to show children, who would not have been portrayed by wax masks in the homes of the aristocracy.

Freedmen of office-holding families would be thoroughly familiar with the *imagines* of their patrons, but that does not mean they felt able to duplicate them. The reverse is more likely to have been the case. The art of freedmen is now being studied in its own right and reveals an eclectic mixture of portrait styles which reflects the particular taste of freedmen and contains archaizing elements of style.[39] Most of the tomb art of freedmen appears to be addressed to their peers. There can be no question of a simple reduplication or exact copy of iconography traditionally reserved for office-holders. Reliefs from the tomb of the Haterii and from Amiternum are discussed below as they depict episodes during a funeral, namely the lying-in-state, the procession, and gladiatorial combats, all of which were especially associated with grand aristocratic funerals. However, the first two subjects were not a usual part of Roman art and they give a simplified picture of what would have been expected at the funeral of an office-holder. At the same time, their use reflects the desire of the freedmen in question to aspire to their own form of especially Roman institutions in order to express their rank as full citizens.[40]

The particular style of profile bust on the relief in Copenhagen can also be found on the tomb stone of Paconius in the Vatican, where the busts appear without cupboards.[41] The motif of a man and woman facing each other in profile can be paralleled on the curule chairs of magistrates.[42] These profile busts have been identified as ancestors, but no ancient account survives to explain this

[37] See esp. Zadoks (1932) pl. 4*b* and 4*c*.
[38] This was demonstrated by Kleiner (1977) 84–7.
[39] Recently, see Kleiner (1992) 40 and Gruen (1992) 168–9.
[40] For further discussion, see Ch. 4 §§ 1 and 2.
[41] Vatican Museum Cat. Vat. 2. 435*b*, Zadoks (1932) 43 with pl. 5*a*, Helbig (1963) no. 210 , and *CIL* 6. 23687. The inscription reads *T. Paconius T. f. Col. Caledus | Octavia A. l. Salvia* ('Titus Paconius Caledus, son of Titus, of the tribe of Collatina, Octavia Salvia, freedwoman of Aulus'). The relief shows scenes of apiculture suggesting that Paconius was a wax merchant.
[42] For curule chairs, see Schäfer (1989) and Ch. 3 § 2*c*.

distinctive genre of portraiture. The Copenhagen relief, therefore, illustrates a characteristic feature of the art of freedmen. By placing busts recalling those on the curule chairs of magistrates in cupboards like those used for wax *imagines* the artist has created a synthesis which uses traditional elements in a new way to reflect the particular concerns of his patrons.

Since no example or depiction of an *imago* survives, no attempt has been made here to explore the relationship between the *imagines* and Roman portraiture, veristic or otherwise.[43] That there was indeed a relationship seems both logical and likely, but it can not be reconstructed without any actual *imagines*.[44] Moreover, there is at the moment not enough evidence to show when Roman realistic styles of portraiture developed.[45] The *imagines* may well have contributed, perhaps significantly, to the characteristic Roman preference for realistic portraiture.[46] At the same time, they may also have played a part in the dialogue between Roman portrait art and Hellenistic ruler portraits of an idealized kind favoured by those who saw themselves as successors to Alexander.[47] It is possible that the *imagines* were in turn influenced by portrait styles and their evolution.[48]

3. *Methodology*

What was an *imago*? This question will be answered in a more literal sense in Chapter 2. However, a larger question remains. What kind of object was a wax mask of an ancestor for a Roman? The present investigation places the ancestor mask in the category of a

---

[43] The bibliography on Roman portraiture is extensive. Note esp. Courbaud (1900), Swift (1923), Kaschnitz-Weinberg (1926), Vessberg (1941), Boethius (1942), Herbig (1942), Schweitzer (1948), Breckenridge (1968), Bianchi Bandinelli (1961) and (1970), Adriani (1970), Zanker (1976), Smith (1981) and (1988), Jackson (1987), Gruen (1992), and Kleiner (1992).

[44] Cf. Bömer (1958) 67: 'Die Frage des Verhältnisses der *cerae* zum römischen Porträt ist immer wieder erörtert und nicht eindeutig beantwortet; ich halte einen Einfluß der *cera* (sic) für nahezu notwendig.'

[45] See Gruen (1992) 152-82 for a recent argument for an early date, perhaps in the 2nd cent. BC.

[46] This has been argued by Smith (1981) 32.

[47] For a full discussion see Smith (1988) and Gruen (1992).

[48] Cf. Smith (1988) 126: 'It is probably best to imagine a reciprocal connection between life-mask-inspired family portraits and public portraits, seen in a shared objective-looking and "style-less" quality. They should be parallel symptoms of related needs in Roman society.'

'status symbol' closely connected with the holding of magisterial office. Other objects in this group include the curule chair, the *lictors*, and the *fasces*. Senatorial dress was perhaps the most obvious mark of status and comprised a toga with a purple border (*toga praetexta*) and special 'senatorial' shoes, such as the ones worn by the magistrate represented in the Barberini statue. All magistrates who had the right to use a curule chair also wore the *toga praetexta*.[49] The inclusion of the *imagines* with other outward symbols of magisterial status is confirmed by Cicero, who thinks of the ancestor mask as a privilege gained with the office of aedile (*Ver.* 5. 36 = T21). However, a study of Roman status symbols has failed to take any account of *imagines*, perhaps because a man's *imago* was not displayed in his own lifetime.[50]

Interpreting the *imago* as a 'status symbol' helps to account for its use, both in the home and in the funeral procession. It also dismisses the unfounded notion that the *imago* was in some sense a cult object or connected with magic in any way.[51] An *imago* was not a 'religious' mask, although it was made to command respect and admiration for the achievements of past leaders. Nor was the *imago* like a status symbol to be found in a purely hereditary aristocracy. *Imagines* were indeed an important part of inheritance, but their aim was to mark merit and service within an élite caste based on the holding of magisterial office, and not solely on birth.[52] The distinguishing feature of the Roman nobility of office was precisely the constant need of its members to win new offices in each generation in order to maintain a family's status.[53] Otherwise the *imagines* served no purpose and could even become an embarrassment.

[49] This does not seem to have been the case for quaestors, tribunes of the plebs, and lower magistrates. See Cic. *Ver.* 5. 14. 36, Plut. *Q. Rom.* 81, Plin. *Nat.* 9. 137, and Mommsen (1887) 1. 418-20.

[50] Kolb (1977). A helpful comparison can be made with the legal status of the curule chair. Schäfer (1989) 69 has argued persuasively that this symbol of office was the private property of the individual magistrate. He sees a clear distinction between the public right to use the chair during the year of office and the private right to own and keep the chair in the home.

[51] For the non-religious character of the *imagines*, see Bömer (1943).

[52] For *imagines* and inheritance, see Ch. 1. See Hölkeskamp (1993) 20: 'There was an awe-inspiring aura about higher magistrates and holders of imperium, who were literally surrounded by traditional time-honoured symbols of power and might whenever they appeared in public: lictors and *fasces*, the *sella curulis*, and robes of office.'

[53] See e.g. Cic. *Mur.* 16.

The *imagines* were, therefore, more than simple markers of rank. They were used as devices to recall individual lives and specific qualities. They promised a glorious and undying memory to those who served the state. Their didactic purpose in inspiring the young is stressed above all by Polybius (6. 53-4 = T61). At the same time, their message was not crude or strident, but a complex and sophisticated reaffirmation of the whole range of Roman values and of the leading families as prime exponents of those values.

Were the *imagines* tools of 'propaganda'? The difficulty in answering this question lies partly in ambiguities surrounding the concept of propaganda.[54] The *imagines* fit quite neatly into the category of 'integration propaganda' as analysed by sociologists.[55] While evoking a familiar and expected picture of the Roman past, they confirmed and reminded people of what they already knew. They offered simple and very visual messages. Their effect was over the long term and they were especially telling when in a series, or associated with other variations of ancestral images. Their appeal was to the emotions although they may have appeared as rational representations. The success of 'integration propaganda' comes from its support of the status quo, which can make it hard to recognize for those closely involved with the culture itself.[56]

However, the word 'propaganda' carries many overtones from its use in the twentieth century. Detailed explanations would be needed to show how 'integrationist propaganda' works and what it could have meant in a Roman context.[57] Without rejecting the category of 'integrationist propaganda', this study employs the term 'advertising' to describe the effect of the *imagines*.[58] The concept of

[54] The fundamental discussion of propaganda is Ellul (1973). See also Foulkes (1983) and Kennedy (1984).

[55] Crawford (1979) 179 points out that such terminology is alien to the thought of the ancients.

[56] Kennedy (1984) 159: 'Successful integrationist propaganda not only presents images which evoke the appropriate interpretants, it also selects those images which perpetuate the very interpretants that ensure the continued survival of the values on which the initial success of the propaganda has been based.'

[57] Sutherland (1983) 74 thinks that a more neutral interpretation of propaganda is needed. For attempts see e.g. Watson (1987) on Horace as propaganda, Wallace-Hadrill (1987) on Ovid and Augustus, and Evans (1992) who is more technical but less convincing. Wallace-Hadrill (1986) 67 wants to avoid the term as it distracts the debate into a semantic one. M. T. Griffin (1991) 23 sees propaganda as directed from above, while ideology describes a collusion of beliefs.

[58] See Levick (1982) 105-6 who chooses 'publicity' instead of 'propaganda' for similar reasons.

'advertising' suggests the very 'integrationist' qualities of ancestral imagery in Rome.

Successful advertising is most often based on familiar concepts and values, rather than on the completely new or shocking. In turn, advertising also contributes to a society's expectations and standards in a subtle way. Its direct and repeated visual messages shape everyday life and have a subconscious effect. Advertising is especially concerned with name-recognition, and this was certainly a feature of the use of *imagines*. Roman names were repeated within families with very little variation from one generation to the next in a regular pattern typical of their culture.[59] The metaphor of advertising can help us to understand the importance of name recognition in Roman society where rank depended on repeated successes at the elections.[60]

Meanwhile, the effect of the *imagines* went beyond 'advertising' or 'propaganda'. A full analysis of their cultural significance must balance a study of their use by Roman families with an appreciation of the conditions and limits the medium itself imposed on its users. As noted above, the *imagines* appealed more to the emotions than to reason, and this is the quality which inspired Polybius to write about them with such enthusiasm. However, the emotions evoked were not limited to the awe of humbler citizens or to the envy of competing noble families. The feelings described by Polybius, especially in his focus on the young, include a strong element of shame.[61]

The *imagines* defined honour and glory in precise terms, namely the holding of political office coupled with the successful exercise of military command. They made the memory of the ancestors a vivid part of everyday experience. The *imagines* contributed to the creation of a society of overt praise and blame, in which honour was considered the measure of a man's status and the greatest reward for merit.

The recognition of shame as a complex and essentially moral emotion can help to explain the powerful effect of the *imagines*.[62] Shame has been defined in a variety of ways each of which can con-

---

[59] The eldest son was nearly always called after his father. Many families only used two or three first names.

[60] For *imagines* and the importance of name recognition, see Plin. *Ep.* 8. 10. 3 = T58.

[61] Polyb. 6. 53. 6 and 54. 2-3 = T61.   [62] See Taylor (1985) 54 and 84.

tribute to an understanding of the *imagines*. In the first place, shame
has been described as a type of fear, a fear of failing to meet certain
expectations.[63] That fear involves awe and respect, specifically felt
by younger people for older members of society. The *imagines* were
vital in teaching the young to value the ancestors and their way of
doing things.

In a related definition shame has been described as an 'emotion
of self-protection' closely linked with a person's definition of self.[64]
Shame is about one's self-image, and hence one's self-respect.[65] It
involves but goes beyond the esteem of others. It is this feeling of
shame (as a type of fear) which keeps a person within the norms
adopted by his culture and especially his own group within that
culture.[66] The *imagines*, therefore, provide an illustration of how
the emotion of shame can be defined by a culture in its own terms.
The question of whether emotions like shame or guilt are culturally determined has been a debated one.[67] Are we subject to emotions only or particularly as described by the language of our own
culture? In Roman aristocratic circles this seems to have been the
case.

Much has been written about Greece as a 'shame-culture', focusing especially on the shame felt by the hero in Homer or Tragedy.[68]
While the cruder definitions of 'shame-culture' originally borrowed
from anthropology by classicists over forty years ago have been discredited, shame continues to be an important element in the analysis of Greek literature and the aristocratic society it reflects.[69] The
study of Greek values of shame naturally concentrates on the use of
the Greek shame word αἰδώς, together with the absence from

[63] Williams (1993) 79 uses fear to describe the shame felt by the Homeric hero
on the battlefield.
[64] See G. Taylor (1985).   [65] G. Taylor (1985) following Rawls (1971).
[66] G. Taylor (1985) 81: 'The individual member of an honour group in the setting of a shame-culture can be used to illustrate this point: the relevant values provided by the honour-code, and his survival as the person he is—which is determined
by his membership of the group—depends on his accepting and living by these values. His doing so is therefore protective of the person he is.'
[67] For a recent discussion, see Wiezbicka (1986) and Cairns (1993) 8. The most
forceful argument that emotions are social and cultural constructs can be found in
Averill (1980a) and (1980b).
[68] See Hooker (1987). Cairns (1993) and Williams (1993) have reasserted the
importance of shame in the study of Greek literature and culture.
[69] Dodds (1951) first applied ideas of 'shame-culture' and 'guilt-culture' which he
borrowed from Margaret Mead and others. For a critique, see Cairns (1993) 27 ff.

Greek of any term equivalent to our concept of 'guilt'.[70] Shame is often an important ingredient in cultures which are small-scale like city-states. Such societies depend on personal rather than on abstract obligations, as citizens regularly come face-to-face with each other.[71]

It is surprising that shame in Roman culture has not been the subject of more discussion. Rome certainly offers an easily identifiable 'honour group' defined partly by shame. The Roman political élite was expected to perform deeds of valour and personal sacrifice as leaders of the community in ways equivalent to the heroes of Greek literature. Meanwhile, it was the *imagines* which preserved and embodied the honour accorded to leading men in the state.[72] They allowed that honour to be recalled within the home and at every family funeral, not just at the funeral of the man in question as was done for Homeric heroes at their funeral games.

In essence, shame involves being seen or revealed.[73] The element of being seen in an unfavourable light, and of feeling shame as a result, depends on the notion of an audience which watches and judges one's actions. Consequently, much has been written about the audience, imagined, imaginary, or internalized.[74] While the audience poses something of a problem in modern discussions of shame, for the aristocratic Roman the *imagines* played the role of an audience which reflected the norms of his 'honour group'.

It makes sense for a culture based largely on shame to construct for itself an 'audience' which watches its member in his own home. Such an audience is virtually ever present as the conscience of the individual member is also assimilated to it. The audience preserves and hands on the honour-code of the élite, a code which also reflects the values of the society as a whole. The emotions of shame elicited by the special audience preserve the 'honour group' which created it.

---

[70] Similarly, Cairns (1993) 13: 'the study of *aidos* becomes a study of Greek values of honour, for the notion of honour is never far away from the evaluation that is constitutive of *aidos*.' If the term 'shame-culture' is deemed to have been discredited, one might substitute the label 'honour-culture' to express the notion that shame was an important emotion in shaping the values of Roman society.

[71] For discussion, see Cairns (1993) 46.

[72] For shame brought on the *imagines* themselves, see Tac. *Ann.* 2. 43. 6 = T86 where Drusus' (the son of Tiberius) descent from an *eques*, Atticus, is said to bring shame on the *imagines* of the patrician Claudii.

[73] G. Taylor (1985) 53, and Williams (1993) 78 who connects shame especially with nakedness.

[74] G. Taylor (1985) 58 ff., Cairns (1993) 15 ff., and Williams (1993) 82 ff.

The *imagines* always appeared in the role of an audience. Yet this function has remained unexplored and unappreciated in discussions of their meaning. In the home the *imagines* formed an audience for any actions taking place in the *atrium* at those times when their cupboards were open. Their presence was probably felt even when the cupboards were closed. In effect, the masks of the ancestors provided a special, culturally determined, locus of shame for a Roman who had to 'face' his ancestors whenever he entered his own or a relative's house.[75] Similarly, his funeral eulogy would be given to an audience of 'ancestors' impersonated by actors, and would contain an account of their deeds also.[76] His public image could not be separated from that of his ancestors. In order to understand the *imagines* as a cultural phenomenon, rather than merely as art objects, it is necessary to consider the role of shame for the Roman élite.

This study sets out to show how the *imagines* were adapted to changing political and social situations, and how they continued to be significant cultural symbols throughout Roman history. A new and comprehensive collection of evidence about the *imagines* allows both discussion in greater detail and more reliable conclusions than are found elsewhere. The *imagines* will be put in context and evaluated in terms of general information available about Roman culture. The present examination will consider the *imagines* as 'status symbols' which embodied honour and evoked shame in a traditional aristocratic setting. A thorough investigation of ancestor masks in Rome will address their use as advertisements by leading political families, as well as the ways in which their character shaped Roman values and expectations.

---

[75] See Williams (1993) 82 and 98. For coming home to the *imagines*, see Ps.-Quint. *Decl. min.* 388. 35 = T64.
[76] For funeral orations, see Ch. 5.

I

The Significance of *Imagines*

*Maiorum gloria posteris quasi lumen est, neque bona neque mala
eorum in occulto patitur.*

(Sall. *Jug.* 85. 23)

WHY investigate Roman ancestor masks (*imagines maiorum*)? Or, to
put it in a different way, why is the study of *imagines* of general
interest to the student of Roman society and customs? An answer
can be found in two ancient texts which reveal the role and significance of *imagines* in widely differing historical contexts. This chapter offers a reading of Sallust's version (*Jug.* 85 = T66) of the speech
that Marius delivered as consul in 107 BC, and of the senate's decree
condemning Gnaeus Calpurnius Piso in AD 20. Both sources provide
explicit and complex evidence about ancestor masks.

While showing a glimpse of the situation on two particularly dramatic occasions, these texts also have wide-reaching implications
for everyday practices in politics, oratory, and the law. The two passages were written about 60 years apart, and shed light on both
Republic and Principate. The information gleaned about the *imagines* shows two sides of the same coin. Sallust indicates what the
imagines meant for a *novus* consul at his moment of triumph over
the traditional office-holding families: the senate's decree reveals
their import for a distinguished *nobilis*, close to the family of the
emperor, at his moment of ruin.

Sallust's rendering of Marius' public address as consul in 107 BC
has been the subject of extensive scrutiny by those concerned with
the historian's style and intentions.[1] From a purely historical point
of view it is necessary to start by establishing what Sallust can tell

---

[1] Especially interesting are Büchner (1953), Earl (1961) 32–3, Syme (1964), and
Vretska (1970).

us about the rhetoric of Marius himself, especially his use of ancestors to attack political opponents from office-holding families. Both Sallust and Plutarch allude to a series of speeches made by Marius while he was in Rome at the beginning of his consulship in 107 BC (*Jug.* 84. 1). No fragments of speeches by Marius are recognized or included in the collection of the fragments of Latin oratory.[2] Why, then, should we accept any aspect of Sallust's recreation as historically accurate? The question is especially pertinent in light of the way Sallust is using the speech for his own purposes. It serves as the climax to the attacks on the *nobiles* which supply the main theme running through his monograph.[3] At the same time, the speech is constructed to offer a character study of Marius that suggests a number of criticisms, notably an unfavourable comparison with Marius' principal rival Q. Caecilius Metellus.

Regardless of what Sallust himself may have thought of Marius, there is evidence that the speech he wrote does contain some echoes of Marius' own ideas and of the tone of popular oratory in the late second century BC. Parallels can be found in Plutarch (*Mar.* 9. 2–3, cf. T60), which raise the question of whether Plutarch used Sallust or an independent source which shared three points of contact with Sallust's version of Marius' speech.[4] For our purposes the most interesting of the three is the reference to the *imagines*, although it has not received much attention from modern scholars.[5]

It is notable that there are no other echoes of Sallust's *Jugurtha* in Plutarch, either in the *Marius* or the *Sulla*. Plutarch's treatment of the war in Africa is brief and very different from Sallust's in content, tone, and structure.[6] Plutarch places Marius' words firmly in the context of the army reforms, while Sallust uses the speech to stress his overall theme of opposition to the office-holding caste. Marius clearly did target the *nobiles* and this was a factor which

[2] Malcovati (1976).

[3] See esp. Sall. *Jug.* 31 (speech of Memmius) and 40. 1 (Mamilius).

[4] Both authors mention the image of capturing the consulship as spoils from the *nobiles* (84. 1); the specific attack on Albinus and Bestia (85. 16); and the reference to the display of Marius' wounds or scars being equivalent to *imagines* (85. 29-30).

[5] e.g. Koestermann (1971) ad. loc. who comments on general parallels with Plutarch, notably the mention of Albinus and Bestia, as true reflections of Marius' words but does not note the similar treatment of the *imagines*.

[6] Note e.g. the different treatment of T. Turpilius Silanus, the garrison commander at Vaga, who receives hostile treatment in Sallust (*Jug.* 69. 4, cf. 66. 3 and 67. 3), while he appears as the innocent friend of Metellus framed by Marius in Plutarch (*Mar.* 8. 1-2).

influenced Sallust to write his monograph in the first place.[7] Consequently, arguments about the historian's style or his development of 'opposition to the *nobiles*' as a theme can not be used to suggest that Marius' speech is necessarily a literary fiction.

During the imperial period a separate collection of the speeches and letters of Sallust was circulated, probably for use in the schools of rhetoric.[8] However, the date of the collection is not established, and Plutarch shows no knowledge of other speeches from the *Jugurtha*. Moreover, his sources for the *Marius* included several contemporaries of Marius, who could also have been used by Sallust.[9] Therefore, the most economical solution is to posit that both writers were using a common source which preserved some striking points made by Marius.[10] The bulk of the speech in Sallust is surely the historian's own creation, but it appears to have been built around a core of Marius' own sentiments, or at least thoughts attributed to him by a contemporary source. The *imagines* are integral to what Marius seems originally to have said. Sallust perhaps followed Thucydides in aiming to reproduce speeches which reflected the main gist of a speaker's argument.[11]

Other considerations, quite apart from the evidence of Sallust and Plutarch, also make it plausible that Marius mentioned *imagines* on this occasion. The subject of his ancestors was a traditional one for a new consul to address in his first public meeting after election.[12] It was, therefore, logical for Sallust to insert a set speech here in his narrative. As a *novus* himself, Sallust was in a position to appreci-

[7] See esp. *Jug.* 5. 1: Sallust has chosen his subject because the war was great and bloody but also *dehinc quia tunc primum superbiae nobilitatis obviam itum est* ('precisely because that was the first time opposition was mounted against the arrogance of the office-holding caste').

[8] We have some of the collection preserved as Codex Vaticanus Latinus 3864 (V), cf. McGushin (1992) 6 who dates it to the 2nd cent. AD 'probably'.

[9] For Plutarch's sources, see Scardigli (1979) 74–88 and Titchener (1992). Sources include Sulla's memoirs, Rutilius Rufus' *Res Gestae*, Q. Lutatius Catulus' work on his consulship, Posidonius (especially favoured by Von Fritz (1943) 166 for *Marius* 9) and several anonymous authors, at least one of whom was very favourable to Marius.

[10] A similar view, argued by Passerini (1934) 20–2, has received varying degrees of support, e.g. Carney (1959), Earl (1961) 77, and Syme (1964) 169 n. 37.

[11] For Sallust's use of Thucydides, see Scanlon (1980) esp. 151: 'In the discussion of Sallust's stylistic debt to Thucydides we noted that Sallust's use of speeches resembled Thucydides' in that although both historians seem to be concerned with keeping close to the actual content of the particular speech, they both use speeches to reveal broader, historical issues and characterize the speaker himself.'

[12] See Ch. 5 § 5 for a detailed discussion.

ate the significance of Marius' words in their original context. According to custom, a newly elected consul alluded to previous office-holders in his family, and promised to follow in their footsteps. Clearly, a candidate 'without ancestors' had to think of something else to say. In the highly charged political atmosphere before and after Marius' election, it was natural for the ancestors and their *imagines* to become targets. Indeed, it would have been more surprising if Marius had made no allusion at all to the *imagines*.

Stylistic arguments also suggest that Sallust has not composed the speech entirely himself. As has been noted in other analyses, Marius' tone differs from what is usually found in Sallust, especially in its use of sarcasm and irony.[13] The language contains a number of archaisms best paralleled in the fragments of Cato, a famous earlier *novus homo* whose influence on Marius may have been a factor.[14] Nevertheless, even if the speech were viewed as a free composition by the historian, it would still contribute valuable insights about the importance of the *imagines* in Sallust's own time.

The substance of Marius' oration is a comparison between himself and the *nobiles*. Consequently, the structure of the speech is heavily dependent on antitheses, such as deeds/words or toil/self-indulgence. The ancestors are at the heart of the basic contrast in an argument which has two principal features. Firstly, the *nobiles* rely on the deeds of their ancestors for election and to excuse their shortcomings in office. The ancestors are, therefore, closely linked with the characteristic arrogance (*superbia*) of Marius' rivals.[15] Secondly, Marius himself is said to be much more like those famous ancestors because of his merits (*virtus*).[16] According to Sallust, Marius is trying to present himself as the true heir of previous great leaders. Sallust and Plutarch both emphasize the impact of Marius' rhetorical strategy.

Ancestors are mentioned nine times in the speech, while the

[13] Carney (1959) reads the speech as a parody of aristocratic *elogia*, such as those from the tomb of the Scipios discussed in Ch. 6. For stylistic analysis, see Syme (1964) 168.

[14] Cf. Skard (1956) 92–100 for a thorough analysis of the parallels with Cato.

[15] For *superbia* in Marius' speech, see 85. 1; 85. 13; 85. 19; 85. 38; 85. 45; 85. 47. *Superbia* is a feature of Sallust's treatment of the *nobiles* in the *Jugurtha*, see 5. 1; 30. 3; 31. 2; 31. 12; 41. 3; 64. 1; 64. 5; 82. 3.

[16] For the role of *virtus* in Sallust, see Earl (1961). Marius later dedicated a temple to Honor and Virtus. See Platner and Ashby (1929) ad loc. and especially Hinard (1987) who brings out the political importance of Marius' Virtus in comparison with his colleague Catulus' temple to Fortuna Huiusce Diei.

imagines appear five times.[17] This is the densest cluster of references to *imagines* in Latin literature. As the argument develops it is not always easy to separate the ancestors from their *imagines*. In the setting of a public meeting, the *imagines* appear as useful and accessible symbols, evocative of the archaic tone and simple values the speaker is aspiring to. The public and popular context is important in suggesting the political role of the *imagines*. They are used to repeat and vary the main theme of opposition to the 'inherited' status of the *nobiles*.[18]

At important moments in the argument the *imagines* support memorable points, which come to a climax in a passage where they appear twice (85. 29–30=T66b). Marius claims his military decorations and scars are, in fact, 'his *imagines*'. For a Roman this metaphor is a vivid expression of the concept of a self-made man in public life.[19] Under the circumstances it would not be surprising if such a striking image was remembered and later given pride of place by Sallust in his effort to recreate a picture of Marius as an orator. The character and function of the *imagines* implied by Sallust's language in the four relevant passages outline the main themes explored in the present study:

1. bellum me gerere cum Iugurtha iussistis, quam rem nobilitas aegerrume tulit. quaeso, reputate cum animis vostris num id mutare melius sit, si quem ex illo globo nobilitatis ad hoc aut aliud tale negotium mittatis, hominem veteris prosapiae ac multarum imaginum et nullius stipendi, scilicet ut in tanta re ignarus omnium trepidet, festinet, sumat aliquem ex populo monitorem offici sui. (85. 10)

You appointed me to wage war against Jugurtha, a thing which the office-holding caste objected to strongly. I ask you, consider in your hearts whether it would be better to change that, by sending out one of that crowd of 'nobles' on this or some other similar business, a man with an ancient lineage and many masks but no military experience, so that of course being inexperienced in so great an undertaking he would fear everything and would hurry to take some man of the people as a guide in carrying out his commission.

Early in his oration, Marius is speaking about the choice of a member of an office-holding family to take charge of the war against

----

[17] Ancestors are *maiores* at 85. 4; 85. 12; 85. 17; 85. 21; 85. 23; 85. 29; 85. 36; 85. 38; and *patres* at 85. 16. *Imagines* appear at: 85. 10; 85. 25; 85. 29–30 (twice); 85. 38 = T66a–c.

[18] Cf. Val. Max. 3. 8. 7 = T100 for surprise at a 'noble soul' without *imagines*.

[19] The same idea is also to be found in Plutarch (*Mar.* 9. 2 = T60).

Jugurtha or any other campaign. His allegation that the inexperienced aristocrat often relies on the knowledge of the trained subordinate, who is really doing the work, implies that he has been in such a situation himself, a claim not supported by Sallust's previous narrative. The *imagines* are represented as outweighing experience or expertise in the promotion of Roman generals. However, Marius is being less than truthful when he asserts that a general from an office-holding family might have no military experience.[20] In this passage archaic language, apparently echoing Cato, is closely associated with the *imagines*.[21]

2. nunc videte quam iniqui sint: quod ex aliena virtute sibi adrogant, id mihi ex mea non concedunt, scilicet quia imagines non habeo et quia mihi nova nobilitas est, quam certe peperisse melius est quam acceptam corrupisse. (85. 25)

Now see how base they are: what they appropriate for themselves from other people's valour, they do not allow me to acquire from my own merit, obviously because I do not have any masks and because my status as an office-holder is new. But it is better, to be sure, to create one's own élite status than to destroy such status after having inherited it.

Marius is contrasting his own attitude to that of the *nobiles* who, according to him, are jealous of his position and will not give him credit for his achievements, achievements which emulate those of the great Romans of the past. The term *nova nobilitas* ('new nobility') is equated with a state of having no *imagines*. Ancestor masks, therefore, contribute to our understanding of the terms *nobilitas* and *novitas*. They define status and mark boundaries. From Marius' point of view they create prejudice. They are portrayed as the tools of oligarchic corruption and influence, thus making them symbols of and weapons in strife between different sections of society.

3. non possum fidei causa imagines neque triumphos aut consulatus maiorum meorum ostentare, at, si res postulet, hastas, vexillum, phaleras, alia militaria dona, praeterea cicatrices advorso corpore. Hae sunt meae imagines, haec nobilitas, non hereditate relicta, ut illa illis, sed quae egomet plurumis laboribus et periculis quaesivi. (85. 29-30)

[20] Polyb. 6. 19. 4 cites ten military campaigns as a requirement before standing for the quaestorship in the mid-2nd cent. BC; see Wiseman (1971) 143 ff. and Develin (1985) 90. Rosenstein (1990) does not discuss Marius' speech in any detail in his assessment of the careers of defeated generals.
[21] Koestermann (1971) compares *hominem veteris prosapiae* with Cato fr. 9. 6.

I am not able to inspire confidence by parading the masks or triumphs or consulships of my ancestors, but, if need arises, I can show spears and standards presented for valour, medals, other military decorations, and besides the scars on the front of my body. These are my masks, these my 'nobility', not inherited as in their case, but which I myself strove to acquire through many labours and dangers.

The newly elected consul argues against the assertion attributed to his opponents from office-holding families that he should never have been elected and is unsuited to high office. This passage, as much as any, confirms the close connection between the ancestors, especially as represented by their *imagines*, and the rhetoric surrounding the elections, both before and after the actual vote. As a result, the *imagines* are used for publicity. The verb *ostentare* ('parade, put on show') suggests a context of spectacle and display, often with a pejorative sense of ostentation.[22] Ancestor masks are associated most notably with earlier triumphs and consulships. They serve as pledges to win the voters' confidence in future results. The deeds of the ancestors are, it is implied, to be repeated by their descendants. The connection of the *imagines* with *nobilitas* is emphasized by the rhetorical device of anaphora. Perhaps Marius accompanied the reference to his scars with some kind of gesture or display.[23] The *imagines*, although special symbols of rank, can appear at the heart of a message of service which challenges the privileges of the élite.

4. ceterum homines superbissimi procul errant: maiores eorum omnia quae licebat illis reliquere, divitias, imagines, memoriam sui praeclaram; virtutem non reliquere, neque poterant: ea sola neque datur dono neque accipitur. (85. 38)

Their ancestors bequeathed to them everything which they could, wealth, masks, their distinguished reputation; they did not leave them valour, nor could they: it alone is neither given nor received as a gift.

Marius has just presented a picture of himself as an old-fashioned Roman general who shares his troops' duties and dangers, unlike the idle aristocrats who live a life of luxury and study Greek rhetoric

[22] For *imagines* associated with the 'glare of publicity', see Cic. *Leg. Agr.* 2. 1 = T7; Val. Max. 3. 3. 7 = T97; Sil. 17. 12 = T79.
[23] See Livy 45. 39. 17 for Servilius showing the crowd his scars to defend Aemilius Paullus' claim to a triumph in 167 BC.

in order to disguise their true merit and actions.[24] As a part of this contrast of lifestyles, he discussed what ancestors can bequeath to their descendants. Masks of previous office-holders are an essential part of an inheritance. They secure a family's continuity and represent a link between generations. Although a tricolon is used here, the *imagines* cannot be entirely separated from the concept of *memoria* which follows immediately after. The concrete objects of an inheritance are described as money and the *imagines*, which embody reputation. A family's position depends on these two elements. At the same time, the *imagines* are connected with money and with certain aspirations. Even in this context, some idea can be gleaned of the pressure on family members from expectations symbolized by *imagines*.

The impression created by Sallust is that Marius wants to enlist the ancestors for his own purposes. They appear as more than just the advertising tools of a few families, for they exert an independent influence. In other words, the prestige of earlier leaders, which was especially represented to the people by their masks, is a force in Roman politics which Sallust's Marius chooses not to ignore or simply to belittle. However dismissive he is of contemporary political opponents he must take account of their ancestors, to the extent that their deeds live on in the imagination of his audience. It is tempting to suppose that Marius is also thinking of his own future *imago* and reputation, since he is no longer an outsider but a member of the 'nobility of office'.[25] In other words, the *imagines* allow him to visualize for himself and to dramatize for his audience a direct comparison between himself and the ancestors of his aristocratic rivals.

In contrast, the senate's decree of 10 December AD 20 posthumously condemning Cn. Calpurnius Piso on a charge of treason (*maiestas*) is utterly different in style and intent.[26] This recently discovered document from Spain stands out among Latin inscriptions

---

[24] The artful structure and powerful imagery of Marius' own words belie his image as an uneducated rustic. Cf. *Jug.* 44–5 where Metellus, Marius' aristocratic opponent, is praised by Sallust for restoring morale and discipline to the Roman army in Africa by old-fashioned methods and personal supervision. Sallust brings out the slanderous elements in Marius' speech.

[25] For Marius' own *imago*, see Vell. Pat. 2. 27. 5 = T105. For the ideology of *novitas*, see Wiseman (1971) 107–16.

[26] For this new inscription see now Caballos, Eck, and Fernández (1991), *Das Senatus Consultum de Cn. Pisone Patre* (forthcoming), and Eck (1993).

for its length, the excellent condition of its text, and the number of copies that have survived.[27] The *senatus consultum* offers a wealth of insights into general conditions under the Empire and the character of Tiberius' reign. It is unique in providing precise legal information about the *imagines*, particularly in a case of *damnatio memoriae* (the condemnation of a man's memory).

A long rubric recommending the removal of Piso's *imago* demonstrates the importance of this posthumous image for a *nobilis* in the first century AD:

73 . . . itaq(ue) is poenis, quas a semet ipso exegisset, adicere: ne quis luctus mortis eius causa a feminis *eis, quibus* more maiorum, si hoc s(enatus) c(onsultum) factum
75 non esset, lugendus esset, susciperetur; utiq(ue) statuae et imagines Cn. Pisonis
patris, quae ubiq(ue) positae essent, tollerentur; recte et ordine facturos qui qu-
andoq(ue) familiae Calpurniae essent, quiue eam familiam cognatione
adfinitateue contingerent, si dedissent operam, si quis eius gentis aut quis eorum, qui cognatus adfinisue Calpurniae familiae fuisset, mortuos esset, lugen-
80 dus esset, ne inter reliquas imagines, ⟨quibus⟩ exequias eorum funerum celebrare solent,
imago Cn. Pisonis patris duceretur, neue imaginibus familiae Calpurniae i-
mago eius interponeretur; . . .

. . . accordingly to those penalties which he had imposed on himself, the senate adds (the following):
– that no mourning for his death should be undertaken by those women who would be obliged by ancestral custom to mourn, if this decree of the senate had not been passed.
– that the statues and busts of Gnaeus Piso, the father, wherever they have been put up, be removed.
– that it would be right and proper for those who at any time would be members of the family of the Calpurnii, or anyone related to that family either by birth or by marriage, if anyone of that family or anyone related either by birth or marriage to the family of the Calpurnii has died and is to be mourned, to see to it that the mask of Gnaeus Piso the father should not

---

[27] See Eck (1993) for a discussion of where the copies were found and why so many came to light in the region of Seville in the Roman province of Baetica.

be part of the procession amongst the other masks, with which the rites of their funerals are accustomed to be celebrated, and that his mask should not be set up amongst the masks of the Calpurnian family.

The *imagines* are mentioned in a section detailing penalties the senate is imposing on Piso after he had committed suicide. The senate's ruling raises the question of what punishments were usual in a case of *maiestas*. To put it differently, what was Piso trying to avoid when he committed suicide? The penalties prescribed by the *lex maiestatis*, especially Caesar's *lex Julia de maiestate* which was probably still in force at this period, have been the subject of much debate amongst scholars.[28] The senate's decree shows that we are not necessarily dealing with statutory punishments but with *poena* which depend on the *pietas* and *severitas* of the judges, i.e. the senators and the *princeps* (lines 71–3). The law itself seems to have enjoined banishment (*aquae et ignis interdictio*).[29] The new decree arranged for that penalty to be imposed on Piso's subordinates, Visellius Karus and Sempronius Bassus, by the appropriate authorities (lines 121–2).[30] Other cases from the reign of Tiberius suggest that banishment to a named place, often an island, was a customary penalty.[31] Death could also be imposed by the *princeps* or the senate in especially serious cases.[32]

From Piso's point of view suicide was clearly preferable to execution. At the same time, both banishment and execution carried

[28] For Caesar's law in its original context, see Yavetz (1979) 81–7.

[29] This had been suggested by Cic. *Phil.* 1. 23: *quid, quod obrogatur legibus Caesaris, quae iubent ei qui de vi itemque ei qui maiestatis damnatus sit aqua et igni interdici?* ('What of the alteration of Caesar's laws, which enjoin banishment for anyone convicted of violence and likewise of treason?') Cf. Tac. *Ann.* 3. 38. 2 (Antistius Vetus) and 3. 50. 4 (Clutorius Priscus). See e.g. Chilton (1955) for the standard view and Allison and Cloud (1962) who discuss the emperor and senate's power to impose a harsher penalty in severe cases. *Contra* Levick (1976) and (1979) who believes death was the standard penalty.

[30] l. 120: *Visellio Karo et Sempronio Basso, comitibus Cn. Pisonis patris et omnium maleficiorum socis et ministris, aqua et igne interdici oportere ab eo pr(aetore) qui lege{m} maiestatis quaereret, bonaq(ue) eorum ab pr(aetoribus), qui aerario praeesse⟨n⟩t, venire et in aerario redigi placere* ('Visellius Karus and Sempronius Bassus, associates of Gnaeus Piso the father and his allies and accomplices in all his crimes, should be banished by the praetor in charge of the law of treason, and it pleases (the senate) that their property should be sold and the proceeds be deposited in the public treasury by the praetor in charge of the public treasury.')

[31] e.g. Tac. *Ann.* 3. 38. 2 and 3. 68. 2.

[32] This is impled for Libo Drusus (Tac. *Ann.* 2. 31. 2) and Cremutius Cordus (*RE* 2, Sen. *Cons. ad Marc.* 22. 6), but actually happened in the case of Clutorius Priscus (Tac. *Ann.* 3. 51).

with them as additional burdens confiscation of property and loss of civic rights, such as the right to make a will.[33] A condemned man might also expect to be deprived of a proper burial. All or at least some of these additional penalties, which affected the status of a man after death and his ability to bequeath his social position to his heirs, might be avoided in a case of suicide.[34] At a later date property was not saved by suicide in cases of *perduellio*.[35] However, the evidence for such treason trials is much later, nor is it at all clear whether Piso was subject to a charge of *perduellio*. By the end of the Republic egregious cases of high treason, such as those of Brutus and Cassius, attracted punishments which were aimed at preventing a man from being remembered, especially in ways customary amongst Roman aristocrats.[36] Such punishments, in their various forms, are collectively known as *damnatio memoriae*.

The example of Scribonius Libo Drusus, who was condemned for *maiestas* after suicide in AD 16, is both the closest in time and the most relevant to Piso's (Tac. *Ann.* 2. 27–32).[37] Libo suffered confiscation of property, his *imago* was banned from family funerals, his name was no longer to be used by the family, and public thanksgiving was decreed for the anniversary of his death.[38] His case suggests that dishonour and loss of property were the two main considerations for Piso's suicide; in other words, the two aspects of an inheritance mentioned by Marius (Sall. *Jug.* 85. 38 = T66*c*).

[33] For loss of property, see Tac. *Ann.* 2. 32. 1 and 3. 50. 6. Dio 57. 22. 5 credits Tiberius with extending the law to cover wills; cf. *Digest* 28. 1. 8.

[34] Tac. *Ann.* 6. 29. 1 on the subject of the suicide of Pomponius Labeo, governor of Moesia, and his wife Paxaea in AD 34 : *Nam promptas eius modi mortes metus carnificis faciebat, et quia damnati publicatis bonis sepultura prohibebantur, eorum qui de se statuebant humabantur corpora, manebant testamenta, pretium festinandi* ('For fear of the executioner made these modes of death a popular option, and because convicted criminals sufferred confiscation of property and were refused burial. Those who decided their fate themselves had their bodies buried while their wills remained valid, the reward for their haste'). Cf. Dio 58. 15. 4 who explicitly states that under Tiberius it was rare for suicides to lose their property.

[35] *Digest* 48. 4. 11, which defines a *perduellionis reus* as *hostili animo adversus rem publicam vel principem animatus* ('motivated by hostile intent towards the state or the emperor').

[36] See Tac. *Ann.* 3. 76 = T89 for the absence of their *imagines* at Junia's funeral in AD 22.

[37] They were, in fact, related. See the family tree in Boschung (1986). The Calpurnii Pisones of the empire and their *imagines* are further discussed in Ch. 9.

[38] Cf. also the *Fasti Amiterni* for 13 September, the day of his suicide. Lahusen (1983) 127 is mistaken in stating that the *imagines* of Libo's ancestors were banned from family funerals.

The punishments imposed on Piso by the senate fall into six categories, which reflect matters of law and of custom. The other *poena* provide the context for the removal of his *imago*.

1. No women were allowed to mourn his death (lines 73–5).
2. Both public and private portraits of him were ordered destroyed (lines 75–6).[39]
3. The senate enjoined that the family of the Calpurnii not display Piso's *imago*, either at a family funeral or with the other *imagines* in the *atrium* (lines 76–82).[40]
4. Piso's name was to be removed from the inscription on the statue of Germanicus set up by the *sodales Augustales* on the Campus Martius, near the altar of Providentia (lines 82–4).
5. Piso's property was confiscated although most of it was then granted to his children and other descendants on condition that his oldest son Gnaeus change his name (lines 84–105).
6. Additions to Piso's house connecting it with the porta Fontinalis were ordered to be demolished (lines 105–8).[41]

The text we have stresses the dishonour done to Piso's memory. In light of popular unrest in Rome and the mourning for Germanicus in many places abroad it was essential for Tiberius and the senate to be seen to have imposed a severe penalty on Piso.[42] The posting of this decree summarizing the actions taken by the senate and *princeps* was designed to fulfil that very purpose, both in the provinces and by the standards in the winter quarters of the legions.[43] Despite the return of most of Piso's property to his heirs, the punishments are still described as being greater than death

[39] Cf. the case of Silius' portrait which counted against his son, when it was discovered in his house (Tac. *Ann.* 11. 35. 1). The crowds in Rome had apparently already tried to destroy Piso's statues during the trial, expressing their expectation of his impending conviction (Tac. *Ann.* 3. 14. 6).

[40] This can be paralleled in the treatment of Libo Drusus (Tac. *Ann.* 2. 32. 1).

[41] For the splendour of Piso's house and its decoration on his return from the East, see Tac. *Ann.* 3. 9. 3: *fuit inter inritamenta invidiae domus foro imminens festa ornatu conviviumque et epulae; et celebritate loci nihil occultum* ('Among the causes of his unpopularity were his house, decorated as for a feast, which overlooked the Forum and his dinner-parties and banquets. Also nothing was hidden because of the crowded nature of the place'). On the destruction of the house as a traditional penalty for treason, see Cic. *Dom.* 101.

[42] On the mourning for Germanicus, see Versnel (1980) and Eck (1993).

[43] Instructions for posting can be found in ll. 169–72.

alone (line 71).[44] The text reveals the importance attached to preserving or destroying the memory of a Roman from the office-holding caste. Later, in the *lex portorii provinciae Asiae* of AD 62, Piso's
name was changed from Gnaeus to Lucius, as was his oldest son's,
with the result that the father disappeared from the record of magistrates without even leaving the gap created by an erasure.[45]

Are the penalties in the *senatus consultum* listed in order? The
most obvious pattern appears to be according to the chronology of
events after a man's death. For this reason mourning by women,
which would include both family members and hired professionals,
is mentioned first. The mourning of women in the family was a
basic element of Roman funerary ritual.[46] After Augustus' death
men were required to mourn for a few days only but women for a
whole year, as if for the death of a father or husband.[47] Such prolonged mourning reflected the position of Augustus as *pater patriae*
and confirmed the importance attached to traditional observances,
especially when carried out by women.

At times of public rejoicing, such as the secular games of 17 BC,
the state tried to put limits on private mourning.[48] At a later date
mourning was generally forbidden for traitors and for those who
killed themselves through a sense of guilt.[49] In AD 32 the mother of

[44] l. 71: *quas ob res arbitrari senatum non optulisse eum se de⌐b⌐itae poenae, sed maiori
et quam inimin⌐e⌐re sibi ab pietate et severitate iudicantium intellegebant, subtraxisse*
('Wherefore, it is the opinion of the senate that he did not subject himself to the punishment he deserved, but has spared himself a greater one which he realized was
hanging over him because of the sense of duty and the severity of his judges').

[45] The son held the consulship in AD 26. Piso's grandson Lucius, consul in AD 57,
was on a commission to publish the *lex portorii provinciae Asiae* in AD 62. Piso's name
is recorded in this law as Lucius, on the occasion of his joint consulship with the
future emperor Tiberius in 7 BC. This law raises the question of what happened in
cases of *damnatio memoriae* when a man, who had been a consular colleague of an
emperor, had a son and grandson who were also consuls. Their filiation needed to
be represented in some way in inscriptions. See Eck (1990) especially 143-4 who
suggests Piso's name had been changed earlier, although in (1993) n. 42 he attributes the change to the grandson on the commission.

[46] See Price (1987) 62.

[47] Dio 56. 43. 1 alludes to this edict. Cf. Dionysius of Halicarnassus 5. 48. 4; Ov.
Fast. 1. 35-6; *FIRA* 2. 535-6. See Arce (1988*b*) 19 for similar year-long mourning
for Sulla and 54-7 for mourning as part of imperial funerals.

[48] *CIL* 6. 32323 lines 110-14 = Pighi (1965) 115. Cf. Livy 22. 54-5 for public
limitation on mourning after the great Roman losses at the battle of Cannae in 216
BC so that the festivals of the gods could be celebrated as usual.

[49] *Digest* 3. 2. 11. 3 : *non solent autem lugeri, ut Neratius ait, hostes vel perduellionis damnati nec suspendiosi nec qui manus sibi intulerunt non taedio vitae, sed mala con-
scientia* ('As Neratius says, it is not the custom to mourn enemies or those convicted

Fufius Geminus (cos. AD 29) was condemned to death for mourning her son who had been executed, probably after he had been convicted of *maiestas*.[50] A ban on mourning deprived the dead man of proper acknowledgement, especially as a member of his own family. By the early imperial period it may be interpreted as a standard penalty in cases of treason. In this instance, the contrast between widespread mourning for Germanicus and no mourning for Piso was marked. Piso had apparently not been officially charged with the murder of Germanicus, as the senate's decree implies. However, his attitude of open rejoicing at the latter's death, which denied his immediate superior the customary gestures of respect and mourning, weighed heavily against him with the senators.[51] The official message was clear: Piso had not mourned Germanicus when the rest of the Roman world had, now no one would mourn Piso.

Since Piso was clearly subject to other penalties associated with high treason, why was he not also debarred from receiving proper burial? The most obvious answer to this question is that he had already been buried. Such a circumstance would explain why the appearance of his *imago* at his own funeral is not mentioned as an issue, although specific recommendations are made about the funerals of other members of his family. Under the circumstances, it is hard to imagine that he had the customary public funeral ceremonies or a eulogy in the Forum. The family probably arranged for immediate and quiet burial after his suicide to avoid the disgrace of being forced to leave his body unburied.

The *imagines* appear at the centre of the penalties designed to dishonour the memory of Piso. This illustrates their role in creating a picture of the man both for his own family and for posterity in general.[52] The wording adopted by the senate and approved by Tiberius reveals the legal and social position of *imagines* in AD 20. Piso's *imago* seems already to have existed since its manufacture is not mentioned amongst the allusions to mourning or inheritance, the matters which concerned the family immediately after a death. The public appearance of the *imagines* is divided into two spheres by the

of treason or those who hanged themselves or those who took their own lives not because they were tired of life but as a result of a bad conscience').

[50] Tac. *Ann.* 6. 10. 1, Cf. Dio 58. 4. 5 ff.

[51] See esp. l. 28, where Piso's responsibility for Germanicus' death is presented as no more than an allegation, but one made by Germanicus himself.

[52] For the proud displays of *imagines* associated with the Calpurnii Pisones, See Cic. *Pis.* 1 = T13, *Laus Pisonis* = T36, Martial 4. 40. 1–4, Plin. *Ep.* 5. 17. 6 = T57.

senate: the funeral and the home. The chapters which follow set out to examine the role of the *imagines* in these two contexts and in the order of importance adopted in the decree.

The *imago* of Piso is subject to a strongly worded injunction by the senate and emperor, that it should not be publicly displayed either at family funerals or in the houses of relatives. The senate's wording demonstrates that any relative, whether by blood or by marriage, was entitled to display a man's *imago* at his or her funeral. The wider family of the Calpurnii is mentioned by name only in the section about the *imago*. The branch of the Pisones is, therefore, singled out for punishment, while the family in general including its other branches are addressed separately and in a respectful tone.[53]

For a man like Piso his *imago* was, therefore, a vital element in maintaining his position within the family of the Calpurnii. As a member of that family he hoped to contribute to its position and reputation after his death. His *imago* would play a part both on solemn and everyday occasions. Setting up his *imago* in the family *atrium* after his death can be seen as equivalent to other rituals which were banned by the senate, such as mourning. The attention his *imago* might command in public can be likened to the effect of his public statues and the very appearance of his house itself, both also targets of the senate. Therefore, the senators felt the need to order the family to remove Piso's *imago* even within their personal sphere of control.[54] The meticulous and detailed wording of the senate's decree challenges us to take seriously ancestor masks whose privileged position reflects a long history of influence during the Republic.

A careful reading of the senate's decree reveals a feature of Roman political culture, namely its emphasis on overt praise and blame. As noted above, Piso's humbler accomplices were banished and had their goods confiscated, but Piso's own family emerges with its property and social position virtually intact.[55] Moreover, leniency is possible despite the fact that Piso's wife Plancina and his

[53] Other branches included notably the Bestiae, Bibuli, and Frugi.
[54] See Cic. *Fam.* 9. 21 for an example of choosing to exclude the *imagines* of certain relatives who were considered unsuitable.
[55] See Tac. *Ann.* 3. 76 = T89 for Junia, the sister of Brutus and wife of Cassius, who died wealthy although she could not display her brother's and husband's *imagines* at her funeral.

younger son Marcus were heavily implicated in his actions.[56] The favour of the emperor, and especially of his mother Livia, is evident.[57] Yet equally striking is the whole tenor of the text which makes it plain that Piso has suffered a terrible punishment for treason and that his example is being held up as a lesson for all the Roman world. This punishment consists of the destruction of his name and memory as preserved by his portraits, his *imago*, and the records of his offices. Such dishonour is described as being worse than the death penalty. Confirmation of these values comes from Marius' speech which ascribes overwhelming influence to the *imagines* and the memory of past achievements they evoked. The very fact that *imagines* were so central to Roman political culture serves to characterize that culture as based on honour and the public recognition of accepted virtues and behaviour patterns.[58]

[56] See ll. 7-10, 100-4 and 109-20.   [57] See ll. 114-20.
[58] For a discussion of Rome as a 'shame culture', see the preface.

2

Defining the *Imagines?*

> Le plus pauvre quirite, sans ouvrir un livre, pouvait voir à cer-
> tains jours l'histoire romaine passer dans la rue.
>
> (Martha (1883) 58)

A STUDY of the *imagines maiorum* must ask what they actually were.
This question includes both the physical nature of Roman ancestor
masks and their role and meaning as social artefacts. In this chapter the outward appearance of the *imagines* will be addressed first.
Their evolving function in Roman culture is a more complex matter which forms the subject of the rest of this study. However, the
legal position of the *imagines* is so intimately linked with their material definition that both aspects are treated together here. My immediate concern is to show how physical character and legal status
can combine to provide a definition of the *imagines maiorum* in their
original context.

1. *What were the* Imagines?

1a. *The Meaning of the Word* Imago

The Latin word *imago* has many senses, as well as nuances of meaning within different senses. This has proved a major difficulty in
investigating the definition of *imagines maiorum* as the technical
term for Roman wax portraits of male ancestors kept in the *atrium*
and displayed at aristocratic funerals. From meaning 'ancestor portrait' *imago* can be used by extension to mean 'ancestor'.[1] In the

---

[1] e.g. Cic. *Leg. Agr.* 2. 100 = T8; *Cael.* 34 = T5; *Planc.* 51 = T15; *Pis.* 1 = T13;
De Or. 2. 225 = T23; *Sull.* 27 = T18; Sall. *Hist.* 3 fr. 48. 18 = T67; Livy 1. 47. 4
= T38; Val. Max. 3. 3. 7 = T97; Sen. *De Clem.* 1. 9. 10 = T73; Tac. *Hist.* 2. 76.
2 = T94; Plin. *Ep.* 5. 17. 6 = T57.

plural *maiorum* may be added for greater clarification. An alternative word used only in poetry is *cerae* ('wax things').[2]

The uses of the term *imago* have been studied by Daut and by Lahusen. They both subscribe to the view that the original meaning of the word was indeed 'ancestor portrait' (*Ahnenbild*) in the peculiarly Roman sense of wax mask.[3] They draw this conclusion from the use of the word in Cicero and Livy. Further support comes from numerous passages in Sallust, Tacitus, and Valerius Maximus, who are the other principal authors to refer to the *imagines maiorum* with some frequency.

Daut and Lahusen have also shown that *imago* is a flexible term in Roman art, which could be used to describe a representation of a human, whether living or dead, in many media including paintings, representations on gems or coins, reliefs, busts, and shield portraits.[4] When paired with *statuae*, the common and almost formulaic expression *statuae et imagines* refers, in a convenient shorthand, to all representations of persons.[5] In this context the *imago* part of the term has particular reference to busts or reliefs as opposed to statues.

We are not in a position to know whether *imago* ever meant only 'ancestor mask'. Several meanings are attested in Plautus, the earliest extant author to use the word. *Imago* is used to refer to physical appearance in plays dealing with doubles and disguises, in which two characters look identical.[6] It is in this context that our first reference to ancestor mask appears (*Am.* 458 = T53). For Plautus *imago* conveys the idea of 'exact likeness' or 'copy'.[7] In the

---

[2] For *cerae* see Ov. *Am.* 1. 8. 65 = T50; *Fast.* 1. 591 = T51; Mart. 7. 44 = T49; Juv. 8. 19 = T35. It is important to note that *imagines maiorum* were not the only form of wax portraiture, cf. von Schlosser (1910-11). Ov. *Ep.* 13. 149-56; *Rem.* 723-4; and Mart. 11. 102 refer to lifelike wax portraits kept by a lover as a special memento. Horace, *S.* 1. 8. 40-5 and *Epod.* 17. 76-81, mentions wax dolls used by witches in magic rituals; cf. Faraone (1991) for discussion of this widespread practice in Greece and the Near East. Servius, *A.* 8. 634 counts wax as one of several media worked by a *fictor*.
[3] Ernout (1941) 87: 'Le sens le plus ancien est peut-être celui de "portrait d'ancêtre".' Daut (1975) 43; Lahusen (1982) 103 n. 36.
[4] Lahusen (1982) 108 gives a convenient summary. Pliny, *Nat.* 35. 4-13 = T54, illustrates many different uses of *imago* within one passage.
[5] Daut (1975) 49-52 and Lahusen (1982) 101-3. Cf. *S.C. de Cn. Pisone patre* ll. 75-6 = I16 which uses this expression as a legal description to denote all public representations of Piso.
[6] *Am.* 121; 124; 141; 265; *Capt.* 39; *Men.* 1063; *Mil.* 151.
[7] *Men.* 1063: *Tuast imago. tam consimilest quam potest* ('He is your very image. He is as like you as it is possible to be'). Cf. *Cas.* 515.

Pseudolus, imago refers to the portrait of a soldier on his ring, which is given as a pledge with a deposit of money.[8] It seems that *imago* had developed a variety of meanings, both abstract and concrete, by the time Plautus was writing.

Daut has drawn attention to the fact that *imago* is never used as a critical term in any context discussing art during the Republic.[9] Nor is it combined with any aesthetic adjectives. He concludes that its main value is social, gentilicial, and moral. Such an interpretation is especially supported by Pliny's contrast (*Nat.* 35. 6 = T54) between the traditional *imagines* and the more costly and attractive examples of Greek art that were popular in his day. *Imago* is an evocative word used to special effect in speeches and by historians writing in Latin.[10] It seems fair to ask how far its repeated use by Sallust, and especially by Tacitus, carries overtones of conscious archaism or at least of a special focus on republican mores and values.

The adjectives used to qualify *imagines* or *cerae* are *superbus, immodicus, vetus, priscus, subitus, fumosus, senatorius, clarus, generosissimus, inlustris, virilis, domesticus, triumphalis, honoratissimus, vividus, severitate conspicuus* (proud, extravagant, ancient, antique, hastily acquired, smoky, senatorial, distinguished, very high-born, illustrious, manly, belonging to the family, triumphal, highly honoured, lifelike, famous for severity).[11] These words emphasize the traditional and consciously 'antique' character of the *imagines* in our sources, mostly writers of the late Republic and early Empire. Ancestor masks are closely associated with the status and claims of the office-holding aristocracy, mostly in a positive sense, but sometimes with negative connotations of arrogance or of exaggerated pretensions.

The work of Daut and Lahusen is mainly concerned with *imago* as a descriptive term in art (*Bildnisbegriff*). Outside of art its field of meaning is extensive and highly suggestive for the wide range of

[8] *Ps.* 56; 649; 986; 1000; 1097; 1202.   [9] Daut (1975) 53.
[10] These uses are discussed in Ch. 5 § 5.
[11] For *imago* with an adjective see Cic. *Cael.* 33 = T5, *Pis.* 1 = T13; *Sul.* 27 = T18; Livy 3. 58. 2 = T39; Hor. *Ep.* 8. 11–12 = T34; Prop. 1. 5. 23–4 = T62; Val. Max. 2. 9. 6 = T96; 3. 3. 7 = T97; 3. 5 = T98; 5. 8. 3 = T103; Sen. *Dial.* 12. 7 = T72; *Ep.* 44. 5 = T75; 76. 12 = T76; Plin. *Ep.* 8. 10. 3 = T58; Tac. *Hist.* 4. 39. 2 = T95; Mart. 2. 90. 6 = T47; 5. 20. 7 = T48; Sil. 10. 567 = T78; Suet. *Aug.* 4. 1 = T80; Boethius *Con.*1 *pros.*1 = T4. For *cerae* with an adjective see Ov. *Am.* 1. 8. 65 = T50; *Fast.* 1. 591 = T51; Mart. 7. 44 = T49; Juv. 8. 19 = T35.

concepts it could contain. In particular, its more abstract senses surely shed some light on *imago* as 'ancestor portrait'. Such uses include 'ghost',[12] 'reflection'[13], 'imitation',[14] 'simile',[15] 'model',[16] 'example or personification',[17] 'visible form or shape'[18], 'species'.[19] The meaning 'ghost' is a natural development from *imago* as 'what our ancestors actually looked like' or 'how they appear to us now',[20] as well as *imago* as an actual synonym for 'ancestor'. 'Ghost' suggests being in the presence of the dead and yet, at the same time, raises a doubt about the reality of such a vision.

Uses of *imago* also range from 'exact copy'[21] or 'true likeness' to 'mere imitation' or 'outward form'. *Imago* can express ideas of 'reality' and 'truth' as well as notions of 'mere reflection', and especially of 'illusion'. It is not hard to see how such concepts are related to the ancestor portrait, which was lifelike, especially when worn in a funeral procession. It made the dead appear to come to life again and allowed them to enter the city once more, whereas their usual place was outside the *pomerium*.[22] In this way the *imago* enabled Romans to view their past history as a pageant.[23] At the same time the *imagines* were powerful symbols in Roman culture, bringing to mind the ancestors with their deeds and values. The various uses of the word *imago* help to suggest the studied awareness Romans had of the function of ancestor portraits as both symbol and reality within their culture.

---

[12] Cic. *Div.* 1. 63; Verg. *Aen.* 1. 353; Prop. 1. 19. 11, Sen. *Con.* 9. 1. 8: *Steterunt ante oculos meos maiorum imagines emissusque sede sua Miltiades maiestate imperatoria refulsit et iterum meas invocavit manus* ('The ghosts of my ancestors stood before my eyes and Miltiades emerged from his resting place and shone with the glory of a general and again called for my hands to help').

[13] Varro, *Rust.* 3. 16. 12; Lucr. 4. 156.   [14] Livy 3. 16. 5; Tac. *Hist.* 1. 84.

[15] *Rhet. Her.* 4. 62; Cic. *De Or.* 2. 266.   [16] Lucr. 2. 112; Cic. *Q. Rosc.* 47.

[17] Cic. *Sest.* 19; Livy 9. 38. 4.   [18] Verg. *Aen.* 8. 23; Ov. *Met.* 6. 110.

[19] Verg. *Aen.* 2. 369; Tac. *Hist.* 3. 28.

[20] e.g. Africanus' ghost appears to Aemilianus at the beginning of the *Somnium Scipionis* (Cic. *Rep.* 6. 10 = T25).

[21] Plaut. *Am.* 131; Cic. *Q. fr.* 1. 3. 3; *Tusc.* 1. 92. Concentrating mainly on the usage of Cicero, Daut (1975) 54 concludes that *imago* often translates notions of 'exact likeness' or 'true copy'.

[22] Dupont (1987) 170 makes a special point of the fact that the law of the Twelve Tables forbade the burial of the dead within the city.

[23] Novara (1987) has suggested that this spectacle inspired the parade of Roman heroes at the end of *Aeneid* 6. Cf. Ch. 4 § 3, and 8 § 2.

1b. *The Physical Appearance of the* Imagines Maiorum

The exact physical nature of the *imagines maiorum* has been a vexed question in scholarship for over a century.[24] For this there are two main reasons. First, and most importantly, we have no physical remains of any wax masks.[25] Second, and as a consequence of no masks having survived, some scholars have been tempted to adapt the description of *imagines* to fit their theories about the origins of the masks.[26] This procedure can lead to a circular type of argument, in which the descriptions of the *imagines*, as adapted to fit theories of their origins, are then themselves used to support those same theories. We have no direct testimony from the Romans as to where the *imagines* came from or exactly how old they were. Any theory about their origin is necessarily speculative.[27] Moreover, their ultimate derivation is an essentially separate question from their form and function within Roman society. In order to understand the *imagines* in their historical context we must rely on direct evidence from ancient authors who were in a position to know the facts.

Our two longest and most important literary descriptions of the *imagines* are to be found in Polybius (6. 53-4 = T61) and Pliny the Elder (*Nat.* 35. 4-14 = T54).[28] Any interpretation must start with

[24] Definitions found in previous scholarship include the following: Benndorf (1878), followed by von Schlosser (1910-11): the *imago* was a bust reworked from a copy of the death mask covering the face of the corpse at the funeral. Kaschnitz-Weinberg (1926) and Zadoks (1932): the death mask from the *collocatio* was used as an *imago* but later replaced by an ordinary bust. Bethe (1935) followed by Rowell (1940), Vessberg (1941), Boethius (1942), and Schweitzer (1948): the *imagines* were actual wax death masks. Brommer (1953-4): an *imago* is a realistic mask but has no connection with a death mask. Drerup (1980): *imagines* are small life masks exactly reproducing the features of the dead and worn by dressed dolls at the funeral. Lahusen (1985b): the *imagines* are busts closely resembling reliefs on the tombs of freedmen from the Augustan age. Jackson (1987): the *imagines* were probably closely related to death masks.

[25] See Introd. for discussion.

[26] Benndorf (1878) has been most influential in arguing that the *imago* must have originated as a death mask used at a *collocatio*, and therefore was an exact reproduction. He posited an elaborate schema of two death masks and a bust for each ancestor. Bethe (1935) argued that the *imagines* grew out of an early custom of burying the dead within the house. Boethius (1942) was misled by his wish to see the *imagines* as part of heroization or even apotheosis of the dead, following putative Etruscan models, suggested primarily by the Warrior of Capestrano.

[27] Colonna and von Hase's (1986) suggestion of an Etruscan origin is discussed in Appendix D.

[28] It is notable that this passage of Pliny does not appear in Jex-Blake and Sellers' (1896/1968) excerpts of Pliny about the history of art. The sections appear in six

these witnesses, both of whom had wide access to relevant information. Their evidence can now be supplemented by the *S.C. de Cn.
Pisone patre* (I16) which clarifies the legal position of the *imagines* in
the early imperial period. Polybius is the most useful source because
he was a reliable observer of Roman customs of the mid-second century BC,[29] who had the chance to attend funerals of office-holders,[30]
and who frequented various aristocratic houses as an intimate.

Polybius tells us that the *imagines* were 'realistic' masks worn by
actors in the funeral procession,[31] and ordinarily kept in individual
wooden cupboards in the *atrium* of the house.[32] He stresses the lifelike quality both of the way they looked and of the performance
given by the actors in the funeral procession who were carefully
chosen to suit each role.[33] He emphasizes the 'theatricality' of the
parade of ancestors in all its aspects: the actors did actually aim to
impersonate their subjects. The masks they wore were an essential
element in this performance and must therefore have been akin, in
a practical sense, to masks worn in a theatre.[34] They were functional masks, having eye holes and allowing the actor to breathe
and surely also to speak, if that was required or usual.[35] Whether
they covered the whole head or only the face is unclear. How 'lifelike' they were is impossible to say, but they seem to have been

segments in Pollitt (1966). Isager (1991) 116-17 quotes parts without explaining
their meaning in any detail.

[29] In Rome as a hostage for the Achaean League from 167 BC after the Roman
victory at Pydna, Polybius published this part of his work around 150 BC.

[30] e.g. the funerals of L. Aemilius Paullus in 160 BC (Livy, *Per.* 46), the son of
M. Porcius Cato, and of M. Aemilius Lepidus (Livy, *Per.* 48 = T46) in 152 BC.

[31] I cannot accept the assertion of Drerup (1980) 112 that Polybius is really talking about dressed dolls that looked so real they might have been taken for actors,
despite being under life-size.

[32] 53. 5-6 = T61. The only problem of translation in the Polybius passage concerns ὑπογραφή, which may refer to the outline or general shape. According to
Zadoks (1932) 27 Polybius meant the drawing of the face rather than its paint or
make-up.

[33] Smith (1981) 31 questions what Polybius means by ὁμοιότης (close resemblance). Clearly this cannot be taken as the exact equivalent of a modern technical
term in art history such as 'veristic' despite the many attempts of previous scholars,
but close attention to the text can yield some conclusions.

[34] The assumption made here is that masks were usual in the Roman theatre of
the Republic. See Ch. 4 § 4.

[35] For more discussion of the funeral procession see Ch. 4 § 2. Suet. *Ves.* 19. 2 =
T84 tells of the actor imitating Vespasian by speaking in character. Cf. Brommer
(1953-4) 338.

recognizable and differentiated.[36] Not unlike theatrical masks they may well have exaggerated certain expressions or features considered characteristic of each individual ancestor.

It is evident from Polybius that the masks were images of people as they had looked when they were alive. He makes no connection at all with any death mask, even as a prototype or artist's model.[37] Nor does he link the custom of the ancestor masks with the lying-in-state, a mask to cover the face of the corpse, or a model used to replace a corpse (*Scheinleib*). He says that the mask of the newly deceased man would be placed in its cupboard in the most frequented part of the house *after* the funeral.[38] This tells us nothing about what happened to it before, nor whether it was also worn by an actor at the funeral of the man himself. The whole nature of the procession of ancestors makes it clear that they are represented as in the prime of life and at the peak of their dignity as office-holders. Quintilian makes this plain in his reference to a court case in which a woman displayed a wax death mask of her husband to the general hilarity of all present.[39] Indeed wax was chosen as the medium, despite its perishability, precisely for its lifelike qualities.[40] These characteristics were seen to outweigh the effort of maintenance, which must have been considerable and constant if masks always had to be ready at short notice for use in a funeral procession.

Polybius' information about the physical appearance of the *imagines* is confirmed in a striking way by the elder Pliny writing over 200 years later. He also sees wax 'faces' (*vultus*), kept in cupboards in the *atrium* and paraded at funerals, as the most typical form of portrait art practised by his Roman ancestors.[41] His complex discussion has proved controversial because of its polemical character and rapid progression from one subject to the next.[42] His main point

---

[36] Zinserling (1959/60) 422: 'Wenn der Römer die Masken seiner Ahnen imagines nennt, so drückt er damit zumindest aus, daß diese Masken dem Verstorbenen außerordentlich ähnlich waren.'

[37] See Gruen (1992) 155: 'The connection between death masks and ancestral portraits is quite tenuous.'

[38] Poly. 6. 53. 4 = T61.   [39] Quint. *Inst.* 6. 1. 40.

[40] These can be seen in the case of the Cumae head and in modern wax portraits, as well as in those dating from the seventeenth century and earlier.

[41] Plin. *Nat.* 35. 6 = T54 opens the section on traditional Roman art.

[42] Vessberg (1941) thought the whole passage was about painting. One may also cite the untenable assertions of Winkes (1969) and (1979) that virtually the whole passage refers solely to *imagines clipeatae*, when these are actually introduced for the first time in section 12.

is that new standards of luxury and foreign influence have changed Roman tastes and encouraged unprecedented and costly Hellenistic-type works of art at the expense of traditional Roman genres and media. The unifying theme underlying the passage is his moral castigation of fashionable and changing tastes, rather than a focus on any particular type of representative art. The tendency of his narrative needs to be kept in mind and may have led to some exaggeration and simplification. Pliny was, however, thoroughly informed as a result of his energetic and wide-ranging research.[43]

The *imagines* occupy a key position in his argument as the archetypal example of traditional Roman art kept in the home. He opposes them specifically to Greek art, to underline their native origins, and presumably also to suggest a contrast of style and appearance. Such a presentation of opposites would only make sense if the *imagines*, which he also emphasizes as being lifelike representations of recognizably differentiated individuals, were indeed different from the types of portraiture that could be classified by Pliny as typically Greek.[44] The natural conclusion is that even in the later first century AD the realism of the *imagines* had not been changed by Greek idealizing styles in any significant way. His statements cast doubt on any theories that by the late Republic or early imperial age the *imagines* were no longer a separate art form, and had become integrated with portraiture in general.[45]

Pliny's other point of comparison concerns cost, as he contrasts the unpretentious wax masks with newly fashionable portraits, executed in precious metals.[46] Beeswax was a cheap commodity in the Roman world with many uses in everyday life.[47] Pliny contrasts the 'simplicity' of wax with the 'showiness' and glamour of metals. Inherent in both the comparisons of style and of medium is his concern with the moral function of art. For him the *imagines* represent 'real art' because their intention was to show actual likenesses of individuals, and thus to preserve the memory of 'who they were'

[43] Plin. *Ep.* 3. 5 describes his uncle's working methods.
[44] *ut essent imagines* is not an easy phrase to translate. Plin. seems to mean 'so that they really did serve as *imagines*'. Zadoks (1932) 30 is quite wrong in asserting that this shows *imago* was not usually the technical term for ancestor mask.
[45] This has been argued especially by Zadoks (1932), but also by Vessberg (1941), Boethius (1942), and Schweitzer (1948).
[46] Plin. *Nat.* 35. 6 = T54.
[47] Columella 9. 16. 1; Plin. *Nat.* 11. 11; Cf. R. Büll and E. Moser, *RE* Wachs (Suppl. 13. 1347-416).

and 'what they looked like' as an essential part of 'what they stood for'. He sees this aim as completely lost in more modern art. This must mean that the *imagines* were indeed more realistic, if more naïve or primitive, than contemporary Hellenistic art. His writing suggests that the artistic canons associated with the *imagines* were well enough known in his time for him not to need to explain the basis of his comparisons in detail.[48] All this is not to say that a Flavian *imago* would have looked exactly like one dating to the time of the Third Punic War, but they would apparently have shared similar aims and artistic effects. The testimony of Polybius and Pliny, when taken together, points to the likelihood that there was indeed a special artistic vocabulary which Romans associated with their *imagines*, even if it is not recoverable for us now.

1c. *A Variety of Ancestral* Imagines *in the Roman House*

Pliny tells us that by his day a Roman house might contain numerous portraits of ancestors in various genres. Most of them were apparently considered 'traditional' and had probably been introduced at different times. They could all be termed *imagines*. Finds from Pompeii show that bronze busts and portrait herms of ancestors were sometimes found in the *atrium*, in front of the *tablinum*.[49] In his references to the entrance and main reception areas of a Roman house Pliny mentions four different types of *ancestor portraits*, namely:

(a) wax face masks kept in cupboards in the *atrium*,[50]
(b) painted portraits (*imagines pictae*) as part of a family tree, either on a board (*tabula*) or painted on the wall,[51]

---

[48] He claims that the art of painting (35. 4 *imaginum pictura*) has died out, perhaps referring also to the painted portraits of the family tree (35. 6). He nowhere suggests that the *imagines* are an obsolete genre, which is confirmed by literary *testimonia* reaching to the 6th cent. AD.

[49] Maiuri (1937) pl. 19 and Dwyer (1982) 127-8. Such ancestral portraits were carefully differentiated from busts of famous philosophers, poets, mythical figures, or Hellenistic kings, usually kept in the garden. See also the arrangement of statues found at the Villa dei Papyri at Herculaneum, which is discussed by Wojcik (1986), Neudecker (1988), and Warden (1991).

[50] 35. 6: *expressi cera vultus singulis disponebantur armariis, ut essent imagines, quae comitarentur gentilicia funera* ('faces rendered in wax were arranged in separate cupboards, so that they should be "true portraits" to accompany funerals in the extended family').

[51] 35. 6: *stemmata vero lineis discurrebant ad imagines pictas* ('Moreover, the family trees traced their lines to painted portraits'). For family trees see also Mart. 4. 40. 1; 5. 35. 4; Suet. *Gal.* 2 = T82; *Ves.* 12; Plut. *Num.* 21. 4; *H. A. Sev. Alex.* 44. 3; Isid. *Etym.* 9. 6. 28.

(*c*) other images (*aliae imagines*) of specially famous ancestors with trophies which were located outside and around the entrance,[52]

(*d*) shield portraits (*imagines clipeatae*).[53]

As Pliny himself mentions there were even differences in the legal status of these *imagines*. The *aliae imagines* and their associated trophies (*c*) were considered an integral part of the building rather than moveable property, and could therefore not be removed even when a house was sold.[54] Propertius (1. 16. 1–4) confirms that a triumph ended at the house of the general and brought his share of the spoils to his own door.[55] Suetonius (*Nero* 38. 2) tells us that at the time of the great fire in Rome in AD 64 many traditional aristocratic houses were still displaying republican trophies, and much was destroyed then.[56]

Wax *imagines* in cupboards (*a*) formed the largest and most typical of Pliny's four distinct groups. That is also why they head Pliny's list. It should not surprise us that an *atrium* crowded with *imagines* would often be accompanied and explained by a painted family tree (*b*), including individual small portraits. Pliny's other two categories (*c* and *d*) were particularly associated with great military victories,

---

[52] 35. 7: *aliae foris et circa limina animorum ingentium imagines erant adfixis hostium spoliis* ('Outside and around the entrance door there were other portraits of great men, with enemy spoils attached to them').

[53] 35. 12–13: *clupeos.* These were first displayed in a private house by M. Aemilius Lepidus, cos. 78 BC and are discussed in Ch. 3 § 2*b*. Ling (1991) 157–9 notes that portraits are unusual in wall-painting, except copies of *imagines clipeatae* or portraits in tondos mostly found in the *atrium*, *alae*, and *tablinum*. See his Ills. 168–70.

[54] Presumably this situation was a result of the assumption that family property would never be alienated while there were still descendants to inherit. Düll (1962) 133–4 discusses the legal aspects of *imagines*. Wax masks of ancestors were classed as *res privata*. Pliny's language does not indicate that these were outside the house as suggested by Croisille (1985).

[55] See Polyb. 6. 39. 10 and Livy 23. 23. 6 (with Livy 10. 7. 9) for spoils in the houses of ordinary soldiers, who were awarded them as military decorations. Coarelli (1984) discusses an example of an inscribed cuirass which seems to have been taken and displayed as spoils by a Roman in the 4th cent. BC. See Rawson (1990) for a full discussion of spoils and the antiquarian tradition.

[56] Cf. Plut. *C. Gracch.* 15. 1 for the spoils and armour kept in Fulvius Flaccus' house, as well as Prop. 4. 11. 29–32, and Plut. *Q. Rom.* 37. Livy 38. 43. 10 implies that the spoils of Ambracia are at Fulvius Nobilior's house. Plut. *Flam.* 13. 6–14 suggests spoils were also put up to mark some diplomatic successes before Augustus' much heralded settlement with the Parthians. Cf. Cato, *ORF*[4] fr. 97: *ne spolia figerentur nisi de hoste capta* ('that spoils should not be put up unless they have been captured from an enemy').

presenting famous ancestors with their trophies or on portrait shields. They were probably exceptional kinds of *imagines* executed in more costly materials and only put up to commemorate the great victories of certain families. It is notable that trophies had pride of place nearest the door in the entrance and away from the common herd of ancestors in the *atrium*. Both types of martial *imagines* might have been a development after Sulla, as can be demonstrated for the *imagines clipeatae*.

There are still other *imagines*, perhaps of a more local character and not mentioned by Pliny, which could be found in the aristocratic house. Significant finds were made in the Casa del Menandro at Pompeii, dating to the time of the eruption in AD 79 in which Pliny also died (see Figs. 1 and 2).[57] The remains of four simple busts of ancestors have been identified in a special niche (*exedra* 25) at the back of the peristyle garden (see Pl. 2).[58] These rather roughly executed pieces are slightly smaller than life size and were made of an organic matter such as wax or more likely wood. They were found with the statue of a small seated nude boy wearing a garland, who is taken to be a *lar domesticus*. The two large iron nails originally found over the niche suggest it was usually closed off with a wood door or a curtain.[59] The *exedra* is decorated with wall-paintings in the Second Style. Maiuri has postulated a private domestic cult of a traditional nature still flourishing in AD 79. The unique discovery of old *imagines in situ* is at odds with the sophisticated and luxurious house designed and decorated under Hellenistic influence. The contrast provides a striking illustration of what Pliny was talking about.

At the time of its destruction the house appears to have belonged to a branch of the Poppaei, the family of Nero's wife Poppaea Sabina.[60] This was a rich family, related to the two Poppaei who

[57] For a general account of the Casa del Menandro, see Maiuri (1933), Drerup (1959) 155 ff., Ling (1983), Wallace-Hadrill (1988) 64, 79, 83, 88, and Richardson (1988) 159-61.

[58] Maiuri (1933) 98-106 and figs. 47-9. Tav. 2 shows the niche in colour. De Franciscis (1951) 19-51 with figure 1 and 7-9 notes that the ancestor found next to the seated boy is bald and resembles a marble bust from the Casa degli Amorini dorati which belonged to the same family.

[59] These nails were no longer in evidence when I visited the house in August 1993.

[60] M. della Corte (1965) 72-84, 130ff., 292-4 attributes five houses in Pompeii to the Poppaei, including the Casa del Menandro (Q. Poppaeus Sabinus), the Casa degli Amorini dorati (Cn. Poppaeus Habitus) and a school (ludimagister Potitus

were both consuls in AD 9 (*RE* 1 and 2).[61] The house had been recently and sumptuously redecorated apparently at the time of the family's prominence under Nero. The paintings in *exedra* 25 are amongst very few to be preserved from an earlier time.[62] Their conservation indicates the importance of this space to the family, who had probably owned the house for some time.[63]

The contrast with Polybius' and Pliny's *imagines* is clear.[64] The 'ancestors' from the Casa del Menandro are busts, probably of wood and under life size, rather than wax masks. Similar finds of wooden busts from Herculaneum, which remain unpublished, suggest parallels.[65] Although the details of their features are lost, they were certainly not notably realistic and were housed in a niche together rather than in separate cupboards. Unlike Roman *imagines maiorum* these busts were associated with a family cult.[66] Not kept in the *atrium*, they were accorded a place of honour in a fine *exedra*, decorated to recall a rustic sanctuary, and they provided the focus for the west side of the peristyle. Occupants of the sitting room opposite (*oecus* 11) would have had a good overall view of the niche.[67]

Poppaei Sabini). The seal of the freedman procurator of Q. Poppaeus was found in the servants' quarters in the Casa del Menandro; cf. Castrén (1975) 209 no. 320. It is unclear whether he is the same man who was a local aedile in AD 39/40 or 61.

[61] For the wealth of the Poppaei and their position in town, see M. T. Griffin (1984) 101-2. Poppaea Sabina owned brick works near Pompeii (*AE* 1955 no. 199 = *PP* 9 (1954) 56-7; cf. Steinby (1974-5) 82 and 85). She also owned the luxurious seaside villa at Oplontis; cf. de Franciscis (1979) and J. R. Clarke (1991) 21-3, 166-70. Pompeii was made a colony by Nero in honour of his wife (*ILS* 6444, cf. 234). Her father's family, the Ollii, were also prominent locally (Castrén (1975) 199 no. 288) and owned the Casa di Pansa (M. della Corte (1965) nos. 171-3).

[62] See Wallace-Hadrill (1988) 88 who discusses the juxtaposition between old and new with special reference to *exedra* 25. Ling (1983) 45 notes that the Second Style paintings of *exedra* 25 help to date the present layout of the peristyle to 40-30 BC.

[63] M. della Corte (1965) 292-9 discusses the architecture and decoration of the house as it reflects the lifestyle of the family, but without reference to the ancestral portraits in *exedra* 25.

[64] J. R. Clarke (1991) 192-3 wrongly takes these to be actual *imagines*. I find it hard to accept his assertion that copying would have produced ever smaller versions.

[65] Ward-Perkins and Claridge (1978) 76-7. There were also female ones judging from the finds in Herculaneum; therefore they cannot have been associated only with office-holders, or may perhaps have included local priestesses. Maiuri (1937) 400 with fig. 489 for the wooden bust from the Casa del Graticcio at Herculaneum.

[66] There is no evidence for cult associated with the *imagines maiorum*; see Bömer (1943) 104 ff., esp. 115, and Ch. 6 § 4 below for this vital question. J. R. Clarke's (1991) 7 contention that portable altars were used in the *atrium* is based on an argument from silence.

[67] Cf. J. R. Clarke (1991) fig. 6. However, the busts were hidden from a viewer in *oecus* 11.

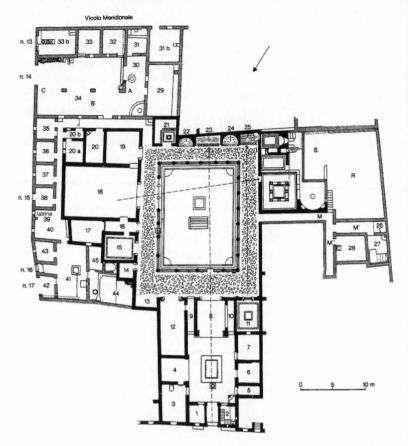

FIG. I. Plan of the Casa del Menandro, Pompeii.

The four busts may represent only the originators of the *gens* Poppaea or distant but famous ancestors of the owner of the house.[68] The Poppaei were certainly entitled to Roman-style *imagines* in the *atria* of their houses, whether in Rome or elsewhere.[69]

[68] This family may be the same as the Poppaei from Interamna Praetuttianorum in Picenum (*ILS* 5671 and 6562). Cf. Syme (1938) 7 n. 23 and Castrén (1975) 209 with *CIL* I². 375. M. della Corte (1965) identifies the last owners as Q. Poppaeus Sabinus and his wife Vatinia Primigenia.

[69] M. della Corte (1965) notes that the family owned many houses and only seem to have come here for short stays. He assumes they would have spent most of their time in Rome.

44

FIG. 2. Vista from the entrance of the Casa del Menandro, Pompeii.

The owner of this house also chose to draw attention to other, perhaps typically local, ancestral portraits. They serve as memorable
reminders of the survival and traditional nature of different genres
of ancestral images to be found alongside the *imagines maiorum* in
the families of Roman office-holders.

1d. *The Tradition of* Imagines *in Rome*

The origins of *imagines* in Rome itself remain obscure and are never
commented on directly by any ancient source. Livy attributes the
custom to the regal period and gives several references in his treatment of the early Republic. Yet these passages are not specific and
mostly occur in speeches at dramatic moments, forming part of the
rhetorical material which the historian has added to enliven his
narrative. During the first century BC families certainly possessed
and displayed *imagines* of ancestors from the early Republic, but the
age of these objects is not documented.[70] The Romans generally
considered this an ancient custom.[71]

In a passage at the end of his prologue to the *Jugurtha* (4. 5–6 =
T63), Sallust speaks of the inspiration drawn from their ancestors'
imagines by earlier statesmen, specifically Fabius Maximus and
Scipio Africanus. This is important to Sallust who is using the whole
notion of the influence and power of historical *exempla* to justify his
writing of history.[72] Indeed, he refers to a general oral tradition for
which he claims to have personal evidence (*saepe ego audivi* 'I have
often heard'). Africanus was born in 236 BC, but Fabius Maximus
probably in the 290s BC. We have firmer evidence for their own
imagines and for others from the Punic War era.[73] The reference to
their ancestors offers a glimpse of a tradition of *imagines* stretching
back into the fourth century BC. Sallust evidently thought of the
imagines as a custom dating back before the third century BC. It is
not possible for us to say how firm a basis he had for this.

The earliest Roman author to mention *imagines* is Plautus at
Amphitryo 458 = T53, probably dating to the 190s BC. The context

---

[70] e.g. M. Junius Brutus cos. 509 BC (Cic. *Phil.* 2. 26 = T12, *De Or.* 2. 225 =
T23), M. Manlius Capitolinus cos. 392 BC (Cic. *Sul.* 27 = T18), L. Papirius
Mugillanus cos. suff. 444 BC (*Fam.* 9. 21 = T24). For a fuller list of named *imagines*
consult Lahusen (1985*b*) 266.

[71] Cf. Dio 47. 19. 2 = T27.

[72] See Steidle (1958) 110 on the meaning of this passage in context.

[73] Punic War era: Cic. *Clu.* 72 = T6; Livy 22. 31. 8–11 = T43; Val. Max. 8. 15.
1–2 = T104; Sil. 10. 566–7 = T78; App. *Iber.* 89 = T2.

shows that he has in mind lifelike *imagines* worn at funerals, perhaps even at a man's own funeral by someone impersonating him
as closely as possible.[74] The slave Sosia has been confronting
Mercury, who is his double. He likens Mercury to an actor wearing
his *imago* after death, a thing that will certainly not happen in his
case. The humour arises from the unexpected picture of a slave
imagining a senatorial ancestor mask of himself.[75] It also depends
on the *imago* being a realistic representation, which could be imagined as someone's 'double'. This joke about *imagines* comes at the
end of the longest scene in Plautus. The brief mention in passing
shows that the custom was well known to his audience by this date.

As discussed above, Plautus makes much of the word *imago*,
playing on its meaning of 'exact likeness' or 'double'. It fits well into
his concern to make his plays topical by parody of Roman aristocratic mores, especially when presented in the mouths of slaves.[76]
The nature of the *imagines* provides Plautus with a chance to allude
to nuances of appearance and reality, transformation and illusion.[77]
He shows that the *imagines*, and the values they stood for, were fully
developed by the end of the Second Punic War. Other second-century evidence for *imagines* comes from Polybius (*c.*150 BC) and
Afranius (*Vopiscus* 12. 364–5 = T2, *c.*130s BC). Titus Manlius
Torquatus' severe treatment of his son D. Junius Silanus under the
influence of his ancestors and their *imagines* in 140 BC fits into this
historical context.[78] Surviving evidence from Roman sources,
therefore, reveals little about the origin of the *imagines*. They appear
fully developed when they are first mentioned by a contemporary
writer.

[74] Plaut. *Am.* 458–9 = T53: *nam hic quidem omnem imaginem meam, quae antehac
fuerat, possidet.* | *vivo fit quod numquam quisquam mortuo faciet mihi* ('For surely this
man has taken possession of my whole appearance | mask, as it was before. I expe-
rience in life what no one will ever do for me once I am dead'). *Possidet* plays on *possessor*, the term for someone who occupies a piece of land without owning it.
[75] The passage implies that the mask is worn at a man's own funeral and that
the actor wearing it would impersonate him. Cf. Ch. 4 for the funeral procession.
[76] Earl (1960) and more recently Gruen (1990) 124–57 discuss Plautus' concern
with Roman institutions. Amphitryo himself serves as a good example of a Roman
general returning home laden with booty, while the humour in Alcmena's situation
comes principally from her portrayal as an archetypal Roman matron (Segal (1987)
178 ff.).
[77] Fraenkel (1960) 28 calls this conceit 'un concetto romano in veste romana'.
[78] Cic. *Fin.* 1. 7. 24.; Livy *Per.* 54; *Oxy. Per.* 54; Val. Max. 5. 8. 3 = T103.

1e. *The* Imago *of Scipio Africanus in the Temple of Jupiter Optimus Maximus*

Within a few years of Plautus' play we have controversial evidence for an *imago* of Scipio Africanus, which was kept in the temple of Jupiter Optimus Maximus on the Capitol. In apparently independent accounts, Valerius Maximus and Appian attest the existence of an image of Scipio Africanus stored in the temple in their own day.[79] In both passages the authors clearly have in mind an *imago* or ancestor mask of Scipio Africanus, rather than a statue, bust, or other type of portrait. The *imago* of Scipio is associated closely with family funerals in a way typical for a Roman ancestor mask. Valerius Maximus confirms this identification in his reference to the *atrium*. In his view, keeping Scipio's *imago* in the *cella* of Jupiter makes the temple, or at least this area of it, like the *atrium* in a family house of the Cornelii. Valerius' testimony is significant because he is an author especially interested in the *imagines*, who was evidently familiar with them and their uses.

Scipio's is the only instance of an *imago* being kept in a temple in our extant evidence. That is not to say that it was the only *imago* of Scipio in existence. Any relative, either by marriage or by blood, would normally be entitled to keep Africanus' *imago* in his or her *atrium*.[80] It does, however, point to specific claims made by the Cornelii after his death. They chose to use the particular medium of the ancestor mask to celebrate and remember their kinsman in a public space in the city. It is tempting to follow Valerius Maximus in interpreting this as a claim that the temple was in some special sense a home to Africanus during his lifetime.[81]

The remarks in both sources are occasioned by the detour involved in family funeral processions, which had to fetch Africanus' *imago* from the temple. As far as we know a funeral procession would go from the house of the deceased to the Forum without any stops on the way. Although our sources are not explicit on this point, they imply that the whole procession started at the house and continued up to the temple of Jupiter on the Capitol to pick up Africanus, before making its way to the Forum. This would have

---

[79] Val. Max. 8. 15. 1–2 = T104 and App. *Iber.* 89 = T2.

[80] Cf. Cic. *Rep.* 6. 10 = T25; *S.C. de Cn. Pisone patre* = 116; Plin. *Nat.* 35. 8 = T54.

[81] Val. Max. 8. 15. 2 = T104: *unique illi instar atrii Capitolium est* ('For him alone the Capitoline temple is like his *atrium*').

made the parade of ancestors more spectacular and longer, while allowing Africanus to take his place in the chronological procession of earlier Cornelii.

A further reason for extending the processional route can be found in the situation of Africanus' own house. Livy tells us that it lay just outside the Forum, behind the Tabernae Veteres near the statue of Vortumnus, on the site subsequently used for the Basilica Sempronia.[82] Any procession originating there would not have had far to go to reach the Forum. The final descent of the funeral procession into the Forum from the temple of Jupiter would have been down the clivus Capitolinus, reversing the route usual for a triumph. This route also passed the arch set up by Africanus in 190 BC, which was adorned with seven gilded statues, two figures of horses, and two marble basins.[83] Coarelli has suggested that the statues represented Africanus himself and his ancestors, perhaps those office-holders buried in the tomb of the Scipios outside the porta Capena by his day.[84] If the arch straddled the clivus Capitolinus, as has been argued, then funerals of the Cornelii would have passed through it on a special processional route.[85]

Why did the Cornelii put an *imago* of Scipio Africanus in the temple of Jupiter on the Capitol? The most logical answer seems to be that it allowed them a very public way of recalling his special connection with Jupiter and this particular temple. Africanus' habit of visiting the temple to communicate with the god and to seek dreams and visions is attested in later sources, notably Livy, Aulus Gellius, Appian, and the anonymous work *De Viris Illustribus*.[86] Gellius mentions that the temple guard dogs did not bark at Scipio, presumably because they knew him well. This evidence points to the practice of sleeping in a temple in the hope of receiving guidance from the god in a dream.

[82] Livy 44. 16. 10, referring to 170 BC. The site has recently been excavated, see Coarelli (1985) 139 with fig. 25 and Carandini (1988).

[83] Livy 37. 3. 7: *P. Cornelius Scipio Africanus, priusquam proficisceretur, fornicem in Capitolio adversus viam qua in Capitolium escenditur cum signis septem auratis et equis duobus et marmores duo labra ante fornicem posuit* ('Before Publius Cornelius Scipio Africanus set out, he put up an arch with seven gilded statues and two horses, and two marble basins in front of the arch, on the Capitol facing the road which goes up to the Capitol'). For arches in general, see Wallace-Hadrill (1990).

[84] Coarelli (1972).

[85] Coarelli (1972) 71–2 and Calabi Limentani (1982) 131. See Hölscher (1990) 80, who sees the most important function of such arches as the display of statues. Cf. Ch. 4 § 2.

[86] Livy 26. 19. 3–9; Gell. 6. 1; *De Vir. Ill.* 49.

Can we assign a secure date to these particular stories about Africanus, amidst the mass of legends about him? Livy records a speech attributed to Tiberius Sempronius Gracchus in 187 BC, claiming that Scipio had refused to allow his *imago* a place in the temple of Jupiter, amongst a list of other extravagant honours offered to him.[87] The same notice can be found in Valerius Maximus, probably taken from Livy. However, Gracchus' speech is generally considered a later invention or at best a school exercise, offering no reliable contemporary testimony.[88]

The earliest secure evidence comes from Polybius book 10 which can be dated to around 150 BC. Twice Polybius alludes to claims that Africanus received special guidance from the gods in dreams.[89] He is clearly aware of a tradition of Africanus as a mystic and is trying to offer an alternative view of him as the cool rationalist, whose success was based on careful calculation, strategy, and talent. The evidence from Polybius is vital in showing that stories of temple visits were current soon after his death. Livy also found these accounts believable.

Such a practice of temple visits fits in with what we know of Scipio's relations with his soldiers, whom he tried to impress with an image of himself as a general specially favoured by the gods and in some way larger than life.[90] At New Carthage he called on Neptune as his special ally in his brilliant, surprise capture of the city. This episode probably marked the beginning of Africanus' fame and the traditions about him.[91] Similarly, after a serious mutiny during his illness in Spain he arranged to appear suddenly in full health, striking fear and awe into his troops. Whether inspired by religious devotion to Jupiter or wishing to make a reputation for himself, it seems likely that Africanus did indeed pay regular visits to the temple on the Capitol.

He was often away from Rome, but when there his temple visits seem to have been a feature of his daily life. They may well have had an effect on the people of the city. Temples were usually only

---

[87] Livy 38. 56. 12–13 = T45 and Val. Max. 4. 1. 6 = T101.

[88] On the question of authenticity, see Walbank (1967) 56, Scullard (1970) 282, and Malcovati (1976) 98. I do not understand Haywood's and Walbank's contention, based on Cic. *Brut.* 79, that no speeches of Gracchus were extant in Cicero's day.

[89] Polyb. 10. 2. 9 and 10. 5.   [90] Polyb. 10. 6 ff., Livy 26. 45 and 28. 26.

[91] So Walbank (1967) 64 ff., *contra* Haywood (1933) 25 ff.

opened to the public on festivals and holidays.[92] Private visits and dedications had to be specially arranged with the *aeditumi*, or temple guardians, who controlled access to temples and were answerable to the aediles.[93] In this way Africanus set himself apart from ordinary worshippers and created an image of himself as the favourite of Jupiter.

No ancient evidence survives to indicate when Scipio's *imago* was first placed in the temple. The installation of his *imago* in the *cella* of Jupiter makes best sense soon after his death, when his habits were still well known and his influence with the *aeditumi* still strong. At a later date there would have been much less motivation for this kind of innovation in the area of the *imagines*, which were objects kept in the family and normally put on display immediately after a man's funeral.[94] By putting Africanus' *imago* in the temple, his family endorsed his claims to a special role there while he was alive. The *imago* made the *cella* of the temple seem like Africanus' own family *atrium*, the room at the heart of family life and at the heart of the image the family offered to the world. At the same time, the *imago* was presumably dedicated to the god and became his property.[95] The choice of the *imago*, rather than a bust or statue, for this public commemoration of Africanus is a gesture which is both bold and intimate.[96]

Some have questioned whether Africanus' *imago* could have been placed in the temple in the tense political atmosphere following the 'trials of the Scipios'.[97] Africanus had been disgraced and had apparently retired to his country estate at Liternum. It appears that he was not buried in the family tomb outside the porta Capena with the other members of his family, but at Liternum, presumably at his own request.[98] On the contrary, the placing of the *imago* in the temple seems natural when interpreted as the reaction of a proud, patrician family to the eclipse of their leading member. Because he was buried at Liternum, they were unable to stage a full funeral for

[92] For the habit of opening temples only on special occasions, see e.g. Livy 30. 17; *S.C. de Cn. Pisone patre* 63–65; Tac. *Ann.* 2. 82. 4; Suet. *Cal.* 6.

[93] Cf. Wissowa (1912) 476–7.   [94] Polyb. 6. 53. 4 = T61.

[95] See Rollin (1979) 88–90 on statues in temple precincts as *res sacrae*.

[96] For the displays associated with Africanus' circle, see Polyb. 32. 12 on the spectacle his wife's lavish jewels and equipment made at festivals.

[97] e.g. Scullard (1970) 21. Haywood (1933) 29 was surely right in seeing this as a family matter. For a reassessment of the background and complex traditions concerning the 'trials of the Scipios', see Gruen (1995).

[98] Coarelli (1972) 73 ff.

him in Rome or to commemorate him in the usual ways at their family tomb on the Appian Way. Their answer to political opponents who had tried to humble Scipio Africanus, and his brother Lucius, was to dedicate his *imago* in the temple of Jupiter Optimus Maximus.

It is true that Scipio's *imago* perhaps needed to be replaced after fire destroyed the temple in 83 BC.[99] Sulla the dictator may have been instrumental in restoring the image of his relative, although the temple was not rededicated until after his death.[100] However, Sulla is not likely to have set up the *imago* in the first place.[101] He was not a direct descendant of Scipio Africanus and was not linked with him in any special way that we know of. Rather, this *imago*, like any other, would have needed regular maintenance and restoration, especially if it appeared at family funerals. The continued use of Africanus' *imago* by the family suggests consistent attention and care, not only at times of crisis such as the fires of 83 BC or of AD 69 in the struggle between Vitellius and Vespasian.[102]

It is logical and reasonable to accept Valerius Maximus' and Appian's testimony that there was an *imago* of Scipio Africanus which was traditionally kept in the *cella* of the temple of Jupiter on the Capitol. It seems most likely that it had been placed there soon after Africanus' death, in the 180s BC. This *imago* was in use at funerals of the Cornelii into the Antonine period. The *imago* in the temple makes sense in light of Scipio's habits during his lifetime. It also reveals the attitude adopted publicly by the family to his claims of special favours from the god. Such innovation in the use of *imagines* shows their importance. The Cornelii used Africanus' *imago* to create a permanent display in the temple of Jupiter as if it were their family *atrium*, and to allow a detour of their funeral processions to the Capitol. The effectiveness of these public displays can be measured in their continued observance by Cornelii of the imperial period over three hundred years after Africanus' death.[103]

[99] Val. Max. 9. 3. 8.
[100] The temple was rededicated in 69 BC by Q. Lutatius Catulus (*RE* 8, cos. 78 BC), cf. *ILS* 35.
[101] This was the argument of de Sanctis (1936) 190; *contra* Walbank (1967) 55.
[102] Tac. *Hist.* 3. 72.
[103] The Cornelii Scipiones Salvidieni Orfiti are attested into the 2nd cent. AD; cf. Ch. 6.

2. *The* Imagines *in Roman Law: Was There a* 'Ius Imaginum'?

No investigation of Roman *imagines* could be complete without considering the vexed question of the so-called *ius imaginum* and the legal status of ancestor masks. For Mommsen the whole position of a *nobilis* rested on an official *ius imaginum* which he gained with curule office.[104] According to his view, there was a law which granted any man who had reached the office of aedile the official rank of '*nobilis*' and the right to have an *imago* of himself displayed after his death. His whole family would be ennobled by his status as magistrate, and this status was represented by his *imago*. This long accepted definition met a challenge from Gelzer's demonstration that in the late Republic *nobilis* was almost without exception applied to descendants of consuls only. Zadoks, echoing Lessing, argued that the term *ius imaginum* was an invention of sixteenth-century scholars without sufficient warrant in the ancient sources.[105] In her view no such law existed in antiquity. The more recent reassertion of Mommsen's position by Brunt has met with scepticism and rebuttal.[106] The time has come for a reassessment, especially in light of the new evidence from the *S.C. de Cn. Pisone patre*.

At the outset the term *ius imaginum* needs to be recognized as a creation of modern scholars. Zadoks traced its origin to Carolus Sigonius' work in 1560. Its use has led to the formulation of a number of false theories about the *imagines* and the status of Roman office-holders (*nobiles*). Most importantly, the whole expression is misleading because the plural of *imago*, in a phrase unsupported by ancient usage, suggests a law applying to many portraits, whether of ancestors or not. There is no reliable ancient evidence that such a general law about ancestor portraits ever existed in Rome. This term should really no longer be used, even as a convenient short-hand in discussion of earlier views.

The expression *ius imaginum* was coined as a sort of corruption

---

[104] Mommsen (1887) 442-7.

[105] Lessing (1769); Zadoks (1932) 97-110. A thoroughgoing criticism was given by Rowell (1940) 134 ff., but see Hopkins (1983) 255-6 for an endorsement of her views. Her negative arguments against previous scholars remain far more valuable than her own reconstruction. The term is still used as a standard one by Nicolet (1977), Rollin (1979) 5-37, Lahusen (1985*a*), and Nista (1988). A full bibliography on this question is given by Lucrezi (1986) 136 n. 20.

[106] Brunt (1982); *contra* Shackleton Bailey (1986) and Burckhardt (1990).

2. Defining the Imagines

of Cicero *Ver.* 5. 14. 36, which is the only passage referring to this 'law'.[107] Cicero, in a *hapax*, refers to a *ius imaginis ad memoriam posteritatemque prodendae* as part of the privileges associated with the office of aedile.[108] In order to understand what he really meant the whole phrase needs to be considered as a unit. Previous interpretations have not given sufficient weight to the singular use of *imago*, while taking virtually no account at all of the force of *prodo*. *Ius* really applies just as much to *prodo* as to *imago*. *Prodo* is frequently found with *memoria* or *exemplum* meaning to hand down or transmit a custom or tradition.[109] The right involved is that of *handing on* a specific *imago* in the singular to future generations.[110] This cannot refer to images of ancestors in general, but only to the officeholder's own *imago*, which his family could display at his death.[111]

Attempts to read this *ius* as a general 'right to be represented in public' (*Bildnisrecht*) of officeholders started with Lessing in 1769 and it has become accepted as a standard interpretation.[112] According to this view the law applied to all statues or portraits of a magistrate, especially those in public places, and must therefore also have included his *imago*. In other words, Cicero is supposed to be saying that a magistrate had a general right to have his portrait in public places and at home. The background to this theory is that images and statues we know of in public places were apparently exclusively of magistrates. A 'law' is invoked in partial explanation. Yet a closer examination should raise serious doubts. Such a reading does not follow naturally from Cicero's words. As stated above the singular *imago* looks like a specific reference to a particular image.[113]

---

[107] The similar phrasing found at *Rab. Post.* 16–17 = T16 is discussed below.

[108] 'Right of handing on a mask to preserve one's memory and for posterity.'

[109] *OLD prodo* 5*a* and *b*.

[110] Cic. uses *prodere* quite frequently to refer to a custom or tradition. For its reference to an historical tradition, see *Planc.* 94; *Tusc.* 1. 100; *Dom.* 134; *Ver.* 1. 48; 4. 103; *Scaur.* 42; *Mil.* 8; *Phil.* 1. 11; 2. 54. For its use with *posteritas* to mean either immediate descendants or future generations in general, see *Mil.* 83 and *Sen.* 25. Similar usages can be found in Caes. *BG* 5. 12. 1; 6. 25. 5; Livy 23. 47. 6; and Tac. *Ann.* 3. 65.

[111] For Cicero's aedileship which appears to have been plebeian, see Taylor (1939) and Brunt (1982). This is overlooked by Rollin (1979) and Lucrezi (1986). Polyb. 6. 53. 9 = T61 refers to all the actors wearing *imagines* as sitting on the ivory chairs of curule magistrates.

[112] e.g. Lahusen (1983) 113–27.

[113] *Memoria* and *posteritas* suggest an effect beyond the immediate family in a wider circle, but this certainly applies equally to the *imagines*. *Posteritas* can refer both to immediate descendants or to future generations in general.

Public permission, usually from the senate and more rarely from the people, was needed for any statue erected in a public place, which is to say outside a home or grave or temple precinct.[114] In fact, there is not much evidence to suggest that statues were frequently awarded by the senate during the Republic.[115] Unauthorized statues were indeed put up but these were removed by the censors, whether at regular intervals or when the situation was considered to be out of hand.[116] Authorized statues were usually of magistrates, but this appears also to have been the case for unofficial ones. The people were theoretically empowered to erect a statue to anyone they chose. One may cite the well-known example of Cornelia, the mother of the Gracchi, who was thus honoured.[117] Within the home, however, someone could display his own portrait at will. As noted above, it was not unusual for an image of the *pater familias*, often a herm, to be found in the *atrium*.[118] There seems no need or sense in a law stating that an office-holder had the right to a public statue *if* one were voted to him.[119] Such redundant legislation is untypical of the Roman legal system, which tended to react to perceived needs by formulating specific solutions. Nor can we seriously consider the notion that such a law gave aediles and others *carte blanche* to put up their own statues all over town only to have them removed later.

There is, therefore, no reason to think that Cicero is speaking of

[114] For a full discussion of Roman laws relating to statues, see Rollin (1979). Statues in public places were public property and subject to senatorial approval. Most statues of living Romans were put up in temples or their precincts and, therefore, belonged to the god in question.

[115] See Wallace-Hadrill (1990) 170-3 which includes a critique of the approach of Lahusen.

[116] e.g. Plin. *Nat.* 34. 30 ff. for the action of the censors in 158 BC; cf. Ch. 3 § 2. Smith (1988) 126 argues for a view that this clearing of the Forum in the mid-2nd cent. BC made way for a new type of Hellenistic statue voted as a political honour. Note, however, a similar clearing of statues in 179 BC (Livy 40. 51. 3).

[117] *CIL* 6. 31610 (*ILS* 68); Plin. *Nat.* 34. 31; Plut. *C. Gracc.* 4. Coarelli (1978) offers an interesting discussion of the statue and inscription in its historical and political context. He considers it to be the first public statue of a woman in Rome and dates it to 100 BC, close to the time of the first public funeral eulogy for a woman. Cf. Ch. 4 § 6, and Flory (1993) 291-2 who argues that statues of women were not regularly put up before Octavian's for his wife and sister in 35 BC (Dio 49. 38. 1).

[118] Brutus kept statues of himself, perhaps given by grateful municipalities, at his Tusculan villa (Cic. *Orat.* 110 = T22). Mau (1907) 255 cites three herms found *in situ* at Pompeii. Cf. Dwyer (1982) 127-8.

[119] Even a law formulated '*ne quis* . . .' (lest anyone . . .) does not make sense in light of the statue of Cornelia.

a formal 'law', when he refers to the *imago* of an aedile. In the passage from the *Verrines ius* is used by Cicero in a non-technical sense to refer to a 'custom' rather than a 'law'. Some scholars have considered the *imagines* as subject to a type of right derived from custom (*Gewohnheitsrecht*).[120] Further information comes from *Rab. Post.* 16–17 = T16 where Cicero says *denique imago ipsa ad posteritatis memoriam prodita*.[121] The wording is very similar to the mention in the *Verrines*, but the omission of *ius* suggests that a concept of 'law' was not essential in this matter. Coming at the end of a list of honours and accomplishments, preceded immediately by *denique* ('finally'), the reference makes most sense when applied to an *imago* appearing at a funeral. The singular *imago* combined with the emphatic *ipsa* must point to a specific image. It seems safe to say that in these two passages Cicero is indeed speaking of the *imago* ('ancestor mask') of an aedile which will be displayed after his death according to traditional custom.

New and decisive evidence about the legal status of the *imagines* comes from the *S.C. de Cn. Pisone patre* (I16). This important inscription demonstrates the separate but parallel legal condition of *imagines* and the more general category of statues and other portraits. As part of the *damnatio memoriae* applied to Cn. Calpurnius Piso, after his posthumous condemnation for *maiestas* in AD 20, all his public images were ordered to be removed, with the implication that they were to be destroyed. This provision is stated directly and unequivocally.[122]

By contrast, the ban on his *imago* is a separate item which is worded in a much more elaborate way. The senators praise any and all relations of Piso who shall do their best to see that his *imago* is never displayed.[123] The official ban is applied to the *imago* in the

---

[120] Boethius (1942) 235 and Rollin (1979) 36: 'ein ungeschriebenes Ehrenrecht'. Berger (1953) 529 s.v. *ius imaginum* suggests that the law applied to the parade of masks in the funeral. Technically this must be correct as the funeral arrangements were subject to permission from the aediles, as discussed in Ch. 3 §§ 1 and 2. Lucrezi (1986) 142 defines the law as the right of a magistrate to bequeath his *imago* to the family, which then had a corresponding duty to maintain and display it.

[121] 'and finally the mask itself, handed on as a memorial to succeeding generations'.

[122] 75–6: *uti(que) statuae et imagines Cn. Pisonis | patris, quae ubiq(ue) positae essent, tollerentur* ('that the statues and busts of Gnaeus Piso, the father, wherever they had been put up, be removed').

[123] 76–82: *recte et ordine facturos qui qu | andoq(ue) familiae Calpurniae essent, quiue eam familiam cognatione | adfinitateue contingerent, si dedissent operam, si quis eius gentis aut quis eo | rum, qui cognatus adfinisue Calpurniae familiae fuisset, mortuos esset,*

funeral procession, as well as specifically to the *imagines* in the *atrium*.[124] The senate's tone might appear tentative, but in fact a clear injunction is being given in phrases addressed specifically to fellow members of the office-holding caste.

Exact parallels can be found in two decrees of similar date which issue orders to public officials, namely in the contemporary *Tabula Siarensis* and in a decree of the senate dating to 11 BC, which deals with the water supply of the city of Rome.[125] In the former case provincial governors or those acting for them are required to post the senate's resolutions honouring Germanicus in the most public place available. In the latter, the officials in charge of aqueducts (*curatores aquorum*) are asked to make sure that the public water supply is constant both day and night. In both instances the senate's instructions must be carried out but the details of their execution are entrusted to the respective officials, who are, in effect, called upon to exercise their own judgement and initiative to achieve an overall goal.

Similarly, in the *S.C. de Cn. Pisone patre* the senate enjoins their fellow *nobiles* to make appropriate arrangements to ensure that Piso's *imago* does not appear in any relative's home or funeral procession. The lengthy formula is needed partly because so many relatives and descendants could be affected by the ban. At the same time, it recognizes what was a family's traditional sphere of influence, equivalent in some ways to the 'province' of an office-holder. The relatives are addressed as social equals and are invited to

lugen | dus esset, ne inter reliquias imagines, ⟨quibus⟩ exequias eorum funerum celebrare solent, | imago Cn. Pisonis patris duceretur, neue imaginibus familiae Calpurniae i | mago eius interponeretur . . . ('—that it would be right and proper for those who at any time would be members of the family of the Calpurnii, or anyone related to that family either by birth or by marriage, if anyone of that family or anyone related either by birth or marriage to the family of the Calpurnii has died and is to be mourned, to see to it that the mask of Gnaeus Piso, the father, should not be part of the procession amongst the other masks, with which the rites of their funerals are accustomed to be celebrated, and that his mask should not be set up amongst the masks of the Calpurnian family.') Cf. Tac. *Ann.* 2. 32 = T85a for the similar case of Scribonius Libo Drusus in AD 16.

[124] This new evidence confirms the general conclusions of Vittinghoff (1936) esp. 13-18, whose theories are endorsed by Lucrezi (1986). The first firm evidence for erasure of a name is generally considered to be that of Antony after Actium but earlier parallels, such as the case of Marius Gratidianus, are suggestive.

[125] *Tabula Siarensis* frag. 2 col. b 26-7 and Frontin. *Aq.* 104. I am greatly indebted to Prof. W. Eck for sharing his discussion of this matter in the first edition of the *S.C. de Cn. Pisone patre* before its publication.

support and approve the senate's condemnation of one of their number. The traditional power of the family was acknowledged even as it was subject to the direct legal control of the senate and the *princeps*.

Meanwhile, there is no mention of the destruction of an *imago* nor an injunction against the manufacture of a mask of Piso. The wording of the *S.C.* further strongly suggests that an *imago* of Piso already existed, presumably made in his lifetime.[126] The implication is that it might still be kept privately by the family in a part of the house other than the *atrium*.[127]

The special nature and significance of the *imagines* is recognized by the senate and the emperor. Their appearance in the funeral procession is described by the verb *solere*, referring to a custom rather than a law. There is no question here of anything resembling a '*ius imaginum*'. Rather, the public display of *imagines* is a traditionally accepted practice, whose age and importance gives it a special place of honour.[128]

The implication of the senate's thoughtful wording is that the *imagines* had traditionally been subject to decisions made within the family. This is suggested by Cicero's letter to Paetus which advises him to pick whose *imagines* to display in his *atrium* according to his own moral and political judgements.[129] In 140 BC T. Manlius Torquatus apparently made his own decision to deprive his disgraced son D. Junius Silanus both of a funeral with *imagines* and of an *imago* of his own in the family *atrium*.[130] Such a place in family law confirms the consistent Roman opinion that the *imagines* were indeed ancient. In early Roman legal practice few penalties were fixed and offenders were subject to the will of the family sitting in council, directed by the *pater familias*.[131] Feelings of shame and hon-

---

[126] This evidence should finally lay to rest the search for a connection between the *imagines* and death masks, cf. Drerup (1980). Further support comes from Diodorus 31. 25. 2 = T30.

[127] Cf. Plin. *Ep.* 1. 17: *mirum est qua religione quo studio imagines Brutorum Cassiorum Catonum domi ubi potest habeat* ('it is admirable with what care and zeal he has put up portraits of Brutus, Cassius, and Cato at home where he is able to do so'), although this refers to busts, not *imagines*.

[128] Similarly, Plut. *Caes.* 5 = T58 tells us of Caesar's impunity in displaying Marius' *imago* for the first time at his widow Julia's funeral in 69 BC, despite his disgrace. Cf. Ch. 4 § 6.

[129] *Fam.* 9. 21 = T24.   [130] Val. Max. 5. 8. 3 = T103.

[131] Cf. Liebenam *RE consilium*; Crook (1955) 4–7 and (1967) 107–8 with Tac. *Ann.* 13. 32. 2 and Suet. *Tib.* 35. 1.

our, combined with the pressure of public scrutiny and approval, could usually have been relied upon to secure the removal of unsuitable ancestors from the *atrium*.[132] Under the renewed political and social conditions of the Principate the *imagines* came to be subject to more frequent and increasingly standardized offical bans, especially in trials involving treason.

3. *Conclusion: The Definition of an* Imago

Our surviving evidence indicates that the traditional *imagines maiorum* of the Roman office-holders were wax masks, closely associated with the nobility of office, which had emerged after the conflict of the orders with the admission of plebeians to magisterial office and therefore to the senate. Judging from our earliest contemporary testimony, dating to the turn of the second century BC, they were lifelike, functional masks and well established in this period. First made during the subjects' own lifetime, the *imagines* represented past family members who had held at least the office of aedile. They were bequeathed and displayed within families as part of a traditional custom, recognized in law. The family which inherited an *imago* had the right to display it publicly, worn by an actor, in subsequent funeral processions. The *imago* was also on show in the *atria* of houses belonging to all relatives of the deceased both on the father's and mother's side of the family. A legal ban on a man's *imago* was a standard ingredient in the public and private limits on recalling his life and achievements imposed in cases of *damnatio memoriae*. The traditional wax mask symbolized the memory of the deceased and his position within the extended family of those related by blood and by marriage.

---

[132] Plin. *Nat.* 35. 8 = T54 records the publicly expressed indignation of M. Valerius Messalla Rufus 'the elder' (*RE* 77, cos. 53 BC) and M. Valerius Messalla Corvinus 'the younger' (*RE* 95, cos. 31 BC) at unauthorized additional *imagines* introduced within their own family and that of the Cornelii. For shame in Roman culture, see the Introd.

3

Ancestors at the Elections: Ancestral Portraits and Magisterial Office

Man kann ohne Übertreibung sagen, daß diese öffentlich für längere Zeit ausgestellten Ahnengalerien das in der pompa funebris Gezeigte gewissermaßen fixierten, indem die dort agierenden Ahnen hier im Bilde gezeigt wurden.

(Zinserling (1959/60) 429)

Ancestral images held a place of high prominence in the political ideology of the Republic.

(Gruen (1992) 154)

THE Roman political caste was a nobility of office which relied on repeated electoral successes to maintain its position of leadership. Yet *nobilitas* as a status was often described in terms of *imagines*. What then was the connection between ancestor masks and the elections, both characteristic features which defined Rome's political élite? Meanwhile, the *imagines* were complemented by many other images of ancestors in various media to be found all over the city. Outside the home and tomb, both private domains in the eyes of the law, ancestral iconography appeared in public spaces in the city as a background to the life of all its citizens. These images reinforced the effect of displays in the *atria* of the political families.[1] The evolution of an aristocracy of office naturally led to the development of a multitude of public advertisements which focused especially on the military successes of the ruling class, and served to justify its

---

[1] For a discussion of *imagines* in the *atrium*, see Ch. 7.

60

position of social privilege.[2] This chapter aims to put the *imagines* in context by exploring the various allusions to ancestors of office-holders which a citizen might encounter in his daily business in the public parts of the city and the effect they might have on the way he voted at the elections.

1. Imagines *and the Concept of* Nobilitas

The close connection of the *imagines* with the office of aedile can be demonstrated from Cicero and Polybius. This raises the old question of what the *imagines* contributed to the definition of the status of a *nobilis*. Was the office-holding élite formally or principally defined in terms of their *imagines*? Mommsen's traditional view that this was indeed the case suffers from excessive legalism and a heavy reliance on the *ius imaginum*, which has been shown to be largely a scholarly construct.[3] Gelzer's theory, which relates *nobilitas* to the consulship rather than to the *imagines*, remains essentially unchallenged, but as Afzelius demonstrated, can only be applied with confidence to Cicero's time.[4] In fact, our information is not full enough before Cicero to trace the exact meaning of *nobilis*, which appears to be an evolving social term. Consequently, Bleicken has more recently put forward an approach eschewing a formal legal definition of *nobilitas* altogether.[5]

Alternatively, *nobilitas* has been described as being the opposite of *novitas*, the condition of having no office-holding ancestors and therefore no *imagines*. Much scholarly debate has actually focused on the meaning of the term *novus*. In different contexts this word has a varying range of senses which has produced the following dual definition.[6] *Novus* may refer to a man who is the first consul

---

[2] A new type of art representative of aristocratic achievements and aspirations emerged in Rome in the late 4th and early 3rd cent. BC. See Hölscher (1978) and (1980*a*) with the discussion in Appendix D. Evidence for public statues has been collected by Vessberg (1941). See also Degrassi (1937) ix–x, Schweitzer (1948) 34 ff., and for statues of women Flory (1993).

[3] For the arguments, see Ch. 2 § 2.

[4] Mommsen (1887); Gelzer (1912/75); Afzelius (1938) and (1945). For recent criticism of this approach, see Hölkeskamp (1993) 13. Compare also Cn. Cornelius Scipio Hispanus' epitaph (*ILLRP* 316 = *ILS* 6 = I5) for the verb *nobilitare* applied to a Scipio who rose no higher than the praetorship.

[5] Bleicken (1981).

[6] Badian in the *OCD*[2] (1970) under *novus homo*, accepted by Wiseman (1971). *Contra* Burckhardt (1990) 83 who applies the term only to equestrian newcomers. See also Cassola (1988) for a general discussion.

in his family, but is also used with quite a different emphasis of a man of equestrian background who is the first Roman office-holder and thus the first senator in his. In practice it is fruitless to try to define *nobilis* in terms of *novus*, as they are not strictly antonyms. A man could be both at the same time. Indeed every *novus* was also a *nobilis* after he became the first to reach a status new to his family. Confusion has perhaps arisen from too much attention being paid to Cicero, who was a *novus* in every sense of the word, but whose career is rather the exception. The term *nobilis*, like the related concept of *novus*, meant something different at different times and was probably also used during the same period with varying degrees of exclusivity according to a man's social standing and pretensions.

It is more relevant to Roman life to think in terms of many gradations of status within the senate, based on an acute sense of hierarchy and constantly reflected in the shape of debate and in decisions reached.[7] Ancestry in terms of previous office-holders was one important factor amongst a number of others including seniority, personal achievement, office held at any given moment, connections at home and abroad, perceived expertise in the area under discussion, etc. Defining a *nobilis* purely in terms of *imagines* or ancestral achievement fails to bring out the constant pressure to maintain a family's status by winning renewed or higher offices within the *cursus honorum*.

Nevertheless, there are many passages from ancient authors which associate *imagines* closely with *nobilitas* and go so far as to equate them in some cases.[8] A wide variety of authors from Cicero to Seneca are involved, comprising different genres of prose and poetry. Although they do not reflect a clear definition in terms of the consulship, they show that the *imagines* were perceived as the most enduring and familiar sign of the office-holding caste and of its values.[9] Unlike many of the trappings of office they were not

[7] See Hölkeskamp (1993) 35.

[8] The following authors equate the two terms: Cic. *Planc.* 18 = T14; Livy 1. 34. 6 = T37; *Per.* 48 = T46; Prop. 1. 5. 23–4 = T62; Val. Max. 3. 8. 7 = T100; Sen. *Ben.* 3. 28. 1–3 = T74; *Ep.* 44. 5 = T75; Suet. *Gal.* 2–3 = T82. A more general association can be found at: Sall. *Jug.* 85. 10 ff. = T66 *a–c*; Livy 10. 7. 11 = T42; 30. 45. 6–7 = T44; Val. Max. 3. 7. 11 = T99; Sil. 17. 12 = T79; Sen. *Con.* 2. 1. 17 = T69; Suet. *Aug.* 4. 1 = T80; *Ves.* 1. 1 = T83.

[9] Hölkeskamp (1993) 25 discusses '. . . a general process of change of values and standards in which the holding of these offices was gradually becoming the most important, if not the only, criterion for rank, reputation and indeed aristocratic status itself'.

temporary, but were a vital part both of the solemn spectacle of the funeral and of everyday life in the home. It was their force as symbols that made Roman writers refer to them so often.

The importance accorded to the *imagines* stems from the nature of the Roman concept of a 'political' élite. As has often been noted, the word *nobilis* is closely connected with *noscere* ('to know/be acquainted with a person').[10] The use of *nobilis* as early as Plautus and Terence, but especially in the Scipionic *elogia*, as well as in contemporary fragments of the orators and historians shows that the concept of 'nobility' was closely associated with being well known.[11] *Nobilis* may originally have meant no more than 'well known'. Cicero plays on this basic meaning when he says of Clodia that she is *muliere non solum nobili verum etiam nota.*[12] As early as the time of Plautus, however, the concept of the office-holding 'nobility' as a 'caste', including the values associated with it, is already in evidence.[13]

The political and social élite consisted of a nobility of office which emerged rapidly at the end of the conflict of the orders. It can be detected in the late fourth century BC.[14] Only office-holding ancestors were represented by *imagines*, since status depended on office. Consequently, aristocratic ambitions were intensely focused on the elections. In order to be elected to a magistracy, and therefore to maintain the status of the family overall, influence with and recognition by the voters was essential. The *imagines* served a key function in making a family well known and keeping its past successes alive in the minds of ordinary citizens. The more previously held offices were associated with a family's name, the more easily its members might expect to obtain future election victories.[15] The *imagines* were powerful visual reminders, whether presented at a

---

[10] e.g. Gelzer (1912/75) 27, Afzelius (1945) 184; Lucrezi (1986) 163, and Hölkeskamp (1987) 220-1.

[11] Gelzer (1912/75) 49-50. Cf. Ennius *scaen. fr.* 200 for *opulentus* ('affluent') as an antonym for *ignobilis* ('humble'). For the *elogia* of the Scipios, see Ch. 6 and Appendix B.

[12] *Cael.* 31: 'a woman not only noble/well-known but also well-known/notorious'.

[13] The historian L. Calpurnius Piso (cos. 133 BC) refers to *nobiles* in 304 BC.

[14] Hölscher (1978) and (1980a) gives a masterly synthesis of the evidence from the monuments.

[15] *Imagines* are associated with the glare of publicity in the following passages: Cic. *Pis.* 53; *Agr.* 2. 1 = T7; Sall. *Jug.* 85. 23 = T66a; Val. Max. 3. 3. 7 = T97; Sil. 17. 12 = T79. Hor. *Serm.* 1. 6. 7-18 = T33 notes that political aspirations invite questions about a man's background.

funeral as living ancestors holding their highest office, or when associated with a tabulation of past achievements and election successes in the *atrium*. A man's own *imago* was his ultimate reward for reaching high office and hence part of an aristocrat's goal; his ancestors' *imagines* served as a means for him to reach that goal.

The controlled nature of the competitive arena undoubtedly made the stakes seem higher. Many sons of office-holders probably failed in their ambitions to match a father's or grandfather's position.[16] It was common for a family to advance slowly, with each generation managing a further step in the *cursus*, since the consulship was always jealously guarded. The significance granted to the ancestors could be decisive, especially in competition with other *nobiles* for individual offices. Factors such as patronage were clearly fundamental, but the ancestors reinforced name recognition and credibility. Ordinary people were represented as still in debt to the ancestors, a debt that could be discharged by voting for a descendant or relative.[17] Families also encouraged the view that the qualities of famous ancestors could be passed down almost as easily as their names.[18]

Cicero speaks with bitterness of the *commendatio maiorum* (recommendation of the ancestors) which he presents as powerful in elections.[19] His views lost some of their earlier stridency once he himself had reached the consulship, but he constantly stressed the need of the *novus homo* to match the prestige of the ancestors with his own *virtus* (merit).[20] In doing so a newcomer could not afford

[16] The research of Hopkins (1983) 31-119 has brought fresh emphasis to this aspect. According to his calculations only two fifths of consuls had consular fathers and one third had a son who became consul. 53% had either a consular father or grandfather. However, we shall never know how many failed or did not try.

[17] Ov. *Am.* I. 8. 65-6 = T50 speaks of a lover being deceived into a relationship of trust by *imagines*. The relations between lover and beloved are represented as similar to those between politician and voter.

[18] Roloff (1938) 8. Note esp. Cic. *Vat.* 28 = T20; Sen. *De Tranq.* 16. 1. For this reason Cato did not record the names of generals, except his own, in his *Origines* (Nep. *Cato* 3. 3-4; Plin. *Nat.* 8. 11). Cf. Val. Max. 3. 7. 11 = T99 for Accius refusing to rise when C. Julius Caesar Strabo (*RE* 135) entered a meeting of poets on the grounds that rank was determined by literary output and not by *imagines*. The anomaly of this situation suggests that men who had *imagines* dominated most social gatherings.

[19] *Ver.* 5. 180-2. The combative tone of this passage sheds light on the politics of 70 BC.

[20] Roloff's discussion (1938) is still fundamental for Cicero's attitudes and their development (with full citation of relevant passages). Note esp. *Ver.* 2. 4. 81; *Agr.* 2. 1 = T7; 2. 100 = T8. For the disadvantages of the new man at the elections, see Wiseman (1971) 100-7.

to condemn the *nobiles* or the Roman system; rather he tried to demonstrate that his own practice of traditional virtues came closest to the standards and values of the ancestors. In this way Cicero serves to illustrate in his own career how each generation of new men who had been admitted into higher office became part of the established system and then emerged, when senior statesmen, as its champions. A newly elected magistrate of equestrian origin was himself a *nobilis* and might even feel superior to the scion of an old family without recent record of offices held. For this reason Cicero always upholds the primacy of *nobilitas*, when combined with *virtus*.

Direct ancient testimony reveals that the influence the ancestors exercised on access to power at the elections was partly due to the *imagines*.[21] For the ordinary Roman citizen who was presumably not in the habit of reading histories, the ancestors of leading families were familiar primarily from their *imagines*, as well as from any public memorials, trophies, buildings or statues, and associated images on coins. The connection of the games held, especially as aedile, and success at future elections is well known. It is remarkable how often such games were given in memory of family members, even those long dead.[22] This was another way in which the general public was reminded of the name and the record of past members of the family. The *imagines* served as constant and powerful advertisements for a family's achievements and eminence: they were the family's public face.[23] Successful families knew how to maintain and exploit these tools, so that their members became synonymous with the proudest moments in Rome's past.

There can be little doubt that the whole election process was influenced by present and past office-holders.[24] A brief overview of

---

[21] For *imagines* and elections see Cic. *Agr.* 2. 100 = T8; *Pis.* 1 = T13; *Planc.* 18 = T14; 51 = T15; Sall. *Jug.* 85. 10 ff. = T66a–c; Hor. *S.* 1. 6. 17 = T33. See Wiseman (1971) 107 on the hurdles facing new men: 'The difficulty was, of course, that the entrance-hall of the noble's house, crowded every morning with visitors and clients, displayed in impressive ranks the wax death-masks of the ancestors of the *gens*, blackened with the smoke of pious sacrifices and no doubt adorned with the insignia of the offices they had held.'

[22] Games given in someone's name: Polyb. 31. 28. 6; Livy 41. 28. 11; *Per.* 16; Augustus *RG* 22; Val. Max. 2. 4. 7; Plut. *Caes.* 5. 9; Suet. *Jul.* 26. 2; 10. 2 ; Dio 37. 8. 2. Q. Aelius Tubero was not elected praetor after giving a meagre funeral banquet for his uncle Aemilianus (Cic. *Mur.* 75). For the games of the aedile, see Develin (1985) 139.

[23] For *imagines* and the morning *salutatio*, see Ch. 7 § 6.

[24] See L. R. Taylor (1966) 113: 'There is no doubt that manipulation was a constant feature of the assemblies.'

how the voting was organized reveals that the *imagines* were one
factor among a number which upheld the established pattern of
office-holding and continuous power for the leading families despite
the fact that each individual office could only be held for one year.
The requirements for candidates, which developed into a regular
period of military service and education in the law and rhetoric, followed by the succession of political offices in a regular pattern (*cursus honorum*), tended to produce men from traditional élite
backgrounds.[25] We do not have ancient evidence to show how
widespread or usual bribery at the elections was before the irregu-
larities to be found at the end of the Republic.[26] The introduction of
the secret ballot by the tribunes of the plebs in the late second century BC (the *Lex Gabinia*) does suggest the use of influence and pressure.[27] The basic structure of the voting assembly gave the élite
classes opportunities to make their choices known.[28]

The wealthiest classes, as assessed by census ratings, voted first
and their votes counted for more as they were allotted a greater
number of voting units (centuries). Within the first class the older
men had their own separate voting units which allowed them more
influence. Of the total number of 193 voting units, 97 were required
for a majority. Voting would cease if and when a majority had
declared for a candidate. If the first class, comprising the senators
and *equites* and those with property worth at least 100,000 asses,
voted together then only 8 units of the second class would be
needed to make a majority. Regularity and predictability in the
field of candidates could foster cohesion within the wealthiest
classes.[29] The degree of aristocratic influence on the elections
depended on the conservative voters of the first class. A split vote
gave the lower orders more say. However, the very predominance
of élite candidates for the higher offices in itself surely tended on

[25] For the background of the candidates, see especially Wiseman (1971) 116–23
and Develin (1985) 89–125.
[26] Note the discussion of Develin (1985) 134–7. For bribery in the late Republic,
see Yacobsen (1992).
[27] On the importance of the *Lex Gabinia* of 139 BC, see Wiseman (1971) 4–5 and
Nicolet (1980) 360–5. For aristocratic control of elections in general, see Rilinger
(1976) 132–41.
[28] The best general discussions of voting procedures in the centuriate assembly
can be found in L. R. Taylor (1966) 85–106, Wiseman (1971) 123–30, Nicolet
(1980) 333 ff., Rilinger (1976) 113–23, and Develin (1985) 17–28.
[29] See Rilinger (1976) 154, Develin (1985) 142–3, 310, and Hölkeskamp
(1993).

many occasions to produce a split vote and a chance for popular participation.

The tone was set by the first unit to vote which was chosen by lot from the first class.[30] This *centuria praerogativa* was thought to bring luck and to indicate both the probable outcome and the will of the gods. The religious atmosphere suggested by the opening prayers and the taking of the auspices was important as the background for the voting itself. Many appear to have followed the lead of the *praerogativa*. The tendency to follow a precedent was encouraged by the practice of announcing the choice of each century as it took its turn to vote. The role of the presiding magistrate, usually one of the consuls, was also a factor.[31] He was in charge of the whole process, including holding the auspices and the announcement of the candidates and of the eventual winners. The actions of the voters were responses to his initiative. Even if he did not directly favour a given candidate, his role as leader set the tone for the assembly. He regulated which procedures were followed and what was acceptable behaviour for candidates and voters alike. His *auctoritas* (influence) both as an individual and as an office-holder had an effect on the assembly.

It has been suggested that voter turn-out was usually low and this seems almost inevitable.[32] The elections were mostly held at times when the city was not crowded with visitors.[33] The consular elections in July would have been hard for farmers to attend. Many of the poorest residents of Rome itself would have been too busy to stay all day. A low number of voters also contributed to the greater influence of the centuries of the first class and to the authority of leading individuals within those groups. The choice of which public space to hold the voting in could also be used to discourage large crowds.

[30] The importance of the *praerogativa* is discussed by L. R. Taylor (1966) 91 ff. and Nicolet (1976) 349-50, 356.
[31] L. R. Taylor (1966) 104-5 and Nicolet (1976) 326, 328, 345 provide the standard treatments. Rilinger (1976) argued at length that the presiding magistrate would not normally exercise much influence. For a recent discussion, see Develin (1985) 132-4.
[32] L. R. See Taylor (1966) 113 and Nicolet (1976) 391 ff. MacMullen (1980) estimates that 2% would be normal. Develin (1985) 317-9 imagines 10% as a high turnout with the first class comprising fewer than one-sixth of the voters.
[33] MacMullen's (1980) discussion is especially good. The *Lex Aelia* and the *Lex Fufia* of the mid-2nd cent. BC made sure the assembly would not be held on a market day or at another time when the city was very crowded. See Rotondi (1912/66) 288-9.

At the same time, real choices between candidates were offered and competition between leading families at the elections was often fierce. Popular participation and a relationship of reciprocity between leaders and voters was fundamental to the ideology and ambiance of the elections.[34] Crowds of humble supporters gave the impression of popularity for a candidate. The support of such ordinary citizens had an important symbolic role to play even when they were not actually able to cast a decisive vote for their chosen candidate (Cic. *Mur.* 70-2). At his first public meeting after election a magistrate would give elaborate thanks to the people for their support and would promise not to disappoint them.[35] The rhetoric of popular choice was plausible because the elections were only very rarely predetermined. It was not really possible for any individual or group to deliver the votes needed for high office.[36] As a result, the public image of a candidate was very important especially in relation to citizens resident in the city, who were more likely to vote. Advertising played a key role in suggesting that a man had the requisite character, qualities, and background to be a suitable leader. Support for the successful candidate had to come from the *equites* and other businessmen, those influential and wealthy citizens who lived in Rome itself, or who could afford to travel to the city, and also from the urban plebs whose influence had grown by the end of the Republic.[37]

The machinery for voting clearly points to the most likely audience for electoral advertising.[38] Although the overall standing and popularity of a candidate within the community was surely an influential factor, on the day itself the opinions and preferences of the voters present carried most weight. Not surprisingly, the more affluent residents of the city were also the group most exposed to aristocratic displays in Rome, including the *imagines*. They would have had plenty of occasions to visit the houses of leading political

[34] For the reality of competition at Roman elections, see Yacobsen (1992) and Millar (1995) esp. 94-5. For an acute analysis of the ideology of the Roman Republic, see Hölkeskamp (1993) esp. 30-9.
[35] For a discussion of speeches at the first *contio*, see Ch. 1 and Ch. 5 § 5.
[36] This point was stressed by Develin (1985) 127-31 and 314-15.
[37] See Yacobsen (1992) especially 50: 'The Roman nobles who, perhaps more than any other social élite in history, were dependent on popular elections for the very definition of their relative status in society, were willing to pay a high price for the votes of the urban plebs.'
[38] See Cic. *Rep.* 2. 22 with the advice about how to campaign for the consulship in the *Commentariolum Petitionis* and Nicolet (1976) 401.

families and to see the displays of spoils and ancestor masks in the *atrium*.[39] At the same time, they would have been active in the Forum and would often have witnessed aristocratic funeral processions and their eulogies from the speaker's platform (*rostra*).[40] They comprised the sections of society who stood to gain the most from the expansion of Rome's empire and her position of power in the Mediterranean, which depended on the military successes and aggressive policies of the *nobiles*.[41] However, the opinions of other residents of the city were also a factor as is revealled by the importance of demonstrated generosity to the people on the part of the candidate.[42]

The role of the *imagines* in elections was inevitably affected by the collapse of the republican system and the emergence of the Principate. In AD 14 Tiberius transferred the elections for magisterial office to the senate and thereby further increased the impact of the emperor's selection of candidates (*commendatio*).[43] The electoral assemblies of the people continued to meet but only to ratify the candidates already chosen in the senate. Competition was still possible but it was reduced by the restricted voting body and the views of the emperor. The function and importance of the *imagines*, therefore, underwent a change as the senatorial aristocracy evolved under the Julio-Claudian emperors. The *imagines* endured as private emblems of rank and reminders of past glory, sometimes serving as symbols of opposition to the imperial system.[44] However, their original purpose of influencing voters in the electoral assemblies had lost its central function of maintaining the status of leading families. Office now depended to a considerable extent on the favour of the *princeps*, who might or might not choose members of traditional office-holding families. His preferences would influence senators even in elections where he had not directly designated a candidate as his own favourite. Alternatively, great power came to be

---

[39] For the *imagines* in the *atrium*, see Ch. 7.

[40] The funeral procession is discussed in Ch. 4, the eulogy in Ch. 5.

[41] See Badian (1972) and Nicolet (1966) and (1974).

[42] See Cic. *Mur.* 75-6 for Q. Aelius Tubero's defeat as a candidate for the praetorship because his contribution to the funeral banquet of Scipio Aemilianus was viewed as insufficient by the people.

[43] Tac. *Ann.* I. 15 and Dio 58. 20. 3-4. The character of imperial elections is discussed by Millar (1977) 300-13, and especially by Talbert (1984) 341-5, whose interpretations I follow here.

[44] For the changing role of the *imagines* in the imperial period, see Ch. 9.

exercised by friends and advisers of the emperor who never held any traditional senatorial offices.[45]

2. Portraits of Ancestors in Public Places

At the end of the fourth century BC trophies marking victories and honorary statues voted to leaders started to become important elements in the adornment of the city.[46] Similarly, temples and other public buildings often contained statues of the individual who had vowed to build them, as well as paintings, trophies, and memorials of the victory which was the occasion for the dedication of the site. The spoils of war provided the funds to pay for many public structures. By the middle Republic, therefore, statues of famous Romans, almost exclusively holders of magisterial office except for the legendary figures of Rome's past, could be found concentrated especially round the Comitium near the Curia and on the Capitol near the temple of Jupiter.[47] These spaces were central to the political and religious life of the city.

A group of statues representing the kings of Rome with Brutus the first consul could be found on the Capitol.[48] It is easy to see why a Roman might want his statue or those of his ancestors associated with these founding fathers to give the impression that he also had played a vital role in the city's history. The proliferation of statues, especially in the Forum, led to the removal of unauthorized ones at intervals by the censors.[49] The right to erect a statue in a public place in the city was carefully controlled because of its political influence.[50] Such images were nearly always put up close to the time of the events commemorated and by the individuals

[45] Maecenas is only the most obvious early example.

[46] These are discussed by Hölscher (1978) and (1980b), and by Hölkeskamp (1993) 27–9. Lahusen (1983) gives a general survey of such statues.

[47] For a survey of portrait galleries of all types in Rome, see Lahusen (1988).

[48] For a discussion of this group and our scant knowledge about them, see Evans (1990).

[49] Plin. *Nat.* 34. 30: *L. Piso prodidit M. Aemilio C. Popilio iterum cos. a censoribus P. Cornelio Scipione M. Popilio statuas circa forum eorum qui magistratum gesserant, sublatas omnes praeter eas, quae populi aut senatus sententia statutae essent . . .* ('Lucius Piso reported that in the consulship of Marcus Aemilius and Gaius Popilius for the second time the statues of magistrates around the Forum were all removed by the censors Publius Cornelius Scipio and Marcus Popilius except those that had been put up by a vote of the people or of the senate').

[50] e.g. Bocchus' dedication of a statue group commemorating the capture of Jugurtha by Sulla mentioned by Plutarch, *Mar.* 32 and *Sulla* 6.

involved.[51] Over time they might then become memorials serving the glory of that man's family rather than his personal political ambitions. As a result, Roman citizens were often reminded of 'ancestors' by public buildings, statues, and monuments throughout the city.

2a. Statues

An impulse parallel to the desire for self-advertisement led to the erection of statues of ancestors by their descendants, sometimes in conjunction with that descendant's own portrait, to stress the continuity of family prominence.[52] We have little direct evidence for ancestral statues, which are principally attested by inscriptions. Only three examples of statues from Rome can be cited which clearly illustrate the setting up of an ancestor portrait.

In 148 BC, Marcus Claudius Marcellus (*RE* 225) put up three statues, of himself with his father (*RE* 222) and grandfather (*RE* 220), near the temple of Honos and Virtus built by his grandfather, the victor of Clastidium and conqueror of Syracuse.[53] The inscription advertises nine consulships held by three Marcelli, thus stressing and quantifying the prestige of the family group in a way reminiscent of an election slogan.

This monument was beside the temple built by the family and also closely associated with the grave of Marcellus' grandfather. The temple of Honos and Virtus was immediately outside the Capena gate on the north side of the Appian way.[54] The situation of the temple just outside the city limits made it accessible while allowing the family a free hand in embellishing their private grave monuments that could be built near it. The inscription preserves a record of the consulship of Marcellus in 215 BC, from which the victor of Syracuse was forced to resign after thunder was heard at the election. Family ambitions are clearly responsible for preserving the

[51] See Ch. 2 § 2 for the legal status of Roman portraits.

[52] Hölscher (1978) 327 suggests that it was the same impulse which led to the setting up of public statues and *imagines*. It is notable that Lahusen (1983) does not distinguish consistently between statues erected in a man's lifetime and statues of ancestors. For statues, especially in programatic groups, see Kellum (1981) 2–38 who stresses that it was always legitimate to celebrate oneself in terms of ancestors.

[53] Asconius 12C = 11KS = 18Stangl = I15. Cf. Ch. 5 § 4 for the family traditions of the Claudii Marcelli. For the statues in their artistic and cultural setting, see Maggiani (1992).

[54] For the position of the temple, see Platner and Ashby (1929), and Richardson (1978) and (1992) 190.

memory of a magistracy held only in a technical sense, but which then passed into the records of the annalistic tradition.[55] Similarly, as Asconius notes, the combined inscription for three family members tends to obscure the fact that the father of the present Marcellus only held one consulship (196 BC). The achievements of three generations of men bearing the same name are presented as a unit. In this context even the outstanding record of the conqueror of Syracuse, who was consul four times, becomes part of a continuous family tradition.

A comparison may be made with the arch of Fabius which was the first victory arch to be erected in or near the Forum.[56] It spanned the Sacred Way at the east end of the Forum and was erected by Q. Fabius Maximus Allobrogicus (*RE* 110) in 121 BC to celebrate his victory over the Allobroges. The arch was restored by his grandson (*RE* 108, suff. cos. 45 BC), probably as curule aedile in 57 BC, to include labelled statues of himself with Aemilius Paullus and Scipio Aemilianus.[57] Clearly the restoration of such a victory memorial in sight of the Forum provided the family with an occasion for erecting statues of their most prominent ancestors, including those by adoption and others, like Aemilianus, who was not a direct ancestor of the Fabii. Again the inscription contains an exaggeration based on family records, perhaps the label (*titulus*) of Aemilius Paullus' *imago*. Paullus is credited with three triumphs,

[55] Livy 23. 12–14; Plut. *Marcellus* 12. 1.

[56] *ILS* 43 and 43a = *ILLRP* 392: [Q.] *Fabius Q. f. Maxsumus | aed. cur. L. Aem[il]ius L. f. Paullus | co[s II] cens. augur | tr[i]umphavit ter P. Cornelius Paulli f. Scipio | Africanus cos. II cens. | augur triumphavit II Q. Fabius Q. f. Maxsumus aed. cur. rest.* ('Quintus Fabius Maximus, son of Quintus, curule aedile, Lucius Aemilius Paullus, son of Lucius, consul twice, censor, augur, he triumphed three times, Publius Cornelius Scipio Africanus, son of Paullus, consul twice, censor, augur, he triumphed twice, Quintus Fabius Maximus, son of Quintus, curule aedile restored [this arch]'). Cf. Cic. *Vat.* 28: *nihil Maximus fecit alienum aut sua virtute aut illis clarissimis Paulis, Maximis, Africanis, quorum gloriam huius virtute renovatam non modo speramus verum etiam iam videmus* ('Maximus did nothing which was foreign either to his valour or to those distinguished men like Paullus, Maximus, and Africanus, whose renown we do not only hope to see but actually do see renewed by this man's excellence'). This can be read as a comment on the restoration of the arch. Lahusen (1983) 61 cites Fabius' as the first securely attested arch with labelled statues of *triumphatores*, although the arch of Scipio is an important earlier example, further up the Sacred Way, about which we are not fully informed (see Ch. 2 § 1e). Hölscher (1990) 80 considers the purpose of such arches to be the display of statues.

[57] L. Aemilius Paullus (*RE* 114) the victor of Pydna was the natural father of P. Cornelius Scipio Aemilianus (*RE* 335) and of Q. Fabius Maximus Aemilianus (*RE* 109, cos. 145 BC), the great-grandfather of the restorer (*RE* 108). Aemilianus, therefore, was the great-great-uncle of the restorer.

whereas he actually only celebrated two. He had, however, been hailed as *imperator* three times by his troops.[58] The family's claims, expressed in the enumeration of offices, could only be boosted by display in such a prominent place. To be effective, public inscriptions needed to agree with the *tituli* labelling the *imagines* in the family *atria*. It seems likely, therefore, that the Fabii kept an *imago* of Scipio Aemilianus as part of the display in their *atria*.

We learn from a letter of Cicero that Q. Caecilius Metellus Pius Scipio Nasica (*RE* 99, cos. 52 BC) erected a whole squadron of gilded equestrian statues of his ancestors on the Capitol around 50 BC.[59] This can be interpreted as a reflection of the highly developed spirit of competition found at the end of the Republic which was frequently expressed in terms of ancestral images and glory.[60] In fact, Metellus publicly revealed his ignorance of the likeness and career of his ancestor P. Cornelius Scipio Nasica Serapio (*RE* 354, cos. 138 BC). His confusion led to the more serious mistake which resulted in

---

[58] There are two triumphs in the *Fasti* (181 and 167 BC). Only Velleius Paterculus 1. 9. 3 refers to a third triumph as praetor, probably meaning Paullus was hailed imperator as propraetor in 189 BC. Note *ter* ('three times') on a coin of 62 BC (M. H. Crawford (1974), *Roman Republican Coinage* (hereafter 'Crawford'), 415).

[59] *Att.* 6. 1. 17: *De statua Africani (ὦ πραγμάτων ἀσυγκλώστων! sed me id ipsum delectavit in tuis litteris), ain tu? Scipio hic Metellus proavum suum nescit censorem non fuisse? atqui nihil habuit aliud inscriptum nisi 'cos.' ea statua quae ab Opis parte postica in excelso est. in illa autem quae est ad Πολυκλέους Herculem inscriptum est 'cos. ⟨cens.⟩'; quam esse eiusdem status, amictus, anulus, imago ipsa declarat. At me hercule ego, cum in turma inauratarum equestrium quas hic Metellus in Capitolio posuit animadvertissem in Sarapionis subscriptione Africani imaginem, erratum fabrile putavi, nunc video Metelli: ὁ ἀνιστορησίαν turpem!* ('What do you think about the statue of Africanus (what a farrago of topics! but that was what pleased me about your letter)? Is this Metellus Scipio ignorant of the fact that his great-grandfather was never censor? Certainly that statue which is on the high ground behind the Temple of Ops has nothing written on it except "consul". But the one near the Hercules of Polykles is labelled "consul, censor". The pose, the dress, the ring, the portrait itself make clear that it is the same man. But good heavens, when I noticed a likeness of Africanus with Serapio's inscription under it amongst the squadron of gilded horsemen which this Metellus put up on the Capitol, I thought it was the workman's mistake, now I see it is Metellus'. What disgraceful ignorance of history!') Cf. Shackleton Bailey (1968) no. 115. For Metellus Scipio's complex coinage, see Crawford 459, 460 and 461 with references to ancestors amongst the Caecilii Metelli and Cornelii Scipiones. At 738 he observes : 'The coinage of Metellus Scipio is pathetically true to its author's belief in the *felix et invictum Scipionum nomen* (Suetonius, *Caes.* 59), overcome at Thapsus by the *felicitas* of Caesar.' Coarelli (1981) 258-9 identifies this group of statues as adapted from Lysippus' group of Alexander at the Granicus which had been brought to Rome by Metellus Macedonicus.

[60] See Coarelli (1969) for the location of these statues near the temples of Fides and Ops Opifera and their political significance both in the 50s BC and as regards Nasica's role in the death of Tiberius Gracchus.

Aemilianus' statue being labeled with Serapio's *cursus*. The nobler a man's birth the more details of family history he was expected to know and the more he laid himself open to correction on the part of others if he made a mistake. Nearly a century after his consulship, Rome apparently contained at least two other statues of Aemilianus before Metellus Scipio added a third. The inscriptions on such public statues were used by Cicero and others as important sources of information about offices held and family status.

Statues of ancestors put up by their descendants, it has been argued, were not subject to the same rigorous rules which applied to statues of living Romans in the city.[61] Yet, if this were true, it is surprising that we do not have more attested examples. The three instances cited above suggest that most ancestral images were associated with family buildings, such as tombs, temples, or arches.[62] Fabius' and Metellus Scipio's ancestral statues within the city limits date to the 50s BC and may not reflect standard republican practice.[63] At the same time, public displays of figures from Rome's past served as a precedent for Augustus' gallery of heroes flanking the temple of Mars Ultor in his new Forum and for copies of these same statues that were to be found in provincial cities.

A similar display of ancestral images could be found in Tarquinii set up in the early imperial age. This series of statues was in the centre of the town and was also associated with an important temple complex. The *Elogia Tarquiniensia* inscriptions found here commemorate leading members of the Spurinna family from the time before Roman conquest. They may be based on records preserved within the family, who decorated their tombs with narrative paintings of past history.[64] Whether they are seen as the product of an authentic local tradition or of more recent elaboration based on the antiquarian interests of the age, their public display mirrors the Forum of Augustus and the type of statues put up by Roman office-

[61] Lahusen (1983) assumes considerable freedom for any *nobilis* to erect statues of his ancestors in public places in the city.

[62] The tomb of the Scipios demonstrates that graves were used for family display in the 2nd cent. BC. See Ch. 6 for discussion.

[63] Lahusen (1988) 365–6 identifies an ambition to go beyond the *imagines* in setting up more permanent public galleries of family portraits, which then developed into 'official' representations of the 'ancestors' of the Roman state.

[64] A full treatment of the *elogia* with arguments for their basis in local traditions and family archives can be found in Torelli (1975); cf. the review by Cornell (1978).

holders during the Republic.[65] The power and prominence of the Spurinnae under the Julio-Claudian emperors was presented in the context of an ancient and glorious family heritage linked closely to episodes in local history. There is no evidence to let us determine whether the statues and inscriptions copied or replaced earlier monuments or were erected in this format for the first time under the influence of the statues in the Forum of Augustus.[66]

2b. Imagines Clipeatae

Reference has already been made to the shield portraits (*imagines clipeatae*) which the elder Pliny mentions as a possible variation of ancestral portraiture to be found in the *atrium* by the late first century AD (*Nat.* 35. 12–14 = T54).[67] Vitruvius (6. 3. 3 = T107) is probably alluding to shield portraits when he mentions *imagines* in the *atrium* and discusses how high on the wall they should be hung. The considerable height he gives as normal makes sense in the case of shields which were hung at an angle for viewing from below.[68] By contrast, wax funeral masks were always kept in cupboards. There is no evidence to suggest that they were ever hung on the wall, especially so high up.

Shield portraits were first displayed by Appius Claudius Pulcher (*RE* 296, cos. 79 BC) in the temple of Bellona built by his ancestor Appius Claudius Caecus.[69] Pliny stresses that he did this as a private citizen (*privatim*). His example was followed by M. Aemilius Lepidus (*RE* 72, cos. 78 BC) who had shields made for the Basilica Aemilia when he restored it, and who kept a second set in his home. It is probably relevant that both these men were patrician adherents of Sulla, and were developing a new fashion for family display at a time of heightened aristocratic confidence.

The temple of Bellona was in the Campus Martius and therefore also not subject to the regulations which applied inside the city. It served as a site for certain senate meetings, especially to discuss

[65] Harris (1971) 28–30 has questioned the historicity of the claims made in the inscriptions.

[66] A further comparison may be made with the founder's statues in Lavinium and Pompeii all dating to this period. Cf. Degrassi (1937) 69–72.

[67] See Ch. 2, § 1c. The origin of this genre of portraiture is unclear: perhaps gods were first represented in this way, cf. *ILLRP* 236.

[68] Winkes (1969) 16 and 49–50 and (1979) 482.

[69] The date and identification of Appius was established by Stark (1876) and accepted by Gross (1954) and Winkes (1969). Kellum (1981) 161–3 still opts for Caecus on the grounds that the consul of 79 BC would have been too poor.

victories and to award triumphs, since a returning general could address the senate here without entering the city and losing his *imperium*. Foreign envoys were also received here. After this date meetings took place in the presence of a display of the most famous ancestors of the patrician Claudii, a powerful reminder of the family's prowess.[70] Presumably these images were labelled and iconographically related to the *imagines* found in the *atrium*.

A coin of Lepidus, the future triumvir, struck in 58 BC, shows the Basilica Aemilia dominated by large shields hung high on the outside of each column, and confirms that the *imagines clipeatae* were a special feature of the building (see Fig. 3 with Pl. 3c).[71] We have little evidence to show how common the public use of ancestral

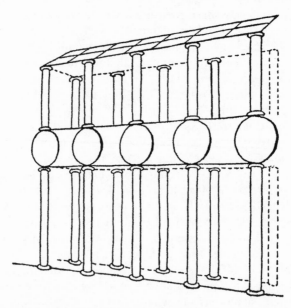

Fig. 3. Reconstruction of the Basilica Aemilia in perspective, based on the coin of M. Aemilius Lepidus illustrated in Plate 3c.

[70] See Ch. 8 for Augustus' similar use of ancestral iconography in the Forum of Augustus, which was a space especially associated with foreign policy and the reception of envoys.

[71] Crawford 419. See also Coarelli (1985) 202–3 for discussion and a reconstruction in figs. 32–4 based on Fuchs (1969) 49–51 with Abb. 1 and 2 and Taf. 2. 23 and 24.

shield portraits was during the Republic.[72] They certainly enjoyed a considerable vogue in private houses under the empire and can be seen in wall-paintings from Pompeii, while Pliny stresses their importance and spectacular effect.[73]

2c. Portraits on Curule Chairs

A further connection between magisterial office and ancestors is provided by the bust portraits of ancestors, both male and female, to be found on curule chairs. A dozen representations of such chairs are extant and date from the second half of the first century BC onwards. The evidence has been collected, illustrated, and evaluated by Schäfer.[74] The ancestors always appear in profile in a pair facing each other to either side on the front of the chair, so that the seated magistrate would be flanked by them as he conducted his business (see Fig. 4). The individualized features of these portraits suggest that they represent ancestors rather than abstract personifications or deities.[75] They provided a constant visual reminder of the magistrate's ancestors and invited a comparison of their achievements in office with his own. The curule chair was in itself a key symbol of power and of the right of a magistrate to sit in judgement. The chair could be legitimately used only by a magistrate during his year of office and by the actor impersonating him at a family funeral.[76] During the late Republic the curule chair also

---

[72] Shields of various kinds, mostly spoils of battle, had been on display in the Forum for much of the Republic. See Livy 9. 40. 16 of 310 BC for Papirius Cursor's Samnite shields, and Cic. *de Or.* 2. 66. 266, Quint. 6. 3. 36, and Plin. *Nat.* 35. 26 for Marius' Cimbrian shields. Coarelli (1985) 203-9 with ills. 32-4 gives a reconstruction of the Basilica Aemilia.

[73] General treatments can be found in Gross (1954) and Winkes (1969) and (1979). Shield portraits of the emperors starting with Augustus adorned the Curia and portraits of authors in libraries may also have been in this form. Ling (1991) 157-9 discusses shield portraits in wall paintings. A particularly fine example comes from the *atrium* in the Villa at Oplontis (Torre Annunziata). For the comparable use of theatrical masks in wall paintings, see Allrogen-Bedel (1974).

[74] Schäfer (1989). See Wanscher (1980) 121-90 for a general treatment which also discusses similar chairs in other cultures, but without comment on the profile busts.

[75] For their imitation on grave reliefs of freedmen in the early imperial period, see the preface. Their appearance on tombs also confirms that they show humans and not gods.

[76] See Cic. *Fam.* 9. 21. 2 = T24 where the history of the Papirii is given in terms of the number of curule chairs between one ancestor and another. In this passage the chair symbolizes a man just as his *imago* does.

Fig. 4. Statue of a Roman magistrate sitting on a curule chair decorated with busts of ancestors, Antonine period.

appeared with increasing frequency on coins which allude to the magisterial authority exercised by an ancestor.[77]

The portraits of female ancestors on curule chairs are especially interesting and have been interpreted as an attempt to stress

[77] Alföldi (1956) 84–5. Such coins are listed and illustrated by Wanscher (1980) 158–66, including imperial issues. For republican coins see Crawford 356, 397, 409, 414, 428, 434, 435, 460, 465, 473, 491, 494, 497.

descent in the female line as well as the male. The Etruscan origin
of the curule chair may account for such a practice, which makes
sense in the context of Etruscan genealogy with its stress on female
ancestors. However, there is no evidence for such bust portraits
before the late Republic: an earlier dating must remain speculative.
Although they were not represented by wax masks, women did
appear on Roman family trees and portraits of female family members, mostly busts, were kept in the house.[78] Cicero (*Cael.* 33 = T5)
has Appius Claudius Caecus cite female ancestors as equally compelling models of behaviour, especially for emulation by a female
descendant. He implies that the women of the family were expected
to share in the prestige and political concerns of the family group.[79]

3. *Ancestors on Coins and Gems*

As discussed above, a citizen was surrounded by reminders of past
Roman office-holders in his visits to aristocratic houses and public
buildings in and around Rome: in the last century of the Republic
he might also be aware of ancestral iconography found on coins.
New coin types were issued in Rome every year by the *triumviri
monetales* and these often advertised ancestral achievements or
offices held. Originally the *denarius* coinage of the Republic had been
dominated by images connected with the state in a limited range of
subjects.[80] Such early coins were designed mainly to identify the
issuing authority which was the city of Rome. A dramatic change
occurred in the 130s BC, which resulted in the minting of a wide
variety of coin types. The reverses of coins became a vehicle for display of ancestral and family themes. The development of coins as a
personal and iconographically complex medium was probably occasioned by the *Lex Gabinia* of 139 BC which provided for the secret
ballot to be used in the centuriate assembly. This important law
reduced the opportunity for candidates and their supporters to exert

[78] See Dwyer (1982) 127-8 for bronze busts, including female ancestors, of the
gens Popidia found in the Casa del Citarista at Pompeii. For statues of women in public places, see Flory (1993).
[79] Close identification with famous ancestors is reflected in the nomenclature of
some aristocratic women in the imperial period, e.g. Mummia Achaica, mother of
the emperor Galba, named for her great-grandfather, the conqueror of Corinth; Fabia
Numantina, daughter of Paullus Maximus cos. 11 BC or his brother cos. 10 BC, named
for Scipio Aemilianus, the natural brother of her ancestor Q. Fabius Maximus
Aemilianus; Poppaea Sabina, daughter of T. Ollius, named for her mother's father.
[80] See Wallace-Hadrill (1986) 74 on the early denarius coinage.

direct pressure on the voters.[81] Such an interpretation also explains the series of rather distinguished politicians who held the office of moneyer in the decade after the electoral reform bill. At the end of the second century BC, therefore, the images on coins came to be used to publicize the ancestors and status of élite families.

The *triumviri monetales* were minor magistrates who formed part of the vigintisexvirate.[82] The office of moneyer does not appear as part of the formal *cursus* during the Republic, but was held by young men before they reached the age at which they were eligible to stand for the quaestorship. Sulla raised the age threshold for the quaestorship to 30, whereas previously it had apparently followed immediately after the completion of military service.[83] He therefore provided a further incentive for young Romans to consider the office of *monetalis* as a convenient step before seeking election to the first senatorial office. The youth of the *monetales* and the need felt by some to gain support for future election campaigns helps to explain why family symbols were important to them. It has also been suggested that the office of *monetalis* was not elective, but that the moneyers were appointed by the consuls and coined under their *imperium*.[84] The men chosen were in a number of cases relatives or clients of the consuls. If correct, this reconstruction shows the organized way in which families influenced and exploited coins for their own purposes.[85] In any case, the *monetales* were directly answerable to the quaestor, a magistrate close to the consuls.[86] At the same time, many *monetales* remain no more than names to us, and their family connections or political allegiances are difficult to assess. A significant number did not go on to have a career of any prominence. It has been noted how often the names of bankers recorded on *tesserae* show a family relationship with *monetales*. It is

[81] Wiseman (1971) 4 and Crawford (1974) 728. Note also the legislation of Marius in 119 BC to narrow the *pontes* (the bridges leading to the voting compartments) and, therefore, to stop inspection of ballots (Cic. *Leg.* 3. 38; Plut. *Mar.* 4. 2).

[82] The office is discussed by Hamilton (1969) and Crawford (1974) 616-19.

[83] Hamilton (1969) 193 and Lahusen (1989) 15.

[84] See Burnett (1977). J. R. Jones (1970) gives a catalogue of mint magistrates from Augustus to Severus Alexander. About half of them were patricians, which shows the importance of the office to them.

[85] *Contra* e.g. Levick (1982) 105-6 who argues that Roman imperial coinage lacked the degree of system and persistence to justify being termed 'propaganda'.

[86] See Lahusen (1989) 15-6 for discussion.

possible that a background in finance was considered important in selecting the moneyers.[87]

Detailed evaluations of the messages on Roman coins depend on precise dating, and interpretations change with each revised chronology.[88] Moreover, the subjects and the significance of many coin types remain highly controversial.[89] Only an overview of the issues can be given here. A detailed study would need to identify and date all coins showing ancestors or ancestral themes before any more definite and precise conclusions could be drawn about their meaning.

About 99 issues in Crawford's collection of all known republican coins can be identified as having some ancestral imagery on them.[90] In the ancient world such iconography was characteristic of the coinage of Rome.[91] The complexity and pervasiveness of ancestral themes raises anew the question of the intended audience. There has been much recent debate about the effectiveness of coins in conveying a message, the nature of that message, and who might be influenced.[92] However, scholars have concentrated mainly on discussing imperial coinage and the role of the emperor in choosing, using, or inspiring coin types.[93] Republican coins are less problematic because we know the *monetales* were responsible for choosing the designs. It is obvious that their tastes and preoccupations are reflected in the resulting issues.[94] The wide variety of types and

[87] See Wiseman (1971) 85-6 and Appendix 4 list C at 199-201, and Lahusen (1989) 17. Zehnacker (1972) 284: 'En tout cas, l'appartenance au monde de la finance expliquerait très bien le mélange caractéristique chez les monetales de noms illustres—des cadets de famille qui ont préféré l'argent aux honneurs—et de noms quasi inconnus—de parvenus.'

[88] The dating system of M. H. Crawford (1974) is followed here, modified by Hersh (1977) and Hersh and Walker (1984). In any case, there is little direct evidence to support the assertion of Zehnacker (1973) 970 that ancestors on coins always convey a religious message.

[89] e.g. Crawford 296 of Cn. Cornelius Blasio which has been interpreted as depicting Scipio Africanus, Cornelius Blasio (pr. 194 BC), or Mars.

[90] These coins are listed in Appendix C showing their distribution patterns.

[91] By far the best treatment of ancestral portraits and images on coins can be found in Zehnacker (1973) 477-627 and 969-1081.

[92] The debate was reopened by A. H. M. Jones (1956/74), whose scepticism about an audience of any size for complex coin messages has been echoed by M. H. Crawford (1974), (1979), and (1983). Hölscher (1982) esp. 277-81 also raises the question without coming to any firm conclusions.

[93] Note esp. Belloni (1974), Sutherland (1976) and (1983), Wallace-Hadrill (1981a) and (1981b), Levick (1982), and M. H. Crawford (1983).

[94] M. H. Crawford's (1974) 726 and (1983) argument that coin types had no effect is unconvincing. See Wallace-Hadrill (1986) for the view that a persuasive function was present.

inscriptions was certainly also a result of the intense political and social competition in Rome during the later Republic.[95] However, the foregoing observations do not solve the problem of the audience, nor do they make it irrelevant. Moreover, they fail to give a sufficient explanation for the change from the earlier denarii which uniformly focused on Rome to the new, more varied and private types.[96] The richness of the iconography in use from the 130s BC onwards and its connections with family prestige suggest that it was not addressed merely to a small circle of the moneyers' family and friends.

Even sceptics are forced to admit that the élite classes did appear to attach importance to coin types.[97] Some issues may have been aimed at the army as new coins were commonly used to pay soldiers, but many messages seem directed at the electorate, the frequent target of ancestral advertisements.[98] As mentioned above, the voting assemblies were influenced by the opinions of the wealthy who voted first and whose votes counted for more.[99] These were also the elements in society with the most education and therefore the most likely to understand the messages on coins. Persuasion on coins with ancestral motifs took the familiar form of the *res gestae* (achievements) of an ancestor, publicly presented for approval and confirmation.[100] Such images were vital to the interests of the educated classes who supported senatorial and aristocratic government.

At the same time, coins may have been designed to mean differ-

[95] See M. H. Crawford (1983) 59 and Wallace-Hadrill (1986) 70. Intense competition between political leaders in the late Republic did not preclude the involvement of other sections of society.

[96] Crawford 728 clearly connects the change in coin designs with new electoral practices, while at the same time denying any political significance to the new coin types.

[97] See M. H. Crawford (1983) 52.

[98] Yavetz (1969/88) 133 hedges on this point.

[99] The importance of ancestral motifs as practical propaganda has been made clear by Zehnacker (1973) 481: 'Même lorsqu'il s'agit d'ancêtres réels, leur glorification répond chez beaucoup de monétaires à des préoccupations parfaitement contemporaines. Les hommes qui ont frappé monaie pour l'État romain ne sont pour la plupart ni des archéologues ni des historiens. Ils évoquent leurs ancêtres pour les proposer en examples, ou du moins pour profiter de leur prestige; ils se réfèrent à certaines situations passées pour juger le présent ou préparer l'avenir.' His arguments are extended and strengthened by Chantraine (1983).

[100] My arguments on the persuasive force of coin types are closest to Wallace-Hadrill (1986). For *res gestae* on coins, see Sutherland (1983) 79: 'The coinage was, apart from its primary economic role, a simple and continuous exercise in self-justification.'

ent things to viewers of differing sophistication. The search for double meanings was a common practice in Roman society. There is ample evidence that ordinary theatre audiences, who represented a cross-section of citizens, were highly politicized and were inclined to see symbolic comments on current affairs in plays on mythological subjects.[101] Similarly, it has been shown how complex iconography on coins, including representations of the gods, conveyed political messages in the age of Sulla and Marius.[102] In light of these considerations it seems rash to assert that ordinary Roman citizens would not have been able to interpret ancestral images on coins which have become obscure to us.

During the last century of the Roman Republic some patterns can be tentatively identified. There seem to have been times when it was particularly fashionable to put ancestral motifs on coins. It is not surprising that certain families tended to feature ancestral themes on their coins at regular intervals, yet there are only a few family badges or motifs that were repeated predictably enough to form a pattern which might have become familiar to the public. The notable example of this practice is the Caecilii Metelli, who used the elephant as their family emblem six times between the 120s and 47/6 BC (see Pl. 3*b*).[103] Similarly the Porcii made regular references to the *leges Porciae*, while the Manlii used the torque as an easy badge of identification.[104] The Julii had used Venus, or Aeneas and Anchises, on their coins since 103 BC.[105] Yet nearly all of the eleven families who repeated ancestral motifs also had family members as moneyers who chose not to use the family's established theme.[106] Some politicians, like Cato Uticensis, simply reproduced the coinage of their fathers without much variation.[107]

Moments of increased interest in ancestors came in the early 120s

---

[101] The evidence is assembled and discussed by Nicolet (1980) 364 ff. See also Dupont (1985) for the background and character of Roman drama.
[102] Luce (1968).   [103] Crawford 262, 263, 269, 369, 374, 459.
[104] Porcii = Crawford 270, 301, 343, 462. Manlii = Crawford 295, 337, 411.
[105] Julii = Crawford 320, 352, 458, 494 3*a-b*.
[106] Families using an ancestral motif consistently: Julii = Crawford 320, 352, 458, 494; Memmii = Crawford 313, 349, cf. 427; Caecilii Metelli = Crawford 262, 263, 269, 369, 374, 459, cf. 335; Servilii = Crawford 264, 370, 423, cf. 239; Manlii Torquati = Crawford 295, 337, 411; Porcii = Crawford 270, 301, 343, 462; Manilii = Crawford 149, 362; Marcii Philippi = Crawford 259, 293, cf. 245, 346, 425; Claudii Marcelli = Crawford 439, 445; Cassii = Crawford 266, 321, 386, 428, cf. 413; Calpurnii Pisones = Crawford 340, 408, cf. 446.
[107] Crawford 462, cf. 343.

BC and then during the career of Marius. The issues throughout the late Republic but especially from the 130s and 120s BC are notable for their competition between moneyers, sometimes on the same board, using parallel ancestral themes apparently to match or rival each other's claims.[108] Brutus' famous coins of 54 BC featuring the portraits of Brutus, the first consul, and Ahala need to be considered in relation to Pompeius Rufus' paired representation of his grandfathers the consuls of 88 BC, Sulla and Pompeius Rufus.[109] The latter issue represents the first portrait coin of more recent ancestors.[110] These coin types mirror strongly opposed feelings about the power of Pompey. The year 88 BC had in turn seen its own contrast of ancestors with L. Titurius Sabinus' coin of Titus Tatius and C. Marcius Censorinus' jugate heads of Numa and Ancus Martius.[111]

There were eleven moneyers using 'ancestor' types in the 80s but only one in the 70s BC. A steady increase can be seen starting with six moneyers in the 60s, and continuing to sixteen in the 50s, and 25 in the 40s BC. It is not correct that family symbols were traditional on coins in the late Republic, but that they were gradually displaced after Sulla by references to contemporary politics and eventually by the representation of living individuals. Many coins surely used family history to comment on present events in a way thoroughly in tune with Roman expectations. In fact, ancestors appear much more frequently at the very end of the Republic. It was not until the 50s BC that portrait heads of historical ancestors, rather than legendary figures of the pre-republican period, could be found on Roman coins, and they enjoyed a considerable vogue.[112]

Seven issues with ancestral motifs were struck in 82–80 BC. After that the highest concentration comes with nineteen examples of issues in the years 47–41 BC. It would appear that ancestral themes

---

[108] Similar and competing themes can be found in the following coins from the 130s and 120s BC: Crawford 242, 243, 245: early corn distribution, Crawford 252, 254: the priesthoods held by the moneyers' fathers, Crawford 258, 259: rival family badges, Crawford 263, 264: motifs using shields, Crawford 267, 268: rival ancestors who were *flamines*, Crawford 269, 270: figures in chariots being crowned by Victory; see also from 114–12 BC, Crawford 291, 293, 295: ancestors on horses or with equestrian statues.

[109] Crawford 433 and 434. Cf. discussion of Brutus in § 4 below. *Contra* Lahusen (1989) 33 who dates both coins to 59 BC

[110] For Roman portrait coins, see Lahusen (1989) with fine illustrations.

[111] Crawford 344 and 346.

[112] The first examples are Crawford 433 and 434.

were prominent at moments of special stress and of heightened competition for power. It is notable that the splendid triumviral gold coins portrayed each of the leaders in person and accompanied by a portrait of an ancestor, Aeneas with Octavian, Hercules with Antony, and the Vestal Aemilia with Lepidus respectively.[113] Ancestral portraits on coins should be seen as complementary to the representation of living individuals.

Coins which combine ancestors from several different time periods are of particular interest to the present study (see Pl. 3*a*).[114] They provide a complex and highly symbolic allusion to cumulative family merit. The scenes created on some coins show an imaginary group of ancestors from various periods seen together in a setting outside historical time. Such a group recalls the meeting of different ancestors as represented by their *imagines* at a family funeral. It is hard to see why so much effort and imagination should have been expended if only very few people with antiquarian interests could understand the coins. Similarly, other coins combine ancestors from two quite separate families which are only linked by the adoption of the moneyer from one to the other.[115] The practice of adoption, which was quite acceptable amongst the Roman élite, meant that a man could keep the ancestors from his previous family and presumably their *imagines*, while he could also make reference to the ancestors of his new family. His new name usually reflected a position in both families.[116]

The growth of a rich and sophisticated iconography of ancestral images on coins shows how ancestors and their achievements were powerful and flexible political tools in Rome. This vocabulary of symbols was aimed at an audience which already had knowledge about ancestors gained from many sources and various artistic media. The resemblance of purpose between the images on coins and the funeral eulogy (*laudatio*) or the wax *imagines* is obvious. The coins were another vehicle for presenting a family's version of a past

[113] See Buttrey (1956) with Crawford 494.
[114] e.g. Crawford 242, 335, 343, 346, 419, 425, 427, 433, 434, 437, 459, 494, 512, 519. Hölscher (1982) 276 also identified Crawford 242 and 243, which shows Minucius' column with two other family members standing at its base, as a timeless combination of ancestors. But see Torelli (1988) 93-4 who takes this as a column and two statues erected by a family member in the late 4th or 3rd cent. BC.
[115] e.g. Crawford 329 and 337.
[116] Cf. the adoptive ties celebrated in the restoration of the Fornix Fabianus or in the coinage of Metellus Scipio (Crawford 459, 460, 461).

event or reminding the public of an historical precedent at a convenient moment. We do not, however, have enough detailed evidence to link particular coin types with a recent family funeral which had rehearsed family history before the public eye.[117] It seems more relevant to consider the role of the *imagines* in everyday life as an inspiration for images on coins. Further reminders of ancestors were provided by monuments and buildings, statues and their inscriptions, games or anniversaries, paintings, triumphs, and rival political claims. Messages about ancestors on coins need to be evaluated in a broad context of related images and themes which may have inspired them or been reinforced by them.[118]

In a genre closely related to coins, ancestors appeared on the personal seals of Roman aristocrats. The number of extant gems suggests that ancestral images were widely used, at least amongst the *nobiles*, and perhaps also in versions mass-produced and distributed to political adherents.[119] Although the portrait styles found on gems do parallel those on coins, the individuals portrayed can only very rarely be identified with any confidence, despite the efforts of generations of scholars.[120] Meanwhile, the problems of dating gems by style alone are legion and inevitably reduce much modern analysis to mere speculation. Nevertheless, it is clear that the gold ring was an important symbol of rank worn by the élite classes and that seals, mostly on these rings, were in common use on legal and state documents.

Plautus tells us that in the second century BC the iron ring of an ordinary citizen might bear his portrait and be used for identification, especially in business dealings (*Ps.* 55 ff.). The symbolic importance of a person's seal is shown by the three symbols used in succession by Augustus (Suetonius *Aug.* 50).[121] His first seal had a sphinx on it, but he later substituted the portrait of Alexander the Great. By the end of his life he was using his own portrait specially

---

[117] Chantraine (1983) 543 sees particular funerals as direct influences on coin types.

[118] See Hölscher (1982) 27 who stresses the importance of coins because they show us the kinds of visual messages that could be produced within the Roman political climate.

[119] Roman gems have been catalogued and evaluated by Vollenweider (1972–4), but most of her conclusions are necessarily based on style alone.

[120] The example of the supposed portrait of Scipio Africanus identified by Vollenweider (1955) is notorious.

[121] See Plut. *Sulla* 3. 4 and *Marius* 10. 5–6 for Sulla's use of a special signet ring, showing his role in the capture of Jugurtha, much to the annoyance of Marius.

commissioned from Dioscurides and this was the ring that was passed on to, and used by, his successors. Archaeological finds confirm that most of the artists responsible for the finest quality stones were Greeks, who sometimes signed their work. Augustus' habits may reflect a republican practice which allowed a contemporary portrait to become an ancestral image after the original owner's death.[122] A close connection between these seal portraits and the *imagines* would help to explain why Augustus never used the head of Caesar as his emblem since Caesar's *imago* had been banned when he became a god (Dio 47. 19. 2 = T27).

In a famous passage from the *Catilinarians* Cicero challenges P. Cornelius Lentulus Sura (*RE* 240) to identify his seal on the fateful letter he had sent to the Allobroges when conspiring with them against the state (*In Cat.* 3. 5. 10). Cicero uses his rhetorical skill to recreate the drama of his confrontation with Lentulus, who had the image of his grandfather on his seal. Apparently this was a well-known image of a particularly prominent ancestor. It is used by Cicero, not unlike an *imago*, as an inspiration for behaviour and a standard to live up to. It represented the political allegiances of the grandfather, P. Cornelius Lentulus (*RE* 202, cos. suff. 162), who had been *princeps senatus* and a notable opponent of the Gracchi. Cicero, speaking as a *novus* consul, made the most of such a potent ancestral symbol against his patrician rival. The seal is familiar partly because it was an heirloom and may have been used by Sura's father before him, but also because it had a key role to play in everyday dealings as a guarantee against forgery. It would be interesting to know how this seal was related iconographically to the *imago* of Sura's grandfather, which was certainly on display in several homes of the Cornelii.

The other main piece of literary evidence about ancestral seals involves the failure of another Cornelius to live up to the image of an ancestor. It is reported that the family deprived a son of Scipio Africanus of a seal with his father's picture on it because he was judged unworthy of it.[123] It remains unclear whether the seal of a

---

[122] Augustus made careful provisions to pass on his ring at times of serious illness, e.g. in 23 BC (Dio 53. 30).

[123] Val. Max. 3. 5. 1: *quam cum propinqui ab eo pollui animadverterent, id egerunt, ne aut sellam ponere aut ius dicere auderet, insuperque e manu eius anulum, in quo caput Africani sculptum erat, detraxerunt* ('When his relatives noticed that [his magisterial office] was being defiled by him, they made arrangements so that he would not dare to hear cases or give judgements, and in addition they took the ring which had

particularly famous ancestor was used as a family badge by many relatives or as a single heirloom passed from father to son. In any case, a seal was linked with the political aims of the family as a whole. In this passage the wearing of the ring is closely connected with a public role and with the exercise of magisterial authority, perhaps because a magistrate used his seal on any official documents and decisions he made in office. Many office-holders may have used ancestral images on seals as early as the time of Scipio. The commissioning of special portrait seals probably came into vogue under Hellenistic influence with the arrival of the first Greek artists in Rome. Seal portraits certainly predated the use of ancestors on coins. It has been proposed that many ancestral images on coins are copied or adapted from gems that were passed down in the family.[124] The poverty of our evidence about ancestors on seals should not lead us to underestimate their role in Rome as symbols of a political heritage and current pretensions.

4. *Brutus and his Ancestors*

A convenient example of aristocratic behaviour which ties together the various themes of this chapter is afforded by the career of M. Junius Brutus, who shaped his political choices with reference to family traditions, notably his connection with the first consul who had driven out the kings.[125] His early upbringing in Cato's house seems to have fostered his sense of a special identity, but he clearly also chose to advertise his heritage publicly. The graffiti scribbled on the statue of the first consul Brutus and on this Brutus' praetorian tribunal in the Spring of 44 BC urged Marcus Brutus to remember his ancestors when he saw Caesar's growing power.[126] Popular sentiment may, however, have been influenced primarily by Brutus' own stress on his descent. He had put his ancestors Brutus and Ahala, whom Cicero saw as his special inspiration, on a coin as

Africanus' head carved on it from his hand'). This incident is thought to apply to Lucius Scipio (praetor 174 BC) rather than to the adopted father of Scipio Aemilianus; see *RE* Cornelius 325. For families weeding out members unsuitable for office, see Develin (1985) 100.

[124] Vollenweider (1955) 104 and (1972–4) 32 n. 46.

[125] Macmullen (1966) 1–18 gives an excellent treatment of the external pressures on Brutus. For the iconography of Brutus the first consul, see Evans (1992) 145–8.

[126] Suet. *Jul.* 80. 3; Plut. *Brut.* 9. 3; App. *BC* 2. 112; Dio 44. 12. 2.

early as 54 BC (see Pl. 3*d*).[127] We know he had their *imagines* in his house in Rome, and probably also at his villa in Tusculum. His friend Cicero makes repeated reference to his long lineage, going back to the first consul, without a shadow of a doubt as to its authenticity. Brutus had consulted Atticus about his family history.[128] Our sources, therefore, accept this pedigree as a natural and laudable inspiration in his betrayal and murder of his former benefactor and long time friend, Caesar.[129] His coins and the pamphlets supporting his actions after the deed returned to the theme of ancestors.[130] His efforts to regain popular favour included a plan to restage Accius' historical drama about the expulsion of the kings, entitled *Brutus*, which had been commissioned by his relative D. Junius Brutus Callaecus (*RE* 57) for games at the dedication of his temple of Mars in 136 BC.[131] He is interesting as a man acting in accord with a family tradition we can trace back 100 years.[132] He presented a carefully calculated and consistent public posture based on the qualities and attributes of early republican ancestors, which he claimed to be heir to. Nevertheless, his actions did not justify themselves to the mass of the people. Since he had no descendants, his memory was kept alive in imperial times mainly within a small circle of aristocratic sympathizers.[133]

5. *Conclusion*

The preceding assessment of the character of Roman elections and their connection with ancestral iconography in various media has tried to illuminate the central role of the *imagines* in the oligarchic culture of the Republic. The *imagines* are a vital factor in explaining

[127] Crawford 433 with Zehnacker (1973) 511. In 54 BC this coin symbolized his opposition to Pompey and was answered by Q. Pompeius Rufus with Crawford 434. Cic. *Att.* 2. 24. 2-3 mentions Brutus' ancestors as early as 59 BC. Crawford 506 of 43-42 BC shows Brutus' own portrait paired directly with that of the first consul in an unrepublican fashion. See § 3 above.

[128] Cic. *Att.* 13. 40; Nep. *Att.* 18. 3.

[129] Cic. *Phil.* 2. 26 = T12; Plut. *Brut.* 1. 1; Dio 43. 45. 3 ff.

[130] Crawford 506 and Dio 44. 12. 2.

[131] Cic. *Arch.* 11. 27 with Schol. Bob.; *Att.* 16. 4; Macmullen (1966) 17.

[132] See also Cic. *De Or.* 2. 225 = T23 for the glorious ancestry of the Junii Bruti used against a family member by the orator Crassus in 91 BC. This passage is discussed in Ch. 5 § 5.

[133] Macmullen (1966) 18-28 discusses the heirs of the liberators in detail. See esp. Tac. *Ann.* 4. 35. 2 = T91; 16. 7; Plin. *Ep.* 1. 17; Suet. *Nero* 37. 1 = T81; Dio 53. 32. 4. For Brutus and his reputation, see Clarke (1981).

how leading families managed to maintain their prominence over many generations.[134] They were used as a pivotal element in a wide array of family advertisements which relied on ancestral images, including statues, shield portraits, reliefs, coins, gems, and related inscriptions.[135] The *imagines* glorified the position of the individual families, while at the same time justifying the Roman system of government itself. They facilitated and articulated competition between leading families, which was often focused on the elections, while encouraging adherence to the traditional norms and rules governing office-holding developed by the ancestors.[136] In other words, they fostered serious competition at frequent elections without danger to the stability of government, especially from individual ambition.[137]

[134] For the domination of established families in the *fasti*, see Scullard (1951) 11, Wiseman (1971) 3, Rilinger (1976) 165-9, and Develin (1979) and (1985) 96-9.

[135] See Kellum (1981) 6 on the overwhelming combined impact of *imagines*, funerals, and public statues.

[136] For a contrast, note the election practices for local magistrates at Pompeii recorded on wall inscriptions of the imperial period. Electioneering stressed the character of the candidates and their personal relationship with the voters in a way comparable with Rome. However, elections for the highest offices seem to have been prearranged and uncontested. The slaves and freedmen of important families played a key role in organizing the vote through their *collegia* (guilds). For analysis, see Jongman (1988).

[137] For a fuller analysis, see Hölkeskamp (1987) and (1993), esp. 37-8.

4

Ancestors at the Funeral: The *Pompa Funebris*

*Odit populus Romanus privatam luxuriam, publicam magnificen-
tiam diligit.*

(Cic. *Mur.* 75)

A chaque culture son théâtre, à chaque culture sa persuasion.
Savoir convaincre à Rome, c'est savoir faire voir.

(F. Dupont (1985) 29)

THE primary use of the *imagines*, which it is the concern of this
chapter to examine, was in the funeral procession of a Roman
office-holder. Their *raison d'être* was to allow the ancestors to be represented as living and breathing Roman magistrates at the height
of their careers, who had reappeared in the city to accompany their
newly-dead descendant on his last journey. On this occasion they
welcomed and received him as one of their number.[1] Polybius (6.
53-4 = T61) is our main source for the Roman funeral. For him
the masks of the ancestors are the most characteristic and important part of the funeral spectacle. He repeatedly stresses the realism
of the masks themselves and the dramatic quality of the ancestors
appearing as magistrates in procession.[2] Their parade was the
largest group of magistrates, accompanied by their symbols of office
and rank, which a Roman citizen was ever likely to see.[3] This

---

[1] See Redfield (1975) 163 who comments: 'Through ceremonies persons are classified and placed in categories; their analogical unity with similar persons is
asserted.'

[2] 6. 53. 6-7 = T61. Polybius states that the *imagines* were real masks, that could
be worn, as discussed in Ch. 2. Drerup's (1980) 112 attempt to reinterpret this passage as referring to realistic dressed dolls has no basis in the text.

[3] Bethe (1935) 3 is the main discussion to focus on the visual effects of the parade.
Cf. Zinserling (1959/60).

chapter will explore in detail the role of the *imagines* on the day of a funeral. Consideration will be given to how the actors wearing the *imagines* appeared in the procession, as well as how such funerals were organized and by whom. A brief history of the development of funerals during the Republic will be outlined. As aristocratic funerals became more elaborate and came to be staged for a wider circle of family members, the *imagines* were seen more often in the streets of Rome and in an increasingly elaborate setting of props and participants.

The funeral procession formed the public climax of several ceremonies surrounding the burial of a Roman office-holder, all of which traditions and rituals could be described by the word *funus*.[4] On the occasion of a death in the family the whole household was in mourning, as indicated by the decoration of the house itself, including foliage fixed to the outside doors to indicate the presence of a corpse inside.[5] Initial mourning took place at the *collocatio* or lying-in-state, during which the body was displayed in fine clothes on a high couch until the day of the funeral. The funeral procession, including musicians, dancers, actors wearing the *imagines*, professional mourners, friends, and relatives, would start at the house and proceed to the Forum for the funeral speech (*laudatio*). This public speech was addressed equally to any citizen who might be present. Consequently, the assembly at the speaker's platform (*rostra*), and the speech delivered there, were both called *contio funebris*, using terminology close to the designation of any other public meeting.[6] More elaborate funerals might be accompanied by a public banquet provided by the family that evening. Games and theatrical performances were mostly held on a separate day, although the earliest gladiatorial contests of the middle Republic seem to have been closely associated with the burial itself and the crowd which had gathered to hear the *laudatio*.

After hearing the praises of the dead, coupled with those of the ancestors, the relatives would leave the city for the cremation or

---

[4] Detailed descriptions of Roman burial rites, including citation of the ancient references, can be found in Marquardt (1905) 340-85, Cuq (1896) 1386-407, Blümner (1911) 482-98, and Toynbee (1971) 43-61.

[5] The doors of houses were closed as a sign of mourning. See Tac. *Ann.* 2. 83. 3, Ch. 7 § 1, and Wallace-Hadrill (1988) 46.

[6] Cicero is our main witness to this terminology which he uses at *De Or.* 2. 341 and *Leg.* 2. 61.

burial at a grave which often served the family as a whole, or at least a particular branch of it. There is no evidence to show that the *imagines* ever left the city and their role was probably over after the *laudatio*. The burial itself was a more private matter. Ancient sources suggest that except in the case of the most celebrated public figures only the family and close friends would proceed to the grave, where various rituals were performed to accompany the burial.[7] A private meal for the family (*silicernium*) was held at the grave to complete the observances of the day. Full mourning would continue until the ninth day when the family returned to the grave for another meal, called the *cena novendialis*, which marked the close of the whole burial rite with a libation to the Manes. Cult and commemoration of the dead by family members would be repeated at the grave on appropriate public feasts, as well as on private anniversaries and birthdays.[8]

1. *Before the Funeral*

The lying-in-state (*collocatio*) was the first part of the mourning rite and formed an essential preparation for the day of the funeral.[9] It provided the occasion when respects might be paid to the dead member of a leading family. The length of the *collocatio* is unclear in our sources and may well have varied considerably. It is hard to believe that any significant delay before burial could have been usual in a Mediterranean climate.[10] By contrast, ordinary people, especially the poor, were apparently buried almost immediately after death.[11] In this, as in so many other features surrounding the funeral, the Roman office-holder aimed to set himself apart in a way for the world to see.

Our best source for the details of a *collocatio* is a relief from the grave of the Haterii in Rome, usually dated to the late Flavian or

[7] According to Suetonius (*Tib.* 32. 1) the emperor Tiberius attended the cremation of a few outstanding figures. The wording implies that he was showing special favour by not leaving the obsequies earlier.

[8] The cult of the dead is treated by Wissowa (1912) 232-5, 434, Toynbee (1971) 61-4, and Harmon (1978) 1600-3. For Greek parallels, especially for meals at the grave, see Alexiou (1974).

[9] On the *collocatio*, see Val. Max. 5. 7 ext. 1, Sen. *Brev. Vit.* 20. 3, *Cons. ad Polyb.* 14. 2, *Vit. Beat.* 28. 1, Lucan 2. 22.

[10] Servius' (*A.* 6. 218) claim that seven days was the normal interval before the funeral is hard to credit.

[11] Cic. *Clu.* 27 speaks of cremation within less than 24 hours.

early Trajanic period (see Pl. 5).[12] This is the only surviving scene of a *collocatio* in Roman art. The reliefs on the elaborate tomb depict the sequence of events after death from lying-in-state to burial. Inscriptions show that the tomb belonged to a family of wealthy freedmen, who seem to have been involved in the building industry.[13] The deceased woman and her husband Q. Haterius Tychicus are represented by bust portraits in small shrines in a style which imitates contemporary court portraiture.[14] The tomb is evidently designed to demonstrate the new status achieved by the family and therefore reflects and echoes some customs of the élite classes in Rome.[15] The dead woman is laid out in splendid array in what appears to be the *atrium* of her house.[16] Her feet are pointing towards the door, showing that she is ready for the funeral procession. The *atrium* has been finely decorated with garlands of fruit and flowers, as well as shells.[17] The scene is brightly lit by torches and candelabra, accompanied by two incense burners in the foreground. Solemnity and splendour characterize what is essentially a very public scene in the entrance of the home.[18]

The relief gives an idea of the numerous attendants and mourners who could be found around the bier. Music was apparently a constant accompaniment to professional and private mourning, while the body is being decked with flowers by a person who is taken to be a professional undertaker's attendant (*pollinctor*). Seated mourning figures wearing the freedman's cap represent slaves who have been freed in the deceased's will. Those filing past the body to pay their last respects have been interpreted as relatives, but they may include friends or clients as well. This is a busy room full of light, music, singing, and splendid decorations and equipment. In an aristocratic household, the

---

[12] For most detail see Jensen (1978) who dates the whole series of sculptures from the Tomb of the Haterii to the end of Domitian's reign in the late 1st cent. AD. For other discussions of this relief, see Blümner (1911) 485, Helbig (1963) no. 1074, Toynbee (1971) 44-5 with pl. 9, and now Kleiner (1992) 196-9 with figs. 164-8.

[13] For the inscriptions, see Jensen (1978) fig. 3 (the dedication tablet) and fig. 4 (Q. Haterius Antigonus).

[14] See Jensen (1978) 269-97 for the social background of Q. Haterius and his sons Q. Haterius Anicetus and Q. Haterius Rufinus.

[15] For a discussion of the art of freedmen, see the Introd. § 2.

[16] The sloping roof is particularly suggestive of the *atrium*.

[17] Toynbee (1971) interprets these as symbols of the journey and happy life after death.

[18] The importance and function of the *atrium* in the Roman house is discussed in Ch. 7.

dead person lay in the presence of the cupboards containing the *imagines*, which were presumably closed in mourning. The masks of the ancestors would be put on by actors on the day of the funeral so that the ancestors 'came to life' again in the *atrium* of the family home immediately before their public procession to the Forum.

An essential reason for a delay in burial, however brief, was the time needed to organize publicity for the funeral itself. Many élite funerals were announced by heralds inviting all citizens both on the day itself and on the previous days.[19] Because of the public nature of aristocratic funerals permission was required during the Republic to hold such a funeral, as it certainly also was under the Empire.[20] The aediles were the officials generally in charge of funerals so they were the logical candidates for this task.[21] The funeral speech (*contio*) was the climax of the public part of the ceremony and permission would have been required to address the crowd in the Forum from the *rostra*. Normally the right to address a public meeting was reserved for magistrates in office, while Polybius indicates that the funeral speech was usually given by a son or other close relative of the deceased, often someone under the age to be eligible for any kind of magistracy.[22]

Whether the public funeral speech originated in the magisterial right to address the people exercised in the past by a son who happened to be in office must remain a matter for speculation in the present state of our evidence.[23] Other public speeches were delivered by magistrates in office, and sometimes by individuals whom they called upon to speak at a public meeting which they had convened.[24] It is a feature of Roman life that the ordinary citizen was

[19] This custom is discussed in most detail by Marquardt (1886) 351.

[20] The only direct testimony for the republican period is Dionysius of Halicarnassus' description of the funeral of Appius Claudius (9. 54. 5). The situation under the Empire is made clear by Tac. *Ann.* 3. 76 = T89.

[21] Cic. *Phil.* 9. 7. 17 and Ov. *Fast.* 6. 663. CIL 6. 1375b (= *ILS* 917b) mentions the aediles' edict regulating tombs. For the aediles' edict which ensured observance of sumptuary legislation, see section 6 below. There is no evidence that the *imagines* were subject to the moral control exercised by the censors; see Baltrusch (1989) 6-30, 191-3.

[22] Polyb. 6. 53. 2 = T61.　　　　　　　　　　　　　[23] Marquardt (1905) 359.

[24] Liebenam (*RE contio*) cites Gell. 13.16 as the basic text for the *ius contionem habendi* ('right to hold a public meeting'). Magistrates and priests could call such a meeting, when a *comitia* was not in session. Cf. L. R. Taylor (1966) 15-16 for the variety of *contiones* held, especially at the *rostra*. An example is L. Aemilius Paullus addressing the people in 167 BC at the *contio* usual for a general after a triumph. This meeting was convened by the tribune M. Antonius for Paullus (Livy 45. 40).

not accorded any right of public speech.[25] Even at meetings of the senate the order of precedence was strictly laid down and no one could speak unless called upon by the presiding magistrate. Therefore, a delay in burial was needed to ensure official approval and make the necessary arrangements for the funeral, while at the same time allowing for a bigger crowd on the day.

Any aristocratic funeral with a *laudatio* and a procession of *imagines* was a public event. It can, therefore, be confusing to speak in terms of a separate category of 'public funeral' when referring to certain exceptional funerals granted to selected individuals by the senate.[26] Such funerals were the exception because they were given 'at public expense' and the state provided the grave, usually on the Campus Martius.[27] However, these funerals were few and are not attested before Sulla.[28] They were a feature of the heightened competition for recognition in the late Republic.[29] They were also unusual for their grandeur since they were not subject to the normal rules which limited lavish displays at funerals. In fact, all families of office-holders were entitled, if not expected, to stage highly public funerals for their members, as long as they kept within the general guidelines of the laws and the aediles' edict.

Aristocratic funerals may originally have been held only for former magistrates, but during the Republic they came to be common for most family members, except young children and infants who were mourned only in a limited way.[30] The public nature of élite funerals is further emphasized by their taking place during the day

[25] Nicolet (1980) 314-41.

[26] The most helpful treatments are by Vollmer (1893) and by Cuq (1896) 1406 who lists the recipients of 'public funerals' (*funus publicum*) during the Republic and notes that they were in vogue under Augustus and Tiberius, but seem to have fallen from use afterwards. Other discussions can be found in Marquardt (1905) 350 and Blümner (1911) 489.

[27] Cicero is our most valuable witness and his proposal before the senate for a public funeral and burial place for Servius Sulpicius Rufus illustrates the procedure in detail (*Phil.* 9. 7. 16). He stresses the rare honour of a public tomb as opposed to the more frequent award of a public statue.

[28] Cf. the public burial of C. Poplicius Bibulus (*ILLRP* 357 = I12) whose grave and inscription have been dated on stylistic grounds to the time of Sulla. Such a rare honour accorded to a man otherwise unknown to us demonstrates our lack of evidence about 'public funerals' during the Republic.

[29] See e.g. the 'public funeral' recorded for L. Volusius Saturninus (cos. suff. AD 3, d. AD 56) in the inscription from the shrine of the Lares at his villa (Boatwright (1982) and Panciera (1982)).

[30] For the funerals of children, see Marquardt (1905) 343, and Blümner (1911) 490 and 510.

in contrast to the funerals of the poor and of children which took place at night.[31] Paupers or slaves were probably buried more conveniently at night, a time when their friends and family might be able to attend.[32] Whatever the religious or legal reasons for burying children at night, it enabled their families to avoid drawing attention to a loss. The burial of children separately and without ceremony is common in cultures which do not regard the child as a full member of the community.[33] Children were always treated differently in Roman burial customs through a recognition of the importance of family status in public. By contrast, in the case of an adult family member, especially an office-holder, the *gens* would strive to make the occasion as memorable and splendid as possible.

2. *The Funeral Procession*

We have no detailed description by any Roman author, let alone one entitled to such a funeral, of a practice which was central to aristocratic life during the Republic. Numerous passing references to be found in the extant sources show how natural it was for Roman writers to assume a knowledge of these customs in their audience.[34]

[31] For the burial of children at night, see Sen. *Brev. Vit.* 20. 5, Servius *A.* 1. 727; 6. 224, and esp. Serv. Dan. 11. 143: *et magis moris Romani ut impuberes noctu efferrentur ad faces, ne funere immaturae subolis domus funestatur . . .* ('And it is particularly the custom of the Romans to carry children out for burial at night by the light of torches so that the house should not be in mourning at the funeral rites of a minor . . .'). Cf. Livy 2. 8. 8; 45. 40 and Tac. *Ann.* 13. 17. 1. Rose (1923) discusses the reasons for these special funerals, adducing parallels from other cultures. Even small children of the imperial house were commemorated only where their remains were cremated (*CIL* 6. 888–893 = *ILS* 172; 181; 181a; 181b; 188). Cf. Platner-Ashby (1929) s.v. *ustrinum domus Augustae*. By way of comparison the Homeric *ekphora* took place by day, but archaic and classical funerals at Athens were before dawn. See [Dem.] 43. 62 with Sourvinou-Inwood (1983) 40.

[32] See Festus 506 L and Martial 8. 75. 9 for the burial of the poor at night. Rose (1923) adduces Hor. *S.* 1.8 as possible counterevidence.

[33] For the burial of children as a purely family concern, see Binford (1971) 232–4, Ariès (1981) 82–92, Sourvinou-Inwood (1981) 34–5, (1983) 44–5, (1994) 430–1, and Morris (1987) 61–2, 181. Children were not buried with adults in Greece *c.*900–725 BC. Their reappearance in Athenian cemeteries in the 8th cent. BC is linked to the hereditary social status of the *Eupatridae*, which made any member of the family important. Cf. Golden (1990) 85 for some possible explanations for Greek children being buried inside the house, such as magic, or the unwillingness to give up a child.

[34] *Imagines* at the funeral: Plaut. *Am.* 458–9 = T53; Polyb. 6. 53 = T61; Cic. *Mil.* 33 = T9; 86 = T10; *De Or.* 2. 225 = T23; Liv. *Per.* 48 = T46; Hor. *Epod.* 8. 11–12 = T34; Prop. 2. 13*b*. 3 = T63; Diod. 31. 25. 2 = T30; Val. Max. 2. 9. 6 = T96; 5. 8. 3 = T103; 8. 15. 1–2 = T104; Sil. 10. 567 = T78; Tac. *Ann.* 2. 32. 1

The procession (*pompa*) was in many ways the most spectacular part of such a funeral and prepared the audience for the climax of the eulogy (*laudatio*). The *laudatio* itself, by including the praise of the ancestors and an account of their careers, served as a type of commentary on the procession which had gone before. The procession formed at the house and then made its way to the Forum for the *laudatio*. It therefore passed through the busiest part of the city and would be obvious to any in the Forum, including those who had come there on other business.[35] Indeed a large funeral procession might take up quite a lot of space and would surely have attracted considerable crowds.

We do not know how direct a route a funeral procession took to reach its destination in the Forum. The patrician Cornelii apparently had at least part of their funeral processions start at the temple of Jupiter on the Capitol, where the *imago* of Scipio Africanus was kept.[36] This special custom of the Cornelii shows that variations in the processional route could be used for additional effect.

A small procession without *imagines* can be seen on a relief from Amiternum, which apparently dates from the late Republic (see Pl. 6).[37] This relief, like the one from the tomb of the Haterii discussed above, is unique in its depiction of a scene not regularly part of Roman iconography.[38] Again we are dealing with the art of freedmen, which is consistently alluding to elements of much grander funerals.[39] The procession scene was probably part of the same monument as a relief showing gladiators fighting and a pediment with Medusa's head which were found nearby. The procession relief illustrates the important role of musicians and hired mourning women who walked before the bier. The torches which accompa-

---

= T85a; 2. 73. 1 = T87; 3. 5 = T88; 3. 76 = T89; 4. 9. 2 = T90; Plin. *Nat.* 35. 6 = T54; Plut. *Caes.* 5 = T59; App. *Hisp.* 89 = T2; Dio 56. 34 = T28.

[35] Cic. *De Or.* 2. 225 = T23 has Crassus point out such a procession to those participating in a trial in the Forum in 91 BC. Hor. *S.* 1. 6. 42-4 comments on the traffic congestion caused by funeral processions in the Forum.

[36] Val. Max. 8. 15. 1-2 = T104; App. *Hisp.* 89 = T2; see discussion in Ch. 2 § 1e.

[37] Toynbee (1971) 46-7 with pl. 11.

[38] See Felletti Maj (1977) 119-25 with bibliography, although she has missed the freedman context, and now Kleiner (1992) 103 with figs. 88-9.

[39] For the inscriptions of the Peducaea and Apisia families, see *CIL* 9. 4454, 4460, 4465-7, 4471, 4477, 4480, 4480a, 4482, 4486, 4487. Franchi (1963-4) esp. 24-7 gives a full discussion of imitation of élite funerals in the relief. His are the best and most detailed illustrations (pl. 5-10).

nied a funeral also attracted further attention and added to the solemnity of the atmosphere. The deceased is shown propped up and may be represented by an actor.[40] The procession was organized by a *dissignator*, who was in charge of orchestrating the whole performance.[41] He has been identified as the figure facing the bier and holding one corner with his right hand as he directs the bearers. The procession is made up of two main parts. The musicians and professional mourners walked ahead of the body, while family and friends followed behind. Presumably the grandeur of a funeral could be measured partly in terms of how many came before the body on its splendid high bier. Those wearing the *imagines* and impersonating the ancestors were part of the group walking in front of the bier.[42] They appeared in chronological order starting with the oldest, often the originator of the family.[43] The general appearance of such a procession of magistrates is suggested by painted processions of men in togas from Etruscan tombs, especially from Tarquinia.[44]

The usual verbs used to describe the procession of the *imagines* are *ducere* or *duci* and *comitari*,[45] which suggest their active part in walking ahead of the bier and acting as an escort for their descendant. The passive of *duco* perhaps alludes to the role of the musicians who led the way or of the *dissignator* in charge of the parade.

Polybius notes that the men wearing the masks were chosen for their likeness in stature and bearing to the particular ancestor they were to represent.[46] His statement should not be taken to indicate that they were family members. This is never suggested by any ancient source and is perhaps disproved by the position of the *imagines* in front of the bier rather than following it with the family members. Perhaps this role originally fell to clients or freedmen of the family, but by the middle Republic actors were employed

---

[40] See Franchi (1963-4) 27.   [41] Sen. *Ben.* 6. 38.

[42] See Ch. 8 § 1*b* for Augustus' funeral, where his body may have been carried in front of his ancestors as a special mark of honour. Hor. *Ep.* 8. 11-12 = T34 refers to the *imagines* leading the funeral procession.

[43] The chronological nature of the procession has been explored by Bettini (1991) 177 ff.

[44] For discussion of Etruscan material, see Appendix D.

[45] e.g. *ducere*, Hor. *Epod.* 8. 11-12 = T34; *duci*, Cic. *De Or.* 2. 225 = T23; *comitari*, Tac. *Ann.* 2. 32. 1 = T85*a*; *anteferri*, Tac. *Ann.* 3. 76 = T89, cf. Polyb. 6. 53. 6 = T61 : ἄγουσιν εἰς τὴν ἐκφοράν.

[46] 6. 53. 6 = T61. Cf. Zinserling (1959/60) 419: 'Diese Schauspieler *waren* dann die Ahnen wirklich—sie hatten deren Antlitz, trugen deren Kleider, wurden wie sie von Liktoren begleitet.'

(Diodorus 31. 25. 2 = T30). Diodorus' description suggests that the family may have had a regular arrangement with certain actors who would then give a realistic portrayal of a man's character, as is the case in the funeral of Vespasian discussed below. The use of actors also makes best sense in terms of the numbers needed for larger funerals. Polybius probably means that actors were chosen according to the character of each ancestor and the role they were to play. He stresses the lifelike quality of the performances and it is this dramatic aspect which seems to have been at the heart of the procession.[47]

Silius Italicus (10. 566-7 = T78) is the only source to mention an alternative tradition of carrying *imagines* on litters. He alludes to this practice in his description of the funeral of Aemilius Paullus, as staged by Hannibal after Cannae (216 BC, Livy 22. 52). It is hard to draw any conclusions about third-century BC customs from what is probably the result of antiquarian research by Silius who lived in the first century AD. Other writers seem to imagine that the *imagines* were always worn and this is implied by their form as masks.

An equally obscure feature of the procession are the *lecti* mentioned by Servius (*A.* 6. 861). These have also been interpreted as litters on which *imagines* or other exhibits were carried.[48] According to this commentator on Virgil, Sulla had 6,000 of these *lecti* at his funeral, while Marcellus had 600 in 23 BC.[49] The reading 'litters' has been used to try to calculate the number of *imagines* at these funerals, and has resulted in controversy over the notion of 6,000 *imagines* even for a patrician Cornelius.[50] In fact, the high figures should warn us that this theory is problematic. It would make better sense to construe *lecti* as 'picked men' or 'invited participants'.[51]

[47] For the *imagines* adding to the theatrical element at funerals, see Arce (1988b) 47-9.
[48] This standard interpretation can be found in *RE*, Schneider and Meyer (1916) 1101. Cf. Plut. *Sulla* 38. 3 for the use of litters at Sulla's funeral. The usual Latin words for a litter are *fercula, feretrum,* or *lectica.*
[49] Servius *A.* 6. 861: *ad funeris huius honorem Augustus sescentos lectos intra civitatem ire iussit: hoc enim apud maiores gloriosum fuerat et dabatur pro qualitate fortunae; nam Sulla sex milia habuit.* ('To enhance his [Marcellus'] funeral rites Augustus ordered 600 picked men to enter the city: for this had been a mark of distinction in the time of our ancestors and was granted according to the distinction of a man's status; for Sulla had 6,000.')
[50] See most recently Drerup (1980) 122.
[51] So Panciera in von Hesberg and Panciera (1994) 89-90 who interprets the *lecti* as persons selected to take part in the procession who might represent different sections of society. As argued below, a military context seems more plausible than a general group of citizens.

According to this translation Servius is alluding to an otherwise unattested, but not implausible, custom of having a picked group of men escorting the procession, either on horseback or on foot.[52] These could be seen as a type of guard of honour and in the case of Sulla perhaps comprised a representative selection of his veterans. Servius' language stresses the appearance of the *lecti* inside the city walls, which was not usually permitted for soldiers except to take part in a triumphal procession.[53] It is, in fact, at Sulla's funeral that we first hear of veterans marching in the parade as they had done in earlier triumphs.[54] They would add to the military atmosphere evoked by many of the *imagines* of previous *triumphatores* and may have accompanied displays from the deceased's own triumphs, if such equipment was on hand.[55] Alternatively, these men may have been drawn from Sulla's 10,000 freedman called Cornelii, who mostly lived in Rome and owed him strong allegiance. They had been specially selected for their strength and youth to represent his interests among the city plebs.[56]

The growing stress on the glory of the individual general increased the significance of his triumph and funeral as presentations of his personal valour and success. His own triumphal imagery could be used to complement that of his *imagines* by using spoils and props from previous processions.[57] The increasing use of triumphal themes also reflects the growing direct role of the army in Roman politics during the last generations of the Republic. The influence of

[52] For *lecti* meaning 'carefully chosen' or 'worthy of selection', see e.g. Sall. *Cat.* 59. 3; Livy 33. 18. 10; Verg. *A.* 11. 60. The term often appears in a military context.

[53] Note Servius *A.* 6. 659 and 11. 142 which are the only examples of the phrase *intra civitatem* before the Vulgate. In every case there is emphasis on something inside the city walls.

[54] App. *BC* 1. 105–6. See below for a discussion of Hellenistic processions and their influence on Roman spectacle.

[55] At Caesar's funeral flute-players and actors wore costumes that had been used at his four triumphs and these were then burned as part of the funeral rites (Suetonius *Jul.* 84. 7). Versnel (1970) 115–29 tries to minimize links between funerals and triumphs, especially during the Republic. His views are developed as a refutation of Brelich (1938).

[56] Cf. *ILLRP* 353 and App. *BC* 1. 100 and 104. Freedmen may have been expected to attend their patron's funeral.

[57] For a refutation of the view that the *fabula praetexta* was a special type of play written to reenact a man's triumph at his funeral, see Flower (1995). Nevertheless, Dupont (1985) 218 has a point: 'En effet dans les prétextes le public romain voit sur la scène, vêtus de toges prétextes, les ancêtres de la noblesse romaine tel qu'ils défilent dans la procession des enterrements aristocratiques.'

the triumph is further illustrated by Augustus' decision to include many more elements from it in his own funeral, presumably because the triumph was the closest ceremony to deification or heroization which was a traditional part of Roman culture.[58]

The ancestors appeared wearing the garb of the highest office they had held in life and accompanied by appropriate lictors and status symbols. Magistrates were never seen in public without *lictors* (Livy 39. 32. 10).[59] In this way also the procession reflected usual practice. Polybius (6. 53. 7 = T61) takes special note of the splendour of the costumes and equipment involved. He describes the ancestors as riding on carriages (6. 53. 8 = T61) which served as further symbols of status since only magistrates could ride in the city by day. The carriages also made them more visible to the crowds. Moreover, it should be noted that current magistrates and senators who took part in a funeral procession would appear in mourning, which is to say in darker togas, or simply with their togas reversed to hide the purple border. Their lictors and those of the deceased wore black and seem to have reversed their fasces.[60] The result was a contrast between contemporary office-holders in mourning and the ancestors who displayed their trappings and status in the most elaborate way. The dignity and importance of the ancestors was, therefore, stressed.

There is nothing in the ancient evidence for the procession or the funeral speech which connects the *imagines* with divine honours for or cult addressed to the dead.[61] Nor was there anything ghostly or macabre about their appearance.[62] Their realistic character means they were made to present each ancestor as he appeared alive and

[58] Richard (1978). Augustus' funeral is discussed in Ch. 8 § 1*b*. Versnel (1970) 122-3 stresses the triumphal imagery which was added to imperial funerals under Hellenistic influences. Hickson (1991) discusses Augustus' use of triumphal imagery without reference to his funeral. Cf. Arce (1988*b*).

[59] See Kübler *RE s.v. lictor*.

[60] See Verg. *A.* 11. 92-3; Hor. *Ep.* 1. 7. 5; *Epicedion Drusi* 142; Tac. *Ann.* 3. 2; Stat. *Theb.* 6. 213-16; with Mommsen (1887) 1. 375.

[61] For further discussion, see Ch. 7 § 4. Bömer (1943) 105-6 argued without ancient evidence that although no cult was associated with the *imagines* in the *atrium*, their use in the procession was essentially religious in character. Cf. Sourvinou-Inwood (1983) 33 ff. for an analysis of Greek death rituals as social rather than religious acts.

[62] A view of the parade of ancestors as macabre or grim was espoused by Martha (1905) 7, Durry (1950) xii, and Skard (1965) 61. Rambaud (1978) 18 argues that the funeral procession expresses a basic human need to see the ancestors live again. For more discussion, see Ch. 10.

at the height of his career. Moreover, they were apparently not present for the cult acts connected with the funeral rites, which took place at the grave outside the *pomerium*. There are no obvious common elements shared with impersonations using masks in other cultures, which served a largely apotropaic or magic function.[63]

Since no detailed description of any individual funeral has come down to us, it is hard to say exactly which *imagines* were expected to appear in any given context. Cicero implies that by his day a wife brought her own *imagines* with her at the time of her marriage.[64] As funerals became more elaborate in the later Republic an increasing number of *imagines* from different families were paraded, as well as more legendary ancestors who had been 'discovered' by antiquarian researches.[65] The *S.C. de Cn. Pisone patre* shows that in AD 20 it was considered usual for any relative, by blood or by marriage (*cognatus adfinisue*), to display a man's *imago*.[66] The wording of this decree can be used as evidence to support the belief that *imagines* were part of a bride's equipment to be taken with her to her husband's house. A son or daughter could, therefore, expect to have their own copies of ancestral *imagines* if they moved from their father's house. Thus *imagines* needed to be reproduced on the occasion of a marriage, or when a son set up his own household. In addition, adoption led to complex interconnections between aristocratic families and these relationships were also represented in terms of *imagines*.[67]

At the same time family members in disgrace and those subject to any type of *damnatio memoriae* were excluded.[68] The importance of the public appearance of *imagines* is underlined by the growth in the last century BC of efforts to ban the images of a political opponent after death. Conversely, Caesar was not represented by an

[63] Breckenridge (1968) 28.

[64] *Vat.* 28 = T20, cf. Schneider and Meyer (1916) 1102–3. There is no ancient evidence about whether or not the *imagines* played a part in the bridal procession (*domum deductio*) on the day of the wedding.

[65] The funeral of Junia, the sister of Brutus and wife of Cassius, in AD 16 included the *imagines* of twenty families (Tac. *Ann.* 3. 76 = T89).

[66] ll. 76–81 = 116.

[67] e.g. Sen. *Con.* 2. 1. 17 = T69. Cf. the restoration of the Fornix Fabianus (*ILLRP* 392) discussed in Ch. 3 § 2a.

[68] See Juv. 8. 17–18 for the breaking of a poisoner's *imago*. *Damnatio memoriae* is discussed in Ch. 2 § 2 and Ch. 1. Cic. *Fam.* 9. 21 = T24 speaks of picking and choosing *imagines* for personal reasons. *Damnatio memoriae* is not firmly attested before Octavian's treatment of Antony, but Sulla had banned Marius' *imago* (Plut. *Caes.* 5 = T58).

imago because he was considered a god.[69] One important function of the funeral procession was to present and hence to define the community of past family members and Roman citizens, while showing their close connection with those still living. Anyone outside the civic body, such as a criminal or a god, could not be accommodated within its framework.

Although the ancient sources available to us do not prove that the dead man was represented by an *imago* at his own funeral, it is most likely that he was. This has been a matter for some debate because the most direct evidence comes from Suetonius describing the funeral of Vespasian in AD 79 (*Ves.* 19. 2 = T84). A mime actor named Favor presented the character of Vespasian to the crowd and made jokes which recalled Vespasian's notorious sense of humour as well as his cautious attitude towards money. This is the only extant reference to an actor speaking during a funeral procession. It is all the more interesting for its fleeting evocation of character improvisation and for the spontaneous interaction between the actor and the bystanders. Yet Suetonius refers to it as a well established custom (*mos*), so that it cannot simply be dismissed as a novelty introduced by the Flavian emperors who did not have their own *imagines*.[70] The incident seems to have been preserved because Favor's performance was especially memorable and amusing. Suetonius suggests that it was usual for the actor to present the words and deeds of the person to the crowd. His evidence tends to confirm an interpretation of the funeral procession as a pageant of Roman history with each ancestor making brief speeches about himself and acting in character for the audience.

Suetonius' testimony can be supported by evidence from Diodorus. A fragment of Diodorus (31. 25. 2 = T30), quoted by Photius, describes actors imitating the dead man and his ancestors at the funeral of L. Aemilius Paullus in 160 BC. Like Suetonius,

[69] Dio 47. 19. 2 = T27 refers to a decree of the triumvirs in 42 BC stating that Caesar should not have an *imago* because he had now been recognized as a god. His *imago* may still have appeared at his funeral, as discussed below in § 6. Similarly, we know that Vespasian's *imago* was part of his funeral although he was deified probably somewhat after being buried (Suet. *Vesp.* 19. 2 = T84).

[70] Dupont (1987) 171 dismisses the evidence of Suetonius as not applicable to the Republic. She does not discuss the fragment of Diodorus treated below. Her contention that the *imago* was only visible when the body of the deceased had been buried is ingenious, but has no basis in the ancient evidence. Vespasian's was the first imperial burial for an emperor not entitled to *imagines*, other than that of his brother.

Diodorus stresses the realism of the character-acting in the procession. His reference to a mid-second-century BC practice is tantalizing as it raises questions about how much more detail Polybius could have provided had he cared to. Polybius had the opportunity to attend the funeral in question, but in his general discussion of aristocratic funerals he does not mention any impersonation of the dead man himself. Despite the limited nature of our evidence, it is altogether probable that every dead office-holder's *imago* was first worn at his own funeral by an actor who aimed to give a lifelike impression of his character.

Suetonius' testimony about Vespasian's funeral also raises interesting questions about the tone and mood of funeral processions in general. Apparently something close to a festival atmosphere was tolerated even at the funeral of an emperor. In addition to flute-players, actors, and much paraphernalia from the triumph, the funeral procession also included comic dancers. Our lone reference comes from Dionysius of Halicarnassus, who claims to have seen these troupes of dancers preceding the bier at the funerals of famous people, and especially the rich.[71] The dance in question was a Greek dance called *sicinnis*, which was particularly associated with the games (*ludi*).[72] Dancers dressed as satyrs and silens parodied the more serious dancers, some of them armed, who went before in the procession at the games.[73] Dionysius' information is drawn from Fabius Pictor's description of the original *ludi Romani* and suggests that satyrs had long been part of public spectacle in Rome.[74]

---

[71] 7.72.12 : εἶδον δὲ καὶ ἐν ἀνδρῶν ἐπισήμων ταφαῖς ἅμα ταῖς ἄλλαις πομπαῖς προηγουμένους τῆς κλίνης τοὺς σατυριστῶν χοροὺς κινουμένους τὴν σίκιννιν ὄρχησιν, μάλιστα δ' ἐν τοῖς τῶν εὐδαιμόνων κήδεσιν ('And even at the funerals of distinguished men I have seen, together with the rest of the procession, choruses of satyrs preceding the bier, dancing the *sikinnis*, and especially at the funerals of the rich').

[72] For the *sikinnis*, see Dion. Hal. 7. 71. 1 ff., Arr. *FGH* 156 F106, Gell. 20. 3, and Ath. 1. 20e.

[73] Rice (1983) 45-6 explains the satyrs as young men and the *silenoi* as older men. Satyrs were used as marshals to control the crowds at the Grand Procession of Ptolemy Philadelphus. For habits of dressing up as satyrs/silens in the Greek world, see Seaford (1984) 5-10, esp. 9: 'It seems that the ambiguity of belief about satyrs is associated with a similar ambiguity of satyrs in festival and ritual. On the one hand they are men and boys, dressed up for frolics at the festival; and on the other hand they are, within the *thiasos*, the attendants of the god and the initiated custodians of a solemn and secret tradition.'

[74] For the importance of satyrs in Hellenistic processions, especially the procession of Dionysus, see Ath. 197c-203b with Rice (1983) ad loc. For satyrs dancing in classical Greece, see Hedreen (1992)155-78 who posits a variety of contexts for

The tone of different parts of the funeral procession apparently varied markedly from patriotic and solemn, to sad, to joyous and festive. Indeed the procession itself seems to have included elements of self-parody, if the dancers followed the *imagines* and mimicked their serious gestures and actions; such a role would be equivalent to the one they played in the circus processions at the games. They presumably had their own music to accompany their part of the action. Dionysius is at pains to stress this combination of serious and comic as a typical feature of Roman spectacle. His comments suggest the established and formalized nature of funerals as the organizers were clearly not worried that last rites would be trivialized by the juxtaposition of very different elements. The presence of the dancers in costume demonstrates the element of public entertainment included in the funeral procession. As the impersonation of Vespasian at his funeral shows, the *imagines* may also have played a variety of roles from solemn to lighthearted within a single parade. Their use illustrates features typical in Roman processions and public spectacle in general.[75]

Similarly, the triumph of a Roman general was a solemn occasion marking religious thanksgiving for victory and the height of the general's career. Yet it also featured ribald songs improvised by the soldiers at the general's expense as they marched with him. The soldiers' songs can be counted as one of the apotropaic elements in a triumph, elements which were designed to set limits on the glorification of the general. It is logical to interpret the role of the satyrs and silens as similarly apotropaic in intention. This would explain why Dionysius associates them particularly with funerals of the rich. The need for a comic element to lighten the tone and to colour the purpose of the funeral *pompa* suggests its affinity with other processions and parades.[76]

performances by satyrs in Greece. *Contra* Lonsdale (1993) 102 who claims there is not enough evidence to distinguish between performance and myth. Szilágyi (1981) traces a chorus of dancing satrys to fifth century Etruria in art. Wiseman (1988) outlines the importance of satyrs and satyr plays at Rome. App. *Pun.* 66 tells of the *sikinnis* being danced at Scipio's triumph in 201 BC. For satyrs on Roman coins, see Crawford 337, 341, 342, 363.

[75] Cf. Cic. *Brut.* 322 for the juxtaposition of humour and seriousness as typical in Roman forensic oratory.

[76] For the soldiers' songs at triumphs, see Bonfante Warren (1970) 65. The elements of parody and mockery in the triumph served an apotropaic function against sacrilege, errors in ceremony, or excess of self-glorification. See de Cazanove (1986) 190–5.

3. The Relationship between Funerals and other Processions

By the late Republic it seems that the funeral *pompa* had absorbed elements of several other processions and presented a full pageant of Roman history accompanied by various entertainments.[77] The other *pompae* in question are the triumphal procession, and to a lesser extent the processions at the games. The funeral procession therefore developed in a pattern parallel with the increasing general importance of spectacle and display in Rome. Whatever the original character and shape of the various public processions, they each came under heavy Hellenistic influence during the middle Republic.[78] From the late fourth or early third century BC the triumph especially developed as the ultimate celebration of individual merit and achievement within a culture typical of the nobility of office.[79] Scipio Africanus' triumph of 201 BC already showed a tendency to make an exhibition of great luxury and wealth while building up the personal prestige of the general himself.[80] This pattern of grandeur and competition in display was characteristic of the great triumphs of the second century BC which celebrated the expansion of Rome's empire in Greece and the East. At the same time, contention over who should be allowed to triumph became a regular part of senatorial politics.[81] The triumph was, therefore, no longer primarily seen as a religious ritual of purification for the army and the community as a whole or of thanksgiving owed to the gods. The significance of the triumph is made clear by the

[77] See Versnel (1970) 115-29 for the influence of the triumph on the funeral.

[78] The triumph and its relations with other *pompae* are treated by Zinserling (1959/60), Versnel (1970), and Künzl (1988). All three appear to have Etruscan roots as can be seen from the depictions of magistrates in procession on Etruscan sarcophagi, see Lambrechts (1959) 188, 193, 195. Scenes combining triumphal and funerary elements suggest that processions may have been part of Etruscan funerals. For Hellenistic influences on the triumph, see Wallisch (1955) esp. 250-8, Bonfante Warren (1970) 64-5, Waurick (1975), and Hölscher (1990) 76 who characterizes the reception of Greek elements as tailored to suit Roman needs.

[79] For discussion and context, see Appendix D and Hölkeskamp (1993) 29. Zehnacker (1983) 47 makes a vivid comparison between the triumph and the funeral: 'c'était un spectacle total: la scène était dans toute la ville, les citoyens participaient intensément à l'action, le triomphateur pour un jour devenait Jupiter, et dans les familles qui avaient le ius imaginum, les masques des ancêtres accompagnaient le défunt dans son dernier voyage. Plus que les inventions de leurs poètes, ces jeux de la mort et du déstin étaient la vraie tragédie des Romains.' Cf. Arce (1988*b*) 35 on the triumph as the grandest Roman procession.

[80] App. *Pun.* 66 with Bonfante Warren (1970) 64.

[81] For 2nd-cent. BC triumphs, see Plut. *Aem.* 34 (Aemilius Paullus in 167 BC).

importance attached to triumphal dress, which was often used as the garb of highest office in the funeral procession of the ancestors.[82]

A triumphal procession glorified the victorious general and his troops in a way which mirrored Hellenistic processions, especially the procession of Dionysus as the conqueror of Asia accompanied by his joyful band of followers. The celebratory procession of Dionysus with his bacchants and satyrs had been a familiar topic for poets and artists in classical Greece.[83] It was used by Alexander the Great to create a powerful image of his success in Asia and his new status as great King and emulator of the gods.[84] His successors encouraged the cult both of Dionysus and of Alexander, and designed splendid spectacles of plundered wealth and military might. Hellenistic kingship defined power through ostentatious displays and conspicuous consumption.[85] The most notable Hellenistic procession we know of is the Grand Procession of Ptolemy II Philadelphus at the second Ptolemaieia in honour of the deified Ptolemy I Soter in 275/4 BC.[86] Like a procession at a traditional Greek festival, Ptolemy's procession seems to have passed through the streets of Alexandria and stopped for offerings at various shrines.

A brief comparison between Ptolemy's new dynastic festival and Roman triumphal and funeral processions illustrates how the Romans came to be influenced when they followed in Alexander's footsteps as conquerors of the East.[87] Ptolemy's procession combined homage to his ancestors and to his deified father with a

---

[82] Triumphal dress was stressed by Augustus in his statues of Roman heroes in the Forum of Augustus; see Ch. 8 § 1. By the late Republic triumphal dress (*toga picta* of purple embroidered with gold along the edges) was distinguished from regal dress (*toga purpurea* of plain purple). See Weinstock (1971) 107-9, 271 and Pelling (1988) 145 on the differences and their use by Caesar. However, in earlier times the Etruscans and Romans equated the two; see Festus 228 L and Bonfante Warren (1970) 59-61 with pl. 6-8.

[83] See e.g. Eur. *Bacch.* 13-16. For black-figure vases, see now Hedreen (1992).

[84] For Alexander's imitation of Dionysus, see Arr. 6. 28 and Curtius 9. 10. 24-28, with Stewart (1993) 257.

[85] For Greek ideas of luxury and their use in Hellenistic processions, see la Rocca (1986) 10. On Hellenistic processions in general, see Caspari (1933) and Wallisch (1955).

[86] Athenaeus (quoting Kallixeinos of Rhodes) 197c-203b = *FGH* 627 F2 = Stewart (1993) T96. For the date, see Foertenmeyer (1988). For discussion and analysis, see Rice (1983) and Stewart (1993) 252-60.

[87] For ancient comparisons, see Varro *Ling.* 6. 68; Dion. Hal. 1. 4-5, 89-90; Plin. *Nat.* 7. 191; Macrob. 1. 49. 4.

celebration of his power and his close connections with Alexander as the New Dionysus and companion of the Olympian gods.[88] The particular hallmark of such a Hellenistic procession was the claim to empire and its spoils, accompanied by a stress on the role and power of the army.[89] The festival illustrated Ptolemy's political programme and aspirations both in Egypt and in the Mediterranean world. The iconography used was purely Greek and was partly aimed at the Greek visitors who had been invited as official observers from many cities. The state was identified with the ruler and his family in a context which also asserted claims abroad.

In a Roman triumph Jupiter Optimus Maximus instead of Dionysus was celebrated as the supreme protector of the state, while the conquering general appeared in his role and image and as the community's mediator with the god.[90] The triumph defined Roman success and power by its display of captured wealth and by territorial claims represented by maps, painted scenes of battles and slogans, captured leaders, and enemy weapons. The soldiers with their equipment played a major role in the procession. Much of the same material, including floats with exhibits, weapons, and soldiers came to be reused at funeral processions. The theatrical imitation and recollection of a triumph took place in the context of the parade of ancestors in front of the bier. The triumph of the deceased, if he had celebrated one, would naturally have furnished the largest number of items. Moreover, spoils and objects from earlier family triumphs could also be used, suggesting an accumulation of merit and the repetition of success across the generations. Both Hellenistic *pompai* and Roman processions presented their audiences with a highly idealized picture of leading families in the state. Each was overtly political in content, even and especially in representing relationships with the gods. Hellenistic rulers and their habits encouraged Roman leaders to use dramatic costumes and enactment to represent their achievements and rank within the city of Rome itself.

4. *Virgil and the Funeral Procession*

Further information about what the *imagines* actually looked like in the funeral procession can be gained by examining the poetic

---

[88] See esp. Ath. 197d, 201d, and 202a with Rice (1983) ad loc.

[89] Rice (1983) 180, 190–1, and Stewart (1993) 254–60.

[90] The role of the triumphator is treated by Wallisch (1955) and Versnel (1970).

fantasy based on such a scene created by Virgil in his parade of Roman heroes at the end of book 6 of the *Aeneid* (*A*. 6. 756–886). Scholars have long recognized certain connections between Virgil's scene and a funeral.[91] The identification with a funeral procession depends on the allusions to the funeral of Marcellus at the end. Yet the full parallels between the parade of heroes and a funeral *pompa* have still to be explored and can be helpful in trying to shed further light on Roman custom.

Virgil's depiction may be influenced by the brief notices of each ancestor to be found at the end of a *laudatio*, although he has actually set the scene during the procession, which is being watched by Anchises and Aeneas as spectators. For our purposes it is especially striking to be presented with a father explaining to his son the meaning of Rome's leading figures and their achievements in a setting which recalls the *imagines* in a funeral procession. Virgil had good reason to use this particular scene as a moment for Aeneas to be inspired for his role in Rome's future greatness and to illuminate the close relationship between father and son, which is a central theme in his poem. At the same time many fathers would surely have been prompted by a funeral procession to explain Roman customs and history to their sons.

Polybius (6. 54. 3 = T61) makes much of the educational value and inspiration drawn from the parades of ancestors at funerals. The close parallels between Virgil and Polybius are striking and are more likely to reflect the actual role of funerals rather than any kind of literary imitation.[92] Polybius (6. 54. 4 = T61) sees the parade of ancestors as a challenge to place the good of the state over private interests. It is precisely this that is being asked of Aeneas as he arrives in Italy. Personal sacrifice appears to have been a standard theme at funerals which created an atmosphere both of glory and of sadness. Both authors stress the visual elements in the parade and the strong sense of community. Virgil illustrates what Polybius meant when he said that the past was constantly made new and the value of praise made clear (6. 54. 2 = T61). Both speak of realism in appearance and bearing as a spectacle unfolds which is deeply moving and familiar to the crowds watching. It is in just such a context that Virgil has placed Anchises' statement of Rome's

---

[91] This comparison was first made by Skard (1965), and has recently been extended by Novara (1987) and Bettini (1991) 144–9.

[92] Their accounts were first compared by Skard (1965).

great mission which is the climax of the parade and a key point in the poem as a whole (6. 847–853).[93] This call is addressed to Aeneas in particular, and in some sense also to Virgil's contemporaries. One of Virgil's most telling and complex passages draws directly on the varied emotions and rich symbolism to be found in the Roman aristocratic funeral procession.

There are also, of course, differences. Virgil does not simply reproduce a funeral procession, since he is creating an imaginary scene in which his characters are about to be born and are being watched by their Trojan ancestors.[94] A sense of fate hangs over them and yet all is perhaps not completely settled. Caesar does appear in the parade despite not having an *imago* after he was declared a god. (6. 826–35). At the same time, Virgil departs from accepted norms in such a way that he can play on his audience's expectations. The whole parade seems unreal until Marcellus suddenly appears and it is as if Aeneas and Anchises are actually at his funeral in 23 BC (6. 868 ff.). His position at the end of the parade of his forebears corresponds to that of the body on a bier, and yet ordinarily spectators at a funeral would know who was to be buried. Moreover, in Virgil Marcellus' early death is mourned by his ancestors Aeneas and Anchises, as if they were indeed simply spectators standing by the roadside to watch the scene. They then become involved by the spectacle and come to share in the grief and sense of common loss which seemed so remarkable a feature of such funerals to Polybius over a hundred years before. Anchises' direct address to Marcellus reflects a custom found both in the *laudatio* and in the laments over the dead in which the crowds sometimes participated.[95]

Throughout the parade, which passes by on foot, Virgil maintains the illusion of Anchises and Aeneas watching and recognizing each individual or group.[96] The language they use has been noted

[93] For discussion, see J. Griffin (1979) 65–6.

[94] Bettini (1991) 147–9 explores how useful the setting of a funeral procession is for Virgil in suggesting a spatial translation of temporal succession. Aeneas who should lead the parade can step outside to watch from a vantage point which seems outside time and yet intimately connected with Virgil's own age through Marcellus. Cf. Ch. 3 § 3 for coins which combine ancestors from different historical periods.

[95] Direct address can be found in the *Laudatio Turiae* and is discussed most usefully by Koenen (1970a) 247–9. Tac. *Agr.* 45. 3 is in the same tradition.

[96] Visual vocabulary can be found at 6. 760; 771; 779; 788; 808; 817; 825; 826; 855. Verbs of motion are introduced at 6. 777; 812; 815; 836 ff.; 855; 863.

by scholars as especially colloquial.[97] It has been compared with comedy, particularly in the phrases which introduce a new character. Although Virgil reminds us of drama, he is mainly concerned to suggest a private conversation between two men watching a funeral procession. This colloquial tone has little in common with the simple but solemn language of the *laudatio*. Considerable stress is given to the visual aspects of each hero in the parade and Anchises points out specific features to Aeneas. Several descriptions, especially of the early figures, recall artistic representations which could be found in Rome and which were well known.[98] Yet, the constant motion of the parade does not evoke a group of statues.

Rather, such features surely reflect how ancestors in a funeral parade were recognized by their dress and attributes, as well as by their masks and bearing. The earliest figures, such as Silvius and the Alban kings, do not seem to be wearing magisterial garb (6. 760 ff.). They were probably dressed in imitation of their statues. Badges of achievement, such as the *hasta pura* (a headless spear presented for valour) and the civic crown of oak, appear as important symbolic elements in the parade (6. 760 and 771-2). Numa is portayed as an elderly priest carrying his sacred emblems (*sacra*), while Marcellus, the victor of Syracuse, is the conquering general with the *spolia opima* (6. 808-12 and 855-9). From Virgil's description we may imagine what the ancestors looked like in an aristocratic funeral and how they were differentiated and characterized. It is easy to see how an actor might be called upon to play a part by presenting a familiar character to the audience, while also stressing the attributes the family wanted remembered and highlighted. It is not certain whether the actors spoke and introduced themselves or whether written labels and placards explained the different parts of the parade.

Virgil's characters from Roman history are in roughly chronological order, but also in groups. They reproduce a pattern reminiscent of a funeral procession, during which the *imagines* of several families would be presented in separate groups, but in chronological order within each group.[99] Virgil skilfully recreates the atmos-

[97] Austin (1977) comments on the passages cited in the previous n.

[98] Delaruelle (1913) made a comparison between some of Virgil's descriptions and statues we know of in Rome.

[99] Novara (1987) 342-3. Tac. *Ann.* 4. 9 = T90 portrays a chronological order within groups. Cf. Bettini (1991) 176 who visualizes this as the genealogical tree coming into the street: 'The inscriptions that faithfully registered their ancient offices came back to life and became purple borders, fasces, and the rest.'

phere of a parade by changing pace as the procession speeds and slows, sometimes spreads out or even seems to halt at an important figure. Some heroes bunch together and pass in quick succession.[100] There is a sense of anticipation and recognition as each figure approaches. The poet draws on the spontaneity and excitement felt by spectators at a parade and confirms for us what such a spectacle might mean to a Roman.[101]

A particular feature of Virgil's procession is the juxtaposition of important figures such as Romulus and Augustus or the two Marcelli (6. 777–807 and 855–86). It is impossible to say whether this pattern is the result of poetic license or whether the order of a funeral was indeed designed to juxtapose and otherwise stress certain key figures. Virgil exploits the arrangement of ancestors in a procession to create a typically Augustan sense of the teleological pattern of history. All past ages of Roman history seem to converge on the figure of the young Marcellus. In addition, Virgil has achieved a sense of special closeness between the founder Aeneas and his descendant living in the time when the poem was written. This pattern of the past suggests cycles rather than a steady decline and decay, as was depicted by Roman historians, notably Sallust and Livy.

Triumphal imagery is repeated throughout, but especially in the two principal similes which offer comparisons with other processions involving triumphal chariots (6. 784–7 and 804–5). Spoils, paintings, and floats made for earlier triumphs were apparently reused at funerals.[102] Virgil's geographic imagery recalls the types of models and maps that were used to illustrate triumphs, giving a sense of Rome's expanding empire. Similarly the special stress on the earliest history and on the origins of customs and family heritage, seems in tune with the competitive antiquarianism of the late Republic.[103] All aspects of the past were not accorded equal treatment; emphasis was laid on the antiquity of the family and on its most recent achievements.

---

[100] This is especially true of 6. 836 ff.

[101] Skard (1965) committed an oversight in comparing Virgil mostly with the *laudatio*. Actually the ancestors were praised after the dead man (Polyb. 6. 54. 1 = T61), so the order is reversed by Virgil. Skard only took notice of Polyb. 6. 53 in his discussion, without mentioning the closely related material to be found in 6. 54.

[102] Dion. Hal. 8. 59. 3 and Marquardt (1905) 354. The evidence for these exhibits is treated in detail by Zinserling (1959/60) 419.

[103] Similar ancestral imagery on Roman coins is treated in Ch. 3 § 3.

Virgil can be used as evidence that by the end of the Republic a funeral procession could be lavish drama and magnificent spectacle, as well as being a medium for popular history. A family's presentation of its past needed to be accessible as well as being impressive. In order to create such a pageant families drew on a large cast of actors and extras, who represented lictors and other attendants. The costumes were varied and colourful. Each ancestor might be equipped with a number of attributes depending on his various offices and achievements. Music was perhaps provided at various stages to help create an appropriate atmosphere and to keep the procession in step. Virgil's description may also suggest that by his time the ancestors no longer rode in carriages, as seems to have been the case at the funeral of Vespasian.

5. Imagines *and Theatrical Masks*

Despite his overall usefulness, Virgil gives us no new information about the ancestor masks themselves. His version of a pageant does, however, support the notion that they were realistic. The use of actors in the funeral procession begs a comparison with masks worn in the theatre. Theatrical masks, however, have been controversial in their own right, especially as regards their use during the Republic. Wiles has recently presented a persuasive case for stock masks in use as early as Plautus.[104] He sees such stock characters, which were influenced both by Hellenistic masks and the types used in Atellan comedy, as integral to the meaning of Plautine theatre as presented on stage. Masks granted license to speak out with greater freedom than usual and also allowed the playwright to meet or defeat the audience's expectation based on their reading of the character's mask. Wiles associates Plautus' theatre and masks closely with the *ludi* and the festive masks worn by flute players on the Ides of June for the festival of Minerva, patron of actors and poets.

Wiles recognizes the central place of the *imago* mask in Roman culture. His interpretation of the ancient evidence presents the two types of mask as opposites in appearance and in use. According to his theory the theatrical mask was an inversion of an *imago* and thus served as a badge of ignobility. Consequently, theatrical masks

---

[104] Wiles (1991) 127-49.

had to be quite different from the *imagines* in order to avoid offending the families of office-holders. A mask worn in a play was a caricature, while an *imago* attempted to be as lifelike as possible.

Wiles's approach has proved fruitful for the whole question of the role of masks in Roman culture. Nevertheless, he seems to have overstated the differences between an *imago* and a theatrical mask. Both were used for a performance in the full sense of the word and to create a sense of character for an audience, whose expectations and reactions were a vital ingredient in the drama.[105] This is not to say that *imagines* looked like the stock figures of Plautine comedy, but they did present characters which could become somewhat standardised over time. It seems plausible to think of ancestor masks in terms of a certain repertoire of characters, such as the wise old censor, the young warrior, the famous orator, or the learned judge. Greater effect could be gained by presenting the audience with types they could recognise, while still keeping alive the memory of certain key family traits, especially those associated with famous individuals. Within the setting of a funeral procession the mask had to work with the costume and props to help the actor bring an individual to life, while also suggesting a recognisable character type.

6. *Organizing an Aristocratic Funeral: Practical Matters and Sumptuary Legislation*

A closer examination of the many features included in a funeral procession reveals the magnitude of the task of organizing such a display, especially at only a few days notice. This job fell to the *libitinarii* (undertakers) who had their headquarters in the grove of Libitina and temple of Venus Libitina, which was probably on the Esquiline near the Porta Esquilina.[106] Here records were kept of those who had died.[107] There are several references in Roman authors to the standard practice of hiring undertakers to organize the funeral (*funus locare*).[108] Similarly, funerals given at public expense were contracted out by a magistrate, usually the

---

[105] *Persona*, the standard Latin word for a mask, is used for an *imago* at Suet. *Ves.* 19. 2 = T84.

[106] Platner-Ashby (1929) s.v. Lucus Libitinae. On sacred groves and the role of the *libitinarii* see Bodel (1994) 13 ff.

[107] Suet. *Nero* 39.

[108] Sen. *Ep.* 99. 22; Tac. *Dial.* 9. 11. 10; Plin. *Nat.* 7. 176.

quaestor.[109] The *libitinarii* are also attested outside Rome by inscriptions from Puteoli and Bergomum.[110] It seems that much of the necessary equipment was kept in the grove, presumably in the storerooms of the temple. We know that the *fasces* needed for the lictors in the procession were kept there because Clodius' gangs broke in to arm themselves from this store in 52 BC.[111]

The *libitinarii* included the *pollinctor* who prepared the body for burial, and the *dissignator* who choreographed the procession itself, as well as the *praefica* who sang the mourning laments (*nenia*).[112] It seems that most of the participants in the procession, as well as their costumes and props, could be hired through the agency of the *dissignator*. The family clearly provided the *imagines* themselves and the spoils, many of which were kept in the house. Some curule chairs may also have been kept in the family, although the number required for all the ancestors in a large procession might seem excessive.[113] The chairs were presumably also carried by attendants to each magistrate represented in the procession as they would have been during his lifetime. Many of the arrangements must have followed a prearranged plan which allowed such an elaborate show to be staged at short notice. This practice helps to explain the tendency to 'borrow' equipment and extras from other processions.

Instructions for elaborate funerals were given well before a death and were sometimes formally written down, perhaps at the same time as the will. Augustus left behind several documents as part of his will, including separate instructions for his funeral. The guidelines for the ceremony were not actually part of the 'will' itself, but were contained in the first of three documents he left at his death. How usual his practice was we cannot tell. Caesar's will entrusted

[109] Dion. Hal. 6. 96. 3; Val. Max. 5. 1. 1c.

[110] *AE* 1971 no. 88 preserves part of a law relating to the *libitinarii*, their staff and duties, including their function as executioners. These activities were leased out by the community (cf. *ILS* 6726 = *CIL* 5. 5128). See Bodel (1994) 72–80 for a new text and photographs.

[111] Asconius 33 C = 29 KS = 32 Stangl.

[112] Van Sickle (1987) 45–7 n. 28 has conveniently collected the ancient evidence for the mourning women, whose laments seem to have been generic. They were probably orally transmitted within the group of women at the lucus Libitinae. See also Kierdorf (1980) 96 ff. and Holst-Warhaft (1992) for comparable women's laments in Greece.

[113] Spoils and curule chairs kept in the home are discussed in Ch. 2 §§ 1c and 7, and Ch. 3 § 2b. Cf. Schäfer (1989) 127 who stresses the close association between the *imago* and the curule chair, both of which were kept in the home as a reminder of the deceased.

his niece Atia, the mother of Octavian, with the organization of his funeral.[114]

No extant fragments of Roman wills allude to arrangements for a funeral, but there is not enough evidence to assume that such instructions were never included. They may often have been oral and informal rather than written.[115] Seneca certainly included definite instructions, in his case for a very simple funeral in accord with his philosophical beliefs, in his will.[116] Similarly, Propertius' instructions (2. 13b. 1–8 = T63) for his simple funeral appear to be quite specific. The public expected a lavish display at a great man's funeral and their disappointment could be felt directly by a family who had failed in their duties. In this context Cicero (*Mur.* 74–5) remarks on the defeat of Q. Aelius Tubero in his bid for the praetorship after the meagre public banquet he had provided as his share of staging the funeral of his uncle Scipio Aemilianus in 129 BC.

Display at noble funerals was carefully controlled both by sumptuary laws and by custom. Cicero in the *De Legibus* 2. 22–6 comments at some length on the restrictions already found in the Twelve Tables, prescripts which he sees as heavily influenced by the laws of Solon. It was a feature of Athenian society from the archaic period that aristocratic funerals were strictly controlled and public funeral orations were only delivered over mixed groups of war dead without regard to social class.[117] The Athenians effectively prevented their aristocratic families from staging anything like the spectacle found in Rome, presumably partly because of the powerful effect such publicity could have within a city-state.[118] At

[114] Nicolaus of Damascus *FGH* 90 F 130. The tablets displayed at the feet of the deceased woman in the *collocatio* relief from the Tomb of the Haterii have been identified as the will (Toynbee (1971) 44).

[115] See Liv. *Per.* 48 = T46 for the oral instructions given by Marcus Aemilius Lepidus to his sons in 152 BC. Cf. Trimalchio's instructions at Petronius *Sat.* 77. 7 ff. *Contra* Champlin (1991) 171: 'In truth, testators were not much interested in their funerals.' In light of the wealth of evidence from sources other than wills, it is hard to agree with this conclusion.

[116] Tac. *Ann.* 15. 64. For Seneca's attitude to display and to the *imagines*, see T72-6.

[117] Toher (1986) collects a wide array of Greek laws from different cities which all put limits on funerals. Convenient discussions of Athenian funerary practices seen in a comparative light can be found in Humphreys (1980) and Loraux (1981). See also Connor (1987) 49 who discusses how Solon sought civic alternatives to lavish aristocratic displays at funerals and on other ocasions.

[118] At *Menexenus* 25a–b Plato has Socrates note the powerful effect of public funeral oratory. See Alexiou (1974) 14–23 for a discussion of Greek funeral legislation which turned a public occasion into a private one. She interprets Solon's laws

Athens, as in Rome, the character of publicly delivered funeral orations reflected the political organization of the state. Polybius
describes Roman funeral practices in detail precisely because they
differed so from contemporary Greek customs. The *imagines* are at
the heart of these differences and they developed within parameters
set by sumptuary legislation.

Roman sumptuary legislation, as applied to funerals, therefore
echoed the outward form but not the spirit of the laws of Solon.[119]
As elsewhere in Roman culture, patterns and forms borrowed and
adapted from the Greeks need to be interpreted as fully 'Roman'
within their new social and political context.[120] In placing restrictions on display and expenditure at funerals Roman law reflected
the concerns of élite legislators to provide norms which would help
their own class to survive and to flourish.[121] The best model for
understanding Roman sumptuary legislation is that of aristocratic
self-preservation within a highly competitive society which valued
overt display of prestige above all else.[122] Despite such laws funerals did become more showy over time, especially with the increase
in social and political tensions in the later Republic. Each generation seems to have seen both the attractions in funerary spectacle
and the dangers inherent in allowing further escalation of rivalry
and expense. Indeed, great funerals given at public expense were
staged by suspending the laws.[123]

Cicero's information about sumptuary laws, including quotations
from the tenth table of the Law of the Twelve Tables, which dealt

as a curb on aristocratic clans and their influential ritual laments. Rituals were therefore transferred from the cult of the clan's ancestor to the state cults for community
heroes. Gabba (1988) 35 notes that in the archaic age the funeral was the main if
not the only exhibition of individual luxury.

[119] *Contra* Toher (1986) who does not see Roman funerals as subject to sumptuary legislation, but to laws close to Greek practices, which were designed to further
the austerity native to Greek religion.

[120] See Hölscher (1990) 74 for this important principle applied to art and material culture.

[121] See esp. Daube (1969) 117-28, Gabba (1988) 34-44, and Baltrusch (1989)
43. At Livy 34. 4. 12 ff. Cato warns the women of Rome against the ravages of competition if sumptuary legislation is repealed. Daube (1969) 124 also suggests that the
Twelve Tables reflect a reaction to lavish Etruscan funerals.

[122] Clemente (1981) has argued persuasively for such an interpretation of sumptuary legislation throughout the middle Republic.

[123] Cic. *Phil.* 9. 17. Sulla was the first to violate his own sumptuary law in the
magnificent funeral he gave for his wife Metella; see Plut. *Sulla* 35. For Sulla's own
funeral, see Plut. *Sulla* 38; App. *BC* 1. 105-6.

with funerals (*Leg.* 2. 22–6), allows us to glimpse the situation in the early Republic. From such evidence we can also deduce something of the evolution of the displays associated with status so typical of the aristocratic funeral. The prohibition against burning or burying a body in the city was designed partly to control the danger of fire as cremation became more common (*Leg.* 2. 23. 58), but partly also to put an end to the earlier aristocratic practice of locating family tombs inside the city.[124] The previous custom had increased family prestige and can be seen reflected in the fame attached at the end of the Republic to those families who could still point to their traditional burial places inside the *pomerium*.[125] The laws carefully controlled the use of purple clothes in the funeral as well as the number of attendants.[126] Evidently, long funeral processions were seen as a problem from the earliest times. Other features of early funerals which were subject to legal restrictions included the use and display of gold, crowns or garlands, incense, and special libations.[127]

These measures reflect the importance of display at funerals; they probably date back to the regal period and are clearly influenced by Greek legislative habits. Attempts to control mourning, especially by women, provide early evidence of bids to play on the emotions of the crowd and to use a sense of common loss for political purposes.[128] The need for such controls is illustrated by the violence

[124] Cf. Sourvinou-Inwood (1981) 36 and (1983) 45 who discusses a similar move of Greek burials outside towns in terms of a new anxiety about death expressed in terms of pollution. Her position has been questioned by Morris (1989). For her powerful reply to his points and methodology, see now Sourvinou-Inwood (1994) 413–44. Ariès (1981) 468–93 gives parallels in Western Europe. Hygiene is the typical excuse offerred in these analogous cases.

[125] For traditional burial places in the city, see Cic. *Leg.* 2. 23; Dion. Hal. 5. 44; Plut. *Mor.* 282f–283a; *Pub.* 23.

[126] *Leg.* 2. 23. 59: *tribus riciniis et tunicla purpurea et decem tibicinibus* ('with three shawls and a purple tunic and ten flute players').

[127] *Leg.* 2. 24. 60: *ne sumptuosa respersio, ne longae coronae, ne acerrae neve aurum addito* ('Let there be no extravagant pouring of wine on the pyre, no long wreaths, no addition of incense or of gold'). Cf. *ILS* 917 and 917a for inscriptions from the tomb of C. Cestius Epulo regarding the money *quae eis per edictum* | *aedilis in sepulcrum* | *C. Cesti ex testamento* | *eis inferre non licuit* ('which the aediles' edict did not allow them to take into the tomb of Gaius Cestius according to the instructions in his will').

[128] *Leg.* 2. 23. 59: *mulieres genas ne radunto neve lessum funeris ergo habento* ('That the women should not tear their cheeks nor therefore have a *lessum* at a funeral'). Cf. Pighi (1965) 115, ll. 110–15 (= *CIL* 6. 32323) for limits on mourning by women during the *ludi saeculares* of 17 BC as set by the *XVviri s. f.* Cf. Alexiou (1974) 14–23 on Greek equivalents and on the connection between ritual laments and vendetta in

which attended the political funerals of the victims of assassination in the last century BC.[129] The laws also banned a delay before the funeral, presumably because of earlier attempts to organize grander funerals or even to stage more than one.

Cicero interprets several of these rules as establishing the principle that display should be limited to the marks of honour actually earned by the dead person (*Leg.* 2. 24. 60). His example is a garland won for bravery by the deceased, which could appear at his funeral, and which his father could also wear. In other words, the laws tried to ban private status symbols which essentially reflected money and social pretensions rather than a position in society earned with the approval of one's peers.[130] It was in the climate created by this legislation that funeral spectacle evolved to focus sharply on offices and achievements that could be measured and recognized by the display of a common vocabulary of symbols. The *imagines* emerged as the ultimate means for representing a family's past achievements and consequently also their present claims to preeminence. The ethos of the Twelve Tables, which were a part of every educated Roman's upbringing, permeated society and created heightened competition within the recognized confines of achievement.[131] Written laws, such as the ones quoted by Cicero, would have been supplemented by the edict of the aediles each year and by any subsequent sumptuary laws such as the *Lex Cornelia sumptuaria* alluded to above.

Meanwhile, the connection between *imagines* and conspicuous consumption as reflected in the ancient sources is complex. Livy quotes M. Aemilius Lepidus (cos. 187 and 175 BC, pontifex maximus since 180 BC), the *princeps senatus* on his deathbed in 152 BC, as instructing his sons to stage a simple funeral which would be magnificent only for the spectacle of the *imagines* (Livy *Per.* 48 = T46). This passage is an excellent illustration of the meaning and func-

---

various societies (e.g. Antony's use of Caesar's funeral discussed below in section 6). For a discussion of Greek legislation to control laments by women, see Holst-Warhaft (1992) 114–26.

[129] At the funeral of Clodius in particular the violence and mass grief threatened the constitution and contributed to the establishment of Pompey as sole consul; see Gruen (1974) 152, 233–4, 337.

[130] Baltrusch (1989) 44–50 and 128 shows how the Tenth Table foreshadows the political purposes and social concerns of later sumptuary laws.

[131] At *Leg.* 2. 23. 59 Cicero says they were all required to learn the Twelve Tables by heart as children.

tion of *imagines* in the middle Republic.[132] They were the supreme status symbols of an aristocracy which based its claim to preeminence on prestige and on a heritage of merit rather than on money. The *imagines* fulfilled their role at a funeral by offering an illustration of a man's greatness and his place in the community and in history. They were intimately linked to the image of ancestral frugality, rustic virtues, and public service which the families of the Roman élite tried to project.[133]

Romans who aspired to traditional practices, like Cato the censor, put on deliberately simple funerals, such as the one he gave for his son who died as praetor designate in the same year as Lepidus.[134] In the mid-second century BC it may already have been a consciously archaic gesture to limit display at a funeral and to highlight the *imagines* as symbols of the ancestors' lifestyle and values. By the early Empire the Augustan poets associated the *imagines*, especially in a grand funeral procession, with money and the ostentatious display of wealth.[135] The feeling of common loss and a shared heritage which Virgil tried to conjure up shortly after 23 BC was perhaps in need of revival. By AD 16 Scribonius Libo Drusus' pretensions to imperial power, which were closely associated with his *imagines*, also led him into an extravagant lifestyle and into debt.[136] The *imagines*, as they appear in imperial writers, are often synonymous with arrogance and conspicuous consumption in a way they were not during the Republic.[137] Indeed, it was the breakdown of an aristocratic consensus to keep display within certain boundaries which gave a new symbolic value to the *imagines* and quite reversed much of their original purpose.[138]

[132] Cf. Daube (1969) 124 on the 'archaizing' character of 2nd-cent. BC frugality.
[133] See Sen. *Dial.* 12. 12. 7 = T72 who still reproduces this republican conceit in writing to console his mother.
[134] Liv. *Per.* 48. Livy's explanation in terms of Cato's poverty should not be taken at face value.
[135] Prop. 1. 5. 23-24 = T62; 2. 13b. 3 = T63; Ov. *Am.* 1. 8. 65 = T50, and see also a similar sentiment in Mart. 2. 90. 6 = T47.
[136] Tac. *Ann.* 2. 27. 2 = T85: Firmius Catus is the senator who tempts Libo into debt partly by making much of his *imagines*.
[137] See Mart. 2. 90. 5-8 = T47 for a picture of the simple life which is contrasted with the *imagines* in the *atrium*.
[138] At the same time writers of the 2nd-cent. AD could refer to the reproaches directed by the *imagines* at descendants who no longer lived up to republican traditions. See esp. Juv. 8. 1-23 = T35 and Plin. *Ep.* 5. 17. 6 = T57.

7. *The Evolution of Aristocratic Funerals during the Republic*

An increase in the splendour associated with funerals can be traced throughout the middle and later Republic. The mounting cost of a funeral and the entertainment provided with it can be measured by the steady rise in the number of pairs who fought in the gladiatorial contests.[139] These were regularly staged at funerals after first being introduced in 264 BC at the funeral of D. Junius Brutus Pera. For example, the three sons of M. Aemilius Lepidus staged funeral games for him in 215 BC with 22 pairs of gladiators, but Caesar's games offered combatants in the hundreds.[140] Such games allowed a funeral celebration to extend over several days, which eventually also included theatrical performances and other entertainments normally associated with regular games (*ludi*). Gladiatorial combats at private funerals were banned early under the Empire because they had been significant advertising tools for families.[141]

The occasions for staging a full aristocratic funeral were significantly increased when women were also given a procession and funeral eulogy.[142] The first woman who is firmly attested as having received this honour is Popilia, who was publicly eulogized by her son Q. Lutatius Catulus, probably during his consulship in 102 BC (Cic. *De Or.* 2. 11. 44).[143] By 91 BC the orator Crassus could refer to the funeral of a Junia, accompanied by the *imagines* of the Junii including the first consul, as if such funerals were a standard occurrence (Cic. *De Or.* 2. 225 = T23). Although the exact content of public funeral speeches for women is not attested, we may assume that they included the same rehearsal of the deeds of the ancestors as might be found at the funeral of a male member of the family.[144]

[139] For gladiatorial contests associated with funerals, see Liv. *Per.* 16; 28. 21. 1; 39. 46; 41. 28. 10; Ter. *Hec.* 31; Plut. *C. G.* 12. 3 with Baltrusch (1989) 111-13.

[140] Livy 23. 30. 15 and Suet. *Jul.* 10.

[141] Permission was needed by law for *munera* after 22 BC and they seem to have stopped completely under Tiberius. See Ville (1981) 121-3 and Wallace-Hadrill (1986) 79.

[142] Women regularly contributed *imagines* to funerals in their husband's families. Bettini (1991) 175 n. 12 : 'carried in procession, the impressive crowd of what I would like to call cognate images constitutes a massive and irrefutable proof of the nobility of the family as a whole, a still further sign of the importance of cognate and maternal relations in a society apparently as rigidly agnatic as the Roman.'

[143] Coarelli (1978) dates the Hellenistic style statue of Cornelia, mother of the Gracchi, to around the same time as Popilia's *laudatio*.

[144] Livy 5. 50. 7 with the remarks of Ogilvie (1965) ad loc.; Plut. *Cam.* 8. References to such a custom existing in the earlier Republic would appear to describe

The public role of women was a constant and developing feature in Roman society during the later Republic. They were seen by ancient authors as sharing in a family's heritage of glory reflected by the *imagines*. They certainly also took part in magnificent public parades of various kinds in their own right. Their appearance in the city was expected to mirror the status and position of their own and their husband's families. Polybius 32. 12 alludes to the splendid equipment used by Scipio Africanus' wife at public festivals, and especially when she appeared in processions of other women. She was noted for her dress, carriage, fine sacrificial vessels, and the number of her entourage. These status symbols were the envy of other Roman women and a distinct part of the family's property to be bequeathed. When Papiria, the natural mother of Scipio Aemilianus, inherited all of this, she made her first appearance at the festivals after many years of absence because she had been unable to maintain the equipment usually associated with someone of her rank. In their own way aristocratic women paralleled the displays of status and rank which were such an important part of their male relatives' public lives as officials of the state.[145]

It was another Lutatius, the son of the man responsible for the first *laudatio* of a woman, who as consul in 78 BC staged the first attested funeral to be held at public expense by decree of the senate when he buried Sulla the former dictator.[146] Although he did not in this case honour a member of his own family, he was clearly serving his political agenda in glorifying Sulla whose constitutional aims he supported. The special funeral honours were opposed by his fellow consul M. Aemilius Lepidus, for whom their celebration was a signal defeat and who led a rebellion later in the same year. Sulla had prevented proper funerals for his political enemies, desecrated their graves, and banned their *imagines*. At the same time, Sulla is the first figure we can identify who added triumphal elements to his funeral, although we may suspect that he was following the

special occasions only, where they are not later inventions. For the extant eulogies of women, see Ch. 5 § 1. However, these speeches seem to come from a private context.

[145] It is interesting that Caesar, whose will probably contained a request for a funeral at public expense, entrusted its organization to a woman, his niece Atia.

[146] App. *BC* 1. 105. Previous public funerals had been for foreign kings such as Syphax and Perseus; see Arce (1988*b*) 25.

example of earlier generals.[147] His funeral was remarkable as a celebration of the Victoria Sullana which he had already made much of in special games.[148] He drew on the traditional image of the *triumphator* as *felix* and a bringer of blessings to the city to create his own vocabulary and imagery of pre-eminence.

Within ten years Caesar launched his political career by staging a magnificent funeral for his aunt Julia, the widow of Marius.[149] As quaestor he dared to show the *imagines* of Marius and his relatives, which had been banned by Sulla. Caesar marked the beginning of his career in the senate with a proud spectacle of his family's earlier political achievements and programme. His actions suggest that a family's use of their *imagines* was not aimed simply at an enumeration of previous offices held, but could identify a specific political programme.

In quick succession to his aunt's funeral, Caesar gave the first funeral eulogy for a young Roman noble woman on the death of his first wife Cornelia, the daughter of Cinna. Once more allusions to the political struggles of the past must have surfaced. Plutarch notes the popular sympathy aroused by the speech Caesar gave for Cornelia. It provided an opportunity for him to gain the goodwill of the crowds by staging a fine show and playing on the pathos of early death and bereavement. His daughter Julia, in turn, received a fine funeral in 54 BC and was buried spontaneously by the crowd on the Campus Martius, as if she had received this special honour from the senate (Dio 39. 64). Caesar fulfilled his promise of splendid funeral games for her in 46 BC, with a grand public banquet, gladiatorial games, and naval battles.[150] Caesar's sister Julia was eulogized from the *rostra* by her grandson Octavian in his first public appearance at the age of 12 in 51 BC.[151]

Powerful individuals and families used funerals for political displays and to increase their standing by innovation. In extending similar honours to women, first the older ones but then also

---

[147] For the innovations in Sulla's funeral which foreshadowed those of the emperors, see Arce (1988*b*) 17–34. A diagram reconstructing Sulla's funeral procession can be found at 20.

[148] Sulla's funeral as a model for Caesar and the emperors is discussed by Weinstock (1971) 348–9 and Richard (1978) 1122.

[149] Plut. *Caes.* 5 = T59 and Nicolet (1980) 349.

[150] Suet. *Jul.* 26. 2; Plut. *Caes.* 55. 3.

[151] Nicolaus of Damascus *FGH* 90 F 127; Quintilian *Inst.* 12. 6. 1; Suet. *Aug.* 8. 1.

younger women, they greatly increased the number of occasions on which such displays could take place. They also enhanced their overall prestige by suggesting that adult family members, even the young and those not entitled to hold political office, shared in the special ethos and heritage of a politically prominent family.[152]

Caesar's own funeral can be seen as the ultimate republican élite funeral and the last step before the funerals of the emperors.[153] In his special position as consul Antony was able, in the absence of Caesar's designated heir Octavian, to stage a public funeral just as Catulus had done for Sulla. He gave the funeral address himself and led the ritual laments. The theatrical nature of the performance was evident, especially as the audience seems to have mourned with him like the chorus of a tragedy or the professional mourning women (*praeficae*).[154] They apparently took turns with Antony in lamenting Caesar and in reciting his achievements.[155] Antiphonal singing of laments was an ancient custom, which was usually performed by relatives and professional mourners.[156] Antony probably cast himself in the role of a relative to stress his claim to be Caesar's heir.[157] One man, whose identity is not revealled by our sources, acted the part of Caesar. He recalled what Caesar had done for each of his murderers and repeated apposite lines from tragedies by Pacuvius and Accius.[158] It is tempting to identify this person as an actor wearing Caesar's *imago*, who had been instructed by Antony on the part he was to play.[159] Caesar's wounded body was also represented

[152] Note, however, that no similar honours were extended to small children who were buried very simply. See § 1 above.

[153] The most comprehensive study is Weinstock (1971) 346-55.

[154] Such antiphonal laments can be compared with the kommos in the *Choephori* 306-478 and are especially associated with women.

[155] Appian BC 2.146 : ἐφ' οἷς ὁ δῆμος οἷα χορὸς αὐτῳ πενθιμώτατα συνωδύρετο καὶ ἐκ τοῦ πάθους αὖθις ὀργῆς ἐνεπίμπλατο ('at this the people like a chorus lamented most sorrowfully with him and they were filled with anger again because of his suffering').

[156] See Alexiou (1974) 10-14 and 131-60 on the antiphonal structure of Greek laments which she traces to an Oriental origin.

[157] Alexiou (1974) 20-1 comments that the right to inherit in Greece was closely linked to the duty to mourn. Cf. Morris (1987) 34 and Paulus ex Festus 68 L.

[158] App. BC 2. 146 : αὐτὸς ὁ Καῖσαρ ἐδόκει λέγειν . . . ('Caesar himself seemed to speak . . .').

[159] Such an identification is not necessarily at odds with Dio's report (47. 19. 2 = T27) of a decree of the triumvirs banning the *imago* of Caesar on the grounds that he was a god. The decree was not passed until 42 BC and may imply that an *imago* of Caesar had been displayed before. The decree also suggests how widely Caesar's *imago* could have been used in the family by others seeking to identify themselves as

by a wax model which could be moved around for viewing by the crowd.

Antony stage-managed the extensive co-operation between the crowd and the members of the funeral procession. He led them in their laments of Caesar and succeeded in presenting the loss as theirs in a special way. The dramatic element which focussed on the actors now included the crowd in an almost equal role. This performance was conceived as a dialogue between the funeral cortège and the crowd, which brought out the full potential of the Roman funeral as political drama.[160] The informal and popular nature of the exchanges is clear; improvisation must have played a large part. The final result was only possible because of the intimate familiarity of Roman citizens with the shape of the aristocratic funeral in which they had not been merely spectators but regular participants on various levels for centuries.[161] Antony used the medium of the funeral and its laments, which had regularly served as a reintegration and restoration of society after a loss, for personal political ends and to further party strife and revenge.[162]

8. *Conclusion*

At an aristocratic funeral, the family used their *imagines* to present Roman history in their own terms, probably giving each procession and speech a different flavour according to their needs and the political climate of the moment. The funerals kept alive the memory of achievements that might otherwise have been forgotten, at the same time as identifying the family as closely as possible with famous episodes from Rome's past. The actors wearing the *imagines* played the role of each ancestor in a studied and realistic way including gestures, and probably also words. Their performance was

his heirs. As noted in Ch. 2, the *S.C. de Cn. Pisone patre* (II6) suggests that an *imago* was normally made during a man's lifetime. See Suet. *Vesp.* 19. 2 = T84 discussed in § 2 above.

[160] See Kierdorf (1980) 102 for Caesar's funeral and its connections with vendetta.

[161] It was the defeat of such expectation for public mourning and pomp that caused widespread outcry when Germanicus' ashes were buried without ceremony (Tac. *Ann.* 3. 5 = T88).

[162] See Alexiou (1974) 21-2 on the strong tradition of ritual lament found in societies where blood feuds are practiced, such as in the Mani and Sicily. For the funeral as a healing for death, see Redfield (1975) 29 and 180 and Morris (1987) 31.

enhanced by the costumes, attributes, and entourage suited to each historical figure at the peak of his career. A man's *imago* seems to have appeared for the first time at his own funeral.[163] Familiarity with the expectations and values of the audience was vital in making the most of a family's display.

When viewed as a pageant of Rome's history, it is hard to imagine a more accessible source of these traditions for the ordinary Roman citizen.[164] Polybius stressed how such funerals made the past seem alive and relevant to present concerns.[165] The spectacle, centred around the *imagines* of the ancestors, acted as a powerful verification of traditional values and especially of the success and prestige of the families represented. The public part of an aristocratic funeral, which comprised the procession of ancestors and the funeral eulogy in the Forum, was reserved for the families of office-holders and set them apart from ordinary citizens in a conspicuous way. The spectators were made to feel an integral part of a celebration of the common heritage they shared with their leaders. A sense of community was created between different layers of society and between generations. The continuity and prestige of the family's overall position was emphasized at a moment of significant change when a member was lost.[166]

[163] Bettini (1991) 179 explores the newly-dead man's position within the funeral cortège as he first appeared immediately in front of the bier and slowly moved ahead of it with each successive death in the family.

[164] Martha (1883) 58 made this point which has not received much attention from more recent scholars.

[165] 6. 54. 2 = T61. Cf. Dupont (1985) 29: 'L'efficacité de ces cérémonies de mémoire que sont les funérailles aristocratiques est uniquement liée à leur qualité spectaculaire.'

[166] This point is well made by North (1983).

5

Praising the Ancestors:
Laudationes and other Orations

Atque etiam, cum apud vos aut in senatu verba faciunt, pleraque oratione maiores suos extollunt, eorum fortia facta memorando clariores sese putant.

(Sall. *Jug.* 85.21)

Non si sottolineerà mai abbastanza la grandezza epica del funerale romano, della sua immaginazione culturale.

(Bettini (1986) 186)

THE climax of the funeral spectacle was the eulogy (*laudatio*) delivered from the speaker's platform (*rostra*) in the Forum. We are poorly informed about funeral speeches because only a few meagre fragments survive and the genre is not discussed in ancient rhetorical writings.[1] Nevertheless, its role and importance within Roman society needs to be explored because it formed a cornerstone of family self-advertisement and influence.[2] The eulogy provided the occasion for the parade of *imagines* into the middle of the city and was the high point of the public part of the funeral ceremonies. It also offered a commentary on the procession of *imagines* and enabled the family to present the career of its newly deceased member in the context of the achievements of his ancestors. The actors wearing the *imagines* re-enacted past events and personalities and illustrated the subject-matter of the eulogy. During the delivery of the speech

---

[1] The fragments were originally collected by Vollmer (1892) with a thorough introduction to the genre. For the few additions since then, see Kierdorf (1980) 137-49, whose approach is assessed by North (1983). The earlier bibliography is given by Schanz-Hosius (1927) 38.

[2] Loraux (1981) 43: 'Réservées à une élite, ces funérailles sont publicitaires et non publiques: exhibition de la toute-puissance des gentes et non célébration civique.' See Ch. 10 for a challenge to her approach.

itself they formed a special audience. Ancestors were also treated in several other types of rhetoric, in both political and judicial contexts. A wide variety of situations in Roman life were suited to a reconsideration of ancestral achievements, which were often recalled in language related to the *imagines*. This chapter examines both funeral eulogies, as revealed by the extant fragments, and other speeches in order to elucidate their relationship with the *imagines*.

1. *The Context of the* Laudatio

The effect of a funeral speech was twofold, at first on the actual day of delivery at the funeral, and later in a published version which might have long-term influence. The small extant fragments of written versions offer only glimpses of the rhetoric of the moment, and may or may not be faithful reflections of what was actually said.[3] The procession with all its sounds and splendour was the essential background to the oration. Both elements combined to create a vivid and characteristically Roman spectacle. The procession set the scene and built up suspense towards the climax of the *laudatio* which expressed the various emotions inspired by the pageant of Rome's past history and by the deceased himself. At the *rostra* the whole parade was present before the eyes of the assembled crowd. The ancestors sat on ivory chairs, apparently in chronological order, to hear the oration.[4] Whether or not they were ever addressed or pointed out by the speaker, they need to be considered as participants in a public drama.[5]

According to Polybius the deceased was often propped up in a

---

[3] Scholars have not commented on the difference between the written and spoken *laudationes* except to surmise that the section dealing with the ancestors was not usually published (e.g. Kierdorf (1980) 66). On the widespread ancient practice of editing speeches for publication, see Humbert (1925), and Stroh (1975) 31-54, who argues persuasively that speeches were published as examples of a rhetorical genre and could only have served that purpose if they faithfully reflected their original form and content.

[4] Polyb. 6. 53. 9 = T61. Cf. Alexiou (1974) 3 on the importance of interpreting Greek ritual laments in context.

[5] Such a reconstruction was suggested by Martha (1883) 52-3. No fragments from *laudationes* enumerate the individual deeds of the ancestors. It is possible to interpret the address by Ap. Claudius Caecus to his descendant Clodia imagined by Cicero (*Cael.* 33-4 = T5) as a reversal of the dramatic action of the eulogy (see section 5 below). It is notable that recent analyses of the fragments of *laudationes* take virtually no account of the setting for the speech, and especially of the *imagines*.

sitting position at the *rostra* (6. 53. 1 = T61).⁶ His assertion has led
some to assume that an effigy was in use from an early period.⁷
Whatever the case, it seems that the dead man was also represented
as one of the ancestors, or as about to join their ranks.⁸ At the
funeral of Drusus in 9 BC his coffin is described as being surrounded
by the *imagines* of his ancestors at the *rostra* in what may have been
the usual configuration showing the ancestors as companions on
the final journey (Tac. *Ann.* 3. 5 = T88).⁹ The close association
between the deeds of the ancestors and the achievements of the
dead man, which can be found in the *laudatio*, was expressed visi-
bly by the presence of the *imagines* as both audience and background for the speech. The speech praised the life and deeds of the
deceased and enumerated the offices and achievements of each
ancestor, starting with the oldest. The proportion of the speaker's
attention devoted to the ancestors must, therefore, often have
exceeded the praises of the deceased, especially in leading families
with many generations of previous office-holders. At the funerals of
women or the young the emphasis on ancestors must have been
striking, if not overwhelming.

Polybius says it was usual for a son to deliver the oration, if one
was present who had already put on his toga of manhood.¹⁰ Even
in the mid-second century BC, therefore, the speaker must often
have been young and would frequently be making his first public
appearance as an orator on such an occasion. As a result, the oration was not specifically designed to show off the rhetorical skills of
older, office-holding family members. This may sometimes have
happened, especially by the first century BC when funerals were
being held for women and presumably also for young family members who may not have held office yet. Nevertheless, it was not a
part of the original purpose of the speech which resembled a rite of

⁶ By contrast, the dead man on the Amiternum relief is propped up on one
elbow.
⁷ e.g. Benndorf (1878) 372. An effigy may have been the norm for those who
died outside Rome, such as the elder Drusus.
⁸ Cf. Ch. 4 § 2 for the question of whether the dead man's *imago* appeared at his
own funeral. Caesar was represented both by an effigy and by an actor, but his
funeral is not necessarily typical; cf. Ch. 4 § 6.
⁹ The term used is *circumfusus*, on which see *OLD* 6 for the meaning 'crowd
around' or 'embrace', often used of a large crowd or of an army. Cf. Tac. *Ann.* 12.
38.
¹⁰ Polyb. 6. 53. 2 = T61. Because Sulla's son was too young, the best orator of
the age was chosen to deliver the eulogy (App. *BC* 1. 106).

passage for the oldest son. The traditional simplicity of the genre can be associated with the youth of the speaker and the potentially large size and diverse character of the crowd in the Forum. It also reflects a desire to evoke an archaic tone associated with the ancestors. The role of the *imagines* as an audience lent authority to the youth of the speaker. The appearance of a new, young orator to praise the dead at a moment of transition for the family could create a balance between themes of loss and the impression of new life. The recent death of a family member was put in perspective by a show of continuity between the ancestors and a new generation represented by the speaker.[11]

The delivery of the funeral speech from the *rostra* in the Forum demonstrates its inherently political nature. Whether it originated as a private speech, which was transferred to the public context of the Forum by an incumbent magistrate, must remain a matter for speculation.[12] For Romans of non-senatorial background private funeral eulogies were probably delivered at the grave, or perhaps at the *silicernium*.[13] An example is the fragment from the eulogy Atticus delivered for his mother Caecilia in 42 BC.[14] This speech comes from an equestrian context and dwells on family life and domestic virtues, as might be expected. It so happens that the longest and most informative fragments of *laudationes* to survive come from speeches delivered for women. Both the 'Laudatio Turiae' and the *Laudatio Murdiae* probably belong to a more private context

---

[11] Cf. Loraux (1981) 269 for the Athenian funeral oration as a praise of the whole city, both the living and the dead. Similarly, at 47 she discusses how the city asserts its abiding reality in the face of death. The Athenian *polis* had taken over much of the role of the aristocratic family.

[12] This theory was advocated by Vollmer (1925) 992 and Durry (1950) 18: 'L'éloge gentilice devenant ainsi éloge public, la politique s'en mêle.' For an alternative argument, first advanced by Mommsen, that originally only magistrates ever received such funerals, cf. Barbieri (1947) 472.

[13] Note the similarities with Greek praises for the dead, which could be found both at the funeral feast and in the context of the symposium; see Alexiou (1974) 104–8. For Greek praises of past heroes, see Rösler (1990) with bibliography. For the equivalent archaic Roman *carmina convivalia*, see Cic. *Brut.* 75, *Tusc.* 1. 3, 4. 3; Val. Max. 2. 1. 10 with Zorzetti (1990).

[14] Nep. *Att.* 17. 1: *cum hoc ipsum vere gloriantem audierim in funere matris suae, quam extulit annorum nonaginta, cum esset septem et septuaginta, se numquam cum matre in gratiam redisse, numquam cum sorore fuisse in simultate, quam prope aequalem habebat.* ('At the funeral of his mother who was 90 [he was 77 at the time] I heard him say the following with genuine pride, that he had never had a reconciliation with his mother nor a quarrel with his sister who was about the same age as himself'). The authenticity of this fragment is doubted by Kierdorf (1980) 114 n. 74 and 138.

than the public speeches on the *rostra*.[15] For this reason they are not easy to use in an examination of aristocratic *mores*. It is not clear whether the detailed information they contain about family affairs, especially financial arrangements, can be seen as at all typical of *laudationes* in general, or whether it reflects the private audience these speeches were designed for. The fact that these eulogies were later rendered as inscriptions, which were presumably accessible to the public, does not change their original character.

Dionysius of Halicarnassus (5. 17. 3) tells us that the public funeral orations of the Romans were of ancient and native origin.[16] As it stands, our first reliable evidence dates from the later third century BC, by which time the habit of public eulogies appears well established. The Romans themselves also believed that this was an old custom and cited the first public oration as that given for Brutus the first consul by his colleague Publicola.[17] This tradition need tell us no more than that they associated the practice closely with the Republic and its institutions. Although Livy does not mention Brutus' eulogy, he does see *laudationes* as current in the early Republic.[18] The *imagines* were closely associated with the structure of the *laudatio*, since their parade only really made sense when elucidated by a funeral speech which included the careers of the ancestors. The public *laudatio* of a typically Roman kind must be at least as old as the *imagines*, and probably existed before them. The *laudatio* was a characteristic feature of the nobility of office which emerged from the conflict of the orders.[19]

From the late third century BC onwards the *laudationes* which we know about are overtly political. On such an occasion an office-holding family set itself apart from ordinary citizens by virtue of past political function and made an exhibition of its history in the most public way available. The funeral speech served to justify the position and leadership of the family, while at the same time celebrat-

[15] For the *Laudatio Turiae*, see Durry (1950) and Wistrand (1976). On its unsuitability for public delivery in the Forum, see Horsfall (1983) 89. The *Laudatio Murdiae* can be found at *ILS* 8394 = *CIL* 6. 10230.

[16] For the emergence of the public *laudatio* in the late 4th/early 3rd cent. BC, partly under Greek influence, see Kierdorf (1980) 94-5, Hölkeskamp (1987) 222, and Hölscher (1990) 78.

[17] Dion. Hal. 5. 17. 2; Plut. *Pub.* 9. 7; *De Vir. Ill.* 10. 7; Lydus, *Mag.* 1. 33.

[18] Livy 2. 47. 11 has Cincinnatus and Q. Fabius praised by M. Fabius Vibulanus in 480 BC.

[19] For further discussion, see Appendix D.

ing and supporting the system of republican government itself. The close connection of such practices with the elections has already been touched upon.[20] By showing the people how often they had voted for earlier family members and with what gratifying results, a strong, if unvoiced, argument was made to vote for a family member in the future, if only through recognition of the name.

2. Laudationes *and Rhetorical Theory*

The principal issues addressed in past studies of the *laudationes* are their absence from books of ancient rhetorical theory, combined with Cicero's apparent ambivalence towards them.[21] These two circumstances have led to a relative devaluation of *laudationes* in comparison with other branches of rhetoric.[22] Funeral orations are represented as an uninspiring type of speech which changed little over time. They are cited as illustrative of the crude, native traditions of the early Romans, maintained because of their close association with highly formalized funeral rituals. One extreme treatment resulted in categorizing them as a type of *Antikunstprosa*, which deliberately flaunted the standards of eloquence expected on other occasions.[23] Alternatively, they are seen as following their own archaic rhetorical conventions.[24]

By contrast, more recent attempts to understand the *laudatio* in a broader social and cultural context, rather than in purely formal, rhetorical terms, have suggested that these speeches, although simple, were effective and followed the oratorical trends of the day.[25] Nevertheless, even such more complex analysis is based on a tacit acceptance of Cicero's apparent dismissal of the genre as crude and uninteresting. Polybius (6. 53–4 = T61), however, portrays funeral speeches as moving and impressive; we should be wary about dismissing them in haste. The most important evidence comes from the

[20] The connection between *imagines* and elections is discussed in Ch. 3.

[21] Cic. *Brutus* 61–2 and *De or.* 2. 341.

[22] Previous scholarship on *laudationes* is summarized and discussed by Kierdorf (1980) 1–9. For an equivalently dismissive modern treatment of Greek funeral orations before the work of Loraux, see her book (1981) 225 ff.

[23] See Durry (1942) and (1950), who is forced to dismiss much of the stylistic evidence from the surviving fragments on the grounds that these were exceptional speeches given by famous orators.

[24] Vollmer (1892).

[25] Already proposed by Martha (1883) 24, this interpretation is developed by Kierdorf (1980).

fragments themselves and the context in which each attested speech was delivered.

The silence of rhetorical handbooks on the subject of funeral eulogies can be accounted for in various ways, not least because they were the narrow preserve of office-holding families. In any classification of rhetorical genres relying on Greek theory funeral orations were never given a full, separate treatment.[26] Cicero, himself a writer of several treatises on rhetoric, tells us that panegyrics do not need rules because the content should be obvious (*De Or.* 2. 46). His view may have been shared by many Romans. Moreover, Cicero had a number of good reasons for not favouring *laudationes*, among which his struggle against the political power of the inner élite at Rome must have played a role. He remarks in the *Brutus* (61–2) on the unreliability of the information preserved in such speeches and on the way they were used for family propaganda. It is clear that he objects in principle to the *laudationes* as sources of a false picture of Rome's past, which frequently went on to become part of written histories and general traditions.[27] Cicero's opinion, confirmed by Livy (8. 40. 4-5 = T41), shows how influential eulogies could be.

At the same time, Cicero's criticisms of the style of *laudationes* need to be seen in context since he is generally dismissive of early Latin rhetoric. In the passage in question, he is talking about panegyrics in general and is very brief in what he says specifically about funeral speeches.

nostrae laudationes quibus in foro utimur aut testimonii brevitatem habent nudam atque inornatam aut scribuntur ad funebrem contionem, quae ad orationis laudem minime accommodata est. (De Or. 2. 341)

Our speeches of praise, which we are accustomed to deliver in the Forum, are either brief depositions by witnesses that are simple and unadorned, or they are written for public delivery at a funeral which is an unsuitable occasion to win acclaim for a speech.

---

[26] Loraux (1981) 42–3 stresses the striking differences between Greek, especially Athenian, and Roman funeral speeches. She does not consider them as part of the same genre in any sense, although both deal especially with virtue and are addressed as an inspiration to the living. Cf. Arist. *Rhet.* 2. 2. 1396ᵃ 12–15 with Loraux (1981) 227.

[27] Cicero's own attempts to have his consulship remembered in the best possible light indicate the pressure he felt from the great aristocratic families who had many more resources for keeping their glorious deeds before the eyes of the public. See *Fam.* 5. 12 for Cicero's letter to Lucceius.

He cites two types of *laudationes* in the Forum, the first of which is the deposition of a character witness in a law suit. It is this which is not surprisingly described as brief, bald, and unadorned. When it comes to the *funebris contio*, he sees it as a poor opportunity for an exhibition of rhetorical brilliance. What he may be referring to is the structure of this type of speech, which stuck closely to the offices held and achievements associated with each ancestor, in chronological order. He goes on to give quite extensive guidelines for praise, focusing especially on virtues in a rather abstract way (*De Or*. 2. 342–8). It is plain even from the sparse surviving fragments of funeral orations that virtues were indeed an important part of such a speech, which could focus on the moral qualities needed for leadership as much as on the actual prizes of office.

Meanwhile it is pertinent that Cicero was himself a writer of *laudationes* and an avowed admirer of certain famous eulogies written by leading statesmen and orators of the past.[28] Cicero's high praise of Fabius Maximus' speech given for his son at the end of the Second Punic War is evidence enough that he did not consider this genre unworthy of the orator.[29] He sees Fabius' speech as brilliantly effective and deeply moving, and noted it as a high achievement even in the career of so famous a figure. Cicero refers to it in passing as a well-known speech of which copies were still available. The fact that he had reservations about the overall possibilities of such speeches, and the style of some of the early ones, should not weigh too heavily in any general assessment of them. They represent some of our earliest examples of Latin oratory and can reveal the public stance adopted by leading Romans.[30]

Funeral speeches followed a pattern familiar to Roman audiences, which was not less significant because it had become somewhat formalized. Well-worn themes were part of the customary

[28] Cic. *Q. fr*. 3. 8. 5 records a speech written by Cicero eulogizing a certain Serranus, who was perhaps the son of L. Domitius Ahenobarbus, delivered by the father on 23 Nov. 54 BC.

[29] *De Sen*. 12: *Multa in eo viro praeclara cognovi sed nihil est admirabilius quam quomodo ille mortem fili tulit clari viri et consularis. est in manibus laudatio quam cum legimus, quem philosophum non contemnimus?* ('I have found out about many outstanding achievements of that man but nothing is more remarkable than the way in which he bore the death of his son who was a distinguished man of consular rank. When we read his eulogy which is extant, what philosopher do we not look down on?')

[30] *Contra* Martha (1883) 6, who claims that most of these speeches were delivered by speakers who were not eloquent.

ceremonies following the death of a leading citizen and their importance was measured partly by people's expectations that certain
topics would be rehearsed in public.[31] Consequently, it was considered a serious matter to deprive a man from an office-holding family of his right to a full funeral.[32] The effectiveness of the seemingly
spare rhetoric, with its lists of careers and awards, can also be
gauged by the apparent reaction against it by popular politicians
during the crisis of the Republic after the Gracchi.[33] Marius seems
to have made such aristocratic rhetoric a target of his scorn and to
have engaged in parodies of it, to judge from the evidence of
Plutarch and Sallust.[34] When attacking the office-holding caste in
the spirit of partisan strife, the particular rhetoric of the funeral oration could provide a readily identifiable object for vituperation.

3. *Ideology and Structure in the* Laudatio

Our oldest fragment comes from the *laudatio* of Q. Caecilius Metellus
(*RE* 81, cos. 206 BC) for his father Lucius (*RE* 72, cos. 251 and 247
BC), delivered in 221 BC.[35] Pliny records the following:

*scriptum reliquit decem maximas res optimasque, in quibus quaerendis sapientes
aetatem exigerent, consummasse eum. voluisse enim primarium bellatorem esse,
optimum oratorem, fortissimum imperatorem, auspicio suo maximas res geri,
maximo honore uti, summa sapientia esse, summum senatorem haberi, pecuniam
magnam bono modo invenire, multos liberos relinquere et clarissimum in civitate
esse. haec contigisse ei nec ulli alii post Romam conditam.*

he [Quintus] left it in writing that he [Lucius] devoted himself to acquiring
the ten greatest and best things which prudent men spend their lives in
search of. For he wanted to be a leading soldier, the most excellent orator,
the bravest general, to do the greatest deeds under his own command, to
hold the highest offices, to display the greatest shrewdness, to be consid-

---

[31] Cf. Loraux (1981) 265 on the significance of repeated *topoi* in Athenian funeral
orations, which served as the model for Athenian discourse about Athens and influenced all other types of civic self-representation.

[32] Cic. *Mil.* 33 = T9 and 86 = T10 makes much of the fact that Clodius received
no proper funeral.

[33] Nicolet (1964) 22: 'Si bien qu'à la fin, au IIe siècle, il pourra servir de repous-
soir à l'éloquence révolutionnaire d'un Caius Gracchus, d'un Marius, qui opposeront,
à la gloire héritée de la noblesse, la gloire individuelle de l'*homo novus*'.

[34] Sall. *Jug.* 85. 10 ff. = T66*a–c*; Plut. *Mar.* 9. 2 = T60 with discussion in Ch. 1.
Cf. also Sallust's version of Macer's speech as tribune in *Hist.* 48 = T67.

[35] Plin. *Nat.* 7. 139 (*ORF*⁴ no. 6 fr. 2). Malcovati (1965) 211–3 and *ORF*⁴ 535
n. 1 refutes the suggestion that this speech was delivered by L. Metellus' grandson.

ered the most senior senator, to make a fortune in a decent way, to leave many children, and to be the most distinguished man in the state. He achieved these goals as no other man since Rome was founded.

This famous passage is the earliest extant piece of Latin oratory, as well as being the longest and richest extract from a public eulogy.[36] It gives a momentary glimpse of a fine, formal oration given by a man who was to become a leading rhetorician of his age.[37] Delivered before the outbreak of the Second Punic War, it illustrates what seems to have been a flourishing genre. The written version of the *laudatio* was probably the main reason why Cicero names Q. Metellus as an orator of note.[38] A young man at the time, Quintus had not yet held public office, so this was probably his first speech from the *rostra*. He is generally taken to be the eldest of Lucius Metellus' three sons, an assumption perhaps partly based on this speech. However, the disgrace of his brother Lucius after Cannae may conceal the fact that Lucius was actually the eldest son and hence the one named after his father.[39] The family's choice of Quintus over his elder brother Lucius suggests the importance attached to eloquence on this occasion.[40] The decision was surely based on Quintus' evident talents as a speaker. Quintus is probably the same man who responded as consul pointedly and wittily when

[36] Cf. Sempronius Asellio fr. 8 P = Aulus Gellius I. 13. 10 on P. Licinius Crassus Mucianus (cos. 131 BC): *Is Crassus a Sempronio Asellione et plerisque aliis historiae Romanae scriptoribus traditur habuisse quinque rerum bonorum maxima et praecipua: quod esset ditissimus, quod nobilissimus, quod eloquentissimus, quod iuris consultissimus, quod pontifex maximus* ('This Crassus is reported by Sempronius Asellio and most other writers of Roman history to have enjoyed the five greatest and most exceptional good things: because he was very rich, from a very distinguished family, very eloquent, highly expert in the law, and he held the office of chief priest').

[37] This oration is commented on by Kierdorf (1980) 10–21. For Q. Caecilius Metellus' career see Münzer *RE* Caecilius 81 and van Ooteghem (1967) 23–44.

[38] *Brutus* 57. Valerius Maximus 7. 2. 3 gives us a paraphrase of his famous speech on the fate of Carthage at the end of the Second Punic War (*ORF*⁴ no. 6 fr. 3).

[39] Lucius (*RE* 73) was quaestor in 214 BC (Livy 24. 18. 3–6), well before his brother Quintus' aedileship of 208 BC. His career is not documented after his tribunate in 213 BC (Livy 24. 43. 2ff.). Cf. Livy 22. 53. 5–13 for Lucius' role at Cannae and 27. 11. 12 for his removal from the senate under the wrong name of Marcus. Quintus' irregular *cursus* somewhat obscures his age.

[40] As the direct ancestor of the leading Metelli in future generations, Quintus easily eclipsed his disgraced and apparently childless brother Lucius. For a family tree of the Metelli see *RE* 3. 1229–30 and Carcopino (1931) where Lucius does not appear at all, whereas Syme (1939) table I starts with the consul of 206 BC. A new family tree with Lucius as the eldest son appears in Appendix E.

attacked by Naevius' famous taunt about how the Metelli achieved consulships.[41]

The speech is significant because it praised the man who was in effect the founder of the family's name and fortunes. Lucius Metellus' funeral had only one *imago* of an ancestor in the male line, namely L. Metellus Denter (*RE* 92, cos. 284 BC), who was killed in a disaster with his army at Arretium (Polybius 2. 19. 8).[42] The son, therefore, worked to stress his father's excellence in comparison with earlier Romans in general. The Caecilii Metelli were especially prominent only in the second century, notably 123-102 BC when they gained six consulships, five triumphs, and four censorships.[43] L. Metellus' exhibition of elephants for the first time in a Roman triumph during the First Punic War was recalled on the coins of his first-century descendants and became a kind of heraldic badge for the Metelli.[44] It is tempting to imagine that his clearly defined role for posterity depended partly on this very oration, which was preserved both within the family and outside it. The written version of a *laudatio* could be a vital link in shaping a family's ancestral iconography and keeping alive the memory of its spectacular funerals and triumphs.

Pliny introduces his quotation from the speech with a summary of the father's career, which probably reflects the shape of earlier

[41] Pseudoasconius Stangl 215: *dictum facete et contumeliose in Metellos antiquum Naevi est: 'fato Metelli Romae fiunt consules'. cui tunc Metellus consul iratus versu responderat senario hypercatalecto, qui et Saturnius dicitur: 'Dabunt malum Metelli Naevio poetae'* ('Naevius long ago composed the following witty and rude verse at the expense of the Metelli: "By fate the Metelli are consuls at Rome". Then Metellus the consul responded angrily to him with a verse in hypercatalectic senarii, which is also called a Saturnian verse: "The Metelli will do a bad turn to Naevius the poet" '). Q. Metellus was elected consul for 206 BC before holding the praetorship, after serving as one of the messengers who reported news of the victory at the Metaurus river. Zorzetti (1991) 314 assigns these exchanges to a genre of vituperative verse. Radke (1981) 65 characterizes Metellus' response as a model Saturnian verse.

[42] Note by comparison the funeral of Q. Caecilius Metellus Macedonicus (*RE* 94, cos. 143 BC) in 115 BC which was attended by his four sons, two of whom were censors, one a consular, and one a praetor soon to be consul. His two daughters were both married to future consuls. His two nephews were also of consular rank and one had held the censorship. See Cassola (1988) 479-80 and the family tree in Appendix E below.

[43] For the family tomb of the Caecilii Metelli on the Via Appia near the Porta Capena, see Cic. *Tusc.* I. 13. The round monument to a Caecilia Metella of the late Republic is about 4 km. from the gate; see Zanker (1988) figs. 14 and 58.

[44] For coins of the Metelli with an elephant, see Crawford 262, 263, and 269 (from the 120s BC), 369 (82-80 BC), 374 (81 BC), 459 (47-46 BC).

material in the oration.[45] The funeral speech set out the offices of the deceased and mentioned special achievements, such as the parade of elephants in the triumph of 250 BC. The tone of this fragment suggests that it is from the last part of the section praising the father, which was clearly supposed to end with a striking vignette or idea for the listeners to take away with them as a memory of the deceased.[46] In this case the summary of the ten most important aristocratic virtues, of which Metellus is made the ultimate example in each category, could not be more telling for any investigation of aristocratic values and their relation to funeral ceremonies.[47] In its very form it points to the development of history written in terms of individual *exempla*, measuring careers throughout the ages by a seemingly absolute standard of excellence.

The climax of the speech is the notion of 'incomparability', a powerful aristocratic ideal in what was already a society permeated at every level by competition for prestige and recognition. Confirmation comes in the marked use of superlatives throughout this short section. The fragment is a reflection of the need felt by leading aristocrats to be seen to 'win' in a 'contest', which already had fixed goals for merit and which was perceived as the characteristic feature of Roman public life since the earliest period. The competition went beyond the present generation to include Rome's past history, represented by the *imagines*.[48] The picture conveyed is of a society in which 'virtue' has been defined in clear terms for those aspiring to the leading role bestowed by politics.

If a scheme is to be found in the sequence of qualities mentioned, it is that each achievement is arranged roughly in the order in which it was aspired to in the highly structured life of the Roman

---

[45] Plin. *Nat.* 7. 139 : *Q. Metellus in ea oratione, quam habuit supremis laudibus patris sui L. Metelli pontificis, bis consulis, dictatoris, magistri equitum, XVviri agris dandis, qui primus elephantos ex primo Punico bello duxit in triumpho, scriptum reliquit . . .* ('Quintus Metellus left a written version of that speech which he delivered as the funeral eulogy of his father Lucius Metellus the high priest, twice consul, dictator, master of the horse, one of fifteen men who gave land alotments, who was the first to lead elephants as booty in a triumph during the First Punic War . . .').

[46] For the use of a *sententia* or authoritative statement in poetic closure, see Herrenstein Smith (1968) 151 ff.

[47] Martha's (1883) 9 dismissal of this fragment as artificial and repetitious misses the point. The best overall analysis is Gabba (1988) 27-31.

[48] Close echoes of this sentiment can be found in the *elogia* of the Scipios. These are discussed in Ch. 6 § 1b. For *primarius* see Cic. *Sen.* 61 = 114 and *Fin.* 2. 35. 116 quoting the tomb inscription of A. Atilius Caiatinus cos. 258 BC.

senator.[49] He started his training as a soldier and progressed to exercising magistracies and their associated military commands, while eventually aiming at a position as leader in the community as a whole. Such an arrangement would be readily recognizable to the audience, who were accustomed to think in terms of a *cursus* as the measure of a man's career. It is further suggested by his introductory phrase *aetatem exigerent* ('spend their lives'). Q. Metellus sets up a *cursus* of his own invention which represents a yet higher standard of achievement, and which is measured across a man's whole life while comparing him with previous generations.

Rhetoric appears as the second ingredient because it was an integral part of that education, together with the military training alluded to at the start, which absorbed the energies of young Romans before they could stand for a first political office in their late twenties.[50] The rhetoric mentioned here was seen as a political means towards the goal of gaining influence and office. Metellus' testimony is the more valuable because he is speaking as a young man rather than a politician who has already become powerful through his oratory. His words reflect society's values and the expectations of his family rather than personal notions of what was important.

The qualities of the general are clearly distinguished from those of the soldier. At this early date themes appear which continued to resound throughout the rest of the Republic and into the Empire. Metellus already stresses the importance attached to achievements won under one's own auspices. No stronger indication could be found of the role of status at every stage in a Roman aristocrat's life. *Honor* is the definition of position and a synonym for offices held. With age more stress is laid on position amongst one's peers and in society at large, which is to say what the Romans called *auctoritas*. It was not enough to do great things; a man's achievements needed to be recognized in a public way in the prestige granted by the community. It is notable that *summus senator* is an expression otherwise unparalleled in Latin.[51]

[49] The structure as interpreted here is more subtle and complex than Durry's (1950) XLII division into public life, followed by private achievements, or Steidle (1963) who characterizes the speech as loosely organized.

[50] Polyb. 6. 19. 4 cites the ten campaigns of military service required before standing for office, cf. Harris (1979) 11–12. The aristocratic ethos and its relationship to war is best explained by Harris (1971) 9–41.

[51] It is interesting as the stated goal of a man whose position as a plebeian probably excluded him from becoming *princeps senatus*. He had not held the censorship which might otherwise qualify him to be deemed *summus senator*.

Metellus twice refers to *sapientia* as the guiding virtue of the noble throughout his career.[52] For him it contains overtones of prudence and shrewdness rather than of philosophical learning.[53] What makes *sapientia* interesting is the fact that it is such a prominent word in the next century. It has been closely associated with the Hellenizing circles of the Scipios, especially Aemilianus.[54] Metellus became a close associate of Scipio Africanus, but at a much later date. The emphasis on *sapientia* as a quality should warn us about the difficulties of dating key words and concepts in Roman society. *Sapientia* was a powerful word with a long history whose meaning changed in Q. Metellus' own lifetime. Customs like the *laudatio funebris* and the inscriptions associated with *imagines* and tombs helped to perpetuate the Roman vocabulary of virtues from one generation to the next.

Money is openly acknowledged as vital in creating a man's position within society. Here we find a classic statement that wealth acquired by certain accepted means was desirable and seen as a goal.[55] Metellus shows us that the senators of his day wanted to be recognized as men of substance beyond what they had inherited, while also living within a society which had strong norms about how aristocrats could make and use money. Money is mentioned late in life because the speaker is referring to the wealth left at his father's death. Making money was not seen as its own reward, rather bequeathing it to future generations was the aim.[56] Similarly, children appear just before the end of the list because the speaker is thinking in terms of the children a man hoped to leave behind him when he died.

The climax of the list expresses the position a man aimed to

[52] *sapientes aetatem exigerent . . . summa sapientia esse.*

[53] Wheeler (1988) has shown that in the 3rd cent. BC and before *sapientia* meant 'trickery', especially with reference to military strategems, while a more general sense of 'wisdom' emerged in the 2nd cent. BC, and later a philosophical meaning with Cicero.

[54] Saladino's (1970) 22 is an example of a misguided attempt to downdate the inscription on L. Cornelius Scipio Barbatus' sarcophagus to the time of Scipio Aemilianus based partly on the appearance of the word *sapiens* inscribed on it. Aemilianus and his circle are treated by Astin (1967) 294-306. For Barbatus as *sapiens*, see Traina (1969) 166.

[55] For senatorial wealth, see Shatzman (1975) 245 who assumes Metellus made a fortune in the First Punic War. See also Harris (1979) 67, D'Arms (1981) 20 ff. and esp. Gabba (1988) 27-9. It was precisely the new wealth of men like Metellus which created the heightened competition reflected in his *laudatio*.

[56] See Plut. *Cat. Mai.* 21. 8 for the importance of increasing one's *patrimonium*.

occupy by the end of his life based on the recognition he had won from all sections of society.[57] This recognition would then be reflected in the size of the crowd at his funeral eulogy where his life's achievements would be rehearsed. It is striking that his peak of glory is expressed by the word *clarissimus* which was to evolve into a technical term designating senatorial rank.[58] This finale to the praises of the deceased illustrates the brevity, simplicity, and formal character which can be described as typical of the *laudatio* as a genre. At the same time it shows how central such an expression could be to the values prized in Roman culture. Funeral rhetoric created the impression and often the conviction of a consensus within society which recognized the achievements of the individual and gave him an absolute position within the social order.

Two other fragments of *laudationes* also seem to come from this same moment of climax at the end of the praise of the deceased, namely Laelius' speech for Scipio Aemilianus and Augustus' for his stepson Drusus.[59] Both end with a '*sententia*' reflecting on the impact of the life of the deceased on the community. The concluding section was mainly addressed to the audience, evoking a shared sense of loss and touching on their role as survivors in a way similar to the ending of Pericles' funeral oration in Thucydides (2. 64).

The only significant fragment from the main body of a speech is that from Augustus' *laudatio* of 12 BC for his son-in-law M. Agrippa, discovered on a papyrus.[60] It reveals that the enumeration of offices and high points in the deceased's career could be addressed directly to him in the second person.[61] This practice, already attested in the *Laudatio Turiae*, confirms an area of connection with the laments, which seem often to have been addressed to the dead person.[62] Brutus' *laudatio* for his stepfather Ap. Claudius Pulcher, which may never have been delivered as Claudius died in Euboea (48 BC), seems to contain an address to himself in the second person by Brutus as the speaker.[63] Changes of address were a characteristic feature of

---

[57] *clarissimum in civitate esse.*

[58] Gaius, *Dig.* 27. 10. 5; Ulpian, *Dig.* 1. 9. 8.

[59] Stangl 118 (*ORF*[4] no. 22 fr. 22) and Suet. *Claudius* 1. 5.

[60] Koenen (1970a) and (1970b).

[61] The use of the second person is discussed in detail by Koenen (1970a) 247-9.

[62] The connections between ritual laments and *laudationes* are treated by Kierdorf (1980) 96-104. For ritual laments in general, see Alexiou (1974). For contemporary laments in the Mani, see Leigh Fermor (1958) 52-63.

[63] *ORF*[4] no. 158 fr. 23: *qui te toga praetexta amicuit* ('who clothed you in your toga of manhood'). Alternatively, the possibility that the dead man could be

this type of oratory, as it tried to involve the audience and could speak to the dead man as one also present. In light of this evidence it is hard to determine whether the section on the careers of the ancestors would have been addressed to them or to the audience. Perhaps they were directly spoken to in a construction parallel to that frequently used for the dead person.

The only fragment which seems to be part of an opening section in a speech is the extract from Caesar's praise of his aunt Julia, the widow of Marius, delivered in 69 BC.[64]

Amitae meae Iuliae maternum genus ab regibus ortum, paternum cum diis immortalibus coniunctum est. Nam ab Anco Marcio sunt Marcii Reges, quo nomine fuit mater; a Venere Iulii, cuius gentis familia est nostra. est ergo in genere et sanctitas regum, qui plurimum inter homines pollent, et caerimonia deorum, quorum ipsi in potestate sunt reges.

My aunt Julia's mother's family is descended from kings, her father's family is related to immortal gods. For the Marcii Reges are descended from Ancus Marcius, and her mother was a member of that family. The Julii, to whose family our branch belongs, are descendants of Venus. Therefore, our family enjoys both the special sacred status of kings, who are the most powerful of men, and the reverence due to gods, who have power over the kings themselves.

It is couched in simple but formal language and is in the third person. The speaker makes his audience aware of his own relationship to the dead woman and of his membership in the same family. Doubtless the person of the speaker was an integral feature of eulogies, which drew their full meaning from the context of a particular family funeral. The fragment gives a description of the family origins of the dead woman, specifically focussed on the age and venerable status of the families on both sides of her background.

From Polybius we learn that in his day the ancestors were praised after the dead person (6. 54. 1 = T61). The first and only evidence for a different procedure is Tacitus' account of the funeral speech written by Seneca for Nero to deliver at the funeral of Claudius in AD 54, in which the origins of the family and the enumeration of the offices and triumphs of the ancestors apparently

---

represented as speaking to his relative, who is delivering the eulogy, has not been considered before.

[64] Suet. *Jul.* 6. 1 (*ORF*[4] no. 121 fr. 29), cf. Ch. 4 § 6.

came first.[65] Customs had perhaps changed since Polybius' day or Tacitus may even have reversed the order of presentation. It is impossible for us to know when such a change might have taken place or whether both practices were admissible. The question of when and how the ancestors were praised is of particular relevance in placing and interpreting the fragment from Caesar's *laudatio*. Tacitus confirms for us that the section about the ancestors contained an exposition of the age of the family followed by a chronological enumeration of its members noting their offices and triumphs. The recitation had the nature of a catalogue but could still engage an audience in Nero's day. In many traditional societies the ritual recital of genealogies plays an important role on public occasions and at moments when power is transferred.[66] The role of the *imagines* in dramatizing the character and deeds of the ancestors helps to explain the impact of this part of the speech.

It is probable, therefore, that the fragment from Caesar's speech represents his introduction to the section about the ancestors, whether this section came first or last in his overall scheme. There is no solid evidence to suggest that the family of the deceased was also discussed at the beginning of the section dealing with his own deeds, as some have assumed.[67] It seems more likely that the parents or nearest relations of the deceased might be indicated just to put him or her in an immediate context. The fragment of Caesar setting out the origins of the Marcii and Julii fits most naturally at the beginning of the section about the ancestors, as described for us by Tacitus. The identification of this fragment as our only direct evidence for praise of the ancestors further increases its significance.

Caesar shows us that he is speaking in his own voice and with reference to a particular funeral. He is obviously not using a standardized introduction from a family 'archive'. His plain style, which made him so effective an orator and writer of political *commentarii*,

[65] Tac. *Ann.* 13. 3 : *Die funeris laudationum eius princeps exorsus est, dum antiquitatem generis, consulatus ac triumphos maiorum enumerabat, intentus ipse et ceteri.* ('On the day of the funeral the emperor [Nero] embarked upon his [Claudius'] eulogy: while he described the venerable age of the family and was enumerating the consulships and triumphs of his ancestors, he himself and the rest were absorbed.')

[66] See Vansina (1965) and (1985).

[67] Vollmer (1892) 476 assumed that the *gens* and *origo* (family background) of the deceased came first in the speech and, therefore, placed Caesar's fragment at the beginning, immediately after the *exordium* (introduction). Later (1925) 993, he suspended judgement on when the ancestors were praised. Peter (1914/67) opted for a discussion of the ancestors at the beginning of the speech.

can be seen at its most typical in the three short sentences which survive. The traditionally spare style of the *laudatio* was an especially suitable vehicle for his talents. He uses the two sides of the family to set up a striking and complementary balance between gods and kings.[68] Consequently, it is logical that the *imagines* present were principally those of the Julii and Marcii Reges, probably arranged in distinct groups to reflect this Julia's particular pedigree.[69] Caesar's preoccupation with the inherited prestige of monarchy and the power of divinity is the more telling in light of his later claims to be a supreme leader, both like a king and like a god.[70] Speaking as quaestor at the start of his senatorial career, he used funeral oratory to help establish his image as an effective speaker and popular politician in the tradition of Marius whose *imago* appeared for the first time at this funeral.[71] His words are direct and easy to understand while they are also bold and striking. Caesar's speech alone makes it hard to endorse Cicero's assertion that funeral speeches did not provide an opportunity for rhetorical display that could make a reputation for the speaker.

4. *Published* Laudationes *and the Roman Historical Tradition*

The surviving fragments illustrate the custom of publishing *laudationes* by the time of our earliest third-century BC evidence.[72] As

[68] On Ancus Marcius, see Badian in Skutsch (1972) 34–5 and Rawson (1975) 153. On Caesar as *pontifex maximus* and his new stress on Romulus, see Classen (1962) especially 193.

[69] Cf. Tac. *Ann.* 3. 5 = T88 and 4. 9. 2 = T90 with discussion in Ch. 8 §§ 1b and 2 for the parallel processions of Julian and Claudian ancestors at imperial funerals.

[70] Steidle (1963) 28 interprets the fragment as an attempt by Suetonius to indicate Caesar's character by quoting words that would have reminded ancient readers of Caesar's desire for kingship. Cf. Suet. *Jul.* 79. 2; Plut. *Caes.* 60. 1; Dio 44. 10 with Weinstock (1971) 270 ff., and Meier (1980) 82–5. For the ideas about kingship, many of them positive, which Caesar inherited, see Rawson (1975).

[71] It is interesting that Marius is treated as one among other senatorial ancestors; cf. Ch. 1 and § 5 below.

[72] The evidence for published *laudationes*, and who read them later, can be summarized as follows: Q. Caecilius Metellus for his father 221 BC (Pliny), M. Claudius Marcellus for his father 208 BC (Coelius Antipater, Livy, Augustus), Q. Fabius Maximus for his son c.207–203 BC (Cicero, Plutarch, Priscian), Laelius for Scipio Aemilianus 129 BC (Cicero and his scholiast), Caesar for his aunt Julia 69 BC (Suetonius, Plutarch), M. Junius Brutus for Ap. Claudius Pulcher 48 BC (Diomedes), Cicero for Cato 45 BC (Macrobius), Atticus for Caecilia 42 BC (Nepos), Augustus for Marcellus 23 BC (Servius, Plutarch), Augustus for Agrippa 12 BC (1st-cent. AD papyrus in Greek from the East), Augustus for Drusus 9 BC (Suetonius). The actual date of publication is rarely known.

Cicero tells us, many of the oldest examples of Latin prose available in his own day, the last generation of the Republic, were funeral speeches (*Brutus* 61). Fabius Maximus' published speech, which he gave for his son in his old age, shows that even in the third century BC *laudationes* were more than exhibition rhetoric produced as exercises by the young. Fabius succeeded in presenting a memorable picture of himself as the bereaved senior statesman, which endured to be quoted for a striking phrase by grammarians of the sixth century AD.[73] The ethos of funeral rhetoric was a vital part of the fabric of Roman life. The *laudationes* represented a branch of oratory highly valued by men who in turn went on to be regarded as famous ancestors themselves. Similarly, speeches which were not actually delivered, often because there had been a problem as a result of a family member dying abroad, came to be published on a regular basis.[74] Sometimes considered purely as a phenomenon of the propaganda contests in the civil wars, this habit can in fact also be traced back to the third century BC.[75]

M. Claudius Marcellus left an *oratio scripta* for his father, the conqueror of Syracuse, who died in an ambush in 208 BC in which the son had also been caught (Livy 27. 27. 13). Conflicting traditions about the fate of Marcellus' body made ancient writers uncertain whether a funeral was ever held for him or not.[76] It seems highly unlikely that a funeral took place, since Livy says that after Marcellus' death Hannibal tried to gain a tactical advantage by using the general's ring to forge instructions to Roman allies (Livy 27. 28. 4-12). Under these circumstances it would have been inconsistent for Hannibal to return the body or ashes, since he was trying to conceal Marcellus' death. It was important for the family to rehabilitate the memory of its leading member, who had been caught in a disgraceful trap and had not received proper funeral rites.[77] This process was started by his son who published a speech

[73] Cic. *De Sen.* 12, Priscian in *ORF*[4] no. 3 fr. 5.

[74] The examples we know of are M. Junius Brutus' speeches for his stepfather Ap. Claudius Pulcher in 48 BC and for his uncle Cato; and Cicero's praises for Cato and Porcia in 45 BC. On Cato see Zecchini (1980) for bibliography and a discussion of the content and context of the work.

[75] Vollmer (1925) 994 argues that *laudationes* which were not delivered were first published as political pamphlets in 48 BC.

[76] These traditions are discussed by Plut. *Marc.* 30 and analyzed by Caltabiano (1975) from an historiographical point of view.

[77] Lack of proper burial was considered a serious matter in the ancient world, and cast doubt on the fate of the soul which might be forced to wander the earth. Denial

like the one he might have delivered, no doubt justifying his father's actions and surely attributing a hero's brave death to him.

Later the family's 'official' history can be glimpsed in the funeral speech of Augustus for his nephew Marcellus in 23 BC, which appears to have attributed a grand funeral to the earlier Marcellus after his ashes were returned in a silver urn.[78] The issue at stake in the presentation of Marcellus' end can be measured in the hostile tradition quoted by Plutarch, which claimed that Marcellus' shameful death had rendered meaningless all the high offices he had previously held.[79] At the time of his death people would have known whether Marcellus had a full funeral or, as seems more likely, none at all. For Augustus, who was eager to present his nephew's ancestor in the best possible light, this difficulty was no longer insurmountable. The *princeps'* eminence gave his version its own authority. The family traditions of the Claudii Marcelli serve to illustrate how published *laudationes* were designed to project a specific image of the family and to explain or justify awkward moments in past history.[80] Layers of rewriting in successive speeches tended over time to produce an ever more elaborated version, which reflected the needs and concerns of each generation.

In the funeral speech, whether spoken or written, strict veracity could hardly be expected and was probably never the original intention. The family wished to present their version of events, which also entailed refuting or displacing other renditions and participants. Over the years the traditions of families which died out often disappeared with them, to be easily replaced by those of more famous or longer lived clans.[81] Certain themes developed as a competition in elaboration between various families.[82] Mythical

of burial might be imposed on an enemy, but could also be considered as a punishment imposed by the gods for impiety or sacrilege.

[78] Plut. *Marc.* 30. His attribution of the same tradition to Livy is perhaps a mistake. Alternatively, this case may illustrate a change of mind on the part of Livy, perhaps under the influence of Augustus' promotion of Marcellus. Cf. the special place of Marcellus in Verg. *Aen.* 6. 855–9 and on a coin of 50 BC, Crawford 439.

[79] Plut. *Comp. Marc. and Pelop* 3. 3–8.

[80] Asconius 12 C = 11 KS = 18 Stangl = I 15 quotes an inscription from the tomb of the Marcelli, as it was renovated by the grandson of the conqueror of Syracuse. Its enumeration of consulships over three generations reflects the material to be found in family *laudationes*. Cf. Ch. 3 § 2a.

[81] Peter (1914/67) 53–4.

[82] Varro wrote *De Familiis Troianis* to justify the claims of certain families to Trojan ancestry; cf. Servius A. 5. 704. Our only fragment is Peter, *HRR²* 2. 9 = Serv. A. 2. 166.

genealogies were tools designed to lay claim to age and prestige or
to specific qualities.[83] All of this could happen gradually as each
generation stressed different achievements of past ancestors, partly
under the influence of the political questions of the day. Similarly,
the rise to power of a new family meant they needed ancestors or
might associate themselves with the highly desirable traditions of
now extinct clans.

A good example to illustrate the ubiquity of tampering by the
family comes from Livy's obituary notice of Fabius Maximus
(22. 31. 8–11 = T43), which draws partly on family sources found
in Coelius Antipater. Livy criticizes the family for claiming that
Fabius was the first dictator to be popularly elected, when his selection was in fact a chance result in the absence of the consul needed
for the customary procedure of direct appointment. Even in the case
of so famous a person, perhaps the best-known member of his illustrious family, exaggeration led to distortion and falsehood. Given
this example, it is to be expected that the same and much more
went on in families with a greater need to make the most of their
past. Competition for prestige in Roman society was intense and
family traditions served as political advertisements. We have no real
evidence that this tendency was more marked in the later Republic.
There is simply more information about that period which can
make its claims appear more egregious.

Cicero tells us that records of funeral speeches were kept by the
families as everyday reminders of their status and past achievements and for use at subsequent family funerals.[84] Whether they
formed part of the records kept in the *tablinum* is not directly
attested by any ancient author.[85] Livy confirms what Cicero has to
say about their effect on history and on traditions about the past.[86]

---

[83] These have been discussed by Wiseman (1974*a*).

[84] Cic. *Brutus* 62: *Et hercules eae quidem exstant: ipsae enim familiae sua quasi ornamenta ac monumenta servabant et ad usum, si quis eiusdem generis occidisset, et ad memoriam laudum domesticarum et ad illustrandam nobilitatem suam* ('And, to be sure, some
of these are extant: for the families themselves preserve them as badges of honour
and memorials, both for use if someone in the same family dies, and to preserve the
memory of their family's renown and to demonstrate their rank as office-holders').

[85] Plin. *Nat.* 35. 7 = T54: *tabulina codicibus implebantur et monimentis rerum in
magistratu gestarum* ('The *tablina* [archive rooms] were filled with ledgers of records
and accounts of deeds done by office-holders'). Cf. Ch. 7 § 1*b*.

[86] Cic. *Brutus* 62: *quamquam his laudationibus historia rerum nostrarum est facta
mendosior. multa enim scripta sunt in eis quae facta non sunt: falsi triumphi, plures consulatus, genera etiam falsa et ad plebem transitiones, cum homines humiliores in alienum
eiusdem nominis infunderentur genus; ut si ego me a M'. Tullio esse dicerem, qui*

As a result of the character of funeral oratory, certain distortions were considered typical, such as extra offices and awards, especially additional consulates and triumphs. The impressiveness of a funeral speech depended partly on the length of the lists of offices and honours. Most histories were written by individuals who were members of a leading family or associated with one in some way. It has been amply demonstrated how extensive such family influence was on the annalistic tradition.[87]

The traditions of office-holding families were shaped to justify and build political power in the present.[88] To this end they might preserve, because of their relevance to the clan, genuine memories of past episodes otherwise obscured. Alternatively, they frequently distorted, exaggerated, and edited the past to create their own eulogistic versions. Livy remarks on the intractability of such material, especially as related to early Rome.[89] A Roman historian was faced with the daunting task of sifting and evaluating family traditions,

patricius cum Ser. Sulpicio consul anno x post exactos reges fuit ('Nevertheless, these funeral orations have caused the historical record of our traditions to be falsified. For many things are written in them which never happened: false triumphs, an exaggerated number of consulships, even invented families and transferals to the plebs, when men of humble birth are insinuated into other families of the same name, just as if I claimed to be descended from Manlius Tullius, a patrician who was consul with Servius Sulpicius ten years after the kings were driven out'). Livy 8. 40. 4–5 = T41: *Vitiatam memoriam funebribus laudibus reor falsisque imaginum titulis, dum familiae ad se quaeque famam rerum gestarum honorumque fallente mendacio trahunt; inde certe et singulorum gesta et publica monumenta rerum confusa. nec quisquam aequalis temporibus illis scriptor exstat quo satis certo auctore stetur* ('I believe that the tradition has been corrupted by funeral eulogies and false labels for masks, while each of the families is claiming for itself by deceptive lies the repute of deeds done and offices held. As a result of this certainly both the achievements of individuals and the public record of events have become confused. Nor is there extant any writer contemporary with that period to provide a sufficiently authoritative voice').

[87] Family influence on the annalistic tradition was amply demonstrated by Peter (1914/67) xxx–lix. Cicero's specific claims have been examined and confirmed by Ridley (1983). Cf. Cornell's remarks about the tradition concerning archaic Rome (1986) 62: 'it incorporated the semi-public traditions of the great noble families, which were solemnly rehearsed at public funerals and legitimated the power and influence wielded by their living representatives.' See Dihle (1986) on the influence of *laudationes* on the development of Roman biography.

[88] Wiseman (1979) 39: 'Funerary orations and the inscriptions on portrait busts were notoriously unreliable for historical fact: masquerading as objective record, they were really a means of persuasion, to convince the Forum crowd or the visitor in the atrium of the greatness of the dead man, and to encourage his descendants to go and do likewise.'

[89] Livy 4. 16. 4; 8. 40. 4–5 = T41. *Contra* e.g. Martha (1905) 15: ' Il avait donc sous les yeux, sous la main, des annales toutes rédigées.' Cf. O. C. Crawford (1941–2) 25–6.

which were often deceptive but could not be dismissed out of hand.

5. Imagines *in Rhetoric outside the Funeral Oration*

The ubiquity of ancestors in Roman public life made them an important subject for orators speaking in a variety of settings. Since so many Roman customs depended on the *mos maiorum*, the example set by individual ancestors was a natural subject for discussion. In a highly conservative society any advocate could further his cause by trying to show it was in harmony with the practices of the ancestors. Outside the formal setting of the *laudatio*, ancestors had a standard role to play in many other branches of oratory, notably in political and legal speeches. Quintilian (*Inst.* 3. 7–11) makes it clear that ancestors and family connections were an essential ingredient in any context involving praise or blame. A man who is to be praised must appear to live up to the example of his ancestors. If he has none, he is said to ennoble his family, partly by the practice of traditional virtues and by imitation of the achievements of famous Romans of the past. Similarly, an opponent from a family of office-holders is attacked on the grounds that he is unworthy of his ancestors, while scorn can safely be heaped on a rival of humble birth. In this context the *imagines* were often evoked as the most powerful symbol of the ancestors and their values, as can be seen from the following examples.

As Quintilian himself points out (*Inst.* 3. 7. 2), elements of praise and vituperation can be found in many speeches outside those on set topics of praise or blame. Both political and legal oratory in Rome depended to a large degree on building up or destroying the credibility and standing of the individuals involved. In the corpus of Cicero a fine example is his speech against L. Calpurnius Piso Caesoninus (*RE* 90) delivered in the senate in 55 BC. This oration is the paradigm of an attack on a *nobilis* by a new man. The opening section of the extant portion of the speech (*Pis.* 1 = T13) contains a classic statement condemning the influence of ancestors on the elections, expressed in terms of the power of *imagines*. Cicero claims that Piso had no merit of his own and had nothing in common with his *imagines* except that his swarthy complexion recalls their smoky colour. Cicero faced in Piso an opponent from the highest ranks of the traditional aristocracy whose family was famous for ancestral displays.[90] The mass of *imagines* was so impressive that Cicero can only discredit Piso by claiming in a variety of rather specious arguments that he is unlike them. Piso's return to Rome from governing Macedonia is compared with a pauper's funeral, which no one attends (*Pis.* 53). Cicero tries to reduce the effect of Piso's birth by claiming he does not behave like or enjoy the standing of a real *nobilis*. The bulk of his bitter attack on Piso is a direct comparison between himself and Piso, and especially of their respective consulships.[91] Similarly, Cicero's attacks on Antony in the *Philippics* are punctuated by references to well-known ancestors his opponent has failed to live up to.[92]

In the courtroom the *imagines* also had a role to play in both praise and blame. Seneca the Elder (*Con.* 2. 3. 6 = T70) sees the *imagines* as an essential part of an emotional appeal to a jury, with whom they were expected to carry some weight. Such a passage was usually to be found in the peroration and can be illustrated from Cicero, who was most famous in his appearances for the defense. In the case of L. Licinius Murena in 63 BC (*Mur.* 88 = T11) Cicero asked the jury how, if he lost his case, Murena could return home to face the *imago* of his father, which had just been opened and decorated with laurel to celebrate the son's election to the consulship. Cicero used the *imago* to stand for the father and, since a mention of both parents was standard in a peroration, balanced this with an allusion to the feelings of Murena's mother who was still alive. Similarly, in the following year, Cicero alluded vividly to the joy his client Sulla might feel if acquitted by imagining his return home to shed his mourning clothes and to open and decorate his *imagines* (*Sulla* 88 = T19).

Cicero also used references to *imagines* in his dealings with advocates on the opposing side. In defending Sulla he claimed that Manlius Torquatus, who was speaking for the prosecution, could not afford to make accusations of tyranny against anyone else in light of the deeds associated with the *imagines* in his own home (*Sulla* 27 = T18). This oblique reference to the disgrace of M. Manlius Capitolinus (*RE* 51) in the fourth century BC suggests

---

90 For the memorable *imagines* of the Calpurnii Pisones, see also the *Laus Pisonis* and Mart. 4. 40. 1-4 with Ch. 9.

91 Cicero and Piso were later reconciled and Cicero spoke warmly of his former rival at the time of the Civil War (*Att.* 7. 13. 1 and *Phil.* 1. 14).

92 e.g. *Phil.* 2. 105; cf. *Ad Her.* 3. 7. 13.

that an active and detailed knowledge of past history was assumed for the average jury member.

Opponents of dubious origin were on two occasions accused by Cicero of appropriating names from the *imagines* of famous families to bolster their credibility.[93] By contrast, in defending Plancius Cicero used references to *imagines* to express his sympathies for the ambitions of the opposing advocate M. Juventius Laterensis, whom Plancius had defeated in the elections (*Planc.* 51 = T15). This was a subtle way of painting Juventius as a young man in a hurry, who was acting from wounded pride and under pressure to live up to his ancestors. Again the jury are expected to do some reading between the lines. Cicero's repeated use of *imagines* to help his argument suggests something of a rhetorical *topos*, which may well have been employed by other orators in forensic speeches not now extant. *Nobiles* who appeared in court had powerful allies in their *imagines*.

An apparently famous use of the *imagines* in forensic oratory is preserved in the longest fragment of the leading orator L. Licinius Crassus (*RE* 55, cos. 95 BC), cited by his pupil Cicero (*De Or.* 2. 225 = T23). Crassus was speaking on behalf of Cn. Plancus against M. Junius Brutus, probably in 91 BC. The funeral of an aged Junia happened to be taking place in the Forum at the same time as the case.[94] Crassus used family spectacle to attack Brutus and to compare him in detail with his ancestors, who were on view for all to see as represented by the actors and to hear about in the *laudatio*.

Crassus asks Brutus what account of himself he could give to Junia to report back to their common ancestors. The devastating effect is heightened by the theatricality of the moment and by a detailed comparison of Brutus' lifestyle with that of his forefathers. The short, clipped sentences and rhetorical questions seem to have been typical of Crassus and reminiscent of the flavour of archaic Latin associated with the style of the ancestors. The *imagines* are used to evoke a catalogue of requirements for an aristocratic lifestyle. They serve as the final measure and are used to frame the episode in a kind of ring composition. This section is quoted by Cicero in the *De Oratore* which he wrote in 55 BC, as he remembered a choice scene from the œuvre of his teacher. The passage was prob-

---

[93] *Clu.* 72 = T6 and *Sest.* 69 = T17. Cicero attacks both Staienus Paetus and Aelius Ligur for taking names from the extinct family of the Aelii.

[94] It remains unclear whether Brutus himself had any hand in staging the funeral or whether he was trying to use it to impress the jurors.

ably all the more memorable as Cicero himself had given what may have been an imitation of it the previous year in his defence of M. Caelius.

It is easy to see how the performance of Crassus speaking for the values of the ancestors and drawing on his own *auctoritas* as censor in 92 BC could suggest the *prosopopoiia* (impersonation) of Appius Claudius Caecus (*RE* 91, cens. 312 BC) to his pupil Cicero (*Cael.* 33-4 = T5). The symbolic importance of the ancestors and their habitual impersonation by actors in the funeral procession explains how they could inspire such a rhetorical display. Quintilian devotes a section to *prosopopoiia* and confirms that the orator was expected to act in character for the rhetorical device to be effective.[95] The impersonation of an ancestor was a special subgroup of *prosopopoiia*. It was classed as a feature of the grand style.[96]

Cicero heightens the effect by a double impersonation first of Caecus and then, in complete contrast, of his dissolute descendant Clodius. The remarks are addressed to Clodia, Clodius' sister, who is being discredited as the inspiration behind the case against Caelius. It is difficult to say which speech is more telling in its effect against her. In his version of Caecus' severe style Cicero also uses the same kind of asyndeton and rhetorical questions that Crassus had. The individual comparison of Caecus' famous deeds with Clodia's vices is also reminiscent of Crassus, while at the same time recalling the *tituli* enumerating the deeds of ancestors so closely associated with the *imagines*. This passage was much admired by ancient critics and represents an important, if not frequently attested, rhetorical device.

In 55 BC, the year after Cicero's memorable performance in defence of Caelius, Helvius Mancia, a freedman's son from Formiae, accused L. Scribonius Libo, a close associate of Pompey, before the censors' court. In reply to Pompey's condescending dismissal of him as someone who looked as if he had come back from the dead, Helvius gave a famous retort which was a variation on a *prosopopoiia* (Valerius Maximus 6. 2. 8). He conjured up a picture of the victims of Pompey from the Sullan age accusing their killer in the underworld and sending Helvius as their messenger from there. It was in this context that Pompey was first called '*adulescentulus*

---

[95] *Inst.* 2. 29-39. It sometimes took the form of speaking for an abstract like the *res publica* or a collective body such as the Roman people, e.g. Cic. *Cat.* 1. 18 and 27; *Planc.* 12.
[96] *Orat.* 85 and *Brut.* 322.

carnifex', a name he had trouble getting rid of. It is possible that Helvius Mancia was partly influenced by the success of Cicero in attempting this bold and emotional accusation against Pompey, who had renewed his position of power through the agreement at Luca in the previous year.

The examples cited so far involve ancestors and *imagines* appearing in speeches on a variety of topics. We also have evidence of one genre of speech, apart from the funeral *laudatio*, which regularly treated the ancestors and their achievements. This was the first public speech to the people (*contio*) given by a magistrate after his election to office. Cicero alludes to the practice only in passing, but Suetonius reports that the emperor Tiberius praised a man for reinstituting this republican custom on the occasion of his election to the praetorship.[97] It seems that the habit had fallen into disuse under Augustus. Sallust has Marius allude to it in his speech attacking the *nobiles* and their self-glorification.[98] Praise of the ancestors can be clearly attested only for consuls and praetors, but has been posited as a right for all curule magistrates.[99] The context of the first *contio* held by the new magistrate implies that it is connected with the right to call such a public meeting. This would suggest that it was only usual for consuls, praetors, and perhaps tribunes of the plebs, to deliver such a speech.

The scant direct testimony about the practice has not attracted the attention of scholars. However, it appears that these speeches were a feature of the start of each magisterial year and were considered *de rigueur* for *nobiles*. The appearance of a successfully elected candidate would confirm the people's choice at the polls in light of the deeds of his ancestors, which had often played a key role in the election. This speech was the first public act of a magistrate in his new garb of office and accompanied by symbols of power and rank. It provided a further regular opportunity for aristocratic family advertisement.

Perhaps the best evidence for the importance of the ancestors at the first *contio* can be found in Cicero's speech *De Lege Agraria II*

---

[97] Cic. *Fin.* 2. 74 and Suet. *Tib.* 32. 1: *praetorem conlaudavit, quod honore inito consuetudinem antiquam ret⟨t⟩ulisset de maioribus suis pro contione memorandi* ('He [Tiberius] commended a praetor because he had reintroduced the ancient custom of talking about his ancestors in a speech to the people at the beginning of his term of office').

[98] *Jug.* 85. 21 = T66*a*, cf. discussion in Ch. 1.   [99] Roloff (1938) 8.

(*Agr.* 2. I = T7),[100] the first one he gave as consul before the people early in 63 BC, which outlined his stance against popular agitation. As the first man of equestrian background to be elected to the highest office in many years he felt the need to excuse his inability to speak about the *imagines* of his ancestors. He makes it clear here that this was an expected topic. He must justify himself once more before the electorate, whom it was customary to thank on this occasion. It is interesting that no similar allusion is found in the published version of his *Pro Lege Manilia* of 66 BC, his first public speech as praetor.

Sallust's version of Marius' speech in 107 BC can be interpreted in the context of this custom (*Jug.* 85. 10 ff. = T66a–c). His speech contains several references to the *imagines*. It has been a matter for some debate how far the speech as given by Sallust could reflect what Marius actually said.[101] The references to *imagines* make sense in a speech where this subject was traditional, thus giving Marius a prime chance to attack the habits and ethos of the *nobiles*. The whole speech can be read as a parody on a catalogue of aristocratic values and achievements as found in *laudationes* or funeral *elogia*. Sallust does not call this speech Marius' first in office and he is apparently drawing on a series of speeches round the time of the levy. Nevertheless, the tone and style of the speech may have identified it as the first *contio* for his readers. It would not be surprising if Cicero knew Marius' actual speech or speeches, particularly as he was also from Arpinum and was connected with Marius' family. He may have composed his own words as a foil to a famous harangue, contrasting his policy of *concordia ordinum* with Marius' strident attacks on the élite.

It is, therefore, possible to identify both the traditional rhetoric of the office-holder who praised his ancestors and presented himself as just like them, as well as a strategy used by some new men to circumvent the expected *topos*.[102] The discussion of the ancestors, often with references to the *imagines*, was paired with the politician's own manifesto of his aims for his year in office. The counter-attack of the *novi homines* may date back to Cato or Marius and can

---

[100] Despite the frequency with which public political speeches were delivered, information about *contiones* in general is poor and only fourteen examples are attested. This makes tracing the rhetoric usual on any particular occasion very hard.

[101] For discussion of this problem and the evidence from Plutarch, see Ch. I.

[102] On the ideology of *novitas*, see Wiseman (1971) 107–16.

certainly be traced in the career of Cicero, while each lent his own colour and tone. The importance of the speech delivered at the first *contio* may well explain why it was an attractive vehicle for Sallust in which to present Marius and his attacks on the aristocracy. A suggestive parallel can be found in the references to *imagines* in the speech of the tribune C. Licinius Macer in 73 BC which appears in the fragments of Sallust's *Histories* (3. 48. 18 = T67). In a speech agitating for the restoration of tribunician rights after Sulla, Macer expresses his contempt for the *nobiles* and their *imagines*. His tone is close to that of Marius and implies that the *imagines* could be a special target of the *populares* in their attacks on leading oligarchs. This speech has been taken as reflecting the overall sentiments of Macer. His history of Rome in sixteen books was very rhetorical and biased in favour of the exploits of his own family. Macer apparently introduced bitter attacks on the *nobiles* into his history, partly in the speeches.

The importance of *imagines* in rhetoric is also reflected in their appearance in the historians who wrote in Latin. Livy includes references to *imagines*, especially in emotional appeals found in speeches incorporated in his early books.[103] This rhetorical *topos*, which is evident in forensic oratory, is here associated with the practices of the ancestors themselves. In his account of the reign of Tiberius, Tacitus introduces the *imagines* into the dramatic speech of Cremutius Cordus who was on trial for praising Brutus and Cassius in his history (*Ann.* 4. 35. 2 = T91). Cremutius is using them to evoke the spirit of republican traditions he is loyal to, even in the face of opposition from the *princeps*. References to *imagines* can be found at the end of several sections in Livy, Sallust, and Tacitus.[104] They provide a conveniently powerful image for an important articulation in the narrative structure. This position at an end point may derive partly from their appearance in the peroration of forensic speeches.[105] At the same time the historians are looking back at republican institutions and are attempting to give some

---

[103] Livy 1. 34. 6 = T37; 1. 47. 4 = T38; 3. 58. 2 = T39; 3. 72. 4 = T40; 10. 7. 2–4 = T42. Ogilvie (1965) ad loc. sees imports from late republican rhetoric in the tone of Livy 1. 34. 6 and 3. 72. 4 .

[104] The end of Livy books 3 = T40, 8 = T41, and 30 = T44 and Tacitus book 3 = T89.

[105] On similar devices in poetic closure, see Herrenstein Smith (1968) especially 33 ff.

flavour of the past and its *mores*.[106] The *imagines* provided a convenient vocabulary, which was both richly evocative and accessible to Roman readers.[107]

6. *Conclusion*

The interpretation of the fragments from *laudationes* offered here suggests that throughout the middle and late Republic, if not earlier, funeral orations were a significant genre in rhetoric, both oral and written. Their essential role in Roman culture is indicated by the fact that they were amongst the earliest, if not the very first, Latin speeches to be published. Examples delivered by famous statesmen survived to be read for centuries to come. They epitomized, and hence helped to hand on, aristocratic values and claims, which justified and explained the function of Rome's political élite in readily accessible terms.[108] Designed as the climax of the whole funeral spectacle, they were central in shaping the citizens' sense of a common past.[109]

The information they communicated was a Roman's essential guide to understanding the complex system of ancestral iconography, centering on the *imagines*; the *imagines*, in turn, served both as the setting and props for the funeral speech while it was being delivered, and as reminders of its message in everyday life at home. The influence of published *laudationes* on the annalistic tradition of Roman history was paralleled and reinforced by the effect of the *imagines* on visitors in the *atrium*. At the same time, the funeral *laudatio* was only one genre of rhetoric, albeit the most important, to rehearse the deeds and offices of the ancestors and to make allusion to the *imagines*. A Roman seeking high office would be most likely to succeed if he had *imagines* of ancestors,

---

[106] The images drawn from a funeral context are useful in encouraging reflection about and comparison of the present in a very Roman way.

[107] So Polyb. (6. 53–54 = T61) follows his account of the Roman funeral with our earliest extant version of the story of Horatius Cocles, the kind of exploit celebrated in a funerary context.

[108] By comparison, Loraux (1981) 175 ff. and especially 224 has shown that in democratic Athens of the 5th cent. BC aristocratic traditions of praise for virtue shaped popular thought and self-definition, especially through public funeral orations for soldiers who died in battle.

[109] Again Loraux (1981) 271 and 172: 'dépositaire de l'histoire idéale d'Athènes, l'oraison funèbre impose par la puissance de la parole des réprésentations plus vraies que la réalité.'

whom he could bring before the voters or the senate in speeches both before and after election. *Imagines, laudationes,* and other rhetorical praises of ancestors were designed to present the same picture of family prestige.

6

Ancestors and Inscriptions:
Elogia and *Tituli*

Cuiqui su(om) cipo(m) graffito near the sarcophagus of L.
Cornelius Scipio Barbatus

(*CIL* 1. 2660)

AFTER the delivery of the funeral oration in the Forum the family
followed the body to the grave outside the city for the burial and its
accompanying rites. Traditional regulations quoted by Cicero confirm that in the earlier republican period graves seem to have been
family plots, in use over a period of some time (*Leg.* 2. 22. 55). This
is supported by the literary and archaeological testimony for early
family burial areas both inside the walls and then spreading along
the main roads from the city gates.[1] Such family burial sites were
placed to attract public attention and to serve as advertisements for
the family's rank, and perhaps even their politics.[2] This chapter is
concerned with the nature of family traditions of memory as preserved in tombs, notably the tomb of the Scipios. Grave inscriptions
associated with tombs contained notices of the deceased's career
and of his position within the family group. Such inscriptions provide vital evidence for the basic information about each family
member which was considered worthy of record for posterity.

---

[1] For burials in the city, see Cic. *Leg.* 2. 23. 58; Dion. Hal. 5. 44; Suet. *Tib.* 1;
Plut. *Mor.* 282f–283a; *Pub.* 23. For tombs on the Via Appia, see Cic. *Tusc.* 1. 7. 13;
Livy 38. 55. 2; 38. 56. 4 and Eisner (1986). For a general introduction to Roman
burials, see now von Hesberg (1994).

[2] Veyne (1985) 168: 'Le tombeau ne s'addresse pas à la famille, aux proches,
mais à tout le monde.' Zevi (1973) remarked on the situation of the Scipionic and
other tombs on the Via Appia as reflecting a new, outward-looking politics directed
towards S. Italy and Sicily. He is followed by Van Sickle (1987) 41. See Panciera in
von Hesberg and Panciera (1994) 66 on the wealth of inscriptions which were to be
found on or near the Mausoleum of Augustus.

Epigraphic evidence from tombs can, therefore, be used as an important source to supplement our understanding of the *laudatio,* and to help in suggesting reconstructions of the labels (*tituli*) under the *imagines* in the *atrium.* In the present discussion the family tomb of the Scipios is considered as analogous to and complementary with a display of *imagines* kept in the *atrium.*[3]

1. *The Tomb of the Scipios*

Our richest evidence for republican family tombs comes from the tomb of the Scipios situated on the Via Appia just outside the Porta Capena.[4] This family grave is discussed below as an example to illustrate practices which were presumably widespread amongst the Roman aristocracy. The elaborate burial complex has been known for over 200 years but has been the subject of much scholarly controversy, partly as a result of poor excavation methods and incomplete records. At the same time, it has been called the most important archaeological site for our understanding of the middle Republic.[5]

In the tomb the ancestors had their permanent residence and were cultivated in a more private and religious way than in the family *atrium.* At the heart of both the *atrium* and the tomb was the memory of the family's past record as it was constructed, tended, and reconstructed over the generations. The inscriptions inside the monument comprised a series of variations on themes of essential concern to the *gens.* It must be borne in mind, however, that the tomb was kept closed, so that the inscriptions were not designed specifically for a public audience.[6] In this sense the epitaphs represent a true family tradition, composed by and for the family to preserve their personal self-image. Similarly, the outside of the tomb

[3] For the *imagines* of the Scipios as a commonplace, see Sen. *Dial.* 12. 12. 7 = T72.

[4] The most authoritative discussion of this tomb complex is by Coarelli, who gives a full bibliography of earlier scholarship (1972) 36–8. The inscriptions are *ILS* 1–10 = *ILLRP* 309–17 (I 1–10). Photographs of the tomb can be found in Nash (1962) 352–6.

[5] Coarelli (1972) 36.

[6] Eck (1984) 133 n. 34. His discussion stresses the importance of reading inscriptions with their particular context and audience in mind. The close connections between family traditions and public self-representation suggested by the Scipionic inscriptions reveal the lack of distinction between public and private inherent in Roman aristocratic culture. Cf. Ch. 7 on the similar character of the Roman house.

changed over time as it reflected the evolving face the family presented to the passing world.

Coarelli's important work on the tomb has demonstrated to us how little we know of even the most famous Roman families. The grave apparently contained nearly all the family members who died during the third and second centuries BC, in over thirty burials, yet we can supply only half that number of names from our record of office-holders.[7] This reminds us that the structure of the family as a whole was far more extensive and complex than a bare list of office-holders might reveal. The family is remembered for those of its members who had the rank to be represented by *imagines* after their death while the others, especially wives and children who died young, lived in their shadow. They all kept company together in a private context inside the tomb.

1a. The Shape of the Tomb

His analysis of the size of the niches relative to the age and type of the sarcophagi allowed Coarelli to demonstrate that burials were made systematically and chronologically, starting in the eastern part with the oldest monolithic sarcophagi (see Fig. 5).[8] The unique sarcophagus of Lucius Cornelius Scipio Barbatus occupied the central place of honour accorded to the oldest family member opposite the entrance. The grotto itself was laid out after the Via Appia was built in 312 BC, and probably within the lifetime of Scipio Barbatus who appears to be the founder of the tomb.[9] Attempts to down-date the tomb into the second century BC have been unconvincing and have created further problems by positing that several early burials were moved from elsewhere to be put here.[10] Those who have argued for a later date in effect claim that the tomb represents family history largely fabricated by later generations to bolster the family's image after their rise to special prominence during the Second Punic War. In fact an examination of the tomb reveals a continuity of family tradition and memory in its structure and ornamentation.

---

[7] Coarelli (1972) 41 and 60. See Appendix E for a family tree of the Cornelii Scipiones.

[8] Coarelli (1972) 48–51.

[9] See Coarelli (1972) 39–43. The date of Barbatus' *elogium* is discussed in § 1b below.

[10] e.g. Saladino (1970) who tries to redate the whole tomb based on the style of Barbatus' sarcophagus. His analysis is refuted by Coarelli (1972) 93–4 n. 133 and by Wachter (1987) 336.

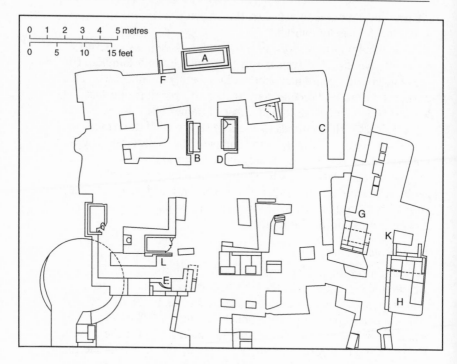

FIG. 5. Plan of the Tomb of the Scipios.

The tomb was planned as a whole and maintained as such throughout its use. It is powerful testimony to the organizational concerns of the family, as each generation added its own contribution in new material and in maintenance. The tomb's brief reuse by the Cornelii Lentuli under the early Empire shows the importance attached to such recognized continuity by a family seeking to associate itself with the Scipios.[11] Coarelli has used the pattern of family burials to suggest a plausible reconstruction of the arch of Scipio Africanus which had seven gilt bronze statues, perhaps represent-

[11] *ILS* 958 and 959 (I 9 and 10). Their family connections are illustrated by Coarelli (1972) 58 n. 60. For an example of a Lentulus Scipio who gave both his sons only the name Scipio, see *PIR* 1398 (P. Cornelius Lentulus Scipio, cos. AD 24) with 1439 (P. Cornelius Scipio, cos. AD 56) and 1440 (P. Cornelius Scipio Asiaticus, cos. AD 68). The Cornelii Scipiones Salvidieni Orfiti are attested until the late 2nd cent. AD.

ing the six office-holders buried in the tomb in his day accompanied by Africanus himself.[12] The tomb also had statues associated with it. Ancient confusion about whom they represented suggests that these were perhaps inside the tomb, for if they had been outside they would surely have been labelled.[13] Presumably both tomb and arch echoed the *imagines* as displayed at funerals and in the *atrium*.

The newer wing, which contained only about six burials, can be securely dated to after the middle of the second century BC, and is convincingly associated with Scipio Aemilianus as the leader of the family at that time.[14] The monumental façade, about which our evidence is poor, seems also to have been his work and required considerable rebuilding to produce a symmetrical effect (see Figs. 6 and 7). The podium in front, which was later expanded to include three symmetrical entrances, was decorated with historical paintings running its full length. The seven layers of paint suggest frequent restorations and renovations of the tomb's façade, both before and after the extension of the podium when the new façade was added.[15] Recent restoration has revealled a continuous tradition of public narrative painting throughout the tomb's use.

There is not enough information to allow a detailed reconstruction of the paintings which must have been the most striking feature of the outside of the tomb. Several series of narrative paintings apparently illustrated family history for passers-by, and showed narratives or summaries of military exploits, probably with labels. This genre of painting is closely related to the pictures carried in triumphs and to the paintings from the third-century BC Esquiline tombs.[16] Each layer of renovation seems to have involved new subjects rather

[12] Livy 37. 3. 7. Cf. Ch. 2 § 1*e* for more discussion with Coarelli (1972) 71–2 and Calabi Limentani (1982).
[13] Livy 38. 56. 1–4. Cf. the contemporary tomb of the Marcelli whose statues were outside and labelled (Asconius 12C = 11KS = 18 Stangl = 115) with Ch. 3 § 2*a*. *Contra* Coarelli (1972) 62–82 with fig. D who places the statues outside because of the narrowness of the passages. Lauter-Bufe (1982) offers a simpler reconstruction of the façade without statues. Richardson (1992) 359–60 imagines the statues crowning the attic of the tomb as on a triumphal arch. See Giuliani (1986) 17–25 for a hypothetical identification of three statues as coming from this tomb.
[14] Coarelli (1972) 58–61. Scipio Hispanus = *ILS* 6/*ILLRP* 316 (I 5) was the earliest burial in the annex, probably around 130 BC.
[15] Coarelli (1972) 69 only mentions three layers of paintings. La Rocca (1984) discusses seven layers of material dating to before and after the extension of the podium. Cf. Felletti Maj (1977) fig. 44 and Coarelli (1988) 173–4.
[16] These tombs and Roman narrative paintings in general are discussed in Ch. 7 § 5. Ling (1991) 10 dates the Esquiline tomb paintings to the 3rd or early 2nd cent. BC.

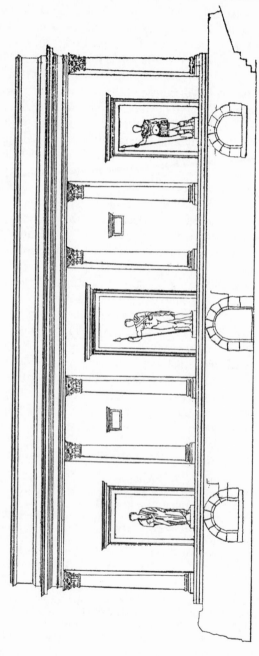

FIG. 6. Reconstruction of the façade of the Tomb of the Scipios.

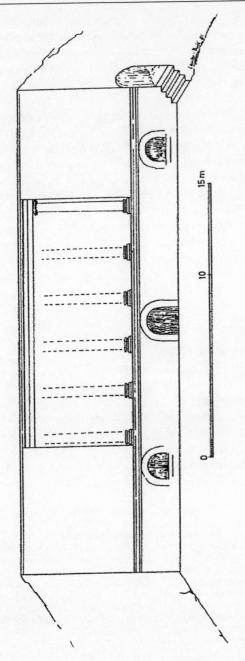

Fig. 7. Reconstruction of the façade of the Tomb of the Scipios.

than simply the refurbishment of paintings exposed to the elements.[17] The paintings can be associated with funerals of leading family members, perhaps those who had been awarded triumphs, of whom seven were buried here. The depictions of battles continued and renewed the family's proud military heritage also recalled in *laudationes, elogia,* and *tituli.*

The relationship between paintings and statues remains a problem which has hardly been addressed for lack of data. According to one theory a series of statues inside the tomb was of a private family character and, therefore, not fully understood by outsiders. In other words, the tomb of the Scipios displayed its paintings outside and thereby reversed the fashion of the contemporary tombs from the Esquiline. The suggestion that family remembrance had both a public and a private aspect would have made it all the more interesting to those contemplating the traditions of this powerful *gens.* Above all it is the loss of interconnections between different traditions of family iconography which hampers our understanding of any individual part of this tomb, which was so clearly conceived and maintained as a whole, and which demonstrated the continuity of the family.

1b. *The Epitaphs of the Scipios*

The extant *elogia* associated with individual burials are a somewhat random group since mainly carved ones have survived. We are largely uninformed about the inscriptions painted on other sarcophagi.[18] The discovery of an older tomb of the Cornelii Scapulae, which dates to the later fourth and early third century BC, has demonstrated that carved inscriptions were in common use at a date before those discovered in the later tomb of the Scipios.[19] As a result attempts to date painted labels as earlier than carved verses,

---

[17] Mansuelli (1979) 52 likens the changing narrative paintings to election slogans.

[18] The *elogia* have been analysed stylistically, revealing their connections with Greek epigramme by Van Sickle (1984), (1987), and (1988). In his view they are the work of professional poets and illustrate the adaptation of a Greek genre to accomodate the needs of the Roman aristocracy. (1984) 23: 'Lungi dall'essere nativi e rudi, questi elogi rappresentano sia per la forma che per la funzione il momento creativo della cultura ellenistico-romana.'

[19] See esp. the inscription of the *pontifex maximus* P. Cornelius P. f. Scapula (*P. Cornelio P. f. Scapola | pontifex maximus,* 'Publius Cornelius Scapola, son of Publius, chief priest') with Blanck (1966–67), Solin (1970), and full publication in Pisani Sartorio and Quilici Gigli (1987/88).

where both were found together, have come to nothing.[20] This grave complex was, therefore, not the first family tomb with monumental sarcophagi and inscriptions; rather it continued an earlier tradition. The tomb of the Cornelii appears to have had a similar design with galleries and niches in an underground chamber. The character of the façade is unclear, while traces of paint inside suggest the interior walls may have been decorated. It seems to have been in use for a period both before and after the late fourth century BC material which has been recovered. Its location near the tomb of the Scipios indicates that this area had special associations for the Cornelii over several centuries, presumably because they owned land here.

Some of the inscriptions in the tomb of the Scipios appear to have been altered at various times either to include additional material or to edit what had been recorded earlier. Indeed the *elogia* may regularly have been composed by members of the family.[21] These texts illustrate how family traditions were rewritten or expanded, even in a private setting. An obvious example is that of the Publius Scipio taken to be the weakling son of Scipio Africanus and adoptive father of Scipio Aemilianus.[22] A seventh verse was added in smaller letters to the standard six-verse set. The addition comes at the beginning and mentions the position of the deceased as *flamen Dialis*. From the lettering it appears that the first line was an addition made not much later than the original inscription.[23] Aemilianus seems the obvious figure to be associated with a change in honour of the man who allowed him to become heir to the family's glorious traditions. He may have composed the additional verse at the time when he enlarged the tomb and remodelled its façade. The new verse changes the whole flavour of the epitaph by introducing the mention of a priesthood, which can be treated as an office, or as an apologia for the lack of a political career.

The original verses simply celebrated the promise of a family member, who had died young. The six lines claimed that he would easily have surpassed the achievements of his ancestors, given more

[20] Zevi (1968–69) 66 and Coarelli (1972) 44.

[21] So Radke (1981) 57 who stresses the importance of the Scipionic inscriptions as examples of the Latin language of their day.

[22] *ILS* 4 = *ILLRP* 311 = I 3. *Contra* Sumner (1973) 36–7 who attributes this inscription to an otherwise unknown grandson of Africanus (accepted by Broughton *MRR* 3).

[23] Coarelli (1972) 94.

time. *Gloria* is the concept which elucidates office (*honos*), public position or reputation (*fama*), moral qualities (*virtus*), and talent (*ingenium*).[24] However, if this man is indeed the son of Africanus he apparently did not die very young, but was in poor health for much of his life.[25] The office of *flamen Dialis* would have suited an invalid as it was subject to numerous restrictions which made a normal career impossible.[26] At this period it seems to have carried with it the rank of senator (Livy 27. 8. 5-8). The original inscription can, therefore, be interpreted as a gloss by the family on a life they did not want individually remembered.[27] The most convenient solution was to present the man as one who had died very young. The additional line in effect challenges this view of him by recognizing a personal achievement and especially by granting him a status equivalent to that of an office-holder. As *flamen Dialis* with the rank of senator P. Scipio may well have been entitled to an *imago*, in addition to his curule chair, *toga praetexta*, and lictors.[28] Consequently, he would have received public recognition at family funerals. His original private epitaph was impersonal and even distorted.

By way of comparison, the tomb offers three republican examples of family members who had indeed died young before holding any office, and one who had only reached the quaestorship.[29] Their epitaphs illustrate the importance attached to representing such young

---

[24] *Contra* Moir (1986) who interprets these terms as referring to P. Scipio's literary talents, a reading not made evident by the Latin. See Till (1970) 282-3 for Hellenistic elements, especially in the last two lines.

[25] *RE* Cornelius 331 (Münzer); Livy 40. 42. 13 with Astin (1967) 12-14. His death has been assumed to come after 167 BC, as it is not recorded in Livy, but before 162 BC when Aemilianus appears as the head of the family. His health was weak but he was remembered as an eloquent speaker, which makes an early death unlikely (Cic. *Brut.* 77; *Sen.* 35; *Off.* 1. 121; Vell. Pat. 1. 10. 3). Moir (1986) dates his flaminate to 176-175 BC in a gap in Livy 41. 19 and his death shortly thereafter.

[26] Wissowa (1912) 505-7 lists the offices held by *flamines*. Cf. Moir (1986) for a thoughtful discussion on this point. Africanus' special cultivation of Jupiter is discussed in Ch. 2 § 1e. If his son was indeed *flamen Dialis*, Africanus and his wife must have been married by *confarreatio*. Suet. (*Jul.* 1. 1) records that Caesar was proposed as *flamen Dialis* at the age of 16.

[27] *Contra* Van Sickle (1988) 150-3 who interprets the sophistication of style as the family's best effort to make up for deficiencies. 151: 'Naming, too, reaches a new peak of elaborateness.' And yet the poem itself does not tell us who this man actually was.

[28] See Plut. *Q. Rom.* 113 and Serv. *A.* 8. 552.

[29] *ILS* 7 = *ILLRP* 312 = I 6 (L. Scipio, younger brother of Hispanus); *ILS* 8 = *ILLRP* 314 = I 7 (Asiagenus Comatus); *ILS* 5 = *ILLRP* 313 = I 4 (L. Cornelius Scipio, son of the conqueror of Antiochus).

men as fully integrated within the family group and as worthy of the political careers they never attained.[30] Not all have verse *elogia* attested, but they are named and fully identified in a way that seems lacking in the case of the Publius who is assumed to be Africanus' son.[31] Although he is assimilated into their number, even the evidence of the epitaphs taken alone indicates that his case may have been different.

The epitaph of Scipio Hispanus (pr. 139), the son of Hispallus, offers an interesting contrast with that of his relatives who died younger.[32] He apparently died soon after his praetorship, but before he could stand for the consulship.[33] This would make him not much older than 40 at the time of his death.[34] His *cursus* is set up to suggest a full career and the two couplets which follow hail his achievements in glowing terms. His life is celebrated above all as a continuation of family tradition.[35] He is presented as one who lived up to the family name by emulating his father and leaving offspring, presumably male, to continue the line.[36] In fact, his father had been consul in 176 BC, so that the son's death could be interpreted as cutting short a promising career just before its peak.[37] The presentation of his life as if it were a full expression of what a Roman office-holder could have hoped for is in itself a piece of window-dressing, which perhaps reflects the tone adopted at his funeral.

He is said to have earned the praise of his ancestors, who are proud to recognize him as their descendant. The recording of such a sentiment reflects the importance of the ancestors, especially as represented at the funeral, in summing up a career and recognizing

[30] I do not understand why Van Sickle (1988) 149 sees this apologetic function as 'unforeseen', rather than an integral part of the genre.

[31] We are not fully informed in this case because the label with his name, which might also have included a list of offices, is missing. The identification must remain unsure.

[32] *ILS* 6 = *ILLRP* 316 = I 5.

[33] Coarelli (1972) 45. This assumption was made by Münzer, *RE* Cornelius 347.

[34] The *Lex Villia Annalis* of 180 BC set the minimum age for a praetor at 40 and for a consul at 43 (Livy 40. 44. 1).

[35] Bettini (1991) 182 cites this *elogium* as the best surviving illustration of the relationship of the individual and the family in Roman culture. Van Sickle (1988) 152 notes that the family has completely replaced the citizen body which was the point of reference in earlier epitaphs.

[36] Till (1970) 286 interprets the stress on descendents as typical of the late 2nd cent. BC when many old families were dying out.

[37] Van Sickle (1987) 53 and Bettini (1991) 182 translate *facta patris petiei* as 'took aim at', but the phrase can be read as cleverly ambiguous in a case where the son of a consular father did not reach the consulship himself.

an individual as a worthy part of a long tradition.[38] In this sense judgement is suspended, at least to some degree, until death on the full meaning of a man's life. Such a theme had been a common place in Greece before, but takes on quite a different tone in an aristocratic Roman context. The *honor* referred to in the last line seems to be his political offices, which are said to renew the family's status as *nobiles*.[39] Such an explicit statement of the connection between a family's rank and its member's political office is in itself unusual. When applied to a man who had advanced no further than the praetorship it raises complex questions about the technical definition of a *nobilis* in the age of the Gracchi.[40] Perhaps the Scipios were stretching a strict or usual definition to make a further claim for their family. This assertion concealed the loss of a potential consular by boldly equating his rank with one at the time of his death.[41]

L. Cornelius Scipio Barbatus' splendid sarcophagus was accorded the place of honour opposite the door of the tomb and served to mark him out as its patriarchal figure (see Pl. 7).[42] The sarcophagus' form and decoration, which recall an altar, have led to speculation about ancestor cult directed to Barbatus as the founder of the family.[43] Without any further evidence the character of the

[38] Traina (1969) 169 sees the happiness of the ancestors mentioned here as made real by the *imagines*. Till (1970) 287 notes the stress on ancestors at a time of decline for the family but also as an echo of themes on contemporary coins (cf. Ch. 3 § 3).

[39] *Contra* Till (1970) 286 who translates *nobilitavit* as 'made famous' rather than 'ennobled'. Cf. *ILLRP* 312 = *ILS* 7 = I6 of L. Scipio who died at 20 with Wheeler (1988) 180–8 and 193, who claims that *sapientia* is there used as equivalent to *nobilis* around 170 BC.

[40] The definition of *nobilitas* is discussed in Ch. 3 § 1.

[41] His son apparently also only reached the rank of praetor (*RE* Cornelius 321).

[42] His elaborate naming in the epitaph in language reminiscent of epic and tragedy supports this; cf. Van Sickle (1988) 145–7 who draws attention to the emphatic use of his *cognomen*. Van Sickle (1987) may well be right in connecting the emergence of the verse *elogia* with the influence of Hellenistic epigramme in Rome. However, the preoccupation with office and rank is essentially Roman and aristocratic. Their private gentilicial context also sets them apart from Greek funerary poetry.

[43] See Saladino (1970) 23 ff., followed by Coarelli (1972) 93–4 n. 133 and (1973) 234. In fact Saladino's argument appears circular since he is positing a special function for Barbatus' sarcophagus based on his later dating scheme and then using this separate function to justify his theory that the body had been moved and was not originally buried in this casket, thus supporting his redating. Zevi (1973) 238 adduces a series of small altars from Sicily as analogous: 'Ma soprattutto indicativo è il tipo stesso di sarcofago, conformato ad ara, non più a forma di casa, secondo una impostazione ideologica che risale chiaramente non alla venerazione, tutta

sarcophagus alone is not sufficient to prove such a theory. This sarcophagus is unique in its ornamentation so that it can not be accurately dated by stylistic comparisons.[44] Barbatus' sarcophagus and that of his son Lucius are the only two monolithic ones to survive from the tomb, which in itself suggests their age, although we do not have accurate information about when either man died.[45]

The *elogia* of Barbatus and Lucius Scipio are at the heart of any interpretation of the tomb as a whole, because of their special position as ancestors of all those attested as being buried in the tomb.[46] The import of these two inscriptions has caused most of the debate among scholars, especially concerning their relative date. For about a century the father's *elogium* has been assumed to be later than the son's for reasons of language, style, and epigraphy.[47] As noted above, the painted name labels on the lids of the two sarcophagi have now been definitely dated to the same period as the verse inscriptions in Saturnians on the main caskets.[48] The visible inscriptions, therefore, present complementary texts by the same hand. However, the erasure of a line and a half of text immediately before the verses inscribed on the sarcophagus of Barbatus has suggested the hypothesis that an original short notice of name and offices was chiselled out at a time when a fuller epitaph was needed for the oldest family member buried in the tomb.[49]

Many recent interpretations of the contents of Barbatus' *elogium* are based on the theory that it is late, perhaps by as much as fifty years after his death.[50] Consequently, it is assumed to be subject to

romana, del capostipite della famiglia, bensi agli *heroa* ellenistici posteriori all'impresa di Alessandro in Asia.' Cf. Van Sickle (1987) 42. Note also that Africanus may have had a similar sarcophagus in Liternum according to Sen. *Ep.* 86. 1.

[44] See the discussion of Wachter (1987) 333-7.

[45] See Coarelli (1972) esp. 48 for a relative dating of the sarcophagi according to their construction techniques. He dates Barbatus' death to around 270 BC and Lucius' to around 230 BC. They are the only two attested 3rd-cent. burials.

[46] Barbatus: *ILS* 1 = *ILLRP* 309 = I 1; his son: *ILS* 2 and 3 = *ILLRP* 310 = I 2.

[47] Coarelli (1972) 89, with earlier bibliography. For bibliography, see also Gordon (1983) 80.

[48] See Coarelli (1972) 87-9.

[49] As Zevi (1968-69) 66 noted, the relative age of the two sarcophagi of father and son is the only tangible indication that we are not dealing with inscriptions contemporary with their subjects. La Regina (1968), followed by Saladino (1970) 15, has interpreted the erasure as representing a second stage of inscription after the original painted label on the lid.

[50] For discussions of the place names in Barbatus' *elogium* and his military campaigns, see Silvestri (1978), Innocenti Prosdocimi (1980/1981), and Marcotte (1985).

distortion and anachronistic rewriting. Barbatus plays a small and relatively undistinguished role in the historical sources now extant, with the result that he has been viewed as something of a creation of the family as they rose to greater fame and prominence in the Second Punic War.[51] The development of scholarship over the last twenty-five years has led to an increasingly rational and scientific approach to these inscriptions, and to a simpler and more plausible account of their character. Instead of three inscriptions of different dates, one painted, one erased, and one carved in verse, Coarelli put forward arguments for two phases, an earlier one represented by the erasure and a later one by the painted and inscribed texts found on the sarcophagus.[52]

In a wide-ranging study of the language of early Latin inscriptions, Wachter has now convincingly challenged the traditional interpretations outlined above.[53] He argues for a single inscription time close to Barbatus' death, which he imagines as being in the 250s BC, and for a single epitaph made up of the painted label on the lid and a carved verse inscription of eight Saturnian lines on the sarcophagus. According to his view, the erasure now visible on the sarcophagus removed the first two verses of the inscribed text at an unknown date after Barbatus' death. Such an unusually long inscription, which would have filled the available space on the front of the sarcophagus, accords well with the character of the decoration and the exceptional workmanship of the whole piece.

As Wachter has shown, there are no linguistic reasons why Barbatus' inscription can not date to the middle of the third century BC at a time when Barbatus might have died in his seventies.[54]

---

[51] For Barbatus' career, see Livy 10. 11. 10–13. 1; 10. 14. 4 ff.; 10. 25; 10. 29. 5; 10. 40. 7; 11. 26. 7 ff. He or his father or uncle may be the *pontifex maximus* of 304 BC in Livy 9. 46. 6. His censorship, only mentioned in the *elogium*, has been restored to 280 BC in a gap in Festus 270L. See Mazzarino (1966) 287–90 for the view that Livy reflects an anti-Cornelian source which supports Barbatus' consular colleague, Cn. Fulvius Maximus Centumalus, who was awarded a triumph for his achievements in 298 BC. Barbatus' inscription can certainly be read as a comment on Fulvius' success, especially as interpreted by Innocenti Prosdocimi (1980/1981). For the reference to *sapiens* meaning the practical wisdom of strategems, see Wheeler (1988) 180–8.

[52] Coarelli's (1972) 88–9 study is based on a critical assessment of Wölfflin (1892).

[53] See Wachter (1987) 301–42, whose complex arguments I only summarize briefly in what follows.

[54] See Wachter (1987) 303–18, who goes on to argue (324–33) for the introduction of the letter 'G', which is found in Barbatus' inscription, into the Latin

There is not enough available evidence to date early epigraphic Latin with any precision. A newly published inscription on a breast-plate formerly in the Getty Museum exhibits many similar features, which were previously considered to be 'modern'.[55] The dedicatory inscription is securely dated to 241 BC, which could put it to within fifteen years or less of Barbatus' text.[56] Both Barbatus' and Lucius' inscriptions show variation of letter forms within each text so that the letters alone can not be said to indicate a specific or even a rel-ative date.[57] A date in the 250s BC is further supported by Lucius' temple to the sea storms which was vowed during his consulship and built somewhere near the family tomb.[58]

The most compelling arguments that suggest the removal of part of the same verse text we now have relate to the shape and char-acter of the erasure itself.[59] In effect, a fine sarcophagus, which was inscribed with a long and carefully executed text, is marred by a rough erasure. If the erasure was made before the new text was cut, why was more trouble not taken to smooth and prepare the stone? Moreover, why does our text start at a distance of a third of a line from the margin? It would have been easy for the mason to produce a better surface so that he could have started at the margin. The whole execution of the inscription itself is very fine and clearly not the work of an amateur.[60] The overall impression is that no expense was spared in the layout of a large tomb and the manufacture of a magnificent sarcophagus for its first occupant.

If a short, earlier text had indeed been inscribed, there would have been no reason to write it in small letters at the very top of the ample space available on the front of the sarcophagus. It would surely have been placed more in the middle and in larger letters. A

alphabet shortly after 272 BC. Radke (1991), however, prefers a date around 304 BC, based partly on the appearance of 'G' in the early calendars which were first pub-lished at that time.

[55] See Zimmermann (1986), Wachter (1987) 313, and Penney (1992) 163.

[56] The text reads: *Q. Lutatio C. f. A. Manlio C. f. consolibus Faleries capto* ('Under [the command of] the consuls Quintus Lutatius, son of Gaius, and Aulus Manlius, son of Gaius, taken [as booty] from Falerii'). The breastplate itself (L80. AC. 37) is from the late 4th cent. BC and was made in a Greek city. It was probably passed down as an heirloom for about three generations before the Romans captured it as booty.

[57] Mommsen (1854) 468 already noted that Barbatus' scribe seems to use *-us* deliberately next to *-os*, as well as Lucius with Loucanam.

[58] This temple is mentioned in his *elogium*, cf. Ov *Fast.* 6. 193-4. See also Platner and Ashby (1929) ad loc. and Richardson (1992) ad loc.

[59] See Wachter (1987) 318-21.

[60] It is, for example, much finer than the inscription for the son.

comparison may be made with the inscription on the sarcophagus of P. Cornelius Scapula from the late fourth century BC. His short inscription is roughly centred and appears about a third of the way down within the space available to the mason.[61] Barbatus' erasure suggests that the letters were the same size and the lines the same length as the extant text.[62] The erasure comprises exactly the length of two of the Saturnian verses below. All these considerations strongly suggest that part of this same text was erased.

In the erasure immediately before CORNELIUS, which is the first word of the extant text, Wachter noticed the faint trace of a horizontal line similar to those which separate the other Saturnian verses (see Pl. 8).[63] This line is especially visible on plate 4 in Diehl (1912) (see Pl. 7)[64] but less so on later photographs, such as Gordon (1983) plate 4 taken in 1963.[65] The left hand section of the line, which is the deepest part, contains a small trace of red paint like the paint which appears in the other letters of the inscription. As the stone is now, the line is not easily seen except with a raking light. There are, of course, many lines of various kinds in the erasure but none is quite like this one. From my own examination of the stone, I am not personally in doubt about the character of the line.[66] If accepted, this line provides proof that the text which was erased was not complete, but ended at the end of a verse with more to come.

It is not possible to prove the exact age of the red paint in the letters, although it has generally been accepted as being ancient.[67]

[61] For a good photograph, see Pisani Sartorio and Quilici Gigli (1987/8) 259.

[62] These considerations were stressed by Mommsen (1854) especially 463. He supposed that the mason had made a mistake in inscribing this same text and had therefore started again. *Contra* Wachter (1987) 320-1 who notes the coincidence that the mistake was noticed after exactly two lines. Mommsen's explanation does not adequately account for the rough erasure and the strange spacing.

[63] Wachter (1987) 320.

[64] Diehl's photograph appears to be the same as Vatican photo XVIII. 19. 12 reproduced as plate 7 here.

[65] This line cannot be compared with the [-] restored by Degrassi between Barbatus and Gnaivod, for which there is no space on the actual stone. In other respects, these two photos do not suggest much general wear on the stone, although the sarcophagus is kept in a rather exposed position at the entrance to the Pio-Clementino Museum in the Vatican.

[66] The existence of the line and the red paint was further confirmed for me by a rubbing kindly provided by Professor Silvio Panciera.

[67] Specks of red paint can also be detected on the decorated area above the inscription, similar to the red and blue paint traces on the sarcophagus lid from the tomb of the Cornelii. Cf. Pisani Sartorio and Quilici Gigli (1987/8) 252-3.

PLATE 1. Marble grave relief showing busts of a man and a woman facing each other in profile in open cupboards, National Museum, Copenhagen (inv. no. 1187).

PLATE 2. Busts of ancestors in exedra 25, Casa del Menandro, Pompeii.

PLATE 3.

a. Minucius' column, reverse of denarius of C. Minucius Augurinus, 135 BC (Crawford 242.1).

b. Elephant, reverse of denarius of C. Metellus, 125 BC (Crawford 269.1).

c. Basilica Aemilia, reverse of denarius of M. Aemilius Lepidus, 58 BC (Crawford 419.3*a*).

d. Busts of Brutus and Ahala, obverse and reverse of denarius of M. Junius Brutus, 54 BC (Crawford 433.2).

PLATE 4.

a. (*left*) Aeneas with Anchises and Ascanius.

b. (*right*) Romulus dressed as a general carrying spoils taken from an enemy general (*spolia opima*), wall-paintings from the façade of a house in Pompeii.

PLATE 5. Marble relief showing a woman lying in state, Tomb of the Haterii, Rome, late Flavian/early Trajanic, Vatican Museum.

PLATE 6. Marble relief showing a funeral procession, Amiternum, late Republic (?), Museo Aquilano, Aquila.

PLATE 7. Sarcophagus of Lucius Cornelius Scipio Barbatus, Museo Pio-Clementino, Vatican.

PLATE 8. Detail of the beginning of the verse inscription on Scipio Barbatus' sarcophagus, Vatican.

When I examined the stone in detail with a magnifying glass I saw a number of small specks of red paint in the erasure, especially in the area above SCIPIO BARBATUS on the right hand side. These small specks are like those to be found around some of the letters in the text itself, notably inside the o of VOS. They can be attributed to small paint specks coming off the brush and it is quite understandable that they would not necessarily have been erased by the person who was aiming to remove the letters from the first line of the stone. My observations serve to confirm those of Wachter that the text in the erasure was part of the text now extant.[68]

The work of Wachter has, therefore, restored Barbatus as the most likely founder and designer of the tomb, whose aims are manifested by the size of the main chamber which seems to have been in use for at least a century before the annex was built. His sarcophagus with its architectural decoration and long inscription sets him apart from other family members who were buried in unadorned sarcophagi with simpler and less well inscribed labels. The choice of site on the Appian Way and the use of a Greek artist, perhaps a Sicilian, for the sarcophagus fit the concerns of the family around the middle of the third century BC, concerns which Barbatus himself probably shared and may well have shaped.[69]

Lucius' inscription can now be read as a complement and reply to his father's. His choice of six Saturnians rather than eight confirms his father's position as the head of the *gens*. The repeated use of *hic* in Lucius' text points a contrast with his father who was buried about two meters away. Recent analysis of the metre and stress of both inscriptions also suggests that the father's text is older than his son's, although their relative age is unclear.[70]

Wachter's research has also revealed that editing could take place in the tomb, even on the oldest text of the most revered family member. Whereas previously the erasure had been explained as the result of a desire to afford Barbatus a longer and more dignified inscription, the new interpretation entails the removal of part of an earlier epitaph. The date of the erasure is unclear but it surely

[68] It is important to note that there are no traces of any letters visible in the erasure now.

[69] See Wachter (1987) 340 who notes the activity in Sicily of Barbatus' son Cn. Cornelius Scipio Asina (cos. 260 and 254 BC). Cf. *SEG* 30 no. 1120 for Tiberius Claudius C. f. Antias as procurator of Entella in Sicily. His role is examined by Corsaro (1982).

[70] See Radke (1991) 79.

belongs to antiquity and can be attributed to a member of this same family. It seems implausible to suggest outside interference in a tomb that was kept shut. It is possible that the erasure makes more sense before the use of the annex for burials towards the end of the second century BC, since the new burial chamber was reached by its own door. Indeed, the last burial in the main chamber, which was that of Paulla Cornelia, was placed immediately behind Barbatus' sarcophagus.[71] It is not clear how often or by whom the main tomb was visited after it was no longer used for new burials.

The question remains as to what was erased by a later family member. Wachter's suggestion that it was the same formula which is to be found at the beginning both of the son's inscription, and of Atilius Caiatinus', is unsatisfactory.[72] It is hard to see why a formulaic opening, which was left intact elsewhere in the tomb, should have prompted erasure here. Whatever was rubbed out must have been controversial or unsatisfactory from the family's point of view. Nor is it plausible to imagine that the inscription was considered 'too boastful' given the tradition of aristocratic inscriptions and the contents of other texts from this same tomb.[73]

Barbatus' full name, a mention of his father, and the *cursus* of political offices held appears on the stone in the part we still have. The first two verses should logically have contained some kind of preamble, but presumably of a more specific nature than what is found for Lucius. The preamble would need to fit in with Barbatus' position as founder and ancestor, which is so clearly illustrated by the rest of his sarcophagus and its overall position within the tomb. It is possible, therefore, to imagine that these two verses contained some general claim to be the 'first' in the family, a claim not apparently related to the tenure of a specific political office.

The early history of the Cornelii Scipiones before Barbatus is vague and confused.[74] His father 'Gnaivos' is unknown and may not have used the name of Scipio at all. Nor do we have any clear information about the relationship between the Scipios and older branches, such as the Scapulae or the Maluginenses. It is reason-

[71] See Coarelli (1972) fig. A.
[72] See Wachter (1987) 321, rebutted by Radke (1991) 79 on the grounds of metrical differences.
[73] So Wachter (1987) 340 n. 804.
[74] See especially Münzer in *RE* 4 s.v. Cornelii Scipiones and early Scipios nos. 328, 329, 322, 315, and 316. Cf. *MRR* for the consul of 328 BC (?dictator 306 BC) who may be a Scapula.

able to see Barbatus as the founder, or one of the very early members, of the Scipio branch of the Cornelii. The Scipios are also known for their continued search for earlier ancestors.[75] This was done partly by invention and partly by substitution of the *cognomen* Scipio for earlier ones of branches that later died out. This family tendency is responsible for much confusion in the early history of the *gens*, which is notable for reduplication of career patterns. It is possible, therefore, that Barbatus' claim to be the first, in whatever precise sense he formulated it, became an obstacle to later family members who were eager to find earlier ancestors and other founders, who could compete with the claims of rival families. Such a reconstruction, while it can not be proved, is at least plausible and in accord with the other available evidence.

Lucius Scipio, the son of Barbatus, is attested as consul in 259 BC and censor in 258 BC, but the year of his death is unknown. His death could, of course, have come early and be quite close to the date of his father's death. If Lucius, like many other Romans of patrician family, held the consulship as early as his mid-thirties, he need not have died until nearer the end of the century.[76] His epitaph is usually dated to the 230s BC, but this is far from being certain as he is not mentioned after his censorship.[77] The spacing between the eldest son in each generation is fairly even with Barbatus consul in 298, his son Lucius in 259, and his grandson Cn. Scipio Calvus in 222 BC.

As noted above, Lucius' epitaph opens with the same lines as that of Atilius Caiatinus (cos. 258 and 254 BC), whose tomb was also in the same area of the Via Appia.[78] Both inscriptions strikingly mention a consensus of Romans that the deceased was the best man (*optimus* or *primarius*) in the community. In two men who were consuls in consecutive years such a claim is evidence of open competition. We do not know whose epitaph is older nor whether they date from the same period.

---

[75] See Münzer in *RE* 4, Cornelius 316.

[76] For the age at which patricians held the consulship in the 3rd cent. BC, see Develin (1979) 58–71, who estimates the mid-to-late thirties as normal.

[77] e.g. Coarelli (1972) 90.

[78] Cic. *Fin.* 2. 35. 116 = I14; *Sen.* 61. He certainly was an outstanding statesman of his day (*RE* Atilius 36, cos. 258, 254, dict. 249, cens. 247). However, Caiatinus is described as *primarius* not *optimus*, probably referring to his offices and achievements, especially in war, rather than to moral qualities of the kind recognized in Nasica.

The specific claim that one man had been agreed upon as the best by most Romans recalls the unparalleled choice by the senate in 204 BC of P. Cornelius Scipio Nasica (cos. 191 BC), the grandson of the present Lucius Scipio and himself the originator of a new *stirps*, as the 'best man' in Rome and therefore as the most suitable to greet the goddess Cybele on her arrival from the East.[79] Many had claimed to excel before. Such rivalry was clearly part of the aristocratic ethos as is suggested by Livy's phrase *vir bonorum optimus* (29. 14. 8) which alludes to an élite caste who shared this man's qualities. However, Nasica is the only man known to have received this title officially during the Republic.[80] Livy is at pains to show how important this competition was at the time and how winning it was valued above any of the usual honours in the *cursus*. The details of how the choice was made were lost by his day, but the result reflects the power of the Cornelii in Rome in the years immediately before Hannibal's defeat. The transfer of the Magna Mater to Rome is clearly associated with hopes for victory, aroused by and focussed on Scipio Africanus' imminent campaign in Africa (Livy 29. 10–14).

A case has been made for thinking that the results of the intense competition of 204 BC produced claims to similar glory on behalf of ancestors of the chosen, as well as those of his peers or rivals.[81] This interpretation is based on the assumption that Lucius' verse epitaph was inscribed a considerable time after his death. As argued above,

---

[79] Livy 29. 10 ff., cf. Diod. 34. 33; Val. Max. 7. 5. 2; 8. 15. 3; App. *Hann.* 56; Dio fr. 57. For a similar instruction from Delphi, see Plin. *Nat.* 34. 26 which records the oracle's advice during the Samnite Wars to erect statues in Rome of the bravest (*fortissimus*) and shrewdest/wisest (*sapientissimus*) of the Greeks.

[80] I am unconvinced by Schmähling's (1938) 6–7 assumption that Nasica was the first official holder of the title of *optimus vir*, which had before been bestowed by the *gens* on a leading member, especially someone active in religious observance. Interestingly, Nasica did not go on to hold any priesthood.

[81] So Münzer *RE* 4.1495 and Vogt (1933) with an excellent analysis showing connections with the Greek ideal of ἄριστος ἀνήρ (best man). *Contra* Degrassi *ILLRP* 310 and Zevi (1968–69) 66 n. 4. Vogt (1933) 87–90 discusses Nasica's moral excellence, as opposed to Atilius Caiatinus' *auctoritas*. Further light could be shed on this matter if we had the epitaph of Cn. Scipio Calvus (cos. 222 BC) the father of the chosen Nasica. (*RE* Cornelius 345; he died in 212 or 211 BC (Livy 25. 36. 14). He was the consular colleague of Marcellus, but did not share in his triumph at the time when Marcellus dedicated the *spolia opima*.) The presence of the Nasicae in this tomb may be inferred from its later reuse by Cornelii Lentuli, who claimed descent from them. Cf. Coarelli (1972) n. 60 for a family tree. Cornelia, the daughter of P. Cornelius Scipio Nasica Serapio (cos. 111 BC) married P. Cornelius Lentulus Marcellinus (tr. mon. *c.*90 BC).

there is no evidence that his inscription is later than his death, while 204 BC would make both Lucius Scipio and Atilius Caiatinus in their late eighties when they died. It is preferable, therefore, to interpret these epitaphs as reflections of the spirit of rivalry and competition which accompanied the rise of the Scipios during the Second Punic War, and which paved the way for an official choice of a 'best man' in Rome by the end of that war. The mention of a consensus sets these two inscriptions apart from the claims made in the *laudatio* of L. Caecilius Metellus, a slightly younger contemporary (cos. 251 and 247 BC), who died in 221.

An important feature of many Scipionic *elogia* is their two-part character. The first part consists of a label in the nominative recording the deceased's full name including *cognomina*, which were not used consistently in other more public texts and inscriptions until the later Republic, followed by a list of his offices, often in order. The second section is the verse *elogium* praising the deceased and covering some of the same material but adding achievements and moral qualities. The earlier verses are Saturnians consisting of six, or in the case of Barbatus apparently eight, lines while the latest example from the 130s BC consists of two elegiac couplets. It is not clear whether most of the Scipios had verse *elogia* and Paulla Cornelia did not. The two-part format appears to have become the norm and is reflected in the shape of the *elogia* from the Forum of Augustus, which surely imitate this republican genre.[82]

The *elogia* as a group suggest the existence of family archives containing biographical material, perhaps in the form of the funeral *laudationes*, which served as an independent source for careers.[83] A direct connection between the *elogia* and *laudationes* can be made partly on the basis of changes of address within the inscriptions. An audience of Roman citizens is imagined in a number of cases as if for a public speech.[84] Words spoken to the deceased are also a feature. The mention of the ancestors is reminiscent of the funeral procession. These characteristics are especially striking because the *elogia* were private, and not directed at passers-by on the Via

---

[82] For a discussion of the Augustan *elogia* and the genre in general, see Degrassi (1937).

[83] The existence of such archives and their use as a source has been accepted by Coarelli (1972) 97.

[84] Hölkeskamp (1993) 30 notes that the Scipionic *elogia* name the audience for the aristocratic art and pomp which developed in the later 4th and 3rd cent. BC.

Appia.[85] They contain a brief résumé of the topics at the heart of the funeral speech: birth, offices held, achievements in office, and virtues.[86] The use of superlatives to make claims is typical of both genres. Common ground is evident. Nevertheless, the *elogia* remain problematic principally because of their brevity. They omit many features which must surely have been stressed in a eulogy and which can be demonstrated to have been part of the common tradition about a family member.[87]

The Scipionic epitaphs can perhaps be best understood as a kind of shorthand, reminding an informed audience which Cornelius was buried where. They appear only to give selected highlights of achievements, notably deeds done in office. At the same time, they do preserve important family information which has not survived in our other sources. It is from the *elogia* that we learn that Asiagenus, not Asiaticus, was the name taken by L. Scipio, the conqueror of Antiochus.[88] Cicero tells us that *laudationes* were often preserved in families, but the *elogia* do not appear to be directly excerpted from them. The link between the *laudationes* and the tomb inscriptions may well be the labels (*tituli*) which accompanied the *imagines* in the *atrium*.

2. *Republican Tomb Inscriptions and the Labels of the* Imagines

In trying to discover the role of the *tituli* which identified the *imagines* in relation to *elogia* on tombs and *laudationes* at funerals, it is helpful to keep in mind that the *tituli* were labels on portraits which were displayed in the most public part of the house. The characteristic simplicity of republican *elogia*, whether inside or outside the tomb, would be anomalous if extensive inscriptions could be found in the *atrium*. Both genres of inscription contained the same core of information

[85] I am not persuaded by Van Sickle (1987) 49 to see the imagined audiences of the *elogia* as mainly a literary commonplace derived from Greek epigramme.

[86] A close connection between the tomb inscriptions and the *laudationes* has been argued for most strongly by Zevi (1968-69) 66-7. *Contra* Van Sickle (1987) and (1988) who shows that the unity and complexity of the *elogia* prove that they are not extracts from larger poems or laments.

[87] As an example one may cite the omission of the triumph of Lucius, son of Barbatus, over the Carthaginians, Corsica, and Sardinia which is mentioned in the triumphal *Fasti*.

[88] It was this name that was passed on for at least two generations to his direct male descendants and yet it was not known by our later sources. Adoption rescued Africanus' line to establish it as the more dominant.

about the deceased. It is logical, therefore, to connect the *tituli* initially with the simplest and oldest form of *elogia*. That is to say, *tituli* probably started as no more than name labels in the nominative with the father's name added. Analogous examples are the painted labels for Barbatus and his son Lucius, which preserve archaisms of language and probably also of style and which reveal the traditional character of such labels.[89] One may also adduce the inscriptions from the tomb of the Furii at Tusculum, which give only names and sometimes also filiation.[90] The highest office might also be mentioned.

The effect aimed at in the late fourth century BC can be seen in the label on the sarcophagus of P. Cornelius Scapula, which gives name, filiation, *cognomen*, and the office of *pontifex maximus*. The omission of other offices has caused some confusion for scholars who have been trying to identify a Scapula who was only *pontifex maximus*. In fact, there is no reason to think the inscription is aiming to give anything like a *cursus* at this early date. The office of *pontifex maximus* was probably mentioned in order to stress Scapula's rank as a patrician at a time when plebeians could not yet hold priesthoods. Within the political context of the time the tone of the inscription was bold and proud, perhaps implying as a matter of course that the man in question had reached the consulship.[91] From such an initial pattern they developed to include as standard features *cognomina*, filiation covering two previous generations, and a basic list of offices held.

The inscriptions from the mausoleum of Augustus show how simplicity remained a norm for *elogia* to the end of the Republic and during the early part of the Empire.[92] Similarly, the grand round

[89] See the comment of Coarelli on the Scipionic inscriptions (1972) 87: 'Il *titulus*, cioè l'elemento più antico, conservò quindi le sue forme originarie, mentre l'elogio, introdotto più di recente, potè atteggiarsi fin dall' inizio in forme più libere, imposte del resto anche dall'uso del metro.' Cf. Wachter (1987) 341.

[90] See *ILLRP* 895-903 with *Roma Medio Repubblicana* (1973) 305-7 for the context of mid-republican tombs.

[91] See Pisani Sartorio and Quilici Gigli (1987/8) 259-60 for this persuasive interpretation of *pontifex maximus*. They date the inscription soon before the *Lex Ogulnia* of 300 BC and suggest it refers to P. Cornelius Scapula consul in 328 BC.

[92] The tomb of Servius Sulpicius Galba (cos. 144 or 108 BC) is decorated with fasces and bears the simple inscription *ILS* 863 = *ILLRP* 339: *Ser. Sulpicius Ser. f. | Galba cos. | ped. quadr. XXX* ('Servius Sulpicius Galba, son of Servius, consul, 30 square feet'). The effect is spare and dignified. For the inscriptions from the mausoleum of Augustus: *ILS* 138; 164; 172; 180; 181; 181*a*; 181*b*; 183; 188, see Panciera in von Hesberg and Panciera (1994) for an exhaustive treatment including previously unpublished material.

tomb of Caecilia Metella bears only the briefest inscription of her name and filiation with her husband's *cognomen*.[93] It may well be that such name labels were by this time a conscious archaism: they also suggested that any reader should know who was buried there without having to be reminded in detail.[94] The case of individuals buried at public expense in special honorific tombs is the most striking illustration that long grave inscriptions were not a regular part of Roman life during the Republic. The public were not even reminded why the special tomb had been decreed.[95]

An example of the most extensive career usual in a republican funerary context comes from the tomb of L. Munatius Plancus (cos. 42 BC).[96] Even this bold inscription, which reflects republican-style rivalry in the claim that Plancus was the founder of two colonies actually named for Caesar and Augustus, is brief and bald. The inscription can be categorized as a standard variation on the model adopted by the Scipios, although three generations are named in Plancus' filiation. His career is given in prose, but only really consists of highlights, with some notable omissions. In a reconstruction of the *tituli* labelling the *imagines* Plancus' inscription can be used to indicate maximum probable length and complexity.[97] The difference between the genre of republican *elogia* and the extensive *cursus* inscriptions which became common under the Empire is marked. It reflects the change in aristocratic opportunities for self-advertisement and a resulting desire for status to be publicly recorded and recognized.[98]

The close association of verse *elogia* with statues in the Forum of Augustus and especially with portraits in books by Varro and

[93] *ILS* 881: *Caeciliae | Q. Cretici f. | Metellae Crassi* ('[The tomb of] Caecilia Metella, daughter of Quintus [Caecilius Metellus] Creticus, wife of Crassus').

[94] For the importance of abbreviated nomenclature in the inscriptions of Roman aristocrats, see Panciera in von Hesberg and Panciera (1994) 92.

[95] *ILS* 862 = *ILLRP* 357 = I 12 (*CIL* 6. 1319) C. Poplicius Bibulus' is a fascinating instance of a public tomb, with a niche for a statue in front, which dates to the Sullan era and honours a man we are not able to identify, cf. Nash (1962) 319–20. The tombs of Hirtius and Pansa (I 13) on the Campus Martius have the simplest inscriptions: *ILS* 8890 = *ILLRP* 421; *ILLRP* 419 and 420. Hirtius' tomb is illustrated by Nash (1962) 341–3.

[96] *ILS* 886 = *CIL* 10. 6087 = I 11.

[97] Cf. Sil. *Pun.* 4. 497 = T77 who portrays late 3rd-cent. BC *tituli* as recording achievements both at home and abroad.

[98] This development can be illustrated by an extensive inscription such as that of Tiberius Plautius cos. AD 74 (*ILS* 986) and is perceptively treated by Eck (1984). See Ch. 8 for more discussion of senatorial self-representation under the Julio-Claudians.

Atticus suggests that the two-part *elogium* could also be found accompanying an *imago* in the *atrium*. If we did not have evidence about the published collections of portraits with verses, which were based on traditional Roman practices and antiquarian research, we might be tempted to assume that the *titulus* was only a plain label, while the verses would be seen as a special funerary genre. Varro and Atticus indicate that verse *elogia* probably also labelled the *imagines* in the *atrium*. That is not to say that verses were the norm. Many seem to have been composed by Atticus to fill gaps where simpler labels were traditional.[99] The powerful impression created by the plain labels should not be underestimated because it is so foreign to our own way of thinking and to the ostentation associated with the Empire.[100]

As argued above, simple labels do make claims, especially regarding the number and nature of offices held, but they cannot have been used as the main source for detailed reconstructions of family history.[101] Like the tomb inscriptions, they probably contained no more than selected highlights from the original *laudatio*. Some families kept careful records of the *laudationes* given by members and also wrote *commentarii*, which gave summaries of family trees and careers.[102] We are not in a position to say how common this practice was, nor whether it was mainly found amongst plebeians or families needing to reconstruct an ancestry because theirs lacked age or prestige. It seems that some families were far more preoccupied with maintaining, creating, and using family 'documents' than others. There is no reliable evidence to support the contention that extensive written 'family records' were kept from an early date by the oldest families. It seems likely that early inscriptions for tombs and *imagines* were brief and assumed a background knowledge of family traditions, which would largely have been passed on orally from one generation to the next. Such traditions were rehearsed in

[99] Nep. *Att.* 18. 5–6; Plin. *Nat.* 35. 8 and 11 = T54 and Vessberg (1941) 72–3.

[100] Note Caesar's deliberate use, especially at the end of books 1 and 7 of the *BG*, of the simple style associated with the reports of generals in the field. See Fraenkel (1956) for a discussion of the power and pathos of the plain style, especially with military overtones, in Roman culture.

[101] A comparison can be made with the brief messages on Roman coins of the last century of the Republic, which also could present a type of *res gestae*. See Ch. 3 § 3 and Sutherland (1983) 79.

[102] The case of the Porcii is noted by Gellius 13. 20, who himself had access to *laudationes* and to a *liber commentarium de familia Porcia*. This important notice is discussed by Taifecos (1979) and Malcovati (1981).

their fullest form at funerals, where citizens would hear them in the eulogy and see them enacted by the *imagines*.

The revisions evident in several *elogia* raise the possibility that the *tituli* in the *atrium* were also rewritten, expanded, or edited over time. What written records, if any, were used to create new versions is obscure. It is plausible to imagine that the changes often had more to do with the claims of rivals or the family's own growing prestige than with research and archives. The past was consistently presented in the form of selected highlights which served a family's present needs.

3. *Conclusion*

The close relationship between the ancestors and more recent family members is manifest in a shared tomb like the tomb of the Scipios, as it was for the living in the *atria* of their houses in everyday life. The need to integrate those who died young and without political achievement was felt especially keenly. Their epitaphs represent them in terms of their office-holding ancestors. Our evidence suggests that the label on the sarcophagus echoed both the *titulus* of the *imago* and the achievements which comprised the core of the *laudatio*. The *elogia* provide our best evidence for reconstructing the format and content of the *tituli*, as well as for documenting the continual process of recreating and editing family traditions about office-holders. Past achievements were kept alive by inscriptions and illustrated by narrative paintings and statues. The house of the dead, therefore, mirrored an aristocratic home in many ways, most importantly in its celebration of the relevance of ancestors, and in a feeling of shared heritage and ambitions which were expressed in prose and verse, painting, architecture, and statuary.

7

Ancestors at Home:
Imagines in the *Atrium*

In pectore amicus, non in atrio quaeritur.

(Sen. *Ben.* 6. 34. 5)

Mireque cupio ne nobiles nostri nihil in domibus suis pulchrum nisi imagines habeant; quae nunc mihi hos adulescentes tacitae laudare adhortari, et quod amborum gloriae satis magnum est, agnoscere videntur.

(Plin. *Ep.* 5. 17. 6)

MOST modern treatments of the *imagines* concentrate on their role in the funeral procession. This is seen as their *raison d'être* and hence as their main function.[1] In addition, however, the *imagines* had more common uses in the everyday life of the home. There is ample testimony in our ancient sources that the *imagines* were often thought of principally as part of a display in the *atrium*.[2] For this reason it makes perfect sense for a love poet, who is contrasting what he has to offer with the allurements of a rival of 'noble' birth, to allude to the *imagines* in the *atrium* rather than at a funeral.[3] This chapter will explore the most frequent contact with the *imagines*, whether for the office-holder or the ordinary Roman citizen, which was in the *atrium* of the Roman aristocratic house. The changing uses of this room will be examined since it was here that the *imagines* were set up and decorated, sometimes as part of extensive displays of ancestral images in various media.

[1] e.g. Schneider and Meyer (1916) 1098.
[2] For *imagines* in the *atrium*, see Polyb. 6. 53. 4 = T61; Cic. *Phil.* 2. 26 = T12; Ov. *Fast.* 1. 591 = T51; Val. Max. 5. 8. 3 = T103; Sen. *Ben.* 3. 28. 2 = T74; *Ep.* 44. 5 = T75; 76. 12 = T76; *Laus Pisonis* 8 ff. = T36; Plin. *Nat.* 35. 6 and 8 = T54; Mart. 2. 90. 5-8 = T47; 5. 20 = T48; Juv. 8. 1-5 and 19-20 = T35.
[3] Ov. *Am.* 1. 8. 65 = T50.

A full understanding of the function of *imagines* depends on an appreciation of their most usual role, when displayed in their cupboards in the *atrium* as an integral part of life in the house both for the family and for any visitor, however humble.[4] It is characteristic of Roman culture that the *imagines* were not stored in some recessed part of the house, only to emerge when a family member died. Because the masks were made of wax they were extremely perishable and needed to be protected from excesses of heat and light. It would have been practical to house them in a storage area designed to make them last longer. Instead aristocratic families chose to keep them in the most public room of the house,[5] with the result that special wooden cupboards were needed to preserve them. Ancient sources reveal that it was typical for them to become blackened with age and exposure to smoke and dirt.[6] The use of individual cupboards for each mask served to underline their importance as part of what was often an extensive display dominating the entrance to the house and occupying the *alae* as well as the *atrium* itself.[7]

1. *The* Atrium: *Its History, Furnishings, and Function*

The strategic position of the *atrium* as the first and most accessible room in an élite Roman town house is attested both by literary sources and archaeological evidence. Vitruvius' handbook on architecture (book 6) is the most direct ancient testimony. He shows clearly the special public nature of the *atrium* and its social importance for those who held magisterial office. Indeed, Vitruvius demonstrates that a particular form of architecture and design was usual for the families of office-holders, precisely because they could expect large numbers of visitors and much public business was

[4] For the house as a status symbol, see Treggiari (1979) 63 ff., Saller (1984), and Wiseman (1987a). For the *imagines* as synonymous with the home, see Ps.-Quintilian 388. 35 = T64.

[5] The public nature of the display of the *imagines* in the *atrium* has been noted by Drerup (1980) 127 and Hölkeskamp (1987) 224.

[6] The smoky colour of the *imagines* is attested by Cic. *Pis.* 1 = T13; Sen. *Ep.* 44. 5 = T75; Juv. 8. 8 = T35; and Boethius, *Consolation of Philosophy* 1 pros. 1.3 = T4.

[7] Budde (1939) 32-4 notes that the 9th cent. AD MSS of Terence include drawings showing theatrical masks kept in cupboards with one cupboard for each play and the masks arranged in the order in which the characters appeared.

transacted in their own houses.[8] The architectural tastes of the élite
also influenced the styles chosen by many of their less prominent
fellow citizens.[9] Vitruvius' words confirm what is suggested by
architectural and decorative features of the grander houses at
Pompeii, namely that these houses were built to recall the atmosphere of public buildings.[10] The owners were consciously
Hellenizing in their emulation of styles considered 'regal' which
were inspired by contacts with the Hellenistic kingdoms of the East.
Hellenistic palace architecture, with its ostentatious displays of
wealth, had itself been influenced by public building and temples.[11]
The notion that Roman senators could consider themselves the
equals of Hellenistic kings had a long history in the Republic.[12]

Conspicuous consumption on domestic architecture was a political necessity for families who aspired to positions of leadership in
the highly competitive society of the Roman Republic.[13] Cicero confirms the evidence of Vitruvius in seeing the *domus* as specially
adapted to the social activities it housed (*Off.* I. 138-9). The *atrium*
was the focus of the Roman town house during the middle Republic.
An appreciation of its uses and character can help to explain why
the *imagines* were kept there and what they were used for on an
everyday basis.

Vitruvius describes the *atrium* as one of the rooms open to

---

[8] 6. 5. 2: *nobilibus vero, qui honores magistratusque gerundo praestare debent officia
civibus, faciunda sunt vestibula regalia alta, atria et peristylia amplissima, silvae ambula-
tionesque laxiores ad decorem maiestatis perfectae; praeterea bybliothecas, basilicas non dis-
simili modo quam publicorum operum magnificentia comparatas, quod in domibus eorum
saepius et publica consilia et privata iudicia arbitriaque conficiuntur* ('But for members of
the office-holding caste, who are required in their exercise of offices and magistracies
to render services to the citizens, regal high entrance halls need to be built, spacious
atria and peristyles, wooded groves, and broad avenues designed to enhance their
prestige. Besides they also need libraries and basilicas (halls) fashioned in the same
grand style as public buildings because both public policy and private lawsuits and
judgements are frequently conducted in their houses').
[9] See Zanker (1979) for a discussion of the influence of luxury villas on ordinary
houses in Pompeii in the imperial period.
[10] For a detailed treatment, see Wallace-Hadrill (1988) 59 ff. and (1994) especially 17-37.
[11] See La Rocca (1986) 10 ff. for the Greek concept of τρυφή as an attribute of
gods or kings, and its effect on Roman ideas of *luxuria* in the private sphere.
[12] See Plut. *Pyrrh.* 19. 5 and App. *Samn.* 10. 3 with Hölscher (1990) for Cineas,
the envoy of king Pyrrhus, addressing the senate as an assembly of kings. Plut. *T.
Gracch.* 1. 4 records king Ptolemy's offer of marriage to Cornelia, the mother of the
Gracchi. For Roman attitudes to kings and kingship, see Rawson (1975) esp. 152-6.
[13] See La Rocca (1986) 8 and Wallace-Hadrill (1988) 45 and (1994) 6-12.

uninvited visitors.[14] We may add that it was the most accessible of these rooms since it was the first to be entered in the house proper. The doors of Roman houses, which were often very large and elaborate, were kept open during the day and were usually only closed as a sign of mourning.[15] A death in the family was marked by closed doors hung with branches of cypress. The *atrium* was a room associated with the morning hours, when most business was conducted, and people called on the master of the house for the traditional *salutatio* (morning greeting).[16] It is, therefore, a space connected with work, especially official business (*negotium*), as opposed to other rooms used for leisure activities (*otium*). The *atrium* accommodated the largest number of callers, who were essentially unsorted according to rank or needs. From here they could be directed in ever smaller and more intimate groups to reception rooms, dining rooms (*triclinia*), or the bedroom (*cubiculum*) of the master where important business was often transacted with two or three people present.[17] The *atrium*, therefore, served to receive all callers and to articulate access to the more secluded areas of the house.

The history of the Roman aristocratic house has often been written in terms of the evolution of the *atrium* (see Figs. 8–11).[18] Evidence for the development of the Roman house comes mainly from Pompeii and Herculaneum, but also from Ostia and some finds in Rome.[19] The earliest dwellings at Pompeii date to the third cen-

[14] 6. 5. 1: *Communia autem sunt, quibus etiam invocati suo iuro de populo possunt venire, id est vestibula, cava aedium, peristylia, quaeque eundem habere possunt usum* ('The communal rooms are those which members of the general public can enter in their own right even without being invited, that is to say the entrance ways, *atria*/inner courts, and peristyles, and the rooms which can have the same function [as these]'). Cf. Varro *L.* 5.161: *Cavum aedium dictum qui locus tectus intra parietes relinquebatur patulus, qui esset ad communem omnium usum* ('The place which is left open in the roofed part inside the house is called the inner court/*atrium*, which was designed for the common use of all').

[15] See Tac. *Ann.* 2. 83. 3 and Wallace-Hadrill (1988) 46 and (1994) 5.

[16] For the *salutatio*, see § 6 below.

[17] Tacitus sets his *Dialogus* in Maternus' bedroom. Cf. Wallace-Hadrill (1988) 94 and (1994) 38–61.

[18] For an overview, see McKay (1975), Boëthius (1978), and Dwyer (1991). Individual houses are treated as detailed examples by Dwyer (1982) and J. R. Clarke (1991).

[19] In Rome, see the Casa dei Grifi dating to around 100 BC and the new excavations of republican houses by Carandini (1988) 359–73, who reconstructs the aristocratic houses on the North slope of the Palatine. He gives evidence for the importance of the *atrium* from the archaic age onwards. Especially notable is the

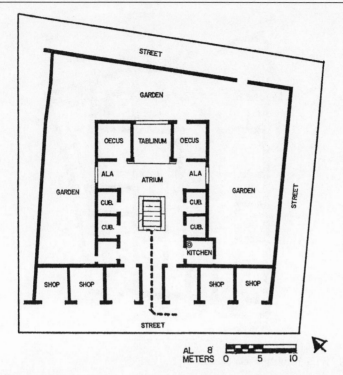

FIG. 8. Reconstructed plan of the Casa di Sallustio *c.*150 BC, Pompeii.

tury BC, by which time the *atrium* was well established as the most
important room in the house and the centre of family life.[20] The
atrium of an early aristocratic house had close connections, both in
form and furnishings, with a similar reception area in the houses of
Etruscan dynasts.[21] Evidence comes from Etruscan tombs built to
look like the insides of houses, which can be dated as early as the

house of M. Aemilius Scaurus (cos. 115) which had a staff of around fifty slaves. For
a reconstruction of his grand *atrium* which later became the core of Clodius' huge
domus, see Coarelli (1989). For an overview, see Patterson (1992).

[20] The best examples are the Casa del Chirurgo and the Casa di Sallustio.

[21] In the absence of direct evidence, many assumptions about early Roman
houses depend on a prototype developed by Patroni and adopted by Wistrand (1970),
McKay (1975), and Boëthius (1978). For a critique of this approach, see Tamm
(1961). For Etruscan culture and the origins of the *imagines*, see Appendix D.

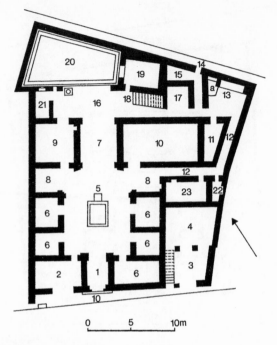

FIG. 9. Plan of the Casa del Chirurgo, Pompeii.

seventh century BC.[22] Etruscan houses from the fourth century BC with *atrium*, *tablinum*, and *alae* have been excavated at Marzabotto.[23] Yet this was not the only house plan available to the Romans, as can be seen from simpler houses at Pompeii, and especially from the third-century BC houses built for the Roman colonists at Cosa.[24] The *atrium* was evidently chosen as the main room in larger houses because it suited the particular purposes of the owners. Pompeii offers several early examples of fine houses with a single *atrium* which indicates the original importance of this room.[25]

[22] See Prayon (1975a) and Steingräber (1979).
[23] Originally published by Mansuelli (1963), these are further discussed by Richardson (1988) 362.
[24] On Cosa, see F. E. Brown (1980) especially 63–9. Cosan houses were adaptations of the *atrium/tablinum* plan made more economical and better suited to colonial life. On Pompeii, see Richardson (1988) 382 ff.
[25] e.g. Casa di Sallustio, Casa del Chirurgo, Casa di Epidio Rufo. For a catalogue, see Richardson (1988) 108–15.

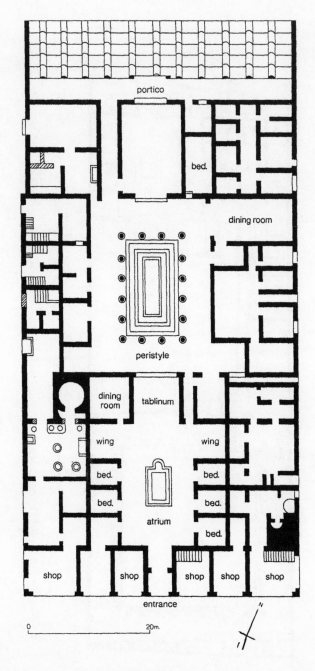

portico

bed.

dining room

peristyle

dining room

tablinum

wing

wing

bed.

bed.

bed.

bed.

bed.

atrium

shop

shop

shop

shop

shop

entrance

N

0   20m.

FIG. 10. Plan of the Casa di Pansa, Pompeii.

191

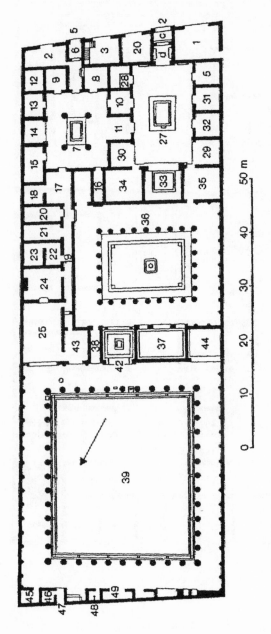

FIG. II. Plan of the Casa del Fauno, Pompeii.

It is assumed that in an early *atrium* house most of the public life of the family would have taken place in the *atrium*, as separate rooms around it were only for sleeping or storing goods.[26] Cooking, eating, and other household activities would all have been in the *atrium*, if not outside. However, the earliest houses in Pompeii already show the development of kitchens, dining rooms, and further reception areas.

Some later houses had two *atria* in order to accommodate both the public and private life of the family.[27] In such a scheme there is a marked contrast between the grander, public *atrium*, which has a *tablinum*, and the simpler, private *atrium*. Around the middle of the second century BC the peristyle was introduced and became widely used as the focus for the more private family rooms which opened off it.[28] The majority of Pompeian houses show this pattern of the original, Roman *atrium* greeting the visitor to the public parts of the house, while newer, more specialized rooms are grouped around a Hellenistic type of peristyle, which reflects a change in the lifestyles of élite Romans as they emulated the luxury and cultivated leisure of the Greek East. Peristyles serve as the setting for the dialogues of Cicero, especially on philosophical subjects.[29]

In the imperial age the *atrium* gradually receded in importance in favour of a more elaborate peristyle, or even several peristyles and gardens. By the high Empire the *atrium* could be omitted completely or become no more than a passageway leading into the grander parts of the house.[30] Such houses may often have been designed for a new class of wealthy patron without the family background to justify the maintenance of an aristocratic *atrium*. Even for traditional aristocrats public life had changed and the newly powerful were now the *amici* of the *princeps*, who did not rely on elections to maintain their rank. Consequently, their life at home

[26] See Cato quoted by Serv. *A.* 1. 726 for dining in the *atrium*. The early importance of the *atrium* is suggested by the name Atrium Vestae given to the dwelling of the Vestal Vigins where the public hearth was kept. See also Platner-Ashby (1929) and Richardson (1992) for *atrium* denoting office or hall, and Stambaugh (1988) 25 for the origin of these names in the Roman aristocratic house.

[27] e.g. Casa del Fauno, cf. Richardson (1988) 116 who dates this development to c.187–175 BC.

[28] e.g. Casa di Pansa, Casa del Menandro, see Richardson (1988) 120 ff. and 394 ff. Diodorus 5. 40 claims the peristyle was also an Etruscan invention. At the time of its destruction the Casa del Fauno had two *atria* and two peristyles.

[29] For the setting of Cicero's dialogues, see Linderski (1989).

[30] See J. R. Clarke (1991) 363-4.

became accessible to the visitor in less traditional and formalized ways.[31] Domitian's new palace on the Palatine was also built without an *atrium*.[32] The younger Pliny still had a traditional *atrium* in his Tuscan villa, but he seems to regard it as a special feature (*Ep.* 2. 17. 4 and 5. 6. 15). Pliny's testimony, which is confirmed by archaeological finds, shows that the traditional *atrium* of the Roman office-holder had become a symbol of an earlier lifestyle and was no longer at the heart of the home.

It seems clear, then, that the *atrium* was the most important and characteristic room in the republican élite town house (*domus*).[33] Its history and decoration reflect the public lives and ambitions of the Roman political caste. The same is true for its contents, which included the *imagines* as an important feature. We are fortunate in possessing a description of the furnishings in the *atrium* of a patrician town house of the late Republic, a description written about a hundred years later.[34]

Post biduum medium quam Clodius occisus erat interrex primus proditus est M. Aemilius Lepidus. Non fuit autem moris ab eo qui primus interrex proditus erat comitia haberi. Sed Scipionis et Hypsaei factiones, quia recens invidia Milonis erat, cum contra ius postularent ut interrex ad comitia consulum creandorum descenderet, idque ipse non faceret, [et] domum eius per omnes interregni dies (fuerant autem ex more quinque) obsiderunt. Deinde omni vi ianua expugnata et imagines maiorum deiecerunt et lectulum adversum uxoris eius Corneliae, cuius castitas pro exemplo habita est, fregerunt, itemque telas, quae ex vetere more in atrio texebantur, diruerunt.

When two days had elapsed since Clodius had been killed, Marcus Aemilius Lepidus was named as first *interrex*. It was not, however, the custom for the man named as first *interrex* to preside over the elections to office. But because Milo's unpopularity was fresh, the supporters of Scipio and Hypsaeus were demanding, contrary to the law, that the *interrex* should come down to the Forum to hold the consular elections. When Aemilius did not do so, they laid seige to his house for the whole period of the *interregnum* (which was usually five days). Then they broke down his door with

[31] For a discussion of this development and the more private character of Third Style wall-paintings, see Wallace-Hadrill (1988) 72-4. Cf. Wallace-Hadrill (1994) 51-4 who explains the retreat of the *atrium* under the Empire in terms of a deeper penetration of the public sphere into domestic space. The proliferation of space for entertainment is characteristic of imperial houses.

[32] For the Flavians as emperors without *imagines*, see Ch. 9 § 2.

[33] See also the use in poetry of the word *atrium* to stand for the house itself: Ov. *Her.* 16. 184; *Met.* 1. 172; 13. 968; Stat. *Thebaid* 1. 197.

[34] Asconius 43C = 37-8 KS = 38 Stangl =T3.

full force and threw down the masks of his ancestors and broke in pieces the symbolic marriage bed of his wife Cornelia, whose chastity was a byword, and in the same way they tore up the cloth which was being woven on looms in the *atrium* according to ancient custom.

In the violence surrounding the elections of 52 BC and after the murder of Clodius by Milo's gangs an attack was made on the house of Marcus Aemilius Lepidus the later triumvir, who was serving as *interrex* at the time. The crowd managed to enter the *atrium* and to destroy its contents. The *atrium* contained the *imagines*, the *lectulus adversus* of Lepidus' wife symbolizing their marriage, and the looms which were kept there according to ancient custom. It is in the *atrium* that Lucretia was pictured as working wool with her maids in Livy.[35] There may have been other items in the room, but these three are singled out as the most important and therefore as targets for the crowd.[36] It is plausible to imagine that by the end of the Republic a family like the Aemilii Lepidi had so many *imagines* that any other furnishings in the room were necessarily limited.[37]

Finds at Pompeii have revealed very few ancestor portraits of any kind in private houses. However, bronze herms of the owner of the house and his father or grandfather were found in several houses, flanking the entrance to the *tablinum*.[38] These special kinds of portraits were visible to anyone as soon as they entered the house and were part of its important first impression. The herms could complement *imagines* or serve in their stead for families which had none.

In Pompeii the traditional place of the *lectus adversus*, opposite the entrance and in front of the *tablinum*, is often taken by the

[35] Livy 1. 57. 9: *ubi Lucretiam haudquaquam ut regias nurus, quas in convivio lusuque cum aequalibus viderant tempus terentes, sed nocte sera deditam lanae inter lucubrantes ancillas in medio aedium sedentem inveniunt* ('where they found Lucretia late at night devoted to wool-working and sitting in her *atrium* amongst her female slaves who were working by lamp light. In complete contrast they had seen the young wives of the royal family and their girl-friends whiling away their time with games at a dinner party'). Note the weaving scenes on the Etruscan 'tintinabulo' from Bologna. Woolworking is an essential part of the life of a *matrona* and is mentioned in the *laudationes* of Turia and Murdia. Cf. *ILS* 8393; 8402; 8403; Columella, *praef.* 1-3; 7-9; Suet. *Aug.* 64. 2 and 73. 1. See D'Ambra (1993) for Domitian's use of domestic images of wool working in the Forum Transitorium.

[36] As is noted by Dwyer (1982), the *atrium* was not a room that was usually furnished in Pompeii except for lights and some small tables.

[37] Cf. Sall. *Hist.* 3 fr. 48. 18 = T67 for the *imagines* appearing like an army.

[38] These are found in front of the *antae* of the *tablinum*. Labelled examples portray L. Caecilius, C. Cornelius Rufus, and Vesonius Primus. See de Franciscis (1951) 30-1, 35, Dwyer (1982) 127-8 and (1991) fig. 1-2, and Richardson (1988) 388.

cartibulum, a type of dining table, frequently of marble.[39] Varro (*L.* 5. 125) tells us that in his boyhood this traditional table could still be found in the *atrium*.[40] The table and the dishes sometimes displayed on it seem to have taken on a symbolic quality once meals were no longer served here. Similarly, a hearth could often be found in the *atrium*, again recalling that meals were originally cooked here. This hearth was used as part of domestic cult, and contributed to the black discolouration typical for older *imagines*.[41]

The shrine of the Lares and Genius, and the Penates could also sometimes be found in the *atrium*, although there were many possible locations for domestic cult within the house, the kitchen being the most typical.[42] Some houses had several shrines scattered throughout.[43] It was usual for the family strong box (*arca*) to be kept in the *atrium* as a repository for money, books, and documents.[44] Massive wooden chests with iron bands and elaborate nails were placed on stone bases in the houses of the affluent.[45] They cannot have been moved around much and certainly dominated the whole *atrium*. Their design and location reveal concerns of security, but also of a conspicuous show of wealth.

Roman houses generally did not contain much furniture by modern standards and what there was was freely moved around according to need.[46] The *atrium* is therefore a typically Roman creation in the sense that it consisted essentially of an open space surrounded

[39] See Pernice (1932) 1-11 who traces these back to the earliest times in Pompeii, Walde and Hoffmann (1938) ad. loc., McKay (1975) 36 and 136, Boëthius (1978) 185.

[40] Varro is the only literary source for the *cartibulum*: *Altera vasaria mensa erat lapidea quadrata oblonga una columella; vocabatur cartibulum. Haec in aedibus ad compluvium apud multos me puero ponebatur et in ea et ⟨cir⟩cum ea⟨m⟩ aenea vasa: a gerendo cartibulum potest dictum* ('There was another table connected with vessels, which was of stone and rectangular with one leg: it was called a *cartibulum*. When I was a boy this table was placed in many people's houses in the *atrium* next to the *conpluvium* and bronze vessels were kept on and around it. It could be called *cartibulum* from its use for putting things on').

[41] Evidence for the smoky atmosphere sometimes met with in the *atrium* can be found in Ov. *Fast.* 6. 301 ff.; Mart. 2. 90. 5-8 = T47; Serv. *A.* 1. 790; 10. 726. Cf. Wistrand (1970) 195-6.

[42] See Fröhlich (1991) for the Lares in the kitchen, in shops, and at crossroads. For a discussion of domestic cult, see § 4 below.

[43] The Casa del Menandro is a good example.

[44] App. *BC* 4. 44; Mau (1907) 255, and J. R. Clarke (1991) 212 and 223.

[45] For a full discussion and catalogue, see Pernice (1932) 71-94.

[46] For a good general discussion, see Veyne (1987) 316. Dwyer (1982) catalogues finds in sample houses.

by smaller rooms with more specific functions. It had little in the way of permanent 'furniture': the looms and the *lectus adversus* were moveable according to circumstances. There is not much evidence for seating arrangements, although folding chairs or benches may have been used.[47] Many who waited here probably did so standing up. The *imagines* therefore take on additional significance as the dominant feature in a large space designed for waiting and for formal social reception, notably but not exclusively for visitors of inferior status and for dependants. The contents of the *atrium* reflected the need felt by republican aristocrats to put on a highly traditional face for the world by preserving an archaizing version of the core of an old Roman town house (*domus*).

The display of prestige and cult objects in the *atrium*, such as spoils from battles, a fine *arca*, and the *imagines*, can be imagined most readily in a setting of First Style wall-paintings. The First Style of painting documented at Pompeii imitated the masonry of public buildings with moulded plaster reliefs in different colours.[48] It also aimed to evoke an atmosphere of something more than a private house, while its effect was severe and dignified.[49] Although it reached its peak in the second and early first centuries BC, this style was then copied and renewed at Pompeii throughout the life of the city, especially in *atria* and other reception rooms.[50] The First Style *atrium* in the Casa di Sallustio was preserved next to more modern styles for close to two hundred years (see Fig. 12).[51] It has therefore been identified as a style associated with the traditions of the ancestors.[52] Consequently, it must also have been a style typically found with a display of *imagines* throughout the middle Republic. The First Style is mainly attested in the larger houses in Pompeii

[47] Wallace-Hadrill (1988) 55 argues for benches but there is not much ancient evidence. See e.g. Ov. *Fast.* 6. 305-6.

[48] For a general discussion, see Ling (1991) 12-22, and J. R. Clarke (1991) 33 ff. The best detailed treatment is Laidlaw (1985).

[49] For the theory that space within the Roman house was differentiated by varying styles of decoration, see Barbet (1985) and Wallace-Hadrill (1988) and (1994).

[50] An illustrated catalogue of the First Style in Pompeii can be found in Laidlaw (1985). The First Style was used in public buildings and tombs long after it was current in houses.

[51] For the deliberate contrast between older and newer styles to be found in many Pompeian houses, see especially Wallace-Hadrill (1994) 50-1 and 160-4.

[52] Laidlaw (1985) 333: 'there is reason to believe that throughout the life of Pompeii the First Style always retained an association with old-fashioned values; consequently it was both renewed and copied up to the final destruction of the town in AD 79, whenever it seemed important to evoke a traditional atmosphere.'

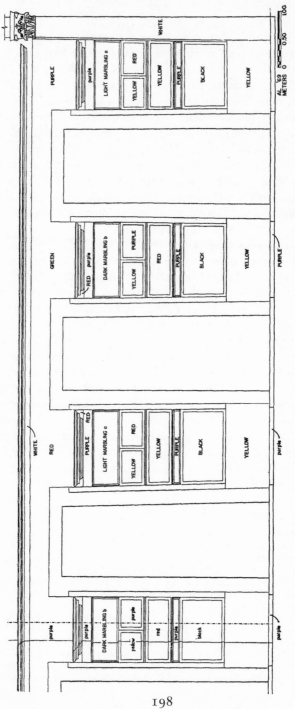

FIG. 12. Reconstruction of First Style wall-painting from the *atrium* of the Casa di Sallustio, Pompeii, N (left) wall with NW corner: pattern and colours.

198

and most extensively in the Casa del Fauno which is the largest. During the Republic small and medium-sized houses were rarely decorated at all, which explains why the houses of the poor in Pompeii do not illustrate more old-fashioned styles of decoration. The close association between conservative decoration of the *atrium* and its function as the traditional reception area was maintained at Pompeii.[53]

The origins of the First Style can be traced back to the fourth century BC and Polybius certainly saw the *imagines* against such a setting in the *atria* of the mid-second century BC.[54] The social importance of the First Style may actually have been linked to its close association with the *imagines*, which could look their best displayed against a background of bright colours in geometric patterns. Spoils and *imagines clipeatae* would have been hung high up on the walls and would have complemented the cupboards (*armaria*) below, which were presumably built to show the masks at eye level, or slightly above.[55]

The Roman house was, therefore, 'a stage deliberately designed for the performance of social rituals, and not as a museum of artifacts'.[56] The aim of social history must be to reconstruct life within the Roman house rather than the house itself as an aesthetic object.[57] Much useful work has been done on the visual impression of a house from the entrance, a concern for architects and owners who aimed to display wealth and status.[58] According to this school of thought, the Roman house is transparent and allows the visitor to look across the brightly illuminated pool (*impluvium*) in the *atrium*, with the *cartibulum* behind it, into the *tablinum* flanked by herms and through into the garden or peristyle beyond. The effect can be seen as a series of constructed tableaux or of symmetrically designed planes inviting the admiration of the viewer standing at

[53] See Wallace-Hadrill (1994) 160-4 who contrasts the careful preservation of the First Style in 'republican' contexts with the rapid diffusion of decoration throughout the city in the Julio-Claudian period.

[54] This was the style that Cicero and Caesar would have grown up with.

[55] For a discussion, see Ch. 2 § 1c. For spoils in Roman houses, see Rawson (1990).

[56] Wallace-Hadrill (1988) 96. Cf. Wallace-Hadrill (1989) 63 for the formal aspect of social relationships focussed on the progress from entrance to *tablinum*.

[57] The best treatment of Roman domestic architecture as a language designed to communicate social distinctions and functions is Wallace-Hadrill (1994).

[58] For an overview, see Wallace-Hadrill (1988) especially 75 ff. and (1994).

the doorway.[59] The view is sometimes enhanced by a sloping entrance ramp or even by mountains visible in the distance over the roof of the house.[60] This series of frames is intended as the setting for the master of the house in his *tablinum,* presiding at the centre of his domain and ready to receive visitors at the *salutatio.*

However, the grand vista from the entrance was quickly lost as soon as the visitor stepped off the central axis into the *atrium* itself.[61] Where the vista gave the important first impression, the *atrium* with its furnishings offered the second and more lasting image of the house, which the visitor could appreciate at leisure while waiting to do his business.[62] The vista is really only the introduction to the *atrium,* which was the scene for many of the social rituals in the house.[63] The presence of the *arca* in the *atrium* also made it the logical place for the distribution of the *sportula* (handout to clients), although this custom is documented mainly in the first century of the Empire.[64]

Beyond its specifically political function as an office and reception area for public business, the *atrium* was traditionally used as the centre of rituals marking the life of the family.[65] These habitual rituals were as important in defining the *atrium* as the daily *salutatio.*[66] At the birth of a child a fire was kindled on the hearth and kept burning for the first days of the new baby's life. The *dies lustricus* would be marked on the eighth or ninth day with a wreath on the door and sacrifices. Sacrifices of thanksgiving would mark birthdays each year.[67] The *atrium* was the setting for ceremonies

[59] Note esp. Drerup (1959), Bek (1980), and Jung (1984), followed by J. R. Clarke (1991).

[60] See Drerup (1959) 157 on the effect of a tilting entrance. Mountains are visible over the doorway to the Casa del Menandro.

[61] It should be noted, however, that we do not know how often or why the view through the *tablinum* and beyond the *atrium* was blocked off by a wooden screen or a curtain, thus giving the house much greater privacy. The grand vistas of Roman houses may well have been associated specifically with certain occasions, such as the *salutatio.*

[62] *Contra* J. R. Clarke (1991) 16 who sees the *fauces-atrium-tablinum* sequence as addressed to the walking spectator and as featuring simple patterns for quick recognition.

[63] See § 6.

[64] For references to and discussion of the *sportula,* see Marquardt (1886) 207 ff. and *RE* s.v. *sportula.*

[65] For a recent general discussion, see J. R. Clarke (1991) 7–12.

[66] For an account of family ritual at different stages of life, see Dixon (1992) 133–59.

[67] See Plut. *Q. Rom.* 102; Suet. *Nero* 6. 2; Macrob. *Sat.* 1. 16. 36; Festus 107 L.

marking a coming of age for both boys and girls. Young men dedicated their first beard shavings and the *bulla* (amulet) worn during
childhood to the Lares when they put on the *toga virilis* of manhood.[68] Similarly, the day before her marriage, a girl dedicated her
dolls, toys, and other symbols of childhood to the household gods at
the shrine of the Lares.[69] Whether in the *atrium* or elsewhere, this
shrine received regular offerings at the kalends, nones, and ides of
each month and on anniversaries when the hearth was also decorated with flowers.[70] The domestic gods received some kind of worship from the family every day and according to the occasion.

On the day of a wedding the bride was accompanied to her new
home by flutes and torches.[71] After she anointed the door posts with
oil and garlanded them with woollen fillets, she was lifted over the
threshold and received fire and water from her new husband in the
atrium, as symbols of her authority within the house.[72] The bride
offered a coin both to the Lar familiaris and to the Lares compi-
tales.[73] A symbolic marriage bed was set up in the *atrium* for the
wedding night, and this is the *lectus adversus* which could be found
in traditional *atria*.[74] The following day the new wife took part in
the household rites in her new home.[75] A marriage was, therefore,
observed in the *atria* of the two houses, as the bride left the one to
take up her official position in the other. The two were linked by the
procession (*domum deductio*) after the marriage rites, which took
place in the bride's home, perhaps partly in the *atrium*. The *imagines* are not attested as having a role to play in the bridal procession, although a wife's *imagines* were also set up in the *atrium* of her

[68] This was done on the Liberalia (17 March), see Prop. 4. 1. 131–2; Persius 5.
30–1; Dion. Hal. 4. 15. 5. For discussion, see Harmon (1978) 1597–8. The archaeological evidence for *bullae* is discussed by Warden (1983).
[69] Varro in Nonius 863. 15 L; Schol. Cruq. ad Hor. *Sat.* 1. 5. 69. For offerings to
Venus, see Persius 2. 70. See D'Ambra (1993) 101 for brides.
[70] See Harmon (1978) 1593–5.
[71] Plaut. *Cas.* 798; Ter. *Adelph.* 905; Serv. *Ecl.* 8. 29. For marriage, see Balsdon
(1962) 181–6 with salutary warnings of how little we know of Roman weddings,
and Harmon (1978) 1598–600.
[72] Plin. *Nat.* 28. 142; Paulus ex Festus 77 L; Serv. *A.* 4. 458.
[73] Nonius 853 L with Fasce (1984) for a discussion of this and other aspects of
Roman marriage customs.
[74] See Catulus 61. 164 ff. and 172 ff.; Hor. *Epist.* 1. 1. 87 ff.; Juv. 10. 334;
Paulus ex Festus 83 L. For representations of the *lectus adversus*, see Kraus and Von
Matt (1973) figs. 119 and 265.
[75] Macrob. *Sat.* 1. 15. 22; cf. Pomeroy (1975) 152 for the wife's participation in
the cult in the husband's house.

new home.[76] As discussed above, a death in the household was marked mainly in the *atrium* behind the doors now closed in mourning. The *atrium* was the scene for the *collocatio* or lying-in-state and was also the point from which the funeral procession with its parade of ancestors departed.[77]

The presence of the *imagines* in the *atrium* allowed the ancestors to appear as spectators for the rituals and activities outlined above. The cupboards would normally be open and the masks decorated for festive or joyous occasions, which would have included a marriage, a birthday, or the birth of a child.[78] To what extent the ancestors were seen as actual participants in any of these rituals is impossible for us to say with any kind of certainty.[79] Even if only as spectators they would have had a strong effect and might appear to be judging the actions of their relatives.[80] Their presence emphasizes in a special way the lack of privacy within the Roman household, which is suggested by the architecture of the houses themselves.[81]

In the *atrium* the ancestors were closely associated with moments of transition within the family, as well as with everyday observances of domestic cult and household rituals such as weaving.[82] In this sense they watched over the traditional work of women in the house just as much as over the official duties of men. At the same time, the public presentation of family life in the *atrium* could in itself serve as advertising. The personal style of politics in the Roman city-state was based to a large extent on the perception of a leading man as fit to govern and command.[83] A convincing picture of character had its basis in the home and the life of the family as a social unit. Traditional family values reflected in the *atrium* could be a powerful political statement, even as the more secluded life in other rooms of the house was increasingly

[76] See Cic. *Vat.* 28 = T20; *S.C. de Cn. Pisone patre* = I16; Plin. *Ep.* 8. 10. 3 = T58. Similarly, the triumphal procession of a general seems to have brought his share of the booty directly to his house after the official ceremonies at the Temple of Jupiter. See Prop. 1. 16. 1–4 with Rawson (1990) 159.

[77] See Ch. 4 § 1 for a full discussion.　　　　　　　　　　　[78] See § 3 below.

[79] For the notion of the ancestors as participants, see Dupont (1987).

[80] See Plin. *Ep.* 5. 17. 6 = T57 quoted above, and § 7 below.

[81] See Wallace-Hadrill (1988) 58 and 81.

[82] For women in the *atrium*, see Nep. *Praef.* 6 and Arnob. *Adv. Gent.* 2. 67 with Balsdon (1962) 270, and Pomeroy (1975) 149, 199–200.

[83] For *imagines* and elections, see Ch. 3.

influenced by Greek taste and by luxuries not known in the
domestic realm of the ancestors.[84]

2. *The* Tablinum

No discussion of the *atrium* can be complete without a consideration of the *tablinum*, the room opposite the entrance which served
as an extension of the *atrium*. Some scholars see this room as the
true focus of the Roman house rather than the *atrium*, which is considered a waiting area and simply a development of the courtyards
found in front of Etruscan and other early Italian houses.[85]
Whatever the original function of the *tablinum* in a very early
period, our concern here is with the nature of this room in the
Republic. Its importance is clearly indicated by its position as the
central point on the vista from the entrance way.[86] Finds at Pompeii
and especially at Herculaneum show that the *tablinum* was also regularly closed off from the *atrium* by a folding wooden screen which
at the same time prevented visitors from seeing through into the
house beyond the *atrium*.[87]

Direct evidence about the *tablinum* is strikingly thin, especially for
so important a room. Ancient testimony comes from Festus (490.
28 L) and the elder Pliny (*Nat*. 35. 7 = T54).[88] They agree in seeing the *tablinum* as a room used to store documents pertaining to
magisterial office. Its character is that of a repository for archives
associated with political office. There is no evidence in our sources
to suggest that the funeral *laudationes* or other material relating to
the *gens* were kept in this room.[89] No ancient writer calls this a
'family' archive room and none of the material stored there is

[84] Note Augustus' emulation of traditional values in his domestic life, especially
in the weaving and woolworking of his female relatives; Suet. *Aug*. 73. 1.

[85] McKay (1975) 34; Boëthius (1978) 185; Grimal in Grimal and Woloch (1983)
205; Jung (1984) 84. According to this interpretation the *tablinum* is actually the
original 'house' and served as the quarters of the master and mistress.

[86] Bek (1980) 182; Jung (1984) 74 and 78.

[87] One has been preserved in the Casa del Tramezzo di legno at Herculaneum.

[88] Festus 490. 28 L : *tablinum proxime atrium locus dicitur, quod antiqui magistra-
tus in suo imperio tabulis rationum ibi habebant publicarum rationum causa factum locum*
('The place next to the *atrium* is called the *tablinum* because in the old days magistrates during their exercise of high office had there a place designed for public documents to store their ledgers of records'). Plin. *Nat*. 35. 7 = T54 : *tabulina codicibus
implebantur et monimentis rerum in magistratu gestarum* ('The *tablina* were filled with
ledgers of records and accounts of deeds done by office-holders').

[89] *Contra* e.g. Besnier (1953).

described as being genealogical in character. Rather, the *arca* in the *atrium* seems to have been the traditional repository for important family papers and books.

The words used to describe the archives in the *tablinum* are *codices, monimenta,* and *tabulae rationum.* It is in just such a context that we should place the reference in Dionysius of Halicarnassus (1. 74. 5) to censorial records preserved in the family and passed down from father to son.[90] One category of records kept there would be legal documents pertaining to citizenship claims settled by the magistrate in question. Other records of legal decisions would probably also fall into this category.[91] *Tabulae rationum* are financial records of all types, including records of fines collected or of war booty. The accountability of a Roman general for his booty was a vexed question, illustrated by the famous scene in the senate when Scipio Africanus tore up his brother Lucius' records rather than render an account of the vast booty taken after the defeat of Antiochus (Livy 38. 54–5).[92] Clearly a general did expect to keep records but these were regarded as essentially private documents even when state funds were involved.[93] *Monimenta* could refer to *commentarii,* speeches, or other more personal accounts as well as to objects. We know that booty or trophies were displayed more prominently in that part of the *atrium* nearest the entrance itself. Objects kept in the *tablinum* and related to magisterial office may have included the magistrate's curule chair which he owned but could not make use of outside his term of office. Such chairs would be needed for the actors wearing the *imagines* to sit on at a family funeral.[94]

The *tablinum* can, therefore, be closely associated with the master of the house whose records were kept there.[95] Its central position and exceptionally good light, coming both from the open roof of the *atrium* in front and from the peristyle or garden behind, suggest that it was used as a reception and work area. It was often one

[90] The discussion of Gabba (1964) is particularly useful.

[91] By the late Republic, and especially during the imperial period, such records came to be stored in public repositories for use by the growing imperial bureaucracy. This development may have helped to make the *tablinum* seem old-fashioned and largely redundant.

[92] The best treatment is still Shatzman (1972).

[93] See *ILLRP* 431, *ILS* 886, and Augustus *RG* 21. 1 for *manubiae* (the general's share of the booty) as his private property.

[94] On the curule chair, see Schäfer (1989). The chairs actually used at the funeral may have been rented with the rest of the equipment, see Ch. 4 § 5.

[95] See Wallace-Hadrill (1988) 75 and J. R. Clarke (1991) 4.

of the most richly decorated rooms in the house[96] and could serve as a background to the objects of prestige or of religious significance kept in the *atrium*. Unlike most Roman rooms, which had ordinary doorways with curtains or wooden doors, the *tablinum* was completely open on one side and could take up almost a whole wall of the *atrium*. Its entrance was often raised slightly, like a stage, and it was flanked by columns or elaborate door posts (*antae*) which framed the master of the house in his own setting.[97]

To describe this space as a 'study' conveys little of its original atmosphere and function. The name *tablinum* is surely derived from the *tabulae* on which records were written, and emphasizes its main character as an archive room. Just as the *imagines* were kept in the most public part of the house, records of official business were not hidden away in a storage area but were also displayed and made as conspicuous as possible.[98] The special work room of the master was named after the records of state housed there rather than after him or after his activity. The impression already given by the architecture and decoration is confirmed, namely that this is more like a public place than a room in a private house. Moreover, the cultivation of records, complemented by spoils, could call to mind functions and achievements of office even after the actual year of magistracy was well passed. Similarly, a candidate would need to present himself in such a setting before the vote, in order to seem worthy of office to the electors.

The *tablinum* and *atrium* were often used as a single space, which formed the characteristic reception area of the Roman office-holder, and of his family. The design and decor of this space created a unified impression of solemnity and public duty, closely associated with the *imagines* of the ancestors. The master of the house appeared in a highly traditional prestige setting, which can be compared to an elaborate stage set. At the same time, the *tablinum* was a practical, well-lit room which offered convenient access to documents and a view of the various parts of the house and of the activities taking place inside it.

[96] See Richardson (1988) 388.

[97] As Jung (1984) 78 notes, two-thirds of *atrium* houses in Pompeii only presented a view of the *tablinum* to those entering, while one-third also showed the *alae* or some side walls.

[98] Note the very large cupboard running the whole length of one wall of the *tablinum* in the Casa del Menandro; Maiuri (1933) 53-6 and Richardson (1988) 159-61.

3. *Imagines in the* Atrium: *Setting up and Opening the* Armaria

Installing *imagines* in the *atrium* was an essential part of decorating and maintaining a house. In a family with many *imagines* they would also be kept in the *alae* or side wings of the *atrium*. Changes came with each death of an office-holder in the family which would occasion the display of a new mask.[99] Copies of masks would be needed by any offspring at the time of setting up his or her own establishment outside the family house. The political importance of *imagines* in securing support at elections suggests that they would be essential furniture for any young man of ambition who was seeking office but was not living at home.[100]

The classic text on the subject of setting up *imagines* is Cicero's letter to his friend Papirius Paetus advising him which *imagines* to install in his *atrium* (*Fam.* 9. 21 = T24). This is especially interesting as Paetus was a man without political ambitions who lived permanently in Naples.[101] The advice Cicero gives cannot, therefore, be intended for a house in town but testifies to the practice of keeping copies of *imagines* at country establishments. Similarly, Brutus had a set of *imagines* at his villa at Tusculum, which was near Cicero's (*Orat.* 110 = T22). Cicero's letter plainly shows that *imagines* could be installed even of branches of the family with which an individual had no known connections. Personal ideas and political tastes could be used to select a group of suitable ancestors from within the clan as a whole.[102] They formed a display of the living history of the family.

The *imagines* were housed in the *atrium* in special cupboards called *armaria*. There is not much evidence to show what these looked like, but they were perhaps related in style to the shrines of the Lares and to depictions of cupboards on funerary reliefs.[103] A comparison can also be made with panel-pictures (*pinakes*) rendered

---

[99] The *S.C. de Cn. Pisone patre* = 116 suggests that masks were usually made in a man's lifetime and not after his death.

[100] For *imagines* and elections, see § 6 below and Ch. 3.

[101] D'Arms (1970) 191–2.

[102] This is also implied by Mart. 2. 90. 6 = T47. Plin. *Nat.* 35. 8 = T54 records the public scrutiny and criticism directed against such displays by two members of the Messalla family.

[103] The evidence for *armaria* was collected by Budde (1939) 46–9. A more recent treatment of the architectural aspects can be found in Hornbostel-Hüttner (1979). The household shrines from Pompeii have been catalogued by Boyce (1937) and now by Fröhlich (1991), and discussed by Orr (1978).

in a number of Second Style wall-paintings from Pompeii; these paintings are shown in frames with folding wooden shutters which could be closed to protect them.[104] Each cupboard was labeled with a *titulus* recording the name of the ancestor and probably the most basic outline of his career as reflected by the offices he had held.[105] No example of a *titulus* has survived so they can only be reconstructed from the *elogia* found on republican graves[106], the versions collected in books by Varro and Atticus at the end of the Republic, and the comparable evidence from the Forum of Augustus.[107] The cupboards containing the masks were normally kept shut, but it seems most likely that the labels were still legible.[108] Therefore, the labels were probably fixed below the folding doors and formed the focus of the display as it was most commonly seen.

Their accessibility is suggested by ancient *testimonia* about how easily any visitor could see which *imagines* a family possessed as he was passing through the *atrium*. Cicero speaks of both Marcus and Decimus Brutus seeing the *imago* of the first consul in their homes every day (*Phil.* 2. 26 = T12). His remark can be interpreted as rhetorical exaggeration or as a reference to the fact that the *titulus* could be read every time either man entered his *atrium*. In order to maximize the effect of the *imagines* it made sense to keep the *tituli* on display even on days when the masks themselves were not on view. In the context of this separate function of the *titulus* it is also easy to see why the traditional simplicity of these inscriptions survived. Their style would have made them readily understood by most who entered the *atrium*, while maintaining a suitable atmosphere of traditional simplicity and archaic *mores*.

On days of rejoicing and celebration the cupboards were opened and for special occasions the *imagines* might also be decorated with

---

[104] See Van Buren (1938), Ling (1991) 112-28, and J. R. Clarke (1991) 64-2 with figs. 16 and 17.

[105] *Tituli* are often mentioned in connection with *imagines* in ancient sources: Livy 8. 40. 4-5 = T41; 10. 7. 2-4 = T42; 22. 31. 11 = T43; 30. 45. 6-7 = T44; Hor. *S.* 1. 6. 17 = T33; Ov. *Fast.* 1. 591 = T51; *Panegyricus Messallae* 28 ff. = T52; Val. Max. 5. 8. 3 = T103; *Laus Pisonis* 13, 21, and 33 = T36; *CIL* 13. 1668. 2. 25 = T26; Tac. *Dial.* 8. 4 = T93.

[106] Republican *elogia* and particularly the tomb of the Scipios are discussed in Ch. 6.

[107] Nep. *Att.* 18. 5-6 and Plin. *Nat.* 35. 11 = T54 tell us about the books on *imagines* written by Atticus and Varro. Messalla's volume *De Familiis* (Plin. *Nat.* 35. 8 = T54) may also have been related to these works. Cf. Varro's *De Familiis Troianis* (Serv. *A.* 2. 166; 5. 704).

[108] This important point is made by Dupont (1987) 170.

laurel. The opening of the cupboards has been a cause of some confusion, mostly as a result of the testimony of Polybius which is not specific (6. 53. 6 = T61). He states that they were opened and decorated for festivals held at public expense but he does not give examples of what he means.[109] His use of the word ναΐδια ('shrines' at 6. 53. 4 = T61) to describe the cupboards suggests cult, while he is probably only referring to the architectural character some cupboards could assume. His testimony has created a false connection in the minds of scholars between the opening of the *imagines* and the opening of public temples for worship on official holidays. Such a connection easily leads to the unsubstantiated assumption that opening the *imagines* was in some way a cult act or associated closely with official religious observances which were regulated by the state.[110]

In fact there is no evidence for any kind of cult, specifically sacrifices, libations, or prayers addressed to the *imagines*.[111] Given the highly traditional character of Roman religion it would be surprising for no traces of an earlier cult of the *imagines* to be found, if such a cult had ever existed. As has been noted, the smoke-blackened colour typical of some old *imagines* is associated with the presence of the hearth in the *atrium* and cannot, therefore, be used as evidence for sacrifices made directly to the masks. The cupboards containing the *imagines* were probably opened on public holidays as a natural expression of joy and a festive mood.[112] Their closing, although apparently normal in everyday life, could also be construed as a sign of mourning.[113] It is quite unclear how often the *imagines* were on view, as that depended largely on the attitude and fortunes of the individual family.[114]

The evidence provided by Roman authors suggests that the open-

---

[109] 6. 53. 6: ἔν τε ταῖς δημοτελέσι θυσίαις ἀνοίγοντες κοσμοῦσι φιλοτίμως ('They open these masks during public sacrifices and compete in decorating them').

[110] Zadoks (1932) 26 and 33-4 sees this as a trace of earlier ancestor worship.

[111] The case has been argued most persuasively by Bömer (1943) 104-23. J. R. Clarke's (1991) 6-7 assumption that there must have been portable altars used to make offerings to the *imagines* in the *atrium* is a classic example of an argument from silence.

[112] This point is well made by Dupont (1987) 170-1. It is not clear how far her assertion that the Romans wanted their ancestors to participate at feasts can be justified.

[113] This is implied by Val. Max. 3. 5 = T98 and Sen. *Con.* 7. 6. 10 = T71.

[114] It is possible that in a great family with members currently in office the closing of the cupboards might become the exception rather than the rule.

ing of the cupboards was in essence a private gesture of celebration on the part of the family. It served to show the house at its best and to use any joyous occasion for a display of prestige. In contrast, Polybius' testimony reveals that in associating the open cupboards only with public festivals he has misunderstood or not fully grasped Roman practice. Cicero's client Murena decorated his father's *imago* with laurel to celebrate his own election to the consulship (*Mur.* 88 = T11).[115] For him this was a private way of signalling a victory rather than a public observance or cult act. Similarly, a defendant who won a lawsuit was expected to return home to change out of his mourning garb into holiday dress and to open his *imagines* to mark the occasion (Cic. *Sulla* 88 = T19).[116] The practice of opening and decorating *imagines* was an important part of life in any aristocratic home and served to indicate changing seasons and moments of solemnity or festive rejoicing for the family. As in so many other matters, this custom was subject to the power of the *pater familias* to regulate, who set the tone for the household and the public face it showed to the world.

4. *The* Imagines *and the Cult of the Ancestors*

The Romans did have cult associated with their ancestors,[117] which was practised at the graveside, either on appropriate public feasts, such as the Parentalia, or on personal anniversaries. For cult purposes the deceased members of the family were thought of collectively as the *di manes* or *di parentes*. The *di manes* were spirits of

---

[115] Cicero's use of *clarissimus* (highly distinguished) to describe Murena's father, who had only reached the praetorship, is rather misleading.

[116] As late as the 3rd cent. AD the accession of the emperor Tacitus was said to have been the occasion for frequent opening of *imagines* and other celebrations in senatorial homes to mark the accession of one of their number to the imperial throne (*H. A. Tac.* 19. 6 = T32 referring to AD 275-6). See Ch. 9 for discussion of this difficult source. Mommsen (1887) 492 and Saller (1984) 351 are mistaken in assuming that the last sentence of T19 shows that under the *Lex Cornelia de ambitu* of 67 BC a conviction carried with it a ban on the exhibition of *imagines* in the *atrium*. Sulla's previous conviction merely meant that he could not return to his house in Rome.

[117] Ancestral cult and the exorcism of spirits is treated by Wissowa (1912) 232-5 and 434, Latte (1960) 98-100, and Toynbee (1971) 48-55, and 61 ff. See Cic. *Phil.* I. 13 on the differences between cult of gods and cult of the dead, with Classen (1962) 202-3. For Greek tomb and hero cults, see Antonaccio (1993) especially 47 where she comments that Greek ancestors received little attention as they did not determine a citizen's rights or duties in the *polis*.

deceased family members lacking in individuality and unconnected with political office. Even at individual grave sites cult seems to have been directed to the ancestors in this collective capacity. Their cult was in no way restricted to any particular social class. Nothing could be further removed from the *imago*, which was always a representation of an individual office-holding family member and a device for recalling his life and character. There is no evidence at all to suggest that the *imagines* were ever present at the grave or played any role there.

Other observances of an apotropaic nature associated with the Lemuria were directed at the appeasement of ghosts and restless or malicious spirits of the deceased. These practices took place in the home because they were designed to protect the house, but were not focused specifically on spirits of individual deceased members of that same family.[118]

Domestic cult could take place in the *atrium* at the shrine of the Lares which was called *sacrarium* or *aedicula* in republican times.[119] These terms denoting domestic shrines are not applied in our extant sources to the cupboards containing the *imagines*. Offerings were made to the Penates, the household Lares, and the Genius of the *pater familias*. The origins of the Lares are obscure but attempts to see them as deified ancestors are unconvincing. There is a rich body of iconographic evidence from Pompeii and Herculaneum showing that they are consistently depicted as youthful, happy figures dancing on tiptoes and holding rhyta full of wine, often in a pastoral setting. It is evident from all we know about Roman society that no aristocrat would have wanted to see his ancestors portrayed in this way.[120] The images of ancestors in all media stress dignity and age, together with social standing and prestige. The Lares are associated with fields and especially with crossroads, suggesting their original role as agricultural deities who protected the boundaries of property.[121] They contrast with the serious pose and Roman costume of the Genius who frequently appears with them. There is, therefore, no evidence, either literary or archaeological, for a cult of the ancestors in the home, let

[118] For the Lemuria, see Wissowa (1912) 235-6, Toynbee (1971) 61-4, and Dixon (1992) 133 ff.
[119] Domestic cult is thoroughly discussed by Orr (1978) and Harmon (1978). For shrines of the Lares in the *atrium*, see the Casa di Epidio Rufo, the Casa di M. Lucretio, and the Villa dei Papyri at Herculaneum.
[120] This is argued by Orr (1978) 1579.
[121] For the Lares and Genius, see Wissowa (1912) 166-81 and Fröhlich (1991).

alone one specifically connected with the *imagines* in the *atrium*. In the earlier Empire there is some evidence for family inscriptions recording the *cursus* of a deceased relative being kept in the shrine of the Lares, but this appears to be a separate usage for which there is not enough evidence at the moment.[122]

5. *Family Trees and other Representations of Ancestors in the Home*

During the Republic the character of the *atrium* as a showplace for the history of the family was developed and enhanced by various allusions to and representations of ancestors. Ancestral trophies, busts, statues, paintings, and shield portraits have been mentioned earlier as part of the evidence of the elder Pliny about the *imagines*.[123] In the context of the *atrium* special stress needs to be given to the painted family trees (*stemmata*) which Pliny also mentions as a feature of the aristocratic house (*Nat.* 35. 6 = T54).[124] These are described by him specifically as including painted portraits joined by lines to show connections within the family.[125] It is easy to see how such painted panels could serve as an explanation for a row of cupboards with their *imagines* and *tituli*. The number of *imagines* amassed by leading families might otherwise present a confusing spectacle. The character of family trees is also a public one since they served to explain family history and relations in more detail to anyone in the *atrium*.

The evidence we have for Roman family trees mostly dates to the imperial period, but their origins may be very ancient.[126] It has

[122] Senatorial *cursus* inscriptions have been found in the shrine of the Lares at the villa of the Volusii near Lucus Feroniae (*AE* 1972, 174-6 and Eck (1972)). At least one of these was set up by freedmen of the family, not by the master of the house. See Moretti and Sgubini Moretti (1977) for illustrations and Boatwright (1982) and Panciera (1982) for the text.

[123] See Ch. 2, § 1c for discussion of these different portraits.

[124] Family trees are best treated by Bettini (1991) 167 ff. Cf. Zinserling (1959/60) 431: 'Die gemalten Rangporträts, von denen die Triumphatordarstellungen nur eine Spielart sind, neben denen ebenso viele andere bestanden, wie es öffentliche Ämter in Rom gab, bilden als Typus das Bindeglied zwischen den 'simulacra' der Triumphzüge und den 'imagines' der pompa funebris.'

[125] Attempts by Mommsen to interpret Pliny's description as referring to the *armaria* containing the *imagines* linked by string to form a kind of three dimensional family tree have been refuted by Zadoks (1932) 108, Vessberg (1941) 103-5, and Boëthius (1942) 230.

[126] Our best *testimonia* about family trees include Sall. *Jug.* 85. 10 = T66; Sen. *Ben.* 3. 28. 2 = T74; Mart. 4. 40. 1; 5. 35; Juv. 8. 1, 6, 40 = T35; Plut. *Numa* 21. 4; Suet. *Ner.* 37. 1 = T81; *Gal.* 2 = T82; *Ves.* 12; *H.A. Sev. Alex.* 44. 3; Isid. *Etym.* 9. 6. 28.

been argued that the Etruscan nobility also had such displays.[127] Persius, who was from Volterra, alludes to the complexity of Etruscan family trees (3. 28). We know that Maecenas had a family tree in his house on the Esquiline, which seems to have presented his maternal ancestors, the Cilnii of Arezzo, on an equal footing with his father's family.[128] Any family tree that was at all extensive would have needed to record marriages and therefore to include the women in the family. To be effective such family trees would have to be kept up to date and might also be redrawn to stress new marriages or alliances.

In a famous satire Juvenal attacks the pomp of ancestral displays and mentions nearly all of Rome's leading families (*Satire* 8 = T35). This poem has caused problems of interpretation as it seems to refer to ancestors represented in different media including traditional *imagines*.[129] The most natural interpretation is to imagine the scene as set in the *atrium* where ancestor masks were accompanied and explained by family trees that could include painted portraits. Such a display could conjure up a whole range of episodes from a family's history in a way that was readily understandable. We have several references to the elaborate display that could be seen in the *atria* of the Calpurnii Pisones.[130]

Ancient literary sources suggest that by the height of the Roman Empire narrative historical paintings could also be a feature of aristocratic houses, often in the peristyle.[131] We do not know at what date such paintings became a regular part of ancestral displays in the home. An interesting analogy is provided by Petronius, at the beginning of the *Cena Trimalchionis*, in his description of the entrance to Trimalchio's house (*Sat.* 29).[132] It was decorated with a continuous narrative of Trimalchio's life, depicted as a series of scenes with explanatory labels and parallels from epic.[133]

---

[127] Heurgon (1964) 258-60.   [128] Prop. 3. 19; Hor. *Carm.* 3. 29. 1.

[129] See Syme (1939) 490-1 for the social context of this satire.

[130] Cic. *Pis.* 1 = T13; *Laus Pisonis* = T36; Mart. 4. 40. 1-4; cf. Ch. 9.

[131] Plin. *Nat.* 2. 17. 4; Sid. Apoll. 22. 150-168; *H.A. Gordian* 3. Rawson (1990) 171 assumes this was a common genre.

[132] For the use of Trimalchio's house as an analogy to real houses of the period, see Maiuri (1945) 243-5, Bagnani (1954), and Wallace-Hadrill (1988) 44 and (1994) 3, 6, 61. Ling (1991) 8 uses Trimalchio's gallery of Greek paintings as evidence for the kinds of paintings which would have inspired Pompeiian artists. The *Cena* is often imagined as taking place at Puteoli.

[133] Rebuffat (1978) sees these labels as a take off of the archaic style. Aelian 10. 10 makes fun of old paintings which are so crude that they need labels to identify each object.

Particularly striking is the theme of the triumph which is exploited in Trimalchio's entry into Rome as a slave about to be sold at the market. The element of parody is evident here.[134] Trimalchio the wealthy freedman boasts of his rise using iconography reminiscent of that commonly used for the exploits of a Roman general.[135] Such an advertisement of his origins makes most sense as a variation on an existing tradition of painting to be found in the houses of the élite, which celebrated the glorious exploits of the family and its ancestors, and which may also have drawn on scenes from myth.[136] Many of Trimalchio's habits are outrageous variations on recognizable practices of the aristocracy or of the imperial household. This series of paintings is imagined as being near the door in the entrance (probably the *vestibulum*) and in the peristyle which seems to come before the *atrium*. The plan of Trimalchio's house is similar to that of the Villa of the Mysteries at Pompeii as it was in the time of Augustus.[137]

A comparison can be made in both style and content between the type of paintings Petronius is envisaging and fragments of tomb paintings, especially those from republican tombs near the Esquiline gate and those from the tomb of the Scipios (see Fig. 13).[138] The so-called 'tomb of the Fabii' is generally dated to the third century BC, although the war referred to in the frescoes has not been securely identified.[139] The paintings in this tomb also appear to convey an historical narrative in a series of interconnected scenes which combine stress on Rome's greatness and the particular role played by an individual or family.[140] The paintings in effect narrate the *res*

[134] Cf. Wallace-Hadrill (1988) 48: 'Trimalchio blunderingly parodies the language of Roman luxury, rather than communicating in it.'

[135] For Trimalchio as a reflection of the life of a freedman, see Veyne (1961).

[136] I am less convinced by Bagnani's (1954) idea that Trimalchio has unwittingly reproduced tomb paintings in a house, despite his obsession with death and with his own grave monument.

[137] It is also possible that a description of the *atrium* has fallen out of the text.

[138] Coarelli (1976) 13–21 and 22–8 remains the basic treatment of the Esquiline tomb paintings, with illustrations and previous bibliography. More recently, see Mansuelli (1979) and La Rocca (1984).

[139] La Rocca (1984) offers an alternative interpretation of the tomb and its paintings as belonging to a Fannius, an infantryman below the rank of *eques*. Cf. Ling (1991) 10. For a cuirass inscribed with the name Novius Fannius, which seems to have been part of a trophy perhaps celebrating victory over the Samnites, see Colonna (1984).

[140] See the narrative frescoes from the François tomb in Vulci (see Fig. 14), showing scenes from Etruscan history, paralleled with episodes from Greek myth and epic. The date of the tomb is disputed but the paintings are now thought to be 4th cent. BC.

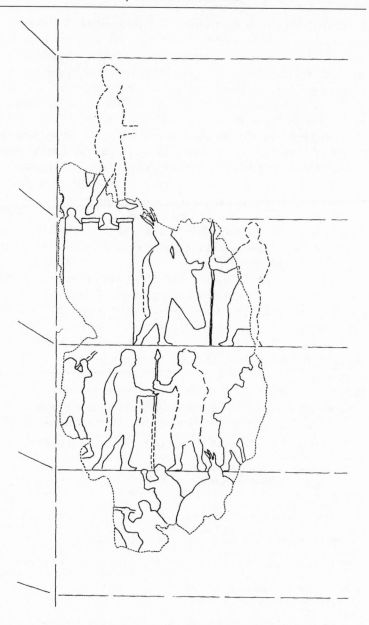

FIG. 13. Painting from the 'Tomb of the Fabii' on the Esquiline, Rome. Dotted and broken lines indicate reconstructions.

gestae of a central figure in a recognizable form like the eulogy at a funeral or the inscription on a sarcophagus.[141] They were visual expressions of the format used in annalistic history.

The meagre fragments from the 'tomb of the Fabii' do not allow any extensive reconstruction of the whole, but it seems as if most of the interior was illustrated and traces of four registers have survived. Similarly, the late second-century BC Arieti tomb discovered nearby has frescoes which apparently illustrate episodes from a triumph stretching across several walls. Scenes of battle were apparently the subject of the paintings on the façade of the tomb of the Scipios.[142] It is tempting to posit links since these frescoes from tombs seem to parallel paintings described as being inside the Roman house, probably in the *atrium* or in the peristyles which took over many functions of the *atrium* in imperial times. Such cycles of paintings could illustrate the elaborate family trees found in the *atrium* or *vestibulum*. The paintings would be more accessible and dramatic than the *imagines*, which were often hidden inside their cupboards.

A current interpretation of Roman tomb paintings is that they can give us a notion of the now completely lost genre of Roman triumphal art.[143] As part of the triumph it was usual, at least as early as the late third century BC, to display pictures illustrating battles, captured cities, maps, and especially the role of generals. Although such paintings are assumed by modern scholars to have had little artistic merit, they were a vital aristocratic genre and were often deposited in temples as a sort of votive, on permanent display after the triumph. Paintings of this type provided direct commentary on recent events and could communicate a powerful political message. Historical frescoes could also be specially commissioned for the interior walls of temples, often those built in fulfillment of a vow by a

Its shape has been interpreted as a reference to the interior of an aristocratic house, suggesting that the paintings are in the *atrium*. See discussions by Mansuelli (1968), Rebuffat (1978), Coarelli (1983), Maggiani (1983), Brilliant (1984) 31-5, La Rocca (1984) 34, and Ling (1991) 9.

[141] See Mansuelli (1979) 50 and La Rocca (1984) 50.

[142] Traces of paint inside the 4th-cent. BC Tomb of the Cornelii suggest that its walls may also have been decorated. Cf. Pisani Sartorio and Quilici Gigli (1987/8) 255.

[143] Zinserling (1959/60) collects the ancient evidence for triumphal paintings. Cf. Frova (1961), Brilliant (1984) 26-7, and now Kleiner (1992) 47-8 who discusses the evolution of triumphal painting as a new Roman genre developed from Hellenistic maps by artists who went on campaign as part of a general's staff.

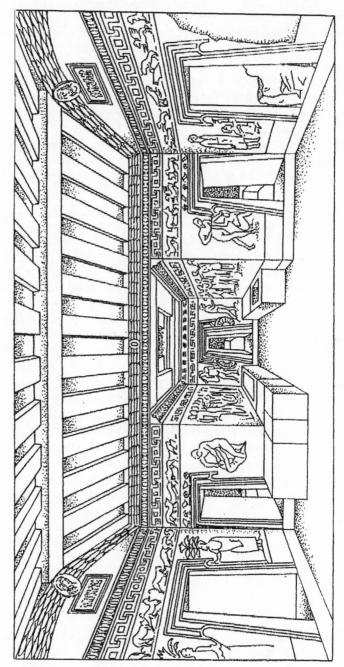

FIG. 14. Reconstruction of the 'atrium' of the François Tomb, Vulci.

victorious general.[144] There is some indication that triumphal paintings may have been exhibited at aristocratic funerals as a part of the same procession in which the *imagines* appeared.[145] The habit of storing some of these paintings in the house, together with trophies and other objects from triumphs, could have encouraged frescoes on similar subjects, specially executed to decorate the house in its own right.

The history of narrative historical painting at Rome is largely unwritten because whole genres, such as triumphal paintings or narrative frescoes on ancestral themes in domestic settings, can only be recovered from scattered references in literary sources of widely differing periods. Meanwhile, the fragments of tomb paintings are meagre and remain controversial in their own context. The connections between these various genres of painting remain elusive and yet shared subjects, style, and purpose suggest a common function in Roman society, a function not unlike that of the *imagines*.[146] Narrative paintings featured the deeds of ancestors or of living family members and expressed aristocratic values in their martial themes and in their emphasis on office and rank. Individuals were identified clearly, usually by labels, and were shown exercising leadership at key moments of success. In effect, narrative paintings of similar style seem to have played an important public role in some houses, and in processions and temples.

6. Imagines *and Visitors to the House: The* Salutatio

The audience for displays in the *atrium* included anyone who entered the house because Roman houses only had one main entrance and it opened onto the street. Yet there can be little doubt that the visitors who came to the morning *salutatio* of the master of the house were a specially targeted group. The habit of receiving

---

[144] Dentzer (1967) has collected the *testimonia* for paintings of historical scenes in temples. Cf. Coarelli (1988) 167 ff., with review by Palmer (1990), on Pacuvius.
[145] Cf. Ch. 3 § 2.
[146] The most convincing attempt to integrate literary and archaeological evidence remains Mansuelli (1979), although he does not discuss frescoes in houses. See esp. 50 : 'Il rituale del funerale gentilizio che impressionò profondamente Polibio al di là della sua macchionosa teatralità e l'elogio oratorio fatto della persona rientra nello stesso ordine di idee e, per le tombe esquiline, la perpetuazione di questo mondo di gesta e di vanti sulle pareti di un sepolcro si pone anche in parallelo con la conservazione delle *imagines* nel sistema genealogico nell' ambito della casa privata.'

callers in the early morning before preceding to the Forum or to other business outside the home was at the centre of the life of a Roman aristocrat.[147] Our evidence for the Roman *salutatio* mostly comes from the late Republic and the Empire.[148] By this time the *salutatio* had taken on a new political significance beyond the fulfilment of obligations by clients in a dependent status. Visitors of any rank might call on a Roman noble in the morning to transact business, gain favours, or show support. In turn, a man seeking election to public office needed to cultivate support and a public image by having a large crowd at his house, thus drawing attention to his importance.

Polybius (31. 29. 8) already alludes to the *salutatio* as an habitual occupation of young aristocrats in Rome in the second century BC. He does not choose to explain this typically Roman institution, nor does he connect it with the *imagines*. Polybius' reference can be supplemented by an inscription from Teos recording a decree of Abdera dated to 166 BC. This text confirms that the *salutatio* was an essential part of Roman political life and a time-consuming duty for the foreign envoys honoured in the decree for their success in diplomatic manœuvres at Rome.[149] Further evidence comes from Valerius Maximus' account of T. Manlius Torquatus' harsh treatment of his son in 140 BC (5. 8. 3 = T103).[150] After the son's suicide the father did not attend the funeral, but rather took up his position in the *atrium*, as was his custom, to receive callers in the presence of his *imagines*, whose example had encouraged him in the severe stance he had adopted. The scene makes best sense at the morning *salutatio*, which would have been cancelled under normal circumstances on the day of a family funeral and perhaps also during mourning before and after.[151] The *salutatio* was, therefore,

[147] This practice is treated by Hug in *RE* s.v. *salutatio*, Friedländer (1919) I. 195 ff., and Kroll (1933) 187–90. The origins of the custom are obscure to us and may lie in the feudal practices of landlords or dynasts in early Roman history and perhaps in the habits of Etruscan warlords. Clients or serfs who were dependent on their lord could be sure to find him in the early morning. Cf. Wallace-Hadrill (1994) 12: 'what is at issue here is more than a specific social ritual; it is the vital interface between public and private in Roman life.'

[148] For the imperial period, see Saller (1982) 11–2, 61–2 and 128–9.

[149] *SIG*³ 656. 26 with Hermann (1971): ἡ καθ᾽ ἡμέραν ἐφοδεία ἐπὶ τῶν ἀτρέων ('the daily round of visiting the *atria*').

[150] T. Manlius Torquatus (*RE* 83, cos. 165 BC) is the father, D. Junius Silanus (*RE* 161) is the son. Their severe ancestor is T. Manlius Torquatus (*RE* 57, cos. 340 BC).

[151] See § 1 above and Ch. 4 § 1 on the closing of the house for mourning.

already a well-established part of Roman life in the second century BC.

According to Seneca, important changes took place in the character of the *salutatio* as a result of the actions of Gaius Gracchus and of Livius Drusus (*Ben.* 6. 34. 1–2). They lived more public lives and sought new ways to gain political support. One was by dividing their callers into three categories of 'friends', presumably to make access to themselves seem more important and special. Only their intimates were allowed a private audience, while callers of the second rank were kept waiting in the *atrium*, being admitted only in groups, and the common man might not even get past the doorkeeper. Seneca disapproved of such practices but reveals that they were still standard in his day. The increasingly formal and elaborate *salutatio* meant more visitors spent longer periods waiting in the *atrium*, a space dominated by the *imagines* and related displays of family prestige.

When Marius returned to Rome after many years of campaigns abroad, he moved near the Forum in order to increase attendance at his house in the morning (Plut. *Marius* 32. 1). Such a move, especially to the Palatine district, became a standard feature of the career of an ambitious Roman. Cicero left his father's house to his brother and moved nearer the centre of political action on his return from his quaestorship in Sicily.[152] He defends a move to the Palatine by his young client Caelius as necessary both in enabling more callers to attend his house and in allowing him easier access to the houses of patrons like Cicero himself (*Cael.* 18). Caelius' accusers were trying to create prejudice against him because he moved away from his father's house, a practice which would have been unusual in an earlier age. Evidence about the role of the *salutatio* in campaigning for high office in the late Republic can be found in the letter of advice addressed to Cicero by his brother Quintus at the time of his campaign for the consulship, although its authorship is disputed.[153] The importance of the *salutatio* in politics, and especially for the elections, helps to explain the significance of the *imagines* as powerful symbols in the minds of Roman voters.

As a boy Cato was taken by his tutor as part of his education to

---

[152] *Planc.* 66 and Plut. *Cic.* 8.

[153] Even at the time of Caesar's dictatorship Cicero could take comfort that his own *salutationes* were still crowded with sympathizers. Atticus urges him to regard this as his own private forum (*Fam.* 9. 20. 3; *Att.* 12. 21 and 23).

attend the *salutationes* of Sulla where he was usually admitted in private and allowed to sit on Sulla's bed.[154] It was in the *atrium* of Sulla's house that he saw a shameless display of the heads of victims of the proscriptions, presumably in sharp contrast to the *imagines* of the patrician Cornelii. This prompted Cato to suggest to Sarpedon his tutor that he should himself take this opportunity to try to kill Sulla with a sword he could smuggle in.[155] Cicero himself was also the target of such an assassination attempt during his consulship by adherents of Catiline.[156] The conspirators planned to attack him at the *salutatio*. The attack on the *atrium* and *imagines* of Lepidus, discussed earlier in the chapter, should be placed in this context of political violence which was no longer confined to public places or to the streets. In this way the *atrium* became more of a waiting area for political followers than a private reception room, and dangers attended a Roman office-holder in this most public part of his house.[157] The increasingly politicized nature of the *salutatio* inevitably set the tone for the *atrium*, and affected the character and purpose of the display of *imagines* and a family tree in this setting.[158] It had become the scene of political rallies and gatherings, with their attendant violence, rather than a room in which much of the family's domestic life still regularly took place. Hence Seneca's dictum quoted below the title of this chapter: a real friend should not be sought amongst the crowd in the *atrium*.

7. *Imagines* and the Aristocratic Family

The *imagines* and their *tituli* kept alive the traditional catalogue of aristocratic virtues and confirmed that politics was the sphere in which a Roman *nobilis* must operate to acquire an identity of his own within his caste. Naturally this created special pressure on the young, for whom the *imagines* served as didactic reminders while

[154] Val. Max. 3. 1. 2: *capita proscriptorum in atrium adlata vidisset* ('He had seen the heads of the proscribed brought into the *atrium*') with Plut. *Cato min.* 3. 2–4.

[155] Similarly, Livius Drusus' assassination amidst the throngs who had followed him home from the Forum probably took place just in front of his house. Vell. Pat. 2. 14 notes the position of Livius' house on the Palatine overlooking the Forum.

[156] Cic. *Cat.* 1. 10; *Sulla* 52; Sall. *Cat.* 28. 1.

[157] For the general increase in violence in the later Republic, see Lintott (1968).

[158] Horace, Martial, and Juvenal provide ample testimony about the continuation of the *salutatio* under the Empire, both for the emperor and leading citizens. This practice was still current in the 3rd cent. AD in the time of Dio. See Ch. 9 below.

they were growing up. From their earliest youth their ancestors, as represented by the *imagines* in the *atrium*, were a part of everyday life, conditioning their self-esteem and expectations, as well as how others treated and viewed them. Polybius tried to suggest this peculiarly aristocratic ethos in his description of the Roman funeral, but similar ideas can already be found in Plautus.[159] Accordingly, the ancestors served as an inspiration or as a daunting standard to live up to.[160] They could even be described as a burden for the young.[161] Their effect was two edged: the achievements of the ancestors were often hard to emulate, while failure carried with it a powerful element of shame.[162] Throughout his life a Roman was expected to act as if constantly in their presence and to consider himself as answerable to them. They were symbolized by the *imagines* which he had to face whenever he entered his house.[163]

During the Republic, therefore, the *imagines* themselves defined the role and values of the *nobilis*, his very sense of self. It is not enough to consider them simply as advertising tools designed for cleverly staged demonstrations of status to impress the humble visitor in the *atrium*. They may often have been used in such a way and many citizens may have felt overawed by them.[164] Yet they also came to embody a standard of behaviour and achievement which was required of a member of an office-holding family, if he was to be accepted by society in general as worthy of his position. Pressure on the *nobiles* themselves was equivalent to and sometimes greater than the influence the *imagines* could exercise over the people.[165]

---

[159] Esp. *Trin.* 642 ff.

[160] Inspiration from *imagines*: Polyb. 6. 53-4 = T61; Afranius *Vopiscus* 12. 364-5 = T1; Cic. *Phil.* 2. 26 = T12; Sall. *Jug.* 4. 5-6 = T65; *Panegyricus Messallae* 28 ff. = T52; Val. Max. 5. 8. 3 = T103; Vell. Pat. 2. 116. 4 = T106; *Laus Pisonis* = T36; Tac. *Ann.* 2. 27 = T85; Cf. Suet. *Ves.* 12.

[161] Plin. *Ep.* 3. 3. 6 = T56 is especially telling. Cf. Plin. *Ep.* 8. 10. 3 = T58 for the strong connection between *imagines* and the careers of children. Val. Max. 5. 5 = T102 speaks of brothers especially sharing their *imagines*.

[162] Not measuring up to one's *imagines*: Cic. *Mur.* 88 = T11; *Cael.* 33-4 = T5; *Pis.* 1 = T13; *Planc.* 51 = T15; *De Or.* 2. 225 = T23; Sall. *Jug.* 85. 10 ff. = T66; Sen. *Con.* 1. 6. 3 = T68; Val. Max. 3. 3. 7 = T97; 3. 5 = T98; Juv. 8 = T35; Plut. *Mar.* 9. 2 = T60. See Ch. 1 for the element of shame in Roman society.

[163] Cic. *Mur.* 88 = T11 and Plin. T57 in the epigraph to this chapter.

[164] Hor. *S.* 1. 6. 17 = T33.

[165] Harris (1979) 10-41 provides the most helpful discussion of the military ethos of the Roman élite. For *imagines* and Empire, see Sall. *Jug.* 4. 5-6 = T65; 85. 10 ff. = T66a-c; Val. Max. 2. 9. 6 = T96; Plin. *Nat.* 35. 7 = T54; Plut. *Mar.* 9. 2 = T60.

8. *Conclusion*

The diverse material surveyed in this chapter indicates the importance of the *atrium* in the Roman republican house and the central role of the *imagines* within that *atrium*. Whether their cupboards were closed and only the *tituli* were to be seen, or whether they were displayed and decorated for some family celebration or public holiday, the *imagines* provided the focus for this sparsely-furnished entrance and reception area. The *imagines* also served as a background, both physical and historical, for the various ceremonies held in the *atrium* on the occasion of birth, coming of age, marriage, or death. They inspired and defined any other ancestral displays such as family trees, busts, shield portraits, trophies, or wall-paintings illustrating exploits of family members. The *imagines* symbolized the continuing role of the ancestors within the household. Their presence had a powerful effect both on the family living in the house and on visitors, especially at the morning *salutatio*. This effect shaped relations between the family and others, notably the ordinary citizen and voter.

8

Imagines and the New Principate: Augustus and Tiberius

> Hostility to the *nobiles* was engrained in the Principate from its military and revolutionary origins.
>
> (Syme (1939) 502)

THERE is not enough evidence to write the history of the *imagines* in any detail after the death of Tiberius. Many scholars have come to believe that *imagines* vanished rapidly from aristocratic funerals under the Julio-Claudian emperors,[1] whereas the sources indicate that they were not restricted to funerals of the ruling house until the third century AD.[2] The present study has concentrated largely on the *imagines* in their original, republican setting, rather than as symbols of the values of an earlier political and social system. However, as the *S.C. de Cn. Pisone patre* shows, evidence from the imperial period, and especially from the reigns of Augustus and Tiberius, is vital to any general understanding of the *imagines* in Roman culture.[3] Much of this chapter aims to explore Augustus' use of *imagines* for his own special purposes.[4] The first *princeps* borrowed and adapted traditional aristocratic ancestor masks to create an iconography for his new political order and to design a series of magnificent funerals which reflected his family's leading position within the community. The precedents he set shaped reactions both by successors and pretenders to the throne, in the Julio-Claudian period and beyond.

---

[1] e.g. Zadoks (1932); Drerup (1980); Lahusen (1985*b*).

[2] Dio 47. 19. 2 = T27 and Pomponius Porfyrio commenting on Hor. *Ep.* 8 = T34*a*. See Ch. 9 for discussion.

[3] This text is discussed in Ch. 1 and 2 § 2*a*.

[4] I have found Rowell (1940) the most helpful discussion of Augustus and *imagines*.

1. *Augustus and the* Imagines

Much surviving information about *imagines* results from Augustus' concern with, and use of, them. Consequently, he is an important figure in their history. The essence of Augustus' use of *imagines* was to help define his position as *princeps*, or 'leading citizen', for his contemporaries and for posterity. At the end of his life the *Res Gestae* confirmed Augustus' personal claim to preeminence based above all on his *auctoritas* (personal influence).[5] Romans would have measured the validity of his assertion in terms of traditional standards of aristocratic excellence, which were symbolized and defined in a special way by the *imagines* and their related inscriptions. Augustus drew most importantly and spectacularly on the *imagines* in the construction of the Forum of Augustus, with its inclusion of republican heroes, and in the development of imperial funerals. These two areas will be explored in the following sections.

1a. *The Forum of Augustus*

Augustus himself was born into the relatively undistinguished family of the Octavii, whose ancestors were mostly equestrian[6] and, therefore, without *imagines*. However, his adoption by Caesar brought him into a patrician house, with pretensions to Trojan origins and a tradition of grand political funerals.[7] Augustus, therefore, worked hard to justify his leadership in competition with the heritage of Rome's greatest families.[8] In his new forum he juxtaposed a record of his own achievements directly with statues and inscriptions honouring famous earlier leaders from his own and other families. These statues have clear affinities with the *imagines* and their *tituli*. The whole complex surrounding the grandiose

---

[5] *RG* 34. 3: *Post id tempus auctoritate omnibus praestiti, potestatis autem nihilo amplius habui quam ceteri qui mihi quoque in magistratu conlegae fuerunt* ('After that time I surpassed all in influence, although I had no more legal power than the others who were my colleagues in each magistracy').

[6] See Suet. *Aug*. 2. 3: *ipse Augustus nihil amplius quam equestri familia ortum se scribit vetere ac locuplete, et in qua primus senator pater suus fuerit* ('Augustus himself writes that he came from nothing grander than an equestrian family, although an old and wealthy one, and one in which his father was the first senator)'. This section is attributed to his biography by Malcovati (1976) fr. 3.

[7] The coinage of the Julii had advertised their Trojan origin in the late 2nd cent. BC, e.g. Crawford 320. For Caesar's political use of funerals, see Ch. 4 § 6.

[8] See Sen. *De Clem*. 1. 9. 10 = T73 for an imaginary scene set in AD 4 in which Augustus tells his would-be assassin Cinna that any *princeps* must answer to the traditional aristocrats who follow the example set by their *imagines*.

temple of Mars Ultor dedicated in 2 BC has been read as the most
complete and systematic presentation of Augustus' vision of a new
Roman order centring on himself as its leading citizen (see Figs. 15
and 16).[9]

The magnificent space was dominated by the huge façade of the
temple of Mars inscribed with Augustus' name, which faced the
honorary statue voted by the senate showing the *princeps* in a four
horse chariot (*quadriga*) with the inscription 'father of his country'.[10] The title of *pater patriae* appears as the culmination of the
honours awarded to Augustus in his lifetime, which was presumably why the inscription was also set up in the entrance to his
house.[11] The bestowal of this singular honour came in his thir-
teenth and last consulship as the climax of the definition of his place
in society which had been evolving since 27 BC. Having been a military ruler with emergency powers, Augustus decided to step down
from his position as warlord and to seek a role within a 'restored'
Roman state along familiar, ancestral lines. It seems that he
intended and planned from his return to Rome after Actium to reestablish many elements of the Roman constitution and to describe
his own pre-eminence in terms of honours rather than of powers.[12]

Augustus' process of self-definition was not completed until 2 BC
and coincided with the dedication of his forum as a new centre to
complement traditional public places in the city.[13] The dynastic
nature of the accompanying celebrations, the first annual *Ludi
Martiales* and the *Lusus Troiae*, was underlined by the roles of Gaius

[9] Zanker (1968) 26 and Bonnefond (1987) 251. Cf. Simon (1986) 46–51 who
notes that no other Augustan building took so long to complete. According to Plin.
Nat. 36. 102 the Forum was the most beautiful building complex in the world.

[10] Anderson (1984) 73 reconstructs the impact of the temple on the Forum as a
whole. See Siebler (1988) for the origins and associations of the statue of Mars and
of its cult.

[11] RG 35: *Tertium decimum consulatum cum gerebam, senatus et equester ordo populusque Romanus universus appellavit me patrem patriae, idque in vestibulo aedium mearum
inscribendum et in curia Iulia et in foro Augusto sub quadrigis quae mihi ex s. c. positae
sunt censuit* ('When I was holding my 13th consulship, the senate and the equestrian
order and the whole Roman people hailed me as "father of the country". And they
resolved that this title should be inscribed in the entrance of my house and in the
Curia Julia and in the Forum of Augustus under the four-horse chariot statue which
had been put up for me by decree of the senate').

[12] Such an evolutionary view of Augustus' constitutional position has been best
developed by Badian (1982).

[13] The dedication date has been established as 12 May by Simpson (1977). Cf.
Siebler (1988) 172 for a discussion of the supplanting of Jupiter on the Capitol.

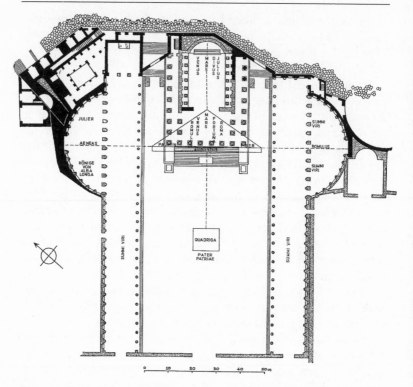

FIG. 15. Ground plan of the Forum of Augustus with a reconstruction of the niches for the statues, Rome.

and Lucius Caesar, both now wearing their *togae viriles*.[14] Bonnefond's important study of the role of the forum in civic life has revealed how it served to replay the message of the *princeps* and his family as leaders in war and peace through a wide array of ceremonies and observances, as well as through much daily business in law and politics.[15] The new forum effectively served as the public *atrium* of the Julii and as the setting for Roman foreign policy as it

[14] *RG* 22. 2; Dio 55. 10. Gaius and Lucius were now first called *principes iuventutis* ('leaders of the youth') and appeared on coins with silver shields and spears which had been presented to them by the equestrian order. Bonnefond (1987) 260-1 remarks on the dynastic setting of the forum.

[15] Cf. Dio 55. 10 for the *lex templi*. This law has been discussed by Anderson (1984) 88-99, and thoroughly reappraised by Bonnefond (1987), whose interpretations I follow here.

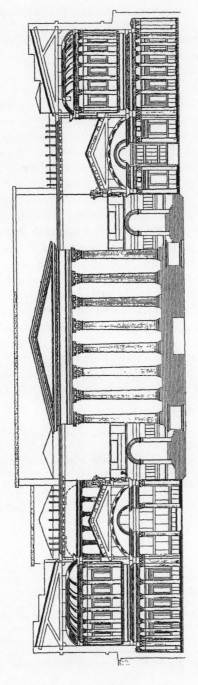

Fig. 16. Proposed reconstruction of the Forum of Augustus, Rome, (NW–SE).

was presented to official visitors to the city. Like an *atrium* in a house it was closely connected with the display of spoils and the memory of past triumphs.[16]

The complex iconography of the Forum of Augustus has been the subject of intensive study since its first systematic excavation in the 1930s. However, the importance of its statues of famous Romans of the past for a consideration of the *imagines* has only been adumbrated rather than fully explored.[17] In many ways the most striking innovation in the whole series of structures was the extensive sculptural programme, presenting great leaders from Roman history with brief descriptions of their careers and achievements.[18] Ovid, who had been in Rome at the time of the dedication of the temple of Mars Ultor, shows us that the comparison with *imagines* and their *tituli* came readily to mind for a contemporary viewer, in this case one who hoped to win favour with the imperial house.[19]

The outer frame for the complex, which contained the statues of Roman heroes, was constructed first and seems to have been in use as a public space for business before the official dedication of the temple itself. Shade and protection from the weather was afforded by the colonnade running down each side of the forum and along the series of statues. This walkway was set apart by being raised slightly above the level of the forum and of the two hemicycles which served as special foci of attention.[20] The statues were ranged

[16] Wistrand (1970) 203 includes a discussion of imperial and provincial fora in his treatment of the *atrium* and its development. See Stambaugh (1988) 55 for Augustus as *pater patriae* in his new *atrium* surrounded by *imagines*, spoils, and examples of Greek art, and Kellum (1981) 126.

[17] Zanker (1968) 16 suggested that the faces of the famous men from the Forum would have been so well known from their *imagines* that the statues must have been modelled on them. He takes this to mean that they were executed in the realistic, 'republican' style.

[18] The most comprehensive treatment of the sculptural programme as a whole can be found in Zanker (1968), supplemented by (1988) 210-15, Kellum (1981) 107-56, and Anderson (1984) 65-100.

[19] Ov. *Fast.* 1. 593-4 = T51: *perlege dispositas generosa per atria ceras:* | *contigerunt nulli nomina tanta viro* ('Survey the wax masks arranged around the *atria* of the well-born: so great a name was bestowed on no other man'). Book 1 of the *Fasti* was revised during his exile and rededicated to Germanicus. This passage can, therefore, be dated to between AD 8 and 17. An informative treatment of the connection of these statues with the *imagines* can be found in Rowell (1940). See Herbert-Brown (1994) 28 and 54-7 and Barchiesi (1994) for a discussion of Ovid's response to Augustus' edict which invited comparison between himself and earlier Romans. Ovid was the only Augustan poet to see the dedication and use of the new forum.

[20] See Kellum (1981) 110-14 for possible models for the *exedrae*, notably the *exedrae* of the Argives at Delphi decorated with statues of Argive kings, their ancestors,

in two tiers and were complemented by shield portraits of deities interspersed by caryatids which formed the entablature in a new variation of *imagines clipeatae*.[21] The statues of republican heroes provided the setting for the temple, for the triumphal statue of Augustus himself, and for the many activities of the new civic space (see Fig. 17). Judging from the few remaining fragments, the statues were finely executed in Luna marble and were slightly over life size.[22] Their appearance was enhanced by the striking pavement of marble in various colours.[23] The impact of this 'series' of Roman statesmen can be gauged from the fact that some or all were reproduced in various provincial towns, from whose inscriptions the *elogia* of the forum itself have been reconstructed.[24]

Augustus himself was closely associated with the planning and building of the forum at every stage, including the private purchase of the land from his own funds to fulfil his vow made on the eve of the battle of Philippi in 42 BC.[25] Ancient authors especially mention his involvement with the composition of the *elogia*, and hence with the selection of the individuals to be represented in his 'hall of fame'.[26] At the same time, it was Augustus who was responsible for removing the statues of famous Romans which had been placed on the Capitol over the years. He moved these to the Campus Martius outside the city walls, where they were subsequently destroyed by Caligula.[27] A number of these older statues portrayed the same figures as those to be found in the new forum. Without going so far as to eliminate all other statues of earlier Romans, Augustus aimed to supersede or replace many. His gallery of heroes was certainly the most impressive and sys-

the heroes who captured Thebes, and Perseus. The present reconstruction follows Anderson (1984) 75 ff. See Ganzert and Kockel (1988) for the statues as a frame for the whole complex, like 'historical' quotations.

[21] Anderson (1984) 77. Cf. Simon (1986) 51, and Ganzert and Kockel (1988) 190-1 with Abb. 82-5. For *imagines clipeatae*, see Ch. 3 § 2*b*.

[22] Tufi (1981) catalogues the statuary finds and notes the fine workmanship. Cf. Kockel (1983), Hofter (1988) nos. 80-92, and Zanker (1988) 211.

[23] This was the first large-scale use of coloured marble in Rome. See Kellum (1981) 109, Anderson (1984) 76, and Ganzert and Kockel (1988) Farbtafeln 1-3.

[24] For evidence from Arretium, Pompeii, and Lavinium, see Degrassi (1937) 7.

[25] *RG* 21. 1: *In privato solo Martis Ultoris templum forumque Augustum ex manubiis feci* ('I built the precinct of Mars the Avenger and the Forum of Augustus on privately owned land from my own share of war booty'). Cf. Suet. *Aug.* 29. 2; 56. 2; Macrob. 2. 4. 9. Note the republican tone of the reference to booty.

[26] Plin. *Nat.* 22. 13 speaks of Augustus as the author of the *elogia*. His close involvement in overseeing the project has been especially stressed by Frisch (1980).

[27] Suet. *Cal.* 34. 2, with the remarks of Bonnefond (1987) 260.

FIG. 17. Reconstruction of a niche with its statue and inscription from the Forum of Augustus, Rome.

tematic ever conceived of up to that time, and may even have included some older statues brought from other public sites.

Partial excavation of the east end of the forum has allowed a reconstruction of the overall scheme, although it remains uncertain how many statues there were.[28] Many of the statues were executed in triumphal garb, although several *elogia* attest the presence of individuals who had not celebrated a triumph.[29] The triumphal theme was central to the complex as the temple of Mars Ultor housed the standards returned by the Parthians, and Augustus himself was depicted in triumphal garb in the centre of the forum. It is no coincidence that by the time of the dedication of the temple triumphs were restricted to members of the imperial house, who would come to deposit their spoils in the new temple, a centre of state and family power.[30] By 2 BC triumphal garb could be recognized by Romans as a badge the imperial family shared in a special way with the historical figures portrayed in the forum.[31]

Other generals could expect no more than triumphal *ornamenta* and a statue in the forum outside the temple. They were also unable to display newly won spoils in their *atria* in the traditional manner.[32] The new hierarchy of achievement can be seen clearly in the arrangement of civic space. Similarly, when Augustus saw to the

[28] Estimates hover around 108, but only 28 names are known. The overall length of the Forum is not established. There is, in fact, no firm evidence that the statues extended beyond the hemicycles although it is generally assumed that they did.

[29] For statues in triumphal garb, see Plin. *Nat.* 22. 6. 13; Dio 55. 10. 3. Those who did not triumph include Marcellus, Augustus' nephew. Suetonius (*Aug.* 31. 5: *Statuas omnium triumphali effigie in utraque fori sui porticu dedicavit.* 'He dedicated statues of all in triumphal dress in both porticoes of his forum.') is probably generalizing and influenced by the fact that recipients of triumphal *ornamenta* under the Empire received a statue here. I am not persuaded by the suggestion of Anderson (1984) 83 that all were portrayed in triumphal garb even when this was not historically justified. Kellum (1981) 124 notes that most of the surviving fragments suggest statues wearing togas. See Hor. *Ep.* 8. 11–12 = T34 for a special stress on ancestors who had triumphed which predates Augustus' forum.

[30] Bonnefond (1987) 257 ff. For a general discussion of senatorial self-representation under Augustus, see Eck (1984).

[31] The last triumph outside the imperial family was celebrated on 27 March 19 BC by L. Cornelius Balbus over the Garamantes. His theatre was also the last public building erected in Rome by a general from his spoils. See Wallace-Hadrill (1986) 79 on Augustus' encouragement of senatorial self-representation in the 20s, followed by a reversal of this pattern with Balbus. Cf. Hickson (1991) for Augustus' use of triumphal themes.

[32] Wiseman (1987a) 394: 'it is important to remember that after paying his vows to Iuppiter Optimus Maximus, the triumphator in his gilded chariot led his procession of captives and wagons of spoil to his own house.' Cf. Rawson (1990) 160 for

inscription of the triumphal *fasti* on an arch in the Roman Forum he did not leave any room for additional names.[33] It seems probable that he did not set aside any empty niches for more statues in his new forum, although he included Marcellus and Drusus, those most recently dead in his own family.[34]

At the time of its dedication in 2 BC Augustus issued an edict explaining the significance of the statues in the new forum.[35] He claimed these past Romans as his personal models, by which the people should measure his successors. Both in his edict and in the design of the forum itself he invited direct comparison between himself and the most illustrious Romans of the past, while he left little doubt about his aim to overshadow them in merit, and hence in *auctoritas*.[36]

Augustus' adopted family, the patrician Julii, did not furnish sufficient *imagines* to match most other office-holding houses; hence his decision to use the ancestors of the traditional ruling oligarchy.[37] The individuals to be represented were apparently chosen either as military leaders to illustrate the theme of empire and conquest, or for achievements that could be interpreted as foreshadowing the deeds and honours of the *princeps*.[38] In true republican fashion the *elogia* stress innovations made by each leader in a way that is then surpassed by Augustus' claims in his *Res Gestae*.[39]

the end of triumphs and the display of spoils in the general's home in the early Augustan period.

[33] Cf. Eck (1984) 138–9.   [34] *Contra* Degrassi (1937) 8.

[35] Suet. *Aug.* 31. 5 : *professus e[s]t edicto: commentum id se, ut ad illorum ⟨. . .⟩ velut ad exemplar et ipse, dum viveret, et insequentium aetatium principes exigerentur a civibus* ('He declared in an edict that he had devised this so that the citizens should hold these men up as a standard of behaviour both for himself, while he was alive, and for emperors in future ages to live up to').

[36] Cf. Zanker (1968) 26 for Augustus' cult here after his death. Anderson (1984) 96 discusses the sacrifices of the Arval brethren to the genius of Augustus, also regularly performed in the Forum of Augustus.

[37] e.g. Consulships held 509–31 BC: Julii 18 (excluding Augustus); Cornelii 77; Fabii 46.

[38] Cf. Suet. *Aug.* 31. 5: *proximum a dis immortalibus honorem memoriae ducum praestitit, qui imperium p. R. ex minimo maximum reddidissent* ('He accorded a place of honour next to the immortal gods to the memory of the leaders who had transformed the empire of the Roman people from a very small to a very big one'). Kellum (1981) 116–23 and Anderson (1984) 83–7 offer a variety of possible criteria for selection such as precedents for Augustus' own career and as ancestors of his supporters and relatives by marriage.

[39] Frisch (1980) 95 and Luce (1990) 127–8. For the epigraphic setting of the *Res Gestae* in relation to the other inscriptions at the Mausoleum of Augustus, see Panciera in von Hesberg and Panciera (1994) 66 and 174–7.

Much careful research produced the *elogia,* which were apparently compilations from several sources and contained details of offices and honours.[40] Augustus drew on antiquarian researches which were available in Rome, many sponsored by him in connection with several of his projects of restoration and enhancement in the city. Such information by its very nature, and especially in the simple but dignified form adopted in the inscriptions, epitomized the spirit of the Roman nobility of office with its characteristic claim to leadership based on merit. The traditional nature of the two-part *elogia* from the forum, including separate label and *cursus,* reminds us of the epigraphical habits found in the tomb of the Scipios.[41] As argued in relation to that tomb, it seems likely that the form and function of these labels was closely reflected in the *tituli* used to identify the *imagines* in the *atrium.*[42] The language of the inscriptions is somewhat antiquated, matching the deliberately archaizing letter forms used to inscribe them.[43] In displaying his own version of past careers, Augustus offered an alternative to the traditions preserved by the annalists and by Livy.[44] He also challenged traditions to be seen at the morning *salutationes* in the homes of the powerful or distinguished. His sponsorship of the project cast him in the role of preserver of Rome's common heritage and glorious past.

At the same time, Augustus could justify his own claim to have held only traditional honours by directly presenting his fellow citizens with historical evidence for earlier parallels.[45] The tone and content of the *Res Gestae* once more linked Augustus with the memory of past Roman generals.[46] His own inscription is on the order of thirty times the length of any *elogium* recovered from the Forum of Augustus. It is surely designed to be read with these *elogia* in mind, as well as republican dedicatory inscriptions he had restored during his renovation of much of the city. He used the very techniques of

[40] The sources for the *elogia* have been thoroughly reevaluated by Luce (1990).

[41] Kellum (1981) 115 links the Augustan *elogia* both to the tomb of the Scipios and to the *tituli* of the *imagines.*

[42] For discussion, see Ch. 6 § 1.   [43] Degrassi (1937) 6.

[44] As Luce (1990) has shown, the many divergences between Livy and the *elogia* are striking, revealing that Livy was not used as a source.

[45] *RG* 6. 1: *nullum magistratum contra morem maiorum delatum recepi* ('I did not accept any political office which did not conform with the custom of our ancestors').

[46] Gagé (1935/77) 31: 'Les Res Gestae se rattachent clairement, par leur inspiration et par leur ton, à cette tradition proprement romaine qui unissait par le lien matériel des *manubiae* les guerres, les triomphes, les libéralités au peuple, les constructions et parfois aussi les spectacles.'

publicity developed by the office-holding families against them by playing on their claim to present a shared history, and yet one which belonged in some exclusive sense to their particular clan. He effectively appropriated the ancestors of other families to enhance his own position as a leader who was exceptional beyond the achievements of his own generation and family. The series of statues with their inscriptions is evidence of Augustus' aim to describe his new position and the role he hoped to establish for his family in terms of the most hallowed traditions of the old political order.[47]

The most important statues on either side were those of Aeneas and Romulus respectively, which were to be found in the central niches of each of the two hemicycles. These statues were monumental and apparently on the order of twice the size of the other figures.[48] Reconstructions based on wall-paintings from Pompeii indicate that Aeneas was represented carrying Anchises and the Penates from Troy with Ascanius, while Romulus was in armour holding the *spolia opima* (see Pls. 4*a* and *b*).[49] Both scenes appear lively and in motion rather than static. Ovid emphasizes the way the two central groups caught the attention of a viewer standing with his back to the temple and looking out over the whole forum (*Fast.* 5. 563-6). They symbolized and introduced the twofold programme of the sculptures, representing the Julii and their relatives led by Aeneas occupying the north side and facing Romulus with the other famous Romans on the south side.

The reference to the *spolia opima* carried by Romulus comes as no surprise in light of Augustus' interest in these supreme honours.[50] His dedication of the Parthian standards in the temple of Mars Ultor served as an equivalent to the *spolia opima* and was enhanced by future triumphal spoils placed in the temple.[51] Romulus was therefore presented as the first to dedicate these spoils, which linked him with the triumphal image of Augustus, the new founder of Rome

[47] Cf. M. T. Griffin (1991) for a similar argument about Augustus' position as benefactor of the people of Rome in the traditional style of republican aristocrats.

[48] Kockel (1983) adduces evidence from fragments of shoes which appear to belong to these statues.

[49] Zanker (1968) 17, (1988) fig. 156, and Hofter (1988) 200.

[50] Propertius 4. 10; *RG* 19. 2; cf. Harrison (1989). Even before Actium he had restored the temple of Jupiter Feretrius, where such dedications had traditionally been made. His refusal of the *spolia opima* to M. Licinius Crassus in 29 BC was in line with his wish to keep triumphal honours and spoils in his own family. Cf. Kellum (1981) 121-3 and Zanker (1988) 203.

[51] Bonnefond (1987) 273-4.

234

and renewer of her traditions.[52] It was through this dominantly triumphal imagery that Augustus connected himself with the series of
famous Romans who were not directly related to him, but were
introduced by the figure of the triumphant general Romulus, the
son of Mars.[53] In this way, Augustus translated into concrete terms
the comparison already invited by Q. Caecilius Metellus in his third-
century BC *laudatio* for his father, which set up a contrast with all
Rome's leaders since the founding of the city.[54] Through his Trojan
ancestry Augustus was able to extend the comparison in time to
start from Aeneas, which enabled him to include the series of Alban
kings amongst his own ancestors.

On the same lines as the central figures, some depictions of individual Roman heroes were more than portraits, in that they also
embodied a visual message to accompany the inscription for each
statue. The surviving fragments are too sparse to enable a detailed
reconstruction of any of the statues.[55] Scattered literary references
suggest figures identified partially by attributes which included honours or symbols of famous deeds and moral qualities. This is
securely attested only in the case of Valerius Maximus Corvinus,
who was shown with a crow on his head (Gellius 9. 11. 10). Scipio
Aemilianus may have been depicted wearing a mural crown (Plin.
Nat. 22. 13). No doubt many attributes used were of a traditional
nature. Such symbolism was in line with the iconography of the
central figures of Aeneas and Romulus as men of action rather than
as static figures.[56]

In setting up a row of statues wearing their garb of highest office
and labelled in this highly traditional way, Augustus was able to
recall both the display of the *imagines* in the *atrium* and their

[52] For a discussion of Augustus as the new Romulus, see Zanker (1968) 20 ff. For
Caesar's interest in Romulus and use of him for political purposes, see Classen
(1962). Herbert-Brown (1994) 48–52 discusses Ovid's presentation of Romulus as a
foil to Augustus in the *Fasti*.
[53] Anderson (1984) sees them as the chosen people of Mars contrasted as a group
with the Julii, the descendants of Venus. Classen (1962) 177–8 discusses the various traditions according to which Romulus was related to Aeneas and the Julii.
[54] This funeral speech is analyzed in detail in Ch. 5 § 3.
[55] See Wünsche (1982) who argues that the Munich 'Marius' and 'Sulla' may be
copies of *summi viri* from the Forum Augustum.
[56] Rowell (1940) 143 was convinced traditional attributes were in use. Horsfall
(1980) 22 suggested the overall effect was like statues of Christian saints, which
were easily identified by the faithful through their dress and symbols. Such an analogy can help to recreate the effect of the series on the viewer.

appearance in the funeral procession.[57] The proposed reconstructions of individual statues fit in with the theory that *imagines* in the funeral procession could be identified by attributes. In turn, the relation between these statues and the *imagines* helps to explain why so many were shown in triumphal dress in the forum. An interpretation of the series of Roman heroes headed by Romulus as intended to present all or most Romans who had celebrated a triumph is problematic. On any reconstruction the series of statues would have been very incomplete.[58] Rather, Augustus was following the rules of attire adopted by the actors who presented the ancestors in a funeral procession. When selecting the dress of highest office triumphal garb would often have been used, since any series of the most famous names in Roman history tended to include many successful generals.

Augustus exploited the potential of the *imagines* as symbols of a unified empire to redefine his own position in Roman society and in relation to Rome's power. In doing so he was acknowledging their importance as symbols of rank and prestige. His use of *imagines* was to a large extent dictated by their influence as it already existed in the minds of citizens at all levels of society. For centuries, previous leaders had defined and presented themselves and their ideas in terms of their ancestral *imagines*, or in opposition to those of others.[59] Augustus developed the claim of a popular politician like Marius to be the true heir to the virtues and achievements of other people's ancestors.[60] Augustus' use of iconography associated with the *imagines* enabled him to match and reshape the nature of aristocratic family self-advertisement, which had been a traditional base of political and social power throughout the Republic.

[57] Bauer (1987) with fig. 1 presents a new reconstruction of parts of the Forum of Augustus based on recent restoration work to the perimeter wall. His findings suggest that the *elogia* cannot have been fixed to the wall which was marked off vertically beneath the niches. I find it hard to accept his notion that the inscriptions were above the niches as they would have been too high to read.

[58] The number of *triumphatores* in the Republic was over 230.

[59] Bloomer (1992) 12 examines how the writings of Valerius Maximus illustrate the denial of a break with the past which was an attitude inherent in the political culture of the principate. 258: 'The marshalling of history owes much to Augustus in whose forum the stone procession of grand republican figures marched into the present.'

[60] For Marius' speech, see Sall., *Jug.* 85. 10 ff. = T64*a–c* and Plut. *Mar.* 9. 2 = T60. The use of *imagines* in rhetoric is discussed in Ch. 1 and 5 § 5.

1b. *The Development of Imperial Funerals by Augustus*

The second important way in which Augustus used the *imagines* was in staging grand funerals for members of his family, at which he himself delivered carefully composed speeches. His innovations with regard to the *imagines* have been especially recognized in his own splendid funeral, for which he left written instructions. This ceremony served as the model and inspiration for later imperial funerals, which fused the traditions of earlier aristocratic burials with new ceremonies to mark the apotheosis of the emperor.[61] At the same time, the appearance in Augustus' funeral cortège of famous Romans who were not related to him vividly reenacted the scene presented to a visitor in his forum, and notably the special leading roles of Aeneas and Romulus.[62] Just as the themes found in the forum were sounded and developed from the start of Augustus' period in power, so his funeral came as the culmination in a scheme that had been rehearsed and redesigned in the funerals of his family throughout his lifetime.[63]

Caesar had shown how effectively a carefully orchestrated display of *imagines* and a powerful funeral oration could boost the popularity of an ambitious young politician at the start of his career.[64] In this same family tradition, Octavian himself delivered the funeral oration for his grandmother Julia, the sister of Caesar, in 51 BC at the age of 12.[65] This was his first experience of speaking in public from the *rostra*, and he appeared as the spokesman of his family. Late in 43 BC, during his first consulship, Augustus held a funeral at public expense for his mother Atia, the daughter of Caesar's sister Julia. His actions recalled the spontaneous burial on the Campus Martius accorded by the crowds to Caesar's daughter Julia in 54 BC and marked out the women of his family for privileged treatment.[66]

---

[61] The development of imperial funerals is traced by Price (1987).

[62] Aeneas and Romulus also appear on the front of the Ara Pacis and as corner acroteria on the temple of Divus Augustus. Rowell (1940) 131 believes that the connections between the iconography of the Forum of Augustus and imperial funerals are essential to any understanding of Augustus' interest in and understanding of *imagines*.

[63] Price (1987) 62 notes the importance of family funerals staged by Augustus as partial models for his own, but does not discuss them in any detail.

[64] Suet. *Jul.* 6; Plut. *Caes.* 5 = T59.

[65] Nicolaus of Damascus *FGH* 90 F 127; Quint. *Inst.* 12. 6. 1; Suet. *Aug.* 8. 1.

[66] Suet. *Aug.* 61 and Dio 47. 17. 6 (Dio dates it to 42 BC). For Julia's funeral, see Dio 39. 64.

Augustus delivered eulogies at family funerals himself during his lifetime. His speeches were published: echoes have come down to us confirming their importance and wide circulation. Servius tells us that Virgil used a striking phrase from Augustus' emotional speech for Marcellus in 23 BC to describe Dido as she falls in love with Aeneas under the influence of Cupid disguised as Ascanius (Serv. *A.* I. 712). Similarly, a papyrus fragment of Augustus' funeral speech for Agrippa in 12 BC has revealed probable echoes of the *princeps's* language in Tacitus, both in the historian's own analysis of Augustus' arrangements for the succession, and in his quotation from an edict of Nero.[67] Points of contact between Augustus' praise of Agrippa and the *Res Gestae* further confirm the relation between Augustus' own position and that of Agrippa as his partner.[68] For Augustus funeral oratory was a useful medium for presenting his ideas to a wide audience in a magnificent setting. These speeches are significant because Augustus was not well known as an orator and rarely addressed large public gatherings.

An examination of imperial family funerals can shed valuable light on Augustus' attitude towards *imagines* and funeral spectacle. Dio tells us that the funeral procession staged by Augustus for M. Agrippa in 12 BC was very similar to what was seen at the *princeps's* own funeral 26 years later.[69] Yet, many new features of Augustus' procession seem to have been honours especially voted to him for the first time by the senate. Examples of such innovations include the redirection of the processional route through the *porta triumphalis*, and the display of boards bearing the titles of his legislation as part of the parade.[70] Which shared elements is Dio alluding to? The striking similarity between the two funerals must have touched on the heart of the procession with the presentation of the *imagines*. Augustus' funeral procession was memorable and spectacular for including the *imagines* of Romans not directly related to

[67] Koenen (1970*a*) and (1970*b*). The phrase in question is *in summum rei publicae fastigium provectus* ('he had risen to a position of supreme eminence in the state'), for which see Tac. *Ann.* 3. 56. 1; 13. 17. 3; 14. 54. 3. Nero may in turn have echoed Augustus' words.

[68] Gagé (1935/77) 211-12.

[69] Dio 54. 28. 5: καὶ τὴν ἐκφορὰν αὐτοῦ ἐν τῷ τρόπῳ ἐν ᾧ καὶ αὐτὸς μετὰ ταῦτα ἐξηνέχθη ἐποιήσατο ('and his [Agrippa's] funeral cortège was arranged in the same fashion in which he himself [Augustus] was later brought out to burial').

[70] Tac. *Ann.* 1. 8. 3 mentions these as special honours voted to Augustus by the senate.

him, in a separate category led by Romulus (Dio 56. 34 = T28). A similar procession may have been organized for Agrippa, who did not have any family *imagines* of his own that he was entitled to display. Indeed, it is hard to see how the two funerals could have been so alike if Agrippa had no procession of *imagines* at all. As a result of his marriage to Augustus' daughter Julia, Agrippa could legitimately use and display the *imagines* of the Julii and others who were related to them.[71] Dio's direct comparison with Augustus' funeral implies that Agrippa's funeral procession included a wide array of what were now considered 'Julian' *imagines*.

The following considerations also make this reconstruction of Agrippa's funeral procession more likely. The fragment of the funeral oration Augustus delivered for Agrippa has revealed that the *princeps* stressed Agrippa as his colleague in empire and power.[72] This point could have been underscored by a fine historical pageant presenting Agrippa as heir to the heritage of earlier great Roman leaders, particularly military heroes. In addition, Dio notes the extensive mourning for Agrippa by a wide section of the population of the city, also a special feature shared with later imperial funerals.[73] Despite the fact that Agrippa had built a private tomb for himself on the Campus Martius, he was buried by Augustus in his own family mausoleum.[74] Such treatment of him as an equal partner in authority, and the father of Augustus' grandsons, fits in with Agrippa's key position as the recipient of

[71] For the wife bringing her own *imagines* to her husband's household, see Ch. 4 § 2. For an analogy, see Tac. *Ann.* 3. 76 = T89 which suggests that Junia would normally have displayed the *imago* of her husband Cassius, and presumably also his family's masks.

[72] Koenen (1970a) and (1970b).

[73] Dio 54. 29. 6. Mourning at imperial funerals is discussed by Price (1987) 62 ff.

[74] The Mausoleum of Augustus is treated by Zanker (1988) 72-7, Arce (1988b) 59-72, and von Hesberg (1988) and in von Hesberg and Panciera (1994). Augustus started work on his impressive new mausoleum in the Campus Martius as soon as he was able and as his reply to Antony's wish to be buried in Alexandria at the side of his foreign queen. Its shape recalled the heroic burial mounds of old, while its designation as the 'tumulus Iuliorum' underlined its dynastic purpose and meaning. The construction of his tomb may be likened to the entrance to his house, which was conceived as a more splendid example of the aristocratic houses to be found along the approach from the old Forum. See von Hesberg (1988) 245-51 and Stambaugh (1988) 53 on the echoes of Etruscan tombs and Hellenistic royal burials. For Augustus' house, see Carettoni (1983) and Wiseman (1987a). For the Casa di Livia which Augustus may have bought from the Hortensii, see Nash (1961) 310-5 and Stambaugh (1988) fig. 5.

Augustus' ring during his serious illness in 23 BC (Dio 53. 30). Whether or not plans for the new forum and its statues had been made by this time, it seems possible that the 'parade of Roman heroes' first appeared in order to meet the special requirements of Agrippa, the imperial colleague who needed the *imagines* of other families at his funeral.[75]

Moreover, Virgil who died in 19 BC well before Agrippa presents a remarkably similar parade of heroes in book 6 of the *Aeneid*, in a scene ostensibly connected with the funeral of Marcellus, Augustus' nephew, in late 23 BC.[76] The points of contact between Virgil's parade and the Forum of Augustus are striking and have given rise to various explanations. It seems evident that the forum had not been started yet at the time when Virgil was writing.[77] Detailed plans can hardly have been available at this early date. Similarly, Virgil wrote with no knowledge of the funerals of Augustus, of Agrippa, or of any other member of the imperial household except for Marcellus. It has long been recognized that the scene at the end of the parade of heroes, as presented by Virgil, is at Marcellus' funeral, which the poet alludes to as being very grand.[78] Marcellus was the first person to be buried in the new mausoleum and was much-mourned since he was both nephew and son-in-law of Augustus.

It seems likely that Marcellus did indeed have an extended procession of *imagines* at his funeral, which was the first funeral of the new ruling clan, and was staged at a key moment in the evolution of the *princeps*'s position.[79] This hypothesis is not susceptible of proof. The political situation in 23 BC had been tense as a result of Augustus' own serious illness; his new role entailed his no longer

---

[75] Dio 54. 29. 4–6 suggests that Agrippa's funeral honours and games met with opposition from the more traditional aristocrats. See Panciera in von Hesberg and Panciera (1994) 96.

[76] *Aeneid* 6. 756–892. I follow the chronology developed by Badian (1982), which places Marcellus' death after mid-September 23 BC and before the trial of M. Primus in 22 BC. Cf. Hanslik (1953) 285. Suetonius–Donatus *Life of Virgil* 32 suggests Virgil read the Marcellus episode to Augustus and his family, presumably before Augustus left Rome for the East in late 22 BC. However, this source is not reliable, nor does it tell us whether the version Augustus heard is the one we now have.

[77] This was established by Degrassi (1945).

[78] e.g. Austin (1977) ad loc. 883 ff.

[79] A direct connection between Virgil's poem and Marcellus' funeral was posited but not explored in any detail by Skard (1965). *Contra* Basson (1975) 40 and Burke (1979) 22.

holding the consulship every year.[80] This year had already been marked by splendid spectacle in the *Ludi Romani* celebrated in September by Marcellus himself as aedile.[81] His death shortly thereafter was the occasion for a major production in terms of funerary publicity. The surviving fragment from Augustus' *laudatio* confirms his bitter feeling of personal loss and doom. It is, however, not possible to give a detailed reconstruction of Marcellus' funeral procession using either Virgil or Dio, whose account is very brief.[82]

Imperial funerals after Marcellus' were for Agrippa (12 BC), Octavia (11 BC), Drusus (9 BC), Gaius (AD 2), and Lucius (AD 4). It was suggested above that Marcellus possibly and Agrippa probably had splendid funerals with a new, extended procession of *imagines*, in addition to eulogies by the emperor and burial in the new family mausoleum. Octavia, the sister of Augustus and mother of Marcellus, is often overlooked in general discussions of imperial funerals.[83] However, the burial of Augustus' beloved sister fits into the development of imperial funerals (Dio 54. 35. 4). Her body lay in state in the temple of Divus Julius her great-uncle, which shows Augustus assimilating the whole of his family with the Julii. This detail helps to confirm the suggestion made above that the funeral of Octavia's son Marcellus had featured a splendid parade of Julian *imagines*, starting with Aeneas. Public mourning seems again to have been a feature, as in the case of Agrippa and probably also of Marcellus. Her burial affords the first example of two funeral orations, only one of which was delivered from the *rostra* in the traditional setting of the Roman Forum. This innovation has been interpreted as presenting two different types of speech: a traditional, public one from the *rostra* given by Drusus and a more private one at the temple of Divus Julius delivered by Augustus.[84] Thus the imperial family was set apart by the public delivery of what was perhaps essentially a family address associated with the *silicernium* or another, private context. Octavia was also buried in the family mausoleum on the Campus Martius. The inclusion of female relatives in the special public spectacle surrounding the *princeps* underlines the dynastic nature of Augustus' public image and his development of

---

[80] The events of 23–22 BC have been elucidated by Badian (1982).
[81] Cf. Prop. 3. 18.
[82] Dio 53. 30. 5 gives a brief account of Marcellus' funeral.
[83] e.g. Price (1987).
[84] For a discussion of funerals for women, see Ch. 4 § 6.

the habits of aristocratic families in the last century of the Republic.[85]

Ancient evidence fails us for the funerals of Gaius and Lucius, which would undoubtedly have revealed further developments of earlier Augustan themes.[86] By contrast several sources remark on the splendour of the funeral of Drusus, the step-son of Augustus, in 9 BC.[87] Tacitus claims that the Roman people still remembered the spectacle in AD 20, on the death of Drusus' son Germanicus, and that it helped to shape their expectations.[88] Drusus was a popular figure and a military hero in his own right; it is not surprising that triumphal themes were stressed in his rites.[89] Again two funeral orations were delivered, although Augustus spoke in the Circus Flaminius to avoid entering the city. The *princeps* was especially fond of his step-son, and after his death he celebrated his achievements in prose and verse (Dio 55. 2. 2). Drusus is the most recent person whose statue is attested in the Forum of Augustus.[90]

The procession of *imagines* at Drusus' funeral must have been notable as his was the first imperial funeral to include the long and illustrious line of patrician Claudii. Tacitus asserts that the Claudii appeared accompanied by the Julii and surrounded Drusus' bier at the *rostra*, where Tiberius delivered a eulogy for his brother.[91] This has caused confusion because Drusus was never adopted into the Julian family. An emendation of the text of Tacitus has been suggested to replace Julii with Livii, the family of Drusus' mother, Livia

[85] Note also the new use of honorific statues for women of the imperial household, especially for Octavia and Livia (Dio 49. 38. 1 in 35 BC) and for Livia alone (Dio 55. 2. 5 in 9 BC). For a full discussion, see Flory (1993). The Porticus Octaviae may have been the location for a gallery of statues of famous mothers, notably Cornelia the mother of the Gracchi. See D'Ambra (1993) for Domitian's use of female imagery to present the imperial message on morals.

[86] Dio 55. 10a. 9 does not include a report of the funerals and is confused about the chronology of their deaths.

[87] Sen. *Cons. ad Marc.* 3. 1; Tac. *Ann.* 3. 5 = T88; Dio 55. 2. 2. Cf. Liv. *Per.* 142 and Suet. *Claud.* 1. 5.

[88] For Tacitus and the *Tabula Siarensis*, see below § 2.

[89] Sen. *Consol. Ad Marc.* 3. 1: *funus simillimum triumpho* ('a funeral very like a triumph').

[90] Degrassi (1937) no. 9 = *AE* 1934 no. 151.

[91] Tac. *Ann.* 3. 5 = T88: *circumfusas lecto Claudiorum Iuliorumque imagines; defletum in foro, laudatum pro rostris; cuncta a maioribus reperta aut quae posteri invenerint cumulata* ('The masks of the Claudii and Julii had surrounded the bier. He had been mourned in the Forum and eulogized from the *rostra*. All the tributes originated by the ancestors or invented by later generations were heaped on him').

Drusilla.[92] However, the evidence for previous imperial funerals, especially those of Marcellus and of his mother Octavia, surely suggests that Tacitus' testimony should be accepted as it stands.[93] The *imagines* of the Julii had probably been a feature of previous imperial funerals, including that of Agrippa, just as earlier family members had been buried together in the new family tomb.

The nature of such a procession is indicated by that at the funeral of Drusus, the son of Tiberius, in AD 23 (Tac. *Ann.* 4. 9. 2 = T90). The younger Drusus, unlike his uncle of the same name, was a member of the Julian family by adoption. In his case also Tacitus comments on a dual procession featuring Claudii and Julii, which included *imagines* of even the earliest ancestors from Trojan times. Aeneas introduced a line of the Alban kings stretching to Romulus.[94] Similarly, the patrician Claudii were apparently not led in procession by Attus Clausus who established the family in Rome, but by his ancestors, the Sabine nobles of Regillum.[95] The elder Drusus' funeral offered Augustus the opportunity to celebrate a grand spectacle in traditional patrician style, as well as marking the glorious death of a military hero. Naturally, he wished to claim Drusus as a full member of his family, as he apparently did in the case of Agrippa. The one surviving fragment from Augustus' funeral oration expresses the hope that the young men of the Julian family will be like Drusus.[96] Since Tacitus says that this funeral

[92] This was suggested by Muretus. See Val. Max. 2. 9. 6 = T96 for the importance of the *imagines* of C. Claudius Nero (*RE* 246) and M. Livius Salinator (*RE* 33) who laid aside their enmity to save their country (Livy 22. 35. 6-9). Their families were joined by Livia and then in Tiberius.

[93] Flory (1993) 298 notes Drusus' Julian *imagines* in her discussion of honours for his mother Livia. Women were used by Augustus to stress links between families, especially the Julii and Claudii.

[94] This passage of Tacitus directly attests the existence of *imagines* of Aeneas and Romulus. By contrast, Dio tells us that in 42 BC the triumvirs banned the display of an *imago* of Caesar on the grounds that he was a god (47. 19. 2 = T27). The same type of decree was passed for Augustus after his death (Dio 56. 46. 4-5b = T29). Apparently, the Romans in general and the Julio-Claudians in particular did not think of Aeneas and Romulus as being in exactly the same category as Caesar and Augustus, although all could be said to have earned divine honours after death by virtue of their achievements. Immortal gods were not represented by *imagines*, although many élite families claimed descent from them. The triumvirs probably set a fashion at a time when they had immediate practical reasons to try to control the political use of Caesar's *imago* by a relative at a family funeral. Suet. *Ves.* 19. 2 = T84 mentions an *imago* of Vespasian at his funeral despite his deification.

[95] For Attus Clausus' ancestors, see *RE* Claudius especially 24.

[96] Suet. *Claud.* 1. 5: *et defunctum ita pro contione laudaverit, ut deos precatus sit, similes ei Caesares suos facerent sibique tam honestum quandoque exitum darent quam illi*

included all traditional features as well as more recent innovations, we may assume that his remark applies to the *imagines* also.

Augustus' own funeral came as a logical climax to the splendid series of family celebrations carefully orchestrated by the *princeps*.[97] In republican fashion Augustus' body lay in state in the entrance to his own house. Two eulogies were delivered, one by the new emperor Tiberius and one by his son Drusus. The traditional *laudatio* from the *rostra* given by Drusus is described as having been read. This raises the possibility that Augustus left a text to be read aloud at his death. The procession of *imagines* was further extended by the inclusion of allegorical images of all the nations he had conquered, with their indigenous characteristics represented in symbol and attribute (Dio 56. 34. 3 = T28). Their names were recorded, presumably on placards, which were also carried in the procession together with a list of laws passed in Augustus' name (Tac. *Ann.* 1. 8. 3). Similarly, the names of the subject peoples had been inscribed above the level of the statues in the Forum of Augustus (Vell. Pat. 2. 39). Augustus himself was represented by three images in the procession, one wax, one gold, and one in a triumphal chariot recalling his statue in the new forum. The statue of Victory housed in the *curia* was used to head the procession, part of which seems to have issued from the senate house before continuing on a novel route through the *porta triumphalis*. By the end of his life Augustus had appropriated the spectacle of the triumph and of the *imagines* to help create a public image of himself as the supreme leader in Rome's history.[98]

Dio appears to claim that Augustus' body in its casket, and his wax funeral portrait as well as the two other likenesses of him, pre-

---

dedissent ('and he praised the dead man [Drusus] in a public speech before the people in the following way, including a prayer to the gods that they should make his own Caesars like him and grant them as honourable a death, whenever it might occur, as they had granted him'). This was perhaps the concluding *sententia* of Augustus' speech.

[97] Our main source is Dio 56. 34 = T28, supplemented by Tac. *Ann.* 1. 8. 3 and Suet. *Aug.* 100. For the funeral ceremonies of the emperors in general, see Arce (1988b) 35–57. Panciera in von Hesberg and Panciera (1994) 111–12 argues that details such as the *imagines* in the procession would have been the subject of specific written instructions by Augustus.

[98] For Augustus' increased use of triumphal imagery in funerals, cf. Versnel (1970) 115–29; Richard (1978) 1122; Price (1987).

ceded the *imagines* in the procession.[99] This in itself would have
been a startling departure from the accepted practice of having the
ancestors lead the deceased. The traditional arrangement was
chronological, adding the deceased as the most recent member in
the category of the ancestors. As time passed a man's *imago* would
gain seniority in the parade and appear at an ever greater distance
from the bier. If Augustus was indeed carried out ahead of his
ancestors and the famous figures from Rome's past, this was a striking dramatization of his claim to outshine the merits of past leaders. It would also have meant that his image appeared next to and
in front of that of Aeneas, as his family preceded the parade of other
Roman heroes. Such a juxtaposition had been suggested in Virgil's
poem, which the poet had read to the *princeps* more than thirty
years before.

It is certain that Augustus' funeral included traditional *imagines*
of many individuals from outside his own family. Dio also makes reference to a portrait of Pompey, whether an *imago* or a statue, whose
presence must have been especially striking in the absence of
Caesar, Augustus' adoptive father. Pompey was, in fact, related to
Augustus through his maternal grandfather, M. Atius Balbus.[100] As
suggested here, it is probable that the practice of using *imagines* of
other people's ancestors had developed over time and had started
with the magnificent funeral of Marcellus. There is little likelihood
that these *imagines* and their equipment were loaned to the Julii by
the descendants of each leader. Many new masks must, therefore,
have been manufactured specially for use in imperial funerals.[101]
However, we have no information as to where these *imagines* were
usually kept and whether they were on permanent display like traditional *imagines*. The fashioning of new masks allowed Augustus to
create his own dramatized image of Rome's great men with their
attributes and characteristics.

How many may have appeared at the funeral of Marcellus is

[99] Dio 56. 34. 2 = T28: καὶ μετὰ ταύτας αἵ τε τῶν προπατόρων αὐτοῦ καὶ αἱ
τῶν ἄλλων συγγενῶν τῶν τεθνηκότων ('and after these the masks of his ancestors
came in procession and those of his other relatives who had died'). This has been
accepted by Bettini (1991) 177 n. 16.
[100] See Appendix E below for a family tree. See Suet. *Aug.* 4. 1 = T80 and 31. 5
for Pompey's statue which Augustus moved from the senate house to a marble arch
facing Pompey's theatre.
[101] Rowell (1940) 143. Augustus probably prepared *imagines* for his funeral early
in his reign, just as he had his mausoleum constructed then.

quite unclear. By 12 BC Agrippa's funeral apparently included a procession long enough for Dio to liken the ceremony to that for the emperor himself. This suggests that the new imperial *imagines* had been conceived of and executed in the early part of Augustus' reign. Such a procession could not have been organized at short notice, and had in the past always relied on a stock of *imagines* in good condition and readily available. The *imagines* of the Roman heroes may, therefore, have predated the statues of the Forum of Augustus. There were surely many links between the two projects. In this way Augustus can be seen to have appropriated the *imagines* directly before any public displays of statues in the city.

In attempting to show the importance of the traditional ancestral *imagines* of the aristocracy for Augustus as the first emperor this discussion has emphasized his need to portray himself—despite and perhaps because of his own obscure background—in terms of the customary political hierarchy of honour in recompense for service and merit. Augustus succeeded, where Caesar had failed, in establishing himself as an absolute ruler; he did so because unlike Caesar, who took no trouble to disguise his absolute power, he found ways to use the accepted methods of the old ruling caste to justify his position. The essence of his claim was that he was no more than the preeminent figure in a social order apparently restored on republican lines. His position of leadership was publicly advertised in terms of merit and honour rather than of power and force. To a significant degree the iconography of the principate drew on the *imagines* as a direct inspiration.[102] The fulfilment of Augustus' programme of public works can be seen in the magnificent new forum which displayed his statue at the height of his prestige in a setting inspired by the *imagines*. Similarly, the evidence for imperial funerals shows that Augustus directly appropriated the *imagines* of Rome's leading families for his own use. The propaganda of subsequent emperors can be measured partly in terms of imitation of, or reaction to, Augustus' use of *imagines*.

2. *Imperial Funerals under Tiberius*

Funerals under Tiberius provide a contrast to imperial funeral spectacle as developed by Augustus. They illustrate a continuing com-

[102] On the general importance of the *imagines*, both for funerals and in the Forum of Augustus, see Panciera in von Hesberg and Panciera (1994) 174–7.

petition of display as the leading family, now represented by a patrician Claudius from the highest ranks of the old aristocracy, sought to define itself for the people, and to react to pressure from traditional office-holding families with continued republican sympathies and ambitions. The reign of Tiberius, as Tacitus claimed, marked the start of the Principate in a certain sense, since the system of government had now been passed on and could no longer be regarded as Augustus' personal arrangement.

It is interesting that the first conspiracy, if it can be accurately described in this way, came from within the ranks of republican office-holding families, who were apparently far from welcoming Tiberius as a leader drawn from their own circles. Scribonius Libo Drusus, who committed suicide after being implicated in a plot against Tiberius in AD 16, was accused of aiming to make himself emperor, rather than of attempting to reestablish a republican type of constitution (Tac. *Ann.* 2. 27-32 = T85 and 85a). He was said to have been tempted into ruin, or perhaps even framed, by Firmius Catus, a senator who was his close friend. It was the *imagines* of his illustrious ancestors which were used by Firmius, both to persuade him to adopt an extravagant lifestyle which resulted in debt, and to imagine that he could aim at imperial power (*Ann.* 2. 27. 2 = T85).[103] Whether this is taken to be a true account of Libo Drusus' motives or not, it is significant that the *imagines* could be presented as playing such a role. For Tacitus writing nearly a century later such ambitions, linked with splendid displays of ancestral iconography in the home, were a natural explanation for treason. Within fifty years of the end of the Republic, the *imagines* had gained new associations with a life of conspicuous consumption and with pretensions to absolute power.

The first funeral of the new reign was that of Germanicus in AD 20, which was notable for its simplicity and tragic circumstances (Tac. *Ann.* 3. 5 = T88). After having died in the East, perhaps as a result of poison, Germanicus was given a simple funeral on the spot and his ashes were brought back to Rome.[104] In the highly charged atmosphere created by the frenzied mourning of the people for their

---

[103] *Contra* Neudecker (1988) who claims the reference to Libo Drusus' *imagines* in the *atrium* is a metaphor at this date. For Libo's family tree, see Koestermann (1965) ad loc., who assumes that Tacitus' source is a family archive.

[104] It is evident from Tac. *Ann.* 2. 73. 1 = T87 that Germanicus did not take his *imagines* to the East with him.

favourite and the impending trial of Piso, who was suspected of his murder, Tiberius made the decision to bury Germanicus' ashes without further ceremony.[105] Dio records no details, while Tacitus paints a vivid picture of the outrage of the people that Germanicus did not receive even the honours usual for any *nobilis*.[106] Tacitus, therefore, suggests that grand funerals were still very much the norm for the aristocracy and that Augustus' expanded funeral spectacle had become an accustomed and appreciated part of the life of ordinary Romans in the city.

The question of the character of Germanicus' funeral rites was reopened by the publication in 1984 of the *Tabula Siarensis*, which contains parts of two senatorial decrees granting posthumous honours to Germanicus in December AD 19.[107] Germanicus had died at Antioch on 10 October AD 19, but the news of his death did not reach Rome until December. In his description of popular feeling Tacitus represents the mood of the people in the following way (*Ann.* 3. 5. 2 = T88):

ubi illa veterum instituta, propositam toro effigiem, meditata ad memoriam virtutis carmina et laudationes et lacrimas vel doloris imitamenta?

What had happened to those practices of former times, the effigy laid out in state on a bier, the songs composed to recall valour, and the eulogies and tears or simulations of grief?

In the first edition of the *Tabula Siarensis*, González sees a contradiction between Tacitus and part of the new text (frag. *2b*. 11–19):

itemque car]men, quod Ti(berius) Caesar Aug(ustus) in eo ordine a(nte) d(iem) XVII k(alendas) Ian(uarias)
[de laudando Germanico mor]tuo proposuisset, in aere incisum figeretur loco publico

---

[105] See Panciera in von Hesberg and Panciera (1994) 120: 'Per la prima volta in questo caso non si organizza una vera e propria pompa funebre, avendo il funerale già avuto luogo ad Antiocha: niente letto funebre, quindi, niente *imagines*, niente *laudatio*.' On the mourning for Germanicus, see Versnel (1980). See Ch. 1 for a discussion of Piso's trial and the *S.C. de Cn. Pisone patre* recording its outcome.

[106] Cf. Dio 57. 18.6 ff. Appian, *BC* 1. 43. 6 records a decree of the senate of 90 BC ordering the burial on the spot of leading Romans who died on the battlefield in order to avoid excessive disturbance and mourning in the city. However, this measure should be interpreted as a response to the crisis of the Social War. The treatment of Drusus' body in 9 BC and his grand funeral illustrate what was the norm under Augustus. Tacitus is surely right that people recalled the funeral of Germanicus' father, who had also died young.

[107] Cf. González (1984) and González and Arce (1988) 307–11.

quo patri eius] placeret; idque eo iustius futurum arbitrari senatum, quod
[libellus Ti(beri)] Caesaris Aug(usti) intumus et Germanici Caesaris f(ili) eius non
magis laudatio-
nem quam uitae totius ordinem et uirtut⟨is⟩ eius uerum testimonium contineret,
aeternae tradi memoriae et ipse se uelle non dissimulare eodem libello testatus
esset et esse utile iuuentuti liberorum posterorumque nostrorum iudicaret.
Item quo testatior esset Drusi Caesaris pietas, placere uti libellus, quem is proxu-
mo senatu recitasset, in aere incideretur eoque loco figeretur quo patri eius ipsique
placuisset.

likewise the poem in praise of Germanicus after his death which Tiberius
Caesar Augustus had given a rendition of in the senate on 16 December
should be inscribed on bronze and put up in a public place which his father
should choose. And the senate judges that this would be the more justifi-
able because the private tribute of Tiberius Caesar Augustus contains not
only a eulogy of his son Germanicus Caesar but rather an account of his
whole life and a true witness to his valour, and he himself declared in that
same tribute that he did not conceal his desire that it should be handed on
as an eternal memorial and he was of the opinion that it was useful for the
youth of our children and descendants.

Likewise, so that Drusus Caesar's feeling of family loyalty should be more
evident, they decided that the pamphlet which he read at the last meeting
of the senate should be inscribed on bronze and put up where his father
and he himself wished.

He believes that the discrepancy refutes Tacitus and reveals that the
historian has deliberately misrepresented the honours for Germanicus, through personal prejudice against the emperor Tiberius and
through a wish to portray him in the worst possible light.[108] If
accepted, this view would have serious consequences for Tacitus'
reputation as an historian who is generally reliable about the facts
he reports in general, and especially about the details of imperial
funerals, for which he is often the only source.

However, a closer examination of the fragmentary text of the
Tabula Siarensis reveals that the contradiction with Tacitus is only
apparent.[109] The *Tabula Siarensis* refers to two eulogies (*libelli*) of
Germanicus, namely a poem (*carmen*) by Tiberius and a prose oration by Drusus, the emperor's son. These were both delivered in the

[108] González (1984) 79: 'observaremos al punto en la palabras de éste una evi-
dente tergiversación de la realidad, un intento de ocultar los hechos o, en palabras
más precisas, una deformación buscada de la verdad, impulsada por la animadver-
sión que Tácito sentía por Tiberio que ya ha sido comentada por diversos autores.'
[109] Cf. Arce (1988a).

senate, Tiberius' on 16 December, and Drusus' at the following senate meeting. The decree records the decision to inscribe both tributes on bronze to be put up in the city. It seems evident that the
people's complaints which Tacitus records refer to a lack of publicly
delivered laments and speeches of the kind usually heard as part of
a funeral ceremony. Eulogies in the senate may also have been traditional, but had never replaced public speeches from the *rostra*.
Tacitus is not denying that eulogies of Germanicus were delivered
in the senate or inscribed on bronze.[110] He is saying that people
were dissatisfied at not hearing such speeches or poems delivered in
public, particularly as this was customary for the republican aristocracy and had been a feature of imperial family funerals under
Augustus. It is in fact unlikely that new evidence could confirm or
disprove such claims about popular opinion.

The more recent discovery of the *S.C. de Cn. Pisone patre* (116) has
served to confirm the general accuracy of Tacitus' account of the
events surrounding the death of Germanicus, especially the trial of
Piso. Popular unrest is suggested by the senate's praise of the plebs
for their willingness to contain their feelings and be swayed by the
emperor and others (lines 155-8).[111] The distribution of this text
throughout the empire and in the winter quarters of every Roman
legion further suggests the political crisis Tiberius faced in the sudden death of Germanicus and the implication of his own friend Piso
(lines 170-2). Our available evidence indicates that there were
indeed political reasons for Tiberius to limit public displays of grief
for Germanicus in Rome itself. It is important to recognize the difference in tone and intention between an official text like the *Tabula
Siarensis* and the text of Tacitus' history. Neither is an unbiased
source, and Tacitus is reacting to the official version of events he
read in laws and other documents. In this case the decrees of the
senate reveal details of posthumous honours for Germanicus, many
outside the city. Tacitus is mainly concerned with events and public feeling in Rome itself.

More problematic is Tacitus' statement about the role of Antonia,
the mother of Germanicus, at *Ann.* 3. 3. 2:

*matrem Antoniam non apud auctores rerum, non diurna actorum scriptura repe-
rio ullo insigni officio functam, cum super Agrippinam et Drusum et Claudium*

---

[110] Cf. Dio 55. 2. 2 for Augustus' praises in both prose and verse of Drusus the
brother of Tiberius, which may well also have been inscribed.
[111] For the plebs and their role after Germanicus' death, see Eck (1995).

ceteri quoque consanguinei nominatim perscripti sunt, seu valitudine prae-
pediebatur, seu victus luctu animus magnitudinem mali perferre visu non toler-
avit. facilius crediderim Tiberio et Augusta⟨e⟩, qui domo non excedebant,
cohibitam, ut par maeror et matris exemplo avia quoque et patruus attineri vider-
entur.

I have not discovered either in the historical writers or in the public records
of daily proceedings that his mother Antonia played any significant part
although, in addition to Agrippina and Drusus and Claudius, the other relatives appear by name in the written records. Perhaps her health failed her
or her spirit was overcome by grief and she could not bear to see the greatness of her misfortune. I would be more inclined to believe that Tiberius
and Augusta (Livia), who were not leaving the house, confined her so that
his grandmother and uncle might appear detained at home by an equal
grief and by the example of his mother.

The *Tabula Siarensis* clearly mentions Antonia as taking part in
decisions about the honours awarded to Germanicus.[112] Her statue
was to appear on an arch honouring Germanicus in the Circus
Flaminius near the representation of her son in a triumphal chariot.[113] Further confirmation of her appearance in official documents
can be found in the *S.C. de Cn. Pisone patre* (lines 140–2), where
Antonia is commended by the senate, albeit more briefly than other
family members appearing in a list of the relatives of Germanicus.
Given the considerable areas of agreement between this document
and the text of Tacitus it is hard to imagine that he had never read
it. In this case Tacitus does seem to be guilty of a deliberate
misrepresentation, or at best a considerable overstatement.[114]
Whatever personal animosity may have existed between Antonia
and Tiberius, her name did appear in the senate's decrees honouring Germanicus. Even if Tacitus is referring to other authors, or

---

[112] Frag. 1. 5–8: . . . *atque is, adsu[e]ta sibi [indulgentia, ex omnibus iis]* | *honoribus,*
quos habendos esse censebat senatus, legerit [eos, quos Ti(berius) Caesar Aug(ustus) et] |
Augusta mater eius et Drusus Caesar materque Germanici Ca[esaris et Agrippina uxore
eius] | *adhibita ab eis et deliberationi, satis apte posse haberi existu[mauerint. d(e) e(a) r(e)*
i(ta) c(ensuere):] ('and that he, with his usual indulgence, should choose from all the
honours which the senate thought appropriate those which Tiberius Caesar
Augustus and Augusta his mother and Drusus Caesar and the mother of Germanicus
Caesar and Agrippina his wife who was also included by them in the discussion, have
judged capable of being considered fitting enough. On this matter the following decisions were reached [by the senate]').

[113] Frag. 1. 20.

[114] Cf. González (1984) 80 and Potter (1987) 270 n. 3. Kokkinos (1992) 23–5
criticizes Tacitus' treatment of Antonia and his persistent confusion of the two sis-
ters of the same name.

official records not now extant, his statements are still seriously misleading in light of the epigraphical texts cited above.

The discovery of new inscriptions, the *Tabula Siarensis* and the *S.C. de Cn. Pisone patre*, supports Tacitus' overall accuracy in his account of the events of AD 19–20 surrounding the death of Germanicus, while at the same time clearly revealing his remarkable prejudice against Tiberius and Livia for their treatment of Antonia. Tacitus has let his guard down over the role of Germanicus' mother and shown that he is quite capable of factual distortion, especially in details which might not be familiar to his readers.

Leaving aside Tiberius' personal feelings towards Germanicus, it seems possible that his general attitude to funerals was somewhat different to that of Augustus.[115] He apparently deliberately avoided the emotional display and pomp connected with such an occasion.[116] In this context we may recall his warning, in an edict at the time of Augustus' death, against excessive public mourning, and the violence that had been associated with it during the Republic (Tac. *Ann.* I. 8. 5). Perhaps he feared that public mourning for a popular leader might cause a riot as had happened in the case of Julius Caesar, especially since rumours were circulating that Germanicus had been poisoned. In an edict Tiberius urged the people of Rome to bear the loss of Germanicus with fortitude and moderation, avoiding excessive or prolonged displays of public grief (Tac. *Ann.* 3. 6). Tiberius' approach provided a marked contrast in style with Augustus, who had openly mourned his family members with emotion. Tiberius, however, did not disapprove of public funerals as such, and on at least one occasion he delivered the funeral oration himself.[117] Dio records this as one of the services he rendered to his friends (57. 11. 7). This particular friend as been tentatively identified as P. Sulpicius Quirinius, who we know from Tacitus received a public funeral at the request of the *princeps* in AD 21.[118] Tiberius' decision in the case of Germanicus is all the more

[115] It is reasonable to suppose that there had been friction between Tiberius and Germanicus, especially over the latter's unauthorized visit to Egypt soon before his death (Tac. *Ann.* 2. 59 ff.). On Tacitus' portrayal of Germanicus, see now Pelling (1993).

[116] Ville (1981) 158–9 dates the end of gladiatorial games at private funerals to the reign of Tiberius.

[117] Augustus and Tiberius were generous with public funerals for individuals outside the imperial family; see Talbert (1984) 370–1.

[118] Tac. *Ann.* 3. 48. 1, as interpreted by Kierdorf (1980) 147.

striking if he did indeed himself speak at a public funeral the following year.

A challenge was issued to the new *princeps* in the magnificent funeral of Junia, the sister of Brutus and wife of Cassius, in AD 22 (Tac. *Ann.* 3. 76 = T89). The form the spectacle would take was made obvious from the start when the deceased mentioned nearly every leading figure in Rome in her will, while omitting to take any notice of the *princeps*. Unlike Scribonius Libo Drusus, her allegiances were firmly with the system of government represented by her ancestors. The figure of Brutus the first consul had served as powerful propaganda for Junia's brother Brutus in his lifetime and could well have been used to recall him after his death, since his own *imago* was not shown in public.[119] This funeral can be seen as a reply, in some sense, to the new imperial funerals exemplified especially by Augustus' own funeral eight years before. The number of related families represented may perhaps have produced a parade that matched Augustus' in length.[120] Many of the Roman heroes whom he had tried to lay claim to in the procession of those not related to him probably appeared here, in what was ostensibly a more traditional setting. Like Augustus, Junia had surely been planning her funeral for some time and a number of new *imagines* may have been needed. We do not know whether her funeral was exceptional or whether it started a new fashion in aristocratic funerals.

Tiberius had the opportunity to give his reply to this challenge the following year, after the death of his son Drusus. Tacitus notes that this funeral was particularly remarkable for the splendour of the procession of *imagines* (Tac. *Ann.* 4. 9. 2 = T90). Employing what was probably a variation on the Augustan theme, Tiberius presented a twofold procession. One section comprised the Julii led by Aeneas, the Alban kings, and then Romulus, the other the Claudii, who were preceded by the Sabine nobility, the ancestors of Attus Clausus.[121] It is not clear from Tacitus' brief allusion whether Romulus was really treated as an ancestor of the Julii. It is perhaps more likely that Romulus introduced the now standard parade of

[119] For Brutus and his *imagines*, see Ch. 3 § 4.

[120] Tac. *Ann.* 3. 76 = T89 alludes to twenty families providing *imagines* but only names two patrician ones. Lahusen (1983) 124 has no reason to assume that Junia's was one of the last family funerals with *imagines*.

[121] The order of the procession is important and has mostly not been noticed at all or been recast to put Attus Clausus at the head of the Claudii, as for example by Bettini (1991) 177–8.

heroes from Rome's past, as seen at previous imperial funerals and in the Forum of Augustus. Drusus' procession may have set up a comparison of sorts between the Julii accompanied by the general category of Roman heroes and the splendid *imagines* of the patrician Claudii, which also stretched back to an age before the foundation of the city. There is no evidence to show whether Tiberius was responsible for expanding the line of Claudii, or whether this represented no more than their traditional *imagines*.[122] Seneca notes that Tiberius appeared before the weeping crowds to deliver the funeral oration, apparently unmoved by his loss.[123] This is evidence for the character and approach of Tiberius. There can be no doubt that Tiberius was deeply affected by the death of his son and heir. His choice not to show grief in public is an indication of his personal attitude towards such displays.[124]

The funeral of Livia in AD 29, which took place after Tiberius had left Rome for Capri, was simple.[125] Gaius, who was 17, delivered the eulogy for his great-grandmother. This ceremony seems to have marked a return to 'traditional' practices by limiting display, especially for the funeral of a woman, and by presenting a young speaker who delivered a single oration. Tiberius' own funeral was perhaps planned by Gaius, who gave a splendid show and a tearful eulogy.[126] However, Dio notes that Gaius used his speech more to celebrate the memory of Augustus and Germanicus, while presenting his own position to the people (59. 3. 8). Such an occasion no doubt enhanced the already popular new *princeps* at the start of his reign.

3. Conclusion

As this chapter has tried to show, the evidence about *imagines* in the early imperial period elucidates their importance during the

[122] As argued above, there were probably connections in content between this funeral and that of Tiberius' brother Drusus as staged by Augustus in 9 BC. But see also Tacitus' concern elsewhere (*Ann*. 2. 43. 6 = T86) with an unfavourable comparison between Drusus and Germanicus; for Drusus' great-grandfather was Cicero's friend Atticus, who was only an *eques*. This pedigree is said to bring disgrace on the *imagines* of the patrician Claudii.

[123] Sen. *Cons. ad Marc*. 15. 3: *flente populo Romano non flexit vultum* ('While the Roman people wept he kept his expression unchanged').

[124] Levick (1976) 162 notes that Tiberius suffered many bereavements in the years AD 20–23. For her comments on his interest in stoicism, see 18 and 82.

[125] Tac. *Ann*. 5. 1. 4: *funus eius modicum* ('her funeral was modest').

[126] Suet. *Cal*. 15. 1: *funeratoque amplissime* ('he was given a very grand funeral'). Cf. Dio 58. 28. 5.

Republic. In creating his new position as *princeps* Augustus employed *imagines* both directly to enhance the funerals celebrated by his family and indirectly as inspirations for the statues of Roman heroes in his new forum. Tiberius followed Augustus' lead in producing magnificent funeral spectacle which rivalled the grandest shows of the old republican aristocracy of office-holders. *Imagines* were a significant ingredient in the public presentation of the Julio-Claudians as a dynasty. As in so many other areas, Augustus' innovations in the use of *imagines* need to be seen as a logical development of aristocratic self-advertisement during the Republic. His precedents were influential both for successors and opponents of the new political order.

9

Imagines in the Later Empire:
The Last *Imagines*

Senators of the time of Boethius were highly conscious of their
descent from the great families the late empire and sometimes maintained their traditions in quite precise terms.

(Matthews (1985*b*) 19)

As has been argued in detail in the previous chapter, the *imagines*
did not die out under the early Empire, nor were they replaced by
busts carried in aristocratic funeral processions.[1] Rather they continued to be powerful symbols of rank and political aspiration, both
within and outside the aristocratic home. Changes in electoral practices and the growing influence of the *princeps* removed much of the
basic function of *imagines* as advertisements aimed directly at the
electors. Nevertheless, their long and venerable history during
the Republic and their place in the iconography developed by
Augustus himself assured that the *imagines* did not quickly become
obsolete. Indeed, they need to be understood as part of the trappings
of the Republic which were tolerated and even encouraged under
the Julio-Claudian emperors. The above considerations raise two
questions about *imagines* in the imperial period: how long were they
still made and what were they used for? What follows attempts to
give an answer on the basis of the available evidence, which is very
thin after the early third century AD.[2]

---

[1] This is the view of Boethius (1942) 229 ff. and Bianchi Bandinelli (1970) 76.
Rollin's theory (1979) 33 ff. that the *imagines* became no more than an empty custom is overstated. Lahusen (1985*b*) 267 thinks they were only used by the imperial
family. Neudecker (1988) 75 interprets *imagines* in first century AD literature as a
topos.

[2] It is notable that the history of *imagines* in the later Empire has not been fully
examined before.

1. Imagines *under the Julio-Claudians*

A consideration of *imagines* after the fall of the Republic must start from a full appreciation of their very public role under Augustus and Tiberius. *Imagines* appeared at funerals of the ruling family and contributed to the new imperial iconography, such as that of the Forum of Augustus, which was designed to establish the leading position of the *princeps* by comparing his achievements with those of earlier heroes, who were the ancestors of Rome's traditional office-holding families. There is reason to believe that the appropriation of ancestral imagery by the ruling clan helped to foster the private use of *imagines* and related images by senatorial families. Many prominent families had been weakened or eliminated as a result of civil wars and proscriptions at the end of the Republic.[3] Survivors and their clans, therefore, clung to traditions and probably inspired new senators to adopt habits common under the Republic, as had been usual for *novi homines* in previous times.[4] The early Principate can be characterized as a period when *imagines* and other ancestral imagery flourished after taking on a new role in justifying the power of one man and his family within the state.

Confirmation of the importance of *imagines* in this period can be found in the family traditions of the Licinii and Calpurnii. Closely involved with but often opposed to the ruling family, the Calpurnii Pisones are noted in the ancient sources for the especially grand display of family portraits and genealogies to be found in their *atria*.[5] The consciousness of a glorious heritage helps to account for their independent and sometimes defiant role in politics.[6] The discovery and analysis of a family tomb of the Licinii and Calpurnii on the Via Salaria outside Rome illustrates their ambitions.[7] The tomb has now been dated to around AD 40 and is an important historical document in its own right. The front of the tomb was decorated with thirteen

---

[3] For the depletion of republican families, see Tac. *Ann.* 1. 2. 1 and Syme (1939) 187 ff., 490 ff., and (1986) 1 ff. and 32 ff.

[4] See Talbert (1984) for a recent account of the imperial senate. For new men during the Republic, see Wiseman (1971).

[5] For the *imagines* of the Calpurnii Pisones, see Cic. *Pis.* 1 = T13; *S.C. de Cn. Pisone patre* 73–82 = I16; *Laus Pisonis* = T36, Mart. 4. 40. 1–4; and esp. Plin. *Ep.* 5. 17 = T57 for the ancestors watching a rhetorical display by the young men of the house.

[6] See e.g. Tac. *Ann.* 2. 43 for Piso, the consul of 23 BC, who maintained an independent position (*PIR* 1. 248). Cf. Syme (1986) 329 ff. and 367 ff. on other Pisones.

[7] See Boschung (1986) for a full description and discussion of the tomb.

sculpted portraits of a similar style showing both recently deceased family members and more distant ancestors, such as Pompey, in the form of busts.[8] The use of portraits accompanied by inscriptions to reconstruct a family's heritage in a public place recalls the display of *imagines* in the *atrium*, as well as the use of statues in the Forum of Augustus and elsewhere in the city. Families such as the Calpurnii felt strong links with their republican ancestors whether by direct descent or by marriage.

This proud display of family portraits at the tomb was erected about twenty years after the disgrace and death of Germanicus' rival Cn. Calpurnius Piso and his relative Scribonius Libo Drusus.[9] It is contemporary with the anonymous poem of praise known as the *Laus Pisonis*, which was probably addressed to the young Piso who subsequently became the figurehead for a conspiracy against Nero in AD 65.[10] The poem is a rare and valuable example of a largely lost genre of praise poetry commissioned directly from dependent poets for an occasion like a birthday or a consulship. The ancestors, represented by their *imagines* and *tituli*, were an essential topic in the praise and glorification of the aristocrat, and particularly of the young man with few achievements of his own to boast about. The promise of future greatness is closely linked by the poet to the merits of the ancestors, as can be paralleled in the *elogia* for young men from the tomb of the Scipios.[11] Genealogical themes may often have served as a convenient opening to such a poem, as is the case for the *Laus Pisonis* and the earlier *Panegyricus Messallae*. Poetry is likened to the *tituli* in perpetuating the renown of both Piso and Mesalla.[12] The cultural significance of habitual praise of

[8] These are best illustrated in *Kaiser Augustus und die verlorene Republik* (1988) nos. 154-66. Boschung (1986) 286: 'Die Büsten vergegenwärtigen den genealogischen Hintergrund der Familie, der gleichzeitig deren Ansicht und politische Stellung begründete.' Pompey had been given pride of place as an ancestor of Augustus in the funeral procession of the first emperor in AD 14 (Dio 56. 34 = T28). For a discussion of the portrait of Pompey, which was based on a public statue (perhaps that from his theatre), and its role at the tomb, see Giuliani (1986) 25-100.

[9] See Ch. 1 for Piso and Scribonius Libo Drusus. Their relationship is shown by the family tree of Boschung (1986) 262.

[10] See Reeve (1984), followed by Champlin (1989).

[11] See *ILLRP* 311, 312, and 316 = I13, 16, and 15 discussed in Ch. 5. Champlin (1989) 124: 'The heritage was crushing. It informs and distorts, it ultimately defeats, a well-meaning panegyric by a young poet who had little material to work with, and it is the only reason why, 25 years later, a man with no qualities was chosen as the handsome and affable figurehead of a conspiracy against the emperor Nero.'

[12] Cf. *Panegyricus Messallae* 28-34 = T52 and *Laus Pisonis* 2 ff. = T36.

the ancestors and their deeds is brought out by the portraits from the tomb, which serve as similar advertisements and affirmations of rank. It was at this time that Caligula destroyed the republican statues of famous Romans which Augustus had moved from the Capitol to the Campus Martius on the excuse that they were taking up too much space.[13]

The *imagines* therefore continued to play a large role in the public presentation of self as cultivated by leading families of the early Empire, especially those with republican ancestors.[14] These families both imitated and rivaled the genealogical claims and iconography of the Julio-Claudian family itself. The emperor Claudius mentioned the *imagines* of the patrician Fabii in a brief aside in a speech to the senate in AD 48 (T26). Seneca (T72–6) stressed the displays of *imagines* in aristocratic houses at the time of Nero and criticized them as symbols of worldly ambition and pride.[15] Major changes only came at the end of the dynasty, and were precipitated by the fire which destroyed many older sections of Rome in AD 64. As Suetonius (*Nero* 38. 2) testifies, it was this fire which destroyed most of the old aristocratic homes together with their traditional decorations, notably spoils which often dated back to famous battles of the Republic.[16] The fire was followed by the construction of Nero's Domus Aurea and later imperial buildings which began to replace what had been private houses and the headquarters for the political families of the republican oligarchy.[17] Tacitus, however, still refers to the great aristocratic households and their ranks of clients and freedmen in his account of the state of the Empire in AD 69.[18]

Further evidence for the influence of *imagines* and the culture they embodied can be found in Valerius Maximus' collection of

[13] (Suet. *Cal.* 34). Cf. *Cal.* 35 for Caligula's attempt to abolish the use of famous *cognomina* from the Republic.

[14] For senatorial self-representation in the early Empire, see esp. Eck (1984).

[15] Propertius (2. 13b. 1–8 = T63) rejects the usual grand funeral with *imagines* since as a lover he is a poor man and a slave of love. For Martial (5. 20 = T48) at the end of the first century AD the *imagines* still represent the pressured life of the great houses of the aristocrats and the Forum with its lawsuits.

[16] For spoils, see Rawson (1990).

[17] For the Domus Aurea, see Platner and Ashby (1929) s.v. Domus Aurea and M. T. Griffin (1984) 133 ff. with more recent bibliography and a plan. For new excavations, see Carandini (1988) 359–73 and Patterson (1992) 203–4, who discuss the problem of where aristocrats lived in imperial Rome and the importance of the fire in destroying the prime aristocratic living area since the early Republic.

[18] *Hist.* 1. 4; cf. Juv. 8 and Plin. *Ep.* 1. 9.

memorable deeds and sayings which he dedicated to the emperor Tiberius. His handbook is written as an anthology of historical *exempla* for use in speeches by lawyers and rhetoricians of all kinds.[19] It also offered easy access to traditional Roman aristocratic culture for the new upwardly mobile classes of the Principate, who served in the army, in the courts, and in the imperial bureaucracy. Valerius' presentation of his material is heavily influenced by the rhetorical exercises of the schools and its content is drawn from orthodox historical sources, such as Cicero and Livy, and reflects the search for 'Romanness' in diction and subject. Valerius allows his readers to appropriate the traditions created by the great Roman families of the Republic.[20] His concern is with differences of status as a new generation of humble or municipal origin sought to imitate the great figures of Rome's past and therefore to become their true descendants.[21] Valerius' work further supported the ethos of the Principate which stressed continuity with the past and a revival of ancestral customs and standards.

2. Imagines *in the Struggle for Empire: AD 69–70*

Imagines emerge as a powerful means of propaganda in the years AD 69–70, when civil wars broke out in the struggle to determine a successor after the suicide of Nero. Power passed for a short time to the elderly senator Galba, the first heir to the Julio-Claudians. His appeal was based on the fact that he was a member of the old aristocracy.[22] He stressed his descent from his great-grandfather Quintus Catulus Capitolinus in the inscriptions on his statues.[23] Suetonius tells us that after he became emperor he advertised his

[19] See Bloomer (1992) for a thorough and enlightening discussion of Valerius' work.

[20] Bloomer (1992) 259: 'The true aristocrat does not feel the need to learn of his past through reading; his methods of acculturation are familial, institutional, and traditional. It is the arriviste who learns of the Roman through a handbook and whose anxieties about the aristocratic culture he seeks to appropriate direct Valerius' work.'

[21] It comes as no surprise that Scipio Africanus is Valerius' favourite example, but nearly 10% of his work pertains to Marius, who is the archetypal 'new man' for Valerius just as he was for the elder Sen. *Con.* 1. 6. 3–4 = T68. Cf. Bloomer (1992) 150.

[22] For the coinage of the rebels of AD 68, which reasserted republican ideas of liberty, see Wallace-Hadrill (1981*b*) 33, 37–8 and (1986) 70.

[23] He was Q. Lutatius Catulus (*RE* 8, cos. 78 BC, cens. 65 BC).

noble ancestry by placing an extensive family tree in his new imperial *atrium* (Suet. *Gal.* 2 = T82). He traced his paternal line back to
Jupiter and his mother's family to Pasiphaë, the daughter of Minos.
Suetonius' brief description of the family tree suggests a traditional
format showing full descent on the side of both parents. Like many
Romans, Galba combined a family of republican office-holders with
mythical and divine ancestors.

Displays of ancestral propaganda were one of the memorable
things about Galba, whose short reign ended in assassination in
January AD 69. Galba had been a close friend and associate of the
Julio-Claudian house and a special favourite of Livia. He showed his
appreciation for their use of *imagines* by emulating their claims to
pre-eminence in republican terms. Shortly before his fall he adopted
L. Calpurnius Piso Frugi Licinianus as his heir and successor.[24] In
doing so he confirmed that his claim to lead depended on the prestige of the old office-holding caste. Piso belonged to the same family of Calpurnii whose tomb was notable for its ancestral portraits
and he was later buried there.[25] He was also an in-law of Galba's
and heir to his private estate before the latter's proclamation as
emperor.

A direct and public link with the Calpurnii Pisones could serve to
connect Galba with the failed conspiracy of AD 65.[26] As noted
above, the conspirator Piso was famous for his family tree and the
proud display to be seen in his *atrium* was celebrated by Martial.[27]
The Licinii and Calpurnii emerged as pretenders to the throne at
points of weakness in the Principate, which is to say at the beginning of the reign of Claudius, after the death of Nero, and under
Nerva.[28]

It is notable that Vespasian, the ultimate victor in the struggle
for empire, had no *imagines* of ancestors, although his brother had
a distinguished career before him and his family was apparently not

[24] Tac. *Hist.* 1. 14-19. Boschung (1986) 260-3 explains the prosopography. Piso
had been Galba's heir for a long time already. He chose him over his own aristocratic relative Cornelius Dolabella; cf. Tac. *Hist.* 1. 88; Suet. *Gal.* 12.
[25] For his inscription found on an altar at the tomb, see *CIL* 6. 31723 = *ILS* 240
= Gordon 1. 126.
[26] Tac. *Ann.* 15. 48 ff.
[27] Mart. 4. 40. 1-4 bears witness to this Piso's family tree in his *atrium*.
[28] The plot of C. Calpurnius Crassus Frugi Licinianus, cos. suff. AD 87 and grandson of the consul of AD 27, against Nerva and Trajan after the murder of Domitian
is attested by Dio 68. 3. 2 and 16. 2; *Epitome de Caesaribus* 12. 6; *H.A. Hadrian* 5.

without pretensions.[29] In his portrayal of Vespasian's decision to allow himself to be acclaimed emperor, Tacitus makes the *imagines* part of Mucianus' argument in encouraging Vespasian (*Hist.* 2. 76. 2 = T94). Licinius Mucianus, the governor of Syria and ally of Vespasian, expresses the opinion that it was reasonable for Vespasian to recognize Galba as emperor because of his illustrious ancestry, represented by his many *imagines*, but that after his murder the way now stands open for Vespasian's own claim.[30] This speech is not an exact transcription of what was actually said, but it does fit in with other ancient testimony about Galba's use of ancestral propaganda. Tacitus thought it was eminently plausible for Galba to present himself in terms of his ancestors and for others to support him on these grounds. In the end Vespasian's claim to power presented him partly as an avenger of Galba's murder, as well as being a favourite of the gods.[31] At the start of rule by an emperor without the traditional qualifications of descent, it was important to find new ways to make the candidate seem especially suitable for the job. The rise to power of the Flavians inaugurated a new age of emperors without their own family traditions of *imagines* and heralded a transformation in both public and private iconography. Vespasian also helped to change the ethos of society with his simple life-style and frugal habits. Both Tacitus and Pliny comment on the luxury and extravagance common under the Julio-Claudians, but which was very much out of fashion by their day at the end of the first century AD.[32] Such luxury had been associated especially with the great aristocratic households, and with their splendid *imagines*.[33] The new men from the municipalities and provinces who replaced them in power did not emulate their

[29] Suetonius sketches the family background in his biography. Syme (1958) x: 'In armed competition for the purple, the premium on ancestors fell sharply.' Vespasian's brother was the first to reach the consulship and must have been represented by an *imago* after his death.

[30] Note the expression *cedere imaginibus* used at Tac. *Hist.* 2. 76. 2 = T94 and at Prop. 1. 5. 23-4 = T62.

[31] For the religious policy of the Flavians, see especially Tac. *Hist.* 2. 2. 2 for Titus' visit to Venus on Paphos at a key moment in the civil war; 2. 78 for Vespasian's prodigies and his visit to Carmel; and Josephus *BJ* 7. 5. 4 for Vespasian and Titus sleeping in the Temple of Isis before their joint triumph after the capture of Jerusalem. For Galba's and Vespasian's use of religion, see Potter (1994) 172-3.

[32] Note Tac. *Ann.* 3. 55, 16. 5, and Plin. *Ep.* 7. 24 with Sherwin-White (1966) 430-1.

[33] See Ch. 1 for the pretensions and life-style of Scribonius Libo Drusus.

grandeur but looked back to a more traditional Roman austerity.[34] Moreover, the Roman house itself had changed so that the *atrium* was no longer necessarily the central room and many newer houses were built without *atria*.[35]

3. *The Second and Third Centuries* AD

The second century AD offers ample primary evidence about *imagines*. Many references reveal that they were still familiar objects, needing no additional explanation for the reader of histories or letters. Our sources are Plutarch, Tacitus, Pliny the Younger, Suetonius, and Appian.[36] Appian is significant because he is the latest in the group, writing in retirement and publishing his histories by about 165 AD. He writes as an eyewitness to the public use of *imagines* in funeral processions by the patrician Cornelii of his day (*Iber.* 89 = T2). There seems little doubt that the Cornelii were not alone in this practice. Rather, *imagines* were still worn and public eulogies still delivered in the Antonine age. It is after this that the evidence for the *imagines* changes and becomes obscure.

Imagines are attested in the early third century AD by the historian Dio and by the commentator on Horace, Pomponius Porfyrio.[37] Both sources assert that *imagines* were now only to be seen in the streets of Rome at funeral ceremonies for emperors. Dio is a particularly important witness as he was a senator of consular rank, close to the ruling family, and himself entitled to *imagines* according to traditional custom.[38] He was in a position to know the facts and has been appreciated above all for the information he recorded about his own day.[39] By the time of the Severans, therefore, the public role of the *imagines* had been severely curtailed and can only have been

[34] See Ch. 4 § 6 and Ch. 8 § 2 for discussion of sumptuary legislation during the Republic and the changing relationship between *imagines* and displays of wealth.
[35] This development can be traced at Pompeii which was destroyed in AD 79. For a fuller discussion, see Ch. 7 § 1. Domitian's new palace was built without an *atrium*.
[36] The relevant passages from these authors can be found in Appendix A: Plutarch = T59-60, Tacitus = T85-95, Pliny = T55-8, Suet. = T80-4, and Appian = T2.
[37] Pomponius Porfyrio is usually dated to the early 3rd cent. AD, although dates as late as the 5th cent. have been suggested. See Helm *RE* ad loc.
[38] Dio shared his second consulship with the emperor Severus Alexander in AD 229. For his career and background, see *PIR* 2. 493.
[39] For Dio as an historian of his own times, see Millar (1964) esp. 171-3 and Bering-Staschewski (1981).

very limited. Without the spectacle of the *pompa funebris* or the explanation of the *laudatio* the very form of the masks had lost its original purpose. Perhaps this change was made by a Severan emperor who decided to complete Augustus' appropriation of the ancestors by banning *imagines* from private funerals. How many families still kept *imagines* at home after they could no longer be displayed at funerals?

4. Imagines *in the later Roman Empire*

After the Severan period the sources mentioning *imagines* are few and of widely differing reliability. However, the poor quality and scarcity of the evidence is no justification for a view that *imagines* became entirely the property of emperors in the third century AD. Only four references to *imagines* have survived from the later imperial period; in chronological order these are an edict of Constantine quoted in the Justinian Code (*Cod. Just.* 5. 37. 22. 3 = I17), HA *Severus Alexander* 29. 2 = T31 and HA *Tacitus* 19. 6 = T32, and Boethius *Con.* 1 *pros.* 1. 3 = T4. The gaps in the evidence are considerable. There could be close to a century between Dio and Constantine's edict of AD 326. Again about 125 years may separate the anonymous author of the *Historia Augusta* biographies and Boethius. Interpretation of the ancient material therefore depends not only on the reliability of each author but also on the significance we choose to ascribe to the intervening centuries of silence.

Much rests on how one reads the *Codex Justinianus*, which comes from the second and revised law code published by a panel of legal experts on the instructions of the emperor Justinian in AD 534. The collection was made from the edicts of previous emperors which were still considered legally valid at the time. Obsolete legislation was not included and careful attention was paid to the date and authorship of each law.[40] The specific mention of the *imagines* in the house by Constantine shows their continuing importance in the new Christian empire. They are part of the furnishings of a house which must be passed on intact to an heir who is left as a minor upon the death of his father. The identification of *imagines* with inheritance and their role in giving character to the house recall

---

[40] The laws were arranged into books by subject, but chronologically within each category. The *imagines* fall into the sphere of private law (books 2–8).

points made earlier by Sallust and Pliny.[41] The republication of this edict in a code of law over 200 years after its original date is in itself testimony to the abiding presence of *imagines* in the aristocratic household. Since the wording of each ruling was made consistent and up-to-date under Justinian, the term *maiorum imagines* was apparently in no need of any explanation in the sixth century AD.

The date of Justinian's second law code is close to the time when Boethius was writing in prison under suspicion of treason.[42] Boethius uses the colour of antique, smoke-stained *imagines* in a simile to describe the dress worn by the allegorical figure of the Lady Philosophy, who appears to comfort him in prison. The dress was made by the Lady herself of fine thread and is decorated with Greek letters but it has been torn by violent hands.[43] The passing allusion to the *imagines* assumes his audience will not be confused by the reference. His words are close to traditional republican descriptions of *imagines*, notably Cicero's account of their colour.[44] Although the *imagines* appear very near the beginning of his work, just as they do in praise poetry,[45] no earlier parallel is extant for the use of an *imago* in a simile or metaphor. It is tempting to suppose that Boethius is himself innovating with his literary use of *imagines*. His reference to their colour presupposes that they are still made of wax and therefore apt to become stained.

The mention of the *imagines* in a law code published a mere fifteen or so years later[46] puts Boethius' words firmly in context as the testimony of a traditional senator, a native of Rome and close to its heritage, who was entitled to *imagines* in his home.[47] Any

[41] Sall. *Jug.* 85. 38 = T66 and Plin. *Nat.* 35. 7 = T54, also Val. Max. 5. 8. 3 = T103.

[42] Boethius' arrest seems to have come late in AD 523 and he was executed in prison some time later. See Martindale (1980) s.v. Boethius 5, Chadwick (1981), and Gibson (1981).

[43] For the dress and its meanings, see Chadwick (1981) 225–6.

[44] For the smoky colour of the *imagines*, see Cic. *Pis.* 1 = T13, Sen. *Ep.* 44. 5 = T75, and Juv. 8. 8 = T35. The use of the same words by the consul of 63 BC and his successor of AD 510 is striking.

[45] Cf. *Panegyricus Messallae* 28–34 = T52 and *Laus Pisonis* 2 ff. = T36.

[46] In fact, this edict probably also appeared in Justinian's first law code of AD 529, which now survives only in fragments. Its original republication is, therefore, very close to Boethius' death in AD 524 or 525.

[47] Anicius Manlius Severinus Boethius came of a family of office-holders and was consul in AD 510. His father had been consul in AD 487 and his sons were joint consuls for AD 522. As a child he was adopted by the powerful Symmachi and he was also related to the Anicii, who were among the first Christian aristocrats in Rome. Boethius' father is represented in official garb on an ivory dyptich in Brescia, see Matthews (1985b) 27 and Chadwick (1981) 5.

attempt to explain away Boethius' words as no more than a literary reference familiar to his learned readers fails because of the legal pedigree of the term *maiorum imagines*. Boethius' use of the characteristic appearance of the *imagines* in the symbolic language of imagery is revealing of his particular ingenuity, as well as of the concerns of his class and social milieu. The old political traditions of Rome still had meaning and were carefully cultivated even in families which had by now developed a considerable Christian heritage.[48] The continuing power of pagan images, such as the *imagines*, can be especially appreciated in the context of the emotional intensity of Boethius' work of consolation. The *imagines* are associated by him with the comforts and justification offered by 'philosophy' to a traditional Roman senator who opposes the tyranny of an unjust emperor. Clearly there are many historical allusions to earlier Roman writers in Boethius' work. But these also reflect the nature of his troubles and above all the way he perceived himself and his role in society.[49]

The appearance of *imagines* in two biographies written by the anonymous author of the *Historia Augusta* can be dated to a time between Constantine's original edict and Boethius.[50] The biographies, their authorship, and their date have been the source of such controversy that it is hard to use anything in them to support a convincing historical argument.[51] A good example is the description of Severus Alexander's household shrine, which allegedly contained images of Christ and Abraham next to traditional *imagines* of ancestors. Nothing can be gained from this kind of evidence.[52] The information from the life of the emperor Tacitus, who reigned briefly in AD 275, is of greater interest. According to the biographer, Tacitus'

[48] See Matthews (1985a) 484: 'A full study of the Roman aristocracy spanning the entire period of the Roman Empire would bring into prominence a continuity which might be less complete than the aristocrats themselves would have wished, but would still be impressive.'

[49] See Matthews (1985b) 38.

[50] I accept the dating of Syme, following Dessau, to *c.* AD 395 and the assumption of a single author. Cf. Syme (1971) 284: 'Not forgery, therefore. Rather "imposture" or "impersonation".'

[51] The bibliography on the *Historia Augusta* is vast and includes notably Syme (1968), (1971), and (1983). Much discussion can be found in the *Bonner Historia Augusta Colloquia*. For bibliography on the individual lives, see Merten (1986) 177 ff. for Severus Alexander and Merten (1987) 111 ff. for Tacitus.

[52] Syme (1983) 214 dismisses the *lararium* and its contents as one of many 'fables'.

accession occasioned much celebration amongst senators, who valued him as one of their number. As a result their *imagines* were put on display by having their cupboards opened and by being decorated frequently. We can know little of the emperor Tacitus or of his age, but this testimony does show knowledge of a traditional use of *imagines* in the *atria* of private houses. It is tempting to accept this as evidence for practices and habits current in the author's own time near the end of the fourth century AD.[53]

What importance should then be accorded to the gaps in our continuous evidence about *imagines*? Should we posit a period of obsolescence for ancestor masks, followed by a revival prompted by antiquarian research and nostalgia for old Roman customs? Silences cannot necessarily be construed as particularly telling. Nor is it possible to measure the exact extent of the continuity undoubtedly present in aristocratic culture during Late Antiquity. It is characteristic of late Roman families that they tended to stress their links with earlier ancestors and élite circles dating back to the Republic.[54] Nevertheless, leaving aside the questionable evidence of the *Historia Augusta*, the most economical explanation for the appearance of *imagines* in Boethius and in the Justinian Code is that they had indeed survived in the homes of at least some prominent senatorial families. At the same time, a mark of the society of Late Antiquity was its mobility. Many statesmen and emperors were produced by the army and had no connections with earlier office-holders and their customs.[55] In the present state of our evidence it is not possible to give a satisfactory account of the function of the *imagines* in late antique society. It is not even clear whether by this period *imagines* were still kept in the *atrium*, where such a room still existed.[56]

Since the centre of political power had moved from Rome long before, the habits of old senatorial families in the city are less well

---

[53] Syme (1971) 241-2 notes that the *HA* did not really know who Tacitus was or much about him and says: 'The fabrications have their modest utility. They illustrate aspects of life in the author's own time. Thus the importance of the *praefectus urbi* or the copying of manuscripts: about the year 400 the eminent Symmachus supervised a revision of the text of Livy.'

[54] Cf. *H.A. Alexander Severus* 44. 3 for Severus' family tree tracing his descent from the Caecilii Metelli of the Republic. Q. Aurelius Memmius Symmachus, Boethius' father-in-law and adopted father, wrote a history of Rome in imitation of his ancestors, according to Cassiodorus *CCSL* 96, p. v.

[55] See P. Brown (1971) 26 ff., 36, and 38.

[56] See J. R. Clarke (1991) 363-4 for the virtual dissappearance of the *atrium* as it became little more than an entrance to the peristyle in the later imperial period.

documented. It seems unlikely that traditional *imagines* could have had much of a role to play in the highly formal ritual of the Byzantine emperors, nor in the elaborate hierarchy of their courtiers and ministers.[57] Nevertheless, *imagines* did survive at Rome and were not the only ancestral images in senatorial homes of the Late Empire.

Sidonius Apollinaris refers in a letter to statues of office-holding ancestors in full magisterial costume kept in the home.[58] His letter, written in the 450s AD, is addressed to Eutropius, a fellow member of the élite whom Sidonius is urging to come to Rome and engage in public service in imitation of his ancestors. Eutropius was probably related to Sabinus, the consul of AD 316, and seems to have followed Sidonius' advice.[59] The statues of ancestors are used in the same way as *imagines* to inspire political ambition and as an everyday reminder of past achievements. Sidonius encourages Eutropius to consider the city of Rome a familiar environment because of the role his ancestors had played there. Like Boethius after him, Sidonius held high office and enjoyed special imperial favour.[60] Sidonius was also a Christian and became bishop of Clermont later in life.[61] His letter confirms the continuing use of ancestral images in office-holding families in the West and in a Christian context.

The last *imagines* to be found in senatorial homes elude us as there is no more evidence beyond Justinian's Code of the early sixth century AD. It is possible that *imagines* were made as long as there were senators in Rome.[62] It appears likely that such late antique

[57] For an introduction to the structured society of Late Antiquity, see A. H. M. Jones (1964), P. Brown (1971), and Cameron (1993a) and (1993b). On ceremony, see MacCormack (1981). See P. Brown (1971) 150 on the court of Justinian: 'The stage-set of traditional ceremonies inherited from the Roman past was wheeled away to leave the emperor alone in his majesty.'

[58] Sid. Apoll. *Ep.* 1. 6: *senatorii seminis homo, qui cotidie trabeatis proavorum imaginibus ingeritur* ('a man of senatorial descent, who keeps company every day with the images of his ancestors in consular dress'). For the *trabea* as the consul's dress, see Sid. Apoll. 15. 150, 7. 384, 23. 174.

[59] See Sid. Apoll. *Ep.* 3. 6 congratulating Eutropius on his appointment as *praefectus praetorio Galliarum* and taking some credit for his new prominence. For Eutropius' family, see Martindale (1980) s.v. Eutropius 3.

[60] For Sidonius' noble lineage, see *Ep.* 1. 3. 1; Greg. Tur. *HF* 2. 21; and Martindale (1980) s.v. Apollinaris 6. Sidonius married the daughter of the emperor Avitus.

[61] See Van Dam (1985) 157–76 on Sidonius and the Christian culture of 5th cent. Gaul.

[62] The Roman senate is last attested in the late sixth century *Dialogues* of Gregory the Great (d. AD 604); see P. Brown (1971) 181. In AD 541 Justinian abolished the consulship in the East. Wormald (1976) discusses the survival of the aristocracy of Late Antiquity into the early Medieval period.

imagines were indeed part of a continuous tradition of wax ancestor masks of office-holders which stretched back to the Republic. The burden of proof lies with any who want to argue that the later *imagines* were merely an archaizing revival of earlier senatorial habits. The *imagines*, therefore, survived in some homes at least 300 years after they were last paraded at an aristocratic family funeral. Such continuity of practice indicates the cultural significance attached to the *imagines*, a significance going far beyond their role in republican politics. The *imagines* outlived the removal of the last Roman emperor in the West in AD 476.[63] To the very end of the Roman empire they were part of what identified a Roman aristocrat, if no longer for a wider circle, at least for himself and his peers. *Imagines*, then, continued to have emotional and symbolic meaning for an aristocracy which consciously modelled itself on earlier Roman figures, but which was also fully involved with the new cultural and religious life of the Christian empire. Although our knowledge of the role of *imagines* in the world of Late Antiquity is severely limited, their very presence suggests their adaptability, as well as the place assigned to them by senators like Boethius in their own construction of a specifically Roman culture.

[63] See Chadwick (1981) 1: 'Barbarian army commanders and the fainéant emperors whom they made and unmade might come and go, but through it all the senators retained their land and power and made themselves indispensible to the administration.'

IO

Conclusions

> Toutes les sociétés éprouvent le besoin de se donner le specta-
> cle d'elles-mêmes, d'incarner dans des personnages, d'inscrire
> dans des chants, des danses, des images mimées les principales
> forces qu'elle devine en elle.
>
> (Grimal (1975) 249)

> The citizens are not naive bumpkins taken in by the leader's
> manipulation, but participants in a theatricality whose rules
> and roles they understand and enjoy.
>
> (Connor (1987) 46)

THE present study has attempted to explore the role played by traditional *imagines* which contributed to the social standing and influence of office-holding families. A striking feature of the Roman
republican constitution was the consistency with which certain
leading families could be elected to the highest magisterial offices
over several generations. Any student of Roman life must try to
account for this pattern, which shaped the character of Roman
oligarchy. In a basic sense political power depended on a series of
election victories, which defined rank and precedence within the
nobility of office. These victories, in turn, were influenced by the
impression of a candidate's family created by the masks of his ancestors, which explained and justified his election to Roman citizens of
all social levels.

The *imagines* provided a permanent and public means of celebrating and commemorating election victories and the achievements in office of earlier family members. The continual renewal of
power depended to a large extent on an image of status and prestige conveyed by magistrates presently in office, and by the families
of previous office-holders. At the same time, competition for office
between candidates from politically privileged backgrounds was

often intense. Over the long term the *imagines* secured a family's goal of maintaining or enhancing their rank and their influence.

In the mid-second century BC Polybius described the *imagines* at aristocratic funerals because he saw them as a characteristic and essential part of Roman self-perception and political life. He considered them important motivators in creating a feeling of consensus and community which contributed, in his view, to Rome's rapid rise to power in the Mediterranean. His account of such funerals is especially significant because extant Roman authors writing in Latin in various genres and periods signally fail to explain basic facts about the *imagines* to their readers. The *imagines* were apparently so well known that any Roman reader of prose or poetry could be expected to be familiar with them.

The preceding chapters have addressed both the physical nature of ancestor masks and their changing social role in the Republic and early Empire. An *imago* was a wax mask, which represented a man in a realistic way and was probably made in his lifetime. The precise style of the masks eludes us because no example or detailed ancient description is extant. Used as part of a performance by an actor, the *imago* mask may have had features in common with theatrical masks, about which we are even less well informed.

The *imago* mask seems usually to have made its first appearance at a man's own funeral and then at subsequent funerals of any relative. When not in use at a funeral, masks were kept in wooden cupboards (*armaria*) in the *atria* of houses owned by the family, whether in Rome or outside the city. The *imago* was a distinctive mark of the office-holding caste and portrayed a man who had held at least the office of aedile.[1] Many ancient authors associate or equate the *imagines* with *nobilitas*, a term which seems perhaps at one time to have referred to all office-holders and their descendants but, by the late Republic, only to consuls and theirs.

The *imagines* symbolized the competition for offices and honours between different office-holding families. At the same time, they reflected the solidarity of the *nobiles* as a caste, by representing office-holders of different ranks and the relationships between families, including marriages and adoptions. They were subject to the discretionary power of the family and defined that family in the widest sense by including marriage connections. An *imago* was a

---

[1] Originally probably only granted to curule magistrates, by Cicero's day plebeian aediles appear also to have received this honour; cf. Ch. 2.

status symbol which, in the funeral procession of a Roman office-holder, introduced the largest mass display of status symbols.

In contrast to other discussions of *imagines*, the present treatment has tried to strike a balance between the two spheres in which *imagines* were to be found, namely the funeral and the home. In order to reconstruct their appearance in the funeral procession every effort has been made to understand them in their original setting and as part of a performance. Polybius and Virgil in particular, as well as other authors, are useful in helping to suggest the gestures and manner of the actors impersonating the ancestors. It is also possible that the actors spoke in character rather than simply miming their role. Each ancestor appeared in the garb of the highest magisterial office he had held and was accompanied by lictors with *fasces* and other symbols of office.

During the Republic funeral processions were elaborated by borrowing props and participants from other processions, notably the triumph and the processions at the games. The actors who wore the *imagines* presented a spectacle akin to a pageant of Roman history that was staged to present a family in the best light. In the later Republic the grandeur and frequency of such processions increased, especially once women were also honoured with funeral eulogies delivered in public.

The permanent home of the *imagines* was in the family *atrium*, where they played a less dramatic role than in the funeral but were an integral part of everyday life in the household. They dominated the *atrium*, which was a stark space, sparsely furnished in an 'archaic' manner. It served as the traditional public reception area for any visitor to the house. The cupboards containing the *imagines* were opened and the masks were decorated for public feasts and private family celebrations. The usual custom was to keep the doors closed to protect the wax masks, although this was also a sign of mourning. The opening of the cupboards, as described in Roman authors, was a gesture decided upon by the family to mark important moments in the changing seasons and the fortunes of the family. The *imagines* represented the public face that the family showed to their fellow citizens.

The strategic position of the *imagines* in the *atrium* reflected the hierarchy of relationships within Roman society. The *atrium* was particularly associated with the *salutatio* or morning reception of visitors calling to do business with the master of the house. The reception of large numbers of people of all ranks in the home was an integral part of the public life of any Roman politician. This process took place in the presence of the *imagines*. The proud display of ancestor masks in the most public part of the house explains their impact on Roman voters and on younger members of the family, who felt pressure to live up to their example.

There is no ancient evidence linking the *imagines*, either in the home or in the funeral procession, with cult addressed to the individual ancestors they represented. Neither are the *imagines* connected with the Lares or the Genius of the master of the house, whose shrine could often be found in the *atrium*. Nor did the actors representing the ancestors follow the funeral cortège to the grave site outside the city walls for the cult acts customarily associated with burial.

The appearance of the *imagines*, both in the *atrium* and in the funeral, was essentially political. The masks of family members who had held political office defined rank at the intersection of public and private. They were private in the sense that they were subject to the will of the *pater familias* and his family council. The family could decide whose *imago* to display, and when and how such a display should take place, either at home or at a funeral. Conversely, a man's *imago* could be removed by his relatives without consulting anyone else. At the same time, the message and purpose of the *imagines* was public and political in all documented instances of their use. At a funeral they publicly advertised the achievements of the family in a way calculated to attract as much attention as possible. Their display in the *atrium* was similar and attempted to impress visitors to the house, especially on days of celebration when the cupboards were open.

The different roles of *imagines* explored in the preceding chapters highlight the need for a large number of professional workers to maintain and display the masks. Our ancient evidence about these craftsmen is severely limited. We do know that the funeral arrangements themselves were made by hiring professionals, known as *libitinarii*, who choreographed the whole procession and provided many of the participants and props. They probably also included the actors who played the ancestors. Their headquarters were in the Lucus Libitinae, both in Rome and in other towns.

In Rome the meaning of the *imagines* was explained by the funeral speech (*laudatio*) and the inscription accompanying the *imago* (*titulus*). No *imago* ever appeared without being identified for the viewer. The very existence of these glosses and commentaries demonstrates the didactic function of the *imagines*. The *laudatio* was delivered from the *rostra* in the Forum and was also known as the *contio funebris*. Both setting and language reveal the political purpose of this speech since it was delivered in the traditional location for speeches by magistrates and was termed a *contio*, like any public meeting.

The scanty fragments of eulogies need to be considered in the context of their delivery at a funeral. The speech included, with the praise of the deceased, an enumeration of the deeds and offices of his ancestors, presented in chronological order. The *laudatio* served as a commentary on the parade of ancestors which had preceded it. The actors wearing the *imagines* were seated on ivory curule chairs, and provided both audience for and illustration of the speaker's words. The fragments reveal that the form and content of these speeches were direct and powerful. Funeral speeches were the first Latin speeches to be regularly published.

The labels for the *imagines*, a genre related to the funeral oration, have not survived. An attempt has been made in Chapter 6 to reconstruct them using *elogia* from republican family tombs, particularly the tomb of the Scipios, and the inscriptions under the statues of the Forum of Augustus. To judge from such analogous epigraphical texts, the *tituli* were probably brief name labels, accompanied by lists of offices held and special honours or achievements. Some *tituli* may also have included verses, as is suggested by the collections of portraits and poems published by Atticus and Varro. The brevity and simplicity of the labels made them accessible to most citizens who entered the *atrium*. There is reason to believe that they were permanently on display, even when the masks themselves were hidden inside closed the cupboards. Their terse format represents a type of shorthand addressed to an audience with a background knowledge of Roman history. It is not plausible to imagine that such labels could have preserved extensive details of family history.

Laudationes and *tituli*, as interpreted here, had important points in common although much detail is lost to us now. Both illustrate the continuous rehearsing and reconstructing of family traditions which took place, often under pressure from contemporary political conditions. Both also suggest the importance of the oral presentation of material, from one generation to another within the family and to a general audience in public at the funeral. The main sources for family traditions probably remained oral. Inscriptions of various types drew on such basic knowledge about past figures.

To sum up: the three literary genres most closely associated with the *imagines* are *laudationes, tituli,* and *elogia* from tombs. Each presented in its own particular style what amounted to a *res gestae* or summary of offices held and honours won in office. For family advertising to be effective the content of its various messages needed to be similar. There is evidence that discrepancies were soon noticed, both by friends and by enemies. The existence and shape of family traditions, as reflected in oratory and inscriptions, can be traced in the annalistic school of Roman historical writing. Latin historiography was composed using the structure of magisterial years and the deeds of individual office-holders as its principal focus. The same episodes were often represented in narrative paintings, also labelled with names and sometimes organized in registers. The genre of historical paintings, now almost entirely lost, played a significant role on tomb façades, in temples, in the *atrium,* at the triumph, and at the funeral. The labels and speeches connected with the *imagines* helped to create a body of historical tradition closely associated with the masks themselves. These summaries of ancestral achievement had a wide-ranging influence on other presentations of history in prose, oratory, and painting.

A full understanding of the importance of *imagines* in Roman culture also depends on an appreciation of their position in relation to other ancestral images. The *imagines* were at the centre of a rich variety of ancestral iconography to be found in Rome during the Republic, which provided a background for everyday life. Most notable were statues, shield portraits, busts on curule chairs, portraits on coins and gems. In this context mention should also be made of the regular appearance of *imagines* in rhetoric, both judicial and political, and in the speeches composed by historical writers. A Roman house could contain many ancestral portraits, especially in the entrance areas, including family trees illustrated with painted portraits, shield portraits (*imagines clipeatae*), busts, trophies with portraits, and narrative paintings. None of these other media was as widespread or familiar as the *imagines.*

An idea of the ubiquity of ancestral images during the Republic, and the special place of *imagines* amongst them, can be given by the experience of a senior Roman magistrate in his year of office. While his election depended partly on his ancestors and his name was probably shared with one or more of them, his first public speech in office included a catalogue of his ancestors' achievements that justified his own position and suggested what he was promising the voters. His morning *salutatio*, the setting for much of his business, was dominated by his *imagines*. The ring he wore to indicate his rank and to seal official documents as a guarantee against forgery might bear the portrait of an ancestor. The curule chair he sat on at public appearances could also have bust portraits of ancestors on either side of him as he sat in judgement. The documents recording his decisions and judgements in office would often be stored in the *tablinum* of his house, near the *imagines* in the adjoining *atrium*. Games he gave in office would frequently be in memory of a deceased family member, usually a previous office-holder. Any monuments he might put up or restore in the city could also be adorned with ancestral portraits and inscriptions. To put it in a different way, in public he appeared in the presence of his ancestors, whose most important portraits were the *imagines* in his *atrium* and to whom he was accountable for his behaviour and policies.

The *imagines* represented deceased family members in a particular way by putting them in a separate category of 'ancestor of office-holding rank'.[2] The word *imagines* could be used in Latin to mean simply 'ancestors'. Such 'ancestors' might include figures from early Roman history, and even from the regal period and before. However, they also comprised all other office-holding relatives now deceased: fathers, uncles, brothers, husbands, sons, cousins, and in-laws. Many of these would not be described as 'ancestors' in our own and many other societies.[3] The Roman family group, as represented by its *imagines*, was defined narrowly in terms of gender and rank, but broadly in terms of relationships, whether by descent or by marriage. This definition was designed to maximize social and political advantage.

These 'ancestors' were brought back to life again with the help of the *imagines*, and especially by the actors in the funeral proces-

---

[2] Cf. Humphreys (1981) 268: 'The tendency [is] to try to transform what was a living person and is now a decaying cadaver into something permanent and stable—mummy, monument or memory, ash, ancestors or angel.'

[3] Dio 56. 34 = T28 distinguishes clearly between the ancestors and the relatives in his description of the *imagines* at Augustus' funeral.

sion. Their 'personification' is made clear by the active verbs associated with them and particularly with their role in swaying the
voters at magisterial elections.[4] The ancient evidence we have
reveals that this personification was not 'religious' or 'magical' but
aimed to keep alive their political influence at its peak. A man's
imago marked his status and hence his worth in society. He held a
certain political seniority within the community. An *imago* could
therefore not portray an outcast, a convicted criminal, or someone
subject to *damnatio memoriae*, nor a deified hero who had passed
beyond the ranks of his peers.

In marking rank and merit in Rome, the *imagines* served as a
means of communication.[5] They presented the values and virtues
considered typical for Roman office-holders. At the same time, they
explained the reasons why these men and others like them were
chosen for leadership. The choice of the citizen body was affirmed
by the status granted through the *imago*. Society, both past, present,
and future, was presented as a cohesive whole embodied by the living and deceased family members. The *imagines* and their associated
messages, either spoken or inscribed, handed on traditions, whether
preserved or invented, by rehearsing them. Such typically Roman
traditions were neither crude nor unchanging but complex and
powerful.

A Roman aristocratic funeral was more than simply a family
'show' from the *rostra* directed at citizens who remained passive,
either overawed or uninvolved.[6] Rather, the whole nature of
Roman funerary spectacle invited a dialogue with citizens, both
during the procession and during the eulogy. This dialogue affirmed
a shared view of the past and of the whole community's attitude to
it. Naturally, the funeral presented society in an 'ideal' rather than
a 'real' condition.[7] However, such ideals were influential in shaping attitudes and norms of behaviour, especially in relations
between the powerful and the humble. Roman society continued to
value images of consensus and of cohesion. The funeral ceremony
therefore came close to being a theatrical performance, not least in
its use of masks, actors, and props to recreate an idealized and

[4] e.g. Cicero *Leg. Agr.* 2. 100 = T8, *Pis.* 1 = T13, *Ver.* 5. 180-2.
[5] For the function of civic ritual as communication, see Connor 's (1987) discussion of political spectacle in Archaic Greece. His method is especially influenced by
Muir's (1981) treatment of civic displays in Renaissance Venice.
[6] A limited and simplified view is given by Loraux (1981) 43.
[7] For ideal social roles in the funeral, see Morris (1987) with his bibliography.

edited spectacle of the past which served the needs of the political families, as well as meeting the expectations of ordinary citizens.[8]

The role of the *imagines* illuminates the character of a society governed by sumptuary laws which limited conspicuous public displays of wealth while aiming to preserve the balance of power within the existing social order. In order to be maintained, the position of a leading Roman family needed to be recognized by citizens of all classes, who would repeatedly decide by their vote whether similar honours should be granted again to family members. Competition between leading families within the city-state was intense, especially when it came to *imagines* and related displays at funerals and in the home. An understanding of the *imagines* reveals the nature and function of spectacle within Roman society, a spectacle which represented, celebrated, and justified the social and political hierarchy. The *imagines* expressed both the competition inherent in an honorific, aristocratic culture, and the continuity and consensus reached within that same culture regarding which values were important and how to lead a good and useful life. The fact that the Roman magistracies were more accessible to new men at some times in history than at others has no bearing on the overall point being made.

Consequently, the role of the *imagines* went well beyond a public presentation of aristocratic propaganda aimed at voters. Their function in public ritual can also be seen as an articulation of collective experience and values. The funeral of a Roman office-holder was an elaborate public spectacle, which served as a means of communication between the family and the citizens at large.[9] The procession of ancestors with its colourful pageantry involved the crowd directly in an affirmation of Roman values and of the way the city was governed.[10]

The 'ancestors' in the procession presented an ideal view of the past and of the importance and dignity of magisterial office. They, therefore, reaffirmed a consensus within the city, just as they advertised the status of one family at the expense of another.[11] The ability to describe competition and cooperation within a single cultural

[8] See Redfield (1975) 163–4 on the nature of repeated ceremonies, which are close to the performing arts but go beyond mere imitation in representing realities which cause change.

[9] For public spectacle as communication in archaic Greece, see Connor (1987).

[10] Muir (1981) gives a similar analysis of civic ritual in renaissance Venice.

[11] For a similar view of the function of spectacle at Rome, see Hölkeskamp (1987).

spectacle was characteristic of the strengths of Roman republican government. As Polybius stressed, Roman rule was based on a single-mindedness of purpose within society which was fostered, in his opinion, by rituals such as the aristocratic funeral.

Within the funeral members of society play different parts in the same drama. The participation of the body of citizens watching the procession needs to be understood as an active and supportive one. The distance between office-holders and the public was not the main point of the parade of *imagines*; prestige and status were enhanced by stressing the unity of society and its common goals. The *imagines* reveal the role of symbolic drama in Roman culture. Such drama gives a commentary on society. The audience is aware of the idealizing tendencies of the homily they are being presented with, but can still take pride and pleasure in celebrating past glory.

The traditional catalogue of virtues displayed within the framework of the aristocratic funeral expressed the needs and aspirations of Roman society. These abstract virtues also found their place in Roman religion and many temples were dedicated to them by the nobility of office. The procession of past leaders gave a dramatic embodiment of what it meant to be a Roman. Roman identity was a careful construct in a world accustomed to Greek myths and foundation legends. The Romans did not produce much of a mythology of their own. Their notion of self depended on a more civic pride fostered by a sense of their history and mission.

Roman politics was shaped by drama and pageant, just as politics in turn served to inspire the visual arts. The *imagines* were essential ingredients in a spectacle of self-definition developed by the nobility of office. The funeral ceremony reflected a fine balance between personal gain and the advantage of the community. It also embodied the special ethos of the city-state with its close relationships between fellow citizens. A death was shared by the whole community and was marked by a reaffirmation of values and of continuity.

Finally, this investigation has also examined evidence for *imagines* from the imperial period. The new balance of power under the Principate led to a change in the format and importance of elections to magisterial office. The influence of the *princeps* became predominant, making *imagines* much less significant. The traditional *atrium* receded in favour of the peristyle and of more elaborate gardens. At the same time Augustus found new uses for the *imagines*, notably as an inspiration for the statues of Roman heroes in the Forum of Augustus, and to create a special type of imperial funeral.

The first *princeps* aimed to limit public self-advertisement by the families of office-holders, especially in the form of triumphs, the display of new trophies in the home, and the dedication of public buildings paid for by war booty. Displays of trophies and related republican mementos could still be seen in aristocratic houses under Nero. Many such houses were subsequently destroyed in the great fire of AD 64 (Suet. *Nero* 38. 2). Meanwhile, Augustus appropriated the *imagines* of famous earlier Roman leaders for use in public displays that advertised his own position as a supreme leader. The *S.C. de Cn. Pisone patre* shows that the *imagines* were also within the sphere of direct control by the *princeps* and the senate. The banning of a man's *imago* was a regular feature of punishments imposed for treason and therefore of *damnatio memoriae*, under which an office-holder was deprived of his position in the family after death.

Augustus and his successors used *imagines* to define and advertise the leading position of the Julio-Claudians as a family. Augustus felt the need to compete directly with aristocratic displays in the home and at funerals. His own house was elaborately rebuilt and his new forum was like a public *atrium* in shape and function. Descendants of prominent republican *gentes* deployed their *imagines* as symbols of opposition to the new regime, or to further their own claims to be *princeps*. The large and varied body of texts about *imagines* from the early imperial period testifies to their continued importance. There is, however, not enough evidence to write a history of the *imagines* in any detail after the Julio-Claudians.

At some point in the third century AD the masks apparently no longer appeared at funerals outside the emperor's family, but they were still familiar objects in the sixth century AD. The *imagines* seem, therefore, to have outlived both the republican oligarchy and the western Roman Empire itself, a fact which attests to their adaptability and endurance. They were particularly suited to express Roman ideas about the past, about status, about values, and about their sense of self. For all the qualities outlined above, the *imagines* and their traditional uses were dear to the Romans and continued to be cultivated long after their original cultural setting was no more than a memory.

APPENDIX A

Literary Testimonia

The following passages contain all the instances of *imago* (εἰκών) or *cerae* in Latin and Greek writers which seem to me to denote 'ancestor masks' of the specific Roman type under discussion here. I have not included passages which are seriously in doubt as to their meaning, nor the many instances where *imago* means portrait in a more general sense. The only exception is T107, a passage of Vitruvius which seems to refer to *imagines clipeatae* (shield portraits), but which is included here because it has so often been taken as evidence about the *imagines*. Many of these passages appear in Lahusen's (1984) collection of sources about Roman portraits and statues but there are significant differences between our understanding of these texts, both in the actual readings used and in questions of translation and interpretation. The authors who mention the *imagines* most often are (in order of frequency) Cicero, Livy, Tacitus, Valerius Maximus, Sallust, and Suetonius. Cicero is the most important source with twice the number of references than the next most useful authors. Of these ancient writers, the number who had inherited any *imagines* of ancestors is very small. One may cite Silius Italicus, Dio, and Boethius in this category. Cicero, Sallust, Seneca, and Pliny the Younger are important *novi homines* who give us information about *imagines*. Others such as Tacitus may also fit into this category. Patrician and plebeian families are mentioned with almost equal frequency in cases of named *imagines* of individuals or families. The passages collected here were written between the 190s BC and the 520s AD, but most evidence comes from the late Republic and early Empire. Dates in brackets refer to the time when the text was composed, as opposed to the dramatic date of the events discussed, which appears outside the brackets.

Many references to *imagines* are to be found in authors writing after the death of Augustus. Twenty-three writers of the imperial period after AD 14 mention *imagines*, although a certain number are, of course, referring to earlier periods of history (Seneca the Elder, the emperor Claudius, Ovid, Valerius Maximus, Velleius Paterculus, Silius Italicus, Seneca the Younger, the author of the *Laus Pisonis*, Pliny the Elder, Martial, Plutarch, Ps.-Quintilian, Tacitus, Pliny the Younger, Juvenal, Suetonius, Appian, Dio, Pomponius Porfyrio, the author of *H.A. Tacitus* and *H.A. Severus Alexander*,

Boethius, the *Codex Justinianus*). None of these felt the need to explain to his readers what the *imagines* were. Among them Valerius Maximus, Tacitus, and Suetonius are three of the six ancient writers who mention *imagines* most often. While consciously looking back to republican values and *mores*, they show us what powerful symbols the *imagines* could remain even as new, more professional and bureaucratic forms of government emerged to rule Rome's empire.

Notes:
1. See Bibliography for editions and commentaries of texts listed.
2. Translation: *imago* is translated as 'mask', *titulus* as 'label', and *nobilis* as office-holder or member of the office-holding caste or 'noble'.

T1 L. Afranius, *Vopiscus* 12. 364–5 = Nonius 790 L   (*fl. c.*110 BC)
eius* te suscitat
imago, cuius effigia, quo gnatu's patre.

*cuius (Daviault)

It is his mask and portrait which rouses you (or stirs you to action), that of the father to whom you were born.

Daviault (1981), who dates this play to around 131 BC, translates 'celui dont t'exaltent l'image et le portrait, le père dont tu est né'. He suggests this fragment perhaps comes from a recognition scene at the end of the play.

T2 Appian, *Iberica* 89   (Antonine)
πολλάκις γοῦν ἐς τὸ Καπιτώλιον ἐσῄει μόνος καὶ τὰς θύρας ἐπέκλειεν ὥσπερ τι παρὰ τοῦ θεοῦ μανθάνων. καὶ νῦν ἔτι τὴν εἰκόνα τὴν Σκιπίωνος ἐν ταῖς πομπαῖς μόνου προφέρουσιν ἐκ τοῦ Καπιτωλίου, τῶν δ' ἄλλων ἐξ ἀγορᾶς φέρονται.

At any rate he often used to go alone into the Temple of Jupiter on the Capitol, and he would lock the doors as if he were receiving a message from the god. And it is still the case that Scipio's is the only mask which they carry out in funeral processions from the Capitol. But the masks of the others are brought from the Forum.

Cf. Val. Max. 8.15.1–2 (T104) and Ch. 2, § 1e.

T3 Asconius, (43C = 37–8K-S = 38 Stangl)   52 BC (AD 54–7)
Post biduum medium quam Clodius occisus erat interrex primus proditus est M. Aemilius Lepidus. Non fuit autem moris ab eo qui primus interrex proditus erat comitia haberi. Sed Scipionis et Hypsaei factiones, quia recens invidia Milonis erat, cum contra ius postularent ut interrex ad comitia consulum creandorum descenderet, idque ipse non faceret, [et] domum eius per omnes interregni dies (fuerant autem ex more quinque) obsiderunt. Deinde omni vi ianua expugnata et imagines maiorum deiecerunt et lectulum adversum uxoris eius Corneliae, cuius castitas pro exemplo habita est,

fregerunt, itemque telas, quae ex vetere more in atrio texebantur, diruerunt.

When two days had elapsed since Clodius had been killed, Marcus Aemilius Lepidus was named as first *interrex*. It was not, however, the custom for the man named as first *interrex* to preside over the elections to office. But because Milo's unpopularity was fresh, the supporters of Scipio and Hypsaeus were demanding, contrary to the law, that the *interrex* should come down to the Forum to hold the consular elections. When Aemilius did not do so, they laid seige to his house for the whole period of the *interregnum* (which was usually five days). Then they broke down his door with full force and threw down the masks of his ancestors and broke in pieces the symbolic marriage bed of his wife Cornelia, whose chastity was a byword, and in the same way they tore up the cloth which was being woven on looms in the *atrium* according to ancient custom.

Cf. Ch. 6 § 1. Asconius is the only source to name Lepidus' wife as Cornelia. Later he was certainly married to Junia (*RE* 193), a sister of Brutus. Asconius is perhaps thinking of Cornelia, the wife of his cousin Paullus Aemilius Lepidus (*RE* 82).

T4 Boethius, *De Consolatione Philosophiae* 1 *pros.* 1. 3   (AD 520s)
Quarum speciem, veluti fumosas imagines solet, caligo quaedam neglectae vetustatis obduxerat.

A certain gloom of neglected old age obscured the appearance (of her dress), just as is usual for smoke-stained masks.

Cf. Cic. *In Pis.* 1 (T13).

T5 Cicero, *Pro Caelio* 33-4   (56 BC)
Exsistat igitur ex hac ipsa familia aliquis ac potissimum Caecus ille; minimum enim dolorem capiet qui istam non videbit. Qui profecto, si exstiterit, sic aget ac sic loquetur: 'Mulier, quid tibi cum Caelio, quid cum homine adulescentulo, quid cum alieno? Cur aut tam familiaris fuisti ut aurum commodares, aut tam inimica ut venenum timeres? non patrem tuum videras, non patruum, non avum, non proavum, non *abavum, non* atavum audieras consules fuisse; (34) non denique modo te Q. Metelli matrimonium tenuisse sciebas, clarissimi ac fortissimi viri patriaeque amantissimi, qui simul ac pedem limine extulerat, omnis prope civis virtute, gloria, dignitate superabat? Cum ex amplissimo genere in familiam clarissimam nupsisses, cur tibi Caelius tam coniunctus fuit? cognatus, adfinis, viri tui familiaris? Nihil eorum. Quid igitur fuit nisi quaedam temeritas ac libido? Nonne te, si nostrae imagines viriles non commovebant, ne progenies quidem mea, Q. illa Claudia, aemulam domesticae laudis in gloria muliebri esse admonebat, non virgo illa Vestalis Claudia quae patrem complexa triumphantem ab inimico tribuno plebei de curru detrahi passa non est? Cur te fraterna vitia potius quam bona paterna et avita et usque a nobis cum in viris tum etiam in feminis repetita moverunt? Ideone ego pacem Pyrrhi diremi ut tu

amorum turpissimorum cotidie foedera ferires, ideo aquam adduxi ut ea tu inceste uterere, ideo viam munivi ut eam tu alienis viris comitata celebrares?

Therefore, let someone from that same family come forward, and best of all that Caecus; for he will suffer the least because he will not see her. In my opinion, if he were to appear, he would act and speak in the following way: 'Madam, what have you to do with Caelius, what with such a young man, what with a stranger? Why were you either so intimate with him that you lent him money, or so much his enemy that you were afraid of poison? Have you not seen your father be consul? Have you not heard that your uncle, your grandfather, your great-grandfather, your great-great-grandfather, your great-great-great-grandfather were consuls? (34) Finally did you not know that you were married to Quintus Metellus, an exceedingly distinguished and brave man and a great lover of his country, who on stepping out of his house surpassed almost every one of his fellow citizens in manly qualities, reputation, and renown? Since you were born to a family of the highest rank and had married into a most distinguished one, why was Caelius so intimate with you? Was he your relative, a relation by marriage, a friend of your husband? None of these. What was this then if not some instance of audacity and lust? If our masks of male ancestors did not influence you, then surely my descendant, that famous Quinta Claudia has been urging you to rival her family renown and to further the reputation of our women? What about that Vestal Virgin Claudia who held onto her father during his triumph and would not let him be dragged down from his chariot by his enemy, a tribune of the plebs? Why were you more influenced by your brother's vices rather than the good qualities of your father and grandfather and of all your ancestors, both male and also female, since my time? Was it for this that I tore up the peace treaty with Pyrrhus so that everyday you might strike bargains in the most shameful love affairs? Was it for this that I brought water to Rome, that you might use it in an unclean way? Was it for this that I built the Via Appia, so that you might frequent it in the company of strange men?'

T6 Cicero, *Pro Cluentio* 72   (66 BC)

Tum appellat hilari voltu hominem Bulbus ut blandissime potest: 'Quid tu' inquit 'Paete'?—hoc enim sibi Staienus cognomen ex imaginibus Aeliorum delegerat ne, si se Ligurem fecisset, nationis magis suae quam generis uti cognomine videretur—'qua re mecum locutus es, quaerunt a me ubi sit pecunia'.

Then Bulbus addresses the man with a cheerful expression and in as friendly a way as possible: 'How are you doing, Paetus?' he said—for Statienus had chosen this *cognomen* for himself from the masks of the Aelii, lest if he had called himself Ligur, he would seem to be using the name of

his tribe rather than of his family—'On the subject which you discussed with me, they are asking me where the money might be.'
Cf. Cic. *Brut.* 241 and T17 below.

T7 Cicero, *De Lege Agraria Contra Rullum* 2. 1   (63 BC)
Est hoc in more positum, Quirites, institutoque maiorum, ut ei qui beneficio vestro imagines familiae suae consecuti sunt eam primam habeant contionem, qua gratiam benefici vestri cum suorum laude coniungant. Qua in oratione non nulli aliquando digni maiorum loco reperiuntur, plerique autem hoc perficiunt ut tantum maioribus eorum debitum esse videatur, unde etiam quod posteris solveretur redundaret. Mihi, Quirites, apud vos de meis maioribus dicendi facultas non datur, non quo non tales fuerint qualis nos illorum sanguine creatos disciplinisque institutos videtis, sed quod laude populari atque honoris vestri luce caruerunt.

Roman citizens, it is a matter of custom and a precedent established by the ancestors, that those who as a result of your support [at the elections] have followed in the footsteps of their family's masks should hold this first public meeting, at which they would join their thanks for your favour with a eulogy of their ancestors. On occasion some men are found to be worthy of the rank of their ancestors in giving this speech, but most [new magistrates] manage to give the impression that so much is owed to their ancestors, that even now a residue is left to be paid to their descendants. Roman citizens, I do not have the opportunity of speaking before you on the subject of my ancestors, not because they were not such men as I am, whom you see before you as their descendant by blood, schooled in their values, but because they lacked the praise of the people and the publicity bestowed by your magisterial office.

Cf. Cic. *Fin.* 2.74 and Suet. *Tib.* 32.1. The differences between Cicero's tone and that of Marius speaking on a similar occasion, as conveyed by Sallust (T66*a–c*), is striking. Cf. Ch. 1 and 5 § 5.

T8 Cicero, *De Lege Agraria Contra Rullum* 2. 100   (63 BC)
Nulli populo Romano pro me maiores mei spoponderunt; mihi creditum est; a me petere quod debeo, me ipsum appellare debetis. Quem ad modum, cum petebam, nulli me vobis auctores generis mei commendarunt, sic, si quid deliquero, nullae sunt imagines quae me a vobis deprecentur.

No ancestors of mine gave any pledges to the Roman people on my behalf: I won their confidence myself. You must require of me what I owe; you must make your demands to me myself. Just as when I was seeking office, no family founders commended me to you, likewise, if I fall short in some way, there are no masks who can ask forgiveness for me from you.

T9 Cicero, *Pro Milone* 33   (52 BC)
Tu P. Clodi cruentum cadaver eiecisti domo, tu in publicum abiecisti, tu spoliatum imaginibus, exsequiis, pompa, laudatione, infelicissimis lignis semiustilatum nocturnis canibus dilaniandum reliquisti.

You threw the bleeding corpse of Publius Clodius out of the house. You threw it out in public. You deprived him of his masks, of funeral rites, of a funeral procession, of a eulogy—and you left his body half-burned on an ill-omened pyre, for the dogs to tear at night.

Addressed to Sextus Clodius (*RE* 12), or S. Cloelius (cf. Shackleton Bailey (1976) 27). Cf. Tacitus on the funeral of Germanicus T88.

T10 Cicero, *Pro Milone* 86 (52 BC)

Nec vero non eadem ira deorum hanc eius satellitibus iniecit amentiam ut sine imaginibus, sine cantu atque ludis, sine exsequiis, sine lamentis, sine laudationibus, sine funere, oblitus cruore et luto, spoliatum illius supremi diei celebritate cui cedere inimici etiam solent ambureretur abiectus.

And, in truth, is it not the same anger of the gods which inspired this madness in his henchmen with the result that, after he was deprived of those public tributes of that last day which even enemies are accustomed to grant, [and his body was] smeared with mud and blood, he was thrown out and cremated without masks, without song and games, without funeral rites, without laments, without eulogies, without a funeral.

T11 Cicero, *Pro Murena* 88 (63 BC)

Si, quod Iuppiter omen avertat! hunc vestris sententiis adflixeritis, quo se miser vertet? domumne? ut eam imaginem clarissimi viri, parentis sui, quam paucis ante diebus laureatam in sua gratulatione conspexit, eandem deformatam ignominia lugentemque videat?

If you ruin him with your verdict (may Jupiter avert this evil omen), to whom will the wretch turn? To his home? So that he might see the mask of that most distinguished man, his father, disfigured by his infamy and in mourning, that same mask which a few days before he saw wreathed with laurel to congratulate him?

Cf. Ch. 5 § 5.

T12 Cicero, *In M. Antonium Oratio Philippica* 2. 26 (44–43 BC)

Etenim si auctores ad liberandam patriam desiderarentur illis actoribus, Brutos ego impellerem, quorum uterque L. Bruti imaginem cotidie videret, alter etiam Ahalae?

If indeed models were required to inspire their actions in freeing our country, did I incite the Bruti, each of whom saw the mask of Lucius Brutus every day, and one of them also the mask of Ahala?

Cf. Crawford 433 for a coin of M. Brutus showing busts of these two ancestors and dating to 54 BC and Ch. 3 § 4.

T13 Cicero, *In Pisonem* 1 (55 BC)

Numquam erat audita vox in foro, numquam periculum factum consilii, nullum non modo inlustre sed ne notum quidem factum aut militiae aut domi. Obrepsisti ad honores errore hominum, commendatione fumosarum imaginum, quarum simile habes nihil praeter colorem.

Your voice was never heard in the Forum, you never risked formulating a policy, you performed no distinguished or even notable act either on campaign or in politics. You stealthily insinuated yourself into public office as a result of the voters' mistake, on the recommendation of your smoke-stained masks, with whom you share nothing in common except your [dark] complexion.

Cf. Boethius T4 and Cicero T8 and Ch. 3 § 1.

T14 Cicero, *Pro Plancio* 18   (54 BC)
Est tuum nomen utraque familia consulare. Num dubitas igitur quin omnes qui favent nobilitati, qui id putant esse pulcherrimum, qui imaginibus, qui nominibus vestris ducuntur, te aedilem fecerint? Equidem non dubito. Sed si parum multi sunt qui nobilitatem ament, num ista est nostra culpa?

Your family is of consular rank on both sides. Surely therefore you do not doubt that all who favour the office-holding caste, who think it is the finest thing, who are influenced by your masks and by your names would have elected you aedile? I, for my part, do not doubt it. But if there are not many who are the kind to love the office-holding caste, surely that is not our fault?

T15 Cicero, *Pro Plancio* 51   (54 BC)
Quaeris etiam, Laterensis, quid imaginibus tuis, quid ornatissimo atque optimo viro, patri tuo, respondeas mortuo.

You also ask, Laterensis, what you should reply to your masks, what to that most eminent and excellent man, your dead father?

T16 Cicero, *Pro C. Rabirio Postumo* 16–17   (54 BC)
Delectat amplissimus civitatis gradus, sella curulis, fasces, imperia, provinciae, sacerdotia, triumphi, denique imago ipsa ad posteritatis memoriam prodita; esto simul etiam sollicitudo aliqua et legum et iudiciorum maior quidam metus.

The most elevated rank in the state is a pleasing thing, [as are] the curule chair, the fasces, military commands, governorships of provinces, priesthoods, triumphs, and finally the mask itself, handed on as a memorial to succeeding generations. At the same time there should also be a certain feeling of unease in relation to the laws and some greater fear of law suits.

Cf. T21 and Ch. 2 § 2.

T17 Cicero, *Pro Sestio* 69   (56 BC)
nam ex novem tribunis quos tunc habueram unus me absente defluxit, qui cognomen sibi ex Aeliorum imaginibus arripuit, quo magis nationis eius esse quam generis videretur.

For of the nine tribunes whom I then had on my side, one slipped away in my absence. He stole a *cognomen* for himself from the masks of the Aelii, with the result that he seemed to be from that tribe rather than that family.

T18 Cicero, *Pro Sulla* 27 (62 BC)

Longe abest a me regni suspicio; si quaeris qui sint Romae regnum occupare conati, ut ne replices annalium memoriam, ex domesticis imaginibus invenies.

I am far from being suspected of aiming at absolute power. If you ask what sort of people tried to seize power at Rome, you will find them amongst the masks of your family, so there is no need to look up the account of the chroniclers.

T19 Cicero, *Pro Sulla* 88 (62 BC)

Nam ipse quidem, si erit vestro iudicio liberatus, quae habet ornamenta, quae solacia reliquae vitae quibus laetari ac perfrui possit? Domus erit, credo, exornata, aperientur maiorum imagines, ipse ornatum ac vestitum pristinum recuperabit. Omnia, iudices, haec amissa sunt, omnia generis, nominis, honoris insignia atque ornamenta unius iudici calamitate occiderunt.

As far as he himself is concerned, if he is set free by your verdict, what marks of honour, what compensation will he have, which he could take pleasure in and enjoy for the rest of his life. I believe that his house will be decorated, the masks of the ancestors will be opened, he himself will again put on his former dress and marks of rank. Gentlemen of the jury, all these things have been lost, all the trappings and badges of honour of his family, his name, his rank in political office have fallen victim to the loss of one lawsuit.

T20 Cicero, *In Vatinium* 28 (56 BC)

Ac nunc quidem C. Antonius hac una re miseriam suam consolatur, quod imagines patris et fratris sui fratrisque filiam non in familia sed in carcere conlocatam audire maluit quam videre.

And in fact, as things are, Gaius Antonius assuages his misery with this one thing, that he preferred to hear about rather than to see the masks of his father and of his brother and his niece (brother's daughter) given in marriage not into a household but into a prison.

Cf. I16 *S.C. de Cn. Pisone patre* for confirmation about the wide use of *imagines* by any relative, whether by blood or by marriage.

T21 Cicero, *In Verrem* 5. 36 (70 BC)

ob earum rerum laborem et sollicitudinem fructus illos datos, antiquiorem in senatu sententiae dicendae locum, togam praetextam, sellam curulem, ius imaginis ad memoriam posteritatemque prodendae.

The following rewards are granted to me for the work and care involved
with those matters: a place of greater seniority in giving my opinion in the
senate, the *toga praetexta*, the curule chair, the right to hand on a mask as
a memorial for future generations.

Despite the mention of the curule chair, he seems to have been plebeian aedile
(Taylor 1939). Cf. T16.

T22 Cicero, *Orator* 110 (46 BC)
Demosthenes quidem, cuius nuper inter imagines tuas ac tuorum, quod
eum credo amares, cum ad te in Tusculanum venissem, imaginem ex aere
vidi, nil Lysiae subtilitate cedit, nihil argutiis et acumine Hyperidi, nil levi-
tate Aeschini et splendore verborum.

However, when I visited you at Tusculum I recently saw Demosthenes' portrait in bronze among your portraits and the masks of your family, presumably because you value him highly. He cedes nothing to Lysias in
subtelty, nothing to Hyperides in wit and acuteness, nothing to Aeschines
in smoothness and in his striking choice of words.

Cf. T12 and 24 and Ch. 7.

T23 Cicero, *De Oratore* 2.225–6 91 BC ? (55 BC)
Pro di immortales, quae fuit illa, quanta vis! quam inexspectata! quam
repentina! cum coniectis oculis, gestu omni ei imminenti, summa gravitate
et celeritate verborum 'Brute, quid sedes? Quid illam anum patri nuntiare
vis tuo? Quid illis omnibus quorum imagines duci vides? Quid maioribus
tuis? Quid L. Bruto, qui hunc populum dominatu regio liberavit? Quid te
agere? cui rei, cui gloriae, cui virtuti studere? Patrimonione augendo? At
id non est nobilitatis. sed fac esse, nihil superest; libidines totum dissi-
paverunt. (226) An iuri civili? est paternum. Sed dicet te, cum aedis
venderes, ne in rutis quidem et caesis solium tibi paternum recepisse. An
rei militari? Qui numquam castra videris! An eloquentiae? quae neque est
in te, et, quicquid est vocis ac linguae, omne in istum turpissimum calum-
niae quaestum contulisti! Tu lucem aspicere audes? tu hos intueri? tu in
foro, [tu in urbe], tu in civium esse conspectu? Tu illam mortuam, tu imagines ipsas non perhorrescis? quibus non modo imitandis, sed ne collocan-
dis quidem tibi locum ullum reliquisti.'

By the immortal gods, what was it, that great release of energy! How unexpected! How sudden! When he (Crassus), looking straight at him [Brutus]
and looming over him with his gestures, spoke with the greatest seriousness and speed of expression: 'Brutus, why are you sitting down? What
message do you want that old woman to give to your father? What should
she say to all those whose masks you see being led in procession? What to
your ancestors? What to Lucius Brutus, who freed this people from the
tyranny of the kings? What should she say that you are doing? What business, what honour, what excellence are you intent on pursuing? Are you

busy increasing your wealth? But that is not the accepted practice of the office-holding caste. But even if it were, there is nothing left; wantoness has wasted everything. (226) Are you involved in the law? That is what your father did. But she will say that when you were selling your house you did not keep even your father's chair although you reserved rights to timber and minerals from the estate. Are you involved in military matters? You who will never see a camp! Are you cultivating eloquence? You do not have any and whatever voice and gift of speech you have you put entirely toward that most disgraceful practice of making a profit from false accusation! Do you dare to appear in public? Do you dare to look at these men? Do you dare to appear in the Forum, in the city, in the presence of your fellow citizens? Do you not tremble before that dead woman? Before the masks themselves? You have left yourself no room even for setting them up, much less for imitating them.'

Cf. T5 and Ch. 5 § 5.

T24 Cicero, *Epistulae ad Familiares* 9. 21. 2–3 (47–43 BC)
Sed tamen, mi Paete, qui tibi venit in mentem negare Papirium quemquam umquam nisi plebeium fuisse? fuerunt enim patricii minorum gentium, quorum princeps L. Papirius Mugillanus, qui censor cum L. Sempronio Atratino fuit, cum ante consul cum eodem fuisset, annis post Romam conditam CCCXII; sed tum Papisii dicebamini. Post hunc XIII fuerunt sella curuli ante L. Papirium Crassum, qui primum Papi⟨s⟩ius est vocari desitus. is dictator cum L. Papirio Cursore magistro equitum factus est annis post Romam conditam CCCCXV et quadriennio post consul cum K. Duilio. Hunc secutus est Cursor, homo valde honoratus, deinde L. Masso aedilicius, inde multi Massones. Quorum quidem tu omnium patriciorum imagines habeas volo. (3) Deinde Carbones et Turdi insequuntur; hi plebeii fuerunt, quos contemnas censeo; nam praeter hunc C. Carbonem quem Damasippus occidit civis e re publica Carbonum nemo fuit. Cognovimus Cn. Carbonem et eius fratrem scurram; quid iis improbius? De hoc amico meo, Rubriae filio, nihil dico. Tres illi fratres fuerunt, C., Cn., M. Carbones. Marcus P. Flacco accusante condemnatus, fur magnus, ex Sicilia. Gaius accusante L. Crasso cantharidas sumpsisse dicitur; is et tribunus pl. seditiosus et P. Africano vim attulisse existimatus est. Hoc vero qui Lilybaei a Pompeio nostro est interfectus improbior nemo meo iudicio fuit; iam pater eius accusatus a M. Antonio sutorio atramento absolutus putatur. Qua re ad patres censeo revertare; plebeii quam fuerint importuni vides.

But come now, my Paetus, what persuaded you to deny that any Papirius had ever been anything but a plebeian? For they were patricians of the minor families, and their leading member was Lucius Papirius Mugillanus, who was censor with Lucius Sempronius Atratinus, as he had been consul with that same man 312 years after Rome was founded. But at that time you were called Papisii. After this man there were 13 who held curule office before Lucius Papirius Crassus, who was the first to stop being called Papisius. He was appointed dictator with Lucius Papirius Cursor as his master of the horse 415 years after the foundation of Rome and four years later he was consul with Kaeso Duilius. Another Cursor followed him, a man who held many high offices, then Lucius Masso with the rank of aedile, and afterwards many Massones. I am eager that you should have masks of all these patricians. (3) Then the Carbones and Turdi came next. They were plebeians, whom I think you should disregard. For apart from the Gaius Carbo whom Damasippus assassinated, no Carbo was a citizen worthy of the state. We knew Gnaeus Carbo and his brother the idler; who was more disreputable than they? I am not speaking of that friend of mine, the son of Rubria. There were those three brothers Gaius, Gnaeus, and Marcus Carbo. Marcus, that great thief, was condemned on a charge brought by Publius Flaccus, from Sicily. Gaius is said to have taken poison when Lucius Crassus brought an accusation against him. He was thought to have been a seditious tribune of the plebs and to have assassinated Publius Africanus. But in my opinion no one was more disreputable than the one who was killed by our friend Pompey at Lilybaeum. Already his father is considered to have been acquitted by an underhanded deal of a charge brought by Marcus Antonius. For this reason I think one should look back to the patricians; you see how unsuitable the plebeians were.

Cf. Shackleton Bailey (1977) no. 188, who contends, without argument, that Cicero is joking when he urges Paetus to set up these *imagines*.

T25 Cicero, *De Re Publica* 6. 10   (54–51 BC)
Africanus se ostendit ea forma quae mihi ex imagine eius quam ex ipso erat notior; quem ubi agnovi, equidem cohorrui . . .

Africanus appeared in the guise which was better known to me from his mask than from himself. When I recognized him, I naturally shuddered. . .

Cf. T2 and 104.

T26 Claudius, *CIL* 13. 1668. 2. 25   (AD 48)
Tot ecce insignes iuvenes, quot intueor, non magis sunt paenitendi senatores, quam paenitet Persicum, nobilissimum virum, amicum meum, inter imagines maiorum suorum Allobrogici nomen legere.

Behold all these distinguished young men whom I am looking at. We should no more regret that they are senators than Persicus, a man of the highest lineage and my friend, is sorry to read the name Allobrogicus among the masks of his ancestors.

T27 Dio 47. 19. 2   42 BC (3rd cent. AD)
πρὸς δὲ τούτοις ἀπεῖπον μὲν μηδεμίαν εἰκόνα αὐτοῦ, καθάπερ θεοῦ τινος ὡς ἀληθῶς ὄντος, ἐν ταῖς τῶν συγγενῶν αὐτοῦ ἐκφοραῖς πέμπεσθαι, ὅπερ ἐκ τοῦ πάνυ ἀρχαίου καὶ τότε ἔτι ἐγίγνετο·

Appendix A

In addition to these measures they banned any mask representing him [Julius Caesar], just as if he was truely a god, from taking part in the procession at the funerals of his relatives, a custom which began in very ancient times and was still practised then.

Cf. Ch. 8 § 1b. For *imagines* of others who received divine honours, see T29 and 84.

T28 Dio 56. 34   AD 14 (3rd cent. AD)

ταῦτα μὲν αἱ ἐντολαὶ εἶχον, μετὰ δὲ τοῦτο ἡ ἐκφορὰ αὐτοῦ ἐγένετο. κλίνη ἦν ἔκ τε ἐλέφαντος καὶ χρυσοῦ πεποιημένη καὶ στρώμασιν ἁλουργοῖς διαχρύσοις κεκοσμημένη· καὶ ἐν αὐτῇ τὸ μὲν σῶμα κάτω που ἐν θήκῃ συνεκέκρυπτο, εἰκὼν δὲ δή τις αὐτοῦ κηρίνη ἐν ἐπινικίῳ στολῇ ἐξεφαίνετο. καὶ αὕτη μὲν ἐκ τοῦ παλατίου πρὸς τῶν ἐς νέωτα ἀρχόντων, ἑτέρα δὲ ἐκ τοῦ βουλευτηρίου χρυσῆ, καὶ ἑτέρα αὖ ἐφ᾽ ἅρματος πομπικοῦ ἤγετο. καὶ μετὰ ταύτας αἵ τε τῶν προπατόρων αὐτοῦ καὶ αἱ τῶν ἄλλων συγγενῶν τῶν τεθνηκότων, πλὴν τῆς τοῦ Καίσαρος ὅτι ἐς τοὺς ἥρωας ἐσεγέγραπτο, αἵ τε τῶν ἄλλων Ῥωμαίων τῶν καὶ καθ᾽ ὁτιοῦν πρωτευσάντων, ἀπ᾽ αὐτοῦ τοῦ Ῥωμύλου ἀρξάμεναι, ἐφέροντο. καί τις καὶ τοῦ Πομπηίου τοῦ μεγάλου εἰκὼν ὤφθη, τά τε ἔθνη πάνθ᾽ ὅσα προσεκτήσατο, ἐπιχωρίως σφίσιν ὡς ἕκαστα ἀπηκασμένα ἐπέμφθη. κἀκ τούτου καὶ τὰ ἄλλα αὐτοῖς, ὅσα ἐν τοῖς ἄνω λόγοις εἴρηται, ἐφέσπετο. προτεθείσης δὲ τῆς κλίνης ἐπὶ τοῦ δημηγορικοῦ βήματος, ἀπὸ μὲν ἐκείνου ὁ Δροῦσός τι ἀνέγνω, ἀπὸ δὲ τῶν ἑτέρων ἐμβόλων τῶν Ἰουλιείων ὁ Τιβέριος δημόσιον δή τινα κατὰ δόγμα λόγον ἐπ᾽ αὐτῷ τοιόνδε ἐπελέξατο·

These were his instructions. After that his funeral took place. The bier was made of ivory and gold and it was adorned with covers of purple embroidered with gold. And in it the body was hidden below in a coffin, while a wax portrait of him in triumphal dress was on display. And this portrait was carried from the Palatine by the magistrates elected for the following year, but another of gold came from the senate house, and yet another on a triumphal chariot. And after these the masks of his ancestors came in procession and those of his other relatives who had died, except for the mask of Caesar as he had been enrolled amongst the deified heroes, and then the masks of the other Romans who had excelled in some way, beginning with Romulus himself. And a mask/likeness of Pompey the Great was also to be seen, and portraits of all the peoples whom he had conquered, each adorned with its own native attributes. And after this the other peoples followed them, as described in the account above. The bier was put on view at the speakers' platform (rostra), and from there Drusus gave a reading, while at the Julian *rostra* Tiberius gave a public address over him according to the decree and said the following sorts of things.

Cf. Suet. *Aug.* 100 with the detailed discussion in Ch. 8 § 1b and Suet. T75 and 31. 5 for Pompey's statue which Augustus moved from the senate house to a marble arch facing his theatre.

T29 Dio, 56. 46. 4–5B   AD 14 (3rd cent. AD)

ταῦτά τε αὐτῷ ἐψηφίσθη, καὶ ὅπως μήτ᾽ εἰκὼν αὐτοῦ ἐν ἐκφορᾷ τινος
πομπεύῃ, καὶ τὰ γενέσια οἱ ὕπατοι ἐξ ἴσου τοῖς ᾿Αρείοις ἀγωνοθετῶσι,
τά τε Αὐγουστάλια οἱ δήμαρχοι ὡς καὶ ἱεροπρεπεῖς ὄντες διατιθῶσι.

And these things they decreed about him, and that no mask representing
him should appear in procession at any funeral: and that the consuls
should hold games to commemorate his birthday just like those for Mars
(Ludi Martiales), while the tribunes of the plebs should organize the
Augustalia since they were sacrosanct.

Like Caesar in T27, Divus Augustus also has no *imago* because he is a god.

T30 Diodorus 31. 25. 2   160 BC (60–30 BC)

῞Οτι περὶ Λευκίου Αἰμιλίου τοῦ Περσέα καταπολεμήσαντος τῆς ταφῆς
διερχόμενος, καὶ λαμπρὰν αὐτὴν ἐς τὰ μάλιστα γενέσθαι λέγων ἐπάγει·
᾿τῶν γὰρ Ῥωμαίων οἱ ταῖς εὐγενείαις καὶ προγόνων δόξῃ διαφέροντες
μετὰ τὴν τελευτὴν εἰδωλοποιοῦνται κατά τε τὴν τοῦ χαρακτῆρος
ὁμοιότητα καὶ κατὰ τὴν ὅλην τοῦ σώματος περιγραφήν, μιμητὰς ἔχοντες
ἐκ παντὸς τοῦ βίου παρατετηρηκότας τήν τε πορείαν καὶ τὰς κατὰ μέρος
ἰδιότητας τῆς ἐμφάσεως. παραπλησίως δὲ καὶ τῶν προγόνων ἕκαστος
προηγεῖται τοιαύτην ἔχων διασκευὴν καὶ κόσμον ὥστε τοὺς θεωμένους
διὰ τῆς ἐκ τούτων ἐμφάσεως γινώσκειν ἐφ᾽ ὅσον ἕκαστοι τιμῆς
προήχθησαν καὶ μετέσχον τῶν ἐν τῇ πολιτείᾳ καλῶν.᾿

When describing the funeral of Lucius Aemilius who conquered Perseus,
and saying that it was organized in the most magnificent way, [Diodorus]
adds: 'Those of the Romans who are the most well-born and are distinguished by the glory of their ancestors are portrayed after death in a way
which is most like their features and which represents their whole bodies.
They use actors who have observed a man's bearing and the details of his
individual appearance throughout his whole life. In the same way also each
of the ancestors marches in procession having such dress and emblems of
office so that the spectators can tell from their appearance how far each
had advanced in rank and had enjoyed his share of honours in the realm
of politics.

This fragment of Diodorus is quoted by Photius (*Bibliotheke* 383B). Cf. Vespasian's
funeral T84.

T31 *H.A. Alex. Sev.* 29. 2   AD 222–35 (late 4th cent. AD?)

primum ut, si facultas esset, id est si non cum uxore cubuisset, matutinis
horis in lar⟨ar⟩io suo, in quo et divos principes sed optimos electos et ani-
mas sanctiores, in quis Apollonium et, quantum scriptor suorum temporum
dicit, Christum, Abraham et Orfeum et huius ⟨modi⟩ ceteros habebat ac
maiorum effigies, rem divinam faciebat.

First that, if he had the opportunity, which is to say if he had not slept with
his wife, in the early morning he used to address cult at his shrine of the

Lares, in which he had images of the deified emperors, of whom the best had been chosen, and of the holier souls, amongst whom Apollonius and, according to a writer of his time, Christ, Abraham and Orpheus and others of this kind and the masks (?) of his ancestors.

Cf. Ch. 9 § 3.

T32 *H.A. Tacitus* 19. 6   AD 275 (late 4th cent. AD)

Longum est omnes epistulas c[u]onectere, quas repperi, quas legi. tantum illud dico senatores omnes ea esse laetitia elatos, ut in domibus suis omnes albas hostias c⟨a⟩ederent, imagines frequenter aperi⟨r⟩ent, albati sederent, * convivia sumptuosiora prae*b*[en]erent, * antiquitatem sibi redditam crederent.

It is a long task to put together all the letters which I found and all which I read. This much I will say: all the senators were affected with such joy that they sacrificed only white animals in their houses, they opened [the cupboards for] the masks more frequently, they received visitors in white clothes, they provided more sumptious banquets, they believed that the old days had been restored to them.

Cf. T27 and 34a. The passage is quite corrupt containing two lacunae of 20 and 30 letters respectively at the points marked *. The mention of the *imagines* is largely unaffected, although its general context is.

T33 Horace, *Sermones* 1. 6. 7–18.   (*c.*37–30 BC)

cum referre negas quali sit quisque parente   7
natus, dum ingenuus, persuades hoc tibi vere,
ante potestatem Tulli atque ignobile regnum
multos saepe viros nullis maioribus ortos   10
et vixisse probos, amplis et honoribus auctos;
contra Laevinum, Valeri genus, unde Superbus
Tarquinius regno pulsus fugit, unius assis
non umquam pretio pluris licuisse, notante
iudice quo nosti populo, qui stultus honores   15
saepe dat indignis et famae servit ineptus,
qui stupet in titulis et imaginibus. Quid oportet
nos facere a vulgo longe longeque remotos?

When you say that it does not matter what kind of a person a man is and who his parents were, as long as he was born free, you convince yourself rightly of this, that before the dominion of Tullius and his low-born reign, many men without ancestors often both lived uprightly and were promoted to distinguished offices. By contrast Laevinus, a descendant of Valerius at whose hands Tarquin the Proud was thrown from power and went into exile, was never considered to be worth more even by an as, by that harsh judge you know well, the people, who often are stupid in giving office to unworthy men and are silly in being slaves to reputation, who are amazed at the labels and masks. What should we do who are far far removed from the common herd?

T34 Horace, *Epode* 8. 11–12   (*c*.40–31 BC)

> esto beata, funus atque imagines
> ducant triumphales tuum,

May you be blessed and may triumphal masks lead your funeral procession.

T34a Pomponius Porfyrio   (early 3rd cent. AD?)
placeas tibi licet generositate ac divitiis inquit, dum modo deformitatem hanc effugere non possis. In funere autem nobilissimi cuiusque solebant praeferri imagines maiorum eius, quod adhuc observari videmus in funeribus principum.

He says you may rejoice in your high birth and wealth, but at the same time you cannot escape this ugliness. And indeed, in the funeral procession of each most prominent member of the office-holding caste it was the custom for the masks of his ancestors to be displayed, which we can see to this day is the practice in the funerals of emperors.

T35 Juvenal 8. 1–23   (after AD 118)

> Stemmata quid faciunt? quid prodest, Pontice, longo   1
> sanguine censeri, pictos ostendere vultus
> maiorum et stantis in curribus Aemilianos
> et Curios iam dimidios umeroque minorem
> Corvinum et Galbam auriculis nasoque carentem,   5
> [quis fructus, generis tabula iactare capaci
> Corvinum, posthac multa contingere virga
> fumosos equitum cum dictatore magistros,]
> si coram Lepidis male vivitur? effigies quo
> tot bellatorum, si luditur alea pernox   10
> ante Numantinos, si dormire incipis ortu
> luciferi, quo signa duces et castra movebant?
> cur Allobrogicis et magna gaudeat ara
> natus in Herculeo Fabius lare, si cupidus, si
> vanus et Euganea quantumvis mollior agna?   15
> si tenerum attritus Catinensi pumice lumbum
> squalentis traducit avos emptorque veneni
> frangenda miseram funestat imagine gentem?
> tota licet veteres exornent undique cerae
> atria: nobilitas sola est atque unica virtus.   20
> Paulus vel Cossus vel Drusus moribus esto:
> hos ante effigies maiorum pone tuorum,
> praecedant ipsas illi te consule virgas.

What good are family trees? What do you gain, Ponticus, in being appraised by your long lineage, in displaying the painted portraits of your ancestors, Aemiliani standing in chariots and already half-missing Curii and Corvinus missing a shoulder and Galba without ears or a nose? [What profit is there to boast of a Corvinus on the huge board recording his family tree, afterwards to claim kinship through many branches with smoky masters of the horse and their dictators] if you live badly in the presence of the Lepidi? What is the point of so many portraits of generals, if you play at dice all night in front of the Numantini, if you go to bed at sunrise, when they as generals struck camp and advance their standards? Why should Fabius, born to the family cult of Hercules, rejoice at the Allobrogici and the great altar, if he is greedy and untrustworthy and so much softer than a Euganean lamb? If his loin is polished smooth with Catinensian pumice it caricatures the hairy ancestors, and as procurer of poison he defiles his miserable family with murder by the enforced breaking of his mask? Although antique wax masks may adorn all your *atria* on all sides, valour alone and uniquely comprises 'nobility'. Be a Paullus or Cossus or Drusus in your way of life: set these up instead of the portraits of your ancestors, let them walk ahead of the very rods themselves when you are consul.

Cf. Seneca (T72–76).

T36 *Laus Pisonis* 1–24 (AD 39–40 ?)

    Unde prius coepti surgat mihi carminis ordo
    quosve canam titulos, dubius feror. hinc tua, Piso,
    nobilitas veterisque citant sublimia Calpi
    nomina, Romanas inter fulgentia gentes;
    hinc tua me virtus rapit et miranda per omnes   5
    vita modos: quae, si deesset tibi forte creato
    nobilitas, eadem pro nobilitate fuisset.
    nam quid imaginibus, quid avitis fulta triumphis
    atria, quid pleni numeroso consule fasti
    profuerint, cui vita labat? perit omnis in illo   10
    gentis honos, cuius laus est in origine sola.
    at tu, qui tantis animum natalibus aequas,
    et partem tituli, non summam, ponis in illis,
    ipse canendus eris: nam quid memorare necesse est,
    ut domus a Calpo nomen Calpurnio ducat   15
    claraque Pisonis tulerit cognomina prima,
    umida callosa cum 'pinseret' hordea dextra?
    nec si cuncta velim breviter decurrere possim;
    et prius aetheriae moles circumvaga flammae
    annua bis senis revocabit mensibus astra,   20
    quam mihi priscorum titulos operosaque bella
    contigerit memorare; manus sed bellica patrum

> armorumque labor veteres decuere Quirites,
> atque illos cecinere sui per carmina vates.

I am in doubt as to where the sequence of the poem I have undertaken should start from and which inscriptions I should sing of. On the one hand your 'nobility', Piso, and the exalted names of old Calpus summon me, names that shine amongst the Roman families; on the other your manly virtue carries me along and your life admirable in all its aspects; if by chance you had been born without the rank of office-holder, your qualities would have served in its stead for you. For what use are masks, or *atria* supported by the triumphs of forefathers, or lists full of many consuls to the man whose life is going to ruin? The family's whole honour perishes in him, whose renown consists only in his birth. But you, who are the equal in spirit to your illustrious birth, and record it as a part of your inscription, not the climax, you yourself will be the subject of song. For why is it necessary to call to mind how your house takes its name of Calpurnian from Calpus and how first the famous *cognomen* of Piso was bestowed, when the tough right hand 'was pounding' the moist barley. Even if I wanted to run through everything briefly I would not be able. And the sphere encircled with heavenly flames will recall in twice six months the annual constellations before I have the chance to recall the careers of the men of old and the toils of war. But the warlike hand of their fathers and the labour of weapons were suited to the Roman citizens of earlier days and to sing of them in songs suited their bards.

T36a 32–4

> quin age maiorum, iuvenis facunde, tuorum
> scande super titulos et avitae laudis honores,
> armorumque decus praecede forensibus actis.

Why come then, eloquent youth, climb above the labels of your ancestors, and the offices of your ancestral renown, outstrip the glory of arms with your deeds in the Forum.

T37 Livy i. 34. 6   Regal period (Augustan)

Roma est ad id potissima visa: in novo populo, ubi omnis repentina atque ex virtute nobilitas sit, futurum locum forti ac strenuo viro; regnasse Tatium Sabinum, arcessitum in regnum Numam a Curibus, et Ancum Sabina matre ortum nobilemque una imagine Numae esse.

Rome seemed the best place for this: in a new people, where all 'nobility' would be hastily acquired and based on valour, there would be a place for a brave and energetic man. Tatius the Sabine had been king, Numa had been summoned to reign from the Curii, and Ancus was born of a Sabine mother and made 'noble' by the one mask of Numa.

Cf. Appendix D.

T38 Livy 1. 47. 4   *c.*530s BC (Augustan)
Non tibi ab Corintho nec ab Tarquiniis, ut patri tuo, peregrina regna moliri
necesse est: di te penates patriique et patris imago et domus regia et in
domo regale solium et nomen Tarquinium creat vocatque regem.

[She said] It is not necessary for you to strive for a foreign kingdom from
Corinth or from Tarquinii, as your father did: your household and family
gods and the mask of your father and your royal house and the royal
throne in the house and the name Tarquinius makes and calls you king.

Ogilvie (1965) connects the ideas in this speech with Sophocles *Electra* 267-70.

T39 Livy 3. 58. 2   449 BC (Augustan)
Virum honoratissimae imaginis futurum ad posteros, legum latorem condi-
toremque Romani iuris, iacere vinctum inter fures nocturnos ac latrones.

[He said] A man destined to bequeath a most respected mask to posterity,
a legislator and founder of Roman law, was lying bound among nocturnal
thieves and brigands.

T40 Livy 3. 72. 4   446 BC (Augustan)
Scaptione hoc, contionali seni, adsignaturos putarent finitimos populos?
clarum hac fore imagine Scaptium; sed populum Romanum quadruplatoris
et interceptoris litis alienae personam laturum.

[He said] Did they think that the neighbouring peoples would credit this to
Scaptius, an old man who hangs about the assemblies? Scaptius would be
made famous by this mask; but the Roman people would play the part
(wear the mask) of a double-crosser and a profiteer from other people's legal
affairs.

Cf. Ogilvie (1965) ad loc. for textual problems and sense.

T41 Livy 8. 40. 3-5   (Augustan)
Nec facile est aut rem rei aut auctorem auctori praeferre. vitiatam memoriam funebribus laudibus reor falsisque imaginum titulis, dum familiae ad
se quaeque famam rerum gestarum honorumque fallente mendacio
trahunt; inde certe et singulorum gesta et publica monumenta rerum confusa. Nec quisquam aequalis temporibus illis scriptor exstat quo satis certo
auctore stetur.

And it is not easy to choose between different versions of events or different authorities. I believe that the tradition has been corrupted by funeral
eulogies and false labels for masks, while each of the families is claiming for
itself by deceptive lies the repute of deeds done and offices held. As a result
of this certainly both the achievements of individuals and the public record
of events have become confused. Nor is there extant any writer contemporary with that period to provide a sufficiently authoritative voice.

Cf. Ch. 5 § 4. Familiae = Madvig, familia = MSS.

T42 Livy 10. 7. 11   300 BC (Augustan)

Cuius ⟨in⟩ imaginis titulo consulatus censuraque et triumphus aequo animo legetur, si auguratum aut pontificatum adieceritis, non sustinebunt legentium oculi?

People are content to read of a consulship and censorship and triumph on the label for such a man's mask. If you added the augurate or pontificate, will the eyes of the readers not put up with it?

T43 Livy 22. 31. 8–11   216 BC (Augustan)

Omnium prope annales Fabium dictatorem adversus Hannibalem rem gessisse tradunt; Caelius etiam eum primum a populo creatum dictatorem scribit. sed et Caelium et ceteros fugit uni consuli Cn. Servilio, qui tum procul in Gallia provincia aberat, ius fuisse dicendi dictatoris; quam moram quia exspectare territa iam clade civitas non poterat, eo decursum esse ut a populo crearetur qui pro dictatore esset; res inde gestas gloriamque insignem ducis et augente titulum imaginis posteros, ut, qui pro dictatore ⟨creatus erat, dictator⟩ crederetur, facile obtinuisse.

Nearly all the annals record that Fabius was in charge of operations against Hannibal as dictator. Caelius also writes that he was the first dictator chosen by the people. But both Caelius and the others failed to recognize that only the consul Gnaeus Servilius, who was at that time far away in his command in Gaul, had the right of naming a dictator. Because the people, already panic striken by defeat, could not wait for this delay, recourse was had to an option whereby a man should be chosen by the people who would fulfil the functions of a dictator. The deeds then done and the celebrated glory of the general and the editing of the label on his mask by later generations easily resulted in the man who was chosen as acting dictator being considered dictator himself.

Cf. Ch. 5 § 4.

T44 Livy 30. 45. 6–7   201 BC (Augustan)

Africani cognomen militaris prius favor an popularis aura celebraverit an, sicuti Felicis Sullae Magnique Pompeii patrum memoria, coeptum ab adsentatione familiari sit, parum compertum habeo; primus certe hic imperator nomine victae ab se gentis est nobilitatus; exemplo deinde huius nequaquam victoria pares insignes imaginum titulos claraque cognomina familiarum fecerunt.

I have not found out whether it was the acclaim of the soldiers or the favour of the people that first made known the *cognomen* of Africanus or whether it was started from family flattery (or the flattery of friends) just as our fathers remembered was the case for Sulla Felix (the Lucky) and Pompeius Magnus (the Great). Certainly he was the first general to gain public recognition from the name of the people he conquered. Afterwards following his example others in no way equally distinguished in victory composed the labels of the masks and the famous *cognomina* of families.

Cf. T2, 45 and 104.

T45 Livy 38. 56. 12-13   187 BC (Augustan)

Prohibuisse statuas sibi in comitio, in rostris, in curia, in Capitolio, in cella Iovis poni; prohibuisse, ne decerneretur, ut imago sua triumphali ornatu e templo Iovis optimi maximi exiret.

He forbade statues of himself from being put up in the *comitium*, at the speakers' platform (*rostra*), at the senate house, on the Capitol, in the shrine of Jupiter. He forbade any decree authorizing the actor wearing his mask from proceeding in triumphal garb from the precinct of Jupiter Optimus Maximus.

Cf. Val. Max. 4. 1. 6 = T101 which is probably derived from this passage but worded less carefully. Cf. App. T2 and Val. Max. T104. Cf. Ch. 2 § 1e.

T46 Livy, *Periochae* 48   152 BC (Augustan)

M. Aemilius Lepidus, [qui] princeps senatus sextis iam censoribus lectus ⟨erat⟩, antequam expiraret, praecepit filiis, lecto se strato [sine] linteis, sine purpura efferrent, in relicum funus ne plus quam aeris decies consumerent: imaginum specie, non sumptibus nobilitari magnorum virorum funera solere.

Marcus Aemilius Lepidus, who had now been chosen to be the leader of the senate by the sixth pair of censors, before he died, gave instructions to his sons that they should carry him out for burial on a bier made up with linen without purple and that for the rest of his funeral they should spend no more than a million asses. [He said that] the funerals of great men are accustomed to be made renowned/'noble' not by their cost but by the spectacle of the masks.

T47 Martial 2. 90. 5-8   (AD 86-98)

> differat hoc patrios optat qui vincere census
> atriaque immodicis artat imaginibus.
> me focus et nigros non indignantia fumos
> tecta iuvant et fons vivus et herba rudis.

Let the man delay this who wishes to surpass his family's social rank and who crowds his *atria* with extravagent masks. I delight in the hearth and the roof not disdainful of black smoke and the living spring and the uncultivated grass.

Cf. T46 above for the very different ethos of the mid-2nd cent. BC.

T48 Martial 5. 20   (AD 86-98)

> Si tecum mihi, care Martialis,
> securis liceat frui diebus,
> si disponere tempus otiosum
> et verae pariter vacare vitae:

nec nos atria nec domos potentum   5
nec litis tetricas forumque triste
nossemus nec imagines superbas;
sed gestatio, fabulae, libelli,
campus, porticus, umbra, Virgo, thermae,
haec essent loca semper, hi labores.   10
nunc vivit necuter sibi, bonosque
soles effugere atque abire sentit,
qui nobis pereunt et imputantur.
quisquam vivere cum sciat, moratur?

Dear Martial, if I might enjoy carefree days with you, if I might map out
my leisure time and equally be free of real life, we would not have known
the *atria* or the houses of the powerful, nor gloomy lawsuits nor the sad
Forum nor the proud masks: but the promenade, plays, books, the campus,
the arcade, the shade, the cold baths of the Aqua Virgo, the warm baths,
these would always have been our haunts, this our work. As things are
neither of us lives for himself, and each feels the good days fleeing and
going away, which are lost to us and are charged to our account. When
any man knows how to live, does he delay?

T49 Martial 7. 44   (AD 86–98)

Maximus ille tuus, Ovidi, Caesonius hic est,
cuius adhuc vultum vivida cera tenet.
hunc Nero damnavit; sed tu damnare Neronem
ausus es et profugi, non tua, fata sequi:
aequora per Scyllae magnis comes exulis isti,   5
qui modo nolueras consulis ire comes.

Ovid, this is your great Caesonius, whose face the living wax still shows. Nero
condemned him; but you dared to condemn Nero and to escape to follow a
fate not your own. You went through the waters of Scylla, the comerade of
a great exile, you who once had refused to go as the comerade of a consul.

Cf. Mart. 7.5; Sen. *Ep.* 13. 2. 2; Tac. *Ann.* 15. 71.

T50 Ovid, *Amores* I. 8. 65–6   (Augustan, before AD 8)

nec te decipiant veteres circum atria cerae:
tolle tuos tecum, pauper amator, avos.

Do not let the antique wax masks around the *atria* beguile you: carry off
your ancestors with you as you go, poor lover.

T51 Ovid, *Fasti* I. 589–92   (AD 8–17)

redditaque est omnis populo provincia nostro
et tuus Augusto nomine dictus avus.
perlege dispositas generosa per atria ceras:
contigerunt nulli nomina tanta viro.

And the whole empire was returned to our people and your grandfather was given the name Augustus. Survey the wax masks arranged round the *atria* of the well-born: so great a name was bestowed on no other man. Cf. Ch. 8 § 1a.

T52 *Panegyricus Messallae* 28–34 (Augustan)

nam quamquam antiquae gentis superant tibi laudes,
non tua maiorum contenta est gloria fama,
nec quaeris quid quaque index sub imagine dicet, 30
sed generis priscos contendis vincere honores,
quam tibi maiores maius decus ipse futuris:
at tua non titulus capiet sub nomine facta,
aeterno sed erunt tibi magna volumina versu

For although you have renown in abundance in your ancient family, your reputation is not content with the renown of your ancestors, nor do you ask what the label says under each mask but you strive to surpass the ancient offices of your family whose greater glory you yourself will be rather than your ancestors: but your label will not encompass your deeds under your name, rather you will have great papyrus rolls of eternal poetry Cf. Sallust T65.

T53 Plautus, *Amphitryo* 458–9 (*c.*195 BC)

nam hicquidem omnem imaginem meam, quae antehac fuerat, possidet.
vivo fit quod numquam quisquam mortuo faciet mihi.

For surely this man has taken possession of my whole mask/appearance, as it was before, I experience in life what no one will ever do for me once I am dead.

Possidet plays on *possessor* meaning a squatter, someone who occupies land which is not his own. Cf. Ch. 2 § 1b and 1d.

T54 Pliny, *Naturalis Historiae* 35. 4–14 (Flavian)

(4) Imaginum quidem pictura, qua maxime similes in aevum propagabantur figurae, in totum exolevit. aerei ponuntur clipei argenteae facies, surdo figurarum discrimine; statuarum capita permutantur, volgatis iam pridem salibus etiam carminum. adeo materiam conspici malunt omnes quam se nosci. Et inter haec pinacothecas veteribus tabulis consuunt alienasque effigies colunt, ipsi honorem non nisi in pretio ducentes, ut frangat heres furisque detrahat laqueus. (5) itaque nullius effigie vivente imagines pecuniae, non suas, relinquunt. iidem palaestras athletarum imaginibus et ceromata sua exornant, Epicuri voltus per cubicula gestant ac circumferunt secum. natali eius sacrificant, feriasque omni mense vicesima luna custodiunt, quas icadas vocant, ii maxime qui se ne viventes quidem nosci volunt. ita est profecto: artes desidia perdidit, et quoniam animorum imagines non sunt, negleguntur etiam corporum. (6) aliter apud maiores in atriis

haec erant, quae spectarerunt; non signa externorum artificum nec aera aut marmora: expressi cera vultus singulis disponebantur armariis, ut essent imagines, quae comitarentur gentilicia funera, semperque defuncto aliquo totus aderat familiae eius qui umquam fuerat populus. stemmata vero lineis discurrebant ad imagines pictas. (7) tabulina codicibus implebantur et monimentis rerum in magistratu gestarum. aliae foris et circa limina animorum ingentium imagines erant adfixis hostium spoliis, quae nec emptori refigere liceret, triumphabantque etiam dominis mutatis aeternae domus. erat haec stimulatio ingens, exprobrantibus tectis cotidie inbellem dominum intrare in alienum triumphum. (8) exstat Messalae oratoris indignatio, quae prohibuit inseri genti suae Laevinorum alienam imaginem. similis causa Messalae seni expressit volumina illa quae de familiis condidit, cum Scipionis Pomponiani transisset atrium vidissetque adoptione testamentaria Salvittones—hoc enim fuerat cognomen— Africanorum dedecori inrepentes Scipionum nomini. sed—pace Messalarum dixisse liceat—etiam mentiri clarorum imagines erat aliquis virtutum amor multoque honestius quam mereri ne quis suas expeteret. (9) Non est praetereundum et novicium inventum, siquidem non ex auro argentove, at certe ex aere in bibliothecis dicantur illis, quorum immortales animae in locis iisdem loquuntur, quin immo etiam quae non sunt finguntur, pariuntque desideria non traditos vultus, sicut in Homero evenit. (10) quo maius, ut equidem arbitror, nullum est felicitatis specimen quam semper omnes scire cupere, qualis fuerit aliquis. Asini Pollionis hoc Romae inventum, qui primus bibliothecam dicando ingenia hominum rem publicam fecit. an priores coeperint Alexandreae et Pergami reges, qui bibliothecas magno certamine instituere, non facile dixerim. (11) imaginum amorem flagrasse quondam testes sunt Atticus ille Ciceronis edito de iis volumine, M. Varro benignissimo invento insertis voluminum suorum fecunditati etiam septingentorum inlustrium aliquo modo imaginibus, non passus intercidere figuras aut vetustatem aevi contra homines valere, inventor muneris etiam dis invidiosi, quando immortalitatem non solum dedit, verum etiam in omnes terras misit, ut praesentes esse ubique ceu di possent. et hoc quidem alienis ille praestitit. (12) Verum clupeos in sacro vel publico dicare privatim primus instituit, ut reperio, Appius Claudius qui consul cum P. Servilio fuit anno urbis CCLVIIII. posuit enim in Bellonae aede maiores suos, placuitque in excelso spectari et titulos honorum legi, decora res, utique si liberum turba parvulis imaginibus ceu nidum aliquem subolis pariter ostendat, quales clupeos nemo non gaudens favensque aspicit. (13) post eum M. Aemilius collega in consulatu Quinti Lutatii non in basilica modo Aemilia, verum et domi suae posuit, id quoque Martio exemplo. scutis enim, qualibus apud Troiam pugnatum est, continebantur imagines, unde et nomen habuere clupeorum, non, ut perversa grammaticorum suptilitas voluit, a cluendo. origo plena virtutis, faciem reddi in scuto cuiusque qui fuerat usus illo. (14) Poeni ex auro factitavere et clupeos et imagines secumque in castris vexere, certe captis talem Hasdrubalis invenit Marcius, Scipionum in Hispania ultor, isque clupeus supra fores Capitolinae aedis usque ad incendium primum fuit. maiorum quidem nostrorum tanta securitas in ea re adnotatur, ut L. Manlio Q. Fulvio cos. anno urbis DLXXV M. Aufidius tutelae Capitolio redemptor docuerit patres argenteos esse clupeos, qui pro aereis per aliquot iam lustra adsignabantur.

At any rate realistic portraiture, by which exact likenesses were handed down for all time, has gone completely out of fashion. Silver plating is applied to bronze shields with a vague rendering of human figures; the heads of statues are exchanged, about which before now satirical poems were spread. To this extent everyone prefers that the material be admired than that they be known themselves. And meanwhile, they embroider their picture galleries with old paintings and they esteem the portraits of strangers, themselves ascribing value only to price so that the heir breaks it and the noose of the thief drags it away. (5) Consequently, they bequeath images (*imagines*) of money which depict the living features of noone, rather than their own. These same people adorn their palaestra and gymnasia with statues of athletes, they put up busts of Epicurus in their bedrooms, and carry these around with them. They make sacrifices on his birthday, and they observe holidays on the twentieth of every month, which they call *eikas*, those especially who do not even want to be known themselves while they are alive. This surely is the situation: idleness has destroyed the arts, and since there are no portraits of their spirits, representations of their bodies are also neglected. (6) These matters were different in the *atria* of the ancestors where portraits offered a spectacle to behold, not the statues by foreign artists either of bronze or of marble; but faces rendered in wax were arranged in separate cupboards, so that they should be 'true portraits' (*imagines*) to accompany funerals in the extended family. And whenever someone died the whole crowd of his family members who had ever lived was present. Moreover, the family trees traced their lines to painted portraits. (7) The *tablina* (archive rooms) were filled with ledgers of records and accounts of deeds done by office-holders. Outside and around the entrance door there were other portraits of great men, with enemy spoils attached to them, which any buyer of the house was not allowed to remove and the houses celebrated triumphs forever even when their owners had changed. This was a great inducement, since every day the houses themselves reproached an unwarlike master with entering into the triumph of another. (8) An indignant speech by the orator Messala is extant, which forbade the introduction into his family of a mask of the Laevini which did not belong to them. A similar sentiment is expressed by the elder Messala in those volumes he wrote 'About Families', since he had walked through the *atrium* of Scipio Pomponianus and seen the Salvittiones—for this was their *cognomen*—usurping the name of the Scipios

after being adopted in a will to the disgrace of Africanus' family. But—if
the Messalae will allow me to say so—even laying a false claim to the
masks of famous men shows some love of excellence and is much more
respectable than not deserving that anyone should seek one's own (mask).
(9) And a new kind of portrait should not be passed over, even if not of gold
or of silver but certainly of bronze [these portraits] in libraries are devoted
to those men whose immortal souls speak in those same places, so that
indeed even likenesses that have not survived are invented, and a sense of
loss gives birth to faces not handed down by tradition, as happened in the
case of Homer. (10) So that, at least as I see it, there is no greater mark of
happiness than for everyone always to want to know what kind of a man
someone was. Asinius Pollio introduced this practice at Rome, who first by
dedicating a library made the great works of men public property. I could
not easily say whether the kings of Alexandria and Pergamum, who
founded libraries in great competition with eachother, had started this earlier. (11) That a strong love of portraits existed in former times is demonstrated by Atticus, that friend of Cicero, in his book about them and by a
very pleasing invention of Marcus Varro, who even included in the rich
output of his writings portraits of seven hundred men who were famous in
some way. He did not allow their likenesses to disappear or the passage of
time to prevail against men. He invented a gift which even the gods envy,
since he did not only give immortality, but also sent it all over the world,
so that men could be present everywhere like the gods. And in this way he
helped men he did not know. (12) But the first man to start the dedication
of portrait shields in a temple or public place by a private act was, as I discover, Appius Claudius who was consul with P. Servilius in the 259th year
of the city. For he put up his ancestors in the temple of Bellona, and decided
that they should be on display in a high spot and that the inscriptions
recording their offices should be read. This is a suitable thing, especially if
a crowd of children is equally displayed in small portraits like some nest of
offspring. There is nobody who does not see such shields with pleasure and
approval. (13) After him Marcus Aemilius, Quintus Lutatius' colleague in
the consulship, set up shields not only in the Basilica Aemilia, but also in
his house, and this also by a warlike example. For portraits were applied to
shields, like those which were used in the Trojan War, and thence they
have their name of *clupei* and not from *cluo* (to be celebrated) as the misguided pedantry of philologists would have it. It is a strong inducement to
moral excellence, for the portrait of the man who once used it to be rendered on a shield. (14) The Carthaginians were accustomed to making both
shields and portraits of gold and to taking these with them on campaign.
Certainly Marcius, the avenger of the Scipios in Spain, found such a shield
when he captured Hasdrubal, and this portrait shield hung over the doors
of the Capitoline temple until the first fire. It is a matter of record that our
ancestors were so unconcerned about this question that in the consulship

of L. Manlius and Q. Fulvius in the 575th year of the city M. Aufudius the contractor in charge of the safety of the Capitol, informed the senate that the shields were silver which had been marked down as bronze for several census periods.

Cf. Ch. 2 § 1*b* and 1*c* and. Stark (1876) with Ch. 3 § 2*b*.

T55 Pliny, *Epistulae* 2. 7. 7, C. Plinius Macrino suo s.   (*c.* AD 97)
etenim, si defunctorum imagines domi positae dolorem nostrum levant, quanto magis hae quibus in celeberrimo loco non modo species et vultus illorum, sed honor etiam et gloria refertur! vale.

Gaius Plinius greets his dear Macrinus
And indeed, if the masks of the dead put up at home console our grief, how much more do these by which not only the appearance and faces of those men are recalled in a most public place, but also their official dignity and reputation. Farewell.

T56 Pliny, *Epistulae* 3. 3. 6, C. Plinius Corelliae Hispullae suae s.
                                                                    (early 2nd cent. AD)
Nihil ex hoc viro filius tuus audiet nisi profuturum, nihil discet quod nescisse rectius fuerit, nec minus saepe ab illo quam a te meque admonebitur, quibus imaginibus oneretur, quae nomina et quanta sustineat.

Gaius Plinius greets his dear Corellia Hispulla
Your son will not hear anything from this man except what will benefit him, he will learn nothing that it would have been better for him not to know, and he will be reminded just as often by him as by you and by me, by what masks he is burdened and what great names he bears.

T57 Pliny, *Epistulae* 5. 17. 6, C. Plinius Vestricio Spurinnae suo s.
                                                                    (early 2nd cent. AD)
Faveo enim saeculo ne sit sterile et effetum, mireque cupio ne nobiles nostri nihil in domibus suis pulchrum nisi imagines habeant; quae nunc mihi hos adulescentes tacitae laudare adhortari, et quod amborum gloriae satis magnum est, agnoscere videntur. Vale.

Gaius Plinius greets his dear Vestricius Spurinna
For I am eager that our age should not be unproductive and sterile, and I am greatly desirous that our 'nobles' should not turn out to have nothing fine in their houses except the masks which seem to me now to be silently encouraging the praises of these young men, and to be recognizing them as descendants, a thing which is enough of a tribute in itself to both. Farewell.

T58 Pliny *Ep.* 8. 10. 3, C. Plinius Fabato prosocero suo s.   (*c.* AD 107)
Neque enim ardentius tu pronepotes, quam ego liberos cupio, quibus videor

a meo tuoque latere pronum ad honores iter et audita latius nomina et non subitas imagines relicturus. nascantur modo et hunc nostrum dolorem gaudio mutent! vale.

Gaius Plinius greets his dear Fabatus, his wife's grandfather.

For you are no more eager for great-grandchildren than I am for children, for whom I imagine both from my and from your side the bequest of a swift path to public office and widely known names and no hastily improvised masks. Only let them be born and let them change this grief of ours into joy! Farewell.

T59 Plutarch, *Caesar* 5   69 BC (early 2nd cent. AD)

Τοῦ δὲ δήμου πρώτην μὲν ἀπόδειξιν τῆς πρὸς αὐτὸν εὐνοίας ἔλαβεν, ὅτε πρὸς Γάϊον Ποπίλιον ἐρίσας ὑπὲρ χιλιαρχίας πρότερος ἀνηγορεύθη· (2) δευτέραν δὲ καὶ καταφανεστέραν, ὅτε τῆς Μαρίου γυναικὸς Ἰουλίας ἀποθανούσης, ἀδελφιδοῦς ὢν αὐτῆς, ἐγκώμιόν τε λαμπρὸν ἐν ἀγορᾷ διῆλθε, καὶ περὶ τὴν ἐκφορὰν ἐτόλμησεν εἰκόνας Μαρίων προθέσθαι, τότε πρῶτον ὀφθείσας μετὰ τὴν ἐπὶ Σύλλα πολιτείαν, πολεμίων τῶν ἀνδρῶν κριθέντων. (3) ἐπὶ τούτῳ γὰρ ἐνίων καταβοησάντων τοῦ Καίσαρος, ὁ δῆμος ἀντήχησε, λαμπρῷ δεξάμενος κρότῳ καὶ θαυμάσας ὥσπερ ἐξ Ἅιδου διὰ χρόνων πολλῶν ἀνάγοντα τὰς Μαρίου τιμὰς εἰς τὴν πόλιν. (4) τὸ μὲν οὖν ἐπὶ γυναιξὶ πρεσβυτέραις λόγους ἐπιταφίους διεξιέναι πάτριον ἦν Ῥωμαίοις, ⟨ἐπὶ⟩ νέαις δ' οὐκ ὂν ἐν ἔθει, πρῶτος εἶπε Καῖσαρ ἐπὶ τῆς ἑαυτοῦ γυναικὸς ἀποθανούσης. καὶ τοῦτ' ἤνεγκεν αὐτῷ χάριν τινα καὶ συνεδημαγώγησε τῷ πάθει τοὺς πολλοὺς ὡς ἥμερον ἄνδρα καὶ περίμεστον ἤθους ἀγαπᾶν.

He received the first demonstration of the people's goodwill towards him when he was elected in first place in his contest with Gaius Popilius for the military tribunate. (2) But the second instance was more obvious, when he delivered a brilliant eulogy in the Forum, when Marius' wife Julia died, who was his aunt. And in the funeral procession he dared to display the masks of the Marians, seen then for the first time after the administration of Sulla and the condemnation of these men as enemies. (3) For when some made an outcry against Caesar on these grounds, the people in turn took his side, greeting him with splendid applause and admiring him for bringing back, as if from Hades, Marius' honours to the city after such a long time. (4) Although, it is a traditional custom of the Romans to deliver funeral orations over older women, it was not a practice in the case of younger ones. Caesar was the first to do so by delivering one for his wife when she died. And this won him some favour and helped him, because of his misfortune, to win the support of the people so that they loved him for his gentleness and depth of feeling.

Cf. Ch. 4 § 6.

T60 Plutarch, *Marius* 9. 2   107 BC (early 2nd cent. AD)

Οὐ μὴν ταῦτά γε μάλιστα διέβαλλε τὸν Μάριον, ἀλλ' οἱ λόγοι θρασεῖς ὄντες ὑπεροψίᾳ καὶ ὕβρει τοὺς πρώτους ἐλύπουν, σκῦλόν τε βοῶντος αὐτοῦ τὴν ὑπατείαν φέρεσθαι τῆς τῶν εὐγενῶν καὶ πλουσίων μαλακίας, καὶ τραύμασιν οἰκείοις πρὸς τὸν δῆμον, οὐ μνήμασι νεκρῶν οὐδ' ἀλλοτρίαις εἰκόσι νεανιεύεσθαι.

But actually it was not these things which gave Marius an especially bad name, but his bold speeches full of contempt and insult harrassed the élite, as he claimed loudly that he had carried off the consulship as spoils of the cowardice of the 'noble' families and the wealthy, and that he made a show of his own wounds to the people, not of memorials of the dead or of masks belonging to other people.

Cf. Sall. T66a-c and Ch. 1 and 5 § 5.

T61 Polybius 6. 53-4   (c.150 BC)

(53.1) Ὅταν γὰρ μεταλλάξῃ τις παρ' αὐτοῖς τῶν ἐπιφανῶν ἀνδρῶν, συντελουμένης τῆς ἐκφορᾶς κομίζεται μετὰ τοῦ λοιποῦ κόσμου πρὸς τοὺς καλουμένους ἐμβόλους εἰς τὴν ἀγορὰν ποτὲ μὲν ἑστὼς ἐναργής, σπανίως δὲ κατακεκλιμένος. (2) πέριξ δὲ παντὸς τοῦ δήμου στάντος, ἀναβὰς ἐπὶ τοὺς ἐμβόλους, ἂν μὲν υἱὸς ἐν ἡλικίᾳ καταλείπηται καὶ τύχῃ παρών, οὗτος, εἰ δὲ μή, τῶν ἄλλων εἴ τις ἀπὸ γένους ὑπάρχει, λέγει περὶ τοῦ τετελευτηκότος τὰς ἀρετὰς καὶ τὰς ἐπιτετευγμένας ἐν τῷ ζῆν πράξεις. (3) δι' ὧν συμβαίνει τοὺς πολλοὺς ἀναμιμνησκομένους καὶ λαμβάνοντας ὑπὸ τὴν ὄψιν τὰ γεγονότα, μὴ μόνον τοὺς κεκοινωνηκότας τῶν ἔργων, ἀλλὰ καὶ τοὺς ἐκτός, ἐπὶ τοσοῦτον γίνεσθαι συμπαθεῖς ὥστε μὴ τῶν κηδευόντων ἴδιον, ἀλλὰ κοινὸν τοῦ δήμου φαίνεσθαι τὸ σύμπτωμα. (4) μετὰ δὲ ταῦτα θάψαντες καὶ ποιήσαντες τὰ νομιζόμενα τιθέασι τὴν εἰκόνα τοῦ μεταλλάξαντος εἰς τὸν ἐπιφανέστατον τόπον τῆς οἰκίας, ξύλινα ναΐδια περιτιθέντες. (5) ἡ δ' εἰκών ἐστι πρόσωπον εἰς ὁμοιότητα διαφερόντως ἐξειργασμένον καὶ κατὰ τὴν πλάσιν καὶ κατὰ τὴν ὑπογραφήν. (6) ταύτας δὴ τὰς εἰκόνας ἔν τε ταῖς δημοτελέσι θυσίαις ἀνοίγοντες κοσμοῦσι φιλοτίμως, ἐπάν τε τῶν οἰκείων μεταλλάξῃ τις ἐπιφανής, ἄγουσιν εἰς τὴν ἐκφοράν, περιτιθέντες ὡς ὁμοιοτάτοις εἶναι δοκοῦσι κατά τε τὸ μέγεθος καὶ τὴν ἄλλην περικοπήν. (7) οὗτοι δὲ προσαναλαμβάνουσιν ἐσθῆτας, ἐὰν μὲν ὕπατος ἢ στρατηγὸς ᾖ γεγονώς, περιπορφύρους, ἐὰν δὲ τιμητής, πορφυρᾶς, ἐὰν δὲ καὶ τεθριαμβευκὼς ἢ τι τοιοῦτον κατειργασμένος, διαχρύσους. (8) αὐτοὶ μὲν οὖν ἐφ' ἁρμάτων οὗτοι πορεύονται, ῥάβδοι δὲ καὶ πελέκεις καὶ τἆλλα τὰ ταῖς ἀρχαῖς εἰωθότα συμπαρακεῖσθαι προηγεῖται κατὰ τὴν ἀξίαν ἑκάστῳ τῆς γεγενημένης κατὰ τὸν βίον ἐν τῇ πολιτείᾳ προαγωγῆς. (9) ὅταν δ' ἐπὶ τοὺς ἐμβόλους ἔλθωσι, καθέζονται πάντες ἑξῆς ἐπὶ δίφρων ἐλεφαντίνων. οὗ κάλλιον οὐκ εὐμαρὲς ἰδεῖν θέαμα νέῳ φιλοδόξῳ καὶ φιλαγάθῳ· (10) τὸ γὰρ τὰς τῶν ἐπ' ἀρετῇ δεδοξασμένων ἀνδρῶν εἰκόνας ἰδεῖν ὁμοῦ πάσας οἱονεὶ ζώσας καὶ πεπνυμένας τίν' οὐκ ἂν παραστήσαι; τί δ' ἂν

Literary Testimonia

κάλλιον θέαμα τούτου φανείη; (54.1) πλὴν ὅ γε λέγων ὑπὲρ τοῦ
θάπτεσθαι μέλλοντος, ἐπὰν διέλθῃ τὸν περὶ τούτου λόγον, ἄρχεται τῶν
ἄλλων ἀπὸ τοῦ προγενεστάτου τῶν παρόντων, καὶ λέγει τὰς ἐπιτυχίας
ἑκάστου καὶ τὰς πράξεις. (2) ἐξ ὧν καινοποιουμένης ἀεὶ τῶν ἀγαθῶν
ἀνδρῶν τῆς ἐπ᾽ ἀρετῇ φήμης ἀθανατίζεται μὲν ἡ τῶν καλόν τι
διαπραξαμένων εὔκλεια, γνώριμος δὲ τοῖς πολλοῖς καὶ παραδόσιμος τοῖς
ἐπιγινομένοις ἡ τῶν εὐεργετησάντων τὴν πατρίδα γίγνεται δόξα. (3) τὸ
δὲ μέγιστον, οἱ νέοι παρορμῶνται πρὸς τὸ πᾶν ὑπομένειν ὑπὲρ τῶν κοινῶν
πραγμάτων χάριν τοῦ τυχεῖν τῆς συνακολουθούσης τοῖς ἀγαθοῖς τῶν
ἀνδρῶν εὐκλείας. (4) πίστιν δ᾽ ἔχει τὸ λεγόμενον ἐκ τούτων. πολλοὶ μὲν
γὰρ ἐμονομάχησαν ἑκουσίως Ῥωμαίων ὑπὲρ τῆς τῶν ὅλων κρίσεως, οὐκ
ὀλίγοι δὲ προδήλους εἵλοντο θανάτους, τινὲς μὲν ἐν πολέμῳ τῆς τῶν
ἄλλων ἕνεκεν σωτηρίας, τινὲς δ᾽ ἐν εἰρήνῃ χάριν τῆς τῶν κοινῶν
πραγμάτων ἀσφαλείας. (5) καὶ μὴν ἀρχὰς ἔχοντες ἔνιοι τοὺς ἰδίους υἱοὺς
παρὰ πᾶν ἔθος ἢ νόμον ἀπέκτειναν, περὶ πλείονος ποιούμενοι τὸ τῆς
πατρίδος συμφέρον τῆς κατὰ φύσιν οἰκειότητος πρὸς τοὺς
ἀναγκαιοτάτους.

For whenever one of the leading men amongst them dies, when the funeral has been arranged the body is brought with the rest of the adornment to the place called the ship's prows (*rostra*) in the Forum where it is usually propped up for all to see, but rarely it is laid out. (2) If a grown-up son is left behind and happens to be present, he mounts the *rostra* with all the people standing around. But if not, then another family member who is available delivers a speech about the virtues of the dead man and his achievements during his lifetime. (3) As a result of this the people remember what happened and picture it before their eyes, not only those who shared in the deeds, but also those who did not. Both share the same feelings to such an extent that the misfortune does not appear as the private concern of the family, but as a public matter for the people. (4) After that they bury the body and perform the customary rites. Then they place a likeness of the dead man in the most public part of the house, keeping it in a small wooden shrine. (5) The likeness is a mask especially made for a close resemblance both as regards the shape of the face and its colouring. (6) They open these masks during public sacrifices and compete in decorating them. And whenever a leading member of the family dies, they introduce them into the funeral procession, putting them on men who seem most like them in height and as regards the rest of their general appearance. (7) These men assume their costume in addition, if the person was a consul or praetor, a toga with a purple border, if a censor, the all-purple toga, but if someone had celebrated a triumph or done something like that, a gold embroidered toga. (8) These men now ride on wagons, and the rods and axes and the other customary equipment of those in power accompanies them according to the dignity befitting the rank and station achieved by

309

each man in politics during his lifetime. (9) And when they reach the *rostra*, they all sit in order on ivory stools. It is not easy for an ambitious and high minded young man to see a finer spectacle than this. (10) For who would not be won over at the sight of all the masks together of those men who had been extolled for virtue as if they were alive and breathing? What spectacle could appear nobler than this? (54.1) None except the man who is speaking over the one who is about to be buried, who, when he has finished the eulogy about him, begins praising the others present starting with the oldest one, and recounts the successes and deeds of each. (2) As a consequence of this, since the reputation for virtue of good men is always being made new, the renown of those who did some noble deed is immortal and the glory of those who rendered service to their country becomes well-known to the many and an inheritance for those who come after. (3) But the greatest result is that the young men are encouraged to undergo anything for the sake of the common cause in the hope of gaining the good reputation which follows upon the brave deeds of men. (4) This is verified by the following considerations. For many Romans have willingly entered single combat for the sake of deciding a whole battle. A number have also chosen certain death, some in war to further the safety of the others, and some in peace for the sake of the security of the state. (5) And indeed a few, as magistrates, have put their own sons to death against all custom and practice, because they preferred the good of their country to their natural feelings of closeness with their nearest relatives.

Cf. T11 and 19.

T62 Propertius 1. 5. 23-4   (before 28 BC?)
>   nec tibi nobilitas poterit succurrere amanti:
>   nescit Amor priscis cedere imaginibus.

And your family's standing as office-holders will not be able to help you as a lover: the god of love does not know how to defer to antique masks.

T63 Propertius 2. 13*b*. 1-8   (before 2 BC)
>   Quandocumque igitur nostros mors claudet ocellos,
>   accipe quae serves funeris acta mei.
>   nec mea tunc longa spatietur imagine pompa,
>   nec tuba sit fati vana querela mei;
>   nec mihi tunc fulcro sternatur lectus eburno,   5
>   nec sit in Attalico mors mea nixa toro.
>   desit odoriferis ordo mihi lancibus, adsint
>   plebei parvae funeris exsequiae.

Therefore, whenever death shall close my eyes, receive the instructions which you should observe concerning my funeral. Then let my funeral procession not wind its way with many masks, nor let there be a trumpet, a vain lament for my fate; nor let a bed be prepared for me with a pillow of ivory, nor let my body lie on a bier embroidered with gold of Attalus. Let me have no procession of incense-bearers, but let me have the simple rites of a poor man's funeral.

T64 Pseudo-Quintilian *Declamationes minores* 388. 35   (?)
A piratis dimissum, a fortuna—o te, liberte, inofficiosum!—reduxisti non ad imagines, sed ut propius amissam dignitatem aspiceret. 'Etiam,' inquit, 'fortunam meam noveram.' Non est, puer, quod cum liberto queraris: omnia tibi reddidit praeter matrem.

After you were freed by the pirates, by fortune—O you, freedman who have caused further troubles by trying to help!—you brought him back not to his masks but so that he might see at close quarters his lost dignity. He said, 'Even so, I have renewed my fortunes.' Boy, you have no complaint to make against the freedman: he returned everything to you except your mother.

T65 Sallust, *Bellum Jugurthinum* 4. 5-6   (*c.*40 BC)
nam saepe ego audivi Q. Maximum, P. Scipionem, ⟨alios⟩ praeterea civitatis nostrae praeclaros viros solitos ita dicere, quom maiorum imagines intuerentur, vehementissume sibi animum ad virtutem adcendi. scilicet non ceram illam neque figuram tantam vim in sese habere, sed memoria rerum gestarum eam flammam egregiis viris in pectore crescere neque prius sedari quam virtus eorum famam atque gloriam adaequaverit.

For I often heard that Quintus Maximus, Publius Scipio, and other outstanding men in our state besides were accustomed to say the following sorts of things: when they were looking at the masks of their ancestors, their spirits were kindled with an ardent desire for moral excellence. To be sure the wax itself and the likeness did not have such a force in it, but the memory of deeds done caused that flame to grow in the hearts of these excellent men and not to die down before their valour had matched the reputation and renown of those men.

T66 Sallust, *Bellum Jugurthinum* 85. 10   107 BC (*c.*40 BC)
bellum me gerere cum Iugurtha iussistis, quam rem nobilitas aegerrume tulit. quaeso, reputate cum animis vostris num id mutare melius sit, si quem ex illo globo nobilitatis ad hoc aut aliud tale negotium mittatis, hominem veteris prosapiae ac multarum imaginum et nullius stipendi, scilicet ut in tanta re ignarus omnium trepidet, festinet, sumat aliquem ex populo monitorem offici sui.

You appointed me to wage war against Jugurtha, a thing which the office-holding caste objected to strongly. I ask you, consider in your hearts whether it would be better to change that, by sending out one of that crowd of 'nobles' on this or some other similar business, a man with an ancient lineage and many masks but no military experience, so that of course being inexperienced in so great an undertaking he would fear everything and would hurry to take some man of the people as a guide in carrying out his commission.

T66*a* 85. 21–5
atque etiam, quom apud vos aut in senatu verba faciunt, pleraque oratione maiores suos extollunt: eorum fortia facta memorando clariores sese putant. quod contra est; (22) nam quanto vita illorum praeclarior, tanto horum socordia flagitiosior. et profecto ita se res habet: (23) maiorum gloria posteris quasi lumen est, neque bona neque mala eorum in occulto patitur. (24) huisce rei ego inopiam fateor, Quirites, verum, id quod multo praeclarius est, meamet facta mihi dicere licet. nunc videte quam iniqui sint: (25) quod ex aliena virtute sibi adrogant, id mihi ex mea non concedunt, scilicet quia imagines non habeo et quia mihi nova nobilitas est, quam certe peperisse melius est quam acceptam conrupisse.

And also, when they give a speech either to you (the people) or in the senate, they often praise their ancestors: they think that they themselves become more renowned by calling to mind the brave deeds of those men. In fact the reverse is true. (22) For the more illustrious the formers' lives are, the more disgraceful the latters' inaction appears. And certainly this is the way things are: (23) the glory of the ancestors is like a light for their descendants, a light which does not allow either their good or their bad deeds to remain in darkness. (24) Roman citizens, I admit my poverty in this regard but I am in a position to speak of my own deeds, which is a much more admirable thing. Now see how base they are: (25) what they appropriate for themselves from other people's valour, they do not allow me to acquire from my own merit, obviously because I do not have any masks and because my status as an office-holder is new. But it is better, to be sure, to create one's own élite status than to destroy such status after having inherited it.

T66*b* 85. 29–30
non possum fidei causa imagines neque triumphos aut consulatus maiorum meorum ostentare, at, si res postulet, hastas, vexillum, phaleras, alia militaria dona, praeterea cicatrices advorso corpore. (30) hae sunt meae imagines, haec nobilitas, non hereditate relicta, ut illa illis, sed quae egomet plurumis laboribus et periculis quaesivi.

I am not able to inspire confidence by parading the masks or triumphs or consulships of my ancestors, but, if need arises, I can show spears and standards presented for valour, medals, other military decorations, and besides the scars on the front of my body. (30) These are my masks, these my 'nobility', not inherited as in their case, but which I myself strove to acquire through many labours and dangers.

T66c 85. 38

maiores eorum omnia quae licebat illis reliquere, divitias, imagines, memoriam sui praeclaram; virtutem non reliquere, neque poterant: ea sola neque
datur dono neque accipitur.

Their ancestors bequeathed to them everything which they could, wealth,
masks, their distinguished reputation; they did not leave them valour, nor
could they: it alone is neither given nor received as a gift.

Cf. Ch. 1 and 5 § 5.

T67 Sallust, *Historiae* III fr. 48. 18, Oratio Macri tr. pl. ad plebem

73 BC (*c.*30S BC)

gerant habeantque suo modo imperia, quaerant triumphos, Mithridatem,
Sertorium et reliquias exulum persequantur cum imaginibus suis: absit periculum et labos, quibus nulla pars fructus est

Let them hold and exercise commands in their own way, let them seek triumphs, let them attack Mithridates, Sertorius and the rest of the exiles with
their masks: but let there be no danger and hard work for those who do
not share any part of the profits.

Cf. T66*a–c* and Ch. 5 § 5.

T68 Seneca, *Controversiae* 1. 6. 3–4   (55 BC–AD 37/41)

quidam avitas paternasque flagitiis obruerunt imagines, quidam ignobiles
nati fecere posteris genus: in illis non servasse quod acceperant maximum
dedecus, in illis quod nemo dederat fecisse laudabile est. si possent homines
facere sibi sortem nascendi, nemo esset humilis, nemo egens, unusquisque
felicem domum invaderet; sed quamdiu non sumus, natura nos regit et in
quemcumque vult casum quemque mittit: hic sumus aestimandi, cum
sumus nostri. quis fuit *Marius*, si illum suis inspexerimus maioribus? *in multis consulatibus nihil habet clarius quam se auctorem. Pompeium si hereditariae
extulissent imagines, nemo Magnum dixisset.*

Some bury their father's and grandfathers' masks in oblivion through their
disgraceful deeds, others who are low-born establish a family for their
descendants: for the former not preserving what they have inherited is the
greatest disgrace, the latter are worthy of praise for creating what no one
had given them. If men could choose their lot at birth, no one would be
lowly, no one poor, every single person would take his place in a prosperous family; but as long as we have not been born yet, nature controls us
and sends each person into the world into whatever situation she wants:
here we are esteemed when we are our own masters. Who was Marius, if
we consider him in terms of his ancestors? In his many consulships he has
nothing more illustrious than being self-made. If the inherited masks
accompanied the funeral of Pompey (or brought Pompey to the height of
his career), no one would have called him Great.

T69 Seneca, *Controversiae* 2. 1. 17 (55 BC–AD 37/41)
Fabriciorum imagines Metellis patuerunt; Aemiliorum et Scipionum familias adoptio miscuit; etiam abolita saeculis nomina per successores novos
fulgent. sic illa patriciorum nobilitas ⟨a⟩ fundamentis urbis [habet] usque in
haec tempora constitit: adoptio fortunae remedium est.

The masks of the Fabricii were open to the Metelli; adoption mixed the families of the Aemilii and the Scipios; even names lost for centuries shine with
new heirs. In this way that élite caste of patricians has endured from the
founding of the city to the present time. Adoption is the remedy of fortune.
Cf. T12.

T70 Seneca, *Controversiae* 2. 3. 6 (55 BC–AD 37/41)
'Rogo' inquit. nunc? hic? sic? si volebas rogare, admovisses propinquos,
amicos, maiorum imagines, lacrimas, repetitos alte gemitus. testor deos, sic
rogaturus fui puellae patrem.

'I beg' he said. Now? Here? Thus? If you wanted to beg, you should have
introduced relatives, friends, the masks of ancestors, tears, deeply felt
groans. I call the gods to witness, in this way I was to beg the girl's father.
Cf. Cic. in T11 and 19.

T71 Seneca, *Controversiae* 7. 6. 10 (55 BC–AD 37/41)
Indicit festum diem, aperiri iubet maiorum imagines, cum maxime tegen-
dae sunt.

He announces a feast day, he orders the masks of the ancestors to be
opened, at a time when they should above all be closed.

T72 Seneca, *Dial.* 12. 12. 6–7, *Ad Helviam Matrem de Consolatione*
(AD 41–9)
Beatioresne istos putas quorum pantomimae deciens sestertio nubunt quam
Scipionem, cuius liberi a senatu, tutore suo, in dotem aes grave accepe-
runt? Dedignatur aliquis paupertatem, cuius tam clarae imagines sunt?
Indignatur exul aliquid sibi deesse, cum defuerit Scipioni dos, Regulo mer-
cennarius, Menenio funus, cum omnibus illis quod deerat ideo honestius
suppletum sit quia defuerat? His ergo advocatis non tantum tuta est sed
etiam gratiosa paupertas.

Do you think those more fortunate whose daughters are pantomime
actresses and marry with a dowry of a million sesterces than Scipio, whose
children were given a pound of old copper money as a dowry by the senate, their legal guardian? Would someone despise poverty, when she has
such famous masks? Would an exile be indignant at lacking something,
when a Scipio did not have a dowry, Regulus had no hired helper,
Menenius no funeral, when all these gained what they lacked more hon-
ourably because they had not had it? With these men to speak for it poverty
is not so much safe as even agreeable.

T73 Seneca, *De Clementia* 1. 9. 10 AD 4   (AD 55 or 56)
Cedo, si spes tuas solus impedio, Paulusne te et Fabius Maximus et Cossi et Servilii ferent tantumque agmen nobilium non inania nomina praeferentium, sed eorum, qui imaginibus suis decori sint?

I yield, if I alone am in the way of your hopes. Will Paulus and Fabius Maximus and the Cossi and Servilii accept you and the great army of 'nobles' who do not bear empty names, but those who are a credit to their masks?

T74 Seneca, *De Beneficiis* 3. 28. 2   (AD 56-65)
Qui imagines in atrio exponunt et nomina familiae suae longo ordine ac multis stemmatum inligata flexuris in parte prima aedium collocant, non noti magis quam nobiles sunt? Unus omnium parens mundus est; sive per splendidos sive per sordidos gradus ad hunc prima cuiusque origo perducitur. Non est, quod te isti decipiant, qui, cum maiores suos saepe recensent, ubicumque nomen inlustre defecit, illo deum infulciunt.

Those who display masks in their *atrium* and put up the names of their family in a long succession and a family tree entwined with many complex connections in the entrance way of the house, are they not well known rather than 'noble'? The universe is the one parent of everyone; whether he arrives at this first birth of his from a magnificent or base origin. Do not be deceived by them when they often ennumerate their ancestors, and wherever there is no famous name, there they slip in a god.

The meaning of *nobilitas* is discussed in Ch. 3 § 1.

T75 Seneca, *Epistulae* 44. 5   (AD 62-5)
Non facit nobilem atrium plenum fumosis imaginibus; nemo in nostram gloriam vixit nec quod ante nos fuit nostrum est: animus facit nobilem, cui ex quacumque condicione supra fortunam licet surgere.

An *atrium* full of smoke-stained masks does not make a man 'noble'; no one lived before to give us glory nor is what came before us ours: the soul creates 'nobility', for whom it is possible to rise above fortune regardless of its station in life.

T76 Seneca, *Epistulae* 76. 12   (AD 62-5)
Si quis omnia alia habeat, valitudinem, divitias, imagines multas, frequens atrium, sed malus ex confesso sit, improbabis illum; item si quis nihil quidem eorum quae rettuli habeat, deficiatur pecunia, clientum turba, nobilitate et avorum proavorumque serie, sed ex confesso bonus sit, probabis illum.

If someone should have everything else, health, wealth, many masks, a crowded *atrium*, but is by general admission a bad man, you will disapprove of him. Likewise, if someone should have none of the things I mentioned, if he lacked money, a crowd of clients, élite status and a row of

grandfathers and great-grandfathers, but was manifestly good, you will
commend him.

Cf. Ch. 6 § 6.

T77 Silius Italicus, *Punica* 4. 493-7   218 BC (AD 26-*c*.101)
    ecce aderat Trebiaeque simul vicina tenebat
    Trinacrio accitus per caerula longa Peloro
    Gracchorum proles, consul. gens inclita magno   495
    atque animosa viro, multusque in imagine claris
    praefulgebat avus titulis bellique domique.

Behold he has arrived, the descendant of the Gracchi, the consul, summoned over a long sea voyage from Pelorus in Sicily, and at the same
time as his colleague he made his camp near the Trebia. The family of
this great man was famous for its spirit and among their masks many
ancestors were illustrious for their distinguished labels both in war and in
politics.

T78 Silius Italicus, *Punica* 10. 566-9   216 BC (AD 26-*c*.101)
    aut celsis de more feretris
    praecedens prisca exsequias decorabat imago,
    omnibus exuviis nudo iamque Hannibal unus
    sat decoris laudator erat.

nor by custom did the antique mask, going ahead on its high litters, adorn
the funeral, (but) the eulogy of Hannibal alone was a glorious thing in itself
at a funeral stripped of any spoils.

Cf. Ch. 4 § 2

T79 Silius Italicus, *Punica* 17. 11-12   204 BC (AD 26-*c*.101)
    qui, genitus patruo ductoris ad Africa bella
    tunc lecti, multa fulgebat imagine avorum.

He, whose father was the uncle of Scipio then selected as general in charge
of the war in Africa, was distinguished by many masks of ancestors.

Cf. Ch. 6 § 1*b*.

T80 Suetonius, *Augustus* 4. 1   (*c*.AD 121/2)
Balbus, paterna stirpe Aricinus, multis in familia senatoriis imaginibus, a
matre Magnum Pompeium artissimo contingebat gradu functusque honore
praeturae inter vigintiviros agrum Campanum plebi Iulia lege divisit.

Balbus was from Aricia on his father's side and had many masks of senators in his family. On his mother's side he was very closely related to
Pompey the Great. He enjoyed the rank and status of a praetor and as a
member of the board of twenty he divided up the Campanian land amongst
the plebs under the Julian law.

Cf. Dio T28 and Ch. 8 § 1*b*.

T81 Suetonius, *Nero* 37. 1   (*c.*AD 121/2)
sed ne de pluribus referam, Salvidieno Orfito obiectum est quod tabernas tres de domo sua circa forum civitatibus ad stationem locasset, Cassio Longino iuris consulto ac luminibus orbato, quod in vetere gentili[s] stemmate C. Cassi percussoris Caesaris imagines retinuisset, Paeto Thraseae tristior et paedagogi vultus.

But to cite just a few examples, Salvidienus Orfitus was charged with renting out three shops which were part of his house by the Forum as offices to foreign states. Cassius Longinus, the legal expert who was blind, was charged because he retained [or reinstated] the portraits/masks of Gaius Cassius the murderer of Caesar on his old family tree. Thrasea Paetus was condemned for his severe manner suited to a tutor.

Tac. *Ann.* 16. 7 implies that this was a bust with a dedicatory inscription, an object that would have been liable to be destroyed after *damnatio memoriae*. One manuscript (X) has *restituisset* (reinstated) for *retinuisset* (retained), which would make Cassius' offence more deliberate and egregious.

T82 Suetonius, *Galba* 2–3   AD 68–9 (after AD 122)
(2) Neroni Galba successit nullo gradu contingens Caesarum domum, sed haud dubie nobilissimus magnaque et vetere prosapia, ut qui statuarum titulis pronepotem se Quinti Catuli Capitolini semper ascripserit, imperator vero etiam stemma in atrio proposuerit, quo paternam originem ad Iovem, maternam ad Pasiphaam Minonis uxorem referret. (3) Imagines et elogia universi generis exequi longum est, familiae breviter attingam.

Nero's successor was Galba who was in no way related to the house of the Caesars but was without doubt a member of the highest élite with a great and ancient lineage. Accordingly in the inscriptions for his statues he always described himself as the great-grandson of Quintus Catulus Capitolinus. In fact, as emperor he also displayed a family tree in his *atrium* on which he traced his father's family back to Jupiter and his mother's to Pasiphaë the wife of Minos. (3) It is a long project to pursue the masks and laudatory inscriptions of the whole clan; I will touch briefly on the closer family.

Cf. Ch. 9 § 2.

T83 Suetonius, *Vespasianus* 1. 1   (after AD 122)
Rebellione trium principum et caede incertum diu et quasi vagum imperium suscepit firmavitque tandem gens Flavia, obscura illa quidem ac sine ullis maiorum imaginibus, sed tamen rei p. nequaquam paenitenda, constet licet Domitianum cupiditatis ac saevitiae merito poenas luisse.

At length the Flavian family took over and strengthened the empire which had for a long time been unsettled and, as it were, destabilized by the usurpation and slaughter of three emperors. Certainly the family was undistinguished and without any masks of ancestors. Nevertheless, the state had no cause for regret despite the fact that everybody knows Domitian paid the penalty he deserved for his greed and cruelty.

T84 Suetonius, *Vespasianus* 19. 2   AD 79 (after AD 122)
sed et in funere Favor archimimus personam eius ferens imitansque, ut est mos, facta ac dicta vivi, interrogatis palam procuratoribus, quanti funus et pompa constaret, ut audit sestertium centiens, exclamavit, centum sibi sestertia darent ac se vel in Tiberim proicerent.

But also in his funeral procession Favor, the leader of a troup of mime actors, wore his mask and imitated his deeds and words when he was alive, as is the custom. He publicly asked the procurators how much the funeral and procession were costing. When he heard 10 million sesterces, he called out that they should give him 100,000 and even throw his body in the Tiber.

Cf. Dio T27 and 29.

T85 Tacitus, *Annales* 2. 27. 2   AD 16 (early 2nd cent. AD)
Firmius Catus senator, ex intima Libonis amicitia, iuvenem improvidum et facilem inanibus ad Chaldaeorum promissa, magorum sacra, somniorum etiam interpretes impulit, dum proavum Pompeium, amitam Scriboniam, quae quondam Augusti coniunx fuerat, consobrinos Caesares, plenam imaginibus domum ostentat hortaturque ad luxum et aes alienum, socius libidinum et necessitatum, quo pluribus indiciis inligaret.

Firmius Catus a senator and a close friend of Libo influenced the young man, who had little forethought and was easily led astray by vain things, to seek out the promises of the Chaldeans, the rites of magicians, and even the interpreters of dreams. Meanwhile he pointed out that Pompey was his great-grandfather, Scribonia, who had once been the wife of Augustus, his aunt, the Caesars were his cousins, and his house was full of masks. He also encouraged him into extravagence and debt as his companion in vice and loans so that he entangled him in a web of much hostile evidence.

T85a 2. 32. 1
tunc Cotta Messalinus, ne imago Libonis exsequias posterorum comitaretur, censuit, Cn. Lentulus, ne quis Scribonius cognomentum Drusi adsumeret.

Then Cotta Messalinus proposed that Libo's mask should not accompany the funerals of future generations. Gnaeus Lentulus moved that no Scribonius should assume the *cognomen* of Drusus.

Cf. Ch. 2 § 2.

T86 Tacitus, *Annales* 2. 43. 6   AD 17 (early 2nd cent. AD)
contra Druso proavus eques Romanus Pomponius Atticus dedecere Claudiorum imagines videbatur.

On the other hand Drusus' great-grandfather, the Roman knight Pomponius Atticus, seemed to disgrace the masks of the Claudii.

T87 Tacitus, *Annales* 2. 73. 1   AD 19 (early 2nd cent. AD)
Funus, sine imaginibus et pompa, per laudes ac memoriam virtutum eius celebre fuit.

His funeral, without masks or a procession, was distinguished by the eulogies and the memory of his bravery.

T88 Tacitus, *Annales* 3. 5   AD 20 (early 2nd cent. AD)
(1) Fuere qui publici funeris pompam requirerent compararentque quae in Drusum, patrem Germanici, honora et magnifica Augustus fecisset. ipsum quippe asperrimo hiemis Ticinum usque progressum neque abscedentem a corpore simul urbem intravisse; circumfusas lecto Claudiorum Iuliorumque imagines; defletum in foro, laudatum pro rostris; cuncta a maioribus reperta aut quae posteri invenerint cumulata: at Germanico ne solitos quidem et cuicumque nobili debitos honores contigisse. (2) sane corpus ob longinquitatem itinerum externis terris quoquo modo crematum: sed tanto plura decora mox tribui par fuisse, quanto prima fors negavisset. non fratrem, nisi unius diei via, non patruum saltem porta tenus obvium. ubi illa veterum instituta, propositam toro effigiem, meditata ad memoriam virtutis carmina et laudationes et lacrimas vel doloris imitamenta?

There were those who felt the lack of the procession at a public funeral and made a comparison with the splendid last tributes which Augustus had accorded Drusus, the father of Germanicus. Naturally, he had himself gone as far as Ticinum in the harshest time of the winter and did not leave the body but had entered the city with it. The masks of the Claudii and Julii had surrounded the bier. He had been mourned in the Forum and eulogized from the *rostra*. All the tributes originated by the ancestors or invented by later generations were heaped on him. But Germanicus had not even been accorded the customary honours owed to any member of the office-holding caste. (2) It was considered reasonable that the body had been cremated abroad in whatever way was available because of the length of the journey. But that made it all the more fitting that great tribute should be paid afterwards, since the initial circumstances had denied this. His brother had not gone more than a day's journey to meet him and his uncle had not even gone to the city-gate. What had happened to those practices of former times, the effigy laid out in state on a bier, the songs composed to recall valour, and the eulogies and tears or simulations of grief?
Cf. Ch. 8 § 2.

T89 Tacitus, *Annales* 3. 76   AD 22 (early 2nd cent. AD)
Et Iunia sexagesimo quarto post Philippensem aciem anno supremum diem explevit, Catone avunculo genita, C. Cassii uxor, M. Bruti soror.

testamentum eius multo apud vulgum rumore fuit, quia in magnis opibus, cum ferme cunctos proceres cum honore nominavisset, Caesarem omisit. quod civiliter acceptum, neque prohibuit quo minus laudatione pro rostris ceterisque sollemnibus funus cohonestaretur. viginti clarissimarum familiarum imagines antelatae sunt, Manlii, Quinctii aliaque eiusdem nobilitatis nomina. sed praefulgebant Cassius atque Brutus, eo ipso quod effigies eorum non visebantur.

And Iunia died in the 64th year after the battle of Philippi, she who was by birth the niece of Cato, the wife of Gaius Cassius, and the sister of Marcus Brutus. Her will was the subject of much talk amongst the common people, because she was very rich and although she had named nearly all the leading men favourably in it, she omitted the emperor. He accepted this equably and did not forbid the celebration of her funeral rites with a eulogy from the *rostra* and other habitual practices. The masks of twenty of the most illustrious families preceded the bier, Manlii, Quinctii and other names of the same high rank. But Cassius and Brutus were the most conspicuous precisely because their portraits were not to be seen.

T90 Tacitus, *Annales* 4. 9. 2   AD 23 (early 2nd cent. AD)
Funus imaginum pompa maxime inlustre fuit, cum origo Iuliae gentis Aeneas omnesque Albanorum reges et conditor urbis Romulus, post Sabina nobilitas, Attus Clausus ceteraeque Claudiorum effigies, longo ordine spectarentur.

The funeral was especially remarkable for its procession of masks, since Aeneas the founder of the Julian family, and all the Alban kings, and Romulus the founder of the city, afterwards the Sabine nobles, Attus Clausus, and the other the masks of the Claudii, appeared in long succession.

Cf. Ch. 8 § 1*b* and 2.

T91 Tacitus, *Annales* 4. 35. 2   AD 25 (early 2nd cent. AD)
An illi quidem septuagesimum ante annum perempti, quo modo imaginibus suis noscuntur, quas ne victor quidem abolevit, sic partem memoriae apud scriptores retinent?

Or should they, who had died seventy years ago, just as they were known by their masks which even the victor did not destroy, in this way retain a place in the tradition recorded by writers (of history)?

T92 Tacitus, *Annales* 6. 1. 2   AD 32 (early 2nd cent. AD)
Nec formam tantum et decora corpora, set in his modestam pueritiam, in aliis imagines maiorum incitamentum cupidinis habebat.

But his lust was excited not only by beauty and physical attractiveness but in some cases by youthful modesty and in others by the masks of ancestors.

T93 Tacitus, *Dialogus* 8. 4   AD 74 (early 2nd cent. AD)
Minimum inter tot ac tanta locum obtinent imagines ac tituli et statuae, quae neque ipsa tamen negleguntur, tam hercule quam divitiae et opes, quas facilius invenies qui vituperet quam qui fastidiat.

Amongst so many great accomplishments the least place is occupied by masks and inscriptions and statues, which are not indeed themselves to be neglected any more indeed than wealth and riches. You would more easily find the kind of person who criticizes the latter than one who avoids them.

T94 Tacitus, *Historiae* 2. 76. 2   AD 69 (early 2nd cent. AD)
cessisti etiam Galbae imaginibus: torpere ultra et polluendam perdendamque rem publicam relinquere sopor et ignavia videretur, etiam si tibi quam inhonesta, tam tuta servitus esset.

You also deferred to Galba's masks: to remain inactive any longer and leave the state to be defiled and destroyed would appear idle and cowardly, even if to you slavery was as shameful as it was safe.
Cf. Ch. 9 § 2.

T95 Tacitus, *Historiae* 4. 39. 3   AD 70 (early 2nd cent. AD)
Et ferebatur Antonius Scribonianum Crassum, egregiis maioribus et fraterna imagine fulgentem, ad capessendam rem publicam hortatus, haud defutura consciorum manu, ni Scribonianus abnuisset, ne paratis quidem corrumpi facilis, adeo metuens incerta.

And it is said that Antonius urged Scribonianus Crassus, who was illustrious because of excellent ancestors and the mask of his brother, to seize power. There would have been no lack of a crowd of supporters had not Scribonianus refused. He was not easily corrupted even by what was ready to hand because he was so fearful of uncertainty.
Cf. Ch. 9 § 2.

T96 Val. Max. 2. 9. 6   207 BC (Tiberian)
Quibus viris si quis caelestium significasset futurum ut eorum sanguis inlustrium imaginum serie deductus in ortum salutaris principis nostri conflueret, depositis inimicitiis artissimo se amicitiae foedere iunxissent, servatam ab ipsis patriam communi stirpi servandam relicturi.

If one of the gods had indicated to these men that in the future their blood would be joined by the birth of our emperor who watches over us after descent through a line of illustrious masks, they would have put aside their hostilities and joined themselves in the closest bond of friendship, since they were to leave the country they had saved as an inheritance for their shared descendants to preserve.

T97 Val. Max. 3. 3. 7 (Tiberian)

Quo evenit ut et humili loco nati ad summam dignitatem consurgant et generosissimarum imaginum fetus in aliquod revoluti dedecus acceptam a maioribus lucem in tenebras convertant.

As a result it can happen that both men of humble birth rise to the highest rank and the offspring of the most aristocratic masks fall back into some disgrace and turn the light they received from their ancestors into darkness.

T98 Valerius Maximus 3. 5 (Tiberian)

Sequitur duplicis promissi pars adopertis inlustrium virorum imaginibus reddenda, quoniam quidem sunt referendi qui ab earum splendore degeneraverunt, taeterrimis ignaviae ac nequitiae sordibus inbuta nobilia portenta.

The part of my twofold promise follows which must be fulfilled when the masks of distinguished men have been covered. Since in fact I must tell of those who fell away from their standard of eminence, of aristocratic monsters steeped in loathsome idleness and filthy wickedness.

T99 Valerius Maximus 3. 7. 11 Mid-2nd cent. BC (Tiberian)

Quapropter insolentiae crimine caruit, quia ibi voluminum, non imaginum certamina exercebantur.

He was not subject to a charge of insolence because in that place rivalries were indulged in terms of literary output, not of masks.

T100 Valerius Maximus 3. 8. 7 (Tiberian)

Non indignabuntur lumina nostrae urbis, si inter eorum eximium fulgorem centurionum quoque virtus spectandam se obtulerit: nam ut humilitas amplitudinem venerari debet, ita nobilitati fovenda magis quam spernenda bonae indolis novitas est. an abigi debet Titius ab horum exemplorum contextu? qui pro Caesaris partibus excubans, Scipionis praesidio interceptus, cum uno modo salus ab eo daretur, si se futurum Cn. Pompei generi ipsius militem adfirmasset, ita respondere non dubitavit: 'tibi quidem, Scipio, gratias ago, sed mihi uti ista condicione vitae non est opus.' sine ullis imaginibus nobilem animum!

The luminaries of our city will not be offended if the valour of centurions is also put on show beside their outstanding brilliance. For just as the lowly is obliged to revere the mighty, so a member of the office-holding caste should encourage rather than scorn a new man with qualities of natural goodness. Should Titius be removed from the context of these examples? While on guard duty for Caesar's party he was captured by Scipio's soldiers. When Scipio gave him this one way of saving himself, if he promised he would join the army of Gnaeus Pompeius, Scipio's son-in-law, he did not hesitate to give the following answer: 'I thank you, Scipio, but I do not need to go on living under those circumstances.' A 'noble' soul without any masks!

T101 Valerius Maximus 4. 1. 6   (Tiberian)
Voluerunt illi statuas in comitio, in rostris, in curia, in ipsa denique Iovis
optimi maximi cella ponere, voluerunt imaginem eius triumphali ornatu
indutam Capitolinis pulvinaribus adplicare, voluerunt ei continuum per
omnes vitae annos consulatum perpetuamque dictaturam tribuere: quorum
nihil sibi neque plebiscito dari neque senatus consulto decerni patiendo
paene tantum se in recusandis honoribus gessit, quantum egerat in
emerendis.

They wanted to put up statues of him in the comitium, at the *rostra*, in the
senate house, and finally in the very cult room of Jupiter Optimus Maximus.
They wanted to place his mask/portrait (*imago*) in triumphal dress at the
banquet of the gods on the Capitol, they wanted to grant him a continuous consulship for the remaining years of his life and the perpetual dictatorship. He would not allow any of these things either to be granted to him
by the people or to be decreed to him by the senate. So he achieved nearly
as much in refusing the honours as he had in earning them.

Cf. T45. The evidence for his *imago* being kept in the temple of Jupiter on the Capitol
can be found in T2 and 104. Cf. Ch. 2 § 1e.

T102 Valerius Maximus 5. 5   (Tiberian)
Quam copiosae enim suavitatis illa recordatio est: in eodem domicilio antequam nascerer habitavi, in isdem incunabulis infantiae tempora peregi,
eosdem appellavi parentes, eadem pro me vota excubuerunt, parem ex
maiorum imaginibus gloriam traxi!

With how much abundance of pleasure that memory is filled: I lived in the
same house before I was born, I spent my infancy in the same cradle, I
called the same people my parents, they made the same vows for me, I
inherited the same glory from the masks of the ancestors!

T103 Valerius Maximus 5. 8. 3   140 BC (Tiberian)
Peregerat iam Torquatus severi et religiosi iudicis partis, satis factum erat
rei publicae, habebat ultionem Macedonia, potuit tam verecundo fili obitu
patris inflecti rigor: at ille neque exequiis adulescentis interfuit et, cum
maxime funus eius duceretur, consulere se volentibus vacuas aures accom-
modavit: videbat enim se in eo atrio consedisse, in quo Imperiosi illius
Torquati severitate conspicua imago posita erat, prudentissimoque viro suc-
currebat effigies maiorum [suorum] cum titulis suis idcirco in prima parte
aedium poni solere, ut eorum virtutes posteri non solum legerent, sed etiam
imitarentur.

Torquatus now fulfilled his role as harsh and dutiful judge, the state was
satisfied, Macedonia had its revenge, his father's inflexible attitude could
have been softened by the son's suicide which had been inspired by shame.
But he did not attend the young man's funeral, and at the very time when
the funeral rites were being conducted, he made himself available to any

who wanted to ask his advice. Furthermore, he noticed that he was sitting in the *atrium* in which the mask of that Torquatus Imperiosus who was famous for his severity was displayed. It occurred to that very prudent man that the masks of his ancestors with their labels were usually kept in the entrance to the house for the very reason that later generations should not only read about their excellent qualities but should also imitate them.

Cf. Cic. *Fin.* 1.7.24; Liv. *Per.* 54; *Oxy. Per.* 54. *Imperiosus* should probably be construed as a *cognomen* in this text.

T104 Valerius Maximus 8. 15. 1   (Tiberian)

Itaque quod hodieque eximium capit adiciam. imaginem in cella Iovis optimi maximi positam habet, quae, quotienscumque funus aliquod Corneliae gentis celebrandum est, inde petitur, unique illi instar atrii Capitolium est.

Consequently, I shall add what he especially has even today. He has his mask put up in the cult room of Jupiter Optimus Maximus and whenever a funeral is held by the family of the Cornelii, it is fetched from there. For him alone the Capitoline temple is like his *atrium*.

An image was still in use in Appian's day (T2). Cf. Ch. 2 § 1e.

T105 Velleius Paterculus 2. 27. 5   82 BC (Tiberian)

Sunt qui sua manu, sunt qui concurrentem mutuis ictibus cum minore fratre Telesini una obsesso et erumpente occubuisse prodiderint; utcumque cecidit, hodieque tanta patris imagine non obscuratur eius memoria.

Some relate that he died by his own hand, others that he died with the younger brother of Telesinus who was also besieged and trying to escape with him, and that each killed the other. However he fell, today his memory is not overshadowed by the great mask of his father.

T106 Velleius Paterculus 2. 116. 4   (Tiberian)

et A. Licinius Nerva Silianus, P. Silii filius, quem virum ne qui intellexit quidem abunde miratus est, [ne] nihil ⟨quod⟩ non optimo civi, simplicissimo duci superesset praeferens, immatura ⟨morte⟩ et fructu amplissimae principis amicitiae et consummatione evectae in altissimum paternumque fastigium imaginis defectus est.

and Aulus Licinius Nerva Silianus, the son of Publius Silius, a man whom even someone who knew him did not fully admire, in all things acting like an excellent citizen and a thoroughly straightforward general during his life time, failed as a result of an early death to obtain the benefits of a highly distinguished friendship with the emperor and the ultimate achievement of a mask of the highest rank and equal to his father's eminence.

In this very corrupt passage Velleius refers to the career of A. Licinius Nerva Silianus (*RE* 137, *PIR*² 5. 53 no. 224), which was partly inspired by his father's success.

Literary Testimonia

Despite many emendations that have been suggested, little certainty has been reached in establishing a text. Cf. Woodman (1977) ad loc.

T107 Vitruvius, *De Architectura* 6. 3. 6 (early Augustan)
Imagines ita alte cum suis ornamentis ad latitudinem alarum sint constitutae.

The shield portraits (*imagines*) with their insignia should be placed so high that their height corresponds to the width of the *alae* (i.e. the side wings off the *atrium*).

Ferri (1960) suggested *imagines ita altae*. Fensterbusch (1964) takes this to refer to the *imagines* and translates: 'Die Ahnenbilder mit ihrem Schmuck sollen so hoch angeordnet werden, daß die Höhe der Breite der Alae entspricht'. However, the height of the display favours an interpretation of this passage as referring to shield portraits (*imagines clipeatae*) of famous ancestors (Cf. Winkes (1969), with the discussion in Ch. 7). It is notable that there is no mention of the cupboards in which traditional *imagines* were kept. Shield portraits can be seen mounted high along walls in some wallpaintings from Pompeii. Cf. Ch. 2 § 1c and Ch. 3 § 2b.

APPENDIX B

Inscriptions and Laws

A. *The tomb of the Scipios*
(Cf. Traina (1969) 165–170 on I 1–3, 5, and 14.)

I 1 *ILLRP* 309 = *ILS* 1: L. Cornelius Scipio Barbatus (cos. 298 BC, *RE* 343)
[L. CORNELI]O(S) CN. F. SCIPIO*

. . . .

. . . .

Cornelius Lucius Scipio Barbatus,
Gnaivod patre | prognatus, fortis vir sapiensque,
quoius forma virtutei parisuma | fuit;
consol, censor, aidilis quei fuit apud vos;
Taurasia, Cisauna | Samnio cepit,
subigit omne Loucanam opsidesque abdoucit.

Lucius Cornelius, son of Gnaeus, Scipio

Cornelius Lucius Scipio Barbatus, born of his father Gnaeus, a brave man
and a shrewd one, whose good looks were equal to his excellent character,
who was consul, censor and aedile among you; he captured Taurasia and
Cisauna in Samnium, he subdues the whole of Loucana and brings back
hostages.

*Label painted in red on the lid of the sarcophagus.
Taurasia Cisauna could also be read as one name (See Silvestri (1978), Marcotte
(1985), and Radke (1991) 73–4).

I 2 *ILLRP* 310 = *ILS* 2 & 3: L. Cornelius Scipio, the son of Barbatus (cos.
259 BC, *RE* 323)
L. CORNELIO(S) L. F. SCIPIO | AIDILES, COSOL, CESOR.*
Honc oino ploirume cosentiont R[omane *or* Romai]
duonoro optumo fuise viro,
Luciom Scipione. Filios Barbati,
consol, censor, aidilis hic fuet a[pud vos].
Hec cepit Corsica Aleriaque urbe,
dedet Tempestatebus aide mereto[d].

Lucius Cornelius, son of Lucius Scipio, aedile, consul, censor.

Most Romans agree that this one man was the best of the good men: Lucius Scipio, son of Barbatus, he was consul, censor, and aedile among you. He captured Corsica and the town of Aleria, he dedicated a temple to the Storms in return for help.

*Label painted in red.

I 3 *ILLRP* 311 = *ILS* 4 : P. Cornelius, Africanus' son ? (*RE* 331)
Quei apice insigne Dial[is fl]aminis gesistei |*
mors perfec[it] tua ut essent omnia | brevia,
honos, fama, virtusque | gloria atque ingenium.
quibus sei | in longa licuiset tibe utier vita, |
facile facteis superases gloriam | maiorum.
qua re lubens te in gremiu, | Scipio, recipit
terra, Publi, | prognatum Publio, Corneli.

⟨You who wore the illustrious cap of the flamen Dialis,⟩ your death resulted in everything being short-lived for you: office, reputation and excellence, glory and talent. If you had been allowed to enjoy these in a long life, you would easily have surpassed the glory of your ancestors by your achievements. Wherefore, the earth is happy to receive you in her bosom, Publius Scipio, son of Publius, Cornelius.

*Later addition in smaller letters.

I 4 *ILLRP* 313 = *ILS* 5 : L. Cornelius Scipio (q. 167 BC, *RE* 324)
L. Corneli(us) L. f. P. [n.] | Scipio, quaist(or), | tr(ibunus) mil(itum), annos | gnatus XXXIII | mortuos. Pater | regem Antioco(m) | subegit.

Lucius Cornelius, son of Lucius, grandson of Publius, Scipio, quaestor, military tribune, died aged 33 years. His father conquered king Antiochus.

I 5 *ILLRP* 316 = *ILS* 6 : Cn. Cornelius Scipio Hispanus (pr. 139 BC, *RE* 347)
Cn. Cornelius Cn. f. Scipio Hispanus, | pr(aetor), aid(ilis) cur(ulis), q(uaestor), tr(ibunus) mil(itum) (bis), (decem)vir sl(itibus) iudik(andis), | (decem)vir sacr(is) fac(iundis). |
Virtutes generis mieis moribus accumulavi,
    Progeniem genui, facta patris petiei.
Maiorum optenui laudem ut sibei me esse creatum
    laetentur; stirpem nobilitavit honor.

Gnaeus Cornelius, son of Gnaeus, Scipio Hispanus, praetor, curule aedile, quaestor, twice military tribune, a member of the board of ten who judge free status, a member of the board of ten who look after the Sybilline books.

I increased the manly virtues of my family by my character, I begot offspring, I aimed to equal/equalled the achievements of my father. I maintained in my own right the renown of my ancestors so that they are happy that I was their descendant: my official rank ennobled/ made known my family.

I 6 *ILLRP* 312 = *ILS* 7 : L. Cornelius Scipio (a younger brother or son of Hispanus ?)
L. Cornelius Cn. f. Cn. n. Scipio.
Magna sapientia | multasque virtutes
aetate quom parva | posidet hoc saxsum.
Quoiei vita defecit, non | honos honore,
is hic situs, quei nunquam | victus est virtutei.
Annos gnatus (viginti) is | l[oc]eis mandatus.
Ne quairatis honore | quei minus sit mandatus.

Lucius Cornelius, son of Gnaeus, grandson of Gnaeus, Scipio.
This stone marks the grave of a man of great shrewdness/judgement and many excellent qualities but who had a short life.
His life not his worth failed with respect to his rank.
The man buried here was never supassed in manly virtue.
He was laid to rest here having lived twenty years.
Do not ask why office was less entrusted to him.

I 7 *ILLRP* 314 = *ILS* 8 : Cornelius Scipio Asiagenus Comatus (*RE* 339)
[. . . Co]rnelius L.f. L.n. | [Sci]pio Asiagenus | Comatus annoru(m) | gnatus XVI.

. . . Cornelius, son of Lucius, grandson of Lucius, Scipio Asiagenus Comatus aged 16 years.

I 8 *ILLRP* 317 = *ILS* 10 : Paulla Cornelia, wife Cornelius Scipio Hispallus (cos. 176 BC, *RE* 346)
[P]aulla Cornelia Cn.f. Hispalli (uxor).

Paulla Cornelia, daughter of Gnaeus, wife of Hispallus.

I 9 *ILS* 958 Cornelia Gaetulica (*PIR* 1390), daughter of Cn. Cornelius Lentulus Gaetulicus (cos. AD 26, *PIR* 1488)
Cornelia | Gaetulici f. | Gaetulica.

Cornelia, daughter of Gaetulicus, Gaetulica.

I 10 *ILS* 959 M. Junius Silanus Lutatius Catulus (*PIR* 836)
M. Iunius Silanus | D. Silani f., Gaetulici | nepos, Cossi pron., | Lutatius Catulus Xvir | stlitib. iudic., salius Collin., vixit | annis XX mensibus VIIII.

Marcus Iunius Silanus, son of Decimus Silanus, grandson of Gaetulicus, great-grandson of Cossus, Lutatius Catulus, a member of the board of ten who judge free status, a member of the Salii Collini priesthood, he lived 20 years and 9 months.

His grandfather was the above-named consul of AD 26, his greatgrandfather Cossus Cornelius Lentulus (cos. I BC, *PIR* I 380), his father D. Junius Silanus Gaetulicus (*PIR* 835). For a stemma of the Cornelii Lentuli, see *PIR* 2, 329.

B. *Other Tomb Inscriptions*

I 11 *ILS* 886 L. Munatius Plancus (cos. 42 BC, *RE* 30) Monte Orlando, Gaeta

L. Munatius L. f. L. n. L. pron. | Plancus cos., cens., imp. iter., VIIvir | epulon., triump. ex Raetis, aedem Saturni | fecit de manibis, agros divisit in Italia | Beneventi, in Gallia colonias deduxit | Lugudunum et Rauricam.

Lucius Munatius, son of Lucius, grandson of Lucius, great-grandson of Lucius, Plancus, consul, censor, twice hailed imperator, one of the seven priests responsible for sacred feasts, he celebrated a triumph over the Raeti, he dedicated a temple to Saturn from his share of booty, he assigned land (to colonists) in Italy at Beneventum, in Gaul he founded the colonies of Lugdunum and Raurica.

I 12 *ILS* 862 C. Poplicius Bibulus, Rome

C. Poplicio L. f. Bibulo aed. pl., honoris | virtutisque caussa senatus | consulto populique iussu locus | monumento, quo ipse postereique | eius inferrentur, publice datus est.

Gaius Poplicius, son of Lucius, Bibulus, plebeian aedile, was awarded at public expense by recommendation of the senate and by order of the people a place for a tomb, where he and his descendants could be buried, on account of the esteem he was held in and his moral excellence.

I 13 *ILLRP* 421 = *ILS* 8890 C. Vibius Pansa Caetronianus (cos. 43 BC, *RE* 9 died in office) Rome, Campus Martius

Ex s(enatus) c(onsulto) | C. Vibio C. f. Pasae | Caetronian(o) *cos.*

(cos. was added later)

By decree of the senate for Gaius Vibius, son of Gaius, Pa(n)sa Caetronianus consul.

I 14 A. Atilius Caiatinus (cos. 258, 254 BC, *RE* 36) near the Porta Capena, Cic. *Sen.* 61, cf. *Fin* 2. 35. 116; *Tusc.* I. 7. 13

... apex est autem senectutis auctoritas. quanta fuit in L. Caecilio Metello, quanta in A. Atilio Calatino! in quem illud elogium
hunc unum plurimae consentiunt gentes populi
primarium fuisse virum.
Notum est carmen incisum in sepulcro.

... however the high point of old age is the influence of a man's authority. How great that was for Lucius Caecilius Metellus, how great for Aulus

Atilius Calatinus! The latter is the subject of that epitaph: 'This one man most families agree was the chief man of the people.'

The well-known verses are inscribed on his tomb.

I 15 *Tomb of the Marcelli*, Asconius 12 C = 11 KS = 18 Stangl 148 BC
Idem cum statuas sibi ac patri itemque avo poneret in monumentis avi sui ad Honoris et Virtutis, decore subscripsit:
III MARCELLI NOVIES COSS.
Fuit enim ipse ter, avus quinquies, pater semel: itaque neque mentitus est et apud impertiores patris sui splendorem auxit.

The same man when he put up statues of himself and his father together with his grandfather at the tomb of his grandfather near the temple of Honor and Virtus (Military Prestige and Courage), he added a fitting inscription:
    3 Marcelli nine times consul
For he himself was consul three times, his grandfather five times, and his father once. In this way he did not lie and he increased his father's prestige with those who were less well informed.

Add. Bücheler.
M. Claudius Marcellus RE 220: cos. 222, 215, 214, 210 and 208 BC (resigned in 215 after thunder at the election cf. Livy 31.12–14; Plutarch *Marc.* 12.1).
M. Claudius Marcellus RE 222: cos. 196 BC.
M. Claudius Marcellus RE 225: cos. 166, 155, 152 BC.
Cf. Platner-Ashby (1929) and Richardson (1992) for the location of the temple of Honor and Virtus.

C. Legal Texts

I 16 Senatus Consultum de Cn. Pisone patre, 10 Dec. AD 20, Spain.
s(enatus) c(onsultum) de Cn. Pisone patre propositum N(umerio) Vibio Sereno pro c(onsule)

73 . . . itaq(ue) iis poenis, quas a semet ipso exegisset, adicere: ne quis luctus mortis eius causa a feminis *eis, quibus* more maiorum, si hoc s(enatus) c(onsultum) factum

75 non esset, lugendus esset, susciperetur; utiq(ue) statuae et imagines Cn. Pisonis
    patris, quae ubiq(ue) positae essent, tollerentur; recte et ordine facturos qui qu-
    andoq(ue) familiae Calpurniae essent, quiue eam familiam cognatione
    adfinitateue contingerent, si dedissent operam, si quis eius gentis aut quis eo-
    rum, qui cognatus adfinisue Calpurniae familiae fuisset, mortuos esset, lugen-

80 dus esset, ne inter reliquas imagines, ⟨quibus⟩ exequias eorum funerum
celebrare solent,
imago Cn. Pisonis patris duceretur, neue imaginibus familiae
Calpurniae i-
mago eius interponeretur;. . .

74 quibus eis
80 ⟨quibus⟩ celebrare cf. Tacitus Ann. 6. 11. 3 of AD 32: dein Piso. . . publico funere
ex decreto senatus celebratus est. (L. Calpurnius Piso cos. 15 BC, praefectus urbi AD
13–32).
81 imaginibus Calpurnia | [nis? B

Decree of the senate concerning Gnaeus Piso, the father, posted when
Numerius Vibius Serenus was proconsul.
. . . accordingly to those penalties which he had imposed on himself, the
senate adds (the following):
– that no mourning for his death should be undertaken by those women
who would be obliged by ancestral custom to mourn, if this decree of the
senate had not been passed.
– that the statues and busts of Gnaeus Piso, the father, wherever they have
been put up, be removed.
– that it would be right and proper for those who at any time would be
members of the family of the Calpurnii, or anyone related to that family
either by birth or by marriage, if anyone of that family or anyone related
either by birth or marriage to the family of the Calpurnii has died and is
to be mourned, to see to it that the mask of Gnaeus Piso, the father,
should not be part of the procession amongst the other masks, with which
the rites of their funerals are accustomed to be celebrated, and that
his mask should not be set up amongst the masks of the Calpurnian
family.

I 17 Codex Iustinianus 5.37.22.3 Edict of Constantine (AD 326), published
in this version AD 534.
De Administratione Tutorum et Curatorum et de Pecunia Pupillari
Feneranda vel Deponenda
Nec vero domum vendere liceat, in qua deficit pater, minor crevit, in qua
maiorum imagines aut videre fixas aut revulsas non videre satis est
lugubre. ergo et domus et cetera omnia immobilia in patrimonio minorum
permaneant, nullumque aedificii genus, quod integrum hereditas dabit, col-
lapsum tutoris fraude depereat.

About the administrative duties of various legal guardians and about how
the money of wards is to be invested or put on deposit:
Nor in truth should it be permitted to sell a house where a father has died
and a son who is a minor is being raised, in which it is sorrowful enough
to see the masks of the ancestors fixed in position or not to see them when

331

they have been removed. Therefore both the house and all the rest of the fixtures should remain as part of the inheritance of minors and no kind of building which was inherited in good condition should go to ruin or be lost through the deceit of the guardian.

APPENDIX C

Moneyers using Ancestral Themes on their Coins

Crawford number	Moneyer(s)	Date (Crawford date where different)
149	L. Mamilius	189–180 BC

Revised coin order for the 130s and 120s BC (Cf. Hersh (1977) table 2):

234	T. Veturius	(137 BC)
242	C. Minucius Augurinus	(135 BC)
239	C. Servilius M.f.	(136 BC)
243	T. Minucius C. f. Augurinus	(134 BC)
262	Anon. with elephant head (Metelli)	(128 BC)
245	M. Marcius Mn. f.	(134 BC)
266	C. Cassius	(126 BC)
267	T. Quinctius	(126 BC)
268	N. Fabius Pictor	(126 BC)
252	L. Postumius Albinus	(131 BC)*
254	M. Opimius	(131 BC)*
258	S. Julius Caesar	(129 BC)*
259	Q. Marcius Philippus	(129 BC)*
263	M. Caecilius Metellus Q. f.	(127 BC)*
264	C. Servilius Vatia	(127 BC)*
269	C. Metellus	(125 BC)*
270	M. Porcius Laeca	(125 BC)
273	Q. Fabius Labeo	(124 BC)
281	M. Furius L. f. Philus	(119 BC)
282	L. Licinius, Cn. Domitius et al.	118 BC (Narbo)
285	Cn. Domitius, Q. Curtius, M. Silanus	116/115 BC

Note: All coins are minted in Rome unless otherwise indicated.
*These issues all come from the same mint workshop.
Crawford's dates are used in the following tables, except where evidence from new coin hoards has led to a revised chronology; see Hersh (1977) and Hersh and Walker (1984).

Crawford number	Moneyer(s)	Date (Crawford date where different)
286	M. Sergius Silus	116/115 BC
291	Mn. Aemilius Lepidus	114/113 BC
293	L. Marcius Philippus	113/112 BC
295	L. Manlius Torquatus	113/112 BC
301	P. Porcius Laeca	110/109 BC
305	Q. Lutatius Cerco	109/108 BC
306	L. Valerius Flaccus	108/107 BC
308	M. Herennius	108/107 BC
296	Cn. Cornelius Blasio Cn. f.	(112–111 BC) c. 106–105 BC
313	L. Memmius Gal.	106 BC
314	L. Aurelius Cotta	105 BC
319	Q. Minucius Thermus M. f.	103 BC
321	L. Cassius Caecianus	102 BC
322	C. Fabius C. f. (Hadrianus?)	102 BC
329	P. Cornelius Lentulus Marcellinus	100 BC
334	L. Pomponius Molo	?97 BC
335	C. Publicius Malleolus, A. Postumius Albiunus, L. Caecilius Metellus	?96 BC
337	D. Junius Silanus L. f.	91 BC
340	L. Calpurnius L. f. L. n. Piso Frugi	90 BC
343	M. Porcius Cato	89 BC
344	L. Titurius L. f. Sabinus	89 BC
346	C. Marcius Censorinus	88 BC
349	L. & C. Memmius L. f. Gal.	87 BC
362	C. Mamilius C. f. Limentanus	82 BC
366	C. Annius T. f. T. n.	82–81 BC N. Italy and Spain
369	M. Caecilius Metellus Q. f.	82–80 BC
370	C. Servilius	82–80 BC
372	A. Postumius A. f. S. n. Albinus	81 BC
374	Q. Caecilius Metellus Pius	81 BC (N. Italy)
380	C. Publicius Q. f.	80 BC

New coin chronology for 75 to 51 BC (Cf. Hersh and Walker (1984) table 2):

386	L. Cassius Q. f. Longinus	75 BC (78 BC)
403	Q. Fufius Calenus, Mucius Scaevola Cordus	68 BC (70 BC)
404	T. Vettius Sabinus	66 BC (70 BC)

334

Crawford number	Moneyer(s)	Date (Crawford date where different)
415	L. Aemilius Lepidus Paullus	62 BC
416	?L. Scribonius Libo	62 BC
417	Paullus Lepidus & Libo	62 BC
408	C. Calpurnius Piso L. f. Frugi	61 BC (67 BC)
413	L. Cassius Longinus	60 BC (63 BC)
411	L. Manlius Torquatus	58 BC (65 BC)
419	M. Aemilius Lepidus	58 BC (61 BC)
420	P. Plautius Hypsaeus	57 BC (60 BC)
421	?M. Nonius Sufenas	57 BC (59 BC)
425	?L. Marcius Philippus	57 BC (56 BC)
410	Q. Pomponius Musa	56 BC (66 BC)
426	Faustus Cornelius Sulla	56 BC
427	C. Memmius C. f.	56 BC
428	Q. Cassius Longinus	55 BC
429	P. Fonteius P. f. Capito	55 BC
433	M. Junius Brutus (=Q. Servilius Caepio Brutus)	54 BC
434	Q. Pompeius Rufus	54 BC
423	C. Servilius C. f.	53 BC (57 BC)
437	C. Coelius Caldus	53 BC (51 BC)
438	Ser. Sulpicius	51 BC
439	?P. Cornelius Lentulus Marcellinus	50 BC
445	L. Cornelius Lentulus C. Claudius Marcellus	49 BC (Apollonia and Asia)
446	Cn. Pompeius Magnus Cn. Calpurnius Piso	49 BC
450	D. Junius Brutus Albinus	48 BC
454	A. Licinius Nerva	47 BC
455	C. Antius C. f. Restio	47 BC
458	C. Julius Caesar	47–46 BC (Africa)
459	Q. Metellus Pius Scipio	47–46 BC (Africa)
462	M. Porcius Cato	47–46 BC (Africa)
470	Cn. Pompeius Magnus M. Minatius Sabinus	46–45 BC (Spain)
473	Lollius Palikanus	45 BC
477	Sex. Pompeius Magnus Pius	45–44 BC (Spain)
480	L. Aemilius Buca M. Mettius, P. Sepullius Macer C. Cossutius Maridianus	44 BC

Crawford number	Moneyer(s)	Date (Crawford date where different)
487	Petillius Capitolinus	43 BC
490	C. Julius Caesar (= Octavian)	43 BC (Gallia Cisalpina and Italy)
494	L. Livineius Regulus P. Clodius M. f. L. Mussidius T. f. Longus C. Vibius Varus	42 BC (triumviral gold coins)
497	C. Julius Caesar (= Octavian)	42 BC (mint moving)
506	M. Junius Brutus	43–42 BC (mint moving)
511	Sex. Pompeius Magnus Pius	42–40 BC (Sicily)
512	C. Clodius C. f. Vestalis	41 BC
513	M. Arrius Secundus	41 BC
514	C. Numonius Vaala	41 BC
515	L. Servius Rufus	41 BC
519	Cn. Domitius L. f. Ahenobarbus	41 BC (mint moving)

Families with More than One Moneyer Using Ancestral Themes

Caecilii Metelli	7: 262; 263; 269; 335; 369; 374; 459
Aemilii	5: 291; 415; 417; 419; 480
Marcii	5: 245; 259; 293; 346; 425
Cassii	5: 266; 321; 386; 413; 428
Cornelii	5: 296; 329; 426; 439; 445
Pompeii	5: 434; 446; 470; 477; 511
Junii	4: 337; 433; 450; 506
Servilii	4: 239; 264; 370; 423
Julii	4: 258; 458; 490; 497
Fabii	4: 268; 273; 322; 366
Porcii	4: 270; 301; 343; 462
Calpurnii	3: 340; 408; 446
Minucii	3: 242; 243; 319
Domitii	3: 282; 285; 519
Manlii	3: 295; 337; 411
Memmii	3: 313; 349; 427
Mamilii	2: 149; 362
Postumii	2: 252; 372
Licinii	2: 282; 454
Pomponii	2: 334; 410
Publicii	2: 335; 380

Distribution (Crawford distribution in brackets where different)

180s	1
130s and 120s	18
110s	8
100s	10
90s	4
80s	11
70s	1 (3)
60s	7 (9)
50s	16 (12)
40s	23

Coins with Claims to Heritage of Extinct Families

322; 410; 415

Coins and Adoption

329; 337

Several Ancestors on a Single Coin

242; 243; 306; 329; 335; 337; 343; 346; 386; 404; 419; 420; 425; 427; 429; 433; 434; 437; 473; 459; 494; 512; 519.

Father of the Moneyer on his Coin

252; 254; 263; 266; 281?; 282?, 306; 308?; 408; 419; 426; 427; 450?; 455; 470; 473; 477; 490; 497; 511.

Grandfather of the Moneyer on his Coin

267; 268; 273; 286; 343; 434; 437; 480; 513; 514; 515?

Distant Ancestor/Founder of Gens

149; 234; 242; 243; 245; 258; 262; 263; 293; 295; 313; 321; 322; 335; 349; 366; 386; 403; 411; 420; 427; 433; 455; 458; 494; 515.

Kings/Regal Period

334; 344; 346; 404; 425; 433; 446; 506.

Family Monuments on Coins

291; 242; 243; 293; 321; 337; 343; 380; 386; 415; 416; 417; 419; 425; 428; 429; 439; 487; 519.

Games Given by a Family Member

340; 346; 408; 421; 423; 427; 454; 512

Offices and Priesthoods

245; 252; 254; 267; 268; 285; 306; 374; 411; 425; 434; 437; 459.

Coins with Portrait Heads of Ancestors

296; 344; 346; 366; 404; 425; 433; 434; 437; 439; 446; 450; 455; 470; 477; 490; 506; 511; 513; 515; 519.

Scenes Representing Deeds of Ancestors

264; 268; 286; 295; 301; 319; 334; 335; 362; 415; 426; 429; 458; 480; 494; 514.

APPENDIX D

Etruscan Statues of Ancestors and the Origins of the *Imagines*

> *ubi eos, plebis aedificiis obseratis, patentibus atriis principum, maior prope cunctatio tenebat aperta quam clausa inuadendi; adeo haud secus quam uenerabundi intuebantur in aedium uestibulis sedentes uiros, praeter ornatum habitumque humano augustiorem, maiestate etiam quam uoltus grauitasque oris prae se ferebat simillimos dis. Ad eos uelut ad simulacra uersi cum starent, M. Papirius, unus ex iis, dicitur Gallo barbam suam, ut tum omnibus promissa erat, permulcenti scipione eburneo in caput incusso iram mouisse, atque ab eo initium caedis ortum, ceteros in sedibus suis trucidatos; post principum caedem nulli deindi mortalium parci, diripi tecta, exhaustis inici ignes.*

(Livy 5. 41. 7–10)[1]

As already discussed above, we do not have precise information about the origin or age of wax ancestor masks representing Roman office-holders, although debate on this topic continues.[2] Scholars have been divided in their interpretations, partly according to their respective views about the nature and function of the *imagines* in later Roman culture. Earlier this century, it was common to posit an Etruscan origin for the wax *imagines* themselves, often on the assumption that they had developed from masks used

---

[1] 'There the houses of the plebeians were shut up but the *atria* of the leading men lay open and they [the Gauls] were almost more hesitant to enter the open houses than the closed ones. Indeed they came close to feeling reverence as they were looking at the men seated in the entrances to their houses, men who besides wearing clothes and badges of rank more dignified than befitted mortals, were also most like gods in their majestic faces and serious expressions. While they were standing in front of them as if before statues of gods, it is said that one of them, Marcus Papirius, provoked the anger of a Gaul by hitting him on the head with his ivory staff when the Gaul stroked his beard, which he wore long as they all did at the time, and Papirius was the first to be killed. The rest were slaughtered in their seats. After the massacre of the leading men no one else was spared, the houses were looted, and after being laid waste, they were burned.'

[2] See esp. Ch. 2 § 1*d*.

to cover the face of the dead man at the funeral.[3] Such arguments were shaped both by the general influence of the Etruscans on Roman culture, as well as by specific Etruscan objects which were adduced as being suggestive for the origin of the *imagines*.[4] However, most studies tended to be essentially art historical in nature and were concerned rather specifically with similarities of style and consequently with the development of a characteristically Roman portrait style.[5] Since we have neither extant *imagines* nor representations of them in other media, it is not possible to make stylistic comparisons which have any value beyond that of guesswork.

Recently, studies of the emergence of the Roman nobility of office in the fourth century BC after the conflict of the orders have yielded more convincing results, which illustrate the typical aristocratic culture created by office-holding families of both patrician and plebeian origin. Careful study of literary sources has revealed that Roman art and architecture was transformed under the influence of the new nobility of office which relied on elections to maintain status.[6] The leading magistrates were also those responsible for Rome's rapid rise to power and her expansion, first in Italy and then in the Mediterranean at large. Whereas earlier aristocratic culture had put little public stress on individual achievements, Rome now saw the rapid development and proliferation of statues which honoured living individuals for their military successes, of trophies and monuments commemorating their victories, of historical paintings and maps to show Rome's spheres of influence, and of temples vowed by successful generals in the field and paid for by their booty. The city itself was transformed to reflect interests wider than those of a farming community or local market town.[7]

---

[3] For a death mask at the *collocatio*, see Benndorf (1878) and Vessberg (1941). For arguments that the wax masks came directly from the Etruscans, see Courbaud (1900) 403 and Swift (1923) 291. Kaschnitz-Weinberg (1926) 192 proposed that early masks were like the canopics from Chiusi and not realistic. He posited the introduction of realistic wax masks in the 3rd cent. BC.

[4] For the realism typical of both Etruscan and Roman art, see von Schlosser (1910/11) 8 ff. and Kleiner (1992) 31 who notes the importance of the head in both Roman and Etruscan art. The Warrior of Capestrano has been interpreted as representing a corpse propped up for a funeral and wearing a mask; see Boethius (1942) 230-1 and Schweitzer (1948) 22. *Contra* Cianfarani (1968) and (1969) who gives a better account of the statue after its restoration in the late 1960s and dates it to the 6th cent. BC.

[5] See Introd. for Roman portraits and their 'veristic' style.

[6] Note the important studies by Hölscher (1978), (1980a), and (1990), with Hölkeskamp (1993) esp. 27-30.

[7] For an overview of the development of the city during the middle Republic, see Torelli (1988) 92-104 and Stambaugh (1988) 23-35. Cf. also Cristofani (1969) 228-32 who discusses the emergence of painted processions of magistrates in Tarquinia in the late 4th cent. BC, which were parallel with the development of *cursus* inscriptions for magistrates, family tombs used over several generations, and the rebuilding of the city.

Since we know that the *imagines* existed by the end of the third century BC, it is logical to posit that they had developed about a century earlier because their purpose and use is similar to that of the new honorary statues and historical paintings which came into being then.[8] The masks portrayed the same leaders in a public way and also served to recall their deeds, although only after death. They clearly answered a need now felt by both patricians and plebeians to stress family continuity and to keep their name and history before the public eye. For Polybius (6. 53-4 = T61) the *imagines* are associated with realistic representation of past leaders and, therefore, with the characteristic ethic of bravery, frugality, and public service which the office-holding families cultivated with care. The *imagines* enacted a dramatic pageant which illustrated the funeral oration and especially the abstract values which became increasingly important in Roman culture. The third century BC saw the erection of many temples dedicated to abstract values.[9] The desire to commemorate individual deeds led to the creation of new artistic forms and of a style of portrait which aimed to represent who a man was and what he stood for. The first public statues of the kings and other figures from early Roman history have been associated with this revolution in Roman politics and society.[10]

The end of the fourth century BC may also have seen a decisive change in the organization and purpose of the Forum, which was at the centre of political life.[11] As early as 338 BC the speaker's platform was made prominent by being decorated with the beaks of ships captured in war from Antium. In effect, it became a type of trophy or war monument in its own right.[12] A possible reconstruction posits a rearrangement of the Forum around 310 BC to house bankers' quarters rather than shops for selling food, especially meat and fish.[13] In addition, the new shops on three sides of the Forum seem to have been equipped with balconies (*maeniana*) for

---

[8] Our earliest secure contemporary reference, Plaut. *Amph.* 458-9 = T53, can be dated very early in the 2nd cent. BC, but speaks of the *imagines* as familiar objects. Cf. Sall. *Jug.* 4. 5-6 = T65 for a later allusion to *imagines* in the 3rd cent. BC.

[9] The earliest was to Concordia, but later also ones to Salus, Honos, Virtus. There were also a number of temples honouring deities of victory. See Platner and Ashby (1929) 587-8 and Richardson (1992) 446-8 for a chronological table.

[10] See Hölscher (1978) 343.

[11] For a reconstruction of the Forum, see Coarelli (1985) 140-9 with criticisms by Rawson (1990) 165.

[12] See Livy 8. 14. 12; Plin. *Nat.* 34. 20. For its importance, see Plin. *Nat.* 34. 24; Dion. Hal. 1. 87. For the statues there, see Cic. *Phil.* 9. 16; Livy 4. 17; 8. 13; Plin. *Nat.* 34. 23-5; Vell. Pat. 2. 61.

[13] Varro *De Vita Populi Romani* fr. 72 (Riposati) = Nonius 853L: *Hoc intervallo primum forensis dignitas crevit atque ex tabernis lanienis argentariae factae* ('After this time the Forum first gained status and banks replaced the butchers' shops'). It remains problematic whether such a change could have taken place before Rome coined her own money. Cf. Livy 1. 35. 10, 3. 48. 5; Dion. Hal. 3. 67. 10, 11. 37. 5.

watching spectacles in the Forum.[14] The shops were decorated with gold shields which were part of the booty of L. Papirius Cursor from the Samnites.[15] Behind the shops were public *atria* which served as offices where business could be transacted.[16] Many dedications of booty and statues could now be found in the Forum, especially near the Comitium and the *rostra*. The importance of commerce was therefore matched by the stress on politics and military success along the triumphal route of the Via Sacra. Such political spectacle also centred especially on the *rostra* where public speeches were given and Rome's new policies were proclaimed to the people. It is evident that this new Forum, at whatever exact date it took shape in the later fourth to early third century BC, provided a setting well suited and perhaps, therefore, partly designed for the spectacle of the Roman aristocratic funeral with its parade of ancestors, public funeral speech, and gladiatorial or other contests.[17]

The form of the *imagines* as wax masks, which could be worn to impersonate the dead, presupposes their realistic character and their use in the funeral procession. Similarly, their appearance at funerals necessitated a funeral speech which could explain them to the public by providing a career for each ancestor. It seems likely, then, that their use in the funeral did not emerge gradually but was introduced as an innovation at a given moment. The funeral speech itself may well be older, but the *imagines* would have made little sense without it. Similarly, once they were used at funerals they needed to be stored somewhere. A place had to be found which accorded with their importance and function in society. Without more evidence, we cannot determine when they were first made. However, we can say that the setting for their appearance was created, both in the Forum and in the newly developed *atrium* house, during the late fourth and

[14] For *maeniana* and the evidence from Pompeii and Herculaneum, see Wallace-Hadrill (1994) 129-30 with figs. 5.9 and 5.14

[15] Note esp. Livy 9. 40. 16 on the subject of the shields used to decorate the Forum in 310 BC. The balconies, known as *maeniana*, are associated with C. Maenius whose censorship in 318 BC has been identified as important for the development of the Forum. For the *maeniana*, see Cic. *Acad.* 22.70-1; Livy 31. 50. 3; Vitruv. 5. 1. 1-2; Val. Max. 9. 12. 7; Plin. *Nat.* 21. 8; Ps. Asconius on Cic. *Div. in Caec.* 16. 50; Festus 120 L; and Isid. *Or.* 15. 3. 11.

[16] See Torelli (1988) 96-7. Similar *atria* have been found behind shops round the Forum of the 3rd cent. BC Latin colony at Cosa; see F.E. Brown (1980) 31-46.

[17] For discussion of the *imagines* in this historical context, see Hölscher (1990) 76-8 and Hölkeskamp (1993) 29. *Contra* Boethius (1942) 230-1 who sees Polybius describing a rite petrified and maintained from Etruscan Rome. The need to control lavish funerals can already be seen in the Law of the Twelve Tables framed over a century earlier. For discussion, see Ch. 4 § 5. Nearly all these displays were funded in a more or less direct way by war booty. While success was required to maintain status within the ranks of office-holders, the new aristocratic order flourished as a result of its military achievements which brought wealth, land, and prestige in the eyes of fellow citizens.

early third centuries BC.[18] This was also the time when other art forms, notably other portraits with similar functions, originated. It was a time of great change, of expansion, and of confidence, especially for the circle of men who held the highest offices and who helped to create Rome's new oligarchic culture. It makes sense to place the emergence of realistic wax ancestor masks, and their function in the funeral and in the home, in this period.

Nevertheless, many questions remain unanswered regarding the ultimate inspiration for the *imagines* and why they were invented in the first place. Other new art forms, such as honorific statues, were clearly developed from Greek models which were adapted for a Roman cultural context. However, the *imagines* remain without an obvious parallel in other Mediterranean cultures. Moreover, we are largely uninformed about the attitude towards ancestors in Roman culture at an earlier period (before *imagines* were used?). As a result, the reconstruction outlined above can only be partially satisfactory and may misrepresent the relative age or novelty of the *imagines*. The main analyses of the 'Roman revolution' of the fourth and third centuries BC have naturally concentrated on innovations and on contacts with Hellenistic culture, especially as met with in Southern Italy and Sicily. In this sense, the *imagines* remain a poorly explained, if characteristic, feature of the political culture of Rome in the middle Republic.[19]

New evidence for the depiction and status of particular, important ancestors in Etruscan aristocratic culture comes from the Tomba delle Statue near Ceri, an early seventh-century BC site excavated in 1971. Although alluded to in general books since the mid-1970s, this tomb was not fully published until 1986 by Colonna and von Hase.[20] The simple dual-chamber tomb contained two monumental seated male statues holding insignia, carved straight from the rock in the entrance room which leads into the burial chamber (see Fig. 18). These statues are the first which document the development of large-scale sculpture in Etruria under Eastern influence at an early date. Colonna and von Hase contend that the statues are images of ancestors, and that they faithfully reflect similar figures, now no longer extant, which were to be found in the entrance room (*atrium*) of Etruscan aristocratic houses.

It has long been recognized that some Etruscan tombs, notably from the second half of the seventh and the mid-sixth centuries BC, offer simplified

[18] See Torelli (1988) 103.

[19] Hölscher (1990) 77-8 compares the Roman funeral procession with a wall-painting showing a procession of magistrates from the Tomba Bruschi at Tarquinia. However, the painting dates to the late 3rd or first half of the 2nd cent. BC, so it cannot be used to show cultural influences coming from Etruria to Rome around 300 BC or even earlier.

[20] Colonna and von Hase (1986).

FIG. 18. Reconstruction of the two statues from the Tomba delle Statue, Ceri.

reproductions of the main rooms of Etruscan houses, including furniture and other household items.[21] These tombs especially illustrate the importance of the central *atrium* and of the thrones of the master and mistress which were kept there.[22] Such special chairs are prototypes of the *solium* of the *paterfamilias* later found in the Roman *atrium*.[23]

The burials in the Tomba delle Statue consist of a married couple as is often the case in Etruria. The two male statues have been interpreted as representing the fathers of the husband and wife, or perhaps as the husband's father and grandfather. There is no evidence that they have a particularly funerary function or one which was limited to the tomb.

[21] For parallels between Etruscan tombs and houses, see Prayon (1975a) tomb types B and D and Steingräber (1979) esp. 176-7.

[22] For the *atrium* with *tablinum*, see esp. the Tomba della Ripa. Cf. the Tomba della Sedia Torlonia which only had one burial and therefore only one chair (Prayon (1975a) 108-9, 112). Steingräber's (1979) 150-1 throne types 1a and 1b are used in graves and for canopics to denote status, but also appear for both men and women in scenes from everyday life.

[23] See the chairs in the Tomba degli Scudi e delle Sedie. For the development of the Roman *atrium* house and the *solium*'s position in it, see Wistrand (1970) with Schäfer (1989) 25-7 on the *solium* itself.

By analogy, the two Ceri statues have also been used to identify the terracotta figures from the Tomba delle Cinque Sedie and a small bronze figure from Massa Marittima as portraits of ancestors (see Fig. 19).[24] Colonna uses a combination of Etruscan archaeological evidence with passages from Latin authors, especially Livy and Virgil, to suggest that the Etruscans and Romans shared a tradition of monumental statues of ancestors kept in the home.[25] The association of these portraits with thrones and insignia indicate a connection with office and rank.[26] However, women were also represented in the Tomba delle Cinque Sedie, where five 'ancestors' appeared to be seated at a special banquet in a room set aside. The room also contained an altar and the usual two chairs left empty for the married couple buried in the tomb.[27] In addition, a connection has been made with the monumental seated statues of men and women in terracotta which served as roof *acroteria* for the 'palace complex' at Murlo around 600 BC.[28]

[24] For the Tomba delle Cinque Sedie, see Prayon (1974), (1975*a*) 109-13, and (1975*b*) with Taf. 44 and 45, and Steingräber (1979) 130. For the statue from Massa Marittima, see von Hase (1974) and Steingräber (1979) no. 513.

[25] Colonna in Colonna and von Hase (1986) 34-41, esp. 40 where he comments on the passage of Livy quoted at the beginning of this appendix: 'I patrizi romani, che nel racconto liviano attendono, solennemente parati e seduti, l'arrivo dei Galli sembrano l'illustrazione vivente delle *imagines maiorum* di questo tipo antichissimo, oggi archeologicamente documentato dalla splendida serie delle statue acroteriali di Murlo . . . Ma la collocazione normale delle *imagines* era nella zona d'ingresso della casa, che avevano il compito di tutelare. Qui le troviamo nella t. delle Statue, nella t. delle Cinque Sedie e nel tumulo della Pietrera a Vetulonia . . .' Cf. Schäfer (1989) 68 for an interpretation of Livy which stresses that ex-magistrates kept their status symbols at home and were staging their own funeral.

[26] A comparison can be made with the seated figures on the Murlo plaques, although these have sometimes been interpreted as divinities. See Torelli (1981) who sees these plaques as illustrations of aristocratic life, with Macintosh (1974) and Schäfer (1989) 34-5 for the folding stools (*sellae curules*) which the dignitaries are seated on.

[27] For a reconstruction of the room in the Tomba delle Cinque Sedie, see Prayon (1974) Abb. 1. It is important to note that the restorations of the statues are probably inaccurate and that the two heads in the British Museum are female, while the head in Rome is male. The length of the necks and relative positions of the heads are also unclear. See Prayon (1975*b*).

[28] For the Murlo acroterial statues, see Edlund Gantz (1972), Bianchi Bandinelli (1972), and now the full publication in Edlund-Berry (1992) with review by Ginge (1993). These statues are hard to interpret because the objects they held in their hands are now lost. The striking 'sombrero' style hats worn by some are also in need of further elucidation, although the available parallels suggest hats worn by mortals in everyday life. See esp. the Certosa Situla, the helmet of the Warrior of Capestrano, the hat worn by the flute player from the Tomba della Scimmia (480/470 BC), and esp. the soft hats shown hanging in a hunting pavilion depicted on the walls of the Tomba del Cacciatore (= T 3700, *c.*510-500 BC, Steingräber [1986] no. 51 with plates 101-2). The Murlo hats may well be exaggerated in size and proportion, as are other features of these statues, which are designed to be seen from below.

FIG. 19. Terracotta seated figure of an 'ancestor' from the Tomba delle Cinque Sedie, Cerveteri, now in the British Museum, London.

The form of a seated ancestor, sometimes represented at a meal, is reminiscent of the many canopic burial urns from Chiusi, a number of which are seated on chairs.[29] Some of these are associated with a seated banquet, notably the scene on the lid of an urn from Volterra now in the Archaeological Museum in Florence.[30] Similarly, examples of sixth-century cinerary urns include life-sized seated male figures.[31] It appears that both 'ancestors' and recently deceased family members were represented sitting on thrones with insignia or at a banquet.

At the moment there is not enough evidence either to prove or to disprove Colonna's bold theories about ancestors in Etruscan art and society but they have profound implications for the origin and development of ancestral iconography in Rome.[32] There is a growing body of evidence which illustrates ancestral portraiture and the special status of some office-holding ancestors in the homes of leading Etruscan families in the seventh and sixth centuries BC. However, most of these representations are not fully understood in their original Etruscan context. An attempt has also been made to gain a more general picture of Etruscan ancestor cult by collecting all representations of 'ancestors' starting in the Early Iron Age (tenth to ninth centuries BC).[33] Ancestors and notably parents do appear as a special subject of representation for élite Etruscans mostly in a funerary context throughout their history. A seated pose on a throne, often associated with a banquet, is central to Etruscan ancestral iconography. At the same time, Etruscan 'ancestor' portraits do not seem to be individually differentiated before the time of the Roman Republic.

The relevance of most of these representations for Roman culture, especially of a later date, is not evident. As noted above, Livy does mention *imagines* in the context of early Rome under the Etruscan kings.[34] That does not necessarily mean that ancestral iconography was borrowed from Etruria at that time, although such an interpretation is certainly a possible

[29] For canopics, their types, and development, see Gempeler (1974), esp. 246-8 for ones on chairs and 242-3 for ones associated with bronze masks.

[30] Cf. Prayon (1974) Taf. 8.2 and Steingräber (1979) no. 573 Taf. 31.3.

[31] Good examples come from the British Museum (Sculptures D9 in Room 71) and from Palermo; see Edlund Gantz (1972) fig. 39. These seated figures have been compared with the 6th cent. BC stone votive statues of local dignitaries found lining the Sacred Way which led from the port of Panormus to Apollo's shrine at Didyma near Miletus (now in the British Museum). See Pryce (1928) 101-17, B271-80 with Stewart (1990) plates 104-8. Tuchelt (1970) gives a catalogue but is undecided about the function of the statues, which appear to imitate ruler portraits from the East. For similar statues from Miletus itself which were probably made locally, see von Gaeve (1983).

[32] His views have been strongly endorsed by Damgaard Andersen (1993) esp. 47.

[33] For Etruscan ancestor cult and the growing tendency to depict humans in art from the late 8th cent. BC onwards, see Damgaard Andersen (1993).

[34] See Livy 1. 34. 6 = T37 and 1. 47. 4 = T38.

one. Rather, Etruscan material can be adduced cautiously as evidence for an aristocratic culture and outlook which was shared, to a greater or a lesser extent, in other areas of Italy, including Latium and Rome.

It is notable that Etruscan epigraphic texts reveal the emergence of family names used with filiation around Ceri in the second half of the seventh century BC.[35] The naming system so typical of Rome, and so different from Greece, was in fact widespread in Italy from this early period and cannot as yet be identified as the creation of a particular group or area.[36] As regards the pattern of naming the Etruscan texts can be used as analogies for Roman practices and to suggest the importance of the family as a unit in Italy during the seventh century BC.[37]

We do have a general picture of the life-style and interests of Etruscan leading families in the sixth and fifth centuries BC, and it reflects some customs shared with other Italian élites at the time.[38] Evidence is provided by a fine banquet service of the late seventh century BC found buried outside a large dwelling complex in the Latin city of Ficana.[39] The service exactly parallels finds made in Etruscan tombs and suggests the importance of the banquet in everyday society, rather than simply as a reference to an idealized life after death. Within Etruscan aristocratic culture, it is now suggested, ancestors played an important role, in the *atrium* of the home, in the tomb, and in more public structures such as the 'palace complex' at Murlo.[40] There the 'ancestors' on the roof are perhaps associated with deities, as well as with the aristocratic pursuits illustrated by the terracotta wall plaques. They may have had an apotropaic function in watching over the courtyard and the banquetting which seems to have been one of the main functions of the building.[41] Antefixes in the form of human faces have also been found at Murlo and may suggest the use of masks representing dead family members.[42]

After the overthrow of the kings in Etruria, power and prestige came to be associated with leading magistrates who continued to use the trappings

[35] See Torelli (1981) 74 who draws on the work of Cristofani and de Simone.
[36] For a discussion of family names, see Rix (1972).
[37] Cf. Ch. 6 § 5 for the tradition of Etruscan family trees which seem also to have had parallels at Rome, esp. amongst those who claimed Etruscan descent.
[38] For a general discussion of Etruscan aristocratic culture, see Torelli (1981) 69-103, (1988) 53-74, and Roncalli in Steingräber (1986) 69-73. For a convenient summary of the relevant artistic and material evidence, see Menichetti (1988) 75-124.
[39] For publication and analysis, see Rathje (1983).
[40] For Murlo in general, see De Puma and Small (1994).
[41] See Torelli (1981) 98. See Damgaard Andersen (1993) 27-9 with figs. 33a and b and 34 for two hut urns with figures on the roof which appear to offer parallels to the Murlo actroteria.
[42] See Damgaard Andersen (1993) 54-5 who considers ancestor cult as an integral part of domestic cult in Central Italy.

of royal power: the lictors, *fasces* and *toga praetexta* which were so important to magistrates in Rome.[43] Most of our information about Etruscan
magistrates comes from sarcophagi and urns of the fourth century BC and
later. These are decorated with scenes of supreme magistrates in triumphal
processions with their status symbols and attendants. Such iconography
reflects the importance of a spectacle of status through its use in a funerary context to sum up a man's best achievements. Parallels come from
tomb paintings which also show processions of magistrates, often in the
context of a final journey to the Underworld, which are sometimes met by
'ancestors'.[44] Recent ancestors also appear together with the deceased in
scenes of banquets set in the other world.[45]

Tomb paintings reveal ideas about another life, but do so by drawing on
important episodes from Etruscan aristocratic culture, notably magnificent
banquets and solemn processions of magistrates in togas with their trappings of office. The processions often include portrait-like renditions of individual figures. We do not know whether such processions had a role to play
in Etruscan funerals or not. The tomb paintings accompany and illustrate
lengthy inscriptions which record names and careers of deceased family
members. It is important, however, to note that evidence for Etruscan magistrates, in written or iconographic form, comes from the fourth century BC
onwards at a time when Etruria was heavily influenced by Rome and
increasingly eclipsed by her.[46]

A spirit of competition between Etruscans and Romans is especially clear

---

[43] The best analysis of the evidence for Etruscan magistrates is still Lambrechts
(1959), although he underestimates the evidence from wall-paintings which is now
available in Steingräber (1986). The Romans believed that their insignia of office had
come from the Etruscans: see Livy 1. 8. 3; Dion. Hal. 3. 61. 1; and Diod. 5. 40. 1
with Wanscher (1980) 121.

[44] Etruscan tomb paintings have now been described and catalogued by
Steingräber (1986). He discusses processions of magistrates at 60–5. The most
important paintings are/were to be found in the Tomba Bruschi, Tomba Mercareccia,
Tomba del Convegno, Tomba del Cardinale, Tomba degli Scudi, and Tomba del
Tifone. Such a procession also appears in a woman's tomb, the Tomba 5512 of the
2nd cent. BC. Steingräber suggests that this format of representing magistrates in procession originated locally in Tarquinia in the 4th cent. BC, since it cannot be paralleled in Greek iconography. He does not note the coincidence with the growing
importance of spectacle and processions at Rome and at Tarquinia around the same
time. The connections of such processions with later Roman art, esp. the Ara Pacis,
have been the subject of more interest.

[45] e.g. in the late 4th-cent. BC Tomba degli Scudi (Steingräber (1986) no. 109
with plates 145–9) the founder of the tomb and his wife sit at a banquet with his
parents, who are also shown separately on thrones.

[46] See Steingräber (1986) 67 and Roncalli in Steingräber (1986) 72–3 who likens
the processions and meetings in Etruscan Hellenistic tombs to the tomb of the 'Fabii'
on the Esquiline in using an artistic language adopted from Rome. For the relation
of Roman and Etruscan painting see now Ling (1991) 9.

in the François tomb.[47] Here wall-paintings of the second half of the fourth century BC are used to illustrate both historical and mythological combats which match Romans against Vulcians, and their respective ancestors against each other in different historical periods. Both sixth-century BC and more recent conflicts are portrayed along side scenes from the Trojan wars, which show the defeat of the Trojans, who are the ancestors of the Romans. These paintings are typically Etruscan in their cyclical view of history, in much of their iconography, and in their eclectic choice of subject matter from family and local traditions of Vulci. At the same time they reflect the pressure felt from Rome by depicting both direct conflicts and mythical contests drawing on a Trojan past which also recalls Homer. The paintings appear in the '*atrium*' of this large tomb and may indicate a tradition of historical paintings both in Etruscan and in Roman *atria* (see Fig. 14 on p. 216 above).[48]

The increasingly rich and complex evidence for the life of leading Etruscan families can, therefore, be used as an analogy to suggest some practices and cultural patterns also found in early Rome as part of an Etruscan/Latin/Campanian *koine*. While such evidence must only be used with care, it can be neither easily dismissed nor ignored. The early Romans, like the Etruscans and perhaps other Italic peoples, may well have had ancestral statues of office-holders and others which were kept in the *atrium* and which were associated with specific functions in their respective societies.[49] A defined category of 'ancestor' seems to have existed and certain individual deceased family members seem to have been represented in such a guise. Ancestral iconography in this early period also appears to have stressed status and family continuity. As things now stand, any connections with the later and specifically Roman custom of wax ancestor masks is obscured by lack of evidence. However, the impact of Roman magisterial processions, whether these had originally been adapted from Etruscan practices or not, can surely be discerned in Etruscan tomb paintings of the Hellenistic era. It has even been suggested that by the middle of the second century BC Etruscans were using actors to impersonate the dead man in procession at his funeral in imitation of the contemporary Roman practices described by Polybius.[50]

---

[47] See Steingräber (1986) no. 178 with analysis by Coarelli (1983) and Maggiani (1983).

[48] For a related discussion, see Ch. 7 § 5. Note also that the burial chamber at the back of the '*tablinum*' is decorated with wall-paintings in the First Style.

[49] Such a position has been espoused by Damgaard Andersen (1993).

[50] See Cristofani (1969) 228–32 who suggests this interpretation in his comments on the procession scene from the Tomba del Tifone, but then rejects it on the grounds that the lictors should appear behind the magistrate in a funeral procession. Yet this scene, like many others from Etruscan tombs, features the demons of the Underworld.

To sum up: the role of the *imagines* in promoting the nobility of office in the middle Republic is one particularly suited to local conditions and to the *Roman* political culture. However, the original idea of acting out the character of an office-holding ancestor may have been partly inspired by earlier ancestral iconography and by practices already found in patrician families who held power in the early Republic, a power they interpreted as inherited from the kings of Rome. At the same time, there is no evidence to suggest that other élites in Italy used wax ancestor masks of office-holders. In this respect it is evident how far certain new practices of the Roman nobility of office differed from the earlier, more homogenous aristocratic culture which is increasingly in evidence in many Italian towns.

The differences can be explained at a basic level by the need for self-promotion resulting from the Roman system of free elections and open access to offices, which were no longer the exclusive preserve of certain traditional families. Competition fostered constant shows of status and prestige. The central position of the family and its aspirations for continuity were traditional features of Italian life. These features were now combined with a new political system which favoured merit and demanded performance accompanied by at least an appearance of public accountability. Yet the social and artistic innovations of the middle Republic, probably including the use of wax ancestor masks, cannot be studied without reference to earlier attitudes to 'ancestors', especially to prominent citizens who had held political office. In other words, a fuller reconstruction of the origin of *imagines* will probably emerge in time from two sources, namely from further examination of Roman political institutions themselves, especially at the time of the emergence of the nobility of office and its early artistic self-expression, and from our growing understanding of the role and representation of 'ancestors' in the aristocratic culture of the previous centuries in Italian city states, and particularly among the Etruscans.

APPENDIX E

Trees of the Caecilii Metelli, Cornelii Scipiones, and Augustus' Family

Sources for family trees given below (none is exhaustive):

A. Caecilii Metelli

RE Caecilius cols. 1229-30; Van Ooteghem (1967) opposite p. 22; Wiseman (1974) 182-3; Syme (1986) table 1. Cf. Syme (1986) table 18 for the last Metelli.

B. Cornelii Scipiones

RE Cornelius cols. 1429-30 with Coarelli (1972) Fig. R and p. 59; cf. Syme (1986) table 19 and pp. 244-54 for the last Scipiones; cf. *PIR*² C opposite p. 360 for the Scipiones Salvidieni Orfiti. Relationships with the Cornelii Scapulae in the earlier tomb on the Via Appia remain unclear.

C1. & C2. Augustus' Family

NB progeny are not all in chronological order; adoptions are not indicated on these charts.

Syme (1986) table 3, M. T. Griffin (1984) stemma of the Julio-Claudians, and Levick (1990) table 1; Gelzer (1968) 354-5 for Caesar; cf. Palmer (1983) p. 358 for the Atii Balbi and their connections; cf. Syme (1986) table 14 (descendants of Pompey) and table 16 (descendants of Sulla).

A. CAECILII METELLI

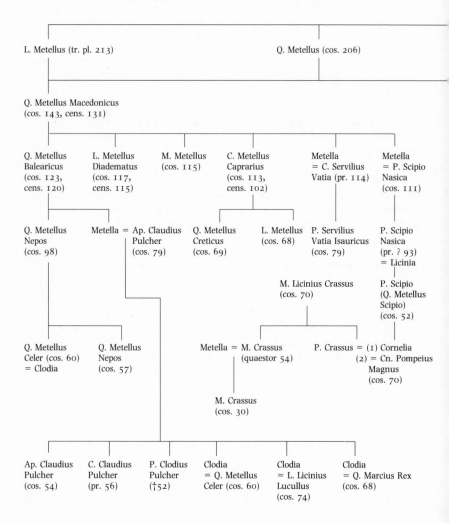

L. Metellus (tr. pl. 213)   Q. Metellus (cos. 206)

Q. Metellus Macedonicus
(cos. 143, cens. 131)

| Q. Metellus Balearicus (cos. 123, cens. 120) | L. Metellus Diadematus (cos. 117, cens. 115) | M. Metellus (cos. 115) | C. Metellus Caprarius (cos. 113, cens. 102) | Metella = C. Servilius Vatia (pr. 114) | Metella = P. Scipio Nasica (cos. 111) |

Q. Metellus Nepos (cos. 98)

Metella = Ap. Claudius Pulcher (cos. 79)

Q. Metellus Creticus (cos. 69)

L. Metellus (cos. 68)

P. Servilius Vatia Isauricus (cos. 79)

P. Scipio Nasica (pr. ? 93) = Licinia

M. Licinius Crassus (cos. 70)

P. Scipio (Q. Metellus Scipio) (cos. 52)

Q. Metellus Celer (cos. 60) = Clodia

Q. Metellus Nepos (cos. 57)

Metella = M. Crassus (quaestor 54)

P. Crassus = (1) Cornelia (2) = Cn. Pompeius Magnus (cos. 70)

M. Crassus (cos. 30)

| Ap. Claudius Pulcher (cos. 54) | C. Claudius Pulcher (pr. 56) | P. Clodius Pulcher (†52) | Clodia = Q. Metellus Celer (cos. 60) | Clodia = L. Licinius Lucullus (cos. 74) | Clodia = Q. Marcius Rex (cos. 68) |

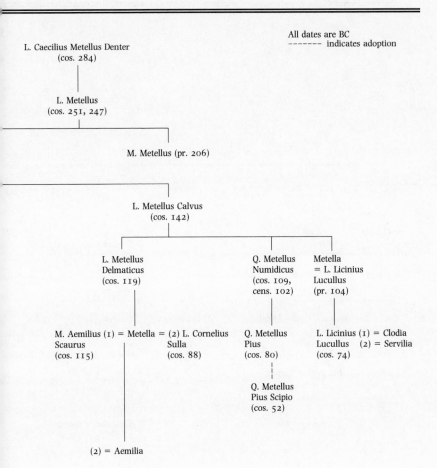

All dates are BC
------- indicates adoption

L. Caecilius Metellus Denter
(cos. 284)

L. Metellus
(cos. 251, 247)

M. Metellus (pr. 206)

L. Metellus Calvus
(cos. 142)

L. Metellus
Delmaticus
(cos. 119)

Q. Metellus
Numidicus
(cos. 109,
cens. 102)

Metella
= L. Licinius
Lucullus
(pr. 104)

M. Aemilius (1) = Metella = (2) L. Cornelius
Scaurus   Sulla
(cos. 115)   (cos. 88)

Q. Metellus
Pius
(cos. 80)

L. Licinius (1) = Clodia
Lucullus   (2) = Servilia
(cos. 74)

Q. Metellus
Pius Scipio
(cos. 52)

(2) = Aemilia

355

B. CORNELII SCIPIONES

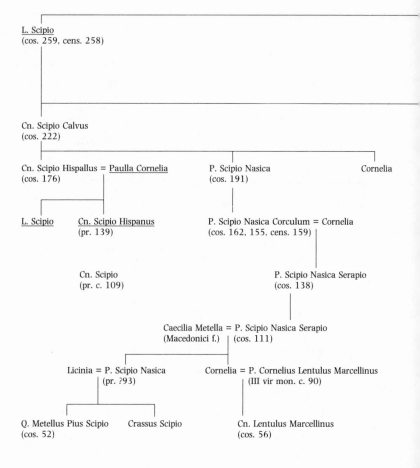

L. Scipio
(cos. 259, cens. 258)

Cn. Scipio Calvus
(cos. 222)

Cn. Scipio Hispallus = Paulla Cornelia   P. Scipio Nasica   Cornelia
(cos. 176)   (cos. 191)

L. Scipio   Cn. Scipio Hispanus   P. Scipio Nasica Corculum = Cornelia
               (pr. 139)   (cos. 162, 155, cens. 159)

               Cn. Scipio   P. Scipio Nasica Serapio
               (pr. c. 109)   (cos. 138)

                         Caecilia Metella = P. Scipio Nasica Serapio
                         (Macedonici f.)   (cos. 111)

               Licinia = P. Scipio Nasica   Cornelia = P. Cornelius Lentulus Marcellinus
                         (pr. ?93)   (III vir mon. c. 90)

Q. Metellus Pius Scipio   Crassus Scipio   Cn. Lentulus Marcellinus
(cos. 52)   (cos. 56)

Family Trees

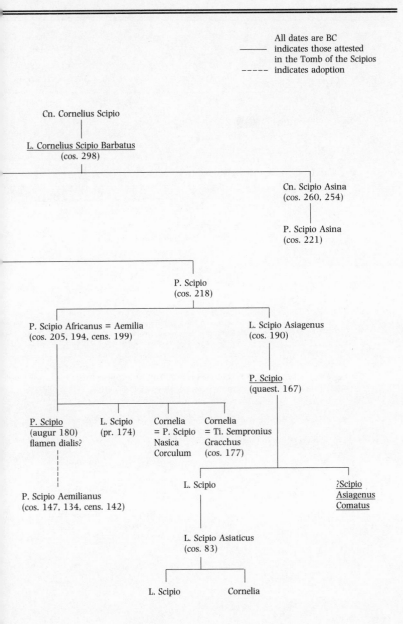

All dates are BC
——— indicates those attested
in the Tomb of the Scipios
- - - - indicates adoption

357

C₁ AUGUSTUS' FAMILY

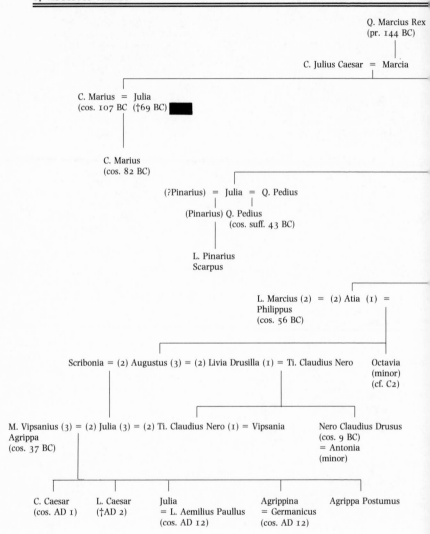

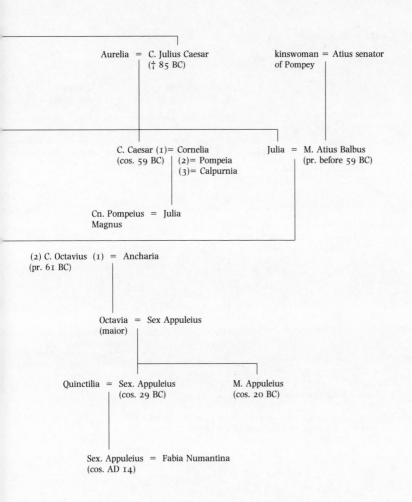

Aurelia = C. Julius Caesar
(† 85 BC)

kinswoman = Atius senator
of Pompey

C. Caesar (1) = Cornelia
(cos. 59 BC) | (2) = Pompeia
| (3) = Calpurnia

Julia = M. Atius Balbus
(pr. before 59 BC)

Cn. Pompeius = Julia
Magnus

(2) C. Octavius (1) = Ancharia
(pr. 61 BC)

Octavia = Sex Appuleius
(maior)

Quinctilia = Sex. Appuleius
(cos. 29 BC)

M. Appuleius
(cos. 20 BC)

Sex. Appuleius = Fabia Numantina
(cos. AD 14)

359

C₂ AUGUSTUS' FAMILY

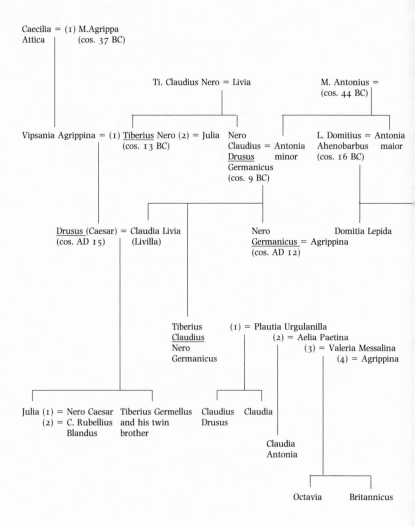

Caecilia = (1) M.Agrippa
Attica   (cos. 37 BC)

Ti. Claudius Nero = Livia

M. Antonius =
(cos. 44 BC)

Vipsania Agrippina = (1) <u>Tiberius</u> Nero (2) = Julia
                         (cos. 13 BC)

Nero
Claudius = Antonia
<u>Drusus</u>   minor
Germanicus
(cos. 9 BC)

L. Domitius = Antonia
Ahenobarbus   maior
(cos. 16 BC)

<u>Drusus</u> (Caesar) = Claudia Livia
(cos. AD 15)   (Livilla)

Nero
<u>Germanicus</u> = Agrippina
(cos. AD 12)

Domitia Lepida

Tiberius
<u>Claudius</u>
Nero
Germanicus

(1) = Plautia Urgulanilla
    (2) = Aelia Paetina
        (3) = Valeria Messalina
            (4) = Agrippina

Julia (1) = Nero Caesar
     (2) = C. Rubellius
           Blandus

Tiberius Germellus
and his twin
brother

Claudius
Drusus

Claudia

Claudia
Antonia

Octavia   Britannicus

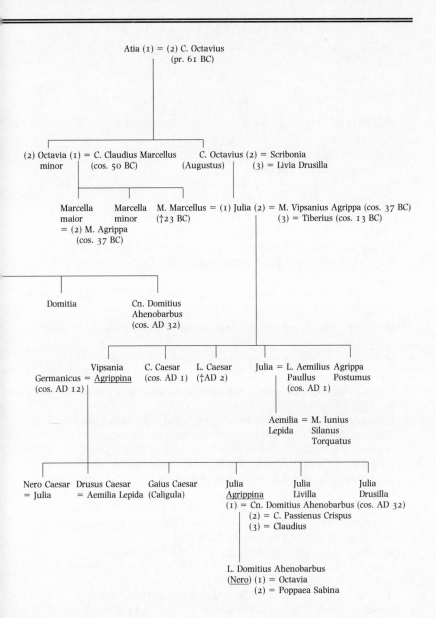

BIBLIOGRAPHY

Editions and Commentaries of Texts Cited in Appendix A

Asconius:

KIESSLING, A. and SCHOELL, R., *Q. Asconii Pediani Orationum Ciceronis Quinque Enarratio* (Berlin, 1875).

CLARK, A. C., *Q. Asconii Pediani Orationem Ciceronis Quinque Enarratio* (Oxford, 1907).

STANGL, T., *Ciceronis Orationum Scholiastae* (Vienna, 1912).

Afranius:

RIBBECK, O., *Scaenicae Romanorum Poesis Fragmenta*, 2 (Leipzig, 1898).

DAVIAULT, A., *Comoedia Togata, Fragments* (Paris, 1981).

Appian:

VIERECK, P., ROOS, A. G., GABBA, E., *Appiani Historia Romana* 1 (Leipzig, 1962).

Boethius:

GRUBER, J., *Kommentar zu Boethius De Consolatione Philosophiae* (Berlin, 1978).

O'DONNELL, J. J., *Boethius Consolatio Philosophiae* (Bryn Mawr, 1984).

Cicero:

CLARK, A. C., *M. Tulli Ciceronis Orationes*, 1, 2, 4, and 6 (Oxford 1905, 1918, 1909, 1911).

PETERSON, G., *M. Tulli Ciceronis Orationes*, 3 and 5 (Oxford, 1911).

POCOCK, L. G., *A Commentary on Cicero In Vatinium* (London, 1926).

WILKINS, A. S., *M. Tulli Ciceronis Rhetorica*, 1 and 2 (Oxford, 1902 and 1935).

AUSTIN, R. G., *M. Tulli Ciceronis Pro M. Caelio Oratio*, 3rd edn. (Oxford, 1960).

JONKERS, E. J., *Social and Economic Commentary on Cicero's De Lege Agraria III* (Leiden, 1963).

YON, A., *Cicéron L'Orateur, du meilleur genre d' orateurs* (Paris, 1964).

KASTEN, H., *Oratio Pro P. Sulla, Oratio Pro Archia Poeta* (Leipzig, 1966).

ZIEGLER, K., *M. Tullius Cicero De Re Publica* (Leipzig, 1969).

KUMANIECKI, K. F., *De Oratore*, Cicero fasc. 3 (Leipzig, 1969).

SHACKLETON BAILEY, D. R., *Cicero Epistulae ad Familiares*, 2 (Cambridge, 1977).

WESTMAN, R., *Marcus Tullius Cicero Orator* (Leipzig, 1980).

BÜCHNER, K., *M. Tullius Cicero De Re Publica* (Heidelberg, 1984).

NISBET, R. G. M., *Cicero In L. Calpurnium Pisonem Oratio* (Oxford, 1987).

LEEMAN, A. D., PINKSTER, H., RABBIE, E., *M. T. Cicero De Oratore Libri III*, 3 (Heidelberg, 1989).

Dio:

BOISSEVAIN, U. P., *Cassi Dionis Cocceiani Historiarum Romanarum Quae Supersunt*, 2 (Berlin, 1898).

CARY, E., *Dio's Roman History*, 5 and 7 (Cambridge, Mass., 1917 and 1924).

MILLAR, F., *A Study of Cassius Dio* (Oxford, 1964).

Diodorus:

WALTON, F. R., *Diodorus of Sicily*, XI (Cambridge, Mass., 1957).

HENRY, R., *Photius Bibliothèque VI* (Paris, 1971).

Historia Augusta:

HOHL, E., SAMBERGER, C., SEYFARTH, W., *Scriptores Historiae Augustae*, 1 and 2 (Leipzig, 1965).

Horace:

WICKHAM, E. C., and GARROD, H. W., *Q. Horati Flacci Opera* (Oxford, 1901).

SHACKLETON BAILEY, D. R., *Q. Horati Flacci Opera* (Stuttgart, 1985).

Juvenal:

CLAUSEN, W. V., *A. Persi Flacci et D. Juni Juvenalis Saturae* (Oxford, 1959).

Laus Pisonis:

WIGHT DUFF, J., and DUFF, A. M., *Minor Latin Poets* (Cambridge, Mass., 1934).

SEEL, A., *Laus Pisonis* (Erlangen, 1969).

Livy:

WEISSENBORN, W., and MÜLLER, H. J., *Titi Livi Ab Urbe Condita, 4th edn.*, 8 (Berlin, 1962).

ROSSBACH, O., *T. Livi Periochae* (Leipzig, 1910).

WALTERS, C. F., and CONWAY, R. S., *Titi Livi Ab Urbe Condita*, 2, 3, and 4 (Oxford 1919, 1929, 1935).

OGILVIE, R. M., *Titi Livi Ab Urbe Condita I–V*, 1 (Oxford, 1974).

—— *A Commentary on Livy books 1–5* (Oxford, 1965).

Martial:

SHACKLETON BAILEY, D. R., post W. Heraeum, *M. Valerii Martialis Epigrammata* (Stuttgart, 1990).

Ovid:

BÖMER, F., *P. Ovidius Naso Die Fasten*, 1 and 2 (Heidelberg, 1957 and 1958).

KENNEY, E. J., *P. Ovidi Nasonis, Amores, Medicamina Faciei Femineae, Ars Amatoria, Remedia Amoris* (Oxford, 1965).

ALTON, E. H., WORMELL, D. E. W., COURTNEY, E., *Ovidius Fasti* (Leipzig, 1978).

Panegyricus Messallae:

POSTGATE, I. P., *Tibulli Aliorumque Carminum Libri Tres*, 2nd edn. (Oxford, 1915).

Plautus:

LINDSAY, W. M., *T. Macci Plauti Comoediae* (Oxford, 1904).

SEDGWICK, W. B., *Plautus Amphitruo* (Manchester, 1960).

Pliny the Elder:
CROISILLE, J.-M., *Pline L'Ancien Histoire Naturelle Livre 35* (Paris, 1985).

Pliny the Younger:
MYNORS, R. A. B., *C. Plinii Caecili Secundi Epistularum Libri Decem* (Oxford, 1963).
SHERWIN-WHITE, A. N., *The Letters of Pliny: A Historical and Social Commentary* (Oxford, 1966).

Plutarch:
ZIEGLER, K., *Plutarchi Vitae Parallelae*, II.2 and III.1 (Leipzig, 1968, and 1971).

Polybius:
BÜTTNER-WOBST, T., *Polybii Historiae*, 2 (Leipzig, 1889).
WEIL, V., and NICOLET, C., *Polybe Histoires Livre VI* (Paris, 1977).

Pomponius Porfyrio:
MEYER, G., *Pomponii Porphyrionis Commentarii in Q. Horatium Flaccum* (Leipzig, 1874).
HOLDER, A., and KELLER, O., *Scholia Antiqua in Q. Horatium Flaccum*, 1 (Innsbruck, 1894, reprinted New York, 1979).

Propertius:
BARBER, E. A., *Sexti Properti Carmina*, 2nd edn. (Oxford, 1960).

Ps.-Quintilian:
WINTERBOTTOM, M., *The Minor Declamations Ascribed to Quintilian* (Berlin/New York, 1984).

Sallust:
MAURENBRECHER, B., *C. Sallusti Crispi Historiarum Reliquiae* (Stuttgart, 1967).
KOESTERMANN, E., *C. Sallusti Crispi Bellum Iugurthinum* (Heidelberg, 1971).
KURFESS, A., *C. Sallusti Crispi Catalina, Iugurtha, Fragmenta Ampliora* (Leipzig, 1981).
REYNOLDS, L. D., *C. Sallusti Crispi Catalina, Iugurtha, Historiarum Fragmenta Selecta, Appendix Sallustiana* (Oxford, 1991).

Seneca the Elder:
WINTERBOTTOM, M., *The Elder Seneca*, 1 and 2 (Cambridge, Mass., 1974).

Seneca:
PRÉCHAC, F., *Sénèque Des Bienfaits*, 1 (Paris, 1926).
REYNOLDS, L. D., *L. Annaei Senecae Ad Lucilium Epistulae Morales*, 1 (Oxford, 1965).
—— *L. Annaei Senecae Dialogorum Libri Duodecim* (Oxford, 1977).

Silius Italicus:
DELZ, J., *Sili Italici Punica* (Stuttgart, 1987).

Suetonius:
IHM, M., *Suetonius I: De Vita Caesarum Libri VIII* (Stuttgart, 1908).

Bibliography

Tacitus:
KOESTERMANN, E., *Germania, Agricola, Dialogus de Oratoribus* (Leipzig, 1962).
—— *Cornelii Taciti Libri Qui Supersunt 2, I Ab Excessu Divi Augusti* (Leipzig, 1965).
—— *Cornelius Tacitus Annalen II* (Heidelberg, 1965).
—— *Cornelius Tacitus Annalen III* (Heidelberg, 1967).
—— *Cornelius Tacitus Annalen IV* (Heidelberg, 1968).
HEUBNER, H., P. *Cornelii Taciti Libri Qui Supersunt, II.1 Historiarum Libri* (Stuttgart, 1978).

Valerius Maximus:
KEMPF, C., *Valerii Maximi Factorum et Dictorum Memorabilium Libri Novem*, 2nd edn. (Leipzig, 1888).
FARANDA, R., *Detti e Fatti Memorabili di Valerio Massimo* (Turin, 1971).

Velleius Paterculus:
STEGMANN DE PRITZWALD, C., *Velleius Paterculus* (Stuttgart, 1965).
WOODMAN, A. J., *Velleius Paterculus The Tiberian Narrative 2.94-131* (Cambridge, 1977).
WATT, W. S., *Velleius Paterculus* (Leipzig, 1988).

Vitruvius:
FERRI, S., *Vitruvio Dai Libri I-VII* (Rome, 1960).
FENSTERBUSCH, C., *Vitruv Zehn Bücher über Architektur* (Darmstadt, 1964).

References

ADRIANI, A. (1970), 'Ritratti dell' Egitto greco-romano', *MDAI(R)* 77: 72-109.
AFZELIUS, A. (1938), 'Zur Definition der römischen Nobilität in der Zeit Ciceros', *C&M* 2: 40-94.
—— (1945), 'Zur Definition der römischen Nobilität vor der Zeit Ciceros,' *C&M* 7: 150-200.
ALEXIOU, M. (1974), *The Ritual Lament in Greek Tradition* (Cambridge).
ALFÖLDI, A. (1956), 'The Main Aspects of Political Propaganda on the Coinage of the Roman Republic', in R. A. G. Carson, and C. H. V. Sutherland (eds.), *Essays in Roman Coinage Presented to Harold Mattingly* (Oxford), 63-95.
ALLISON, J. E., and CLOUD, J. D. (1962), 'The Lex Julia Maiestatis', *Latomus* 21: 711-31.
ALLROGGEN-BEDEL, A. (1974), *Maskendarstellungen in der römischen-kampanischen Wandmalerei* (Munich).
ALTMANN, W. (1905), *Die römischen Grabaltäre der Kaiserzeit* (Berlin).
ANDERSON, J. C. JR. (1984), *The Historical Topography of the Imperial Fora* (Collection Latomus 182, Brussels).
ANTONACCIO, C. (1993), 'The Archaeology of Ancestors', in C. Dougherty and L. Kurke (eds.), *Cultural Poetics in Archaic Greece: Cult, Performance, Politics* (Cambridge), 46-70.

ARANGIO-RUIZ, V., and CARRATELLI, G. P. (1954), 'Tabulae Herculanenses', *PP* 9: 54-74.

ARCE, J. (1988a), 'La tabula Siarensis y los funerales imperiales II', in J. González and J. Arce (eds.), *Estudios sobre la Tabula Siarensis, Anejos de archivo español de arqueologia* 9, (Madrid), 43-50.

—— (1988b), *Funus Imperatorum: Los funerales de los emperadores romanos* (Madrid).

ARIÈS, P. (1981), *The Hour of our Death* (New York).

ASTIN, A. E. (1967), *Scipio Aemilianus* (Oxford).

AUSTIN, R. G. (1977), *P. Vergili Maronis Aeneidos liber sextus* (Oxford).

AVERILL, J. R. (1980a), 'Emotion and Anxiety: Sociocultural, Biological and Psychological Determinants', in A. O. Rorty (ed.), *Explaining Emotions* (Berkeley/Los Angeles).

—— (1980b), 'A Constructivist View of Emotion', in R. Plutchik and H. Kellerman (eds.), *Emotion: Theory, Research, and Experience*, 1. *Theories of Emotion* (New York).

BADIAN, E. (1964), *Studies in Greek and Roman History* (Oxford).

—— (1972), *Publicans and Sinners: Private Enterprise in the Service of the Roman Republic* (Oxford).

—— (1982), ' "Crisis Theories" and the Beginning of the Principate', in G. Wirth (ed.), *Romanitas-Christianitas: Untersuchungen zur Geschichte und Literatur der römischen Kaiserzeit, Johannes Straub zum 70. Geburtstag gewidmet* (Berlin/New York), 18-41.

BAGNANI, G. (1954), 'The House of Trimalchio', *AJP* 75: 16-39.

BALSDON, J. P. V. D. (1962), *Roman Women: Their History and Habits* (London).

BALTRUSCH, E. (1989), *Regimen morum. Die Reglementierung des Privatlebens der Senatoren und Ritter in der römischen Republik und frühen Kaiserzeit* (Munich).

BARBET, A. (1985), *La Peinture murale romaine. Les styles décoratifs pompéiens* (Paris).

BARBIERI, G. (1947), 'Laudatio' and 'Laudatio Turiae' in E. de Ruggiero (ed.), *Dizionario epigrafico di antichità romana* 4 (Rome), 471-5.

BARCHIESI, A. (1994), *Il poeta e il principe. Ovidio e il discorso augusteo* (Bari).

BASSON, W. P. (1975), *Pivotal Catalogues in the Aeneid* (Amsterdam).

BAUER, H. (1987), 'Nuove ricerche sul foro di Augusto', in *L'urbs: espace urbain et histoire (Ier siècle av. J.-C.-IIIe siècle ap. J.-C.)*, Actes du colloque international organisé par le Centre National de la Recherche Scientifique et L'École Française de Rome, 8-12 Mai 1985 (Rome), 763-70.

BECATTI, G. (1959), 'Clipeate immagini', in *Enciclopedia dell'arte antica classica e orientale* 2 (Rome), 718-21.

BEK, L. (1980), *Towards Paradise on Earth: Modern Space Conception in Architecture: A Creation of Renaissance Humanism* (ARom Suppl. 9, Rome).

BELLONI, G. G. (1974), 'Significato storico-politico delle figurazione e delle scrite delle monete da Augusto a Traiano', *ANRW* 2.1 (Berlin), 997-1144.

BENNDORF, O. (1878), *Antike Gesichtshelme und Sepulcralmasken* (Denkschrift der Kaiserlichen Akademie der Wissenschaften Wien, Phil.-Hist. Bd. 28, Vienna), 301-75.

BERGER, A. (1953), *Encyclopedic Dictionary of Roman Law* (Philadelphia).

BERING-STASCHEWSKI, R. (1981), *Römische Zeitgeschichte bei Cassius Dio* (Bochum).

BESNIER, R. (1953), 'Les Archives privées, publiques et religieuses à Rome au temps des rois', in *Studi in memorie di E. Albertario* 2 (Milan), 3-26.

BETHE, E. (1935), *Ahnenbild und Familiengeschichte bei Römern und Griechen* (Munich).

BETTINI, M. (1986), *Antropologia e cultura romana: parentela, tempo, immagini dell'anima* (Rome).

—— (1991), *Anthropology and Roman Culture: Kinship, Time, Images of the Soul*, trans. by J. Van Sickle, (Baltimore).

BIANCHI BANDINELLI, R. (1961), *L'origine del ritratto in Grecia e in Roma* (Rome).

—— (1970), *Rom. Das Zentrum der Macht. Die römische Kunst von den Anfängen bis zur Zeit Marc-Aurels* (Munich).

—— (1972), 'Qualche osservazione sulle statue acroteriali di Poggio Civitate (Murlo)', *DArch* 6: 236-47.

—— (1975), *Die römische Kunst: von den Anfängen bis zum Ende der Antike* (Munich).

BIEBER, M. (1973), 'The Development of Portraiture on Roman Republican Coins', *ANRW* 1.4 (Berlin), 871-98.

BINFORD, L. R. (1971), 'Mortuary Practices: Their Study and Their Potential', in J. A. Brown (ed.), *Approaches to the Social Dimensions of Mortuary Practices* (New York), 6-29.

BLANCK, H. (1966-7), 'Zwei Corneliersarkophage', *MDAI(R)* 73-4: 72-7.

BLEICKEN, J. (1981), 'Die Nobilität der römischen Republik', *Gymnasium* 88: 236-53.

BLOOMER, W. M. (1992), *Valerius Maximus and the Rhetoric of the New Nobility* (Chapel Hill, NC).

BLÜMNER, H. (1911), *Die römischen Privataltertümer*, Handbuch d. Klassischen Altertumswissenschaft, 4.2.2 (Munich).

BOATWRIGHT, M. T. (1982), 'The Lucii Volusii Saturnini and Tacitus', in *I Volusii Saturnini. Una famiglia romana della prima età imperiale* (Bari), 7-16.

BODEL, J. (1994), *Graveyards and Groves: A Study of the Lex Lucerina* (*AJAH* 11 (1986), Cambridge, Mass.).

BOETHIUS, A. (1942), 'On the Ancestral Masks of the Romans', *AArch*, 13: 226-35.

—— (1978), *Etruscan and Early Roman Architecture*, 2nd edn. (Harmondsworth).

BOMATI, Y. (1986), 'Phersu et le monde dionysiaque', *Latomus* 45: 21-32.

BÖMER, F. (1943), *Ahnenkult und Ahnenglaube im alten Rom* (Beihefte zum Archiv für Religionswissenschaft, Heft 1, Leipzig and Berlin).

—— (1957-8), *P. Ovidius Naso Die Fasten*, 1-2 (Heidelberg).

BONFANTE WARREN, L. (1970), 'Roman Triumphs and Etruscan Kings: The Changing Face of the Triumph', *JRS* 40: 49-66.

BONNEFOND, M. (1987), 'Transferts de fonctions et mutation idéologique: le Capitole et le Forum d'Auguste', in *L'urbs: espace urbain et histoire* (*Ier siècle av. J.-C.-IIIe siècle ap. J. C.*), Actes du colloque international organisé par le Centre National de la Recherche Scientifique et L'École Française de Rome, Rome 8-12 Mai 1985 (Rome), 251-78.

BONNEFOND-COUDRY, M. (1989), *Le Sénat de la république romaine* (Rome).

BORDA, M. (1973), 'I ritratti repubblicani di Aquileia', *MDAI(R)* 80; 35-57.

BOSCHUNG, D. (1986), 'Überlegungen zum Liciniergrab', *JDAI* 101; 257-87.

BOYCE, G. K. (1937), *Corpus of the Lararia of Pompeii, MAAR* 14, (Rome).

BRECKENRIDGE, J. D. (1968), *Likeness: A Conceptual History of Ancient Portraiture* (Evanston, Ill.).

—— (1973), 'Origins of Roman Republican Portraiture: Relations with the Hellenistic World', *ANRW* 1.4, (Berlin), 826-54.

BRELICH, A. (1938), 'Trionfo e morte', *Studi e materiali di storia delle religioni* 14: 189-93.

BRILLIANT, R. (1963), *Gesture and Rank in Roman Art: The Use of Gesture to Denote Status in Roman Sculpture and Coinage* (Memoirs of the Connecticut Academy of Arts and Sciences 14, New Haven, Conn).

—— (1984), *Visual Narratives: Storytelling in Etruscan and Roman Art* (Ithaca and London).

BROMMER, F. (1953-4), 'Zu den römischen Ahnenbildern', *MDAI(R)* 60-1: 163-71.

BROWN, F. E. (1980), *Cosa: The Making of a Roman Town* (Ann Arbor).

BROWN, P. (1971), *The World of Late Antiquity* (London).

BRUNT, P. A. (1982), 'Nobilitas and Novitas', *JRS* 72: 1-17.

—— (1988), 'Clientela', in *The Fall of the Roman Republic and Related Essays* (Oxford), 382-442.

BÜCHELER, F. (1895-7), *Carmina Latina Epigraphica* (Leipzig).

BÜCHNER, K. (1953), *Der Aufbau von Sallusts Bellum Jugurthinum* (Hermes Einzelschrift 9, Wiesbaden).

BUDDE, E. (1939), *Armarium und κιβωτός, Ein Beitrag zur Geschichte des antiken Mobilars* (Würzburg-Aumühle).

BURCK, E. (1942), 'Die altrömische Familie', in H. Berve (ed.), *Das neue Bild der Antike* 2 (Leipzig), 5-52.

BURCKHARDT, L. (1990), 'The Political Elite of the Roman Republic: Comments on Recent Discussion of the Concepts Nobilitas and Homo Novus', *Historia* 39: 77-99.

BURKE, P. F. JR. (1979), 'Roman Rites for the Dead and *Aeneid* 6' *CJ* 74: 220-8.

BURNETT, A. M. (1977), 'The Authority to Coin in the late Republic and Early Empire', *NC*7 17: 37-63.

BUTTREY, T. V. (1956), *The Triumviral Portrait Gold of the Quatuorviri Monetales* (Numismatic Notes and Monographs 137, New York).

CABALLOS, A., ECK, W., and FERNÁNDEZ, F. (1991), 'S. C. de Cn. Pisone patre: Informe preliminar', in A. Fraschetti (ed.), *Il Congreso de Historia de Andalucia* (Cordoba).

CAIRNS, D. L. (1993), *Aidos: The Psychology and Ethics of Honour and Shame in Ancient Greek Literature* (Oxford).

CALABI LIMENTANI, I. (1982), 'I fornices di Stertinio e di Scipione nel racconto di Livio (xxxiii,27,1-5 e xxxvii,3,7)', *CISA* 8: 123-35.

CALTABIANO, M. (1975), 'La morte del console Marcello nella tradizione storiografica', *CISA* 3: 65-81.

CAMERON, A. (1993a), *The Later Roman Empire* (London).

—— (1993b), *The Mediterranean World in Late Antiquity A.D. 395-600* (London).

CARANDINI, A. (1988), *Schiavi in Italia. Gli strumenti pensanti dei Romani fra tarda Repubblica e medio Impero* (Rome).

CARCOPINO, J. (1931), *Sylla ou la monarchie manquée* (Paris).

CARETTONI, G. (1983), *Das Haus des Augustus auf dem Palatin* (Mainz).

CARNEY, T. F. (1959), 'Once again Marius' speech after election in 108 B.C.', *SO* 35: 63-70.

—— (1961), *A Biography of Marius* (An inaugural lecture, University College of Rhodesia and Nyasaland, Proceedings of the African Classical Association 1).

CASPARI, F. (1933), 'Studien zu dem Kallixeinosfragment Athenaios 5, 197c-203b', *Hermes* 68: 400-14.

CASSOLA, F. (1988), 'Lo scontro fra patrizi e plebei e la formazione della "*nobilitas*" ', in A. Momigliano and A. Schiavone (eds.), *Storia di Roma 1: Roma in Italia* (Turin), 451-81.

CASTRÉN, P. (1975), *Ordo Populusque Pompeianus: Polity and Society in Roman Pompeii* (Rome, Acta Instituti Romani Finlandiae 8).

CHADWICK, H. (1981), *Boethius: The Consolations of Music, Logic, Theology, and Philosophy* (Oxford).

CHAMPLIN, E. (1989), 'The Life and Times of Calpurnius Piso', *MH* 46; 101-24.

—— (1991) *Final Judgements: Duty and Emotion in Roman Wills 200 B.C.-A.D. 250* (Berkeley).

CHANTRAINE, H. (1983), 'Münzbild und Familiengeschichte in der römischen Republik', *Gymnasium* 90; 530-45.

CHILTON, C. W. (1955), 'The Roman Law of Treason under the Early Principate', *JRS* 45: 73-81.

CIANFARANI, V. (1968), 'Note sul restauro del "Guerriero di Capestrano" ', *RIA* NS 15: 5-19.

—— (1969) *Antiche Civiltà d'Abruzzo* (Roma- Palazzo Venezia-Avr. 1969, Rome).

CLARKE, J. R. (1991), *The Houses of Roman Italy 100 B.C.-A.D. 250: Ritual, Space and Decoration* (Berkeley).

CLARKE, M. L. (1981), *The Noblest Roman: Marcus Brutus and his Reputation* (London).

CLASSEN, C. J. (1962), 'Romulus in der römischen Republik', *Philologus* 106: 174-204.

CLEMENTE, G. (1981), 'Le leggi sul lusso e la società romana tra III e II secolo A.C. ', in A. Giardina and A. Schiavone (eds.), *Società romana e produzione schiavistica, 3, Modelli etici, diritto e trasformazioni sociali* (Bari), 1-14.

COARELLI, F. (1969), 'Le Tyrannoctone du Capitol et la mort de Tiberius Gracchus', *MEFRA* 8: 137-60.

—— (1972) 'Il sepolcro degli Scipioni', *DArch* 6: 36-106.

—— (1973) 'Il sepolcro degli Scipioni', in *Roma Medio Repubblicana: Aspetti culturali di Roma e del Lazio nei secoli IV e III A.C.* (Rome), 234-6.

—— (1976), 'Frammento di affresco dall'Esquilino con scena storica' and 'Cinque frammenti di una tomba dipinta dall'Esquilino (Arieti)', in *Affreschi romani dalle raccolte dell'antiquarium communale* (Rome), 13-21 and 22-8.

—— (1978), 'La Statue de Cornélie, mère des Gracques, et la crise politique à Rome au temps de Saturninus', in *Le Dernier siècle de la république romaine et l'époque augustéenne* (Strasbourg).

—— (1981), 'Alessandro, i Licinii e Lanuvio', in *L'Art décoratif à Rome à la fin de la République et au début du Principat* (Collection de l'École Française de Rome 55, Rome), 229-84.

—— (1983), 'Le pitture della tomba François a Vulci; una proposta di lettura', *DArch* 1: 43-78.

—— (1984), 'Un "trofeo" di Novio Fannio, commandante sannita', in *Studi di Antichità in onore di G. Maetzke* 2 (Rome), 229-41.

—— (1985), *Il Foro Romano: Periodo Repubblicano e Augusteo* (Rome).

—— (1988), *Il Foro Boario, dalle origini alla fine della repubblica* (Rome).

—— (1989), 'La casa dell'aristocrazia romana secundo Vitruvio', in H. Geertman and J. J. de Jong (eds.), *Munus non ingratum: Proceedings of the International Symposium on Vitruvius' De Architectura and the Hellenistic and Republican Architecture* (Leiden), 178-187.

COLONNA, G. and VON HASE, F. W. (1986), 'Alle origini della statuaria etrusca: la tomba delle statue presso Ceri', *SE* 52: 13-59.

CONNOR, W. R. (1987), 'Tribes, Festivals and Processions: Civic Ceremonial and Political Manipulation in Archaic Greece', *JHS* 107: 40-50.

CORNELL, T. J. (1978), review of Torelli (1975) *JRS* 68: 167-173.

—— (1986), 'The Value of the Literary Tradition concerning Archaic Rome', in K. A. Raaflaub (ed.), *Social Struggles in Archaic Rome: New Perspectives on the Conflict of the Orders* (Berkeley), 52-76.

CORSARO, M. (1982), 'La presenza romana a Entella: una nota su Tiberio Claudio di Anzio', *ASNP* 12.3: 993-1032.

COURBAUD, E. (1900), 'Imago' in C. Daremberg and E. Saglio (eds.), *Dictionnaire des antiquités grecques et romaines* 3 (Paris), 402-415.

CRAWFORD, M. H. (1974), *Roman Republican Coinage*, 1 and 2 (Cambridge).

—— (1975), review of Zehnacker (1973), *JRS* 65: 177-9.

—— (1979), review of P. Wallmann, *Münzpropaganda in den Anfängen des Zweiten Triumvirats (43/42 v. Chr.)* (Bochum, 1977), *CR* 29: 179.

—— (1983), 'Roman Imperial Coin Types and the Formation of Public Opinion', in C. N. L. Brooke, B. H. I. H. Stewart, J. G. Pollard, and T. R. Volk (eds.), *Studies in Numismatic Method Presented to P. Grierson* (Cambridge), 47-64.

CRAWFORD, O. C. (1941/2), 'Laudatio Funebris', *CJ* 37: 17-27.

CRISTOFANI, M. (1967), 'Ricerche sulle pitture della tomba François di Vulci. I fregi decorativi', *DArch* 1: 186-219.

—— (1969), *La Tomba del Tifone. Cultura e società di Tarquinia in età tardo etrusca* (Atti della Classe di Scienze morali, storiche e filologiche dell'Accademia dei Lincei, ser. 6 vol. 14 fasc. 4, Rome).

CROISILLE, J.-M. (1985), *Pline L'Ancien Histoire Naturelle Livre 35* (Paris).

CROOK, J. A. (1955), *Consilium Principis: Imperial Councils and Counsellors from Augustus to Diocletian* (Cambridge).

—— (1967), *Law and Life of Rome* (Ithaca).

CUQ, E. (1896), 'Funus' in C. Daremberg and E. Saglio (eds.), *Dictionnaire des antiquités grecques et romaines* 2 (Paris), 1386-1409.

D'AMBRA, E. (1993), *Private Lives, Imperial Virtues: the Frieze of the Forum Transitorium in Rome* (Princeton).

DAMGAARD ANDERSEN, H. (1993), 'The Etruscan Ancestor Cult-Its Origin and Development and the Importance of Anthropomorphization', *ARom* 21: 7-66.

D'ARMS, J. H. (1970), *Romans on the Bay of Naples* (Harvard).

—— (1981), *Commerce and Social Standing in Ancient Rome* (Harvard).

DAUBE, D. (1969), *Roman Law. Linguistic, Social and Philosophical Aspects* (Edinburgh).

DAUT, R. (1975), *Imago. Untersuchungen zum Bildbegriff der Römer* (Heidelberg).

DE CAZANOVE, O. (1986), 'L'association dionysiaque dans les sociétés anciennes', *MEFRA* 89: 190-5.

DE FRANCISCIS, A. (1951), *Il ritratto romano a Pompei* (Naples).

—— (1979), 'Beryllos e la villa di Poppea ad Oplontis', in *Studies in Classical Art and Archaeology—a tribute to P. H. von Blanckenhagen* (New York).

DEGRASSI, A. (1937), *Inscriptiones Italiae* 13, fasc. 3, (Rome).

—— (1945), 'Virgilio e il Foro di Augusto', *Epigraphica* 7: 88-103.

DELARUELLE, L. (1913), 'Les Souvenirs d'œuvres plastiques dans la revue des héros au livre VI de l'Énéide', *RA* 1: 153-63.

DELLA CORTE, F. (1975), 'Maschere e personaggi in Plauto', *Dionisio* 46: 163-93.

DELLA CORTE, M. (1965), *Case e Abitanti di Pompei*[3] (Naples).

DENTZER, J. M. (1967), 'Les Témoinages sur l'histoire de la peinture italique dans la tradition littéraire latine et le problème de la peinture murale en Italie', *MEFRA* 79: 7-27.

DE PUMA, R. D., and SMALL, J. P. (1994), *Murlo and the Etruscans: Art and Society in Ancient Etruria* (Madison).

DE SANCTIS, G. (1936), review of Haywood (1933), *RFIC*: 189-203.

DEVELIN, R. (1979), *Patterns of Office-Holding 366-49 B.C.* (Collection Latomus 161, Brussels).

—— (1985), *The Practice of Politics at Rome 366-167 B.C.* (Brussels).

DE VOS, A. M. (1982), *Pompei Ercolano Stabia, Guide archelogiche Laterza* (Rome/Bari).

DIEHL, E. (1912), *Inscriptiones Latinae* (Bonn).

DIHLE, A. (1986), *Die Entstehung der historischen Biographie* (SHAW 3).

DIXON, S. (1992), *The Roman Family* (Baltimore/London).

DODDS, E. (1951), *The Greeks and the Irrational* (Berkeley).

DRERUP, H. (1959), 'Bildraum und Realraum in der römischen Architektur', *MDAI(R)* 66: 147-74.

—— (1980), 'Totenmaske und Ahnenbild bei den Römern', *MDAI(R)* 87: 81-129.

DREXLER, H. (1988), *Politische Grundbegriffe der Römer* (Darmstadt).

DULL, R. (1962), 'Zum Recht der Bildwerke in der Antike', in *Studi in onore di E. Betti* 3 (Milan), 131-53.

DUPONT, F. (1985), *L'Acteur roi ou le théâtre dans la Rome antique* (Paris).

—— (1987) 'Les Morts et la mémoire: le masque funèbre', in F. Hinard (ed.), *La Mort, les morts et l'au-delà dans le monde romain* (Actes du colloque de Caen, 20-22 Nov. 1985, Caen), 167-72.

DURRY, M. (1942), 'Laudatio funebris et rhétorique', *RPh* 16, ser. 3: 105-14.

—— (1950), *Laudatio Turiae: éloge funèbre d'une matrone romaine* (Paris).

DWYER, E. (1982), *Pompeian Domestic Sculpture: A Study of Five Pompeian Houses and their Contents* (Rome).

—— (1991). 'The Pompeian Atrium House in Theory and in Practice', in E. K. Gazda and A. E. Haekl (eds.), *Roman Art in the Private Sphere: New Perspectives on the Architecture and Decor of the Domus, Villa, and Insula* (Ann Arbor), 25-48.

EARL, D. C. (1960), 'Political Terminology in Plautus', *Historia* 9: 235-43.

—— (1961), *The Political Thought of Sallust* (Cambridge).

ECK, W. (1972), 'Die Familie der Volusii Saturnini in neuen Inschriften aus Lucus Feroniae', *Hermes* 100: 461–84.

—— (1984), 'Senatorial self-representation: developments in the Augustan period', in F. Millar and E. Segal (eds.), *Caesar Augustus, Seven Aspects* (Oxford), 129–67

—— (1990), 'Cn. Calpurnius Piso, cos. ord. 7 v. Chr. und die Lex Portorii Provinciae Asiae', *EA* 15: 139–46.

—— (1993), 'Das s. c. de Cn. Pisone patre und seine Publikation in der Baetica', *Cahiers du Centre G. Glotz* 4: 189–208.

—— (1995), 'Plebs und Princeps nach dem Tod des Germanicus', in I. Malkin and Z. W. Rubinsohn (eds.), *Leaders and Masses in the Roman World. Studies in Honor of Zvi Yavetz* (*Mnemosyne* Suppl. 139, Leiden), 1–10.

EDER, W. (ed.) (1990), *Staat und Staatlichkeit in der frühen römischen Republik* (Akten des Symposiums [12.–15. Juli 1988] Freie Universität Berlin, Stuttgart).

EDLUND GANTZ, I. (1972), 'The Seated Statue Akroteria from Poggio Civitate (Murlo)', *DArch* 6: 167–235.

EDLUND-BERRY, I. E. M. (1992), *The Seated and Standing Statue Akroteria from Poggio Civitate (Murlo)* (Rome).

EISNER, M. (1986), *Zur Typologie der Grabbauten im Suburbium Roms* (Mainz).

ELLUL, J. (1973), *Propaganda: the Formation of Men's Attitudes* (New York).

ERNOUT, A. (1941), 'Les Noms en -ago, -igo, -ugo du latin', *RPh* 67: 85–111.

EVANS, J. D. (1990), 'Statues of the Kings and Brutus on the Capitoline', *ORom* 18.5: 99–105.

—— (1992), *The Art of Persuasion: Political Propaganda from Aeneas to Brutus* (Ann Arbor).

FARAONE, C. A. (1991), 'Binding and Burying the Forces of Evil: the Defensive Use of "Voodoo Dolls" in Ancient Greece', *CA* 70: 165–205.

FASCE, S. (1984), 'I tre assi della sposa', *Studi Noniani* 9: 97–110.

FEENEY, D. C. (1986), 'History and Revelation in Vergil's Underworld', *PCPS* 32: 1–24.

FELLETTI MAJ, B. M. (1977), *La tradizione italica nell'arte romana* I (Rome).

FISHER, N. R. E. (1992), *Hybris: A Study in the Values of Honour and Shame in Ancient Greece* (Warminster).

FLORY, M. B. (1993), 'Livia and the History of Public Honorific Statues for Women in Rome', *TAPA* 123: 287–308.

FLOWER, H. I. (1995), '*Fabulae Praetextae* in Context: When Were Plays on Contemporary Subjects Performed in Rome?', *CQ* 45: 170–90.

FOERTENMEYER, V. (1988), 'The Dating of the Pompe of Ptolemy II Philadelphus', *Historia* 37: 90–104.

FOULKES, A. P. (1983), *Literature and Propaganda* (London).

FRAENKEL, E. (1956), 'Eine Form römischer Kriegsbulletins', *Eranos* 54: 189–94.

Fraenkel, E. (1960), *Elementi Plautini in Plauto* (Florence).

Franchi, L. (1963–4), 'Rilievo con pompa funebre e rilievo con gladiatori al museo dell'Aquila', in R. Bianchi Bandinelli (ed.), Sculture municipali dell'area sabellica tra l'età di Cesare e quella di Nerone, *Studi Miscellanei* 10: 23–32.

Frank, T. (1938), 'Augustus, Vergil and the Augustan Elogia', *AJP* 59: 91–4.

Freedberg, D. (1989), *The Power of Images: Studies in the History and Theory of Response* (Chicago).

Frenz, H. G. (1977), *Untersuchungen zu den frühen römischen Grabreliefs* (Diss. Frankfurt).

Friedländer, L. (1919), *Sittengeschichte Roms⁹* 1–4 (Leipzig).

Frier, B. W. (1979), *Libri Annales Pontificum Maximorum: The Origins of the Annalistic Tradition* (American Academy in Rome, Monograph 27, Rome).

Frisch, P. (1980), 'Zu den Elogien des Augustusforums', *ZPE* 39: 91–8.

Fröhlich, T. (1991), *Lararien und Fassadenbilder in den Vesuvstädten. Untersuchungen zur 'volkstümlichen' pompejanischen Malerei* (Mainz).

Frova, A. (1961), *L'arte di Roma e del mondo romano* (Turin).

Fuchs, G. (1969), *Architekturdarstellungen auf römischen Münzen der Republik und der frühen Kaiserzeit* (Berlin).

Gabba, E. (1964), 'Un documento censorio in Dionigi d'Alicarnasso 1.74.5', in A. Guarino and L. Labruna (eds.), *Synteleia V. Arangio-Ruiz* 1 (Naples), 486–93.

—— (1976), *Republican Rome: the Army and the Allies* (trans. by C. J. Cuff) (Oxford).

—— (1988), 'Ricchezza e classe dirigente romana fra III e I sec. a. C.', in *Del buon uso della ricchezza* (Milan), 27–44.

Gagé, J. (1935/1977), *Res Gestae Divi Augusti³* (Paris).

Ganzert, J., and Kockel, V. (1988), 'Augustusforum und Mars-Ultor-Tempel', in *Kaiser Augustus und die verlorene Republik* (Mainz), 149–200.

Garland, R. (1985), *The Greek Way of Death* (London).

Gazda, E. K., and Haekel, A. E., (1993), 'Roman Portraiture: Reflections on the Question of Context', *JRA* 6: 289–302.

Gelzer, M. (1912/1975), *The Roman Nobility* (Oxford).

Gempeler, R. D. (1974), *Die Etruskischen Kanopen. Herstellung, Typologie, Entwicklungsgeschichte* (Einsiedeln).

Gibson, M. (ed.) (1981), *Boethius. His Life, Thought, and Influence* (Oxford).

Ginge, B. (1993), review of Edlund-Berry (1992), *AJA* 97: 583–4.

Giuliani, L. (1986), *Bildnis und Botschaft. Hermeneutische Untersuchungen zur Bildniskunst der römischen Republik* (Frankfurt).

Giuliano, A., and Buzzi, G. (1992), *Splendore degli Etruschi. Dalle pitture murali agli oggetti in oro, dai bronzi alla ceramica* (Milan).

Goette, H. R. (1990), *Studien zu römischen Togadarstellungen* (Mainz).

374

GOLDEN, M. (1990), *Children and Childhood in Classical Athens* (Baltimore).

GONZÁLEZ, J. (1984), 'Tabula Siarensis, fortunales Siarensis et municipia civium romanorum', *ZPE* 55: 55-100.

—— and ARCE, J. (eds.) (1988), *Estudios sobre la Tabula Siarensis, Anejos de archivo español de arquelogia* 9 (Madrid).

GORDON, A. E. (1958), *Album of Dated Latin Inscriptions* (Berkeley).

—— (1983), *Illustrated Introduction to Latin Epigraphy* (Berkeley).

GRIFFIN, J. (1979), 'The Fourth Georgic, Virgil and Rome', *G&R* 26: 61-80.

GRIFFIN, M. T. (1984), *Nero: the End of a Dynasty* (London).

—— (1991) 'Urbs Roma, Plebs and Princeps', in L. Alexander (ed.), *Images of Empire* (Sheffield), 19-46.

GRIMAL, P. (1953), *Les Jardins romains* (Paris).

—— (1954), 'Le Livre VI de l'Éneide et son actualité en 23 av. J.-C.', *REA* 56: 40-60.

—— (1975), 'Le Théâtre à Rome', in *Actes du IXᵉ Congrès de l'Association G. Budé* 1 (Paris), 249-305.

GRIMAL, P., and WOLOCH, G. M. (1983), *Roman Cities. Les villes romaines* (Madison, Wis.).

GROS, P., and TORELLI, M. (1988), *Storia dell'urbanistica: il mondo romano* (Rome/Bari).

GROSS, W. H. (1954), '*Clipeata imago* und εἰκὼν ἔνοπλος', in *Convivium, Festschrift Konrat Ziegler* (Stuttgart), 66-84.

GRUEN, E. S. (1974), *The Last Generation of the Roman Republic* (Berkeley).

—— (1990), *Studies in Greek Culture and Roman Policy* (Leiden).

—— (1992), *Culture and National Identity in Republican Rome* (Ithaca, NY).

—— (1995), 'The "Fall" of the Scipios', in I. Malkin and Z. W. Rubinsohn (eds.), *Leaders and Masses in the Roman World. Studies in Honor of Zvi Yavetz* (*Mnemosyne* Suppl. 139, Leiden), 59-90.

HAMILTON, C. D. (1969), 'The Tresviri Monetales and the Republican Cursus Honorum', *TAPA* 100: 181-99.

HANSLIK, R. M. (1953), 'Horaz und Varro Murena', *RhM* 96: 282-7.

HARMON, D. P. (1978), 'The Family Festivals of Rome', *ANRW* 16.2 (Berlin), 1592-1603.

HARRIS, W. V. (1971), *Rome in Etruria and Umbria* (Oxford).

—— (1979), *War and Imperialism in Republican Rome 327-70 B.C.* (Oxford).

—— (1990) 'On Defining the Political Culture of the Roman Republic', *CPh* 85: 288-94.

HARRISON, S. J. (1989), 'Augustus, the Poets and the Spolia Opima', *CQ* 39, 408-14.

HAYWOOD, R. M. (1933), *Studies on Scipio Africanus* (Baltimore).

HEDREEN, G. M. (1992), *Silens in Attic Black-Figure Vase-Painting: Myth and Performance* (Ann Arbor).

HELBIG, W. (1963), *Führer durch die öffentlichen Sammlungen klassischer Altertümer in Rom⁴* 1 (Rome).

HERBERT-BROWN, G. (1994), *Ovid and the Fasti: An Historical Study* (Oxford).

HERBIG, R. (1942), 'Die italische Wurzel der römischen Bildniskunst', in H. Berve (ed.), *Das neue Bild der Antike* 2, (Leipzig), 85 ff.

HERMANN, P. (1971), 'Zum Beschluss von Abdera aus Teos, Syll. 656', ZPE 7: 72–7.

HERRENSTEIN SMTIH, B. (1968), *Poetic Closure. A Study of How Poems End* (Chicago).

HERSH, C. A. (1977), 'Notes on the Chronology and Interpretation of the Roman Republican Coinage. Some Comments on Crawford's *Roman Republican Coinage*', NC⁷ 17: 19–36.

HERSH, C., and WALKER, A. (1984), 'The Mesagne Hoard', ANSMusN 29: 103–34.

HEURGON, J. (1964), *Daily Life of the Etruscans* (New York).

—— (1973), *The Rise of Rome to 264 B.C.* (Berkeley).

HICKSON, F. V. (1991), 'Augustus *Triumphator*: Manipulation of the Triumphal Theme in the Political Program of Augustus', *Latomus* 50: 124–38.

HINARD, F. (1987), 'Sur une autre forme de l'opposition entre virtus et fortuna', *Kentron* 3: 17–20.

HOFTER, M. (1988), 'Porträt', in *Kaiser Augustus und die verlorene Republik* (Mainz), 291–343.

HÖLKESKAMP, K.-J. (1987), *Die Entstehung der Nobilität. Studien zur sozialen und politischen Geschichte der Römischen Republik im 4. Jhdt. v. Chr.* (Stuttgart).

—— (1993), 'Conquest, Competition and Consensus: Roman Expansion in Italy and the Rise of the *Nobilitas*', *Historia* 42: 12–39.

HÖLSCHER, T. (1978), 'Die Anfänge römischer Repräsentationskunst', *MDAI(R)* 85: 315–57.

—— (1980a), 'Die Geschichtsauffassung in der römischen Repräsentationskunst', *JDAI* 95: 265–321.

—— (1980b), 'Römische Siegesdenkmäler der späten Republik', in H. A. Cahn and E. Simon (eds.), *Tainia: R. Hampe zum 70. Geburtstag* 1 (Mainz), 351–71.

—— (1982), 'Die Bedeutung der Münzen für das Verständnis der politischen Repräsentationskunst der späten römischen Republik', in T. Hackens and R. Weiller (eds.), *Proceedings of the Ninth International Congress of Numismatics (Berne)* (Louvain-la-Neuve, Luxemburg), 269–82.

—— (1987), *Die römische Bildsprache als semantisches System* (AHAW).

—— (1990), 'Römische Nobiles und hellenistische Herrscher' in *Akten des XIII. Internationalen Kongresses für Klassische Archäologie in Berlin 1988* (Mainz), 73–84.

HOLST-WARHAFT, G. (1992), *Dangerous Voices. Women's Laments and Greek Literature* (London/New York).

HOOKER, J. T. (1987), 'Homeric Society: a Shame-culture', *G&R* 34: 121–5.

Hopkins, K. (1983), *Death and Renewal* (Sociological Studies in Roman History 2, Cambridge).

Horn, R. (1933), Review of Zadoks (1932), *Gnomon* 19: 657-63.

Hornbostel-Hüttner, G. (1979), *Studien zur römischen Nischenarchitektur* (Dutch Archaeological and Historical Society 9, Leiden).

Horsfall, N. M. (1980), 'Virgil, Varro's Imagines and the Forum of Augustus', *AncSoc* 10: 20-3.

—— (1982), 'The structure and purpose of Vergil's Parade of Heroes' *AncSoc* 12: 12-8.

—— (1983), 'Some problems in the "Laudatio Turiae" ', *BICS* 30: 85-98.

Humbert, J. (1925), *Les Plaidoyers écrits et les plaidoiries réelles de Ciceron* (Paris).

Humphreys, S. C. (1980), 'Family Tombs and Tomb Cult in Ancient Athens—Tradition or Traditionalism', *JHS* 100: 96-126.

—— (1981), 'Death and Time', in S. C. Humphreys and H. King (eds.), *Mortality and Immortality: the Anthropology and Archaeology of Death* (London), 261-83.

Innocenti Prosdocimi, E. (1980/1), 'Sull'elogio di Scipione Barbato', *Annali dell'Istituto di Storia* (Firenze) 2: 1-23.

Isager, J. (1991), *Pliny on Art and Society* (London/New York).

Jackson, D. (1987), 'Verism and the Ancestral Portrait', *G&R* 34: 32-47.

Jannot, J.-R. (1984), *Les reliefs archaïques de Chiusi* (Rome).

Jensen, W. M. (1978), 'The Sculptures from the Tomb of the Haterii' 1-2, Ph.D. dissertation (Michigan).

Jex-Blake, K. and Sellers, E. (1896/1968), *The Elder Pliny's Chapters on the History of Art* (Chicago).

Jones, A. H. M. (1956/74), 'Numismatics and History', in P. A. Brunt (ed.), *The Ancient Economy. Studies in Ancient Economic and Administrative History* (Oxford), 61-81.

—— (1964), *The Later Roman Empire A.D. 284-602: a Social, Economic and Administrative Survey* 1-3. (Oxford).

Jones, J. R. (1970), 'Mint Magistrates in the Early Roman Empire', *BICS* 17: 70-8.

Jongkees, J. H. (1956), 'Primitive *Imagines Maiorum* on Coins of the Roman Republic', *AArch* 36: 232-9.

Jongman, W. (1988), *The Economy and Society of Pompeii* (Amsterdam).

Jung, F. (1984), 'Gebaute Bilder', *AK* 27: 71-122.

Kaschnitz-Weinberg, G. (1926), 'Studien zur etruskischen und frührömischen Porträtkunst', *MDAI(R)* 41: 133-211.

—— (1965) *Ausgewählte Schriften* 1-3, ed. P. H. von Blanckenhagen, H. von Heintze, G. Kleiner (Berlin).

Kellum, B. A. (1981), 'Sculptural Programs and Propaganda in Augustan Rome: the Temple of Apollo on the Palatine and the Forum of Augustus', Ph.D. dissertation (Harvard).

Kennedy, D. F. (1984), review of Woodman and West (eds.), *Poetry and Politics in the Age of Augustus* (Cambridge, 1984), *LCM* 9.10 Dec.: 157-60.

Kierdorf, W. (1980), *Laudatio funebris: Interpretationen und Untersuchungen zur Entwicklung der römischen Leichenrede* (Beiträge zur klassischen Philologie 106, Meisenheim am Glan).

Kleiner, D. E. E. (1977), *Roman Group Portraiture: Funerary Reliefs of the late Republic and Early Empire* (New York).

—— (1988), 'Roman Funerary Art and Architecture: Observations on the Significance of Recent Studies', *JRA* 1: 115-18.

—— (1992), *Roman Sculpture* (Yale).

Kockel, V. (1983), 'Beobachtungen zum Tempel des Mars Ultor und zum Forum des Augustus', *MDAI(R)* 90: 421-48.

Koenen, L. (1970a), 'Die 'laudatio funebris' des Augustus für Agrippa auf einem neuen Papyrus', *ZPE* 5: 217-83.

—— (1970b) 'Summum Fastigium: zu der laudatio funebris des Augustus (P. Colon. inv. Nr. 4701)', *ZPE* 6: 239-43.

Koestermann, E. (1965), *Cornelius Tacitus Annalen II* (Heidelberg).

—— (1971), *C. Sallusti Crispi Bellum Iugurthinum* (Heidelberg).

Kokkinos, N. (1992), *Antonia Augusta. Portrait of a Great Roman Lady* (London).

Kolb, F. (1977), 'Zur Statussymbolik im antiken Rom', *Chiron* 7: 239-59.

Kraus, T., and Von Matt, L. (1973), *Lebendiges Pompeji: Pompeji und Herculaneum: Antlitz und Schicksal zweier antiken Städte* (Köln).

Kroll, W. (1933), *Die Kultur der ciceronischen Zeit* 2 (Leipzig).

Krueger, P. (1877/1970), *Corpus Iuris Civilis* 2, *Codex Iustinianus* (Heidelberg).

Künzl, E. (1988), *Der römische Triumph: Siegesfeiern im antiken Rom* (Munich).

La Regina, A. (1968), 'L'elogio di Scipione Barbato', *DArch* 2: 173-90.

La Rocca, E. (1984), 'Fabio e Fannio. L'affresco medio-repubblicano dell'Esquilino come riflesso dell'arte rappresentativa e come espressione di mobilità sociale', *DArch* 3a ser. 2: 31-53.

—— (1986) 'Il lusso come espressione di potere', in M. Cima and E. La Rocca (eds.), *Le tranquille dimore degli dei. La residenza imperiale degli horti Lamiani* (Venice).

Lahusen, G. (1982), 'Statuae et Imagines', in B. von Freytag gen. Löringhoff, D. Mannsperger, F. Prayon (eds.), *Praestant Interna. Festschrift für Ulrich Hausmann* (Tübingen), 101-9.

—— (1983), *Untersuchungen zur Ehrenstatue in Rom. Literarische und epigraphische Zeugnisse* (Rome).

—— (1984), *Schriftquellen zum römischen Bildnis* 1 (Bremen).

—— (1985a), 'Zum römischen Bildnisrecht', *Labeo* 31: 308-23.

—— (1985b), 'Zur Funktion und Rezeption des römischen Ahnenbildes', *MDAI(R)* 92: 261-89.

—— (1988), 'Offizielle und private Bildnisgalerien in Rom', in N. Bonacasa and G. Rizza (eds.), *Ritratto ufficiale e ritratto privato. Atti della II conferenza internazionale sul ritratto romano* (Rome), 361–6.

—— (1989), *Die Bildnismünzen der römischen Republik* (Munich).

LAIDLAW, A. (1985), *The First Style in Pompeii: Painting and Architecture* (Rome).

LAMBRECHTS, R. (1959), *Essai sur les magistratures des républiques étrusques*, Études de philologie, d'archéologie et d'histoire anciennes, Institut historique belge de Rome 7 (Brussels/Rome).

LATTE, K. (1960), *Römische Religionsgeschichte* (Munich).

LAUTER-BUFE, H. (1982), 'Zur Fassade des Scipionengrabes', *MDAI(R)* 89: 35–46.

LEBEK, W. D. (1970), *Verba Prisca. Die Anfänge des Archaisierens in der lateinischen Beredsamkeit und Geschichtsschreibung* (Hypomnemata 25, Göttingen).

LEIGH FERMOR, P. (1958), *Mani: Travels in the Southern Peloponnese* (London).

LESSING, G. E. (1769/1974), 'Über die Ahnenbilder der Römer', in H. v. Heintze (ed.), *Römische Porträts* (Wege der Forschung 348, Darmstadt), 11–25.

LEVICK, B. (1976), *Tiberius the Politician* (London).

—— (1979), 'Poena Legis Maiestatis', *Historia* 28: 358–79.

—— (1982), 'Propaganda and the Imperial Coinage', *Antichthon* 16: 104–16.

—— (1990), *Claudius* (London).

LINDERSKI, J. (1989), 'Garden Parlors: Nobles and Birds', in R. I. Curtis (ed.), *Studia Pompeiana et Classica in Honor of Wilhelmina F. Jashemski, 2 Classica* (New Rochelle, NY).

LINDSAY, W. M. (1913/1965), *Sexti Pompei Festi De Verborum Significatu Quae Supersunt cum Pauli Epitome* (Hildesheim).

LING, R. (1983), 'The Insula of the Menander: interim report', *AntJ* 63: 34–57.

—— (1991), *Roman Painting* (Cambridge).

LINTOTT, A. W. (1968), *Violence in Republican Rome* (Oxford).

LONSDALE, S. H. (1993), *Dance and Ritual Play in Greek Religion* (Baltimore).

LORAUX, N. (1981), *L'Invention d'Athènes. Histoire de l'oraison funèbre dans la 'cité classique'* (Paris).

LUCE, T. J. (1968), 'Political Propaganda on Roman Republican Coins (92–82 B.C.)', *AJA* 72: 25–39.

—— (1990), 'Livy, Augustus, and the Forum Augustum', in K. A. Raaflaub and M. Toher (eds.), *Between Republic and Empire: Interpretations of Augustus and his Principate* (Berkeley).

LUCREZI, F. (1986), 'Ius imaginum, nova nobilitas', *Labeo* 32: 131–79.

MACCORMACK, S. G. (1981), *Art and Ceremony in Late Antiquity* (Berkeley).

McGUSHIN, P. (1992), *Sallust: The Histories, Books 1 and 2 1* (Oxford).

MACINTOSH, J. (1974), 'Representations of Furniture on the Frieze Plaques from Poggio Civitate (Murlo)', *MDAI(R)* 81: 15–40.

McKAY, A. G. (1975), *Houses, Villas and Palaces in the Roman World* (Ithaca, NY).

MACMULLEN, R. (1966), *Enemies of the Roman Order: Treason, Unrest, and Alienation in the Empire* (Cambridge, Mass.).

—— (1980), 'How Many Romans Voted?', *Athenaeum* 58: 454–7.

MACNAMARA, E. (1990), *The Etruscans* (London).

MAGGIANI, A. (1983), 'Nuovi dati per la riconstruzione del ciclo pittorico della tomba François', *DArch* 1: 71–8.

—— (1992), 'Ritrattistica tardo-ellenistica fra Etruria e Roma', *Prospettiva* 66: 36–47.

MAIURI, A. (1933), *La casa del Menandro e il suo tesoro di argenteria* (Rome).

—— (1937), *Herculaneum* (Rome).

—— (1945), *La Cena di Trimalchione di Petronio Arbitro: saggio, testo e commento* (Naples)

MALCOVATI, E. (1965), 'Per una nuova edizione degli *ORF*', *Athenaeum* 43: 209–16.

—— (1976), *Oratorum Romanorum Fragmenta Liberae Rei Publicae*[4] (Turin).

—— (1981), 'Una laudatio funebris recuperata', *Athenaeum* 59: 185–7.

MANSUELLI, G. A. (1963), 'La casa etrusca di Marzabotto: constatazioni nei nuovi scavi', *MDAI(R)* 70: 44–62.

—— (1968), 'Individuazione e rappresentazione storica nell'arte etrusca', *SE* 36: 3–19.

—— (1979), "Γραφαὶ καὶ Σχήματα τῶν Γεγνότων (App. *Punic.* 66)", *RdA* 3: 45–58.

MARCOTTE, D. (1985), 'Lucaniae: Considérations sur l'éloge de Scipion Barbatus', *Latomus* 44: 721–42.

MARQUARDT, J. (1905), *Das Privatleben der Römer*[2] (Leipzig).

MARTHA, C. (1905), 'L'Éloge funèbre chez les romains', in *Études morales sur l'Antiquité*[4] (Paris), 1–59.

MARTINDALE, J. R. (1980), *The Prosopography of the Later Roman Empire A.D. 395–527* 2 (Cambridge).

MATTHEWS, J. F. (1985*a*), 'Continuity in a Roman Family: the Rufii Festi of Volsinii', in *Political Life and Culture in Late Roman Society* (London), 484–509.

—— (1985*b*), 'Anicius Manlius Severinus Boethius', in *Political Life and Culture in Late Roman Society* (London), 15–43.

MAU, A. (1907), *Pompeii: Its Life and Art* (trans. K. W. Kelsey, New York).

MAZZARINO, S. (1966), *Il pensiero storico classico*, 2.1 (Bari).

MEIER, C. (1980), *Die Ohnmacht des allmächtigen Diktators Caesar* (Frankfurt).

MENICHETTI, M. (1988), 'Le aristocrazie tirreniche: aspetti iconografici', in A. Momigliano and A. Schiavone (eds.), *Storia di Roma 1: Roma in Italia* (Turin), 75–124.

MERTEN, E. W. (1986), *Stellenbibliographie zur Historia Augusta* 2 (Bonn).
— — (1987), *Stellenbibliographie zur Historia Augusta* 4 (Bonn).
MIELSCH, H. (1987), *Die römische Villa: Architektur und Lebensform* (Munich)
MILLAR, F. (1964), *A Study of Cassius Dio* (Oxford).
— — (1977), *The Emperor in the Roman World* (Cornell).
— — (1984*a*), 'State and Subject: the Impact of Monarchy', in F. Millar and E. Segal (eds.), *Caesar Augustus: Seven Aspects* (Oxford), 37–60.
— — (1984*b*), 'The Political Character of the Classical Roman Republic 200–150 B.C.', *JRS* 74: 1–19.
— — (1986), 'Politics, Persuasion and the People before the Social War (150–90 B.C.)', *JRS* 76: 1–11.
— — (1988), 'Imperial Ideology in the Tabula Siarensis', in J. González and J. Arce (eds.), *Estudios sobre la Tabula Siarensis, Anejos de archivo español de arquelogia* 9 (Madrid), 11–19.
— — (1989), 'Political Power in Mid-Republican Rome: Curia or Comitium?', *JRS* 79: 138–50.
— — (1995), 'Popular Politics at Rome in the Late Republic', in I. Malkin and Z. W. Rubinsohn (eds.), *Leaders and Masses in the Roman World. Studies in Honor of Zvi Yavetz* (*Mnemosyne* Suppl. 139, Leiden), 91–113.
MOIR, K. M. (1986), 'The Epitaph of Publius Scipio', *CQ* 36: 264–6.
MOMIGLIANO, A. (1957), 'Perizonius, Niebuhr and the Character of Early Roman Tradition', *JRS* 47: 104–14.
MOMMSEN, T. (1854), 'Die ältesten Scipionengrabschriften', *RhM* NF 9: 461–68.
— — (1887), *Römisches Staatsrecht*³ 1 (Leipzig).
MORETTI, M., and SGUBINI MORETTI, A. M. (1977), *La Villa dei Volusii a Lucus Feroniae* (Rome).
MORRIS, I. (1987), *Burial and Ancient Society: the rise of the Greek city state* (Cambridge).
— — (1989), 'Attitudes towards Death in Archaic Greece', *CA* 8: 296–320.
MUIR, E. (1981), *Civic Ritual in Renaissance Venice* (Princeton).
MÜNZER, F. (1897), *Beiträge zur Quellenkritik der Naturgeschichte des Plinius* (Berlin).
MUSTAKALLIO, K. (1994), *Death and Disgrace: Capital Penalties and Post Mortem Sanctions in Early Roman Historiography* (Helsinki).
NASH, E. (1962), *Pictorial Dictionary of Ancient Rome* 2 (London).
NEUDECKER, R. (1988), *Die Skulpturenausstattung römischer Villen in Italien* (Mainz).
NICOLET, C. (1964), *Les idées politiques à Rome sous la République* (Paris).
— — (1966–1974), *L'ordre équestre à l'époque républicaine 312–43 av. J.-C.* 1–2 (Paris).
— — (1976), *Le métier de citoyen dans la Rome republicaine* (Paris).
— — (1977), *Rome et la conquête du monde méditerranéan 264–27* 1 (Paris).
— — (1980), *The World of the Citizen in Republican Rome* (London).

NISTA, L. (1988), 'Ius imaginum and Public Portraiture', in M. L. Anderson and L. Nista, *Roman Portraits in Context. Imperial and Private Likenesses from the Museo Nazionale Romano* (Rome).

NORTH, J. A. (1983), 'These He Cannot Take', *JRS* 73: 169–74.

—— (1990), 'Politics and Aristocracy in the Roman Republic', *CPh* 85: 277–87.

NOVARA, A. (1987), 'Imagines de l'Élysée virgilien', in F. Hinard (ed.), *La Mort, les morts et l'au-delà dans le monde romain* (Actes du colloque de Caen, 20–22 Nov. 1985, Caen), 321–49.

OGILVIE, R. M. (1965), *A Commentary on Livy, Books 1–5* (Oxford).

ORR, D. G. (1978), 'Roman Domestic Religion: the Evidence of the Household Shrines', *ANRW* 16.2 (Berlin), 1557–91.

PALMER, R. E. A. (1983), 'On the Track of the Ignoble', *Athenaeum* 61: 343–61.

—— (1990), 'Cults of Hercules, Apollo Caelispex and Fortuna in and around the Roman Cattle Market', *JRA* 3: 234–44.

—— (1993), 'Paen and Paenists of Serapis and the Flavian Emperors', in R. M. Rosen and J. Farrell (eds.), *Nomodeiktes. Greek Studies in Honor of Martin Ostwald* (Ann Arbor), 355–65.

PANCIERA, S. (1982), 'Volusiana. Appunti epigrafici sui Volusii', in *I Volusii Saturnini. Una famiglia romana della prima età imperiale* (Bari), 83–95.

PARIS, R. (1990), *Persona. La maschera nel teatro antico* (Rome).

PASSERINI, A. (1934), 'Caio Mario come uomo politico', *Athenaeum* 12: 10–44, 109–43, 257–97, 348–80.

PATTERSON, J. R. (1992), 'The City of Rome: From Republic to Empire', *JRS* 82: 186–215.

PELLING, C. B. R. (1988), *Plutarch: Life of Antony* (Cambridge).

—— (1993), 'Tacitus and Germanicus', in T. J. Luce and A. J. Woodman (eds.), *Tacitus and the Tacitean Tradition* (Princeton).

PENNEY, J. H. W. (1992), review of Wachter (1987), *CR* 42: 162–4.

PERNICE, E. (1932), *Hellenistische Tische, Zisternenmündungen, Beckenunter-sätze, Altäre und Truhen* (Berlin/Leipzig).

PETER, H. (1914/67), *Historicorum Romanorum Reliquiae*[2] I (Stuttgart).

PIGHI, I. B. (1965), *De Ludis Saecularibus Populi Romani Quiritium Libri Sex*[2] (Amsterdam).

PISANI SARTORIO, G., and QUILICI GIGLI, S. (1987/8), 'A proposito della Tomba dei Corneli', *BCAR* 92.2: 247–64.

PLATNER, S. B., and ASHBY, T. (1929), *A Topographical Dictionary of Ancient Rome* (Oxford).

POLLITT, J. (1966), *The Art of Rome c. 753 BC–337 AD; Sources and Documents* (Englewood Cliffs, NJ).

POMEROY, S. B. (1975), *Goddesses, Whores, Wives, and Slaves: Women in Classical Antiquity* (New York).

POTTER, D. S. (1987), 'The *Tabula Siarensis*, Tiberius, the Senate, and the Eastern Boundary of the Roman Empire', *ZPE* 69, 269–76.

—— (1994), *Prophets and Emperors. Human and Divine Authority from Augustus to Theodosius* (Cambridge, Mass.).

POULSEN, V. (1973), *Les Portraits romains 1, république et dynastie julienne*[2] (Copenhagen).

PRAYON, F. (1974), 'Zum ursprünglichen Aussehen und zur Deutung des Kultraumes in der Tomba delle Cinque Sedie bei Cerveteri', *Marburger Winckelmann-Programm*: 1-15.

—— (1975*a*), *Frühetruskische Grab-und Hausarchitektur* (Heidelberg).

—— (1975*b*), 'Zur Datierung der drei frühetruskischen Sitzstatuetten aus Cerveteri', *MDAI(R)* 82: 165-79.

PRICE, S. R. F. (1987), 'From Noble Funerals to Divine Cult: the Consecration of the Roman Emperors', in D. Cannadine and S. Price (eds.), *Rituals of Royalty: Power and Ceremonial in Traditional Societies* (Cambridge), 56-105.

PRYCE, F. N. (1928), *Catalogue of Sculpture in the Department of Greek and Roman Antiquities of the British Museum, 1.1 Pre Hellenic and Early Greek* (London).

—— (1931), *Catalogue of Sculpture in the Department of Greek and Roman Antiquities of the British Museum, 1.2 Cypriote and Etruscan* (London).

PUTNAM, M. C. J. (1986), *Artifices of Eternity: Horace's Fourth Book of Odes* (Ithaca, NY).

RADKE, G. (1981), *Archaisches Latein. Historische und sprachgeschichtliche Untersuchungen* (Darmstadt).

—— (1991), 'Beobachtungen zum Elogium auf L. Cornelius Barbatus', *RhM* 134: 69-79.

RAMBAUD, M. (1978), 'Masques et *imagines*. Essai sur certains usages funéraires de l'Afrique Noire et de la Rome Ancienne', *LEC* 46: 3-21.

RATHJE, A. (1983), 'A Banquet Service from the Latin City of Ficana', *ARom* 12: 1-29.

RAWLS, J. (1971), *A Theory of Justice* (Cambridge, Mass.).

RAWSON, E. (1972), 'Cicero the Historian and Cicero the Antiquarian', *JRS* 62: 33-45.

—— (1975), 'Caesar's Heritage: Hellenistic Kings and their Roman Equals', *JRS* 65: 148-59.

—— (1990), 'The Antiquarian Tradition: Spoils and Representations of Foreign Armour', in Eder (1990), 158-73.

REBUFFAT, D. and R. (1978), 'De Sidoine Appollinaire à la Tombe François', *Latomus* 37: 88-104.

REDFIELD, J. M. (1975), *Nature and Culture in the Iliad: the Tragedy of Hector* (Chicago).

REECE, R. (ed.) (1977), *Burial in the Roman World* (Council for British Archaeology Research Report 22, London).

REEVE, M. D. (1984), 'The addressee of the Laus Pisonis', *ICS* 9: 42-8.

RIBBECK, O. (1962), *Scaenicorum Romanorum Fragmenta 1*[2] (Hildesheim).

RICE, E. E. (1983), *The Grand Procession of Ptolemy Philadelphus* (Oxford).

RICHARD, J. C. (1978), 'Recherches sur certains aspects du culte imperiale; les funérailles des empereurs romains aux deux premiers siècles de notre ère', *ANRW* 16.2 (Berlin), 1121-34.

RICHARDSON, L. (1978), 'Honos et Virtus and the Via Sacra', *AJA* 82: 240-6.

—— (1988), *Pompeii: an Architectural History* (Baltimore).

—— (1992), *A New Topographical Dictionary of Ancient Rome* (Baltimore).

RICHTER, G. M. A. (1955), 'The Origin of Verism in Roman Portraits', *JRS* 45: 39-46.

RIDLEY, R. T. (1983), 'Falsi triumphi, plures consulatus', *Latomus* 42: 372-82.

RILINGER, R. (1976), *Der Einfluß des Wahlleiters bei den römischen Konsulwahlen von 366 bis 50 v. Chr.* (Munich).

RIX, H. (1972), 'Zum Ursprung des römisch-mittelitalischen Gentilnamensystems', *ANRW* I.2 (Berlin), 700-58.

ROLLIN, J. P. (1979), *Untersuchungen zu Rechtsfragen römischer Bildnisse* (Bonn).

ROLOFF, H. (1938), *Maiores bei Cicero* (Göttingen).

Roma Medio Repubblicana. Aspetti culturali di Roma e del Lazio nei secoli IV e III A. C. (Rome, 1973).

ROSE, H. J. (1923), 'Nocturnal Funerals in Rome', *CQ* 17: 191-4.

ROSENSTEIN, N. (1990), *Imperatores Victi: Military Defeat and Aristocratic Competition in the Middle and Late Republic* (Berkeley).

RÖSLER, W. (1990), 'Mnemosyne in the *Symposium*', in O. Murray (ed.), *Sympotica: a Symposium on the Symposion* (Oxford), 230-7.

ROTONDI, G. (1912/66), *Leges Publicae Populi Romani. Elenco cronologico con una introduzione sull'attività legislitiva dei comizi romani* (Hildesheim).

ROWELL, H. T. (1940), 'The Forum and Funeral Imagines of Augustus', *MAAR* 17: 131-43.

—— (1941), 'Vergil and the Forum of Augustus', *AJP* 62: 261-76.

RYBERG, I. SCOT (1955), *Rites of the State Religion in Roman Art* (*MAAR* 22, Rome).

SAGE, M. (1979), 'The Elogia of the Augustan Forum and the De Viris Illustribus', *Historia* 28: 192-210.

SALADINO, V. (1970), *Der Sarkophag des Lucius Cornelius Scipio Barbatus* (Würzburg).

SALLER, R. (1982), *Personal Patronage under the Early Empire* (Cambridge).

—— (1984), 'Familia, Domus, and the Roman Conception of the Family', *Phoenix* 38: 336-55.

SCANLON, T. F. (1980), *The Influence of Thucydides on Sallust* (Heidelberg).

SCARDIGLI, B. (1979), *Die Römerbiographien Plutarchs* (Munich).

SCHÄFER, T. (1989), *Imperii Insignia: Sella curulis und Fasces, zur Repräsentation römischer Magistrate* (*MDAI(R)* Ergänzungsheft 29, Mainz).

SCHANZ-HOSIUS, (1927), *Römische Literaturgeschichte*[4] I (Munich), 38-40.

SCHMÄHLING, E. (1938), *Die Sittenaufsicht der Censoren. Ein Beitrag zur Sittengeschichte der römischen Republik* (Stuttgart).

SCHNEIDER, K., and MEYER, H. (1916), *RE* "Imagines Maiorum", 9.1097-1104.

SCHWEITZER, B. (1948), *Die Bildniskunst der römischen Republik* (Weimar).

SCULLARD, H. H. (1930), *Scipio Africanus in the Second Punic War* (Cambridge).

—— (1951), *Roman Politics 220-150 BC* (Oxford).

—— (1970), *Scipio Africanus, Soldier and Politician* (London).

—— (1973), *Roman Politics 220-150 BC*² (Oxford).

SEAFORD, R. (1984), *Euripides Cyclops* (Oxford).

SEGAL, E. (1987), *Roman Laughter: The Comedy of Plautus*² (Oxford).

SHACKLETON BAILEY, D. R. (1976), *Two Studies in Roman Nomenclature* (ACS 3, University Park, Pa).

—— (1977), *Cicero: Epistulae ad Familiares* 2 (Cambridge).

—— (1986), 'Nobiles and Novi Reconsidered', *AJP* 107: 255-60.

SHATZMAN, I. (1972), 'The Roman's General's Authority over Booty', *Historia* 21: 177-205.

—— (1975), *Senatorial Wealth and Roman Politics* (Coll. Latomus 142, Brussels).

SHERWIN-WHITE, A. N. (1966), *The Letters of Pliny: A Historical and Social Commentary* (Oxford).

SIEBLER, M. (1988), *Studien zum augusteischen Mars Ultor* (Munich).

SILVESTRI, D. (1978), 'Taurasia Cisauna e il nome antico del Sannio', *PP* 33: 167-80.

SIMON, E. (1986), *Augustus: Kunst und Leben in Rom um die Zeitwende* (Munich).

SIMPSON, C. J. (1977), 'The Date of the Dedication of the Temple of Mars Ultor', *JRS* 67: 91-4.

SKARD, E. (1956), *Sallust und seine Vorgänger, eine sprachliche Untersuchung* (*SO* Suppl. 15, Oslo).

—— (1965), 'Die Heldenschau in Vergils Aeneis', *SO* 40: 53-65.

SKUTSCH, O. (ed.) (1972), *Ennius* (Fondation Hardt 17, Geneva).

SMALLWOOD, E. M. (1967), *Documents Illustrating the Principates of Gaius, Claudius and Nero* (Cambridge).

SMITH, R. R. R. (1981), 'Greeks, Foreigners, and Roman Republican Portraits', *JRS* 71: 24-38.

—— (1988), *Hellenistic Royal Portraits* (Oxford).

SOLIN, H. (1970), 'Analecta epigraphica', *Arctos* 6: 110-12.

SOURVINOU-INWOOD, C. (1981), 'To Die and Enter the House of Hades: Homer, Before and After', in J. Whaley (ed.), *Mirrors of Mortality: Essays on the Social History of Death* (London), 15-39.

—— (1983), 'A Trauma in Flux: Death in the Eighth Century and After', in R. Hägg (ed.), *The Greek Renaissance of the Eighth Century B.C.: Tradition and Innovation* (Stockholm), 33-48.

—— (1994), *'Reading' Greek Death* (Oxford).
STAMBAUGH, J. E. (1988), *The Ancient Roman City* (Baltimore).
STARK, (1876), 'Über die Ahnenbilder des Appius Claudius im Tempel der Bellona', *Verhandlungen der 31. Philologenversammlung in Tübingen*: 38–50.
STEIDLE, W. (1958), *Sallusts historische Monographen. Themenwahl und Geschichtsbild* (*Historia* Einzelschrift 3, Wiesbaden).
—— (1963), *Sueton und die Antike Biographie*² (Munich).
STEINBY, M. (1974–5), 'La cronologia delle figlinae doliari urbane dalla fine dell'età repubblicano fino all'inizio del III secolo', *BCAR* 84: 7–132.
STEINGRÄBER, S. (1979), *Etruskische Möbel* (Rome).
—— (1986), *Etruscan Painting. Catalogue Raisonné of Etruscan Wall-Paintings* (New York).
STEWART, A. (1990), *Greek Sculpture: An Exploration* 1–2 (New Haven).
—— (1993), *Faces of Power: Alexander's Image and Hellenistic Politics* (Berkeley).
STRASBURGER, H. (1937), '*Nobiles*' *RE* 17: 785–91.
STROH, W. (1975), *Taxis und Taktik. Die advokatische Dispositionskunst in Cicero's Gerichtsreden* (Stuttgart).
STRONG, S. A. (1914), 'A note on two Roman Sepulchral Reliefs', *JRS* 4: 153–6.
STUART, D. R. (1928), *Epochs of Greek and Roman Biography* (Princeton).
SUMNER, G. V. (1973), *The Orators in Cicero's Brutus: Prosopography and Chronology* (*Phoenix* Suppl. 11, Toronto).
SUTHERLAND, C. H. V. (1976), *The Emperor and the Coinage* (London).
—— (1983), 'The Purpose of Roman Imperial Coin Types', *RN* ⁶ 25: 73–82.
SWAN, M. (1966), 'The Consular Fasti of 23 B.C. and the Conspiracy of Varro Murena', *HSCP* 71: 235–47.
SWAN, E. H. (1923), 'Imagines in Imperial Portraiture', *AJA* 27: 286–301.
SYME, R. (1938), 'Caesar, the Senate and Italy', *PBSR* 14: 1–31.
—— (1939), *The Roman Revolution* (Oxford).
—— (1958), *Tacitus* 1 (Oxford).
—— (1964), *Sallust* (Cambridge).
—— (1968), *Ammianus and the Historia Augusta* (Oxford).
—— (1971), *Emperors and Biography: Studies in the Historia Augusta* (Oxford).
—— (1983), *Historia Augusta Papers* (Oxford).
—— (1986), *The Augustan Aristocracy* (Oxford).
SZILÁGY, J. C. (1981), 'Impletae modis saturae', *Prospettiva* 24: 2–23.
TAIFECOS, I. G. (1979), *Una laudatio funebris di M. Catone Nepote dalla testimonianza di Aulo Gellio* (Rome).
TALBERT, R. J. A. (1984), *The Senate of Imperial Rome* (Princeton).
TAMM, B. (1961), 'Le Temple des Muses à Rome', *ORom* 3; 157–67.

—— (1973), 'Some Notes on Roman Houses', *ORom* 9: 53-60.

TAPLIN, O. (1977), *The Stagecraft of Aeschylus: the Dramatic Use of Exits and Entrances in Greek Tragedy* (Oxford).

—— (1978), *Greek Tragedy in Action* (London).

TAYLOR, G. (1985), *Pride, Shame and Guilt: Emotions of Self-Assessment* (Oxford).

TAYLOR, L. R. (1931), *The Divinity of the Roman Emperor* (Middletown, Conn).

—— (1939), 'Cicero's Aedileship', *AJP* 60: 194-202.

—— (1949), *Party Politics in the Age of Caesar* (Berkeley).

—— (1966), *Roman Voting Assemblies from the Hannibalic War to the Dictatorship of Caesar* (Ann Arbor).

THÉBERT, Y. (1987), 'Private Life and Domestic Architecture in Roman Africa', in P. Veyne (ed.), *A History of Private Life: 1. From Pagan Rome to Byzantium*, 316-405.

THOMAS, R. (1989), *Oral Tradition and Written Record in Classical Athens* (Cambridge).

TILL, R. (1970), 'Die Scipionenelogien', in D. Ableitinger and H. Gugel (eds.), *Festschrift Karl Vretska* (Heidelberg), 276-89.

TITCHENER, F. (1992), 'Critical Trends in Plutarch's Roman Lives 1975-1990', *ANRW* 33.6 (Berlin), 4128-53.

TOHER, M. (1986), 'The Tenth Table and the Conflict of the Orders', in K. A. Raaflaub (ed.), *Social Struggles in Archaic Rome: New Perspectives on the Conflict of the Orders* (Berkeley), 301-26.

TORELLI, M. (1975), *Elogia Tarquiniensia* (Florence).

—— (1981), *Storia degli Etruschi* (Rome/Bari).

—— (1984), *Lavinio e Roma* (Rome).

—— (1988), 'Le popolazioni dell'Italia antica: società e forme del potere', in A. Momigliano and A. Schiavone (eds.), *Storia di Roma 1: Roma in Italia* (Turin), 53-74.

TOYNBEE, J. M. C. (1971), *Death and Burial in the Roman World* (London).

TRAINA, A. (1969), *Comoedia: antologia della palliata*[3] (Padua).

TREGGIARI, S. (1979), 'Sentiment and Property: some Roman Attitudes', in A. Parel and T. Flanagan (eds.), *Theories of Property: Aristotle to the Present* (Waterloo, Ontario).

TUCHELT, K. (1970), *Die archaischen Skulpturen von Didyma. Beiträge zur frühgriechischen Plastik in Kleinasien* (Istanbuler Forschungen 27, Berlin).

TUFI, S. (1981), 'Frammenti delle statue dei "summi viri" nel Foro di Augusto', *DArch* 3: 69-84.

VAN BUREN, A. W. (1938), 'Pinacothecae, with especial reference to Pompeii', *MAAR* 15: 70-81.

VAN DAM, R. (1985), *Leadership and Community in Late Antique Gaul* (Berkeley).

VAN OOTEGHEM, J. (1967), *Les Caecilii Metelli de la république* (Brussels).

Van Sickle, J. (1984), 'Stile ellenistico-romano e nascita dell'epigramma a Roma', in E. Flores (ed.), *Dall' epigramma ellenistico all' elegia romana* (Naples), 9-26.

—— (1987), 'The Elogia of the Cornelii Scipiones and the Origin of Epigram at Rome', *AJP* 108: 41-55.

—— (1988), 'The First Hellenistic Epigrams at Rome', *BICS* suppl. 51: 143-56.

Vansina, J. (1965), *Oral Tradition* (Chicago).

—— (1985), *Oral Tradition as History* (Madison).

Versnel, H. S. (1970), *Triumphus: An Inquiry into the Origin, Development and Meaning of the Roman Triumph* (Leiden).

—— (1980), 'Destruction, Devotio and Despair in a Situation of Anomy: the Mourning for Germanicus in Triple Perspective', in *Perennitas: studi in onore di Angelo Brelich* (Rome), 541-618.

Vessberg, O. (1941), *Studien zur Kunstgeschichte der römischen Republik* 1-2 (Lund).

Veyne, P. (1961), 'Vie de Trimalchio', *Annales ESC* 16: 213-47.

—— (1985), in P. Ariès and G. Duby (eds.), *Histoire de la vie privée: de l'empire romain à l'an mil* (Paris), 168-71.

—— (ed.) (1987), *A History of Private Life 1: From Pagan Rome to Byzantium*

Ville, G. (1981), *La Gladiature en occident des origines à la mort de Domitien* (Rome).

Vittinghoff, F. (1936), *Der Staatsfeind in der römischen Kaiserzeit: Untersuchungen zur 'damnatio memoriae'* (Berlin).

Vlad Borelli, L. (1962), 'Imagines maiorum', in *Enciclopedia dell'arte antica classica e orientale* 4 (Rome), 118-19.

Vogt, J. (1933), 'Vorläufer des Optimus Princeps', *Hermes* 68: 84-92.

Vollenweider, M.-L. (1955), 'Verwendung und Bedeutung der Porträtgemmen für das politische Leben der römischen Republik', *MH* 12: 96-111.

—— (1972-4), *Die Porträtgemmen der römischen Republik* 1 and 2 (Mainz am Rhein).

Vollmer, F. (1892), *Laudationum funebrium romanorum historia et reliquiarum editio (Fleckeisens Jahrbuch für class. Phil.* Suppl. 18), 445-528.

—— (1893), 'De funere publico Romanorum', *Fleckeisens Jahrbuch für classische Philologie*, Suppl. 19, 321-64.

—— (1925), '*Laudatio funebris*' in *RE* 12.992-4.

Von Fritz, K. (1943), 'Sallust and the Attitude of the Roman Nobility at the Time of the Wars against Jugurtha (112-105 B.C.)', *TAPA* 74: 134-68.

Von Blanckenhagen, P., and Alexander, C. (1962), *The Paintings from Boscotrecase* (Heidelberg).

Von Graeve, V. (1983), 'Archaische Plastik in Milet. Ein Beitrag zur Frage der Werkstätten und der Chronologie', *MJBK* 34: 7-24.

Von Hase, F. W. (1974), 'Eine unbekannte etruskische Sitzstatuette in Massa Marittima', *Marburger Winckelmann-Programm*: 16-23.

Von Hesberg, H. (1988), 'Das Mausoleum des Augustus', in *Kaiser Augustus und die verlorene Republik* (Mainz), 245-51.

—— (1994), *Römische Grabbauten* (Darmstadt).

—— and Panciera, S. (1994), *Das Mausoleum des Augustus. Der Bau und seine Inschriften* (Bayerische Akademie der Wissenschaften, Phil.-Hist. Klasse, Heft 108, Munich).

Von Premerstein, A. (1905), '*Elogium*' in *RE* 5.2440-52 .

Von Schlosser, J. (1910/11), 'Geschichte der Porträtbilderei in Wachs', *JbKS* Wien 29: 171-85, reprinted in H. von Heintze (ed.), *Römische Porträts* (Darmstadt, 1974), 76-101.

Vretska, K. (1970), 'Studien zu Sallusts *Bellum Jugurthinum*' in V. Pöschl (ed.), *Sallust* (Darmstadt).

Wachter, R. (1987), *Altlateinische Inschriften. Sprachliche und epigraphische Untersuchungen zu den Dokumenten bis etwa 150 v. Chr.* (Bern).

Walbank, F. W. (1957), *Polybius* 1 (Oxford).

—— (1967), 'The Scipionic Legend', *PCPS* 193: 54-69.

Walde, A., and Hoffmann, J. B. (1938), *Lateinisches etymologisches Wörterbuch*[3] (Berlin).

Walker, S. (1985), *Memorials to the Roman Dead* (London).

Wallace-Hadrill, A. (1981*a*), 'The Emperor and his Virtues', *Historia* 30: 298-323.

—— (1981*b*), 'Galba's Aequitas', *NC* 141: 20-39.

—— (1986), 'Image and Authority in the Coinage of Augustus', *JRS* 76: 66-87.

—— (1987), 'Time for Augustus: Ovid, Augustus and the Fasti' in M. Whitby, P. Hardie, and M. Whitby (eds.), *Homo Viator, Classical Essays for John Bramble* (Bristol), 221-30.

—— (1988), 'The Social Structure of the Roman House', *PBSR* 56: 43-97.

—— (1989), 'Patronage in Roman Society: from Republic to Empire', in *Patronage in Ancient Society* (London/New York), 63-87.

—— (1990), 'Roman Arches and Greek Honours: the Language of Power at Rome', *PCPS* 216: 143-81.

—— (1994), *Houses and Society in Pompeii and Herculaneum* (Princeton).

Wallisch, E. (1955), 'Name und Herkunft des römischen Triumphes', *Philologus* 99: 245-58.

Walters, H. B. (1903), *Catalogue of Sculpture in the Department of Greek and Roman Antiquities of the British Museum, Terracottas* (London).

Wanscher, O. (1980), *Sella Curulis. The folding Stool. An Ancient Symbol of Dignity* (Copenhagen).

Ward-Perkins, J., and Claridge, A. (1978), *Pompeii A. D. 79* (London and New York).

WARDEN, P. G. (1983), 'Bullae, Roman Custom and Italic Tradition', *ORom* 14: 69–75.

—— (1991), 'The Sculptural Program of the Villa of the Papyri', *JRA* 4: 257–61.

WATSON, L. (1987), 'Epode 9 or the Art of Falsehood' in M. Whitby, P. Hardie, and M. Whitby (eds.), *Homo Viator, Classical Essays for John Bramble* (Bristol), 119–29.

WAURICK, G. (1975), 'Kunstraub der Römer. Untersuchungen zu seinen Anfängen anhand der Inschriften', *JRGZ* 22: 1–46.

WEINSTOCK, S. (1957), 'The Image and the Chair of Germanicus', *JRS* 67, 144–54.

—— (1971), *Divus Julius* (Oxford).

WHEELER, E. L. (1988), 'Sapiens and Stratagems: The Neglected Meaning of a Cognomen', *Historia* 37: 166–95.

WIERZBICKA, A. (1986), 'Human Emotions: Universal or Culture-Specific?', *American Anthropologist* 88: 584–94.

WILES, D. (1991), *The Masks of Menander: Sign and Meaning in Greek and Roman Performance* (Cambridge).

WILLIAMS, B. (1993), *Shame and Necessity* (Berkeley).

WINKES, R. (1969), *Clipeata Imago: Studien zu einer römischen Bildnisform* (Bonn).

—— (1979), 'Pliny's Chapter on Roman Funeral Customs in the Light of Clipeatae Imagines', *AJA* 83: 481–4.

WISEMAN, T. P. (1971), *New Men in the Roman Senate 139 B.C.—A.D. 14* (Oxford).

—— (1974a), 'Legendary Genealogies in Late-Republican Rome', *G&R* 21: 207–19.

—— (1974b), *Cinna the Poet and other Roman Essays* (Leicester).

—— (1979), *Clio's Cosmetics: Three Studies in Greco-Roman Literature* (Leicester).

—— (1982), '*Pete Nobiles Amicos*: Poets and Patrons in Late Republican Rome', in B. K. Gold (ed.), *Literary and Artistic Patronage in Ancient Rome* (Austin), 28–49.

—— (1985), 'Competition and Co-operation', in *Roman Political Life 90 B.C. to 69 A.D.* (Exeter), 13–19.

—— (1987a), '*Conspicui postes tectaque digna deo*: the Public Image of Aristocratic and Imperial Houses in the Late Republic and Early Empire', in *L'Urbs: espace urbain et histoire (Ier siècle av. J.-C.—IIIe siècle ap. J.C.)*, Actes du colloque international organisé par le Centre National de la Recherche Scientifique et L'École Française de Rome (Rome, 8–12 Mai 1985), (Rome), 393–413.

—— (1987b), 'Their History Intact', in *Roman Studies: Literary and Historical* (Liverpool), 367–70.

—— (1988), 'Satyrs in Rome? The Background to Horace's Ars Poetica', *JRS* 78: 1–13.

WISSOWA, G. (1912), *Religion und Kultus der Römer*² (Munich).

WISTRAND, E. (1970), 'Das altrömische Haus nach den literarischen Quellen', *Eranos* 68: 191–223.

—— (1976), *The So-called Laudatio Turiae* (Göteborg).

WOJCIK, M. R. (1986), *La villa dei Papiri ad Ercolano. Contributo alla riconstruzione dell'ideologia della nobilitas tardorepubblicana* (Rome).

WÖLFFLIN, E. (1890), 'De Scipionum elogiis', *RPh* NS 14: 113–22.

—— (1892), 'Die Dichter der Scipionenelogien', *SB München*, Heft 2: 188–219.

WORMALD, P. (1976), 'The Decline of the Western Empire and the Survival of its Aristocracy', *JRS* 66: 217–26.

WÜNSCHE, R. (1982), '"Marius" und "Sulla". Untersuchungen zu republikanischen Porträts und deren neuzeitlichen Nachahmungen', *MJBK* 32, 7–38.

YACOBSEN, A. (1992), 'Petitio et Largitio: Popular Participation in the Centuriate Assembly of the Late Republic', *JRS* 82: 32–52.

YAVETZ, Z. (1969/88), *Plebs and Princeps* (Oxford).

—— (1979), *Caesar in der öffentlichen Meinung* (Düsseldorf).

ZADOKS-JOSEPHUS JITTA, A. N. (1932), *Ancestral Portraiture in Rome and the Art of the Last Century of the Republic* (Amsterdam).

ZANKER, P. (1968), *Forum Augustum; das Bildprogramm* (Tübingen).

—— (1975), 'Grabreliefs römischer Freigelassener', *JDAI* 90: 267–315.

—— (1976), 'Zur Rezeption des hellenistischen Individual-Porträts in Rom und in den italienischen Städten', in *Hellenismus in Mittelitalien* 2 (Göttingen), 581–605.

—— (1979), 'Die Villa als Vorbild des späten pompejanischen Wohngeschmacks', *JDAI* 94: 460–523.

—— (1983), 'Zur Bildnisrepräsentation führender Männer in mittelitalischen und campanischen Städten zur Zeit der späten Republik und der Julisch-Claudischen Kaiser', in *Les 'Bourgeoisies' municipales italiennes aux IIᵉ et Iᵉʳ siècles av. J. C.* (Naples), 251–66.

—— (1988), *The Power of Images in the Age of Augustus* (Ann Arbor).

ZECCHINI, G. (1980), 'La morte di Catone e l'opposizione intellettuale a Cesare e ad Augusto', *Athenaeum* 58, 39–56.

ZEHNACKER, H. (1972), 'La Numismatique de la République romaine: bilan et perspectives', *ANRW* 1.1 (Berlin), 266–96.

—— (1973), *Moneta. Recherches sur l'organisation et l'art des émissions monétaires de la république romaine (289–31 av. J. C.)* 1–2, Bibl. des Écoles franç. d'Athènes et de Rome 222 (Paris).

—— (1983), 'Tragédie prétexte et spectacle romain', in *Théâtre et spectacles dans l'antiquité* (Strasbourg), 31–48.

ZEVI, F. (1968/9), 'Considerazioni sull'elogio di Scipione Barbato', *Studi Miscellanei* 15: 65-73.

—— (1973), 'Sarcofago di L. Cornelio Scipione Barbato', in *Roma Medio Repubblicana: Aspetti culturali di Roma e del Lazio nei secoli IV e III A.C.* (Rome), 236-9.

ZIMMERMAN, J.-L. (1986), 'La Fin de Falerii Veteres: un témoinage archéologique', *GMusJ* 14: 37-42.

ZINSERLING, G. (1959/60), 'Studien zu den Historiendarstellungen der römischen Republik', *WZJena* 9: 403-48.

ZORZETTI, N. (1990), 'The *Carmina Convivalia*', in O. Murray (ed.), *Sympotica: a Symposium on the Symposion* (Oxford), 289-307.

—— (1991), 'Poetry and Ancient City: the Case of Rome', *CJ* 86: 311-29.

INDEX OF PERSONS

All dates are BC unless otherwise indicated

Numa 84, 112

Octavia 241, 242 n. 85, 243
Octavia A. l. Salvia 8 n. 41
Ollii 43 n. 61
Ollius T. 79 n. 79

Paconius Caledus T. 8 n. 41
Papiria, mother of Aemilianus 123
Papirius Cursor L. 77 n. 72, 342
Papirius Mugillanus L. (cos. suff. 444) 46 n. 70
Papirius Paetus L. 206
Paulla Cornelia 176, 179
Paxaea 26 n. 34
Perseus 123 n. 146
Plancina, wife of Piso 30–1
Plancius Cn. 152
Plautius Tib. (cos. AD 74) 182 n. 98
Pompeius Magnus Cn. (cos. 70, 55, 52) 153, 245, 258
Pompeius Rufus Q. 84
Pomponius Labeo 26 n. 34
Popilia, mother of Q. Lutatius Catulus 122
Poplicius Bibulus C. 96 n. 28, 182 n. 95
Poppaea Sabina 42–3, 79 n. 79
Poppaeus Habitus Cn. 42 n. 60
Poppaeus Q., freedman procurator 42 n. 60
Poppaeus Sabinus Q. 42 n. 60, 44 n. 68
Porcia 146 n. 74
Porcius Cato M. (cos. 195) 19, 64 n. 18, 88, 121, 193 n. 26
Porcius Cato Uticensis M. 58 n. 127, 83, 146 n. 74, 219–20
Potitus, Poppaei Sabini ludimagister 42 n. 60
Primus M. 240 n. 76
Ptolemy II Philadelphus 108–9

Quinctius Cincinnatus L. 132 n. 18

Romulus 113, 234–5, 237, 239, 243, 253

Scribonius Libo L. 153
Scribonius Libo Drusus M. 26, 121, 247, 253, 258
Sempronius Bassus 25
Sempronius Gracchus C. (tr. pl. 123–2) 219

Sempronius Gracchus Tib. (cos. 177) 50
Sempronius Gracchus Tib. (tr. pl. 133) 73 n. 60
Serranus 135 n. 28
Servilius Ahala C. (cos. 365, 362) 88–9
Severus Alexander 263 n. 38, 266
Sidonius Apollinaris 268
Silius G. 27 n. 39
Silvius 112
Socrates 117 n. 118
Spurinnae 74–5
Staienus Paetus (C. Aelius Paetus Staienus q. 77) 152 n. 93
Sulpicius Galba Ser. 181 n. 92
Sulpicius Quirinius P. 252
Sulpicius Rufus Ser. (cos. 51) 96 n. 27
Symmachus 276 n. 54
Syphax 123 n. 146

Tacitus, emperor 266–7
Tatius T. 84
Terentius Varro M. 182, 207, 274
Tiberius 156, 257–60
    and elections 69, 154
    and funerals 93 n. 7, 96 n. 26, 242–3, 246–55
    and Piso's trial 24–31, 58
Titurius Sabinus L. 84
Titus 262 n. 31
Trimalchio 212–13
Turpilius Silanus T. 17 n. 6

Valerius Maximus Corvinus M. (cos. 312, 289, 286) 235
Valerius Messalla Corvinus M. (cos. 31) 59 n. 132, 258
Valerius Messalla Rufus M. (cos. 53) 59 n. 132
Valerius Publicola P. (cos. suff. 509, 508, 507, ?506, ?504) 132
Vatinia Primigenia 44 n. 68
Vesonius Primus 195 n. 38
Vespasian 52, 104, 106, 114, 243 n. 94, 261–2
Vibius Pansa Caetronianus C. (cos. 43) 182 n. 95
Vipsanius Agrippa M. 142–3, 238–41, 243, 246
Visellius Karus 25
Vitellius 52
Volusius Saturninus L. (cos. suff. AD 3) 96 n. 29

INDEX OF ANCIENT SOURCES

Literary *testimonia* appear in Appendix A, inscriptions are in Appendix B

Authors

Aelian
  10. 10   212 n. 133

Aeschylus
  Choe.
    306-478   125 n. 154

Afranius
  Vop.
    12. 364-5 = T1   221 n. 160

Appian
  BC
    1. 43. 6   248 n. 106
    1. 100 & 104   101 n. 56
    1. 105-6   101 n. 54, 118 n.
    123, 123 n. 146, 130 n. 10
    2. 112   88 n. 126
    2. 146   125 n. 155 & 158
    4. 44   196 n. 44
  Hann.
    56: 178 n. 79
  Iber.
    89 = T2   46 n. 73, 48 n. 79,
    98 n. 34 & 36, 263
  Pun.
    66   106 n. 74, 107
  Samn.
    10. 3   187 n. 12

Aristotle
  Rhet.
    2. 2. 1396^a 12-15   134 n. 26

Arnobius
  Adv. Gent.
    2. 67   202 n. 82

Arrian
  FGH
    156 F 106   105 n. 72

Asconius
  12C = 11K-S = 18Stangl = I 15
    71 n. 53, 147 n. 80, 63 n. 13
  33C = 29K-S = 32 Stangl   116
    n. 111

43C = 37-8K-S = 38 Stangl = T3
  194-5

Athenaeus
  1. 20e   105 n. 72
  197c-203b   105 n. 74, 108 n. 86,
    109 n. 88

Augustus
  RG
    6. 1   233 n. 45
    19. 2   234 n. 50
    21. 1   204 n. 93, 229 n. 25
    22   65 n. 22, 226 n. 14
    34. 3   224 n. 5
    35   225 n. 11

Boethius
  Con.
    1 *pros.* 1. 3 = T4   34 n. 11,
    186 n. 6, 264-7

Caesar
  BG
    5. 12. 1   54 n. 110
    6. 25. 5   54 n. 110

Cassiodorus
  CCSL 96 p. v   267 n. 54

Cato
  fr. 9. 6   21 n. 21
  97   41 n. 56

Cicero
  Acad.
    22. 70   342 n. 15
  Arch.
    11. 27   89 n. 131
  Att.
    2. 24. 2-3   89 n. 127
    6. 1. 17   73 n. 59
    7. 13. 1   151 n. 91
    12. 21 & 23   219 n. 153
    13. 40   89 n. 128
    16. 4   89 n. 131
  Brut.
    57   137 n. 38

Inscriptions

5671   44 n. 68
6562   44 n. 68
8393   195 n. 35
8402   195 n. 35
8403   195 n. 35
8890 = *ILLRP* 421   182 n. 95

Laudatio Murdiae (ILS 8394 = CIL
    6.10230)   131-2, 195 n. 35

Laudatio 'Turiae'   111 n. 95, 131-2,
    142, 195 n. 35

S. C. de Cn. Pisone patre = I16: 2 n. 4,
    23-31, 33 n. 5, 37, 48 n. 80,
    51 n. 92, 53, 56-9, 103, 126
    n. 159, 202 n. 76, 206 n. 99,
    223, 250-2, 257 n. 5, 280

SEG
    30 no. 1120   175 n. 69

*SIG*3
    656. 26   218 n. 149

Tabula Siarensis 57, 248-52

GENERAL INDEX